International Perspective Boxes

Summarizing the Core Concepts

Case Studies and Boxes of Special Interest

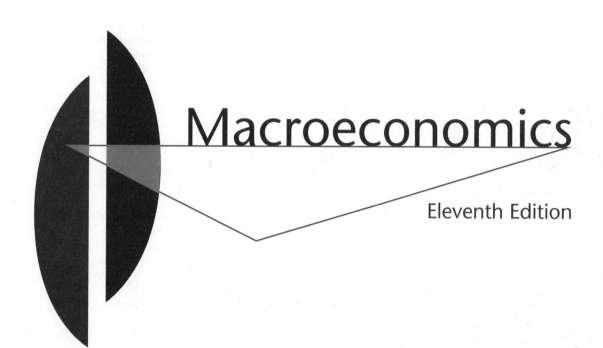

Macroeconomics

Eleventh Edition

The Addison-Wesley Series in Economics

Abel/Bernanke/Croushore
*Macroeconomics**

Bade/Parkin
*Foundations of Economics**

Bierman/Fernandez
Game Theory with Economic Applications

Binger/Hoffman
Microeconomics with Calculus

Boyer
Principles of Transportation Economics

Branson
Macroeconomic Theory and Policy

Bruce
Public Finance and the American Economy

Byrns/Stone
Economics

Carlton/Perloff
Modern Industrial Organization

Caves/Frankel/Jones
World Trade and Payments: An Introduction

Chapman
Environmental Economics: Theory, Application, and Policy

Cooter/Ulen
Law and Economics

Downs
An Economic Theory of Democracy

Ehrenberg/Smith
Modern Labor Economics

Ekelund/Ressler/Tollison
*Economics**

Fusfeld
The Age of the Economist

Gerber
International Economics

Ghiara
Learning Economics

Gordon
Macroeconomics

Gregory
Essentials of Economics

Gregory/Stuart
Russian and Soviet Economic Performance and Structure

Hartwick/Olewiler
The Economics of Natural Resource Use

Hoffman/Averett
Women and the Economy: Family, Work, and Pay

Holt
Markets, Games and Strategic Behavior

Hubbard
Money, the Financial System, and the Economy

Hughes/Cain
American Economic History

Husted/Melvin
International Economics

Jehle/Reny
Advanced Microeconomic Theory

Johnson-Lans
A Health Economics Primer

Klein
Mathematical Methods for Economics

Krugman/Obstfeld
*International Economics**

Laidler
The Demand for Money

Leeds/von Allmen
The Economics of Sports

Leeds/von Allmen/Schiming
*Economics**

Lipsey/Ragan/Storer
*Economics**

Melvin
International Money and Finance

Miller
*Economics Today**

Miller
Understanding Modern Economics

Miller/Benjamin
The Economics of Macro Issues

Miller/Benjamin/North
The Economics of Public Issues

Mills/Hamilton
Urban Economics

Mishkin
*The Economics of Money, Banking, and Financial Markets**

Mishkin
*The Economics of Money, Banking, and Financial Markets, Alternate Edition**

Murray
Econometrics: A Modern Introduction

Parkin
*Economics**

Perloff
*Microeconomics**

Perloff
Microeconomics: Theory and Application with Calculus

Perman/Common/McGilvray/Ma
Natural Resources and Environmental Economics

Phelps
Health Economics

Riddell/Shackelford/Stamos/ Schneider
Economics: A Tool for Critically Understanding Society

Ritter/Silber/Udell
Principles of Money, Banking, and Financial Markets

Rohlf
Introduction to Economic Reasoning

Ruffin/Gregory
Principles of Economics

Sargent
Rational Expectations and Inflation

Scherer
Industry Structure, Strategy, and Public Policy

Sherman
Market Regulation

Stock/Watson
Introduction to Econometrics

Stock/Watson
Introduction to Econometrics, Brief Edition

Studenmund
Using Econometrics

Tietenberg
Environmental and Natural Resource Economics

Tietenberg
Environmental Economics and Policy

Todaro/Smith
Economic Development

Waldman
Microeconomics

Waldman/Jensen
Industrial Organization: Theory and Practice

Weil
Economic Growth

Williamson
Macroeconomics

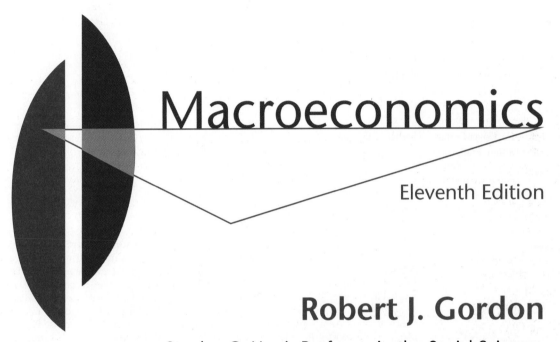

Macroeconomics

Eleventh Edition

Robert J. Gordon

Stanley G. Harris Professor in the Social Sciences
Northwestern University

PEARSON

Addison
Wesley

Boston   San Francisco   New York
London   Toronto   Sydney   Tokyo   Singapore   Madrid
Mexico City   Munich   Paris   Cape Town   Hong Kong   Montreal

Editor-in-Chief:	Denise Clinton
Sponsoring Editor:	Noel Kamm
Assistant Editor:	Courtney E. Schinke
Managing Editor:	Nancy Fenton
Photo Researcher:	Beth Anderson
Supplements Coordinator:	Heather McNally
Media Producer:	Melissa Honig
Senior Marketing Manager:	Roxanne McCarley
Marketing Assistant:	Ashlee Clevenger
Rights and Permissions Advisor:	Dana Weightman
Senior Manufacturing Buyer:	Carol Melville
Cover Design:	Barbara Atkinson
Text Design, Production Coordination, Composition, and Illustrations:	Elm Street Publishing Services

Cover image: Veer, Inc.

Photo credits: page **v** photo of Robert J. Gordon by Julie P. Gordon; Chapter 3, page **76** left: © Tim Sloan/AFP/Getty Images; page **76** right: © Kevin Fleming/Corbis; Chapter 7, page **216**: © Bettmann/Corbis; Chapter 9, page **289**: © AP/Wide World Photos; page **291**: © The Kobal Collection; Chapter 10, page **327**: © AP/Wide World Photos; Chapter 11, page **366**: © AP/Wide World Photos; page **367**: © AP/Wide World Photos; page **369**: © Michael S. Lewis/Corbis; Chapter 12, page **403**: Courtesy Robert J. Barro, Harvard University; Chapter 13, page **433**: Yale University Office of Public Affairs; page **438**: Digital Vision; Chapter 14, page **454**: PhotoDisc Blue; page **478**: Medio Images/Getty Royalty Free; Chapter 15, page **497**: © Owen Franken/Corbis; page **503**: PhotoDisc; Chapter 16, page **532**: © Jerry Laizure/Getty Images; page **538**: © Bettmann/Corbis; Chapter 17, page **554**: © Roger Ressmeyer/Corbis; page **555**: Photograph by Fournier; page **557**: © Ralf-Finn Hestoft/Corbis; Chapter 18, page **600**: © Reuters/Corbis.

ISBN   978-0-321-55207-5

1 2 3 4 5 6 7 8 9 10—CRK—12 11 10 09 08

About the Author

Robert J. Gordon

Robert J. Gordon is Stanley G. Harris Professor in the Social Sciences and Professor of Economics at Northwestern University. He did his undergraduate work at Harvard and then attended Oxford University in England on a Marshall Scholarship. He received his Ph.D. in 1967 at M.I.T. and taught at Harvard and the University of Chicago before coming to Northwestern in 1973, where he has taught for 35 years and was chair of the Department of Economics from 1992 to 1996.

Professor Gordon is one of the world's leading experts on inflation, unemployment, and productivity growth. His recent work on the rise and fall of the New Economy, the U.S. productivity growth revival, and the recent stalling of European productivity growth has been widely cited. He is the author of *The Measurement of Durable Goods Prices*, which has become known as the definitive work showing that government price indexes substantially overstate the rate of inflation. His book of collected essays, *Productivity Growth, Inflation, and Unemployment*, was published in 2004. He is editor of *Milton Friedman's Monetary Framework: A Debate with His Critics*, *The American Business Cycle*, and *The Economics of New Goods*. In addition he is the author of more than 100 scholarly articles and more than 60 published comments on the research of others. In addition to his main field of macroeconomics, he is also a frequently quoted expert and author on the airline industry, and is the founder and president of an Internet chat group on airline management.

Gordon is a Research Associate of the National Bureau of Economic Research, a Research Fellow of the Centre for Economic Policy Research (London), a Research Fellow of OFCE in Paris, a Guggenheim Fellow, a Fellow of the American Academy of Arts and Sciences, and a Fellow of the Econometric Society. He has served as the coeditor of the *Journal of Political Economy* and as an elected at-large member of the Executive Committee of the American Economic Association. He serves currently as senior advisor to the Brookings Panel on Economic Activity and on the economic advisory panels of the Congressional Budget Office and the Bureau of Economic Analysis. He has served as a member of the Technical Panel on Assumptions and Methods of the Social Security Administration, and on the national "Boskin Commission" to assess the accuracy of the U.S. Consumer Price Index.

Gordon lives in Evanston, Illinois, with his wife, Julie, and their two dogs, Lucky and Toto (see the box on p. 291 for more about Toto).

with love, for Julie

Brief Contents

Contents

Preface: To the Instructor

Every time we teach macroeconomics, the business and political climate changes from what it was in last year's class and from the last textbook edition. Since the previous edition there has been a sharp change in the macroeconomic landscape. Soon after the economy began a solid recovery from the stock market and dot.com bubble and bust of 1997–2002, it experienced a second bubble and bust, this time in the housing market. A new theme in this edition is the sources and consequences of the housing bubble and the possible role of the Federal Reserve in creating it. As the economy appeared headed toward a recession in 2008, Congress and the administration reacted quickly to provide a fiscal stimulus, returning short-term fiscal policy actions to the front burner of stabilization policy debates.

Several new events of the past few years reinforce the relevance of this book's emphasis on supply shocks as a cause of inflation and stagflation, including a sharp jump in oil prices, the depreciation of the dollar, and slowing productivity growth. Longer-term issues at the top of the macroeconomic agenda are the future of the Social Security and Medicare systems and the rapid growth of the large emerging market economies sometimes called the "BRICs" (standing for Brazil, Russia, India, and China).

This book stems from the belief that all macroeconomic questions relate to a core set of basic macro puzzles, and that those puzzles have solutions. This text guides students to the most direct solution of each puzzle and implements that approach by introducing a few basic models. These models are then applied immediately in Case Study sections and International Perspective boxes.

I have found it most effective to begin the course with business cycles and inflation because my students relate to what is happening today, and what will happen in the near future. Later in the course, we turn to a unified discussion of growth theory, the failure of many poor nations to achieve economic growth, and take a closer look at policy and the sources of economic instability.

Economics has become increasingly empirical, and it is critical that students learn to interpret data and use it to evaluate macroeconomic questions. This text uses two strategies to reinforce the connection between theory and data. First, the text includes a unique set of data that provide capsule illustrations of how recent research explains, or challenges, the macro puzzles. The data set goes far beyond what is available on government data Web sites, was developed exclusively for this text, and is available online for use in your course. Second, color is used strategically to reinforce macroeconomic theory by linking theoretical models to the corresponding real-world data.

Guiding Principles of the Text

This text has been guided by five organizing principles since its inception, and the Eleventh Edition develops them further.

1. **Macro questions have answers.** The use of traditional macro models can be enormously fruitful in developing answers to macro puzzles. Unlike other texts, this book introduces the natural level of output and natural rate of unemployment in the first few pages of Chapter 1. Students learn from the beginning that the output and unemployment gaps move in opposite directions, and that to understand why output is so low is the same as understanding why unemployment is so high. Similarly, the fully developed dynamic inflation model of Chapter 8 shows that we have a solid answer to the puzzle of why inflation was so high in the 1970s and so low in the 1990s.

   When an economic model fails, this is not swept under the rug, but rather is used to highlight what the model misses, as in the lively treatment in Chapter 10 of "Puzzles That Solow's [Growth] Theory Cannot Explain" (see pp. 333–39). The Solow failure opens the way to a unique treatment of the debate between the new institutional economics, and the exponents of a tropical geography explanation of the failure of poor countries to converge to the income level of rich countries (pp. 360–71). This is a departure from other intermediate macro texts, which barely mention the theory's failures or the modern research that takes us beyond these failures.

2. **Up-front treatment of business cycles and inflation.** Students come to the macro classroom caring most about today's issues, starting with how they and their family members can avoid unemployment. Responding to this basic curiosity of students, a core principle of this book is that students should be taught about business cycles first, instead of beginning the text with the dry abstractions of classical economics and growth theory. This allows us to begin with topical issues that interest students, such as the role of monetary policy in creating the housing bubble of 2004–06 and the housing meltdown of 2006–08, the renewed interest in short-term fiscal stabilization policy evident in 2008, and the symbiotic relationship between Chinese exports to the United States funded in part by Chinese accumulation of U.S. dollars.

   Accordingly, this text introduces the *IS-LM* model immediately after the first two introductory chapters, with a goal in each edition of having the *IS* and *LM* curves cross by p. 100 (it happens on p. 103 of this edition). An integrated treatment covers monetary and fiscal policy stabilization, fiscal and foreign deficits and national saving, and the interplay between the balance of payments and exchange rates. The *AS-AD* model then allows an in-depth treatment of the Great Depression, and a dynamic version of the *AS-AD* model directly implies the Phillips Curve and the sources of high and low inflation. By the end of Chapter 9, students have learned the core theory of business cycles and inflation, and the text then turns to growth theory, the puzzles that Solow's theory cannot explain, and the big issues of economic growth and the non-convergence of so many poor countries.

3. **Integration of models.** The challenge many instructors face is that most intermediate macro texts overload the simple models, offering a new model every chapter or two without telling students how the models connect and work together. This book adopts the core distinction between short-run macro devoted to explaining business cycles and their prevention, and long-run macro dedicated to explaining economic growth and the long-run consequences of debt and deficits.

   This text is unique in its focused, cohesive presentation of the macro concepts. The aggregate demand curve is explicitly derived from the *IS-LM* model (pp. 198–202), and then the short-run Phillips Curve is explicitly derived from the short-run aggregate supply curve (pp. 236–39). In discussing the biggest question of economic growth—why so many nations are still so poor—the text provides an integration of the production function in the Solow growth theory with the added elements of human capital, political capital (i.e., legal systems and property rights), geography, and infrastructure (pp. 360–71).

4. **Simple graphs can convey important research results.** The graphs in this book go beyond those in the typical macro textbook in several dimensions, including the use of original data, the double-stacking of graphs plotting related concepts (see pp. 235 and 253), the extensive use of shading between lines to convey concepts like a positive and negative output gap, and the integrated use of color. A unique feature of this text is its use of graphs on the natural level of real GDP and the natural rate of unemployment to illustrate the key concepts like the output and unemployment gaps (pp. 5–14), the Okun's Law relation linking the gaps (pp. 264–68), the structural budget deficit (pp. 134–39), the role of supply shocks and demand shocks in causing the diametrically opposite behavior of inflation in the 1970s and 1990s (pp. 252–61), and why the natural rate of unemployment declined in the 1990s (p. 311).

Research results and data transformations are also used to illustrate changes in monetary policy lags and efficacy over time (pp. 457–62), apparent changes in the Fed's weights applied to inflation and output in the context of the Taylor Rule (pp. 469–71), the contradiction between the official measure of the U.S. saving rate and the vast increase in the wealth of U.S. households (pp. 510–15), and the role of computer price changes in amplifying the high-tech boom and bust of the late 1990s (pp. 540–44).

5. **The economy is open from the start.** Students come to their macroeconomics classroom concerned about the open economy. They carry iPods made in China, and they worry about whether their future jobs will be out-sourced to India and whether a further slump in the dollar will make future trips to Europe unaffordable. This text avoids the false distinction between the closed and open economy. As early as pp. 34–35, the linkage between saving, investment, government budget, and foreign lending or borrowing is emphasized by the label "magic equation" to dramatize the importance of a basic accounting identity. In the *IS-LM* model of aggregate demand, net exports can be a source of instability (pp. 72–73). Fiscal deficits can be financed by foreign borrowing, but international crowding out and growing international indebtedness reduce the future standard of living (pp. 139–44).

The emphasis on international macro is reinforced by International Perspective boxes, which explore policy paralysis in Japan in the past decade, the motivation for massive dollar accumulation by Asian central banks, why the Great Depression was more severe in the U.S. than in Europe, how the euro eliminates monetary policy autonomy and constrains fiscal policy for individual European nations, and numerous other topical international comparisons.

A Tour of the Highlights

Introduction and Measurement

There are three strong points of the introductory Chapter 1. First is the unifying kick-off with the three major concepts of macro, followed second by the early introduction of the concept of natural real GDP and the natural rate of unemployment linked to data on the past century. Third, the section "Macroeconomics at the Extremes" illustrates the Great Depression, the German hyperinflation, and the growth explosion of Korea compared to the Philippines. Chapter 2 on measurement includes several flow diagrams with consistent use of color, a Case Study on the conflict between the payroll and household measures of employment, and a useful topic box (p. 41) that shows how to calculate the annual growth rate of *anything* over any period, ranging from one day to five centuries.

The *IS-LM* Model and the Open Economy

Chapters 3 and 4 introduce the Keynesian expenditure model and the *IS-LM* model. The usefulness of the *IS-LM* model is motivated by a box on the role of consumer confidence and household wealth (p. 80) and on policy paralysis in the long slump in Japan (pp. 118–19). Chapters 5 and 6 discuss fiscal debt and deficits, national saving, and the links between international deficits, national saving, and the exchange rate. A centerpiece of Chapter 6 is the unifying idea of the "trilemma."

Inflation and Unemployment

The next section covers flexible prices and the determinants of inflation. Chapter 7 derives the *AD* curve from the *IS-LM* model and motivates the short-run and long-run *AS* curves. The *AD-AS* model is then applied to controversies surrounding the Great Depression, including a box on why the U.S. suffered a much deeper slump than Europe or Japan. Chapter 8 begins with an explicit derivation of the short-run Phillips Curve (*SP*) from the *AD-AS* model, and then builds a dynamic inflation model to illustrate the effects of demand and supply shocks, supported by case studies and examples. A core strength of the text since its inception has been the explicit *SP-DG* model of inflation, which is capable of explaining all the ups and downs of postwar inflation. This is presented using graphs in the body of Chapter 8 and as an explicit algebraic model in the Appendix to Chapter 8. The costs of inflation and unemployment in Chapter 9 conclude this section.

The Long Run

Chapter 10 on growth theory goes beyond traditional expositions by emphasizing the "puzzles that Solow's theory cannot explain," leading the way in Chapter 11 to explore more modern explanations of the failure of many poor nations to converge to the living standards of rich nations. This chapter also includes unique material on the modern debate about political institutions versus geography as a source of slow growth of the poorest nations. The section on long-run issues concludes with a treatment of the public debt, theories of fiscal policy, and the debate about Social Security.

Stability and Instability in an Open Economy

Stabilization policy is the focus of Chapters 13 and 14, including basic material on money supply and theories of money demand, and an updated discussion of monetary policy discretion, rules, and the recent debate about inflation targeting vs. Taylor Rules that targets both inflation and the output gap. The sources of *IS*-curve instability are then examined in Chapter 15 on consumption and Chapter 16 on investment. A novel feature of the consumption chapter is its focus on the contrast between the low U.S. saving rate and rising household wealth. The investment chapter examines the role of instability in high-tech investment as a cause of the boom of the 1990s and slump after 2000, and it also includes a new box on the behavior of investment during the Great Depression and World War II.

Debates at the Macro Frontier

The book concludes with a two-chapter part on where we stand today. Chapter 17 on doctrinal disputes begins with the Friedman-Phelps-Lucas model of "fooling" or incorrect expectations and the real business cycle model. These are criticized and contrasted with various new Keynesian models based on menu costs, efficiency wages, and other ideas. Chapter 18 explores "the effect of events on ideas," tracing the economy's evolution since 1923 and the effects of major events like the Great Depression, postwar inflation, and the twin peaks of inflation and unemployment on the rise and fall of alternative theories. The book concludes with a summary of what we know and the remaining puzzles.

New to the Eleventh Edition

The Eleventh Edition reflects today's macroeconomic debates and controversies. It features organizational and pedagogical improvements, the latest data, and a myriad of new case studies and boxes.

Organizational and Substantive Changes

My goal in this revision has been to tighten and clarify the exposition of each theory and to motivate the discussion by providing more examples. While the chapter order remains the same, substantial revisions have been made throughout.

As before, the book begins with an introduction in Chapter 1 and measurement issues in Chapter 2. The details of how chain-weighted real GDP and the GDP deflator are calculated have been moved into a new Appendix to Chapter 2. The income-expenditure and *IS-LM* models are developed as before in Chapters 3 and 4, but the discussion of the balance of payments, the current account, and international indebtedness has been moved from Chapter 6 to Chapter 5, in order to provide a more unified treatment of the "twin deficits."

New to this edition is the recognition that net international indebtedness responds not only to the current account deficit but also to revaluations of assets held abroad (see pp. 150–52). The text highlights the fact that the U.S. net international indebtedness position did not become larger during 2001–06 even though the cumulative current account deficit during those years was 30 percent of GDP. It also poses the puzzle of "Why Is U.S. Income from Abroad Still Positive?" (p. 152).

The greater stability of the U.S. economy after 1984 is highlighted by new sections on the "Great Moderation" at the beginning of the income determination chapter (pp. 58–59) and as a main focus of the monetary policy chapter (pp. 462–67). The treatment of the interaction between monetary and fiscal policy, including monetary accommodation and the monetary-fiscal policy mix, is improved with an explicit treatment of government investment in infrastructure and the example of the 2007 Minneapolis bridge collapse (p. 117).

Housing is also a unifying theme throughout this revision. Chapter 4 examines how easy money created the boom and bust in housing; a new linkage strengthens the connection between capital market instruments and the

2007–08 mortgage market crisis (pp. 421–22); Chapter 14 includes the housing collapse in its discussion of Fed policy; and Chapter 15 analyzes the wealth explosion, capital gains, and low interest rates.

New examples offer additional motivation, such as the new sections on "Intermediate Goods, Final Goods, and Value Added" and "GNP Versus GDP" (pp. 29–30); "Why We Care About Real GDP and the GDP Deflator" (p. 39); and a presentation of policy impacts in the small and large open economy that deletes the previous use of *IS* and *LM* curves (pp. 185–88).

Pedagogy is improved with several new set-off lists, such as "Other Factors That Shift the Demand for Money Schedule" (p. 97), and the new summary box "Types of Supply Shocks and When They Mattered" (p. 254). The Eleventh Edition also includes a clearer step-by-step presentation of the components of the current account (p. 147) and simplified presentations of the negative interest responsiveness of autonomous spending (pp. 78–80) as well as the Solow growth theory (pp. 326–27) and the burden of the fiscal debt (pp. 392–93).

New Case Studies, Boxes, and Applications

The following four elements reinforce the connection between theory and real-world application.

- *Case Studies* apply the theory immediately after it is introduced. For instance, a new Case Study in this edition is "Why Did Inflation Creep Up After 2003?" (pp. 259–61).

- *International Perspective boxes* compare economic performance in the United States with selected foreign nations. New boxes include a comparison of European versus U.S. unemployment and productivity growth (pp. 20–21), "A Symptom of Poverty: Urban Slums in the Poor Cities" (p. 363), and "Institutions Matter: South Korea Versus North Korea" (pp. 366–67).

- *Topic boxes* provide illustrations that are not explicitly international. New boxes include "Shifts in Consumer Confidence and Household Wealth as Sources of Demand Shocks" (pp. 80–81), "How Easy Money Created a Boom and Bust in Housing" (pp. 104–05), "Plastic Replaces Cash, and the Cell Phone Replaces Plastic" (pp. 438–39), "How the Fed Reinvented Instability in Residential Construction" (pp. 478–79), and "Investment in the Great Depression and World War II" (pp. 538–39). "Where to Find the Numbers: A Guide to the Data" (p. 28) includes an updated and expanded list of the key Web sites providing economic data.

- *Data graphs* include many data series created especially for this book and are fully updated through 2007. These data series include the natural unemployment rate, natural output, the output and unemployment gaps, and the productivity growth trend (p. 372). Several unique graphs are based on the author's research, including the lags of monetary policy (p. 459) and alternative weighting schemes for Taylor's Rule (pp. 469–71).

Pedagogy

The Use of Color

This book has always been unique in its use of double-framed data graphs to show related concepts like inflation and the output ratio, or inflation and oil prices. The graphs in the Eleventh Edition continue to use consistent colors to connect macro concepts and discussions, thereby strengthening conceptual ties throughout the text.

The supply curve of money, the *LM* curve, and plots of short-term interest rates are always shown in green. Government expenditures are red and revenues are green, a government surplus is shown by green shading and a deficit by red shading. The government debt and long-term interest rates appear in purple. Data on inflation and the *AD* curve are plotted in orange. The *SAS* and *SP* curves are plotted in blue. Long-run "natural" concepts like natural real GDP, the natural rate of unemployment, the *LAS* curve, and the *LP* curve are all plotted in black.

Color is also used consistently for country-specific data. The U.S. is always red, the U.K. (or EU) is blue, Canada is gray, Japan is orange, Germany is black, France is purple, and Italy is green.

Continuing Pedagogical Features

The Eleventh Edition retains the main pedagogical features of the previous editions that aid student understanding.

- *Key terms* are introduced in bold type, defined in the margin, and listed at the end of each chapter.
- *Self-Test questions* appear at intervals within each chapter, so that students can immediately determine whether they understand what they have read. Answers are provided at the end of every chapter.
- *Learning About Diagrams boxes.* Each of these boxes covers on a single page every aspect of the key schedules—*IS, LM, AS, AD,* and *SP*—and discusses why they slope as they do, what makes them rotate and shift, and what is true on and off the curves.
- *End-of-chapter elements* include a summary, a list of key terms, a revised and expanded set of questions and problems, and answers to the self-test questions.
- The *Glossary* at the end of the book lists definitions to every key term, with a cross-reference to the sections where they are first introduced.
- *Data Appendixes* provide annual data for the U.S. back to 1875, quarterly data for the U.S. back to 1947, and annual data since 1960 for other leading nations. This data can now be downloaded from the book's Companion Web site for use in your course. Appendix C lists data sources and Web sites that offer the latest data on key macroeconomic variables.
- *Data diagrams* have been replotted electronically to ensure accuracy, and include annual and quarterly data to the end of 2007.

Supplements

With each edition, the supplements get more robust with the aim of helping you to prepare your lectures and your students to master the material.

- *Online Instructor's Manual.* Subarna Samanta of the College of New Jersey revised the manual for this edition, providing chapter outlines, chapter overviews, a discussion of how the Eleventh Edition differs from the Tenth Edition, and answers to the end-of-chapter questions and problems. The manual is available for download as PDF or Word files on the Instructor's

Resource Center (www.pearsonhighered.com/irc) and on the Instructor's Resource CD-ROM.

- *Online Test Bank.* Completely revised by Andrew Foshee of McNeese State University and Mihajlo Balic of Palm Beach Community College, the Online Test Bank offers more than 2,000 questions specific to the book. It is available in both PDF and Word format on the Instructor's Resource Center and on the Instructor's Resource CD-ROM.

- *Online Computerized Test Bank.* The Computerized Test Bank reproduces the Test Bank material in the TestGen software that is available for Windows and Macintosh. With TestGen, instructors can easily edit existing questions, add questions, generate tests, and print the tests in a variety of formats. It is available in both Mac and PC formats, on the Instructor's Resource Center and on the Instructor's Resource CD-ROM.

- *Online PowerPoint with Art, Figures, and Lecture Notes.* PowerPoint presentations, revised by Richard Stahnke of Bryn Mawr College, contain the figures and tables in the text, as well as new lecture notes that correspond with the information in each chapter. The PowerPoint presentations are available on the Instructor's Resource Center and on the Instructor's Resource CD-ROM.

- *Instructor's Resource CD-ROM.* The Instructor's Resource CD-ROM offers instructors electronic supplements conveniently packaged on a CD-ROM. It includes the PowerPoint presentations, Instructor's Manual, Test Bank, and Computerized Test Bank with TestGen software for simple test preparation.

- *Study Guide.* Prepared by Andrew Foshee and Mihajlo Balic, this manual breaks each chapter into a series of key questions, with each question covering a specific topic. Students test their understanding by answering short-answer, numerical, and short essay questions, as well as problems that ask students to draw graphs and use current data. All solutions to Study Guide questions are provided as well.

- *Companion Web Site.* The open-access Web site (www.aw-bc.com/gordon) offers the following resources:
  - Online glossary review and links to related sites for macroeconomic data and research.
  - Online quizzes to practice the major concepts of every chapter that have been revised for this edition by Andrew Foshee and Mihajlo Balic.
  - *eThemes of the Times,* which are *New York Times* articles with discussion questions, completely revised by Mihajlo Balic.
  - The Data Appendixes from the text are available for download, as is the robust data set created explicitly for the text that includes the historical data and natural level of output.
  - New! Excel®-based problems, written by David Ring of SUNY College at Oneonta, offer students one to two questions per chapter using the Excel program and data. Solutions to all Excel-based problems are available on the Instructor's Resource Center.

Acknowledgments

I remain grateful to all those who have given thoughtful comments on this book over the years. In recent years, these colleagues include:

Terence J. Alexander, *Iowa State University*
Jeffrey H. Bergstrand, *University of Notre Dame*

William Branch, *University of California, Irvine*
John P. Burkett, *University of Rhode Island*
Henry Chen, *University of West Florida*
Andrew Foshee, *McNeese State University*
Donald E. Frey, *Wake Forest University*
John Graham, *Rutgers University*
Luc Hens, *Vesalius College, Vrije Universiteit Brussel*
Tracy Hofer, *University of Wisconsin, Stevens Point*
Brad R. Humphreys, *University of Illinois, Urbana-Champaign*
Alan G. Isaac, *American University*
Thomas Kelly, *Baylor University*
Barry Kotlove, *Edmonds Community College*
Ilir Miteza, *University of Michigan, Dearborn*
Gary Mongiovi, *St. John's University*
Jan Ondrich, *Syracuse University*
Chris Papageorgiou, *International Monetary Fund*
Walter Park, *American University*
Michael Reed, *University of Kentucky*
Kevin Reffett, *WP Cary School of Business, ASU*
Charles F. Revier, *Colorado State University*
David Ring, *State University of New York, Oneonta*
Wayne Saint Aubyn Henry, *University of the West Indies*
Subarna K. Samanta, *The College of New Jersey*
Richard Stahnke, *Bryn Mawr College*
Manly E. Staley, *San Francisco State University*
Mark Thoma, *University of Oregon*
David Tufte, *Southern Utah University*
Kristin Van Gaasbeck, *California State University, Sacramento*

An expanded set of questions and problems was provided by David Ring of SUNY at Oneonta. In addition, the book contains a great deal of data, some of it originally created for this book, both in the text and the Data Appendix. Neil Sarkar created all the data, tables, and graphs, as well as the Data Appendix.

Many thanks go to the staff at Addison-Wesley. I am extremely grateful to Denise Clinton for suggesting and then implementing the development of the Eleventh Edition. A delight in my long experience in writing this textbook has been the upbeat attitude, talent, and wisdom of Noel Kamm, the sponsoring editor who has managed this project from the initial discussion of themes for the Eleventh Edition, through the reviews and then the back-and-forth of nagging and tolerance for the author's endless delays, from the first delivery of manuscript in summer 2007 to the last word of the preface, which arrived in late January 2008. Courtney Schinke handled her role as assistant editor with enthusiasm and accuracy. The final stages of handling proof and other pre-publication details were managed efficiently, with new heights of tact and courtesy, by Nancy Fenton of Addison-Wesley and Karin Kipp of Elm Street Publishing Services.

Finally, thanks go to my wife, Julie, for putting up with the overwhelming litter of manuscript and proofs that often spilled out of my home office onto kitchen counters and the kitchen table. As always, her unfailing encouragement and welcome diversions made the book possible.

Robert J. Gordon
Evanston, IL
February 2008

Preface: To the Student

Macroeconomics is one of the most important topics for you as a college student because the health of the economy will have an influence on your whole life. The overall level of employment and unemployment will determine the ease with which you find a job after college and with which you will be able to change jobs or obtain promotions in the future. The inflation rate will influence the interest rate that you receive on your savings and that you pay when you borrow money, and also the extent to which the purchasing power of your savings will be eroded by higher prices.

This macroeconomics text will equip you with the principles you need to make sense out of the conflicting and contradictory discussions of economic conditions and policies in newspapers and news magazines. You will be better able to appraise the performance of the President and Congress, and to predict the impact of their policy actions on your family and business.

You will also be able to understand why people your age in many other countries are so poor, and why some poor countries succeed in the transition to being like the rich countries, while many others fail.

Who Should Read This Book?

Most college students taking this course will have taken a course in economic principles. But this book has been written to be read by *all* students, even those who have not previously enrolled in an economics course. How is this possible? In Chapters 1–3 we review material covered in every principles course. By the end of Chapter 3, all students will have learned the concepts essential to understanding the new material to be developed.

This book has been carefully designed to look and read like a principles text. The entire presentation is graphic, with simple algebra used only in the review of elementary ideas. Examples are used frequently. Most chapters have at least one Case Study that gives you a breather from the analysis and shows how the ideas of the chapter can be applied to real-world episodes. "International Perspective" boxes show you how U.S. economic performance compares with that in other nations, such as Germany and Japan. To help with vocabulary problems, new words are set off in boldface type and defined both in the margins and in the Glossary in the back of the book. Many end-of-chapter questions provide numerical examples for you to solve in order to cement your understanding of the theory. Finally, end-of-chapter appendixes for Chapters 2, 3, 4, 8, and 10 provide optional algebraic treatments of the theory, available for assignment by instructors or for those students who want to do independent work that will deepen their command of the material.

A unique feature of this textbook is the set of Self-Test questions. These questions, which appear three or four times in each chapter, test your understanding of the main point of the preceding section. Write down your answers on a sheet of paper and compare them with those provided at the end of each chapter. You will quickly see whether you have understood what you have been reading, or whether you need to review the material.

How to Read This Book

Each chapter begins with an introduction linking it to previous chapters and ends with a summary. When you begin a chapter, first read the introduction to make sure you understand how the chapter differs from the previous ones. Then plan to read each chapter twice. On the first reading, use the Self-Test questions and answers to check whether you understand what you have been reading. Then, after completing your first reading of the chapter, study the Summary and try to answer the end-of-chapter questions and problems, marking those points you do not understand. Finally, go back for a second reading, paying attention to the discussion of issues you may not have grasped fully at first.

Always try to write out answers to the questions and problems. Those who have purchased the accompanying *Study Guide* find that the path to greater comprehension has been laid out for you in detail.

If you should get lost in the course of reading the text, remember that there are built-in study aids to help, in addition to the Self-Test questions. If you don't understand a particular section, turn to the Summary at the end of the chapter. If you forget the meaning of a word, turn to the Glossary. (The Glossary will also help you tackle any outside readings assigned by your instructor.) A Guide to Symbols on the back inside covers of the book will help you with the alphabetical symbols that are used in equations or in diagrams as labels.

Optional Material

Footnotes and chapter appendixes have been provided as a place to put more difficult or less important material. Your instructor will decide whether an appendix is to be assigned, but even if not assigned, tackle it on your own when you have mastered the ideas in the chapter. Footnotes contain qualifications, bibliographical references (valuable if you ever need to write a term paper on these topics), and cross-references to related material and diagrams in the book.

Notice that tables in the appendix contain historical data starting with 1875 and updated to 2007. These figures can help you determine what was going on in periods not covered by the case studies or can be used in outside assignments and term papers. Don't forget possible applications in history, political science, and sociology courses.

The World Wide Web has made it much easier for you to locate recent data to update the graphs and tables in this book. For information on using the Web to find data, turn to p. 28 and several specific Web sites listed in Appendix C.

Supplements

This text includes two resources to help you prepare for your exams and projects.

- *Study Guide.* Students praise the unique format of this *Study Guide* because it helps them focus on the concepts that are most important. Prepared by Andrew Foshee of McNeese State University and Mihajlo Balic of Palm Beach Community College, this manual breaks each chapter into a series of key questions you need to understand in that chapter. In addition, each chapter includes short-answer, numerical, and short essay questions, and problems that let you draw graphs and use current data.

- *Companion Web Site.* The open-access Web site (www.aw-bc.com/gordon) offers the following resources:
  - Online glossary review and links to related sites for macroeconomic data and research.
  - Online quizzes to practice the major concepts of every chapter that have been revised for this edition by Andrew Foshee and Mihajlo Balic.
  - *eThemes of the Times,* which are *New York Times* articles with discussion questions, completely revised by Mihajlo Balic.
  - The Data Appendixes from the text are available for download, as is the robust data set created explicitly for the text that includes the historical data and natural level of output.
  - New! Excel®-based problems, written by David Ring of SUNY College at Oneonta, offer students one to two questions per chapter using the Excel program and data.

Finally, I would value any feedback from you in the form of comments, suggestions, corrections, and questions at rjg@northwestern.edu.

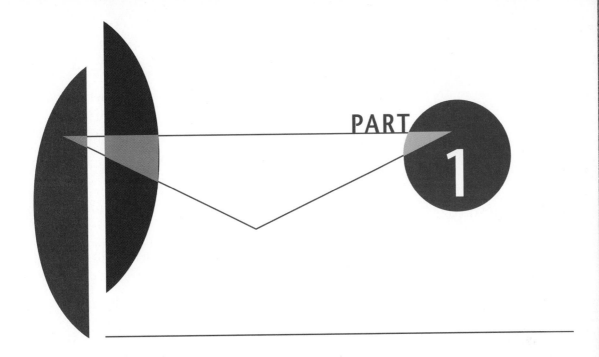

Introduction and Measurement

CHAPTER

1

What Is Macroeconomics?

Business will be better or worse.
—Calvin Coolidge, 1928

1-1 How Macroeconomics Affects Our Everyday Lives

Macroeconomics is concerned with the big economic issues that determine your own economic well-being as well as that of your family and everyone you know. Each of these issues involves the overall economic performance of the nation rather than whether one particular individual earns more or less than another.

The nation's overall macroeconomic performance matters, not only for its own sake but because many individuals experience its consequences. For instance, the economy experienced a recession in the year 2001, and more than two million people lost their jobs. They were among the victims of the downturn in the overall economy. Other victims besides job losers were students who found it difficult to find a summer job or a good job after graduation. Macroeconomic performance can also determine whether inflation will erode the value of family savings, and whether today's students in their future lives will have a higher standard of living than their parents.

> **Macroeconomics** is the study of the major economic totals, or aggregates.

The "Big Three" Concepts of Macroeconomics

Each of these connections between the overall economy and the lives of individuals involves a central macroeconomic concept introduced in this chapter—unemployment, inflation, and economic growth. The basic task of macroeconomics is to study the causes of good or bad performance of these three concepts, why each matters to individuals, and what (if anything) the government can do to improve macroeconomic performance. While there are numerous other less important macroeconomic concepts, we start by focusing just on these, which are the "Big Three" concepts of macroeconomics:

1. The **unemployment rate.** The higher the overall unemployment rate, the harder it is for each individual who wants a job to find work. College seniors who want permanent jobs after graduation are likely to have fewer job offers if the national unemployment rate is high, as in 2001–03, than low, as in 2005–2007. All adults fear a high unemployment rate, which raises the chances that they will be laid off, be unable to pay their bills, have their cars repossessed, lose their health insurance, or even lose their homes through mortgage foreclosures. In "bad times," when the unemployment rate is high, crime, mental illness, and suicide also increase. It is no wonder that many

> The **unemployment rate** is the number of persons unemployed (jobless individuals who are actively looking for work or are on temporary layoff) divided by the total of those employed and unemployed.

people consider unemployment to be the single most important macroeconomic issue. And this is nothing new. Robert Burton, an English clergyman, wrote in 1621 that "employment is so essential to human happiness that indolence is justly considered the mother of misery."

The **inflation rate** is the percentage rate of increase in the economy's average level of prices.

2. **The inflation rate.** A high inflation rate means that prices, on average, are rising rapidly, while a low inflation rate means that prices, on average, are rising slowly. An inflation rate of zero means that prices remain essentially the same, month after month. In inflationary periods, retired people, or those about to retire, lose the most, since their hard-earned savings buy less as prices go up. Even college students may lose as the rising prices of room, board, and textbooks erode what they have saved from previous summer and after-school jobs. While a high inflation rate harms those who have saved, it helps those who have borrowed. Great harm comes from this capricious aspect of inflation, taking from some and giving to others. People want their lives to be predictable, but inflation throws a monkey wrench into individual decision making, creating pervasive uncertainty.

Productivity is the average output produced per hour.

3. **Productivity** growth. "Productivity" is the average output per hour of work that a nation produces in total goods and services; it was about $55 per worker-hour in the United States in 2008. The faster average productivity grows, the easier it is for each member of society to improve his or her standard of living. If productivity were to grow at 3 percent from 2008 to the year 2028, U.S. productivity would rise from $55 per worker-hour to $100 per worker-hour. When multiplied by all the hours worked by all the employees in the country, this extra $45 per worker-hour would make it possible for the nation to have more houses, cars, hospitals, roads, schools, and even to combat greenhouse gas emissions that worsen global warming.

But if the growth rate of productivity were zero instead of 3 percent, U.S. productivity would remain at $55 in the year 2028. To have more houses and cars, we would have to sacrifice by building fewer hospitals and schools. Such an economy, with no productivity growth, has been called the "zero-sum society," because any extra good or service enjoyed by one person requires that something be taken away from someone else. Many have argued that the achievement of rapid productivity growth and the avoidance of a zero-sum society form the most important macroeconomic challenge of all.

The first two of the "Big Three" macroeconomic concepts, the unemployment and inflation rates, appear in the newspaper every day. When economic conditions are poor, daily headlines announce that one large company or another is laying off thousands of workers. In the past, sharp increases in the rate of inflation have also made headlines, as when the price of gasoline jumped during 2006–07. The third major concept, productivity growth, has received widespread attention in the past decade as a source of an improving American standard of living compared to that in Europe and Japan.

Macroeconomic concepts also play a big role in politics. Incumbent political parties benefit when unemployment and inflation are relatively low, as in the landslide victories of Lyndon Johnson in 1964 and Richard Nixon in 1972. Incumbent presidents who fail to gain reelection often are the victims of a sour economy, as in the cases of Herbert Hoover in 1932 and Jimmy Carter in 1980. The recession of 1990–91 and the weak recovery of 1992 helped Bill Clinton defeat George H. W. Bush in the presidential election of 1992. The defeat of Al Gore by George W. Bush in 2000 was an exception since the strong economy of 2000 should have helped Gore's incumbent Democratic party win the presidency. Rapid GDP growth in 2003–04 helped to reelect George W. Bush, restoring the tradition that a strong economy favors the election of the incumbent party.

1-2 Defining Macroeconomics

How Macroeconomics Differs from Microeconomics

Most topics in economics can be placed in one of two categories: macroeconomics or microeconomics. *Macro* comes from a Greek word meaning large; *micro* comes from a Greek word meaning small. Put another way, macroeconomics deals with the totals, or **aggregates,** of the economy, and microeconomics deals with the parts. Among these crucial economic aggregates are the three central concepts introduced in the last section.

> An **aggregate** is the total amount of an economic magnitude for the economy as a whole.

Microeconomics is devoted to the relationships among the different *parts* of the economy. For example, in micro we try to explain the wage or salary of one type of worker in relation to another. For example, why is a professor's salary more than that of a secretary but less than that of an investment banker? In contrast, macroeconomics asks why the total income of all citizens rises strongly in some periods but declines in others.

Economic Theory: A Process of Simplification

Economic theory helps us understand the economy by *simplifying complexity*. Theory throws a spotlight on just a few key relations. Macroeconomic theory examines the behavior of aggregates such as the unemployment rate and the inflation rate while ignoring differences among individual households. It reaches striking conclusions by pretending that there is just one interest rate, instead of the many rates reported in daily newspapers.

It is this process of simplification that makes the study of economics so exciting. By learning a few basic macroeconomic relations, you can quickly learn how to sift out the hundreds of irrelevant details in the news in order to focus on the few key items that foretell where the economy is going. You also can begin to understand which national and personal economic goals can be attained and which are "pie in the sky." You can learn when it is fair to credit a president for strong economic performance or blame a president for poor performance.

1-3 Actual and Natural Real GDP

We have learned that the "Big Three" macroeconomic concepts are the unemployment rate, the inflation rate, and the rate of productivity growth. Linked to each of these is the total level of output produced in the economy. The higher the level of output, the lower the unemployment rate. The higher the level of output, the faster tends to be the rate of inflation. Finally, for any given number of hours worked, a higher level of output automatically boosts output per hour, that is, productivity.

The official measure of the economy's total output is called **gross domestic product** and is abbreviated GDP. As you will learn in Chapter 2, real GDP

> *Nominal*
> **Gross domestic product** is the value of all currently produced goods and services sold on the market during a particular time interval.

includes all currently produced goods and services sold on the market within a given time period and excludes certain other types of economic activity. As you will also learn, the adjective "real" means that our measure of output reflects the quantity produced corrected for any changes in prices.

Actual real GDP is the value of total output corrected for any changes in prices.

Actual real GDP is the amount an economy actually produces at any given time. But we need some criterion to judge the desirability of that level of actual real GDP. Perhaps actual real GDP is too low, causing high unemployment. Perhaps actual real GDP is too high, putting upward pressure on the inflation rate. Which level of real GDP is desirable, neither too low nor too high? This intermediate compromise level of real GDP is called "natural," a level of real GDP in which there is no tendency for the rate of inflation to rise or fall.

Figure 1-1 illustrates the relationship between actual real GDP, natural real GDP, and the rate of inflation. In the upper frame the red line is actual real GDP. The lower frame shows the inflation rate. The thin dashed vertical lines connect the two frames. The first dashed vertical line marks time period t_0. Notice in the bottom frame that the inflation rate is constant at t_0, neither speeding up nor slowing down.

Figure 1-1 **The Relation Between Actual and Natural Real GDP and the Inflation Rate**

In the upper frame the solid black line shows the steady growth of natural real GDP—the amount the economy can produce at a constant inflation rate. The red line shows the path of actual real GDP. In the blue region in the top frame, actual real GDP is below natural real GDP, so the inflation rate, shown in the bottom frame, slows down. In the region designated by the red area, actual real GDP is above natural real GDP, so in the bottom frame inflation speeds up.

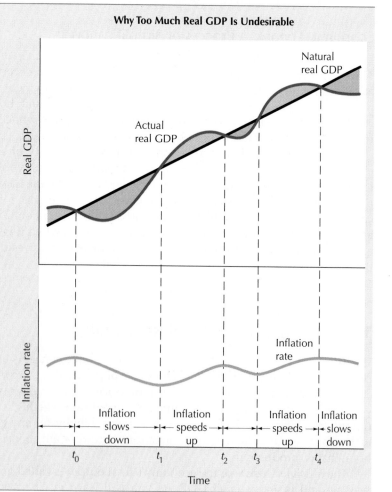

By definition, **natural real GDP** is equal to actual real GDP when the inflation rate is constant. Thus, in the upper frame, at t_0 the red actual real GDP line is crossed by the black natural real GDP line. To the right of t_0, actual real GDP falls below natural real GDP, and we see in the bottom frame that inflation slows down. This continues until time period t_1, when actual real GDP once again is equal to natural real GDP. Here the inflation rate stops falling and is constant for a moment before it begins to rise.

This cycle repeats itself again and again. *Only when actual real GDP is equal to natural real GDP is the inflation rate constant.* For this reason, natural real GDP is a compromise level to be singled out for special attention. During a period of low actual real GDP, designated by the blue area, the inflation rate slows down. During a period of high actual real GDP, designated by the shaded red area, the inflation rate speeds up.

Natural real GDP designates the level of real GDP at which the inflation rate is constant, with no tendency to accelerate or decelerate.

Unemployment: Actual and Natural

When actual real GDP is low, many people lose their jobs, and the unemployment rate is high, as shown in Figure 1-2. The top frame duplicates Figure 1-1

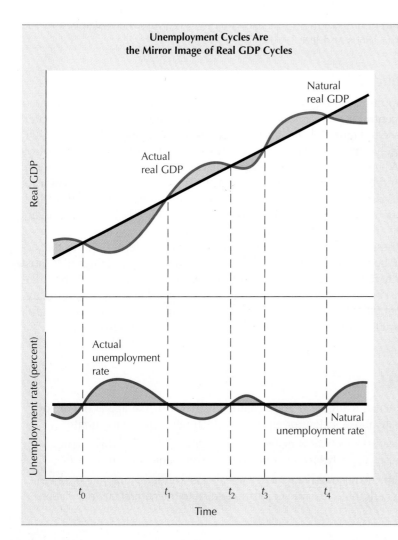

Unemployment Cycles Are the Mirror Image of Real GDP Cycles

Figure 1-2 The Behavior Over Time of Actual and Natural Real GDP and the Actual and Natural Rates of Unemployment

When actual real GDP falls below natural real GDP, designated by the blue shaded areas in the top frame, the actual unemployment rate rises above the natural rate of unemployment as indicated in the bottom frame. The red shaded areas designate the opposite situation. When we compare the blue shaded areas of Figures 1-1 and 1-2, we see that the time intervals when unemployment is high (1–2) also represent time intervals when inflation is slowing down (1–1). Similarly, the red shaded areas represent time intervals when inflation is speeding up and unemployment is low.

exactly, comparing actual real GDP with natural real GDP. The blue line in the bottom frame is the actual percentage unemployment rate, the first of the three central concepts of macroeconomics. The thin vertical dashed lines connecting the upper frame and lower frame show that whenever actual and natural real GDP are equal in the top frame, the actual unemployment rate is equal to the **natural rate of unemployment** in the bottom frame.

The definition of the natural rate of unemployment corresponds exactly to natural real GDP, describing a situation in which there is no tendency for the inflation rate to change. When the actual unemployment rate is high, actual real GDP is low (shown by blue shading in both frames), and the inflation rate slows down. In periods when actual real GDP is high and the economy prospers, the actual unemployment rate is low (shown by red shading in both frames) and the inflation rate speeds up.

Figures 1-1 and 1-2 summarize a basic dilemma faced by government policymakers who are attempting to achieve a low unemployment rate and a low inflation rate at the same time. If the inflation rate is high, lowering it requires a decline in actual real GDP and an increase in the actual unemployment rate. This happened in the early 1980s, when inflation was so high that the government deliberately pushed unemployment to its highest level since the 1930s. If, to the contrary, the policymaker attempts to provide jobs for everyone and keep the actual unemployment rate low then the inflation rate will speed up, as occurred in the 1960s and late 1980s.

> The **natural rate of unemployment** designates the level of unemployment at which the inflation rate is constant, with no tendency to accelerate or decelerate.

$U^* =$ Natural Rate of Unemployment

Real GDP and the Three Macro Concepts

The total amount that the economy produces, actual real GDP, is closely related to the three central macroeconomic concepts introduced earlier in this chapter. First, as we see in Figure 1-2, the *difference* between actual and natural real GDP moves inversely with the *difference* between the actual and natural unemployment rates. When actual real GDP is high, unemployment is low, and vice versa.

The second link is with inflation, since inflation tends to speed up when actual real GDP is higher than natural real GDP (as in Figure 1-1). The third link is with productivity, which is defined as actual real GDP per hour; data on actual real GDP are required to calculate productivity.

Each of these links with the central macroeconomic concepts requires that actual real GDP be compared with *something else* in order to be meaningful. It must be compared to natural real GDP to provide a link with unemployment and inflation, or it must be divided by the number of hours worked to compute productivity. Actual real GDP by itself, without any such comparison, is not meaningful, which is why it is not included on the list of the three major macro concepts.

SELF-TEST

1. When actual real GDP is above natural real GDP, is the actual unemployment rate above, below, or equal to the natural unemployment rate?

2. When actual real GDP is below natural real GDP, is the actual unemployment rate above, below, or equal to the natural unemployment rate?

3. When the actual unemployment rate is equal to the natural rate of unemployment, is the actual rate of inflation equal to the natural rate of inflation?

1-4 Macroeconomics in the Short Run and Long Run

Macroeconomic theories and debates can be divided into two main groups: (1) those that concern the "short-run" stability of the economy, and (2) those that concern its "long-run" growth rate. Much of macroeconomic analysis concerns the first group of topics involving the short run, usually defined as a period lasting from one year to five years, and focuses on the first two major macroeconomic concepts introduced in Section 1-1, the unemployment rate and the inflation rate. We ask why the unemployment rate and the inflation rate over periods of a few years are sometimes high and sometimes low, rather than always low as we would wish. These ups and downs are usually called "economic fluctuations" or **business cycles.** Much of this book concerns the causes of these cycles and the efficacy of alternative government policies to dampen or eliminate the cycles.

The other main topic in macroeconomics concerns the long run, which is a longer period ranging from one decade to several decades. It attempts to explain the rate of productivity growth, the third key concept introduced in Section 1-1, or more generally, **economic growth.** Learning the causes of growth helps us predict whether successive generations of Americans will be better off than their predecessors, and why some countries remain so poor in a world where other countries by contrast are so rich.

2 phases
expansion + contracting

Business cycles consist of expansions occurring at about the same time in many economic activities, followed by similarly general recessions and recoveries that merge into the expansion phase of the next cycle.

Economic growth is the topic area of macroeconomics that studies the causes of sustained growth in real GDP over periods of a decade or more.

The Short Run: Business Cycles

The main short-run concern of macroeconomists is to minimize fluctuations in the unemployment and inflation rates. This requires that fluctuations in real GDP be minimized.

Figure 1-3 contrasts two imaginary economies: "Volatilia" in the left frame and "Stabilia" in the right frame. The black "natural real GDP" lines in both frames are *absolutely identical.* The two economies differ only in the size of their business cycles, shown by the size of their **real GDP gap,** which is simply the difference between actual and natural real GDP shown by blue and red shading.

In the left frame, Volatilia is a macroeconomic hell, with severe business cycles and large gaps between actual and natural real GDP. In the right frame, Stabilia is macroeconomic heaven, with mild business cycles and small gaps between actual and natural real GDP. All macroeconomists prefer the economy depicted by the right-hand frame to that depicted by the left-hand frame. But the debate between macro schools of thought starts in earnest when we ask how to achieve the economy of the right-hand frame. Active do-something policies? Do-nothing, hands-off policies? There are economists who support each of these alternatives, and more besides. But everyone agrees that Stabilia is a more successful economy than Volatilia. To achieve the success of Stabilia, Volatilia must find a way to eliminate its large real GDP gap.

The hallmark of business cycles is their pervasive character, which affects many different types of economic activity at the same time. This means that they occur again and again but not always at regular intervals, nor are they the same length. Business cycles in the past have ranged in length from one to

The **real GDP gap,** sometimes called the *output gap,* is the percentage difference between actual and natural real GDP.

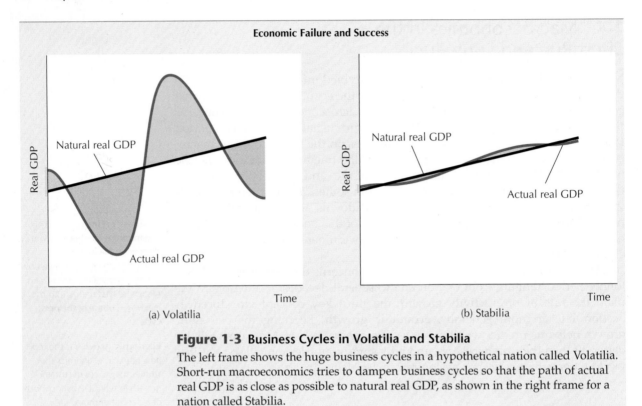

Figure 1-3 Business Cycles in Volatilia and Stabilia
The left frame shows the huge business cycles in a hypothetical nation called Volatilia. Short-run macroeconomics tries to dampen business cycles so that the path of actual real GDP is as close as possible to natural real GDP, as shown in the right frame for a nation called Stabilia.

twelve years.[1] Figure 1-4 illustrates two successive business cycles in real output. Although a simplification, Figure 1-4 contains two realistic elements that have been common to most real-world business cycles. First, the expansions last longer than the recessions. Second, the two business cycles illustrated in the figure differ in length.

The Long Run: Economic Growth

For a society to achieve an increasing standard of living, total output per person must grow, and such economic growth is the long-run concern of macroeconomists. Look at Figure 1-5, which contrasts two economies. Each has mild business cycles, like Stabilia in Figure 1-3. But in Figure 1-5, the left frame presents a country called "Stag-Nation," which experiences very slow growth in real GDP. In contrast, the right-hand frame depicts "Speed-Nation," a country with very fast growth in real GDP. If we assume that population growth in each country is the same, then growth in output per person is faster in Speed-Nation. In Speed-Nation everyone can purchase more consumer goods, and there is plenty of output left to provide better schools, parks, hospitals, and other public services. In

---

[1] A comprehensive source for the chronology of and data on historical business cycles, as well as research papers by distinguished economists, is Robert J. Gordon, ed., *The American Business Cycle: Continuity and Change* (Chicago: University of Chicago Press, 1986). A discussion of the 2001 recession and contrasts with previous recessions can be found at www.nber.org/cycles/main.html.

Figure 1-4 Basic Business-Cycle Concepts

The real output line exhibits a typical succession of business cycles. The highest point reached by real output in each cycle is called the *peak* and the lowest point the *trough*. The *recession* is the period between peak and trough; the *expansion* is the period between the trough and the next peak.

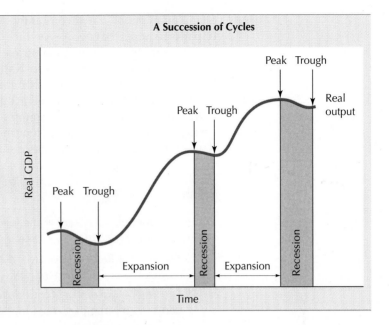

A Succession of Cycles

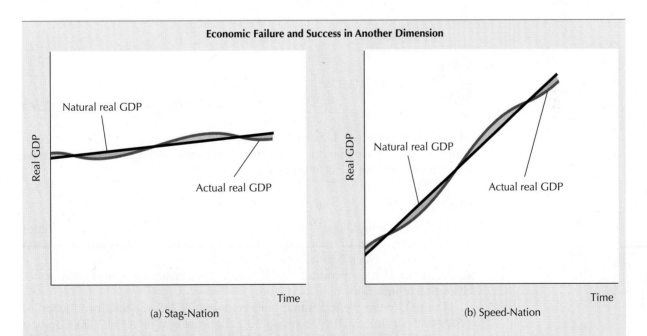

(a) Stag-Nation

(b) Speed-Nation

Figure 1-5 Economic Growth in Stag-Nation and Speed-Nation

In both frames the business cycle has been tamed, but in the left frame there is almost no economic growth, while economic growth in the right frame is rapid. For Speed-Nation there can be more of everything, while Stag-Nation in the left frame is a "zero-sum society," in which an increase in one type of economic activity requires that another economic activity be cut back.

Stag-Nation people must constantly face debates, since more money for schools or parks requires that people sacrifice consumer goods.

Over the past decade, countries like Stag-Nation include Germany, Italy, and Japan. Countries like Speed-Nation include China and India. The United States has been between these extremes.

How do we achieve faster economic growth in output per person? In Chapters 10–12 we study the sources of economic growth and the role of government policy in helping to determine the growth in America's future standard of living, as well as the reasons why some countries remain so poor.

 SELF-TEST

Indicate whether each item in the following list is more closely related to short-run (business cycle) macro or to long-run (economic growth) macro:

1. The Federal Reserve reduces interest rates in a recession in an attempt to reduce the unemployment rate.

2. The federal government introduces national standards for high school students in an attempt to raise math and science test scores.

3. Consumers cut back spending because news of layoffs makes them fear for their jobs.

4. The federal government gives states and localities more money to repair roads, bridges, and schools.

 1-5 Case Study

A Century of Business Cycles

This section examines U.S. macroeconomic history since the early twentieth century. You will see that unemployment in the past four decades did not come close to the extreme crisis levels of the 1930s.

Real GDP

Figure 1-6 is arranged just like Figure 1-2. But whereas Figure 1-2 shows hypothetical relationships, Figure 1-6 shows the actual historical record. In the top frame the solid black line is natural real GDP, an estimate of the amount the economy could have produced each year without causing acceleration or deceleration of inflation.

The red line in the top frame plots actual real GDP, the total production of goods and services each year measured in the constant prices of 2000. Can you pick out those years when actual and natural real GDP are roughly equal? Some of these years were 1900, 1910, 1924, 1963, 1977, 1987, 1997, and 2005.

In years marked by blue shading, actual real GDP fell below natural real GDP. A maximum deficiency occurred in 1933, when actual real GDP was only 64 percent of natural GDP; about 36 percent of natural real GDP was thus "wasted," that is, not produced. Before 1929 and since 1950, these intervals of substantial output deficiency have been much less serious than in the Great Depression but nevertheless have added up to billions in lost output.

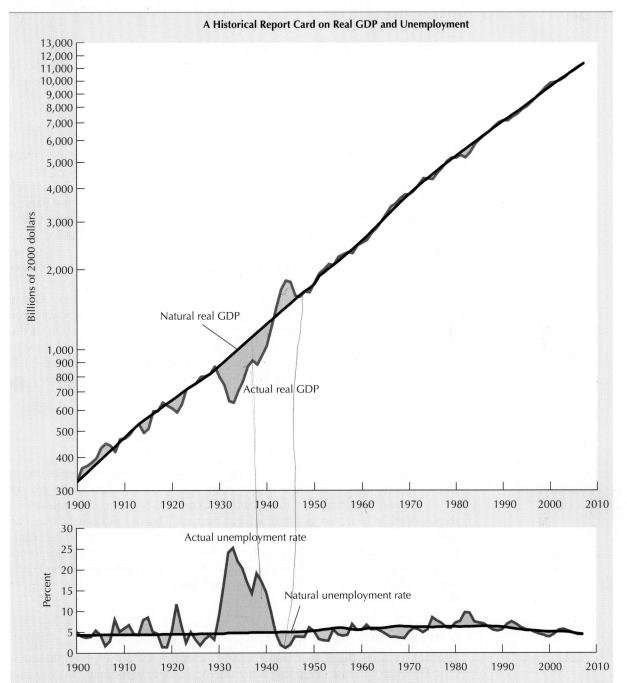

A Historical Report Card on Real GDP and Unemployment

Figure 1-6 **Actual and Natural GDP and Unemployment, 1900–2007**

A historical report card for two important economic magnitudes. In the top frame the black line indicates natural real GDP. The red line shows actual real GDP, which was well below natural real GDP during the Great Depression of the 1930s and well above it during World War II. In the bottom frame the black line indicates the natural rate of unemployment, and the blue line indicates the actual unemployment rate. Actual unemployment was much higher during the Great Depression of the 1930s than at any other time during the century. Notice how periods of high actual unemployment like the 1930s, designated by blue shaded areas in the bottom frame, occur simultaneously with periods of low actual real GDP in the top frame. Red shaded areas indicate times when the economy was "overheated," with high actual real GDP and low unemployment.

Sources: See Appendix A-1 and C-4.

In some years actual real GDP exceeded natural real GDP, shown by the shaded red areas. This occurred mainly in wartime, particularly during World War I (1917–18), World War II (1942–45), the Korean War (1951–53), and the first half of the U.S. involvement in the Vietnam War (1965–69).

Unemployment

In the bottom frame of Figure 1-6, the blue line plots the actual unemployment rate. By far the most extreme episode was the Great Depression, when the actual unemployment rate remained above 10 percent for ten straight years, 1931–40. The black line in the bottom frame of Figure 1-6 displays the natural rate of unemployment, the minimum attainable level of unemployment that is compatible with avoiding an acceleration of inflation. The red shaded areas mark years when actual unemployment fell below the natural rate, as in 1917–19 and 1966–69. The blue shaded areas mark years when unemployment exceeded the natural rate.

Notice now the relationship between the top and bottom frames of Figure 1-6. The blue shaded areas in both frames designate periods of low production, low real GDP, and high unemployment, such as the Great Depression of the 1930s and the "Great Recessions" of 1975 and 1981–82. The red shaded areas in both frames designate periods of high production and high actual real GDP, and low unemployment, such as World War II and other wartime periods. ●

1-6 Macroeconomics at the Extremes

Most of macroeconomics treats relatively normal events. Business cycles occur, and unemployment goes up and down, as does inflation. Economic growth registers faster rates in some decades than in others. Yet there are times when the economy's behavior is anything but normal. The normal mechanisms of macroeconomics break down, and the consequences can be dire. Three examples of unusual macroeconomic behavior involving our "Big Three" concepts are the Great Depression of the 1930s, the German hyperinflation of the 1920s, and the stark difference in economic growth between two Asian nations over the past 50 years.

Unemployment in the Great Depression, 1929–40

The first of our "Big Three" macroeconomic concepts is the unemployment rate. The most extreme event involving unemployment in recorded history was the Great Depression of the 1930s. As is clearly visible in Figure 1-6 in the previous section, real GDP collapsed between 1929 and 1933, and the unemployment rate soared. A closer look at the decade of the 1930s is provided in Figure 1-7. For contrast with the 1930s, the blue line displays the unemployment rate from 1995 to 2007, which fell as low as 4.0 percent during the prosperity year of 2000 and was never higher than 6.0 percent, the rate reached in 1995. The unemployment rate during the Great Depression behaved quite differently, as shown by the purple line, soaring from 3.2 percent in 1929 to 25.2 percent in 1933, and never falling below 10 percent until 1941.

In the United States, the Great Depression caused many millions of jobs to disappear. College seniors could not find jobs. Stories of job hunting were unbelievable but true. For example, men waited all night outside Detroit employ-

Figure 1-7 **The Unemployment Rate from 1929–41 Compared with 1995–2007**

The blue line displays the unemployment rate from 1995 to 2007, which was never higher than 6.0 percent or lower than 4.0 percent. In contrast the purple line exhibits the unemployment rate during the Great Depression; this never fell below 14 percent during the ten years from 1931 to 1940.

Source: Bureau of Labor Statistics. See Appendix C-4.

ment offices so they would be first in line the next morning. An Arkansas man walked 900 miles looking for work. So discouraged were Americans of finding jobs that for the first (and last) time in American history, there were more emigrants than immigrants. In fact, there were 350 applications per day from Americans who wanted to settle in Russia. Since there was no unemployment insurance, how did people live when there were no jobs? Wedding rings were sold, furniture pawned, life insurance borrowed against, and money begged from relatives. Millions with no resources moved aimlessly from city to city, sometimes riding on freight cars; some cities tried to keep the wanderers out with barricades and shotguns.[2]

The Great Depression affected most of the industrialized world but was most serious in the United States and in Germany. The Great Depression in Germany led directly to Hitler's takeover of power in 1933 and indirectly

---

[2] Details in this paragraph are from William Manchester, *The Glory and the Dream: A Narrative History of America, 1932–72* (Boston: Little-Brown, 1973), pp. 33–35.

caused the 50 million deaths of World War II. What caused the disastrous depression and what could have been done to avoid it? We need to study basic macroeconomics first, and then we can examine the causes of the Great Depression in Chapter 7.

The German Hyperinflation of 1922–23

A *hyperinflation* can be defined as an inflation raging at a rate of 50 percent or more *per month*. If a Big Mac cost $2 in January, a 50 percent monthly inflation would raise the price to $3 in February, $4.50 in March, $6.75 in April, and onward until it reached $173 in December! There were several examples of hyperinflation in the twentieth century, most of them involving the experience of European countries after World Wars I and II. The best known is the German hyperinflation, which proceeded at 322 percent per month between August 1922 and November 1923; in its final climactic days in October 1923, it rose at 32,000 percent per month! Figure 1-8 displays the German price level from 1920 to 1923. The price level goes from slightly above 1.0 in 1920 and early 1921 to 550 by the end of 1922 and about 100,000,000,000 at the end of 1923.

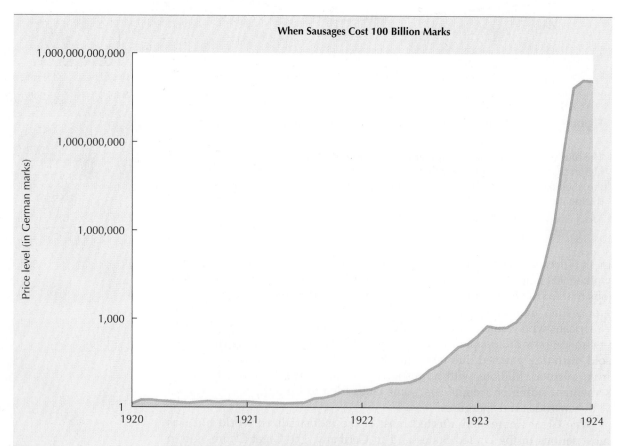

Figure 1-8 The German Price Level, 1920–23

The orange line shows the German price level, which increased from a little above 1 in 1920 and 1921 to 550 at the end of 1922 and to 100,000,000,000 in November 1923.

The basic cause of the German hyperinflation was the Versailles Peace Treaty, which ended World War I and required payment of massive reparations by Germany to Britain and France. The Germans were unwilling to obtain funds to pay the reparations by raising taxes, so instead they ran huge government budget deficits financed by printing paper money. When people realized the implications of these deficits, they became less willing to hold money; it was both the rapid increase in the supply of money and the ever-declining demand for money that combined to fuel the hyperinflation.[3]

The inflation decimated the savings of ordinary Germans. A farmer who sold a piece of land for 80,000 marks as a nest egg for his old age could barely buy a sandwich with the money a few years later. Elderly Germans can still recall the days in 1923 when:

> People were bringing money to the bank in cardboard boxes and laundry baskets. As we no longer could count it, we put the money on scales and weighed it. I can still see my brothers coming home Saturdays with heaps of paper money. When the shops reopened after the weekend they got no more than a breakfast roll for it. Many got drunk on their pay because it was worthless on Monday.[4]

Just as the Great Depression helped to create resentments about the existing government that turned voters to Hitler's Nazi party, so bitter memories of lost savings in the hyperinflation ten years earlier added to Hitler's growing support. Very rapid inflation is not an ancient artifact lacking relevance for today. Throughout the 1980s and 1990s several Latin American countries suffered from inflation rates of 1,000 percent per year or more. Recently, a devastating inflation broke out in the southern African nation of Zimbabwe, where the inflation rate in 2007 reached 5,000 or more percent per year. Because the government failed to raise the wages of teachers and hospital workers by even remotely the percentage by which prices had gone up, the nation in 2007 was in a state of collapse, with schools and hospitals closing down. We return in Chapter 9 and Chapter 11 to the sad story of Zimbabwe, which has become a poster child of macroeconomic mismanagement.

Fast and Slow Growth in Asia

Neither the Great Depression nor the German hyperinflation had any significant effect on the American or German standard of living a decade or two later. For effects that really matter over the decades, we need to look at the third of our "Big Three" macroeconomic concepts: productivity growth. Differences in growth rates that may appear small can compound over the decades and create enormous differences in the standard of living of any economic unit, from individuals to nations. A classic example of the importance of rapid growth is illustrated in Figure 1-9, which displays real GDP per capita in South Korea and the Philippines over the period 1960 to 2008.

In 1960, real GDP per capita in the Philippines was actually 20 percent higher than in South Korea, with values of $2,034 and $1,690, respectively. But between 1960 and 2008, real GDP per capita grew at 5.7 percent per year

---

[3] Data from Philip Cagan, "The Monetary Dynamics of Hyperinflation," in Milton Friedman, ed., *Studies in the Quantity Theory of Money* (Chicago: University of Chicago Press, 1956), Table 1, p. 26.

[4] Alice Siegert, "When Inflation Ruined Germany," *Chicago Tribune,* November 30, 1974.

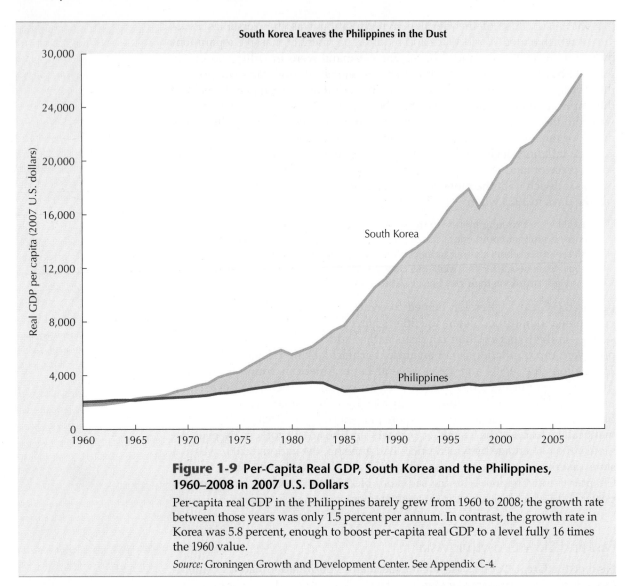

Figure 1-9 Per-Capita Real GDP, South Korea and the Philippines, 1960–2008 in 2007 U.S. Dollars

Per-capita real GDP in the Philippines barely grew from 1960 to 2008; the growth rate between those years was only 1.5 percent per annum. In contrast, the growth rate in Korea was 5.8 percent, enough to boost per-capita real GDP to a level fully 16 times the 1960 value.

Source: Groningen Growth and Development Center. See Appendix C-4.

in South Korea compared to only 1.4 percent in the Philippines. Figure 1-9 shows the wide gap that opened up between the Korean and Philippine standards of living, with 2008 values of only $4,195 for the Philippines and $26,894 for South Korea. As a result of its superior economic growth record, the average Korean in 2008 could save or consume almost seven times as much as the average citizen of the Philippines. Stated another way, the Korean could consume everything enjoyed by the Philippine citizen and then have almost six times as much left over. This extra output in Korea is shown by the orange shading in Figure 1-9.

The outstanding achievement of South Korea has been duplicated in several other countries in East Asia, notably Hong Kong, Singapore, and Taiwan, and more recently by China. What secrets have the Koreans learned about economic growth that the Philippine government and population have not learned? The story of growth successes and failures is a fascinating one that awaits us in Chapters 10 and 11.

1-7 Taming Business Cycles: Stabilization Policy

Macroeconomic analysts have two tasks: to analyze the causes of changes in important aggregates and to predict the consequences of alternative policy changes. In policy discussions the group of aggregates that society cares most about—inflation, unemployment, and the long-term growth rate of productivity—are called goals, or **target variables**. When the target variables deviate from desired values, alternative **policy instruments** can be used in an attempt to achieve needed changes. Instruments fall into three broad categories: **monetary policies**, which include control of the money supply and interest rates; **fiscal policies**, which include changes in government expenditures and tax rates; and a third, miscellaneous group, which includes policies to equip workers with skills they need to qualify for jobs.

> **Target variables** are aggregates whose values society cares about.

How are target variables and policy instruments related to the three central macroeconomic concepts introduced at the beginning of this chapter? All three concepts—the unemployment rate, inflation rate, and productivity growth—are the key target variables of economic policy, the goals society cares most about.

> **Policy instruments** are elements that government policymakers can manipulate directly to influence target variables.

The goal of policymakers regarding productivity growth is simple—just make productivity growth as fast as possible. There are no negatives to rapid productivity growth, and virtually every country in the world admires the growth achievement of South Korea (and some other East Asian countries) displayed in Figure 1-9 in the previous section. However, the goal of policymakers regarding the unemployment rate is not so simple. An attempt to reduce unemployment to zero would be likely to cause a significant acceleration of inflation, and moderation of inflation may be impossible if policymakers attempt to maintain the unemployment rate too low. A compromise goal for policymakers is to try to set the actual unemployment rate equal to the natural unemployment rate, since this would tend to maintain a constant inflation rate that neither accelerates nor decelerates.

> **Monetary policy** tries to influence target variables by changing the money supply or interest rate or both. – Benjamin Benacky
>
> **Fiscal policy** tries to influence target variables by manipulating government expenditures and tax rates.

The Role of Stabilization Policy

Macroeconomic analysis begins with a simple message: Either type of **stabilization policy**, monetary or fiscal, can be used to offset undesired changes in private spending. The effects of monetary and fiscal policy on the price level and on real GDP are the main subjects of Parts Two and Three of this book.

> A **stabilization policy** is any policy that seeks to influence the level of aggregate demand.

There are many problems in applying stabilization policy. It may not be possible to control aggregate demand instantly and precisely. A policy stimulus intended to fight current unemployment might boost aggregate demand only after a long and uncertain delay, by which time the stimulus might not be needed. The impact of different policy changes may also be highly uncertain. These and other limitations of policy "fine-tuning" or "activism" are central themes in the consideration of monetary and fiscal policy in Part Five.

Most policy disagreements stem from the incompatibility of worthy economic goals. Most people would like the price level to be stable and the unemployment rate to be close to zero. But this state of nirvana cannot be achieved instantly, if ever. Macroeconomics, like economics in general, is the science of *choice* in the face of limitations for each of the possible alternatives. Choices emphasized in this book include whether to reduce the inflation rate at the cost of higher unemployment during a transition period that may last five years or longer and whether to boost investment and economic growth at the cost of higher tax rates.

International Perspective

Puzzles in the Economic Performance
of the United States Versus Europe

One result of the internationalization of macro-economics is the increased attention to the relative economic performance of major countries or regions in the world, such as the United States versus Europe or Asia. We learn from these comparisons that performance differs over time. Compared to Europe, the United States did not perform well from 1960 to 1985 but then started to improve and performed much better than Europe after 1995.

Good performance means the achievement of low unemployment, low inflation, and rapid productivity growth. The two charts in this box compare the United States and Europe on the unemployment rate and rate of productivity growth.[a] We do not include the third big concept, the inflation rate, because differences between the U.S. and European inflation rates are minor.

The chart below shows Europe's unemployment rate as lower than the U.S. rate throughout the 1960s and 1970s, but higher after 1980. In fact, in the mid-1990s the European unemployment rate was almost double that in the United States. The graph shows that the U.S. unemployment rate was actually lower in 2006 than in 1960,

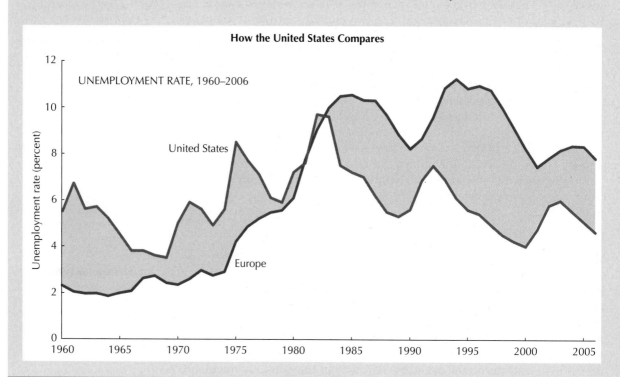

How the United States Compares

UNEMPLOYMENT RATE, 1960–2006

SELF-TEST

1. Is it the task of stabilization policy to set the unemployment rate to zero? Why or why not?

2. Is it the task of stabilization policy to set the inflation rate to zero? Why or why not?

3. What are the two big problems in applying stabilization policy to control aggregate demand?

whereas the European unemployment rate was four times as high. The reasons for the big increase in the European unemployment rate constitute one of the most important and exciting research topics in macroeconomics—what policies could the European countries adopt to reduce the European unemployment rate? We return to this puzzle in Chapter 9.

The chart below shows the growth rate of productivity in the United States and the same group of European countries. European productivity growth was more rapid than in the United States until 1997, after which the U.S. growth rate sped up and the

European rate slowed down. The U.S. speedup after 1995 is often attributed to its rapid adoption of computer and Internet technology, but this creates a big puzzle because there are plenty of computers and Internet use within Europe. We return to this puzzle in Chapter 11.

---

[a] All data on Europe refer to the fifteen members of the European Union prior to its enlargement to twenty-five nations on May 1, 2004.

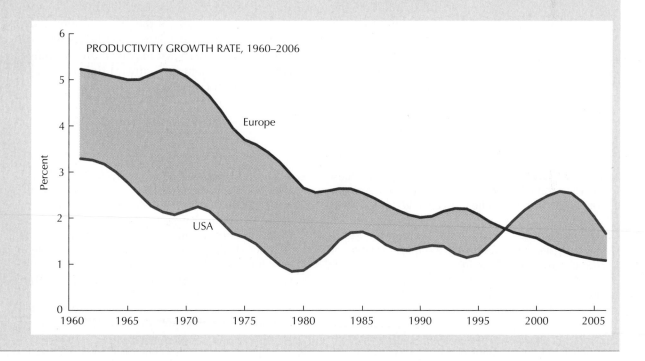

PRODUCTIVITY GROWTH RATE, 1960–2006

1-8   The "Internationalization" of Macroeconomics

More than ever before, macroeconomics is an international subject. The days are gone when the effects of U.S. stabilization policy could be analyzed in isolation, without consideration for their repercussions abroad. This old view of the United States as a **closed economy** described reality in the first decade or so after World War II. In the 1940s and 1950s, trade accounted for only about 5 percent of the U.S. economy, exchange rates were fixed, and financial flows to and from other nations were restricted.

A **closed economy** has no trade in goods, services, or financial assets with any other nation.

An **open economy** exports goods and services to other nations, imports from them, and has financial flows to and from foreign nations.

The United States has increasingly become an **open economy**. Imports now equal 17 percent of U.S. GDP. The exchange rate of the dollar has been flexible since 1973 and has fluctuated far more widely than anyone had predicted prior to that time. International financial flows are massive and often instantaneous, with computers sending messages to buy or sell stocks, bonds, and foreign currencies at the speed of light among the major financial centers of Tokyo, London, New York, and Chicago.

As the economy has become internationalized, so has macroeconomic analysis. For instance, during the years of persistent government deficits (1980–97 and 2001–08), the depressing effect of government deficits on private domestic investment was partly offset by capital inflows from abroad, as foreigners purchased U.S. stocks, bonds, factories, and hotels. Further, in an open economy there are additional impacts of monetary and fiscal policy to consider. When it reduces interest rates, the Federal Reserve Board must take into account the likelihood that the value of the dollar will decline, which tends to boost U.S. exports and stimulate the economy while also causing inflation to accelerate.

Along with a new analysis of fiscal and monetary policy and of the determinants of inflation, the internationalization of macroeconomics brings new attention to American efficiency and competitiveness. If the U.S. economy is doing so well, why are we so "hooked" on imports of foreign goods? As we shall see early in the book, America's current account deficit may be more of a reflection of its low private saving rate and persistent government deficits than of any unique enthusiasm for foreign goods and services.

Summary

1. The three central macroeconomic concepts are those that most affect everyday lives. They are the unemployment rate, inflation rate, and productivity growth.

2. Macroeconomics differs from microeconomics by focusing on aggregates that are summed up over all the economic activities in the economy. Theory in macroeconomics is a process of simplification that identifies the most important economic relationships.

3. Gross domestic product (GDP) is a measure of the overall size of the economy. While it does not affect everyday life directly, the behavior of GDP helps us to understand the behavior of the three central macroeconomic concepts that do influence everyday life.

4. Neither too much nor too little real GDP is desirable. The best compromise level is called natural real GDP and is consistent with a constant inflation rate. When the economy is operating at its natural level of real GDP, it is also by definition operating at its natural rate of unemployment.

5. The topic of "business cycles" studies short-run phenomena in macroeconomics over a period of one to five years. The topic of "economic growth" studies long-run phenomena over a period lasting a decade or more.

6. While most macroeconomic analysis concerns relatively normal events, a challenge for macroeconomists is to explain how extreme and unusual events can occur. Two of these were the Great Depression of the 1930s and the German hyperinflation of 1922–23. Another challenge is to understand how the rate of economic growth can be so different between two countries like South Korea and the Philippines that are located in the same region of the world.

7. In this century, periods of high unemployment have coincided with those of low real GDP. The Great Depression clearly scored worst on both counts.

8. The three central macroeconomic aggregates, (unemployment rate, inflation rate, and productivity growth) are the main targets of stabilization policy. Stabilization policy may not be effective in improving well-being if both unemployment and inflation are too high, and stabilization policy may operate with a long delay or have effects that are highly uncertain.

9. Macroeconomics is now an international subject. International repercussions influence the way fiscal and monetary policy work and how the inflation process operates. The current account deficit raises new concerns about U.S. competitiveness.

Concepts

macroeconomics
unemployment rate
inflation rate
productivity
aggregate
gross domestic product
actual real GDP

natural real GDP
natural rate of unemployment
business cycles
economic growth
real GDP gap
target variables
policy instruments

monetary policy
fiscal policy
stabilization policy
closed economy
open economy

Questions

1. Read either an entire week of the *Wall Street Journal* or a business-oriented weekly magazine such as *Business Week* or *The Economist*. Identify three stories that deal with topics related to microeconomics and another three stories that discuss topics related to macroeconomics. Explain why you have put each story in either the microeconomics or macroeconomics category.

2. Using the quarterly data in Table A-2 for the period 1947–2007 in Appendix A, attempt to identify the recession phases and the expansion phases of the basic business cycle depicted in Figure 1-4.

3. Using your answer to question 2, compare the lengths of recessions and expansions for the period 1947–1982 with the years since 1983.

4. How are the natural real GDP and the natural real unemployment rates related to the rate of inflation?

5. Between June 2003 and June 2005, U.S. unemployment fell from 6.3 percent to 5.0 percent of the labor force. The Federal Reserve, the nation's monetary policy-making authority, took active measures beginning in June 2004 to raise short-term interest rates. What might have motivated policymakers to raise interest rates and what were they hoping to accomplish?

6. In April 2000, the seasonally adjusted unemployment rate was 3.8 percent. By June 2001, the unemployment rate had increased to 4.5 percent. Yet the measures by the Federal Reserve to reduce short-term interest rates were taken in stages, and in fact the unemployment rate continued to rise. What might have motivated the policymakers' cautious behavior?

7. (a) The "big three" concepts of macroeconomics are the unemployment rate, the inflation rate, and productivity growth. Discuss which of these concepts primarily relate to the behavior of the economy (i) in the short run and (ii) in the long run.

   (b) Using Figures 1-3 and 1-5 as guides, discuss how natural real GDP is used to evaluate the behavior of the economy in both the short run and the long run.

8. Explain why productivity growth not only allows a society to have higher living standards in the form of more goods and services, but also allows it to increase the percentage of an average person's life that is spent in school, on vacation, in retirement, or in other non-work related activities.

9. Explain how the value of real GDP relative to natural real GDP can be used by policymakers to decide how to change the values of the target variables.

10. How does the performance of the U.S. economy contrast with the performance of the European economy since 1960?

Problems

1. (a) Suppose that real GDP is currently $97 billion per year and natural real GDP is currently $100 billion. Measured as a percentage, what is the real GDP gap?

   (b) Suppose natural real GDP is growing by $4 billion per year. By how much must real GDP have risen after two years to close the real GDP gap?

2. The sum of exports and imports as a percent of gross domestic product is sometimes used as a measure of how open an economy is. In particular, the greater the percent, the more open the economy is considered.

Using the following data, compute this measure of the openness of the U.S. economy in 1960, 1970, 1980, 1990, 2000, and 2006. Discuss what the data show in terms of the "internationalization" of the U.S. economy since 1960.

	1960	1970	1980	1990	2000	2006
GDP	2,501.8	3,771.9	5,161.7	7,112.5	9,817.0	11,319.4
Exports	90.6	161.4	323.5	552.5	1,096.3	1,304.1
Imports	103.3	213.4	310.9	607.1	1,475.8	1,928.6

SELF-TEST ANSWERS

p. 8 (1) When actual real GDP is above natural real GDP, the actual unemployment rate is below the natural unemployment rate. (2) In this opposite case, the actual unemployment rate is above the natural unemployment rate. (3) There is no such thing as the natural rate of inflation. When the economy is operating at its natural rate of unemployment, the inflation rate does not change. But it does not change from whatever level is inherited from the past, and this could be zero, 10 percent per year, or 100 percent per year.

p. 12 (1) short-run, (2) long-run, (3) short-run, (4) both (the money can create jobs during a recession but also will stimulate long-run productivity growth).

p. 20 (1) Stabilization policy cannot set the unemployment rate to zero or any other rate below the natural rate of unemployment without causing accelerating inflation. (2) Stabilization policy can set the inflation rate to zero only at the cost of a recession and a substantial cost in terms of lost output. (3) The two big problems are lags and uncertainty. A policy change may affect aggregate demand only after a long and uncertain delay, and the impact of different policy changes may also be highly uncertain.

For additional practice and exploration, exercises that require the use of Excel are available at www.aw-bc.com/gordon.

CHAPTER

2

The Measurement of Income, Prices, and Unemployment

It has been said that figures rule the world; maybe. I am quite sure that it is figures which show us whether it is being ruled well or badly.

—Johann Wolfgang Goethe, 1830

Our first task is to develop a simple theoretical model to explain real output (gross domestic product, or GDP) and the price level. Before we can turn to theory in Chapter 3, however, we must stop in Chapter 2 for a few definitions. What are GDP and the price level? How are they measured? What goods and services are included in or excluded from GDP? How are private saving, private investment, the government deficit, and the current account deficit related to one another? How are the inflation rate and unemployment rate measured?

2-1 Why We Care About Income

In Chapter 1 we identified two key links between real GDP and the three central concepts of macroeconomics. First, in Figure 1-2 we noted that movements in the unemployment rate (the first central concept) are closely related to the parallel movements of the gap between actual and natural real GDP. Thus the key to understanding changes in unemployment is the change in actual real GDP.

Second, the level and growth rate of our standard of living are measured by productivity (the third central concept), defined as the ratio of output to the number of hours worked. Output is the same as real GDP. Thus any discussion of U.S. productivity performance in comparison with the country's history or with other nations requires an understanding of the data on real GDP.

This chapter begins by asking what is included in GDP and why. We then learn about the different sectors of the economy that purchase portions of the total GDP and how that GDP is the source of different types of income. We learn how the price level and rate of inflation are measured. Finally, we learn how the unemployment rate is measured and how the unemployment rate is related to real GDP.

2-2 The Circular Flow of Income and Expenditure

We begin with a very simple economy, consisting of households and business firms. We will assume that households spend their entire income, saving

25

Figure 2-1 The Circular Flow of Income and Consumption Expenditures

Circular flow of income and expenditure in a simple imaginary economy in which households consume their entire income. There are no taxes, no government spending, no saving, no investment, and no foreign sector.

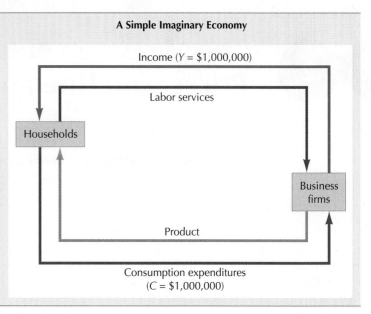

A Simple Imaginary Economy

Income (Y = $1,000,000)

Labor services

Households

Business firms

Product

Consumption expenditures
(C = $1,000,000)

nothing, and that there is no government.[1] Figure 2-1 depicts the operation of our simple economy, with households represented by the box on the left and business firms by the box on the right. There are two kinds of transactions between the households and the firms.

First, the firms sell goods and services (product)—for instance, bread and shoes—to the households represented in Figure 2-1 by the lower orange line, labeled product. The bread and shoes are not a gift, but are paid for by a flow of money (C), say $1,000,000 per year, represented by the solid red line, labeled **consumption expenditures.**

Consumption expenditures are purchases of goods and services by households for their own use.

Second, households must work to earn the income to pay for the consumption goods. They work for the firms, selling their skills as represented by the upper purple line, labeled labor services. Household members are willing to work only if they receive a flow of money, usually called wages, from the firms for each hour of work. Wages are the main component of income (Y), shown by the upper green line.

Since households are assumed to consume all of their income, and since firms are assumed to pay out all of their sales in the form of income to households, it follows that income (Y) and consumption expenditures (C) are equal. For the same reason, the labor services provided in return for income are equal to the goods and services (product) sold by the firms to households in return for the money flow of consumption expenditures:

$$\begin{aligned} \text{income } (Y) &= \text{labor services} \\ &= \text{consumption expenditures } (C) \\ &= \text{product} \end{aligned}$$

[1] Because households do no saving, there is no capital or wealth, and all household income is in the form of wages for labor services.

Each of the four elements in the preceding equation is a **flow magnitude,** any economic magnitude that is measured per unit of time, like U.S. GDP *per year.* A flow is distinguished from a **stock,** which is measured at a particular point in time, such as the amount of paper money in your wallet or purse at noon on September 11, 2008.

A **flow magnitude** is an economic magnitude that moves from one economic unit to another at a specified rate per unit of time.

A **stock** is an economic magnitude in the possession of a given economic unit at a particular point in time.

SELF-TEST

1. Imagine that a student named Eric purchases a haircut, priced at $10, with a $10 bill. Describe in words how the student's haircut will be included in each of the four flows of Figure 2-1.

2. Imagine that a student named Alison obtains a job as a lifeguard at a summer camp paying $8 per hour for July and August, and that the camp obtains the money to pay Alison from fees paid by parents for their children to go to the camp. Describe in words how the fees and the lifeguard job will be included in each of the four flows of Figure 2-1.

2-3   What Transactions Should Be Included in Income and Expenditure?

The **National Income and Product Accounts** (also called NIPA, or national accounts, for short) is the official U.S. government accounting of all the flows of income and expenditure in the United States. Historical data for GDP and other macro concepts are listed in Appendix A for the United States and in Appendix B for other major nations. A guide to government data sources is provided in the box on p. 28.

National Income and Product Accounts is the official U.S. government economic accounting system that keeps track of GDP and its subcomponents.

Defining GDP

In our free market economy, the fact that a good or service is sold is usually a sign that it satisfies certain human wants and needs; otherwise, people would not be willing to pay a price for it. So by including in the GDP only things that are sold through the market for a price, we can be fairly sure that most of the components of GDP do contribute to human satisfaction. There are three major requirements in the rule for including items in the total **final product,** or GDP: *Final product consists of all currently produced goods and services that are sold through the market but not resold during the current time period.*

Final product includes all currently produced goods and services that are sold through the market but are not resold.

Currently produced.   The first part of the rule—*to be included in final product, a good must be currently produced*—excludes sales of any used items such as houses and cars, since they are not currently produced. It also excludes any transaction in which money is transferred without any accompanying good or service in return. Among the **transfer payments** excluded from national income in the United States are payments from the government to persons, such as Social Security, Medicare, and unemployment benefits. Also excluded are capital gains accruing to persons as the prices of their assets change.

Transfer payments are those made for which no goods or services are produced in return.

Sold on the market.   The second part of the rule—*goods included in the final product must be sold on the market and are valued at market prices*—means that we measure the value of final product by the market prices that people are willing

Where to Find the Numbers: A Guide to the Data

The first place to look for macroeconomic data is the appendixes in the back of this textbook. There you will find annual data covering more than a century (from 1875 on) and quarterly data since 1947 on major macroeconomic concepts. Also included are several important annual data series for Japan, Canada, and the major European nations for the period since 1960.

Time Passes and Revisions Occur: How to Cope

You will need to know where to find macroeconomic data that are not included in the textbook appendixes or data for more recent periods that were released after the textbook was printed. For these head to the Internet. There you can find the most recent and comprehensive sources of economic data.

The "Big Three" Agencies

Using the Internet is by far the easiest way to gather economic data; whether it be rather simple data, such as real GDP or the most recent Consumer Price Index, or more detailed data, such as the unemployment rate for males aged 20–24 or how much U.S. consumers spend on funerals. For these and many other series, turn to one of the Web sites of the government agencies that actually produce the data. The three most important are the Bureau of Economic Analysis (BEA, a branch of the Commerce Department), the Bureau of Labor Statistics (BLS, a branch of the Labor Department), and the Federal Reserve Board (usually called by its nickname, the Fed).

BEA: National Income Data All the data on GDP, and related income and product series, are produced by the BEA in an organized system of tables called the National Income and Product Accounts (NIPA). These extend back to 1929 for annual data and to 1947 for quarterly data and are updated regularly on the BEA Web site **www.bea. gov.** Here you can find not only NIPA tables, but recent news releases, industry data, and international and regional series.

BLS: Labor Market, Price, and Wage Data The BLS is a primary producer of data on employment, unemployment, consumer and producer prices, and wage rates. The BLS runs several large surveys, contacting thousands of families each month to learn about their employment and unemployment experience and contacting thousands of retail outlets to track price changes. All of the BLS data series are available at **www.bls.gov.**

The Fed: Financial Market Data The Federal Reserve compiles data on interest rates, the money supply, and

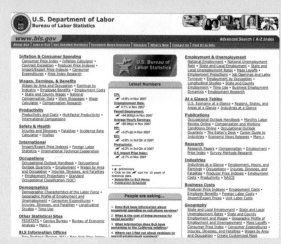

The opening screen of the Bureau of Labor Statistics Web site.

other figures describing the banking and financial system. One of the regional Feds, the Federal Reserve Bank of St. Louis, supports an online database known as FRED (**research.stlouisfed.org/fred2**). This database provides historical U.S. economic and financial data, including daily interest rates, monetary and business indicators, exchange rates, balance of payments, and select regional economic data. The Federal Reserve Board of Governors Web site (**www.federalreserve.gov**) is also useful.

The preceding list does not even include the grandfather of all statistics agencies, the Bureau of the Census, which conducts the decennial Census of Population and, every five years, economic censuses of business establishments. The Census data form the raw material for much of the BEA's work in creating the national accounts, not to mention much research by economists on both macro and micro topics. See **www.census.gov.**

International Web Sites to Know:
Org. for Economic Cooperation and Development
   www.oecdwash.org/DATA/online.htm
World Bank
   www.worldbank.org/data
International Monetary Fund
   www.imf.org/external/data.htm
Groningen Growth and Development Center
   www.ggdc.net/index-dseries.html

Many more sites are available through such search engines as google.com, yahoo.com, and ask.com.

to pay for goods and services. We assume that a Mercedes gives 10,000 times as much satisfaction as a package of razor blades because it costs about 10,000 times as much. Excluded from GDP by this criterion is the value of personal time spent engaged in activities that are not sold on the market (time spent commuting, baking a cake, and so on). Also excluded is any allowance for the costs of air pollution, water pollution, acid rain, or other by-products of the production process for which no explicit charge is made.

But not resold.   The third part of the rule—*to be included in final product, a good must not be resold in the current time period*—further limits the inclusion of items. The many different goods and services produced in the economy are used in two different ways. Some goods, like wheat, are mainly used as ingredients in the making of other goods, in this case, bread. Any good resold by its purchaser is an **intermediate good** and is not included in GDP.

An **intermediate good** is resold by its purchaser either in its present form or in an altered form.

Intermediate Goods, Final Goods, and Value Added

The opposite of an intermediate good is a **final good,** one that is not resold. Bread sold at the grocery is a final good, used by consumers, as are the many other products that consumers buy. Take a simple example of a loaf of bread that sells for $2.00. We assume that the only ingredient in the bread is wheat, which the bakery buys from the wheat farmer for $0.50 per loaf. The remaining $1.50 represents the wages of the bakery employees, the rent on the bakery building, and the profits of the owner. Only the $2.00 spent for the final good, a loaf of bread, is included in GDP.

A **final good** is part of final product.

We cannot include intermediate goods in GDP, because that would be double counting. The value of the wheat is already included in the price of bread, so we don't want GDP to include *both* the $0.50 value of the wheat and the $2.00 value of the bread, since the resulting sum of $2.50 would be more than consumers pay for the bread.

Another way to compute GDP is to add up the **value added** at each stage of production, defined as the value of a firm's output minus the amount paid for intermediate goods. Assuming there are no intermediate goods involved in growing wheat, in this example the wheat farmer has a value added of $0.50 and the bread bakery has a value added of $1.50 (consisting of wages, rent, and profit). Total GDP is the sum of the value added of each firm, $0.50 for the farmer and $1.50 for the bread bakery. By definition, the final product of $2.00 is equal to value added of $2.00. GDP is equal to *both* total final product and total value added.

Value added is the value of a firm's output minus the value of the intermediate goods that the firm produces. It includes wages paid to the firm's employees, rental of buildings and equipment, and the firm's profit.

GNP Versus GDP

Until 1991, the main aggregate in the national income accounts was **gross national product (GNP),** not gross domestic product (GDP). Once we know GDP, we can calculate GNP by adding receipts of factor income (wages, rent, and profits) by Americans from the rest of the world and subtracting payments of factor income to the rest of the world:

Gross national product (GNP) is GDP plus factor payments received from the rest of the world minus factor payments sent to the rest of the world.

$$\text{GNP} = \text{GDP} + \text{Factor Payments from Rest of World}$$
$$- \text{Factor Payments to Rest of World} \qquad (2.1)$$

For instance, Procter & Gamble makes Tide detergent and Crest toothpaste in factories around the world. The value of the detergent and toothpaste is included in the GDP of the countries where the foreign plants are located, from

Japan to Britain, and is not part of U.S. GDP. But Procter & Gamble brings some of the profits from these plants back to the United States, and these are included in "Factor Payments from Rest of World" and raise U.S. GNP relative to GDP. Conversely, Japanese factories produce millions of cars inside the United States, and the value of these cars is included in U.S. GDP. But these factories are profitable, and some of their profits are sent back to Japan. These profits are treated as a factor payment to the rest of the world, which is subtracted from GNP and makes it smaller than GDP.

Overall, the factor payments received by the United States, such as profits earned abroad by McDonald's and Procter & Gamble, and those sent from the United States, such as profits earned by Honda and Toyota, are roughly equal in size, and so GNP is very similar in size to GDP. But in some other countries, such as Ireland, GNP is much smaller than GDP because many of the factories are owned by foreign-owned companies. In other countries, such as Kuwait, GNP is much larger than GDP because Kuwaiti residents own large amounts of bank deposits and other assets in other countries and receive large flows of interest and dividend income on those assets.

2-4 Components of Expenditure

Types of Investment

The goods and services produced by business firms, which are not resold as intermediate goods to other firms or consumers during the current period, qualify by our rule as final product. But the business firm does not consume them. Final goods that business firms keep for themselves are called **private investment** or private capital formation. These goods add to the nation's stock of income-yielding assets. Private investment consists of *inventory investment* and *fixed investment.*

Private investment is the portion of final product that adds to the nation's stock of income-yielding physical assets or that replaces old, worn-out physical assets.

Inventory investment includes all changes in the stock of raw materials, parts, and finished goods held by business.

Inventory investment. Bread produced by the baker but not resold to consumers in the current period stays on the bakery's shelves, raising the level of the bakery's inventories. Since all the bread that is produced is included in GDP, we must define expenditure so as to include the bread, whether it is sold to consumers or whether it remains unsold on the shelf. *By including the change in inventories as part of expenditure, we guarantee that GDP (that is, total product) by definition equals total expenditure.* When inventories increase, the inventory investment component of GDP is positive. When inventories decrease, the inventory investment component of GDP is negative.

 SELF-TEST

Imagine that a bakery has 10 loaves of bread at the close of business on December 31, 2007. Valued at the baker's price of $2.00, the value of the bakery's inventory is $20.00. At the close of business on March 31, 2008, the baker has 15 loaves or $30.00 of bread on the shelves.

1. What is the level of the baker's inventory on December 31, 2007, and on March 31, 2008?

2. What is the change in the baker's inventories in the first quarter of 2008?

3. What is the implication of these numbers for the contribution of the baker's inventories to GDP in the first quarter of 2008?

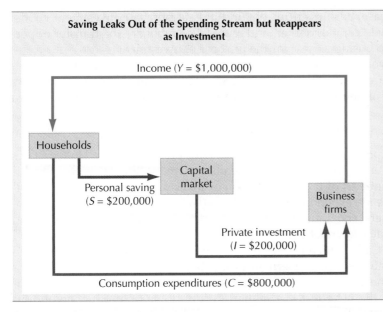

Saving Leaks Out of the Spending Stream but Reappears as Investment

Income (Y = \$1,000,000)

Households

Personal saving
(S = \$200,000)

Capital market

Business firms

Private investment
(I = \$200,000)

Consumption expenditures (C = \$800,000)

Figure 2-2 Introduction of Saving and Investment to the Circular Flow Diagram
Starting from the simple imaginary economy (Figure 2-1), we now assume that households save 20 percent of their income. Business firms' investment accounts for 20 percent of total expenditure. Again, we are assuming that there are no taxes, no government spending, and no foreign sector.

Fixed investment.   **Fixed investment** includes all final goods purchased by business, other than additions to inventory. The main types of fixed investment are structures (factories, office buildings, shopping centers, apartments, houses) and equipment (refrigerated display cases, computers, trucks). Newly produced houses and condominiums sold to individuals are also counted as fixed investment—a household is treated in the national accounts as a business firm that owns the house as an asset and rents the house to itself.[2]

> **Fixed investment** includes all final goods purchased by business that are not intended for resale.

Relation of Investment and Saving

Figure 2-1 described a simple imaginary economy in which households consumed all of their total income. Figure 2-2 introduces investment into that economy. Total expenditures on final product are the same as before, but now they are divided into consumption expenditures by households (C) and business purchases of investment goods (I). Households spend part of their income on purchases of consumption goods and save the rest.

The portion of household income that is not consumed is called **personal saving.** What happens to income that is saved? The funds are channeled to business firms in two basic ways:

> **Personal saving** is that part of personal income that is neither consumed nor paid out in taxes.

1. Households buy bonds and stocks issued by the firms, and the firms then use the money to buy investment goods.
2. Households leave the unused income (savings) in banks and other financial institutions. The banks then lend the money to the firms, which use it to buy investment goods.

---

[2] An individual who owns a house is treated as a split personality in the national accounts: as a business firm and as a consuming household. My left side is a businessperson who owns my house and receives imaginary rent payments from my right side, the consumer who lives in my house. The NIPA identifies these imaginary rent payments as "Imputed rent on owner-occupied dwellings," which makes rent payments the most important exception to the rule that a good must be sold on the market to be counted in GDP.

In either case, business firms obtain funds to purchase investment goods. The box labeled "capital market" in Figure 2-2 symbolizes the transfer of personal saving to business firms for the purpose of investment.

In other words, saving is a "leakage" from the income used for consumption expenditures. This leakage from the spending stream must be balanced by an "injection" of nonconsumption spending in the form of private investment.

Net Exports and Net Foreign Investment

Exports are goods produced within one country and shipped to another.

Imports are goods consumed within one country but produced in another country.

Net exports and **net foreign investment** are both equal to exports minus imports.

Exports are expenditures for goods and services produced in the United States and sent to other countries. Such expenditure creates income in the United States but is not part of the consumption or investment spending of U.S. residents. **Imports** are expenditures by U.S. residents for goods and services produced elsewhere and thus do *not* create domestic income. For instance, an American-made Chevrolet exported to Canada is part of U.S. production and income but is Canadian consumption. A German-made Mercedes imported to the United States is part of German production and income but is U.S. consumption. If income created from exports is greater than income spent on imported goods, the net effect is a higher level of domestic production and income. Thus the difference between exports and imports, **net exports,** is a component of final product and GDP.

Another name for net exports is **net foreign investment,** which can be given the same economic interpretation as domestic investment. Why? Both domestic and foreign investment are components of domestic production and income creation. Domestic investment creates domestic capital assets; net foreign investment creates U.S. claims on foreigners that yield us future flows of income. An American export to Japan is paid for with Japanese yen, which can be deposited in a Japanese bank account or used to buy part of a Japanese factory. The opposite occurs as well. When the United States imports more than it exports, as it has in every year since 1981, net foreign investment is negative. U.S. payments for imports provide dollars that foreign investors use to buy American factories, hotels, and other assets including bank accounts in the United States.

The Government Sector

Up to this point we have been examining an economy consisting only of private households and business firms. Now we add the government, which collects taxes from the private sector and makes two kinds of expenditures. Government purchases of goods and services (tanks, fighter planes, schoolbooks) generate production and create income. The government can also make payments directly to households. Social Security, Medicare, and unemployment compensation are examples of these transfer payments, given the name *transfer* because they are payments from the government to the recipient without any obligation for the recipient to provide any services in return. As you learned in Section 2-3, transfer payments are not included in GDP.

Figure 2-3 adds the government (federal, state, and local) to our imaginary economy of Figures 2-1 and 2-2. A flow of tax revenue (R) passes from the households to the government.[3] The government buys goods and services (G).

---

[3] In the real world, both households and business firms pay taxes. Here we keep things simple by limiting tax payments to personal income taxes.

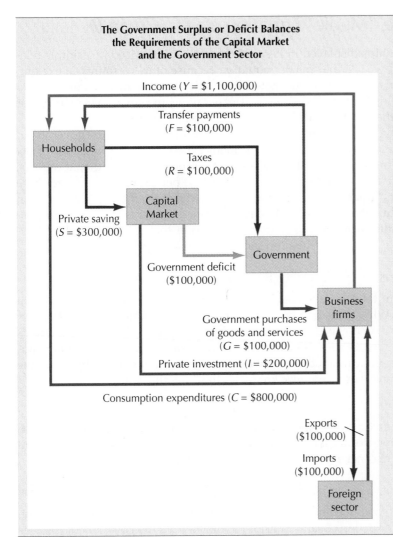

The Government Surplus or Deficit Balances the Requirements of the Capital Market and the Government Sector

Income (Y = $1,100,000)

Transfer payments
(F = $100,000)

Households

Taxes
(R = $100,000)

Capital Market

Private saving
(S = $300,000)

Government

Government deficit
($100,000)

Government purchases
of goods and services
(G = $100,000)

Business firms

Private investment (I = $200,000)

Consumption expenditures (C = $800,000)

Exports
($100,000)

Imports
($100,000)

Foreign sector

Figure 2-3 Introduction of Taxation, Government Spending, and the Foreign Sector to the Circular Flow Diagram

Our simple imaginary economy with the addition of a government collecting $100,000 in tax revenue, paying households $100,000 in transfer payments, and purchasing $100,000 of goods and services. Its total expenditures ($200,000) exceed its tax revenues ($100,000), leaving a $100,000 deficit that is financed by selling government bonds to the households.

In addition the government sends transfer payments (F), such as welfare payments, to households, leaving a deficit that must be financed. To do this, the government sells bonds to private households through the capital market, just as business firms sell bonds and stock to households to finance their investment projects.

Also shown in Figure 2-3, in the bottom right corner, is the foreign sector. Imports are already included in consumption and investment spending, so imports are shown as a leakage by the blue arrow pointing down toward the foreign sector box. Exports are spending on domestic production, as shown by the red arrow going from the foreign sector to the business firms. To keep the diagram simple, exports equal imports.[4]

---

[4] If imports exceed exports, there is a flow equal to the difference going from the foreign sector box to the capital market box. This is the inflow of foreign capital available to finance private investment or the government deficit.

2-5 The "Magic" Equation and the Twin Deficits

The **magic equation** states that private saving plus net tax revenue must by definition equal the sum of private domestic investment, government spending on goods and services, and net exports.

The relationships displayed in Figure 2-3 can be summarized in a simple relationship that we call the "magic" equation because of its versatility in explaining central macroeconomic concepts. The **magic equation** helps us understand the relationships among investment, private saving, the government surplus or deficit, and the surplus or deficit of exports versus imports.

A central phenomenon of the current U.S. economy is that the government is running a large deficit, with government expenditures far in excess of tax revenue. At the same time, the U.S. economy imports far more than it exports, implying a large international deficit (negative net exports). How are these "twin deficits" financed? What difference would it make if the government ran a surplus while the international deficit remained the same? What would happen if the international deficit were zero while the government deficit remained large? The magic equation can help us to answer these questions.

Implications of the Equality Between Income and Expenditures

By definition, total income created (Y) is equal to total expenditure on final product (E). Why is this true by definition? Because income is created from total production, and expenditures include both the production that is sold to final users, as well as the production that is not sold (i.e., the change in inventories). We can indicate that this relationship is true by definition by using the three-bar equals sign, otherwise known as the "identity sign":

$$Y \equiv E$$

There are four types of expenditure on final product: consumption expenditures (C); private domestic investment (I); government purchases of goods and services (G); and net exports (NX):

$$E \equiv C + I + G + NX \tag{2.2}$$

The total personal income that households receive consists of the income created from production (Y) and transfer payments from the government (F). This total ($Y + F$) is available for the purchase of consumption goods (C), private saving (S), and the payment of taxes (R):

$$Y + F \equiv C + S + R$$

An equivalent expression is obtained if we subtract F from both sides:

$$Y \equiv C + S + R - F \tag{2.3}$$

Transfer payments (F) can be treated as negative taxes. Accordingly, we define net tax revenue (T) as taxes (R) minus transfers (F), converting equation (2.3) into the simpler expression:

$$Y \equiv C + S + T \tag{2.4}$$

Leakages and Injections

Since $Y \equiv E$, the right side of equation (2.4) is equal to the right side of equation (2.2), and we obtain:

$$
\begin{array}{rl}
C + S + T \equiv & C + I + G + NX \\
-C & -C \qquad \text{(subtracting } C \text{ from both sides)} \\
\hline
S + T \equiv & I + G + NX
\end{array}
\tag{2.5}
$$

The bottom line of (2.5) can be translated to a general rule:

> Since income is equal to expenditure, the portion of income not consumed (saving plus net taxes) must be equal to the nonconsumption portion of expenditure on final product (investment plus government spending plus net exports).

In other words, **leakages** out of the income available for consumption goods $(S + T)$ must be exactly balanced by **injections** of nonconsumption spending $(I + G + NX)$.

Leakages describe the portion of total income that flows to taxes or saving rather than into purchases of consumer goods.

Equation 2-5 is one of the most important relationships in macroeconomics and reappears often in the next few chapters. We call it the magic equation; its more technical name is the leakages–injections identity. The importance of this relationship is that it shows how some of the most basic concepts in macroeconomics—private saving, government spending and taxes, domestic investment, and net exports—are connected *by definition*. As we see in the next section, for instance, the fact that the government is running a budget deficit ($T - G$ less than zero) implies that investment plus net exports must be less than saving ($I + NX - S$ less than zero). Subsequently in Chapters 5 and 6 we shall return to the magic equation and learn that any change in the sum of private and government saving requires a change in the sum of domestic and foreign investment, and how changes in foreign borrowing alter the balance between domestic saving and investment.

Injections is a term for nonconsumption expenditures.

The Government Budget and the Twin Deficits

The magic equation shows how the funds resulting from a government budget surplus are used, and it is equally useful in showing how the government finances a budget deficit. We can arrange equation (2.5) to show the uses of a government budget surplus:

$$T - G \equiv (I + NX) - S \qquad (2.6)$$

On the left side of this definition is the government budget surplus. If the left side is negative, the government is running a budget deficit. Shown on the right side is the excess of total investment, both domestic (I) and foreign (NX), over private savings (S). The definition indicates that there are three ways that a government budget surplus can be used. First, a budget surplus allows private saving to decline without any need for a decline in total investment. Second, a government budget surplus can stimulate domestic investment. Third, a government budget surplus can boost foreign investment or, if foreign investment is negative, reduce the amount of borrowing from foreigners.

If government spending is greater than net tax revenue, the government is running a deficit, and equation (2.6) shows that there are three possible implications. First, the government budget deficit could make domestic investment (I) smaller than otherwise. Second, the government budget deficit requires that private saving must rise to avoid any downward pressure on the sum of domestic and foreign investment ($I + NX$). Third, if there is no increase in private saving, then to avoid a decline in domestic investment there must be more borrowing from foreigners (larger negative NX) or a decline in lending to foreigners.

We can use a numerical example from recent years to illustrate how the right-hand side of equation (2.6) changed as the government shifted from its 1993 deficit to its surplus in 2000 and then back to deficit in 2007:

$$T - G \equiv (I + NX) - S$$

1993	$-1.8 \equiv (17.6 - 1.0) - 18.4$	
2000	$4.4 \equiv (20.8 - 4.0) - 12.4$	
2007	$-2.9 \equiv (15.5 - 5.1) - 13.3$	

In 1993, there was a budget deficit equal to −1.8 percent of GDP. This was financed by foreign borrowing (negative NX) of −1.0 percent of GDP, requiring that domestic saving (18.4 percent) be larger than domestic investment (17.6 percent). In contrast, in the year 2000 there was a budget surplus equal to 4.4 percent of GDP, together with even greater foreign borrowing of −4.0 percent of GDP. The funds from the government surplus together with the large amount of foreign borrowing allowed domestic investment to be much larger (20.8 percent) than domestic saving (12.4 percent). By 2007, the government budget had returned to deficit (−2.9 percent). In effect, foreign borrowing (−5.1 percent) allowed domestic investment (15.5 percent) to be larger than domestic saving (13.3 percent).

The magic equation (2.5 or 2.6) can be rearranged in several additional ways, as we shall see in Chapter 5. Because it is true by definition, it does not identify the direction of causation among the interrelated variables. For instance, in the year 2000 did the government run a budget surplus because domestic investment was so strong, or was investment so strong because the government ran a surplus? Did the sharp decline in investment between 2000 and 2007 cause the government to run a deficit, or did the government deficit occur for other reasons?

During most of the period since 1980, the United States has experienced "twin deficits," with a government budget deficit accompanied by foreign borrowing (negative NX). The year 2000, with its budget surplus accompanied by foreign borrowing, was the exception rather than the rule, but the year 2000 shows that the deficits are not guaranteed to be "twins." Is the experience of the United States unusual? Turn to the box on pp. 154–55 to see how the magic equation operates in Europe and Japan.

2-6 How Much Income Flows from Business Firms to Households?

Income, Leakages, and the Circular Flow

An important lesson of circular flow diagrams like Figure 2-3 (see p. 33) is that the expenditures on GDP (consumption, investment, government spending, and net exports) create income, and this income is available to be spent on another round of expenditure. Households receive only part of the GDP generated by business firms; the rest leaks out of the circular flow in the form of tax revenue for government and saving that provides funds to the capital market. Recall from equation (2.5) that total leakages (taxes and saving) must by definition equal total nonconsumption spending, also called *injections*.

Table 2-1 provides a concise summary of the steps by which income travels from business firms to households. Down the left-hand side are the various concepts of total income; these differ depending on which tax and saving leakages are included. The three remaining columns identify the major types of saving and tax leakages, as well as transfer payments (which work like taxes in reverse).

Line 1 starts with GDP, the total amount of income created by domestic production. The first leakage, on line 2, is for **depreciation,** sometimes called consumption of fixed capital, which is the amount that business firms must set aside to replace structures and equipment that wear out or become obsolete (like old jet aircraft that still work but use too much fuel or make too much

Depreciation (consumption of fixed capital) represents the part of the capital stock used up due to obsolescence and physical wear.

Table 2-1   **Households Get What Remains After All the Leakages**

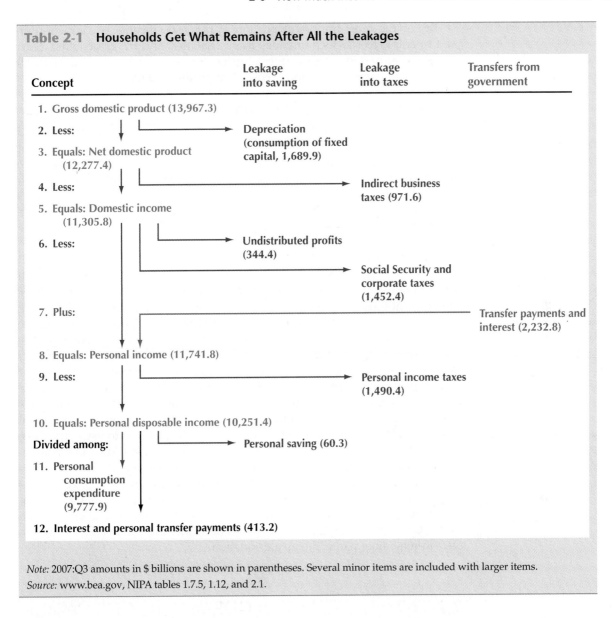

Concept	Leakage into saving	Leakage into taxes	Transfers from government
1. Gross domestic product (13,967.3)			
2. Less:	Depreciation (consumption of fixed capital, 1,689.9)		
3. Equals: Net domestic product (12,277.4)			
4. Less:		Indirect business taxes (971.6)	
5. Equals: Domestic income (11,305.8)			
6. Less:	Undistributed profits (344.4)		
		Social Security and corporate taxes (1,452.4)	
7. Plus:			Transfer payments and interest (2,232.8)
8. Equals: Personal income (11,741.8)			
9. Less:		Personal income taxes (1,490.4)	
10. Equals: Personal disposable income (10,251.4)			
Divided among:	Personal saving (60.3)		
11. Personal consumption expenditure (9,777.9)			
12. Interest and personal transfer payments (413.2)			

Note: 2007:Q3 amounts in $ billions are shown in parentheses. Several minor items are included with larger items.
Source: www.bea.gov, NIPA tables 1.7.5, 1.12, and 2.1.

noise). Since depreciation deductions are not counted as corporate profits, such deductions do not count as income. What remains after depreciation deductions appears on line 3, and is called **net domestic product (NDP)**. This represents how much we produce each year after setting aside enough to replace worn-out and obsolete capital.

The terms **gross** and **net** in economics usually refer to the inclusion or exclusion of depreciation. Thus the difference between "gross investment" and "net investment," or between "gross saving" and "net saving," is exactly the same type of distinction as that between GDP and NDP.

Next, line 4 in Table 2-1 deducts indirect business taxes, which include state and local sales and property taxes. These tax payments are not available as income to households or business firms. Only what is left over, called **domestic income** (line 5), is available to provide net income to the domestic factors of production (labor and capital) that produce current output.

Net domestic product (NDP) is equal to GDP minus depreciation.

In economics, **gross** refers to the inclusion of depreciation; **net** refers to the exclusion of depreciation.

Domestic income is the earnings of domestic factors of production, computed as net domestic product, minus indirect business taxes, which are taxes levied on business sales.

By far the most important portion of domestic income is compensation paid to employees (which includes wages, salaries, and fringe benefits). Next in order of importance are net interest income, proprietors' income (from small businesses like farms and shops), corporate profits, and rental income.

From Domestic Income to Personal Income

Not all of domestic income is paid out to households as personal income, and personal income also includes some receipts by households that are not counted in GDP or domestic income. Lines 6 and 7 in Table 2-1 explain these differences. First, part of domestic income is kept by corporations in the form of undistributed profits—that is, the part of corporate profits that is not paid as dividends to stockholders or as corporate taxes to the government. Undistributed profits are a type of saving leakage, providing funding for the capital market to finance investment spending.

Next, large amounts flow to the government in the form of corporate and Social Security tax payments, then back from the government to households in the form of transfer payments like Social Security and unemployment benefits. Government funds also are paid out for interest on the national debt. Adjusting domestic income for these deductions and additions yields **personal income,** the sum of income payments to households (line 8). Personal income represents the current flow of purchasing power to households coming from *both* the productive activities of business firms *and* transfers from the government sector.

All personal income is not available to households to spend, first because they must pay personal income taxes to the government (line 9). What remains is one of the most important concepts in national income accounting, **personal disposable income** (line 10). This is available for households to use in the three ways shown at the bottom of Table 2-1: consumption expenditure, personal interest and transfer payments, and personal saving (lines 11 and 12).

The total saving and tax leakages (with transfers treated as a negative tax) are symbolized as $S + T$ in equation (2.5) on p. 34, which shows that, by definition, they must be equal to nonconsumption spending (injections), symbolized by $I + G + NX$. This is the leakages–injections identity, for which we use the easy-to-remember name, the magic equation.

Personal income is the income received by households from all sources, including earnings and transfer payments.

Personal disposable income is personal income minus personal income tax payments.

2-7 Nominal GDP, Real GDP, and the GDP Deflator

Thus far, all the terms and relationships of national income accounting apply to a particular time period (a quarter or a year) and are measured at the prices actually paid by households and firms. Any economic magnitude measured at the prices actually paid is described by the adjective **nominal.** For instance, **nominal GDP** is the total amount of current product valued at the prices actually paid on the market.

Nominal is an adjective that modifies any economic magnitude measured in current prices.

Nominal GDP is the value of gross domestic product in current (actual) prices.

Real and Nominal Magnitudes

Nominal amounts are not very useful for economic analysis because they can increase either when people buy more physical goods and services—more cars, steaks, and haircuts—or when prices rise. An increase in my nominal spending on consumption goods from $40,000 in 2007 to $50,000 in 2008 might indicate that I became able to buy more items, or it could simply mean that I had to pay higher prices in 2008 for the same items purchased in 2007. Changes in nominal magnitudes hide more than they reveal. So economists focus on changes in real magnitudes, which eliminate the influence of year-to-year changes in prices and reflect true changes in the number, size, and quality of items purchased.

Real GDP and Real Output

To focus on changes in production and eliminate the influence of changing prices, we need a measure of real gross domestic product, or real GDP. Like any real magnitude, real GDP is expressed in the prices of an arbitrarily chosen base year. The official measures of GDP in the United States currently use 2000 as the base year. Real GDP for every year, whether 1929 or 2008, is measured by taking the production of that particular year expressed at the constant prices of 2000. For instance, 2008 real GDP measured in 2000 prices represents the amount that the actual 2008 production of goods and services would have cost if each item *had been sold at its 2000 price.*

Since prices usually increase each year, nominal GDP is higher than real GDP for years after 2000. Similarly, nominal GDP is lower than real GDP for years before 2000. You can see this regular pattern in Figure 2-4, which displays nominal and real GDP for each year since 1900. Only in 2000 are nominal and real GDP the same.

The ratio of nominal GDP to real GDP is a price index called the **GDP deflator,** and this is displayed as the orange line in Figure 2-4. The GDP deflator measures the ratio of the prices actually paid in a particular year to the prices paid in the base year 2000. For instance, in 1959 nominal GDP was about one-fifth of real GDP, indicating that prices actually paid in 1959 were about one-fifth of the prices that would have been paid in 2000 for the same goods and services.

The **GDP deflator** is the economy's aggregate price index and is defined as the ratio of nominal GDP to chain-weighted real GDP.

Later on we will consider other real magnitudes, such as real consumption and the real money supply. An alternative label for real magnitudes is constant-dollar; in contrast, nominal magnitudes are usually called current-dollar. To summarize:

Alternative labels for magnitudes			
Items measured in prices of a single year	Constant-dollar	or	Real
Items measured in actual prices paid in each separate year	Current-dollar	or	Nominal

Why We Care About Real GDP and the GDP Deflator

We care about real GDP because its movements create a mirror image movement in the opposite direction in the unemployment rate, one of the three key macroeconomic concepts introduced in Chapter 1. Further, we care about accurate measurements of real GDP, since they are essential to measuring productivity, or output per hour, the third of our central macro concepts.

We care about the GDP deflator because it is the basis for measuring the inflation rate. Recall from the beginning of Chapter 1 that the inflation rate is the percentage rate of increase in the economywide average price level, which we measure by the GDP deflator. To convert the GDP deflator into the inflation rate, we use the universal formula for calculating growth rates shown in the box on p. 41.

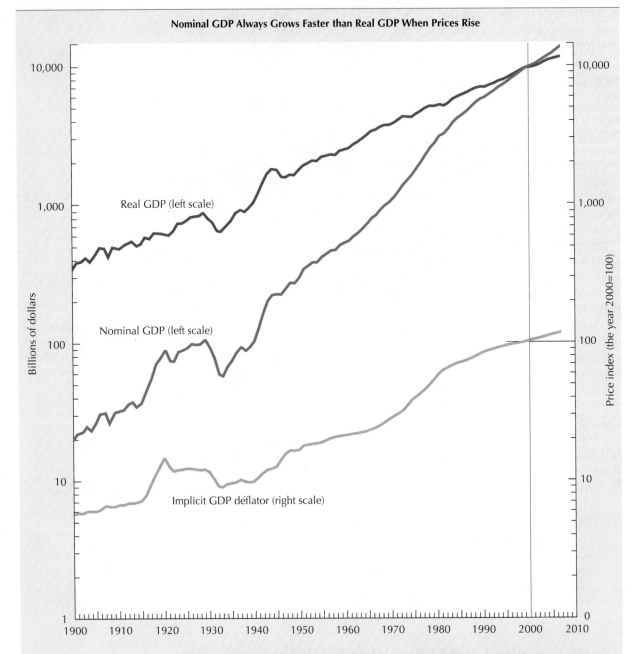

Figure 2-4 Nominal GDP, Real GDP, and the GDP Deflator, 1900–2007.
Notice how the nominal GDP line lies below the real GDP line before 2000 but lies above the real GDP line after 2000. This reflects the fact that before 2000 the current prices used to measure nominal GDP were lower than the 2000 prices used to measure real GDP. After 2000, the current prices used to measure nominal GDP were higher than the 2000 prices used to measure real GDP. Notice how the nominal GDP line crosses the real GDP line in 2000, the same year that the GDP deflator attains the value of 1.0.

Source: Appendix Table A-1. See explanation in Appendix C-4.

How to Calculate Inflation, Real GDP Growth, or Any Other Growth Rate

Often you will want to calculate a percentage growth rate, whether of the U.S. rate of inflation, real GDP, or even your own income over a period of years. In this section we will learn a very simple formula that will allow you to calculate the growth rate of *anything* over any period, no matter how long or short, and convert it to an annual rate.

In this book we will use lowercase letters, say *x*, to designate the growth rate of a variable, the level of which is called the same uppercase letter *X*. Let's say that we have been given the value of the GDP deflator for 1974 as 34.7 and for 1975 as 38.0, and we have been asked to calculate the inflation rate for 1975. (You will find GDP deflator data for these and many other years in Appendix Table A-1 in the back of this book.)

The general formula to calculate the percentage annual growth rate of any variable *X* at a time period *t* from another period *s* years earlier (call this *t-s*) is as follows:

General Form
$$x_t = 100 \, LN(X_t/X_{t-s})/s$$
Numerical Example
$$9.08 = 100 \, LN(38.0\,/34.7)/1.0$$

Here *LN* means "natural logarithm" and is a function found on any scientific calculator. The answer to the example is found simply by taking the ratio 38.0/34.7 = 1.0951 and then pushing the "LN" button, which yields 0.0908, and finally multiplying that result by 100.

Exactly the same formula can be used to calculate the annual rate of inflation between two adjacent quarters. Let us take the level of the GDP deflator for the first quarter of 2007, abbreviated "2007:Q1" from Appendix Table

A-2, which is 118.75. The value for the next quarter, 2007:Q2, is 119.53. What is the annual rate of inflation between those two quarters?

General Form
$$x_t = 100 \, LN(X_t/X_{t-s})/s$$
Numerical Example
$$2.64 = 100 \, LN(119.53/118.75)/0.25$$

The method is exactly the same. The only difference is that now we are comparing two adjacent quarters rather than two adjacent years, and so *s* = 0.25 instead of *s* = 1 as before.

Our final exercise is to calculate the average annual growth rate of U.S. real GDP from 1875 to 2006, using the data in Appendix Table A-1:

General Form
$$x_t = 100 \, LN(X_t/X_{t-s})/s$$
Numerical Example
$$3.45 = 100 \, LN(11,319/123)/131$$

Again, this is exactly the same formula, now with *s* = 131 since there are 131 years between 1875 and 2006. Despite the fact that real GDP in 2004 was 92.0 times larger than in 1875, such a long period elapsed between those two years that the annual growth rate was a mere 3.45 percent.

The extremely useful formula discussed in this box can be used for any calculation involving growth rates, not just for such macroeconomic concepts as the price level or real GDP, but to calculate the annual rate of return of an investment over any period of time, even for a single day.

Further, we care about the GDP deflator because very fast inflation can destroy a society, as in the German hyperinflation (see pp. 16–17). Even in the United States, inflation was so rapid in the 1970s and early 1980s that draconian measures were taken to stop it. As a result, interest rates rose to unprecedented heights, decimating the auto and construction industries, and the unemployment rate rose in 1982 to its highest level since the 1930s. Fast inflation is bad because of the direct harm it causes, and because of the indirect harm done by measures taken to stop it. And to measure the inflation rate, we need to start with the GDP deflator.

The Appendix to Chapter 2 provides the details that you need to understand how to calculate real GDP and the GDP deflator from specific prices and quantities of individual products.

SELF-TEST

Without looking at Figure 2-4, you should now be able to answer the following:
1. Is the implicit GDP deflator greater or less than 1.00 in every year before 2000? In every year after 2000?
2. In what year is the implicit GDP deflator equal to exactly 1.00?

2-8 Measuring Unemployment

The unemployment rate is the first of the central macro concepts introduced in Chapter 1. Families dread the financial and emotional disruption caused by layoffs, so news of an increase in the unemployment rate creates public concern and plummeting popularity ratings for incumbent politicians. Because of widespread public awareness, the unemployment rate is generally considered the most important of the central macro concepts. In this section we learn how the unemployment rate is measured.

The Unemployment Survey

Many people wonder how the government determines facts such as "the teenage unemployment rate in November 2007 was 16.3 percent," because they themselves have never spoken to a government agent about their own experiences of employment, unemployment, and time in school. It would be too costly to contact everyone in the country every month; the government attempts to reach each household to collect information only once each decade when it takes the decennial Census of Population. However, it would not be enough to collect information just once every ten years, because then policymakers would have no guidance for conducting current policy.

As a compromise, each month 1,500 Census Bureau workers interview about 60,000 households, or about 1 in every 1,400 households in the country. Each month one-fourth of the households in the sample are replaced, so that no family is interviewed more than four months in a row. The laws of statistics imply that an average from a survey of a sample of households of this size comes very close to the true figure that would be revealed by a costly complete census.

Questions asked in the survey. The interviewer first asks each separate household member, "What were you doing most of last week—working, keeping house, going to school, or something else?" Anyone who has done any work at all for pay during the past week, whether part-time (even one hour per week), full-time, or temporary work, is counted as employed.

For those who say they did no work, the next question is, "Did you have a job from which you were temporarily absent or on layoff last week?" If the person is awaiting recall from a layoff or has obtained a new job but is waiting for it to begin, he or she is counted as unemployed.

If the person has neither worked nor been absent from a job, the next question is, "Have you been looking for work in the last four weeks, and if so, what have you been doing in the last four weeks to find work?" A person who has not been ill and has searched for a job by applying to an employer, registering with an employment agency, checking with friends, or other specified job-search activities is counted as unemployed. The remaining people who are nei-ther employed nor unemployed, mainly homemakers who do not seek paid work, students, disabled people, and retired people, fall in the category of "not in the labor force."

Definitions based on the interview. Despite the intricacy of questions asked by the interviewer, the concept is simple: People with jobs are employed; people who do not have jobs and are looking for jobs are **unemployed;** people who meet neither labor-market test are not in the labor force. The **total labor force** is the total of the civilian employed, the armed forces, and the unemployed. Thus the entire population aged 16 and over falls into one of four categories:

1. Total labor force
   a. Civilian employed
   b. Armed forces
   c. Unemployed
2. Not in the labor force

The actual **unemployment rate** is defined as the ratio

$$U = \frac{\text{number of unemployed}}{\text{civilian employed } + \text{ unemployed}}$$

Example: In November 2007, the BLS reported an unemployment rate of 4.7 percent. This was calculated as the ratio

$$U = \frac{\text{number of unemployed}}{\text{civilian employed } + \text{ unemployed}} = \frac{7,167,000}{146,703,000 + 7,167,000}$$

or

$$U = 4.7 \text{ percent}$$

The labor force participation rate is the ratio of the total labor force (civilian employed, armed forces, and the unemployed) to the population aged 16 or over. Those who do not participate in the labor force include those above age 15 who are in school, retired individuals, people who do not work because they are raising children or otherwise choose to stay at home, and those who cannot work because they are ill, disabled, or have given up on finding jobs. In November 2007 this rate was 66.1 percent.

Flaws in the definition. The government's unemployment measure sounds relatively straightforward, but unfortunately it disguises almost as much as it reveals:

1. *The unemployment rate by itself is not a measure of the social distress caused by the loss of a job.* Each person who lacks a job and is looking for one is counted as "1.0 unemployed people," whether the person is the head of a household responsible for feeding numerous dependents or a 16-year-old looking only for a 10-hour-per-week part-time job to provide pocket money. Only a minority of the unemployed can be described as workers who have lost one job and are looking for another.
2. *The government's unemployment concept misses some of the people hurt by a recession.* Some suffer a cut in hours, being forced by their employers to shift from full-time to part-time work. Still counted as employed, these "involuntary part-time" workers never enter the unemployment statistics.

The **unemployed** are those without jobs who either are on temporary layoff or have taken specific actions to look for work.

The **total labor force** is the total of the civilian employed, the armed forces, and the unemployed.

The **unemployment rate** is the ratio of the number unemployed to the number in the labor force, expressed as a percentage.

3. *A person lacking a job must have performed particular specified actions to look for a job during the past four weeks.* What about people who have looked and looked and have given up, convinced that no job is available? They are not counted as unemployed at all. They simply disappear from the labor force, entering the category of "not in the labor force." Those out of the labor force who would like to work but have given up on the job search are sometimes called "discouraged workers" or the "disguised unemployed."

Do the flaws matter? Since the official concept of the unemployment rate omits those who are involuntarily working part-time when they would prefer full-time employment, and also omits the discouraged workers, it is generally agreed that the official concept understates the total amount of unemployment. Yet this does not turn out to be very important, since a broader measure of unemployment, which includes the effect of involuntary part-time work as well as the discouraged workers, exhibits cyclical fluctuations similar to those of the official concept of the unemployment rate. Recessions and expansions occur at the same time. The primary impediment to achieving low unemployment, which is the tendency of the economy to generate accelerating inflation when the unemployment rate becomes too low, is completely independent of the particular unemployment measure that is used.

2-9 Case Study

Conflicting Measurements: Was the 2002–04 Recovery "Jobless" or Not?

A frequent point of contention in the 2004 presidential election campaign between George W. Bush and John Kerry was whether the economy was strong or weak. While real GDP had grown at a relatively rapid rate of 3.4 percent per annum during the first three years after the 2001 recession, employment had actually declined.

Or at least one measure of employment had declined, but another had increased. The government keeps track of two different measures of employment, and these were in sharp conflict in tracking the evolution of employment from 2001 to 2004.

The previous section described the "household" survey, also called the "Current Population Survey." As we have seen, interviewers ask questions that allow each member of the household to be counted as employed, unemployed, or not in the labor force. The total level of employment from the household survey is plotted as the blue line in Figure 2-5.

A different story is told by the orange line, which shows the level of employment reported by the "payroll" employment survey, also known as the "establishment" survey. In contrast to the household survey, which interviews 60,000 households, the payroll survey is based on 400,000 establishments that submit more than 8 million records of employees. Here are the key differences between the two measures of employment.

- **People versus jobs.** The household survey counts the number of people with jobs, while the payroll survey counts the number of jobs. People who have two jobs are counted as two employed people in the payroll survey but only as one employed person in the household survey.

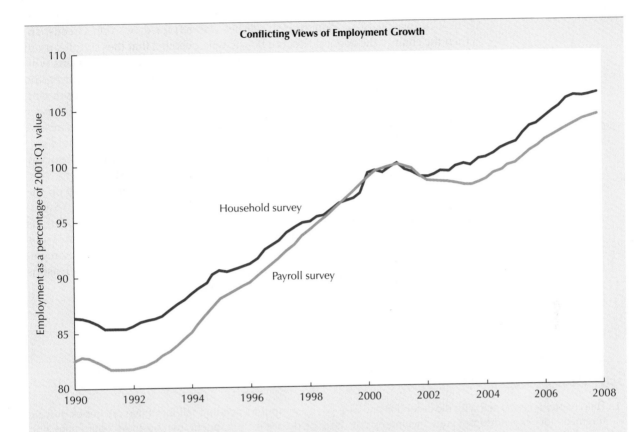

Figure 2-5 Employment from the Household and Payroll Surveys, 1990–2007
The blue line displays total employment as measured by the household survey. The orange line displays total employment as measured by the payroll survey. Both series are set equal to 100 in the first quarter of 2001 in order to highlight that the payroll measure grew faster in the 1990s but grew more slowly between 2001 and 2004.

Source: Bureau of Labor Statistics.

- **Sample size.** The payroll survey is much larger, leading many observers to think that it is more accurate.
- **Sources of error.** The household survey may miss new immigrants who may have a different pattern of employment than native Americans or previous immigrants. The payroll survey may miss newly created firms, particularly in the early stages of a business cycle expansion as in 2001–04.

The disagreement between the surveys was particularly acute in 2001–04, as shown in Figure 2–5. Between the start of the recession in 2001:Q1 and 2004:Q3, the quarter before the election, the household survey reported that employment had increased by 1.8 million. But the payroll survey disagreed, stating that employment had *declined* by almost 1 million jobs. Democratic candidates used the payroll survey number to gloat that, "George Bush is the only president since Herbert Hoover to have employment decline during his administration." Republicans retorted that employment had increased, citing the household survey.

Who was right? A nonpartisan verdict was rendered by Alan Greenspan, then the chair of the Federal Reserve Board, who believed that the payroll survey was more accurate because of its larger sample. But there are two reasons why the household survey could register a faster increase in employment during the 2002–04 recovery. First, many employees of large firms who lost their jobs during the 2001 recession went into business for themselves as consultants. No longer employees of firms covered by the payroll survey, they would have been missed by that survey but would have been reported as employed by the household survey. Second, as stated above, the sample of establishments in the payroll survey becomes increasingly obsolete as businesses fail and new ones start up.

For the years since the 2004 election, the two surveys agree closely on the growth of employment, which over the period 2004:Q3–2007:Q4 was 6.8 million for the household survey and 6.6 million for the payroll survey. But, as shown in Figure 2-5, the two surveys still disagree on the total number of jobs created since the start of the recession in 2001:Q1. The household survey registered 8.6 million new jobs versus 5.7 million for the payroll survey; the reasons for this disagreement still have not been resolved. ●

Summary

1. This chapter is concerned with the definition and measurement of expenditures and income—what is included and excluded, and why, as well as with the measurement of real GDP, inflation, and the unemployment rate.

2. A flow magnitude is any money payment, physical good, or service that flows from one economic unit to another per unit of time. A flow is distinguished from a stock, which is an economic magnitude in the possession of an individual or firm at a moment of time.

3. Final product (GDP) consists of all currently produced goods and services sold through the market but not resold during the current time period. By counting intermediate goods only once, and by including only final purchases, we avoid double-counting and ensure that the value of final product and total income created (value added) are equal.

4. GNP equals GDP plus factor payments received from the rest of the world minus factor payments sent to the rest of the world.

5. Leakages out of income available for consumption spending are, by definition, exactly balanced by injections of nonconsumption spending. This equality of leakages and injections is guaranteed, by definition, to be true.

6. In the same way, by definition, total income (consumption plus leakages) equals total expenditure (consumption plus injections). Injections of nonconsumption spending fall into three categories: private domestic investment (on business equipment and structures, residential housing, and inventory accumulation); foreign investment or net exports; and government spending on goods and services. The definitions require private saving to exceed private investment (domestic and foreign) by the amount of the government deficit.

7. Net domestic product (NDP) is obtained by deducting depreciation from GDP. Deduction of indirect business taxes from NDP yields domestic income, the sum of all net incomes earned by domestic factors of production in producing current output. If we deduct corporate undistributed profits, corporate income taxes, and Social Security taxes, and add in transfer payments, we arrive at personal income, the sum of all income payments to individuals. Personal disposable income is personal income after the deduction of personal income taxes.

8. The GDP deflator is defined as nominal GDP in actual current prices divided by real GDP.

9. Those aged 16 and over are counted as unemployed if they are temporarily laid off or want a job, and take specified actions to find a job. The unemployment rate is the number of unemployed expressed as a percent of the total number of persons employed and unemployed.

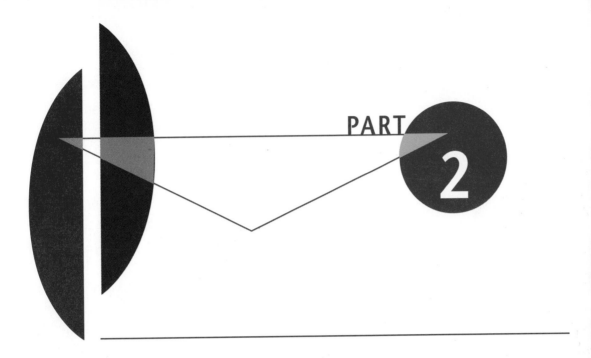

Income, Interest Rates, Policy, and the Open Economy

CHAPTER

3

Spending, Income, and Interest Rates

*An honest man is one who knows that he can't consume more than
he has produced.*
—Ayn Rand, 1966

Our introduction to macroeconomics in Chapter 1 distinguished two main groups of issues: those that concern *short-run* business cycles or economic fluctuations and those that concern the economy's *long-run* growth rate and the sources of differences in the standard of living of rich and poor nations. This chapter begins a two-part unit, spanning Chapters 3–9, that develops the theory of business cycles and examines the potential role of monetary and fiscal policy in dampening the amplitude of these cycles. Thus we will be concerned with the *short-run* behavior of the economy for the next several chapters and will return to the sources of *long-run* growth starting in Chapter 10.

Autonomous –

3-1 Business Cycles and the Theory of Income Determination

As we learned in Chapter 1, a business cycle refers to the alternation of periods of rapid or slow growth in real GDP. Figure 1-3 contrasts two hypothetical nations to demonstrate the importance of minimizing fluctuations in real GDP, with "Volatilia" showing large swings in real GDP, and "Stabilia" showing much smaller swings because of its more stable economy. Figure 1-4 defines the key terminology of business cycles, describing an economy that starts from a trough in real GDP, proceeds through an expansion that usually lasts several years until real GDP reaches its peak, followed by a recession that only lasts a few quarters until the next trough. In this chapter we start to learn about the origins of business cycles; we put together into a simple economic model the numerous factors that contribute to economic volatility.

The Reduced Volatility of Business Cycles: "The Great Moderation"

The goals of monetary and fiscal policy are to dampen business cycles and move toward an ideal world in which real GDP grows steadily from one quarter to the next. The real world as shown in Figure 3-1 is far from that ideal world. Plotted along the red line are changes in real GDP compared with the same quarter one year earlier. Since 1950, the four-quarter growth rate of real GDP has been as high as 12.6 percent and as low as −3.1 percent.

A notable feature of Figure 3-1 is that real GDP was much more volatile before 1985 than after. In fact, real GDP growth showed remarkable steadiness

*monetary
money Supply
Interest Rates*

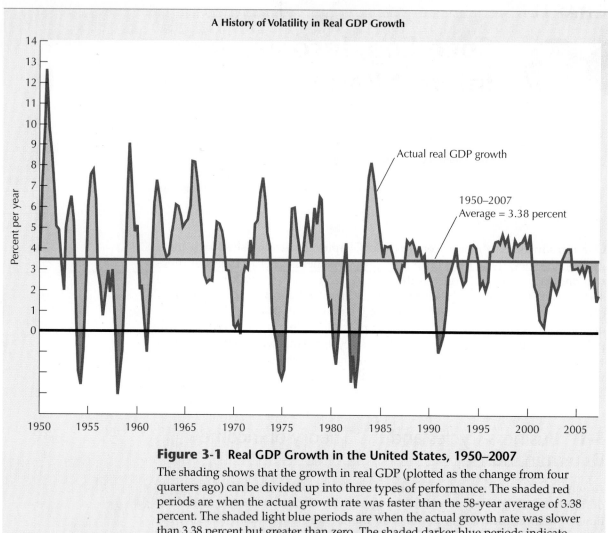

Figure 3-1 Real GDP Growth in the United States, 1950–2007

The shading shows that the growth in real GDP (plotted as the change from four quarters ago) can be divided up into three types of performance. The shaded red periods are when the actual growth rate was faster than the 58-year average of 3.38 percent. The shaded light blue periods are when the actual growth rate was slower than 3.38 percent but greater than zero. The shaded darker blue periods indicate periods of negative real GDP growth.

Aggregate demand is the total amount of desired spending expressed in current (nominal) dollars.

A **demand shock** is a significant change in desired spending by consumers, business firms, the government, or foreigners.

between 1992 and 2000, with most quarters relatively close to the 1950–2007 average growth rate of 3.4 percent. The improved stability of the economy since 1985 has been called the "Great Moderation," and there has been much debate among macroeconomists about its causes. Were there fewer or smaller "shocks" that caused changes in real GDP? Did monetary or fiscal policy simply do a better job at offsetting shocks that were similar in frequency and size to those before 1985? To understand this debate, we begin with a simple model showing how real GDP is determined and how monetary and fiscal policy can be used to offset shocks that affect real GDP.

In this chapter, we begin the process of identifying what some of those shocks may be. Among these are changes in consumer confidence, business optimism, government spending, and foreign events that influence U.S. exports and imports. These shocks to **aggregate demand** (also known as **demand shocks**) are the basic source of business cycles and economic volatility.

One possible reason for the improved performance since 1985 might be that demand shocks have become smaller and less important. Another reason might be that monetary and fiscal policies have become more effective, countering demand shocks without delay. A third reason might be some change in conditions that makes monetary and/or fiscal policy more powerful. Our model of income determination allows for all of these possibilities. We learn how demand shocks have a multiplier effect, exacerbating the impact of any given demand shock on real GDP. We learn that the stabilizing impact of monetary and fiscal policy can be strong or weak, depending on particular relationships in the economy.

3-2   Income Determination, Unemployment, and the Price Level

We learned at the beginning of this book that the three central macroeconomic concepts are unemployment, inflation, and productivity growth. Yet our theory in this chapter concerns the level of real GDP and real income, not the unemployment rate, inflation, or productivity growth. Why? We postpone our treatment of the determinants of productivity growth as part of our examination of long-run economic growth later in the book; also we postpone our treatment of inflation until Chapters 7–9. Finally, we do not need a separate theory of fluctuations in the unemployment rate, since unemployment is the mirror image of business cycles in real GDP, or more precisely of changes in the difference (gap) between actual and natural real GDP (see Chapter 1, Figure 1-2). When that gap rises into positive territory as the economy expands, the unemployment rate falls; when that gap becomes negative as the economy slides into a recession, the unemployment rate rises. *Thus the key to understanding the causes of fluctuations in unemployment is to develop a theory of fluctuations in real GDP.*

Income Determination and the Price Level

Shocks to aggregate demand can change either real GDP, the price level (GDP deflator), or both. Later we will learn that the division of changes in aggregate demand between changes in real GDP and the price level depends both on shocks to aggregate demand and to **aggregate supply,** the amount that firms are willing to produce at a given price level. Changes in aggregate supply depend on such factors as the costs of production for business firms, including wages and the prices of raw materials such as oil. It makes sense to discuss changes in aggregate demand and in aggregate supply separately. We cover aggregate demand in Chapters 3 and 4 and aggregate supply in Chapters 7 and 8.

As we have learned, economic theory is a process of simplification that allows us to study parts of a problem, one at a time, and then bring together those parts into a more complete model of the economy. In order to focus on changes in aggregate demand, we will make a bold but extremely useful simplifying assumption: *The price level is fixed in the short run.* Because the price level is fixed, *all changes in aggregate demand automatically cause changes in real GDP by the same amount in the same direction.*

> **Aggregate supply** is the amount that firms are willing to produce at any given price level.
> Short-Run

$$\text{Changes in Real GDP} = \frac{\text{Changes in Aggregate Demand}}{\text{Fixed Price Level}} \quad (3.1)$$

Many features of the real world support our assumption that the price level is fixed in the short run and that changes in aggregate demand are translated directly into changes in real GDP. Prices in restaurants are printed on menus that are expensive to reprint. Price labels for many products on supermarket shelves are changed infrequently. Prices in mail-order catalogues are set for the entire season until the next catalogue is printed. The most important cost for many business firms is the cost of the wages and salaries paid to workers, and the wage or salary level usually changes only once each year, and some wages are set by labor union contracts that last for as long as three years.

True, the prices of vegetables at the supermarket and of gasoline at the pump can change from day to day, but we gain insight by adhering to the useful simplification that all prices are like those in mail-order catalogues, fixed for a set period of time. Once we have used this simplification to learn about shocks to aggregate demand and the potential role of monetary and fiscal policy in stabilizing the economy, we then will be ready to turn to the role of aggregate supply in determining the division of aggregate demand changes between changes in real GDP and in the price level.

What We Explain and What We Take as Given

Endogenous variables are those explained by an economic theory.

Exogenous variables are those that are relevant but whose behavior the theory does not attempt to explain; their values are taken as given.

money supply
Gov't spending

Any theoretical model in economics sets limits on what it tries to explain. The limited number of variables to be explained are called **endogenous variables.** The large number of variables that are taken as given and are not explained are called **exogenous variables.**

In macroeconomic theory we begin with a short list of endogenous variables and treat most as exogenous. Gradually, we move some from the exogenous list to the endogenous list as our theory becomes more realistic. In the first part of Chapter 3, we develop a simple model that explains only two endogenous variables, consumption and real GDP. All the other important macroeconomic variables are not explained, that is, they are treated as exogenous variables. This includes not just the price level, which is treated as fixed (as discussed in the previous section), but also investment and interest rates. In the last part of Chapter 3, we move investment to the list of endogenous variables. Then in Chapter 4 a more complete model shifts the interest rate to the list of endogenous variables. In Chapter 7, we complete our process of model building by shifting the price level to the list of endogenous variables.

Throughout our study of business cycles in Chapters 3–9, the key instruments of monetary and fiscal policy will continue to be treated as exogenous, or taken as given. These include the money supply, government spending, and tax rates. Also taken as exogenous is the real GDP of foreign nations that determine the quantity of U.S. exports, as well as potential causes of demand shocks, such as changes in the confidence of consumers about future incomes and jobs and the confidence of business firms about future sales and profits. Now we turn to the simplest version of the theory of income determination that treats only consumption and income (or real GDP) as endogenous and everything else as exogenous.

3-3 Planned Expenditure

Our study of national income accounting in Chapter 2 identified four types of expenditure on GDP. By definition, total expenditure on GDP (E) is equal to the sum of these four components: consumption (C), investment (I), government spending on goods and services (G), and net exports (NX).

$$E \equiv C + I + G + NX \qquad (3.2)$$

The Consumption Function

At the beginning, we treat only consumption spending (C) as endogenous, or explained by the theory, and treat the other three types of planned spending as exogenous. An obvious way to explain consumption is that people spend more when their incomes go up and vice versa. The income that matters for consumption decisions is income after taxes, or disposable personal income. This can be written as total real income (Y) minus personal taxes paid (T), or $Y - T$.[1]

How do households divide their disposable income between consumption and saving? Households consume a fixed amount that does not depend on their disposable income, plus a fraction of each dollar of disposable income:

General Linear Form

$$C = C_a + c(Y - T) \qquad (3.3)$$

The fixed amount is called **autonomous** consumption, abbreviated (C_a), and this is completely independent of disposable income. The amount by which consumption expenditures increase for each extra dollar of disposable income is a fraction called the **marginal propensity to consume,** abbreviated (c). This equation (3.3) says, in words, that consumption spending (C) equals autonomous consumption (C_a) plus the marginal propensity to consume times disposable income [$c(Y - T)$]. Another name for this last term is **induced consumption.**

The *consumption function* is any relationship that describes the determinants of consumption spending. This function can be written as a general expression, as in equation (3.3), or as a numerical example. For instance, if we choose $500 billion to be the value of autonomous consumption and 0.75 to be the value of the marginal propensity to consume, the consumption function can be written

Numerical Example

$$C = 500 + 0.75 (Y - T)$$

An **autonomous** magnitude is independent of the level of income. $\left(F_{ixed}^{c} \right)$

The **marginal propensity to consume** is the dollar change in consumption expenditures per dollar change in disposable income.

Induced consumption is the portion of consumption spending that responds to changes in income.

The consumption function using this numerical example can also be shown graphically, as in Figure 3-2. The thick red line shows on the vertical axis the amount of consumption for alternative values of disposable income (measured along the horizontal axis). When disposable income is zero, total consumption consists just of the autonomous component ($500 billion). For each extra $1,000 billion of disposable income, as we move to the right on the graph, the red consumption function line rises by $750 billion, since its slope (the marginal propensity to consume) is 0.75. For instance, at point D disposable income is $8,000 billion and total consumption is $6,500 billion (consisting of $6,000 billion of induced consumption and $500 billion of autonomous consumption).

---

[1] The notation T in this chapter continues, as in Chapter 2, to mean "total taxes minus transfer payments."

Figure 3-2 A Simple Hypothesis Regarding Consumption Behavior

The red line passing through *F* and *D* illustrates the consumption function. It shows that consumption is 75 percent of disposable income plus an autonomous component of $500 billion that is spent regardless of the level of disposable income. The blue shaded area shows the amount of positive saving that occurs when income exceeds consumption; the pink area shows the amount of negative saving (dissaving) that occurs when consumption exceeds income.

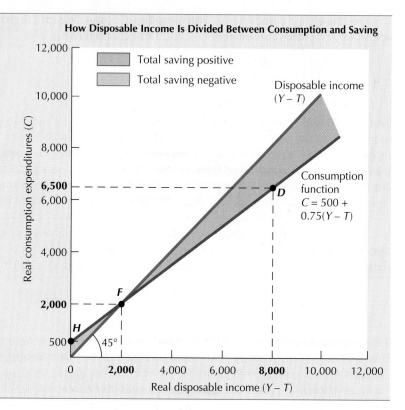

How Disposable Income Is Divided Between Consumption and Saving

---

SELF-TEST

1. If a person's disposable income is zero, what is that person's level of consumption spending in the general linear form of equation (3.3)? In the numerical example?

2. How can that person consume a positive amount with a zero disposable income? Think of yourself—what options are open to you to buy something even if you have no income?

Induced Saving and the Marginal Propensity to Save

The simplest way to show the amount of saving is to use a graph like Figure 3-2. The thick green line shows the amount of disposable income in both a horizontal and a vertical direction; this line is often called the "45-degree" line. Since the thick red line shows the consumption function, the distance between the two lines indicates the total amount of saving.

To the right of point *F*, total saving is positive because disposable income exceeds consumption; this is indicated by the blue shading. To the left of point *F*, total saving is negative because consumption exceeds disposable income; this is indicated by the pink shading. How can saving be negative? Individuals can consume more than they earn, at least for a while, by withdrawing funds from a savings account, by selling stocks and bonds, or by borrowing. Negative saving is quite typical for many college students who borrow to finance their education.

The blue shaded vertical distance between the green and red lines represents saving (S), that is, the difference between disposable income and consumption:

General Linear Form

$$S = Y - T - C = Y - T - C_a - c(Y - T)$$
$$= -C_a + (1-c)(Y - T)$$

Numerical Example

$$S = Y - T - C = Y - T - 500 - 0.75(Y - T)$$
$$= -500 + 0.25(Y - T) \qquad (3.4)$$

This *saving function* starts with the definition of saving as personal disposable income minus consumption; then it substitutes the consumption function from equation (3.3). The last line simplifies the saving function, which now states that personal saving equals minus the amount of autonomous consumption ($-C_a$) plus the **marginal propensity to save** $(1 - c)$ times disposable income $(Y - T)$.

Marginal propensity to save is the change in personal saving induced by a $1 change in personal disposable income.

Notice the three points in Figure 3-2 marked with letters corresponding to different levels of disposable income. At H, disposable income is zero, so consumption is C_a, or 500, and saving from equation (3.4) is $-C_a$, or -500. At F, disposable income and consumption are equal, so saving is zero. At D, consumption of 6,500 is less than disposable income of 8,000, so saving is a positive 1,500.

SELF-TEST

1. Can you derive a general expression showing how the level of consumption and disposable income at point F depend on autonomous consumption (C_a) and the marginal propensity to consume (c)?

2. If disposable income is 5,000 rather than 8,000, the economy in Figure 3-2 will be at a point between points F and D. Calculate the values of consumption (C) and saving (S) when disposable income is 5,000.

Autonomous Consumption, the Interest Rate, and the Stock Market

Thus far we have seen that the total amount of consumption spending will change if there is a change in income, but also if any factor causes a change in autonomous consumption (C_a). What are these factors? One of the most important is the interest rate; as we learn in the last part of this chapter, autonomous consumption rises when the interest rate falls and vice versa. Low interest rates in 2001–04 stimulated consumption of automobiles and houses, and these low interest rates (working through their stimulus to autonomous consumption) help to explain why the recession of 2001 was so mild.

Similarly, the increase of interest rates in 2004–06 put a squeeze on consumer purchases of cars and houses, and by 2007 many households that could not afford the higher interest rates charged on their mortgages were "foreclosed" by banks, meaning that they were forced to move out of their homes due to their inability to pay the higher monthly mortgage interest payments.

The other major factor affecting autonomous consumption is **household wealth.** This consists of all the assets of households, particularly the market value of houses, stocks, bonds, and bank accounts, minus any mortgage loans, credit card balances, or other liabilities. When wealth increases, households can spend more even if their income is fixed, thus boosting autonomous consumption and reducing saving. As discussed in the next section, the boom in the stock market in the late 1990s raised household wealth and helps to explain why the household saving rate decreased so much. The collapse in the stock market in 2000–03 did not cause a reversal of the household saving rate, because household

Automosis Comsumption ↑ when wealth ↑'s.

Household wealth is the total value of household assets, including the market value of homes, possessions such as automobiles, and financial assets such as stocks, bonds, and bank accounts, minus any liabilities, including outstanding mortgage and credit card debt, automobile loans, and other loans.

wealth was held up by a boom in house prices and thus in the component of wealth consisting of the value of houses minus the value of mortgage debt.

3-4 Case Study

Why Did U.S. Saving Almost Vanish in This Decade?

Figure 3-3 is arranged exactly like Figure 3-2 and shows the actual values of disposable income and consumption spending in the United States during the years 1929–2007. As in Figure 3-2 the amount of personal saving[2] is shown by the light blue shaded area between the green and red lines.

Four major conclusions can be drawn from the evidence. First, consumption increased as disposable income grew during the years since World War II. Second, in the worst years of the Great Depression, in 1932 and 1933, households consumed more than their entire disposable incomes, so the fraction saved was negative (−1.0 percent in 1932 and −1.5 percent in 1933). Third, these usual peacetime relationships were interrupted during World War II (1942–45), when consumer goods were unavailable or rationed. In that period, households were forced to consume much less and save much more than is normal in peacetime, fully 26 percent of disposable income in 1944. After the war, consumers rushed out to spend their accumulated savings, helping to maintain prosperity.

The fourth conclusion is quite surprising. In the late 1980s and throughout the 1990s, real personal saving decreased, from 11.2 percent of personal disposable income in 1982, to 4.8 percent in 1994, and then hitting a minimum of 0.4 percent in 2006. The gradual shrinking of saving in the 1990s was generally attributed to the long stock market boom following 1982, during which the average value of stock prices increased tenfold. Consumers were able to raise their consumption relative to their disposable income by selling some of their stocks that had enjoyed large capital gains.

The saving rate stayed low after 2000 even though the boom in the stock market ended. Why didn't the saving rate recover after the stock market collapse? The most important reason was the sharp decline in interest rates achieved by monetary policy. Many households took advantage of low interest rates to refinance the mortgages on their homes. Because low interest rates imply lower monthly payments, households could use the money released by lower monthly payments to boost their consumption relative to their income. Further, many households "took cash out" in the refinance, boosting the amount financed from, say, $150,000 to $200,000. The extra $50,000 could be used to pay off credit card or other high-interest debt, in which case it would have no impact on the personal saving rate. But any households that spent part or all of that $50,000 on consumption goods and services reduced the personal saving rate, since their consumption increased without any change in their disposable income.

---

[2] Be careful to distinguish "savings" (with a terminal "s"), which is the *stock* of assets that households have in savings accounts or under the mattress, from "saving" (without a terminal "s"), which is the *flow* per unit of time that leaks out of disposable income and is unavailable for purchases of consumption goods. It is the flow of *saving* that is designated by the symbol *S*. For review, see the definitions of flows and stocks on p. 27.

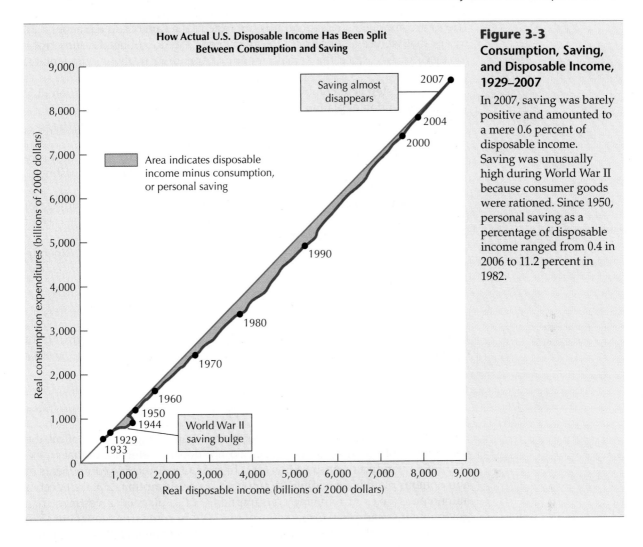

Figure 3-3
Consumption, Saving, and Disposable Income, 1929–2007

In 2007, saving was barely positive and amounted to a mere 0.6 percent of disposable income. Saving was unusually high during World War II because consumer goods were rationed. Since 1950, personal saving as a percentage of disposable income ranged from 0.4 in 2006 to 11.2 percent in 1982.

3-5 The Economy In and Out of Equilibrium

Until now, we have seen that the level of consumption spending depends both on autonomous consumption and on disposable income. But so far we have no idea what the level of income will actually be: $5,000 billion? $10,000 billion? We need an extra element, besides the consumption function, to construct our theory of income determination.

This extra element is that expenditure is not always what is desired or planned, and if some expenditure is unplanned, business firms will adjust production until the unplanned component of expenditure is eliminated. The total amount of spending that people want to do includes only the planned component, called planned expenditure (E_p). The rest of expenditure ($E - E_p$) is *unplanned* and *undesired*. To simplify, we assume that investment (I) is the only component of total expenditure that can contain an unplanned component, whereas consumption (C), government spending (G), and net exports (NX) *are always equal to the planned amount.*

$$E_p = C + I_p + G + NX \qquad (3.5)$$

The four components of expenditure are exactly the same as in equation (3.2), except that we use a subscript p for investment. We do not need a subscript p for C, G, or NX, since the actual amount of spending is always the amount planned.

The next step is to combine the consumption function from equation (3.3) with the definition of planned expenditure from equation (3.5):

$$E_p = C_a + c(Y - T) + I_p + G + NX \tag{3.6}$$

In words, this states that planned expenditure equals autonomous consumption, plus induced consumption, plus the fixed values of planned investment, government spending, and net exports.

A **parameter** is a value taken as given or known within a particular analysis.

The word **parameter** means something that is taken as given, including not only exogenous variables but also fixed elements of a function. In the case of the consumption function, there are two such fixed elements (C_a and c), and we will take both as given. In addition, the three components of planned expenditure other than consumption (I_p, G, and NX) can be considered as both exogenous variables and parameters.

Autonomous Planned Spending

It helps to simplify the subsequent analysis if we take all the elements of equation (3.6) that do not depend on total income (Y) and call them *autonomous planned spending* (A_p):

General Linear Form

$$A_p = E_p - cY = C_a - cT_a + I_p + G + NX \tag{3.7}$$

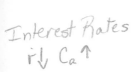

In words, this states that autonomous planned spending consists of all the components of planned spending that do not depend on income, that is, excluding only induced consumption (cY). To summarize, the five components of autonomous planned spending are autonomous consumption (C_a), the effect of autonomous taxes in reducing consumption ($-cT_a$), planned investment (I_p), government spending (G), and net exports (NX). In comparing equations (3.6) and (3.7), notice that we have replaced the tax component (T_a), reflecting our assumption that all taxes are autonomous.

As our numerical example, we will continue to assume that autonomous consumption (C_a) equals 500 and the marginal propensity to consume (c) equals 0.75, and add assumed values of 1,200 for planned investment (I_p) and −200 for net exports (NX). Government spending and autonomous taxes are set to zero. These imply that autonomous planned spending is equal to a total of 1,500:

Numerical Example

$$A_p = 500 - 0.75(0) + 1,200 + 0 - 200 = 1,500$$

Overall, we have learned that total planned expenditure (E_p) has two parts, autonomous planned spending (A_p) and induced consumption (cY).

General Linear Form   Numerical Example

$$E_p = A_p + cY \qquad\qquad E_p = 1,500 + 0.75Y \tag{3.8}$$

When Is the Economy in Equilibrium?

A basic lesson of Chapter 2 was that *actual* expenditure (E) and total income (Y) are always equal by definition. But there is no reason for income (Y) always to equal *planned* expenditure (E_p). Only when the economy is in **equilibrium** is income equal to planned expenditure. Only then do households, business firms, the government, and the foreign sector want to spend exactly the amount of income that is being generated by the current level of production.

Equilibrium is a state in which there exists no pressure for change.

Equilibrium is *a situation in which there is no pressure for change.* When the economy is *out of equilibrium,* production and income are out of line with planned expenditure, and business firms will be forced to raise or lower production. When the economy is *in equilibrium,* production and income are equal to planned expenditure, and on the average, business firms are happy to continue the current level of production.

This idea is illustrated in Figure 3-4. The thick green line, as in Figure 3-2, has a slope of 45 degrees; everywhere along it the level of income plotted on the horizontal axis is equal to the level of expenditure plotted on the vertical axis. Hence the green line is labeled $E = Y$. The red line is the total level of planned expenditures (E_p) given by equation (3.8), namely, 1,500 plus 0.75 times income (Y).

The "Keynesian Cross" Model

Only where the green and red lines cross at point *B* is income equal to planned expenditure, with no pressure for change. Because the economy is in equilibrium at the crossing point of the green 45-degree line and the red planned expenditure line, this theory of income determination is often called the "Keynesian Cross" model after the great English economist John Maynard Keynes. We learn more about Keynes in Chapter 7, where you will find his photo on p. 216.

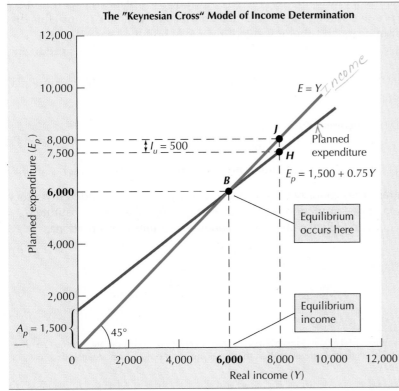

The "Keynesian Cross" Model of Income Determination

Figure 3-4 How Equilibrium Income Is Determined

The economy is in equilibrium at point *B,* where the red planned expenditure (E_p) line crosses the 45-degree income line. At any other level of income, the economy is out of equilibrium, causing pressure on business firms to increase or reduce production and income.

The economy is in equilibrium at point B in Figure 3-4 because households and business firms want to spend $6,000 billion when income is $6,000 billion. And this amount of income is created by the $6,000 billion of production of the goods and services that households and firms want to buy.[3]

What Happens Out of Equilibrium?

The economy is out of equilibrium at all points other than B along the 45-degree line. For instance, at point J, income is $8,000 billion. How much do households and business firms want to spend when income is $8,000 billion? The two components of planned expenditure are:

$$\text{autonomous planned spending } (A_p) = 1,500$$
$$\underline{\text{induced consumption } (0.75Y) = 6,000}$$
$$\text{planned expenditure } (E_p) = 7,500$$

Thus at an income level of $8,000 billion, planned expenditure (E_p) is only $7,500 billion (point H on the E_p line), leaving business firms with $500 billion of merchandise that nobody wants to purchase.

The $500 billion of unsold production is counted as inventory investment in the official national income accounts. But businesses do not desire this inventory buildup (if they did, they would have included it in their planned investment, I_p). To bring inventories back to the original desired level, businesses react to the situation at J by cutting production and income, which moves the economy left toward point B. In the diagram, the distance between points J and H, amounting to $500 billion, is labeled I_u, which stands for **unintended inventory investment.**

The distance JH measures the excess of income over planned expenditure—that is, the positive value of I_u. Production and income will be cut until this discrepancy disappears and the unwanted inventory buildup ceases $(I_u = 0)$. This occurs only when the economy arrives at B. Only at B are businesses producing exactly the amount that is demanded.

At point J, as in every situation, income and actual expenditure are equal by definition:

$$\text{income } (Y) \equiv \text{ependiture } (E)$$
$$\equiv \text{ planned expenditure } (E_p) +$$
$$\text{unintended inventory investment } (I_u) \qquad (3.9)$$

By contrast, the economy is in equilibrium only when unintended inventory accumulation or decumulation is equal to zero $(I_u = 0)$. When we substitute $(I_u = 0)$ into the equation (3.9), we obtain the economy's equilibrium situation:

$$Y = E_p \qquad (3.10)$$

Unintended inventory investment is the amount business firms are forced to accumulate when planned expenditure is less than income.

---

[3] Note that the horizontal axis in Figure 3-4 is income (Y) rather than disposable income $(Y - T)$ as in Figure 3-2. This reflects our assumption that taxes are autonomous and are included in A_p on the vertical axis.

Table 3-1   Comparison of the Economy's "Always True" and Equilibrium Situations

	Always true by definition	True only in equilibrium
1. What concept of expenditure is equal to income?	Actual expenditure including unintended inventory accumulation	Planned expenditure
2. Amount of unintended inventory investment (I_u)	Can be any amount, positive or negative	Must be zero
3. Which equation is valid, (3.9) or (3.10)?	(3.9) $Y = E = E_p + I_u$	(3.10) $Y = E_p$
4. Where does the economy operate in Figure 3-4?	Any point on 45-degree income line (example: point J)	Only at point B where E_p line crosses 45-degree income line
5. Numerical example in Figure 3-4 of nonequilibrium and equilibrium situations.	At point J, $$Y(8{,}000) = E(8{,}000)$$ $$= E_p(7{,}500) + I_u(500)$$	At point B, $$Y(6{,}000) = E_p(6{,}000)$$

Table 3-1 summarizes the differences between what is always true and what is true only in equilibrium.

 SELF-TEST

1. What happens in Figure 3-4 when income is only $4,000 billion?
2. Describe the forces that move the economy back to equilibrium at B.

Determining Equilibrium Real GDP

How do we calculate the equilibrium level of real GDP? We have already used one method by drawing the Keynesian Cross diagram as in Figure 3-4. However, it is much faster to calculate equilibrium real GDP using a simple equation. We start with the definition of equilibrium in equation 3.10, that income (Y) is equal to planned expenditure (E_p), and we combine it with the definition from equation (3.8) that planned expenditure is equal to autonomous planned spending (A_p) plus induced consumption (cY):

$$Y = A_p + cY$$

Then we subtract induced consumption from both sides of this equation and obtain:

$$(1 - c)Y = A_p \qquad (3.11)$$

Because the marginal propensity to save equals 1.0 minus the marginal propensity to consume ($s = 1 - c$), we can rewrite (3.11) as

General Linear Form

$$sY = A_p$$

Numerical Example

$$0.25Y = 1{,}500 \qquad (3.12)$$

This states that **induced saving** (sY) equals autonomous planned spending. Now it is easy to solve for equilibrium income by dividing both sides of equation (3.12) by the marginal propensity to save (s):

Induced saving is the portion of saving that responds to changes in income.

General Linear Form	Numerical Example	
$$Y = \frac{A_p}{s}$$	$$Y = \frac{1,500}{0.25} = 6,000$$	(3.13)

In the numerical example, $6,000 billion of income is required to generate the $1,500 billion of induced saving needed to balance $1,500 billion of autonomous planned spending.

3-6 The Multiplier Effect

Our conclusion thus far that equilibrium income equals $6,000 billion is absolutely dependent on our assumption that autonomous planned spending (A_p) equals $1,500 billion. Any change in autonomous planned spending will cause a change in equilibrium income. To illustrate the consequences of a change in A_p, we shall assume that business firms become more optimistic, raising their guess as to the likely profitability of new investment projects. They increase their investment spending by $500 billion, boosting A_p from $1,500 billion to $2,000 billion. In each situation where a change is described, a numbered subscript is used to distinguish the original from the new situation. Thus A_{p0} denotes the original level of A_p ($1,500 billion), and A_{p1} denotes the new level ($2,000 billion).

Calculating the Multiplier

We can use equation (3.13) to calculate the equilibrium level of income in the new and old situations. Note that only A_p changes; there is no change in the marginal propensity to save (s).

	General Linear Form	Numerical Example	
Take new situation	$$Y_1 = \frac{A_{p1}}{s}$$	$$Y_1 = \frac{2,000}{0.25} = 8,000$$	
Subtract old situation	$$Y_0 = \frac{A_{p0}}{s}$$	$$Y_0 = \frac{1,500}{0.25} = 6,000$$	
Equals change in income	$$\Delta Y = \frac{\Delta A_p}{s}$$	$$\Delta Y = \frac{500}{0.25} = 2,000$$	(3.14)

The top line of the table calculates the new level of income when A_{p1} is at the new value of 2,000. The second line calculates the original level of income when A_{p0} is at the old value of 1,500. The change in income, abbreviated ΔY, is simply the first line minus the second. The **multiplier** (k) is defined as the ratio of the change in income (ΔY) to the change in planned autonomous spending (ΔA_p) that causes it:

The **multiplier** is the ratio of the change in output to the change in autonomous planned spending that causes it. It is also 1.0 divided by the marginal propensity to save.

General Linear Form	Numerical Example	
$$\text{multiplier } (k) = \frac{\Delta Y}{\Delta A_p} = \frac{1}{s}$$	$$\frac{\Delta Y}{\Delta A_p} = \frac{1}{0.25} = 4.0$$	(3.15)

In Figure 3-5 we can see why the multiplier (k) is $1/s$, or 4.0. Figure 3-5 reproduces from Figure 3-4 the original situation, with A_p at its original value of $1,500 billion.

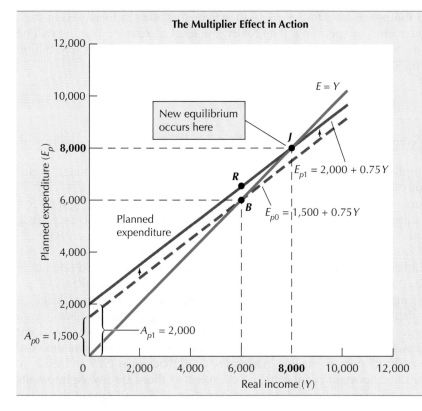

The Multiplier Effect in Action

Figure 3-5 The Change in Equilibrium Income Caused by a $500 Billion Increase in Autonomous Planned Spending

The increase in autonomous planned spending (A_p) by $500 billion is shown by the increase in the vertical intercept of the red planned expenditures line from $1,500 billion to $2,000, as shown in the lower left corner of the diagram. The upward shift in the red line moves the equilibrium position where the red planned expenditures line crosses the green 45-degree line from point B to point J. This $500 billion change in A_p has a multiplier effect, raising real income by $2,000 billion.

The $500 billion increase in A_p causes the E_p line to shift upward by $500 billion and to intersect the 45-degree line at point J. Because only 25 percent of extra income is saved, income must rise by $2,000 billion to generate the required $500 billion increase in induced saving. In terms of the line segments:

$$\text{multiplier } (k) = \frac{\Delta Y}{\Delta A_p} = \frac{RJ}{RB} = \frac{1}{s} \left(\text{since } s = \frac{RB}{RJ} \right)$$

Example of the Multiplier Effect in Action

How does the magic of the multiplier work? An answer is provided by a real-life example. Let us consider Southwest Airline's decision in 2007 to increase planned investment with the purchase of $4 billion of Boeing 737 aircraft. Initially the $4 billion of new investment spending would raise income by the $4 billion earned by Boeing workers in Seattle, where the aircraft plant is located. But, using our example of a marginal propensity to consume (c) of 0.75, the Boeing workers would soon spend 0.75 of the $4 billion, or $3 billion, on goods and services at Seattle stores. The stores would have to reorder $3 billion of additional goods, causing production and income to rise at plants all over the country that supply the goods to the stores in Seattle. Workers at these supplying plants also have a marginal propensity to consume of 0.75, adding another $2.25 billion of spending and income. So far, in the first three rounds of spending, income has gone up by $4.0 plus $3.0 plus $2.25 billion, or $9.25 billion. But the process continues, as induced consumption is increased in each successive round of spending. Eventually, the total increase in income will be four times the initial increase in planned investment, or $16 billion (= $4 billion times 1/0.25).[4]

3-7 Sources of Shifts in Planned Spending

Is a multiplier expansion or contraction of output following a change in autonomous planned spending desirable or not?

Assume that the *desired* level of real GDP is $8,000 billion. In Figure 3-5, a level of autonomous planned spending (A_p) of $2,000 billion would be perfect, for it would bring about an equilibrium level of actual real GDP of $8,000 billion at point *J*, the desired level. On the other hand, a decline in A_p by $500 billion would cut equilibrium income to $6,000 billion at *B* and would open up a gap of $2,000 billion between *actual* and the *desired* level of real GDP.

What might cause actual real GDP to decline below the desired level? A drop in planned investment, a major component of A_p, can be and has been a major cause of actual real-world recessions and depressions. In the Great Depression, for instance, fixed investment dropped by 81 percent, and this contributed to the 27 percent decline in actual real GDP between 1929 and 1933.

The most important point of this section is that there are five components of autonomous planned spending, as in equation (3.7), and any of these can change. Real GDP can increase or decrease through a multiplier response to changes in autonomous consumption, planned investment, and net exports, an example of the "demand shocks" that create business cycles. At least in principle, if it can act fast enough, the government can offset any undesirable shift in autonomous consumption, planned investment, or net exports by creating an

---

[4] It is possible to use an algebraic trick to prove that the sum of ΔA_p plus the induced consumption at each round of spending is exactly equal to the multiplier $\dfrac{1}{1-c}$ times ΔA_p. The first round of consumption is $c\Delta A_p$. The second is c times the first, $c(c\Delta A_p)$, or $c^2 A_p$. Thus the total ΔY is the series of all the infinite number of rounds of spending:

$$\Delta Y = \Delta A_p + c\Delta A_p + c^2\Delta A_p + \cdots + c^\infty \Delta A_p \tag{a}$$

Factor out the common element ΔA_p on the right-hand side of equation (a):

$$\Delta Y = \Delta A_p(1.0 + c + c^2 + \cdots + c^\infty) \tag{b}$$

Multiply both sides of equation (b) by $-c$:

$$-c\Delta Y = \Delta A_p(-c-c^2-\cdots-c^\infty) \tag{c}$$

The difference between lines (b) and (c) is

$$(1-c)\Delta Y = \Delta A_p \tag{d}$$

We can neglect the c^∞ term, since any fraction raised to the infinity power is zero. Dividing both sides of equation (d) by $(1-c)$, we obtain the familiar:

$$\Delta Y = \frac{\Delta A_p}{1-c} = \frac{\Delta A_p}{s}$$

offsetting movement in autonomous planned spending *in the opposite direction* through its control over government spending and autonomous taxes.

Government Spending and Taxation

The government can adjust its expenditures on goods and services as well as its tax revenues in an attempt to offset fluctuations in real GDP caused by movements in autonomous consumption, in planned investment, and in net exports. Our definition of autonomous planned spending (A_p) in equation (3.7) already includes government spending (G) and the effect of autonomous taxes (T_a) on consumption. For convenience we repeat equation (3.7):

General Linear Form

$$A_p = C_a - cT_a + I_p + G + NX \qquad (3.7)$$

 SELF-TEST

1. Why is I_p written with a p subscript, but the other components of autonomous planned spending (C_a, $-cT_a$, G, and NX) are not?
2. Why does the (cT_a) term appear with a minus sign but all the other sums appear with a plus sign?
3. Why is T_a multiplied by c but the other terms are not?

Equation (3.7) states that autonomous planned spending equals the sum of five components. It also implies that the *change* in autonomous planned spending equals the sum of the *change* in each of the same five components. We can state this as an equation if we insert the "change" symbol, Δ, in front of each element in equation (3.7). The only remaining element without a Δ symbol is the marginal propensity to consume (c), which we are assuming to be fixed throughout this discussion:

$$\Delta A_p = \Delta C_a - c\Delta T_a + \Delta I_p + \Delta G + \Delta NX \qquad (3.16)$$

In sum, the five causes of changes in A_p are:

1. A \$1 change in autonomous consumption (C_a) changes A_p by \$1 in the same direction.
2. A \$1 change in autonomous tax revenue (T_a) changes A_p by c (the marginal propensity to consume) times \$1 *in the opposite direction.*
3. A \$1 change in planned investment (I_p) changes A_p by \$1 in the same direction.
4. A \$1 change in government spending (G) changes A_p by \$1 in the same direction.
5. A \$1 change in net exports (NX) changes A_p by \$1 in the same direction.

Once the change in A_p has been calculated from this list, our basic multiplier expression from equation (3.14) determines the resulting change in equilibrium income:

$$\Delta Y = \frac{\Delta A_p}{s} \qquad (3.14)$$

SELF-TEST

1. Notice that there is no Δ in front of the *c* in equation (3.16). Why?
2. Notice that there is no Δ in front of the *s* in equation (3.14). Why?
3. How is *s* defined in terms of *c*?

Fiscal Expansion

To provide an example of a situation in which higher government spending can expand real income, let us assume that initially the level of autonomous planned spending (A_p) is 1,500. This means that the level of real income will be 6,000, as shown at point *B* in Figure 3-5. This is unsatisfactory, because we have assumed that the desired level of real GDP is at the higher level of $8,000 billion. Thus point *B* represents a situation in which actual real GDP and real income are $2,000 billion lower than desired. How can government fiscal policy correct this situation through its control over the level of government expenditure?

It is clear from our basic income-determination formula (3.14) that the required $2,000 billion increase in real income and real GDP can be achieved by any action that raises autonomous planned spending (A_p) by $500 billion. Two possibilities are (1) a $500 billion increase in *G* (government spending on goods and services) and (2) a $667 billion reduction in autonomous tax revenue.[5]

The $500 billion change in government spending ($\Delta G = 500$) in Figure 3-5 has exactly the same effect on income as any other $500 billion increase in A_p. The economy reaches a new equilibrium at point *J*. The multiplier (*k*) for ΔG is also the same, already given by equation (3.15) in the preceding section.

The Government Budget Deficit and Its Financing

Any change in government expenditure or tax revenue has consequences for the government's budget. The government budget surplus has already been linked to other key magnitudes in Section 2-5 on p. 35 as the magic equation. Tax revenue minus government expenditure, ($T - G$), by definition equals investment plus net exports minus private saving.[6]

$$T - G \equiv I + NX - S$$

Similarly, the change in the left side of the magic equation must balance the change in the right side:

$$\Delta T - \Delta G \equiv \Delta I + \Delta NX - \Delta S \qquad (3.17)$$

---

[5] Why $667 billion? Because according to equation (3.16), a reduction in taxes raises A_p by *c* times the reduction. If $c = 0.75$, as in our numerical example, then

$$\Delta A_p = -c\Delta T_a = -0.75(-667) = 500$$

Recall that transfer payments (Medicare, Social Security, and unemployment benefits) are equivalent to negative taxes, so that a $667 billion *reduction* in taxes has the same impact on A_p as a $667 billion *increase* in transfer payments.

[6] See equation (2.6) on p. 35. Page 35 also provides examples of the real-world values of the magic equation for the years 1993, 2000, and 2007.

When the government boosts its spending by 500, the movement in Figure 3-5 from point B to point J assumes that autonomous consumption, investment, and net exports are fixed ($\Delta C_a = \Delta I = \Delta NX = 0$) and that tax revenue remains at zero ($\Delta T = 0$). Thus the only elements of (3.17) that are changing are ΔS and ΔG. The value of ΔG is the fiscal stimulus of 500. But what is the value of ΔS? Saving changes by the marginal propensity to save times the change in disposable income, $\Delta S = s\,(\Delta Y - \Delta T)$. Using this expression for saving, we can substitute the numbers for this example into equation (3.17) and obtain:

$$\Delta T - \Delta G = \Delta I + \Delta NX - s(\Delta Y - \Delta T)$$
$$0 - \Delta G = 0 + 0 - s(\Delta Y - 0)$$
$$0 - 500 = 0 + 0 - 0.25(2{,}000) = -500$$

The $2,000 billion increase in output induces $500 billion of extra saving. Each extra dollar of saving is available for households to purchase the $500 billion of government bonds that the government must sell to finance its $500 billion government budget deficit. The payoff of this government deficit is the $2,000 boost in income needed to raise income to its desired amount.

The Tax Multiplier

As an alternative to stimulating the economy by raising government spending by $500 billion, it could choose to reduce autonomous taxes by $667 billion. As we have seen, these two actions have exactly the same effect, which is to boost autonomous planned spending by $500 billion and to raise income through the multiplier effect by $2,000 billion.

The tax multiplier is $-c/s$ or -3.0 in our example, compared to a multiplier of $1/s$ or 4.0 for government spending and the other components of autonomous planned spending. The tax multiplier is less simply because taxes are not part of expenditures; taxes change expenditures only by the amount they change consumption, -0.75 times the change in tax revenue. Thus the tax multiplier is $-c/s$ or -0.75 times the 4.0 multiplier for other components of planned spending. When autonomous taxes are reduced by $667 billion, real GDP rises by -3.0 times $667 billion, or $2,000 billion.

SELF-TEST

1. If government spending is reduced by $500 billion and the marginal propensity to save is 0.25, how much does total saving change?

2. What is the government doing when it runs a surplus, and how do private savers react?

3. If taxes are raised by $667 billion and marginal propensity to save is 0.25, how much does saving change? How do private households pay for the higher taxes?

The Balanced Budget Multiplier

In the previous example, the government could boost income by $2,000 billion either by raising government spending by $500 billion or by cutting taxes by $667 billion. Yet either method would create a large increase in the government deficit, which may be undesirable. Yet, surprisingly, the government can stimulate the

International Perspective

How the United States and Japan Use Fiscal Policy

One method to stabilize the economy by reducing the amplitude of business cycles is to use "countercyclical" fiscal policy. Such a policy operates "counter" or "against" the business cycle by using fiscal stimulus (higher spending or lower taxes) when the economy is weak and using the reverse when the economy is strong. However, fiscal policy in practice runs up against major problems. If government spending is used, then government spending on what? If the government takes a long time to develop plans for projects such as highways, hospitals, or schools, the economy's condition in the meantime may have changed from too weak to too strong. If tax cuts are used, they may be delayed by political debates, and households may decide to save the tax cut money rather than spending it.

Countercyclical fiscal policy in the United States has primarily used tax changes, and spending changes have rarely been used since the New Deal era of the 1930s. Tax reductions were used to stimulate the economy in 1964–65, for restraint in 1968, and again for stimulus in 1975 and 1981–83. However, the tax cuts of the early 1980s left the government budget mired in persistent deficits until the late 1990s, and this experience gave fiscal policy a bad name.

This changed in 2001 when Congress ratified the Bush administration's proposal for significant cuts of income tax rates to be spread over the next half-decade. Skepticism seemed to be warranted when the personal saving rate jumped, indicating that a substantial fraction of the payments had been saved rather than spent. Further tax cuts occurred in 2003 and were extended in 2004.

Since the early 1990s, the Japanese economy has been depressed, and numerous forms of fiscal stimulus have been employed as the Japanese government struggles to find a route back to prosperity. In contrast to the United States, the Japanese place much more emphasis on public works projects. To avoid time lags in starting new projects, the Japanese have a set of plans ready and vary fiscal expenditures to speed up or slow down completion of particular projects. For instance, the 115-mile Tokyo Coastal Bay Expressway was under construction for two decades. Many observers are skeptical of the usefulness of many of these public works projects, pointing to roads that lead to nowhere and a report that 60 percent of the Japanese coastline is encased in concrete. However, the Chapter 3 multiplier for government projects spending does not require that the projects must be useful to stimulate spending, and recent evidence has supported that textbook view.

Although tax cuts have also been introduced in Japan, these have been ineffective, as they have been announced as temporary and have soon been followed by even larger tax increases. Overall, Japanese policymakers continue to struggle to extricate their economy from its 15-year slump. In 2004–07, the Japanese economy seemed to be reviving somewhat, but this mainly reflected increased demand for Japanese exports from the United States and China, rather than any new-found potency of fiscal policy. We return in Chapter 5 to a deeper look at the Japanese policy dilemma, and at some of the mistakes and misconceptions that have plagued policymakers.

economy even if it needs to maintain a balanced budget. To see this, we simply add the multipliers for government spending ($k = 1/s$) and that for a change in taxes (*tax change multiplier = $-c/s$*):

$$\text{Balanced budget multiplier} = \frac{1}{s} + \frac{-c}{s} = \frac{1-c}{s} = 1.0 \qquad (3.18)$$

This states that the multiplier for a balanced-budget fiscal expansion is always 1.0, no matter what the value of *c!* Why? The positive multiplier occurs because one dollar of government spending raises autonomous planned expenditure by exactly one dollar, whereas the extra dollar of taxes only reduces autonomous planned expenditure by *c* times one dollar, and *c* (the marginal propensity to consume) is normally substantially less than unity. Thus, the government can achieve any desired increase in income and real GDP by a sufficiently large increase in government spending accompanied by exactly the same increase in tax rates.[7]

3-8   How Can Monetary Policy Affect Planned Spending?

Thus far fiscal policy seems to be the only tool that the government can use to fight against demand shocks caused by changes in autonomous consumption, planned investment, and net exports. Where does monetary policy fit in? Now we are ready to drop our simplifying but unrealistic assumption that autonomous consumption and planned investment are exogenous. In the next two sections we learn how and why interest rates can influence planned autonomous spending, raising spending when interest rates are low as in years such as 2001–04 and cutting spending in years when interest rates are high such as 1981 and 1989.

Functions of Interest Rates

Interest rates help the economy allocate saving among alternative uses. For savers, the interest rate is a reward for abstaining from consumption and waiting to consume at some future time. The higher the interest rate, the greater the incentive to save. For borrowers, the interest rate is the cost of borrowing funds to invest or buy consumption goods. At a higher interest rate, people will borrow fewer funds and purchase fewer goods. Thus if the desire to borrow exceeds the willingness to save sufficient funds, the interest rate tends to rise.

   Interest rates are central to the role of monetary policy. Since the government, through the Federal Reserve Board (the Fed), can influence the interest rate, it can affect the cost of borrowed funds to private borrowers.

Types of Interest Rates

Banks offer a variety of interest rates on checking and savings accounts. Some types of accounts allow customers to earn interest instantly; others require

---

[7] The appendix to this chapter shows that this simple expression for the balanced budget multiplier does not apply to a more realistic world in which tax revenues and imports depend on income.

customers to leave funds on deposit for a year or more. The phrase "short-term interest rate" refers to interest that is paid on funds deposited for three months or less; "long-term interest rate" refers to interest on funds deposited for a year or more.

In addition to short-term interest rates on bank deposits, there are short-term interest rates that apply to funds borrowed by the government (the Treasury bill rate), by businesses (the commercial paper rate), and by banks (the federal funds rate). Similarly, in addition to long-term rates on bank deposits, there are long-term interest rates that apply to funds borrowed by the government (the Treasury bond rate), by businesses (the corporate bond rate), and by households (the mortgage rate). The business sections of most newspapers publish the daily values of these rates.

The hallmark of a good theory is its ability to spotlight important relationships and to ignore unnecessary details. For most purposes, the differences between alternative interest rates fall into that category of detail, in contrast to the important overall *average* level of interest rates. Thus "the" interest rate discussed in this chapter can be regarded as an average of all the different interest rates listed in the previous paragraph.

3-9 The Relation of Autonomous Planned Spending to the Interest Rate

We begin by asking why planned investment (a component of autonomous planned spending) depends on the interest rate. Business firms attempt to profit by borrowing funds to buy investment goods—office buildings, shopping centers, factories, machine tools, computers, airplanes. Obviously, firms can stay in business only if the earnings of investment goods are at least enough to pay the interest on the borrowed funds (or to attract enough investors to warrant a new issue of stock).

Example of an Airline's Investment Decision

Rate of return on an investment project is its annual earnings divided by its total cost.

American Airlines calculates that it can earn $15 million per year from one additional Boeing 777 jet airliner after paying all expenses for employee salaries, fuel, food, and airplane maintenance—that is, all expenses besides interest payments on the borrowed funds. If the 777 costs $100 million, that level of earnings represents a 15 percent **rate of return,** defined as annual earnings divided by the cost of the airplane. If American must pay 10 percent interest to obtain the funds for the airplane, the 15 percent rate of return is more than sufficient to pay the interest expense, and the plane will be purchased.

But American Airlines only has a few routes that can earn a 15 percent rate of return. If American buys a second plane, it must fly that plane on routes with less traffic or lower fares, and the rate of return is only 10 percent, just barely enough to pay the interest expense on the second plane. If American buys a third plane, the rate of return is only 5 percent, insufficient to pay the interest expense, and the plane will not be bought. The key fact is that, for any firm, each successive unit purchased has a lower rate of return and eventually that rate of return is too low to pay the interest expense. As long as the interest rate remains at 10 percent, American will buy two planes but not three.

In the American Airlines example, if the interest rate should decline from 10 to 5 percent, then the third plane will be bought. If the interest rate should rise from 10 to 15 percent, then only the first plane will be bought. The overall economy behaves just as in the American Airlines example—the amount of planned investment spending (I_p) depends inversely on the interest rate.

Autonomous consumption (C_a) depends on the interest rate, just as does planned investment spending. Households will buy new cars more often—and will purchase bigger and more expensive cars—if the interest rate is low because this reduces the monthly payment for any given car. Similarly, high interest rates on car loans will force some households to buy smaller cars or to buy a used car instead of a new car. Overall, both planned investment and autonomous consumption are negatively related to the interest rate.

The Demand for Autonomous Planned Spending

You learned earlier that there are five components of autonomous planned spending (A_p): planned investment, autonomous consumption, government spending, the effect of autonomous taxes on consumption, and net exports. We have now seen that planned investment and autonomous consumption both depend on the interest rate; both types of spending are stimulated by a lower interest rate.

In Figure 3-6 we plot the relationship of the components of autonomous planned spending on the horizontal axis to the interest rate on the vertical axis. The total amount of government spending, the effect of autonomous taxes on consumption, and net exports ($G - cT_a + NX$) do not depend on the interest rate and so are plotted as a black vertical line in Figure 3-6.

Total autonomous planned spending also consists of autonomous consumption (C_a) and planned investment (I_p), both of which depend negatively on the interest rate, so *the amount of these two components added to the first three depends on the interest rate.* The lower the interest rate, the larger C_a and the larger I_p. The total of all five components is shown by the red line on the right

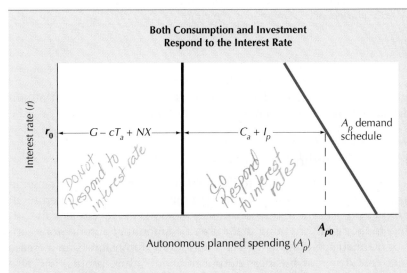

Both Consumption and Investment Respond to the Interest Rate

Figure 3-6 Relation of the Various Components of Autonomous Planned Spending to the Interest Rate

The vertical black line shows that three components of autonomous planned spending do not depend on the interest rate. These are government spending (G), the effect of autonomous taxes ($-cT_a$), and net exports (NX). The sloped line shows that autonomous consumption (C_a) and planned investment (I_p) depend inversely on the interest rate. Hence, the total demand for autonomous planned spending, as shown by the "A_p demand schedule," also depends inversely on the interest rate.

Shifts in Consumer Confidence and Household Wealth as Sources of Demand Shocks

The text lists five causes of shifts to the right or left in the A_p demand schedule of Figure 3-6. These are changes in autonomous consumption, planned investment, government spending, autonomous taxes, or net exports. The text shows that changes in business optimism or pessimism about future profits can shift planned investment spending. This box examines causes of shifts in autonomous consumption.

Just as business firms spend more when they are optimistic about the future, so do consumers. Consumer optimism, or high consumer confidence, promotes a willingness to make large expenditures on houses, cars, and appliances, and to do the borrowing often needed to finance such purchases. The opposite situation, economic uncertainty, breeds pessimism and a desire to curtail spending and rebuild financial resources needed to cope with possible future job losses or other adverse events.

Two alternative indexes of consumer confidence are compiled regularly, and one of these, the University of Michigan Consumer Sentiment Index, is shown by the blue line in the graph. This index is based on at least 500 telephone interviews each month with a sample of American households. The ups and downs of the index reflect answers to questions about expected changes in personal finances, household income, and business conditions in the economy as a whole.

Research has shown that consumers are able to anticipate adverse future events such as higher interest rates, higher inflation, and higher unemployment, each of which is reflected in a drop in the consumer sentiment index. A particularly striking example in the graph is a sharp drop in consumer sentiment in the third and fourth quarters of 1990, a direct result of the Iraqi invasion of Kuwait in early August that led to fears of a bloody war and severe interruptions in the supply of oil imported from the Middle East. There was also a sharp drop in confidence in the first quarter of 2001, nine months *before* the September 11 terrorist attacks, in part due to a decline in the stock market and a rise in expected future unemployment.

The graph compares the blue consumer sentiment index with a red line plotting the change in real GDP over the previous two years. In some episodes, the consumer sentiment index predicts the change in real GDP well in advance. For instance, the index began to decline in late 1977, more than two years in advance of the decline in GDP growth that occurred in early 1980. In 2000–01, the index declined about one year in advance of the decline in GDP growth.

When households respond to the survey about their personal finances, they report positively when their household wealth has increased, due for instance to success in paying off a loan, an increase in the value of the stock market, or an increase in the value of equity in a family's home. Economists have long deduced that autonomous consumption rises by a fraction, perhaps 3 to 5 percent, of any increase in wealth. Thus, if a household's stock market or housing wealth increases by $10,000, that household might raise its consumption expenditures by $300 to $500.

Does the consumer sentiment index provide independent evidence beyond the behavior of stock market and housing wealth? Recent research suggests that consumer confidence is indeed a separate cause of changes in autonomous consumption.[a] Negative events such as the

---

labeled "A_p demand schedule." This schedule shows that the total of all autonomous planned spending depends on the interest rate.

Shifts in the A_p Demand Schedule

The A_p demand schedule will shift to the right whenever there is a change in any component of planned autonomous spending. Increases in government spending or net exports and reductions in autonomous tax revenues will shift the schedule to the right. Anything that raises the amount of autonomous consumption or planned spending at a given interest rate, for instance, an increase in consumer confidence or business optimism about future profits, will also shift the A_p demand schedule to the right. Changes in any component of planned autonomous spending in the opposite direction will shift the A_p demand schedule to the left.

gasoline shortages of 1973–74 or the Iraqi invasion of Kuwait in 1990 can undermine confidence of consumers who do not own stocks in the stock market and whose house price is unchanged.

[a] See Nicholas Souleles, "Expectations, Heterogeneous Forecast Errors, and Consumption: Micro Evidence from the Michigan Consumer Sentiment Surveys, *Journal of Money, Credit, and Banking,* vol. 34, no. 1 (February 2004), pp. 39–72.

Consumer Sentiment Versus Growth in Real GDP

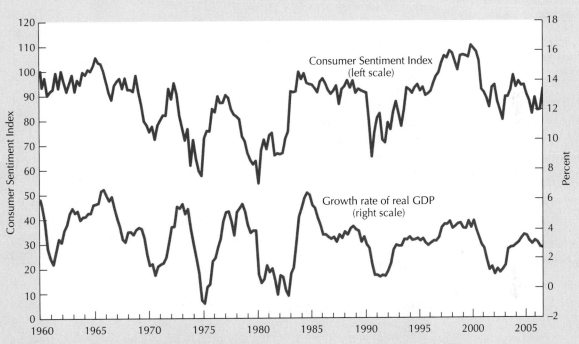

Source: Consumer sentiment from www.sca.isr.umich.edu/.

 SELF-TEST

Explain how the A_p demand schedule will shift to the left, right, or not at all in response to the following events:

1. A reduction in auto imports from Japan as the quality of American-built cars improves.

2. The stimulus to housing given by lower mortgage interest rates.

3. Higher taxes levied by the government in an attempt to reduce the budget deficit.

4. Higher government spending on security at airports.

5. A reduction in consumer confidence after the September 11, 2001, attacks.

3-10 The *IS* Curve

As shown in Figure 3-6, autonomous planned spending (A_p) depends on the interest rate. And Figure 3-5 has shown that real GDP and real income depend on autonomous planned spending. Now, if we put these two relationships together, we conclude that real GDP and real income must depend on the interest rate. In this section we derive a graphical schedule that shows the different possible combinations of the interest rate and real income that are compatible with equilibrium, given the state of business and consumer confidence, the marginal propensity to save, and the level of government spending, taxes, and net exports. This schedule is the *IS* **curve.**

*The **IS curve** is the schedule that identifies the combinations of income and the interest rate at which the commodity market is in equilibrium; everywhere along the IS curve the demand for commodities equals the supply.*

How to Derive the *IS* Curve

The left frame of Figure 3-7 displays the "A_p demand schedule." This shows how the demand for autonomous planned spending varies at different levels of the interest rate. Notice that at a 10 percent interest rate (point C), A_p is assumed to be $1,500 billion.[8]

What will be the equilibrium level of real income if A_p equals $1,500 billion? We answer this question, just as we did earlier in the chapter, by using a multiplier of 4.0. When we are at point C in the left frame with A_p equal to $1,500 billion, then in the right frame real GDP is plotted at point C with a value of $6,000 billion (4 times $1,500 billion).

Two other possibilities are shown in Figure 3-7. At point B, the interest rate is 15 percent. As shown in the left frame by the A_p demand schedule, this high interest rate cuts autonomous planned spending back from $1,500 billion at point C to $1,000 billion at point B. Since the multiplier is 4.0, real GDP is 4.0 times $1,000 billion, or $4,000 billion as shown in the right frame at point B. Similarly, at the low interest rate of 5 percent, real GDP in the right frame is $8,000 billion at point D.

> **SELF-TEST**
>
> 1. What interest rate is compatible with an $8,000 billion level of equilibrium real income?
> 2. At what point does this equilibrium occur in the right frame of Figure 3-7?

Because A_p depends on the interest rate, equilibrium income does also. The *IS* curve in Figure 3-7 plots the values of equilibrium real income when the marginal propensity to save is 0.25 and the multiplier is 4.0, as we have assumed throughout this chapter. Notice that points B, C, and D along the *IS* curve are all plotted at a horizontal distance exactly 4.0 times the value of the A_p line in the left-hand frame.

What the *IS* Curve Shows

The *IS* curve shows all the different combinations of the interest rate (r) and income (Y) at which the economy's market for commodities (goods and services)

---

[8] The equation of the A_p demand schedule in the left quadrant of Figure 3-7 is:

$$2,500 - 100r$$

Thus, when the interest rate is at 10 percent, the level of autonomous planned spending along the A_p demand schedule is $2,500 - (100 \times 10) = 1,500$.

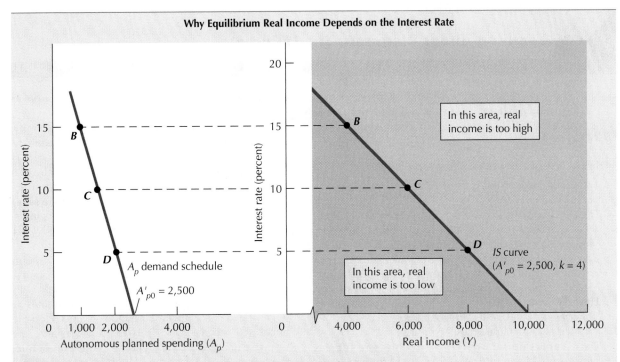

Figure 3-7 Relation of the *IS* Curve to the Demand for Autonomous Spending

In the left frame, the "A_p demand schedule" shows that the demand for autonomous planned spending depends on the interest rate. For instance, at a 10 percent interest rate the level of A_p is $1,500 billion at point C. Because the multiplier (k) is 4.0, the equilibrium level of income is $6,000 billion and is plotted in the right frame at point C, opposite the 10 percent interest rate.

is in equilibrium, which occurs only when income equals planned expenditures. At any point off the *IS* curve the economy is out of equilibrium.

It will be convenient to have a label for the horizontal position of the A_p line, since this in turn will affect the horizontal position of the *IS* curve.[9] *Let us define A'_p as the value of autonomous planned spending that would take place at an interest rate of zero.* In Figure 3-7, the A_p line intersects the horizontal axis at $2,500 billion, so our label for this A_p line will be $A'_{p0} = 2,500$. The *IS* curve always lies at a horizontal distance 4.0 times the A_p line, because the multiplier (k) is 4.0. Notice in Figure 3-7 that the *IS* curve intersects the horizontal axis at $10,000 billion, exactly 4.0 times the level of $A'_{p0} = 2,500$.

3-11 Conclusion: The Missing Relation

The *IS* curve is like a menu, providing us with innumerable combinations of interest rates and income that are consistent with equilibrium in the commodity market. But which item on the menu should we choose? There is not enough

---

[9] We call the *IS* schedule a "curve," even though we have drawn it as a straight line, because in the real world the relationship might be a curve. Also the term "*IS* curve" has been familiar to generations of economists since its invention by the late Sir John Hicks in a classic article, "Mr. Keynes and the Classics: A Suggested Interpretation," *Econometrica*, vol. 5 (April 1937), pp. 147–159.

Learning About Diagrams: The *IS* Curve

Since the *IS* curve is so important and useful, we pause here to study it more closely. (A full algebraic treatment of the *IS-LM* model is given in the Appendix to Chapter 4.)

Diagram Ingredients and Reasons for Slope

The vertical axis is the interest rate and the horizontal axis is the level of income.

The *IS* curve takes information from two other graphs, the A_p demand schedule and the equilibrium between induced saving and autonomous planned spending. Because A_p depends on the interest rate, and because equilibrium income is a multiple (k) of A_p, equilibrium income becomes a negative function of the interest rate.

The horizontal position (equilibrium income) along the *IS* curve is equal to the horizontal position along the A_p demand schedule times the multiplier k.

The *IS* curve slopes down because income is a multiple of A_p, and A_p depends negatively on the interest rate.

The *IS* curve becomes flatter, the more responsive is A_p to the interest rate, and the larger the multiplier. The *IS* curve becomes steeper, the less responsive is A_p to the interest rate, and the smaller the multiplier.

What Shifts and Rotates the *IS* Curve?

The *IS* curve is equal to the interest-dependent level of A_p times the multiplier (k). Anything that shifts the A_p demand schedule will shift the *IS* curve in the same direction. The factors that shift the *IS* curve to the right include an increase in business or consumer confidence, an increase in government spending or net exports, and a decrease in taxes (or increase in

transfers). Opposite changes will shift the *IS* curve to the left.

A rightward shift in the A_p demand schedule causes a rightward shift in the *IS* curve by an amount equal to the A_p shift times the multiplier.

The multiplier (k) transforms the A_p demand schedule into the *IS* curve. An increase in the multiplier (due, for instance, to a smaller marginal propensity to save) rotates or twists the *IS* curve outward around its intercept on the vertical interest rate axis. Thus the higher the multiplier, the flatter the *IS* curve.

Anything that makes investment or consumption demand less sensitive to the interest rate (for instance, a tendency for firms to pay for investment goods with internal funds rather than borrowed funds) rotates or twists the *IS* curve upward around its intercept on the horizontal income axis. Thus the less sensitive the response of autonomous spending to the interest rate, the steeper the *IS* curve.

What Is True of Points That Are Off the *IS* Curve?

The entire area to the left of each *IS* curve is characterized by too low a level of production and income for the economy to be in equilibrium. There is undesired inventory decumulation (negative unplanned investment, I_u).

The entire area to the right of each *IS* curve is characterized by too high a level of production and income for the economy to be in equilibrium. There is undesired inventory accumulation (positive unplanned investment, I_u).

At any point off the *IS* curve there is pressure for business firms to adjust production until the economy returns to the *IS* curve.

---

information here to make a choice. We need to find another relationship to link income and the interest rate in order to tie down the economy's position along the *IS* curve. In the familiar language of elementary algebra, we have two unknowns but only one equation. In the next chapter, we supply the missing equation and arrive at a complete theory of how income and the interest rate are determined.[10]

---

[10] Despite its name, the *IS* curve has no unique connection with investment (*I*) or saving (*S*). It shifts whenever there is a shift in the A_p demand schedule, which can be caused by a change in government spending, in taxes or transfers, or in net exports, as well as by changes in business and consumer confidence.

The missing relation between real income and the interest rate (in addition to the *IS* curve), occurs in the "money market," a general expression for the financial sector of the economy. The operation of the money market provides the crucial missing link that explains how the interest rate is determined. At the beginning of the next chapter, we will learn how the money market creates a second, positively sloped relationship between real income and the interest rate. We will learn that the Fed, through its control of the money supply, can shift this positive relationship back and forth and offset some or all of the effects of the demand shocks (such as changes in business and consumer confidence) that shift the position of the *IS* curve. We will also learn how monetary and fiscal policy can be used together to determine both the interest rate and the level of real income.

Summary

1. This chapter presents a simple theory for determining real income. Important simplifying assumptions include the constancy of the price level.

2. Disposable income is divided between consumption and saving. Throughout the chapter consumption is assumed to be a fixed autonomous amount, $500 billion in the numerical example, plus 0.75 of disposable income. Saving is the remaining 0.25 of disposable income minus the $500 billion of autonomous consumption.

3. During the twentieth century, U.S. consumption was a roughly constant fraction of disposable income. Exceptions were during World War II, when rationing prevented households from obtaining the goods they desired and forced them to save an abnormal fraction of their income, and in the period 2005–07 when saving almost vanished.

4. Output and income (Y) are equal by definition to total expenditures (E), which in turn can be divided up between planned expenditure (E_p) and unintended inventory accumulation (I_u). We convert this definition into a theory by assuming that business firms adjust production whenever I_u is not zero. The economy is in equilibrium, with no pressure for production to change, only when there is no unintended inventory accumulation or decumulation ($I_u = 0$).

5. Autonomous planned spending (A_p) equals total planned expenditure minus induced consumption. The five components of autonomous planned expenditure are autonomous consumption (C_a), planned investment (I_p), government spending (G), net exports (NX), and the effect on consumption of autonomous tax revenue ($-cT_a$).

6. Any change in autonomous planned spending (ΔA_p) has a multiplier effect: An increase raises income and induced consumption over and above the initial boost in A_p. Income must increase until enough extra saving has been induced ($s\Delta Y$) to balance the injection of extra autonomous planned spending (ΔA_p). For this reason, the multiplier, the ratio of the change in income to the change in autonomous planned spending ($\Delta Y/\Delta A_p$), is the inverse of the marginal propensity to save ($1/s$).

7. The same multiplier is valid for a change in any component in A_p. Thus, if private spending components of A_p are weak, the government can raise its spending (G) or cut taxes (T) to maintain stability in A_p and thus in real output.

8. Interest rates allocate the supply of funds available from savers to alternative borrowers. Not only do private households and firms borrow in order to buy consumption and investment goods, but the government also borrows to finance its budget deficit.

9. Private autonomous planned spending (A_p) depends partly on the interest rate. The higher the interest rate, the lower is A_p.

10. Private autonomous planned spending (A_p) also depends on the optimism or pessimism of investors and consumers about the future. An increase in optimism tends to raise A_p for any given level of the interest rate.

11. The *IS* curve indicates all the combinations of the interest rate and real income at which the economy's commodity market is in equilibrium. At any point off the *IS* curve, the commodity market is out of equilibrium.

Note: Asterisks designate Concepts, Questions, and Problems that require the Appendix to Chapter 3.

Concepts

aggregate demand
demand shock
aggregate supply
endogenous variables
exogenous variables
autonomous magnitude
marginal propensity to consume

induced consumption
marginal propensity to save
household wealth
parameter
equilibrium
unintended inventory investment
induced saving

multiplier
rate of return
IS curve
*marginal leakage rate
*automatic stabilization

Questions

1. Explain the distinction between exogenous variables and endogenous variables. Explain the distinction, if any, between a parameter and an exogenous variable. For the most complete model used in this chapter, which of the following variables are endogenous? Which are exogenous?
   (a) autonomous taxes
   (b) consumption
   (c) marginal propensity to consume
   (d) exports
   (e) net exports
   (f) GDP
   (g) price level
   (h) interest rate
   (i) investment
   (j) tax revenue
   (k) disposable income
   (l) saving
   (m) foreign trade surplus (deficit)
   (n) government budget surplus (deficit)

2. Why do we distinguish between autonomous consumption and induced consumption?

3. How do changes in the interest rate and household wealth from the late 1980s to the present help explain why the real personal saving rate has declined over that same period?

4. Explain why inventories would tend to rise just before the start of a recession and again tend to rise once businesses become more confident that the economy is expanding.

5. What moves the economy toward equilibrium when unintended inventory investment is positive? negative?

6. Assume that there is an increase in autonomous investment of $100 billion. Will the effect on the level of equilibrium real GDP be greater with a relatively high or a relatively low marginal propensity to consume? Explain.

7. Explain why government action that increases the deficit is expansionary fiscal policy. What about action that decreases the surplus?

8. Explain why the *IS* curve slopes down and to the right. Explain the difference between a movement along the *IS* curve and a shift of the *IS* curve.

9. Explain how each of the following will shift the *IS* curve.
   (a) The decline in sales of American agricultural products to foreign countries resulting from a strong U.S. dollar in the early-to-mid 1980s.
   (b) The collapse in consumer confidence that occurred in the fall of 1990 following the rapid rise in energy prices after Iraq's invasion of Kuwait in August 1990.
   (c) The decline in the personal saving rate from 4.8 percent in 1994 to 0.4 percent in 2006.
   (d) The drop in business confidence following the collapse of the stock market and the Internet bust in 2000.

10. One of the hypotheses for the increased stability of the U.S. economy since 1985 is that demand shocks have become smaller and less important. Explain why a demand shock can be thought of as a shift of the *IS* curve. Then discuss the hypothesis concerning demand shocks and the increased stability of the U.S. economy in terms of shifts of the *IS* curve.

The following three questions assume knowledge of the Appendix to Chapter 3.

*11. Given a consumption function of the form $C = C_a + c(Y - T)$ and $T = T_a + tY$, write the formula for the expanded consumption function. Write the formula for the expanded saving function that is implied by the stated consumption function.

*12. How would your answer in question 6 change if the alternatives read with a relatively high or with a relatively low marginal leakage rate? Explain.

*13. When all taxes and net exports are autonomous, the balanced budget multiplier is one. Find the balanced budget multiplier when all taxes are autonomous, but net exports have an autonomous and induced component. Is this new balanced budget multiplier less than, greater than, or equal to one?

Problems

1. Consider an economy in which all taxes are autonomous and the following values of autonomous consumption, planned investment, government expenditure, autonomous taxes, and the marginal propensity to consume are given:

$$C_a = 1,400 \; I_p = 1,800 \; G = 1,950 \; T_a = 1,750 \; c = 0.6$$

(a) What is the level of consumption when the level of income (Y) equals $10,000?

(b) What is the level of saving when the level of income (Y) equals $10,000?

(c) What is the level of planned investment when the level of income (Y) equals $10,000? What is the level of actual investment? What is the level of unintended inventory investment?

(d) Show that injections equal leakages when income (Y) equals $10,000.

(e) Is the economy in equilibrium when income (Y) = $10,000? If not, what is the equilibrium level of income for the economy described in this question?

(f) Is there a surplus or deficit in the government budget at the equilibrium level of income? How much?

2. Consider an economy is which taxes, planned investment, government spending on goods and services, and net exports are autonomous, but consumption and planned investment change as the interest rate changes. You are given the following information concerning autonomous consumption, the marginal propensity to consume, planned investment, government purchases of goods and services, and net exports:

$$C_a = 1,500 - 10r \quad c = 0.6 \quad T = 1,800$$
$$I_p = 2,400 - 50r \quad G = 2,000 \quad NX = -200$$

(a) Compute the value of the marginal propensity to save.

(b) Compute the amount of autonomous planned spending, A_p, given that the interest rate equals 5.

(c) Compute the equilibrium level of income, given that the interest rate equals 5.

(d) Suppose that autonomous consumption changes by 4 percent of any change in household wealth and that the decline in the housing market in 2006–07 and drop in the stock market in the summer of 2007 reduces household wealth by $750 billion. Compute the decrease in autonomous consumption that results from the decline in household wealth.

(e) Calculate the new amount of autonomous planned spending, A_p, and the new equilibrium level of income, given that the interest rate equals 5.

(f) Using your answers to parts c–e, compute the value of the multiplier.

(g) Fiscal and monetary policymakers can respond to the decline in household wealth by taking actions that restore income to its initial equilibrium level. Fiscal policymakers can increase government spending or cut taxes or do both. Monetary policymakers can reduce interest rates. Given the values of the multiplier, the tax multiplier, and the balanced-budget multiplier, compute by how much:

Government spending must be increased in order to restore the initial equilibrium level of income, given no change in taxes or the interest rate.

Taxes must be cut in order to restore the initial equilibrium level of income, given no change in government spending or the interest rate.

Government spending and taxes must be increased in order to restore the initial equilibrium level of income, given no change in the government budget balance or the interest rate.

The interest rate must be reduced in order to restore the initial equilibrium level of income, given no change in government spending or taxes.

3. Consider an economy is which taxes, planned investment, government spending on goods and services, and net exports are autonomous, but consumption and planned investment change as the interest rate changes. You are given the following information concerning autonomous consumption, the marginal propensity to consume, planned investment, government purchases of goods and services, and net exports:

$$C_a = 1,500 - 20r \quad c = 0.6 \quad I_p = 2,450 - 60r$$
$$G = 1,980 \quad NX = -200 \quad T = 1,750$$

(a) Compute the value of the marginal propensity to save.

(b) Compute the amounts of autonomous planned spending, A_p, when the interest rate equals 0, 2, 4, and 6.

(c) Compute the equilibrium levels of income when the interest rate equals 0, 2, 4, and 6. Graph the IS curve.

(d) Suppose that policymakers decide to reduce the number of troops in Iraq, which results in a reduction in government spending of $160 billion. Compute the new amounts of autonomous planned spending, A_p, when the interest rate equals 0, 2, 4, and 6.

(e) Compute the equilibrium levels of income when the interest rate equals 0, 2, 4, and 6 and graph the new IS curve.

(f) Suppose that policymakers decide to expand health care to those currently without health insurance, which results in an increase in government spending of $80 billion from $1,980 billion to $2,060 billion. Compute the new amounts of autonomous planned spending, A_p, when the interest rate equals 0, 2, 4, and 6.

(g) Compute the equilibrium levels of income when the interest rate equals 0, 2, 4, and 6 and graph the new IS curve.

(h) Suppose that initially the interest rate equals 4 and the economy is in equilibrium at natural real GDP, which equals 10,900. If monetary policymakers want to maintain income at natural real GDP, explain by how much they will change the interest rate as a result of either the Iraqi troop reduction or the expanded health care coverage.

*4. Assume an economy in which the marginal propensity to consume, c, is 0.8, the income tax rate, t, is 0.2, and the share of imports in GDP, nx, is 0.04. Autonomous consumption, C_a, is 660; autonomous taxes, T_a, are 200; autonomous net exports, NX_a, are 300; planned investment, I_p, is 500; and government spending, G, is 500.

(a) What is the value of autonomous planned spending (A_p)?

(b) What is the value of the multiplier?

(c) What is the equilibrium value of income (Y)?

(d) What is the value of consumption in equilibrium?

(e) Show that leakages equal injections.

(f) Suppose government expenditures decline by 150. Describe the economic process by which the new equilibrium value of Y is attained.

(g) What is the new equilibrium value of Y?

5. Consider an economy in which taxes, planned investment, government spending on goods and services, and net exports are autonomous, but consumption and planned investment change as the interest rate changes. You are given the following information concerning autonomous consumption, the marginal propensity to consume, planned investment, government purchases of goods and services, and net exports: $C_a = 1,400 - 15r$; $c = 0.5$; $I_p = 2,350 - 35r$; $G = 1,940$; $NX = -200$; $T_a = 1,600$.

(a) Compute the value of the multiplier.

(b) Derive the equation for the autonomous planned spending schedule, A_p.

(c) Derive the equation for the IS curve, $Y = kA_p$.

(d) Using the equation for the IS curve, calculate the equilibrium levels of income at interest rates equal to 0, 3, and 6.

(e) Using your answers to part d, calculate the slope of the IS curve, $\Delta r / \Delta Y$.

(f) Suppose that autonomous consumption rises by $40 billion, so that $C_a = 1,440 - 15r$. Explain whether this increase in autonomous consump-

tion is caused by a rise or fall in consumer confidence. Derive the new equation for the IS curve.

(g) Using the equation for the new IS curve, calculate the new equilibrium levels of income at interest rates equal to 0, 3, and 6.

(h) Using your answers to parts d and g, explain whether the IS curve shifts to the left or right when autonomous consumption rises. Explain why the horizontal shift of the IS curve equals the multiplier times the change in autonomous planned spending.

6. The purpose of this problem is to study how the slope of the IS curve changes as the multiplier changes and the responsiveness of autonomous planned spending to interest rate changes. Initially, use the same information as given in problem 5.

(a) Suppose that the marginal propensity to consume increases from 0.5 to 0.6. Compute the new value of the multiplier.

(b) Derive the equation for the new autonomous planned spending schedule, A_p.

(c) Derive the equation for the new IS curve, $Y = kA_p$.

(d) Using the equation for the new IS curve, calculate the new equilibrium levels of income at interest rates equal to 0, 3, and 6.

(e) Using your answers to part d, calculate the slope of the new IS curve, $\Delta r / \Delta Y$.

(f) Given that $c = 0.6$, suppose that the equation for planned investment expenditures is now $I_p = 2,350 - 45r$. Derive the equation for the new autonomous planned spending schedule, A_p.

(g) Derive the equation for the new IS curve, $Y = kA_p$.

(h) Using the equation for the new IS curve, calculate the new equilibrium levels of income at interest rates equal to 0, 3, and 6.

(i) Using your answers to part h, calculate the slope of the new IS curve, $\Delta r / \Delta Y$.

(j) Using your answers to part e of problem 5, and parts e and i of this problem, explain whether the IS curve gets flatter or steeper as (1), the multiplier increases, and (2), the responsiveness of autonomous planned spending to the interest rate increases.

*7. Consider an economy in which consumption, taxes, and net exports all change as income changes. In addition, consumption and planned investment change as the interest rate changes. You are given the following information concerning autonomous consumption, the marginal propensity to consume, planned investment, government purchases of goods and services, and net exports: $C = C_a + 0.85(Y - T)$; $C_a = 225 - 10r$; $I_p = 1,610 - 30r$; $G = 1,650$; $NX = 700 - 0.08Y$; $T = 100 + 0.2Y$.

(a) Compute the value of the multiplier.

(b) Derive the equation for the autonomous planned spending schedule, A_p.

(c) Derive the equation for the *IS* curve, $Y = kA_p$.
(d) Using the equation for the *IS* curve, calculate the equilibrium level of income at an interest rate equal to 3.

(e) At the equilibrium level of income at an interest rate of 3, show that leakages equal injections.

 SELF-TEST ANSWERS

p. 62 (1) $C = C_a$ in the general linear form, $C = 500$ in the numerical example. (2) Your options are to borrow, reduce your savings account, and sell stocks, bonds, or any other assets you may own.

p. 63 (1) At point F consumption and disposable income are equal. Thus consumption, $C_a + c(Y - T)$, equals disposable income, or $Y - T$. Setting these two equal, we can subtract $c(Y - T)$ from $Y - T$ to obtain $C_a = (1 - c)(Y - T)$. Dividing by $1 - c$, we obtain the answer that disposable income $(Y - T)$ is equal to $C_a/(1 - c)$ and so is consumption. Thus at point F consumption equals 500/0.25, or 2,000, while saving equals zero. (2) When disposable income is 5,000, consumption $C = 500 + 0.75\,(5,000) = 4,250$. Saving $= Y - T - C = 5,000 - 4,250 = 750$.

p. 69 (1) When income is only 4,000, planned expenditure is equal to autonomous spending $(1,200 + 500 - 200)$ plus induced consumption (0.75 times $4,000 = 3,000$), for a total of 4,500. Thus planned expenditure exceeds income, forcing firms to reduce their inventories in order to meet demand. (2) Unintended inventory investment is −500, and firms raise production in order to provide goods to meet planned expenditures; this increase in production moves the economy toward the equilibrium income level of 6,000.

p. 73 (1) We write planned investment as I_p with a p subscript, to reflect our assumption that *consumers, the government, and exporters and importers are always able to realize their plans*, so that there is no such thing as autonomous unplanned consumption, autonomous unplanned tax revenues, unplanned government spending, or unplanned net exports. Only business firms are forced to make unplanned expenditures, as occurs when investment (*I*) is not equal to what they plan (I_p), but also includes unplanned inventory (I_u).

(2) cT_a appears with a minus sign because an increase in taxes will reduce, rather than increase, autonomous planned spending by the amount of the tax times the fraction of the tax that would have been consumed rather than saved. (3) T_a is multiplied by c because taxes are not part of GDP. A change in taxes only alters GDP if it alters consumption. The effect on consumption is given by $-T_a$ times the marginal propensity to consume.

p. 74 (1) We are assuming that the marginal propensity to consume does not change. (2) When we assume the marginal propensity to consume does not change, the marginal propensity to save will not change either.[a] (3) $s = 1 - c$.

p. 75 (1) Income will decline by 2,000 and saving will decline by one quarter of 2,000, the exact amount of the decline in government expenditures. (2) Tax revenues exceed government spending. Private savers no longer purchase government bonds. Saving will equal the amount that total investment exceeds the surplus. (3) If taxes are raised by $667 billion, saving declines by exactly $667 billion. Private households pay for the higher taxes by reducing their level of saving.

p. 81 (1) A reduction of imports raises net exports and shifts the A_p demand schedule to the right. (2) A change in interest rates moves the economy *along* the schedule but does not shift it. (3) Higher taxes reduce consumption and thus shift the A_p demand schedule to the left. (4) Higher government spending shifts the A_p demand schedule to the right. (5) A reduction in consumer confidence shifts the A_p demand schedule to the left.

p. 82 (1) An interest rate of 5 percent is compatible with a $8,000 billion level of equilibrium real income. (2) This occurs at point D on the *IS* curve in the right-hand frame of Figure 3-7.

For additional practice and exploration, exercises that require the use of Excel are available at www.aw-bc.com/gordon.

[a] Using the calculus formula for the change in a ratio, the change in income when both A_p and s are allowed to change is

$$\Delta Y = \Delta A_p/s - A_p\Delta s/s^2$$

Equation (3.14) in the text simply sets Δs equal to zero in this expression.

Appendix to Chapter 3

Allowing for Income Taxes and Income-Dependent Net Exports

Effect of Income Taxes

When the government raises some of its tax revenue (T) with an income tax in addition to the autonomous tax (T_a), its total tax revenue is:

$$T = T_a + tY \tag{1}$$

The first component is the autonomous tax, for which we continue to use the symbol (T_a). The second component is income tax revenue, the tax rate (t) times income (Y). Disposable income ($Y - T$) is total income minus tax revenue:

$$Y_D = Y - T = Y - T_a - tY = (1 - t)Y - T_a \tag{2}$$

Leakages from the Spending Stream

Following any change in total income (Y), disposable income changes by only a fraction ($1 - t$) as much. For instance, if the tax rate (t) is 0.2, then disposable income changes by 80 percent of the change in total income. Any change in total income (ΔY) is now divided into induced consumption, induced saving, and induced income tax revenue. The fraction of ΔY going into consumption is the marginal propensity to consume disposable income (c) times the fraction of income going into disposable income ($1 - t$). Thus the change in total income is divided up as shown in the following table.

Fraction going to:	General Linear Form	Numerical Example
1. Induced consumption	$c(1 - t)$	$0.75(1 - 0.2) = 0.6$
2. Induced saving	$s(1 - t)$	$0.25(1 - 0.2) = 0.2$
3. Induced tax revenue	t	0.2
Total	$(c + s)(1 - t) + t$ $= 1 - t + t = 1.0$	1.0

As in equation (3.10) on p. 68, the economy is in equilibrium when income equals planned expenditures:

$$Y = E_p \tag{3}$$

As before, we can subtract induced consumption from both sides of the equilibrium condition. According to the preceding table, income (Y) minus induced consumption is the total of induced saving plus induced tax revenue. Planned expenditure (E_p) minus induced consumption is autonomous planned spending (A_p). Thus the equilibrium condition is

$$\text{induced saving} + \text{induced tax revenue} = \text{autonomous planned spending } (A_p) \tag{4}$$

From the table just given, equation (4) can be written in symbols as:

$$[s(1 - t) + t]Y = A_p \tag{5}$$

The **marginal leakage rate** is the fraction of income that is taxed or saved rather than being spent on consumption.

The term in brackets on the left-hand side is the fraction of a change in income that does not go into induced consumption—that is, the sum of the fraction going to induced saving $s(1 - t)$ and the fraction going to the government as income tax revenue (t). The sum of these two fractions within the brackets is called the **marginal leakage rate.** The equilibrium value for Y can be calculated when we divide both sides of equation (5) by the term in brackets:

General Linear Form

Numerical Example

$$Y = \frac{A_p}{s(1 - t) + t} \qquad Y = \frac{2,000}{0.25(0.8) + 0.2} = \frac{2,000}{0.4} = 5,000 \qquad (6)$$

The numerical example shows that if autonomous planned spending (A_p) is \$2,000 billion, income will be only \$5,000 billion, rather than \$8,000 billion as in the example used in Chapter 3. Why? A greater fraction of each dollar of income now leaks out of the spending stream—0.4 in this numerical example—than occurred due to the saving rate of 0.25 by itself. This allows the injection of autonomous planned spending ($A_p = 2,000$) to be balanced by leakages out of the spending stream at a lower level of income.

Income Taxes and the Multiplier

The change in income (ΔY) is simply the change in autonomous planned spending (ΔA_p) divided by the marginal leakage rate:

$$\Delta Y = \frac{\Delta A_p}{s(1 - t) + t} \qquad (7)$$

The multiplier ($\Delta Y / \Delta A_p$) is simply 1.0 divided by the marginal leakage rate. The multiplier was $1/s$ when there was no income tax. Now, with an income tax:

$$\text{multiplier} = \frac{1}{\text{marginal leakage rate}} = \frac{1}{s(1 - t) + t} \qquad (8)$$

In Chapter 3, where the income tax rate is assumed to be zero, the numerical example of the multiplier was 4. This was a special case of equation (8), valid when $t = 0$, so that the marginal leakage rate equals simply s, or 0.25.

Now that we have introduced an income tax rate of 0.2, the marginal leakage rate is 0.4 [see equation (6)] and the multiplier is $1/0.4$ or 2.5. Thus raising the income tax rate reduces the multiplier and vice versa. This gives the government a new tool for stabilizing income. When the government wants to stimulate the economy and raise income, it can raise income in equation (6) and the multiplier in equation (8) by cutting income tax rates. This occurred most recently in 2001 and again in 2003. And, when the government wants to restrain the economy, it can raise income tax rates, as occurred most recently in 1993.

The Government Budget

The government budget surplus is defined as before; it equals tax revenue minus government spending, $T - G$. Substituting the definition in equation (1), which expresses tax revenue (T) as the sum of autonomous and induced tax revenue, we can write the government surplus as:

$$\text{government budget surplus} = T - G = T_a + tY - G \qquad (9)$$

Thus the government budget surplus automatically rises when the level of income expands. This consequence of the income tax is sometimes called **automatic stabilization.** This name reflects the automatic rise and fall of income tax revenues as income rises and falls. When income rises, income tax revenues rise and siphon off some of the income before households have a chance to spend it. Similarly, when income falls, income tax revenues fall and help minimize the drop in disposable income. This is why the presence of an income tax makes the multiplier smaller.

Automatic stabilization is the effect of income taxes in lowering the multiplier effect of changes in autonomous planned spending.

Autonomous and Induced Net Exports

The theory of income determination in equation (6) states that equilibrium income equals autonomous planned spending (A_p) divided by the marginal leakage rate. When the United States trades with nations abroad, U.S. producers sell part of domestic output as exports. Households and business firms purchase imports from abroad, so part of U.S. expenditure does not generate U.S. production.

How do exports and imports affect the determination of income? We learned in Chapter 2 that the difference between exports and imports is called net exports and is part of GDP. When exports increase, net exports increase. When imports increase, net exports decrease. Designating net exports by NX, we can write the relationship between net exports and income (Y) as:

$$NX = NX_a - nxY \tag{10}$$

Net exports contains an autonomous component (NX_a), reflecting the fact that the level of exports depends mainly on income in foreign countries (which is exogenous, not explained by our theory) rather than on domestic income (Y). Net exports also contains an induced component ($-nxY$), reflecting the fact that imports rise if domestic income (Y) rises, thus reducing net exports. The meaning of nx can be stated as "the share of imports in GDP."

Because we now have a new component of autonomous expenditure, the autonomous component of net exports (NX_a), we can rewrite our definition of A_p as the following in place of equation:

$$A_p = C_a - cT_a + I_p + G + NX_a \tag{11}$$

Because imports depend on income (Y), the induced component of net exports ($-nxY$) has exactly the same effect on equilibrium income and the multiplier as does the income tax. Imports represent a leakage from the spending stream, a portion of a change in income that is not part of the disposable income of U.S. citizens and thus not available for consumption. The fraction of a change in income that is spent on net exports (nx) is part of the economy's marginal leakage rate.

Types of leakages	Marginal leakage rate
Saving only	s
Saving and income tax	$s(1 - t) + t$
Saving, income tax, and imports	$s(1 - t) + t + nx$

Full Equations for Equilibrium Income and the Multiplier

When we combine equation 6, equation 11, and the table, equilibrium income becomes:

$$Y = \frac{A_p}{\text{marginal leakage rate}} = \frac{C_a - cT_a + I_p + G + NX_a}{s(1 - t) + t + nx} \tag{12}$$

The change in income then becomes

$$\Delta Y = \frac{\Delta A_p}{\text{marginal leakage rate}}$$

where $\Delta A_p = \Delta C_a - c\Delta T_a + \Delta I_p\, \Delta G + \Delta NX_a$ and the marginal leakage rate is the same as the denominator of equation (12).

The Balanced Budget Multiplier

The balanced budget multiplier may be generalized from equation (3.18) in Chapter 3 by replacing s in the denominator by the marginal leakage rate:

$$\text{balanced budget multiplier} = \frac{1 - c}{\text{marginal leakage rate}}$$

Monetary and Fiscal Policy in the *IS-LM* Model

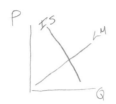

Money is always there, but the pockets change.
—Gertrude Stein

IS = Investment + Savings

LM = money/supply

4-1 Introduction: The Power of Monetary and Fiscal Policy

The last chapter examined the determinants of the demand for commodities, that is, the goods and services that make up total real GDP. We learned that the economy is in equilibrium when total output or real GDP is equal to what households, business firms, the government, and foreigners want to buy, that is, planned expenditures. When any of the determinants of planned expenditures change, business firms will react by raising or reducing output, and the economy will experience business cycles rather than smooth and steady growth of real GDP.

The last chapter summarized the relationship between equilibrium real GDP and the interest rate in a downward-sloping graphical schedule called the *IS* curve. Everywhere along the *IS* curve, the commodity market is in equilibrium and there is no unplanned inventory accumulation or decumulation. The position of the *IS* curve depends on the components of planned autonomous spending and the multiplier, and its slope depends on the multiplier and the responsiveness of planned spending to changes in the interest rate. However, this single graphical schedule, the *IS* curve, cannot determine two unknown variables: real GDP and the interest rate. We cannot determine real GDP without knowing the value of the interest rate, and the reverse is true as well: We cannot determine the interest rate until we have determined real GDP.

To determine *both* real GDP and the interest rate simultaneously, we need a second, separate relationship between them. This second relationship, called the *LM* curve, is provided by the money market, where the supply of money controlled by the Federal Reserve Board interacts with the demand for that money by households and business firms. The economy's equilibrium real GDP and its equilibrium interest rate are simultaneously determined at the intersection of the *IS* curve and the *LM* curve, where both the commodity market and money market are in equilibrium.

This *IS-LM* model allows us to understand more fully the sources of business cycles and what can be done by the government to dampen or, ideally, to eliminate business cycles. Monetary policy, controlled by the Federal Reserve Board, can be used to change interest rates and hence equilibrium real GDP. Fiscal policy, controlled by Congress and the president, can also be used to change equilibrium real GDP and the interest rate by means of changes in government spending, autonomous tax revenue, and the income tax rate. We will learn that both the level of real GDP and the interest rate can be affected by monetary and by fiscal policy, working separately or in combination.

This chapter greatly improves our understanding of the determination of real GDP and the causes of business cycles, going well beyond Chapter 3 in which there was no monetary policy and no indication of how the interest rate is determined. In this chapter we can begin our investigation of the key questions at the heart of recent debates:

1. How does monetary policy work? By what mechanism did the Federal Reserve Board (the Fed) reduce the interest rate from 6.5 to 1.0 percent between late 2000 and mid-2003? How did the Fed raise the interest rate from 1.0 percent in June 2004 to 5.25 percent in June 2006?

2. What difference did it make that the federal government ran persistent budget deficits from 1980 to 1997, followed by budget surpluses during 1998–2001, followed by deficits in 2002–08? Why did this shift from deficit to surplus back to deficit occur?

3. Does the multiplier effect of fiscal policy, previously examined in Chapter 3, depend on the conduct of monetary policy? Does the multiplier effect of monetary policy depend in turn on the conduct of fiscal policy?

4. If real GDP is higher or lower than desired, so that a policy action restraining or stimulating the economy is needed, should that policy action be carried out in the form of monetary or fiscal policy, or by a combination of the two?

4-2 Why People Use Money

The money market is a general expression for the financial sector of the economy. In reality, the financial sector consists of many assets in addition to money, including short-term debt of corporations and the government, as well as bonds, stocks, and mutual funds. In this chapter we will limit our attention to the segment of the financial sector generally referred to as "money."

The **money supply** (M^s) consists of two parts: currency and checking accounts at banks and thrift institutions. At this stage in the book, the money supply may be considered to be a policy instrument that the Fed can set exactly at any desired value, just as we have been assuming that the government can precisely set the level of its fiscal policy instruments—that is, its purchases of goods and services and tax revenues. Later, in Chapter 13, we will learn how the Fed achieves its control over the money supply in actual practice.

The theory developed in this chapter establishes a link between the money supply, income, and interest rates. In order to understand the hypothesis underlying the demand for money, we begin by examining the three traditional functions of money: its roles as a medium of exchange, a store of value, and a unit of account.

A Medium of Exchange

The most important function that differentiates money from other assets is its role as a **medium of exchange.** Money is one of the most important inventions in human history because it has allowed society to rise above the cumbersome method of exchange known as the barter system. With barter, one good or ser-

---

The **money supply** consists of currency and transactions accounts, including checking accounts at banks and thrift institutions.

A **medium of exchange** is used for buying and selling goods and services and is a universal alternative to the barter system.

vice is exchanged directly for another. If, as a professor, I want a leaky faucet fixed, I must find a plumber who wants to learn about economics. It might take weeks or months to find such a plumber, since the matching of services requires a "double coincidence of wants."

A barter society remains primitive because people have to spend so much time arranging exchanges that they have little time remaining to produce efficiently. As a result, to avoid arranging exchanges they must become self-sufficient (I would have to fix my own leaking faucet), thus failing to take advantage of the essential role of specialization in the development of an advanced economic system. Money eliminates the need for barter and the double coincidence of wants.

Which types of assets serve as a medium of exchange? Thirty years ago almost all exchanges in the United States involved coins, currency, or checking accounts that paid no interest. Gradually other methods of exchange have developed, including interest-bearing checking accounts, savings accounts, and money market mutual funds against which checks can be written. The requirements for an asset to qualify as a medium of exchange include ready acceptability, protection from counterfeiting, and divisibility (ability to use for small transactions).

A Store of Value

People do not always spend the entirety of their income the instant they receive it. Some receipts may be spent a day or two later, but others may be saved for a substantial period of time. People need some way of storing the purchasing power of their receipts until a later time. Any asset that performs this function is called a **store of value.** There are many financial instruments that serve as a store of value but not as a medium of exchange, including savings accounts that do not provide check-writing services, as well as bonds and stocks. Money can be used both as a medium of exchange and as a store of value.

A **store of value** is a method of storing purchasing power when receipts and expenditures are not perfectly synchronized.

A Unit of Account

Money is also used for accounting purposes. How much your employer will pay you in wages, how much you owe the bank, how much a firm has earned, and how much a bond is worth are all recorded in some **unit of account.** This unit is called dollars in the United States, pounds sterling in the United Kingdom, yen in Japan, euro in thirteen of the European Union countries, and so on. The dollars entered on accounting records do not physically exist, in the sense that no coin or piece of currency corresponding to each one exists in a particular location. Some dollars that serve as bookkeeping entries can also serve as a medium of exchange without any piece of paper actually changing hands, as in wire transfers between bank accounts.

A **unit of account** is a way of recording receipts, expenditures, assets, and liabilities.

4-3 Income, the Interest Rate, and the Demand for Money

The hypothesis that links the money supply, income, and the interest rate states that *the amount of money that people demand in real terms depends both on income and on the interest rate.* Why do households give up interest earnings to hold money balances that pay no interest? The main reason is that at least *some* holding of money is necessary to facilitate transactions, due to the role of money as a medium of exchange.

Income and the Demand for Money

Funds held in the form of stocks or bonds pay interest but cannot be used for transactions. People have to carry currency in their pockets or have money in their bank accounts to back up a check before they can buy anything. (Even if they use credit cards, they need money in their bank accounts to keep up with their credit card bills.) Because rich people make more purchases, they generally need a larger amount of currency and larger bank deposits. Thus the demand for **real money balances** increases when everyone becomes richer—that is, when the total of real income increases.

> **Real money balances** equal the total money supply divided by the price level.

Changes in real income alter the demand for money in real terms—that is, adjusted for changes in the price level. Let us assume that the demand for real money balances (M/P) equals half of real income (Y):

$$\left(\frac{M}{P}\right)^d = 0.5Y$$

The superscript *d* means "the demand for."

If real income (Y) is \$8,000 billion, the demand for real money balances $(M/P)^d$ will be \$4,000 billion, as shown in Figure 4-1 by the vertical line (L') drawn at \$4,000 billion. The line is vertical because we are assuming initially that the demand for real balances $(M/P)^d$ does not depend on the interest rate (r).

Figure 4-1 The Demand for Money, the Interest Rate, and Real Income

The vertical line L' is drawn on the unrealistic assumption that the demand for real balances is equal to half of real income (\$8,000 billion in this case), but does not depend on the interest rate. The L_0 curve maintains income at \$8,000, but it allows the demand for real balances to decrease by \$1,000 billion for each 5 percent increase in the interest rate. The shaded area shows the amount shifted into other assets, an amount that grows as the interest rate rises, leaving a smaller and smaller amount to be held as money.

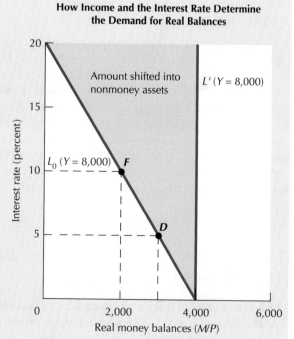

How Income and the Interest Rate Determine the Demand for Real Balances

The Interest Rate and the Demand for Money

The L' line is unrealistic, however, because individuals will not hold as much money at a 10 percent interest rate as at a zero interest rate. Why? Because the interest rate plotted on the vertical axis is paid on *assets other than money*, such as bonds and savings certificates. The higher the reward (r) for holding interest-earning financial assets (that are not money), the less money will be held.

If the interest rate (r) paid on nonmoney assets were less than the interest paid on money, there would be no point in holding them. Individuals would hold all of their financial assets in the form of money to take advantage of its convenience. But if the interest rate on them were higher than the interest paid on money, individuals would cut down on their average money holding in order to earn the higher interest available on alternative assets. They would consider these higher interest earnings sufficient compensation for the nuisance of periodically converting these assets into money.

In Figure 4-1 the downward slope of the L_0 line through points F and D indicates that when real income is $8,000 billion and the interest rate is zero, the demand for real balances is $4,000 billion. But when the interest rate rises from zero to 5 percent, people suffer inconvenience to cut down their money holdings from $4,000 billion to $3,000 billion (point D). When the interest rate is 10 percent, only $2,000 billion of money is demanded (point F). The new L_0 line can be summarized as showing that the real demand for money $(M/P)^d$ is half of income minus $200 billion times the interest rate:

$$\left(\frac{M}{P}\right)^d = 0.5Y - 200r$$

A change in the interest rate moves the economy up and down its real money demand schedule, whereas a change in real output (Y) shifts that schedule to the left or right, as shown in Figure 4-2. At any given interest rate, the change in the amount of money demanded is given by

$$\Delta\left(\frac{M}{P}\right)^d = 0.5\Delta Y$$

Between points F and C, the interest rate is the same, output falls by 2,000, and the demand for money declines by $1,000.

SELF-TEST

1. What are the two determinants of the real demand for money?

2. What is the effect of each determinant on the real demand for money?

3. Does a change in either determinant shift the *IS* curve?

Other Factors That Shift the Demand for Money Schedule

Thus far we have allowed for only one factor, real income, that shifts the money demand schedule as in Figure 4-2. In reality, there are several other factors besides real income that can shift that schedule. Recall that we use the word "money" in this chapter to include currency and checking accounts and treat all other assets, including savings accounts, stocks, and bonds, as "nonmoney assets." Here we introduce some of these additional shift factors and return at the end of this chapter to examine their impact on the determination of income and interest rates.

Figure 4-2 Effect on the Money Demand Schedule of a Decline in Real Income from $8,000 to $6,000 Billion

The L_0 line is copied from Figure 4-1 and shows the demand for real balances at different rates of interest, assuming that real income is $8,000 billion. A $2,000 billion drop in the level of income to $6,000 billion causes the demand for real balances to drop by half as much, or $1,000 billion, at each interest rate level. For instance, at an interest rate of 10 percent the demand for real balances falls from $2,000 billion at point F to $1,000 billion at point C.

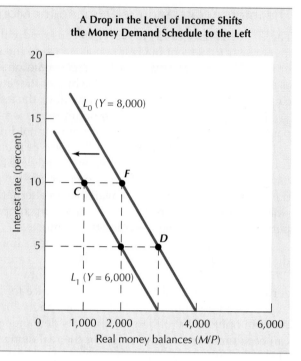

A Drop in the Level of Income Shifts the Money Demand Schedule to the Left

Handwritten margin note: M↑, M^d↓ as people switch to other forms

Interest rate paid on money.   Before 1978, only checking accounts could be used for transactions and no interest was paid on checking accounts. Today, a low interest rate is paid on some types of checking accounts. An increase in the interest rate paid on checking accounts will increase the demand for money. In reality, the interest rate paid on checking accounts is so low and varies so little that this factor can be ignored.

Wealth.   If people become wealthier by saving a lot or through higher prices on their houses and holdings in the stock market, then some of that wealth may be held in the form of extra holdings of money. In reality, however, most increases in wealth are held in nonmoney assets such as savings accounts, stocks, and bonds. Recall from Chapter 3 (pp. 63–64) that higher wealth also raises autonomous consumption and shifts the *IS* curve to the right.

Expected future inflation.   If people expect the price level to rise rapidly in the future, they know that their money will buy less in the future and will try to hold as little as possible. They will try to convert their money into nonmoney assets that will rise in price as a result of high inflation, including stocks and houses.

Payment technologies.   Any technological development that alters how people pay for goods and services, or the ease of switching between money and nonmoney assets, can influence the demand for money. For instance, ATM cash machines now are everywhere, enabling people to carry less cash because it is so easy to obtain extra cash when it is needed. Before the invention of ATMs, people had to carry more cash because money could be obtained only in person at a bank branch during business hours. Equally important was the invention of credit cards that allow most transactions to be paid for without us-

ments found that they could not sell them at a higher price, causing a collapse in the demand for homes as investments. Second, adjustable-rate mortgages, especially in the subprime market, were reset at higher rates, which overextended and unqualified borrowers could not afford. Banks began to foreclose when borrowers fell behind on their monthly mortgage payments. By mid-2007, troubles in the subprime mortgage market caused the bankruptcy of several mortgage lenders and a general tightening of credit standards as lenders scrutinized more carefully mortgage applicants' incomes and credit histories.

Higher interest rates and tighter credit standards also caused a sharp decline in residential construction activity. The number of new housing units started that had climbed from 1.6 million in 2001 to 2.1 million in 2005 dropped by 30 percent to 1.5 million in 2007; some home builders went bankrupt and some construction workers lost their jobs. In 2006–07, house prices began to decline in many parts of the United States, further reducing the demand for housing for investment purposes.

Was monetary policy too easy in 2002–04? The Fed was strongly criticized by economic analysts for creating a boom-bust cycle in the housing market by keeping interest rates too low for too long. If interest rates had not been pushed down so far, the post-2001 economic recovery would have been slower but more balanced between housing and other components of GDP. Housing prices would not have risen so fast, there would have been less speculative demand for houses, and the economic dislocation caused by too much building followed by bankruptcies and foreclosures would have been partly avoided. Further, if the Fed had regulated the subprime mortgage market more closely, so many mortgages would not have been made to borrowers who ultimately could not afford them, which would have reduced the number who suffered the economic and personal dislocations caused by foreclosure.

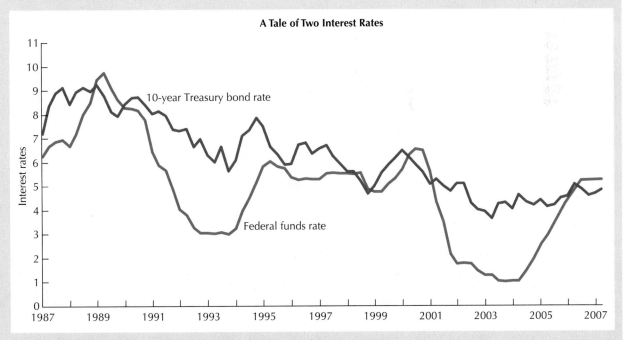

A Tale of Two Interest Rates

Source: Federal Reserve Board of Governors *H.15 Selected Interest Rates.*

Assume that the Fed now raises the nominal money supply from $2,000 billion to $3,000 billion. As long as the price level stays fixed at 1.0, the real money supply increases by the same amount. The *LM* curve shifts to the right

Figure 4-5 The Effect of a $1,000 Billion Increase in the Money Supply with a Normal *LM* Curve

The real money supply rises from $2,000 billion along the old LM_0 curve to $3,000 billion along the new LM_1 curve. In order to maintain equilibrium in both the commodity and money markets here, two effects occur: equilibrium income rises and the interest rate declines, as indicated by the movement from E_0 to E_1.

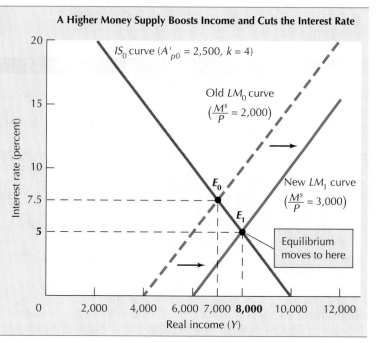

A Higher Money Supply Boosts Income and Cuts the Interest Rate

IS_0 curve ($A'_{p0} = 2,500$, $k = 4$)

Old LM_0 curve ($\frac{M^s}{P} = 2,000$)

New LM_1 curve ($\frac{M^s}{P} = 3,000$)

Equilibrium moves to here

Interest rate (percent)

Real income (Y)

by $2,000 billion. Now, at the new, higher real money supply of $3,000 billion, there is an "excess supply of money" of $1,000 billion. How can the economy generate the $1,000 billion increase in the real demand for money needed to balance the new higher supply?

Finding themselves with more money than they need, individuals transfer some money into savings accounts and use some to buy stocks, bonds, and commodities. This raises the prices of bonds and stocks and reduces the interest rate. The lower interest rate raises the desired level of autonomous consumption and investment spending, requiring an increase in production. Only at point E_1, with an income level of $8,000 billion and interest rate of 5 percent, are both the money and commodity markets in equilibrium. Compared to the starting point E_0, the increase in the real money supply has caused both an *increase* in real income and a *reduction* in the interest rate.

The *LM* Curve Can Also Be Shifted by Changes in the Demand for Money

So far we have interpreted the rightward movement of the *LM* curve in Figure 4-5 as being caused by an *increase* in the money supply. But exactly the same rightward shift in the *LM* curve can be caused by *reduction* in the demand for money. Some of the factors that could reduce the demand for money at a given interest rate and level of real income were introduced on pp. 97–99. These include a decrease in the interest rate paid on money, a decrease in wealth, an increase in expected future inflation, and new payment technologies such as ATMs and credit cards that reduce the need for people to carry currency in their purses and wallets. Any of these changes would shift the *LM* curve to the right and the opposite changes would shift the *LM* curve to the left.

If the Fed wants to avoid a change in real GDP and the interest rate when these shifts in money demand occur, then it needs to change the money supply in the same direction. Thus if the invention of ATMs and credit cards reduces the demand for money, the Fed must reduce the supply of money by the amount needed to keep the LM curve from shifting to the right.

4-7 How Fiscal Expansion Can "Crowd Out" Investment

In the last section we examined the effects on real income and the interest rate of changes in monetary policy by shifting the LM curve along a fixed IS curve. Now we shall do the reverse and shift the IS curve along a fixed LM curve. The original IS curve is copied from Figure 4-4 and is labeled in Figure 4-6 as the "old IS_0 curve."

Expansionary Fiscal Policy Shifts the IS Curve

An expansionary fiscal policy taking the form of a $500 billion increase in government purchases shifts the IS curve to the right. Note that the horizontal distance between the old and new IS curves is not $500 billion but $2,000 billion,

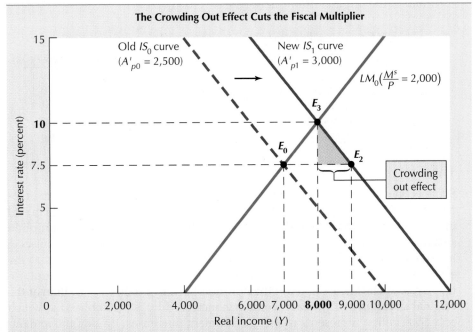

Figure 4-6 The Effect on Real Income and the Interest Rate of a $500 Billion Increase in Government Spending

Along the original IS_0 curve, the autonomous spending desired at a zero interest rate (A'_{p0}) is 2,500 and the economy's equilibrium occurs at point E_0. A $500 billion increase in government spending boosts spending from $A'_{p0} = 2,500$ to $A'_{p1} = 3,000$, and shifts the IS curve rightward to IS_1. The economy's equilibrium slides up the LM curve from point E_0 to E_3. In contrast to Chapter 3's multiplier of 4.0, now the government spending multiplier is only 2.0. But, since income increases from E_0 to E_3, crowding out is partial, not complete.

since the horizontal shift of *IS* is $500 billion times the multiplier, still assumed to be 4.0.

Figure 4-6 demonstrates that the effect of an expansionary fiscal policy on real income is not indicated by our original Chapter 3 multiplier ($k = 4.0$) once the money market is taken into consideration. The full fiscal multiplier of $k = 4.0$ would move the economy horizontally from the initial equilibrium position at E_0 to point E_2, where income is $2,000 billion higher. At E_2, however, the money market is not in equilibrium, because E_2 is off the LM_0 curve. Income is higher than at E_0, raising the demand for money, but the real supply of money remains unchanged at the original assumed value $M^s/P = 2,000$. There is an excess demand for money.

To cut the demand for money back to the level of the fixed supply, the interest rate must rise. But an increase in the interest rate makes point E_2 untenable by reducing planned consumption and investment expenditures. *Only at point E_3 are both the commodity and money markets in equilibrium.* Real income does not increase by the full $2,000 billion, but only by half as much, $1,000 billion.

The higher interest rate accounts for the fact that the fiscal policy multiplier is 2.0, rather than 4.0, when the requirement for money market equilibrium is taken into account. The increase in the interest rate from 7.5 to 10 percent cuts private autonomous planned consumption and investment spending by $250 billion, fully half of the $500 billion increase in government spending. Thus fully half of the original multiplier of 4.0 is "crowded out."

Comparison of Equilibrium Positions E_0 and E_3

	Initial E_0	New E_3
Interest rate (r)	7.5	10.0
Private autonomous spending ($I_p + C_a = 2,500 - 100r$)	1,750	1,500
Government spending (G)	0	500
Total autonomous spending ($A_p = I_p + C_a + G$)	1,750	2,000
Income ($Y = 4.0A_p$)	7,000	8,000

The Crowding Out Effect

The **crowding out effect** describes the effect of an increase in government spending or a reduction of tax rates in reducing the amount of one or more other components of private expenditures.

Some economists and journalists use the phrase **crowding out effect** to compare points such as E_2 and E_3 in Figure 4-6. The $1,000 billion difference in real income between points E_2 and E_3 results from the investment and consumption spending crowded out by the higher interest rate. Point E_2, used in calculating the size of the crowding out effect, is a purely hypothetical position that the economy cannot and does not reach. Actually, far from being crowded out, total private spending is higher in the new equilibrium situation at E_3 than at the original situation at E_0—real income has increased by $1,000 billion, of which only $500 billion represents higher government purchases, leaving the remaining $500 billion for extra private expenditures. The composition of private spending changes, however, as a result of the higher interest rate. Induced consumption spending increases, but autonomous private spending decreases. Expenditures are divided up as follows in the two situations:

	At E_0	At E_3
Government purchases	0	500
Autonomous private spending ($I_p + C_a$)	1,750	1,500
Induced consumption	5,250	6,000
Total real expenditures	7,000	8,000

Can Crowding Out Be Avoided?

The fundamental cause of crowding out is an increase in the interest rate that is required whenever income rises and the supply of money is fixed while the demand for money responds positively to an increase in income. To offset the increase in the demand for money caused by higher income, it is necessary for the interest rate to rise by enough to offset the effects of higher income on the demand for money.

The simplest way to avoid crowding out would be for the Fed to increase the money supply, thus allowing the LM curve to shift rightward by the same amount as the IS curve. Another possible exception to crowding out would be if the demand for money did not depend on income. Other hypothetical situations in which crowding out would be avoided are when the IS curve is vertical (that is, the interest responsiveness of spending is zero) or when the LM curve is horizontal (that is, the interest responsiveness of the demand for money is infinite).

In the next section we will examine some of these situations in which monetary policy and fiscal policy are unusually strong or weak, then we will study interactions among monetary and fiscal policy. Using monetary and fiscal policy together, the government can achieve the desired (natural) level of real GDP at any level of the interest rate.

4-8 Strong and Weak Effects of Monetary Policy

The IS-LM model that we have developed shows how real income (or GDP) and the interest rate are determined. Previously, in Figure 4-5, we examined the "normal" effects of an increase or decrease in the money supply. With the assumed IS curve and the LM curve labeled LM_0 the economy's equilibrium occurred at a real income of $7,000 billion and was labeled E_0.

We repeat the same assumed equilibrium point E_0 in Figure 4-7. The diagram differs from those in previous sections of this chapter, however, by dropping specific numbers from the vertical and horizontal axes. Now that we have learned how the IS-LM model works, we can simplify our analysis by labeling each point with alphabetical symbols rather than specific numbers. For instance, in Figure 4-7 the equilibrium level of income along the initial LM_0 curve is labeled Y' and the equilibrium interest rate is labeled r'.

Now we will ask how much will real income increase if the Fed raises the money supply enough to shift the LM curve from the old LM curve to the new LM curve? We do not need to calculate the exact numerical value of the change in income and the interest rate, since we will be interested in answers to two simple questions. First, following an increase in the real money supply, does real income increase by a lot, a little, or not at all? Second, does the interest rate decline by a lot, a little, or not at all?

Strong Effects of Monetary Expansion

The answer to these questions depends on the slopes of both the IS and LM curves. With the normal slopes shown in the top frame of Figure 4-7, the economy moves from point E_0 to point E_1. The higher money supply boosts income from Y' to Y_1 and lowers the interest rate from r' to r_1. The economy's equilibrium moves from E_0 to E_1, just as in Figure 4-5. Higher income and

Figure 4-7 The Effect of an Increase in the Money Supply with a Normal *LM* Curve and a Vertical *LM* Curve

The top frame shows the normal effect of an increase in the real money supply, which is to raise real income and to reduce the interest rate. In the bottom frame, the *LM* curve is vertical, and the same increase in the real money supply leads to a greater drop in the interest rate and a greater increase in real income.

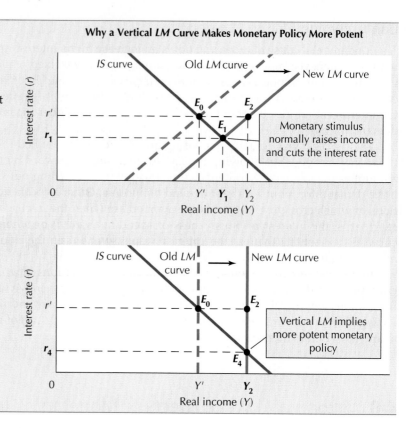

lower interest rates suffice to boost the demand for money by the amount needed in order to match the assumed higher supply of money that the Fed has created.

What would it take for the impact of the same increase in the money supply to differ from this normal case? In one variant, monetary expansion has an unusually strong effect on income. This occurs when the *LM* curve is steep (due to a low interest responsiveness of the demand for money). Shown in the bottom frame of Figure 4-7 is the same starting place at E_0, and exactly the same *IS* curve as in the top frame. But now the old and new *LM* curves are vertical, indicating the extreme case of a zero interest responsiveness of the demand for money. The same increase in the money supply as in the top frame moves the *LM* curve to "new *LM*" (note that the horizontal shift in the *LM* curve in both the top and bottom frames is the identical distance marked from E_0 to E_2). As a result, the economy moves from point E_0 to point E_4 in the bottom frame. Income increases twice as much in the bottom frame as in the upper frame, while the interest rate falls twice as much.

Why does monetary policy exert a greater stimulus in the bottom frame? In both frames the money supply increases by the same amount, and so does money demand. But in the bottom frame the demand for money is totally insensitive to a reduction in the interest rate, *so all the "work" of boosting money demand must be achieved by higher income*. Since the lower interest rate offers no help in boosting money demand, income must rise further than in the top frame. And, to maintain commodity-market equilibrium along the fixed *IS* curve, a greater drop in the interest rate is needed to achieve the required boost in income.

Weak Effects of Monetary Policy

The Fed boosts the money supply when it believes that income is too low. But in some circumstances the effects of monetary policy are so weak that the policy cannot boost real income sufficiently to reach the desired level Y_1. This section reviews two such cases. First, changes in the interest rate may have only weak effects on autonomous planned spending (A_p). Second, money demand might be extremely sensitive to changes in the interest rate, which weakens the Fed's ability to reduce the interest rate.

Steep *IS* curve. The first case is shown in the top frame of Figure 4-8. The zero interest responsiveness of A_p implies that the *IS* curve is vertical. This situation occurs when business firms are so pessimistic about the future that they choose not to boost investment spending in response to lower interest rates. As a result, a lower interest rate does not raise equilibrium income. Income is "stuck" at point Y' in response to the same rightward shift in the *LM* curve that occurs in the top frame of Figure 4-7. The only effect of the higher money supply in the top frame of Figure 4-8 is a lower interest rate as the economy moves from point E_0 down vertically to point E_5. Since real income is stuck at Y', all the work of boosting money demand now must be achieved by a lower interest rate.

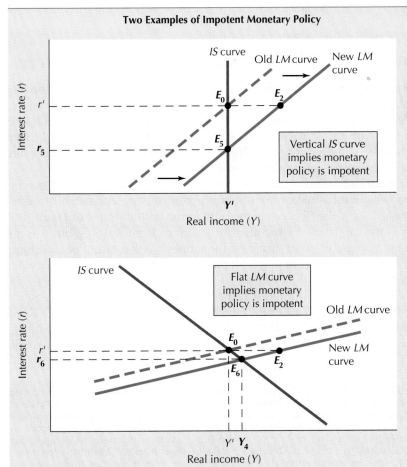

Figure 4-8 Effect of the Same Increase in the Real Money Supply with a Zero Interest Responsiveness of Spending and with a High Interest Responsiveness of the Demand for Money

In the top frame, the higher money supply does not stimulate expenditures because expenditures are assumed to be independent of the interest rate—that is, the *IS* curve is vertical. In the bottom frame, the *LM* curve is so flat that the same increase in the money supply (as in the top frame of this figure and in both frames of Figure 4-7) hardly reduces the interest rate at all, and so real income hardly increases at all.

Flat *LM* curve. The second case of weak monetary policy occurs when the demand for money is extremely responsive to the interest rate, which makes the *LM* curve very flat, as shown in the bottom frame of Figure 4-8. Once again, the money supply goes up by the same amount as before, and the *LM* curve shifts horizontally by the distance shown between E_0 and point E_2. But now, because the *LM* curve is so flat, the economy's equilibrium position hardly moves at all, from E_0 to E_6. Before the interest rate falls enough to stimulate an increase in autonomous planned spending, it is already low enough to boost money demand and falls no further. In the extreme case of a horizontal *LM* curve, the Fed loses control over both output and the interest rate, which remain unchanged in response to a higher money supply. This case is called the **liquidity trap,** signifying a loss of control by the central bank over the interest rate. Some economists have suggested that Japan experienced a liquidity trap in 1998–2002.[3]

The **liquidity trap** is a situation in which the central bank loses its ability to reduce the interest rate.

SELF-TEST

1. If the demand for money is independent of the interest rate, is the *LM* curve vertical or horizontal?

2. Does an increase in the money supply have strong or weak effects when the *LM* curve is steeper than normal?

3. When is it flatter than normal?

4-9 Strong and Weak Effects of Fiscal Policy

As with monetary policy, the effect of a fiscal policy stimulus on real income depends on the slopes of the *IS* and *LM* curves. Fiscal policy is strong when the demand for money is highly interest-responsive, as illustrated in the top frame of Figure 4-9. With this extreme case of a horizontal *LM* curve, the multiplier becomes just the simple multiplier (k) of Chapter 3. There is no crowding out effect, since the interest rate remains constant.

The opposite situation occurs when the interest responsiveness of money demand is zero, which makes the *LM* curve vertical. An increase in government spending shifts the *IS* curve to the right in the bottom frame of Figure 4-9, exactly as in the top frame by the identical distance from E_0 to E_2, but real income cannot increase without throwing the money market out of equilibrium. Why? An increase in real income would raise the demand for money above the fixed money supply.

But because of the zero interest responsiveness of money demand, no increase in the interest rate can keep money demand in balance with the fixed money supply and a higher level of income. Thus as long as the money supply is fixed, real income cannot be any higher than its initial position at Y'. In this

---

[3] Normally an increase in the money supply reduces the interest rate because people try to get rid of the excess money by purchasing bonds and other financial assets, thus raising the price of bonds and other financial assets and reducing the interest rate. In the extreme (and hypothetical) case of the "liquidity trap," people are convinced that the prices of bonds and other financial assets are unusually high and are likely to fall, so they hold on to the extra money and refuse to buy any financial assets. As a result, the Fed (or the Bank of Japan) loses control of the interest rate, and the *LM* curve becomes a horizontal line that no longer shifts its position in response to a higher money supply. For a discussion of policy weakness in Japan, see pp. 118–19.

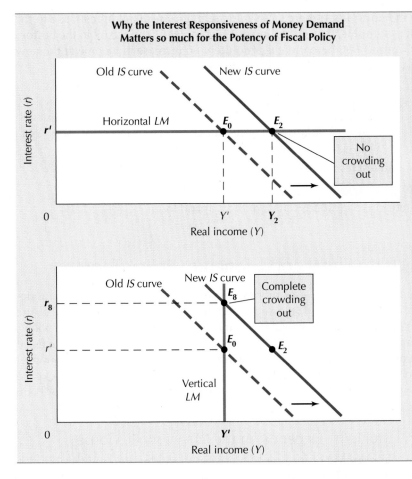

Why the Interest Responsiveness of Money Demand Matters so much for the Potency of Fiscal Policy

Figure 4-9 **Effect of a Fiscal Stimulus When Money Demand Has an Infinite and a Zero Interest Responsiveness**

In the top frame, an infinite interest responsiveness means that the interest rate is fixed, and no crowding out can occur. In contrast, the same fiscal stimulus has no effect on income when the interest responsiveness is zero (bottom frame), because then a higher interest rate releases no extra money to support higher income, and the income level is completely determined by the size of the real money supply. Since the fiscal stimulus causes no growth at all in income from E_0 to E_8, crowding out is complete.

case the only effect of a fiscal stimulus is to raise the interest rate. The crowding out effect is complete, with the higher interest rate cutting autonomous *private* spending by exactly the amount by which government spending increases, leaving total autonomous spending unchanged.

Which diagram is the most accurate depiction of the effects of expansionary fiscal policy with a fixed real money supply—the "normal" case depicted in Figure 4-6 or the extreme cases shown in Figure 4-9? Numerous historical episodes suggest that the original analysis of Figure 4-6 is accurate—the crowding out effect is partial rather than complete or nonexistent. Furthermore, statistical evidence shows that the interest responsiveness of the demand for money is neither zero nor infinity. For this reason we should regard Figure 4-6 as giving a reliable example of the effects of expansionary fiscal policy, while Figure 4-9 depicts two artificial and extreme cases rather than realistic possibilities.

Summary of Crowding Out

The fundamental cause of crowding out is an increase in the interest rate caused by a fiscal policy stimulus. Crowding out can be avoided only if there is no upward pressure on the interest rate when the IS curve shifts rightward; with a fixed money supply this requires a horizontal LM curve as in the top frame of Figure 4-9. In this frame, there is zero crowding out.

Crowding out can be either partial or complete. If there is any increase in real income in response to the fiscal policy stimulus, crowding out is partial, as is shown in Figure 4-6. If there is no increase in income at all in response to the fiscal policy stimulus, then crowding out is complete. This occurs in the bottom frame of Figure 4-9, where there is absolutely no increase in income at the new point E_8, as compared with the initial point E_0.

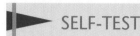

SELF-TEST

Indicate whether crowding out is zero, partial, or complete in the following cases:
1. Zero interest responsiveness of autonomous planned spending.
2. Zero interest responsiveness of the demand for money.
3. Infinite interest responsiveness of the demand for money.

4-10 Using Fiscal and Monetary Policy Together

So far we have used the *IS-LM* model to examine, first, the effects of a monetary expansion and, second, the separate effects of a fiscal expansion. Yet the two types of policy do not always work in isolation. The Fed's monetary policy, formed on the "west side" of Washington, may strengthen or dampen the fiscal policy formed on the "east side" of Washington.[4] An important application of this section is the recent history of Japan, where the potential for fiscal expansion to reinforce monetary expansion, and vice versa, has until recently been ignored.

The Fiscal Multiplier Depends on the Monetary Response

How does the response of income to a fiscal policy stimulus (the fiscal multiplier) depend on the Fed? The basic idea is simple: The more the Fed *expands* the money supply, the larger is the fiscal multiplier; the more the Fed *contracts* the money supply, the smaller is the fiscal multiplier. If the Fed contracts the money supply enough, the fiscal multiplier could even be negative.

Three cases are shown in Figure 4-10. In the upper left frame, we repeat the standard case from Figure 4-6. When the Fed holds the money supply constant, the *LM* curve remains at its original position. A fiscal stimulus consisting of either an increase in government spending or a tax cut shifts the *IS* curve rightward to the "new *IS* curve." Because the money supply is fixed, the higher demand for money created by rising income forces interest rates higher, crowding out some investment and consumption spending. The economy goes from point E_0 to E_3 just as in Figure 4-6.

In the upper right frame is a second possibility. If the Fed's goal is to keep the interest rate fixed, the money supply must be allowed to change passively whenever there is a shift in the *IS* curve (due not only to fiscal policy but also to changes in consumer and business confidence and to changes in net exports). If the Fed allows the money supply to change by the amount needed to keep the interest rate constant at r', it must shift the *LM* curve rightward. The result of

---

[4] Monetary policy is formulated in the Federal Reserve building, about seven blocks west of the Washington Monument. Fiscal policy is formulated not just in the White House (near the Washington Monument) but in the Capitol and nearby Senate and House office buildings, which are about fifteen blocks east of the Washington Monument.

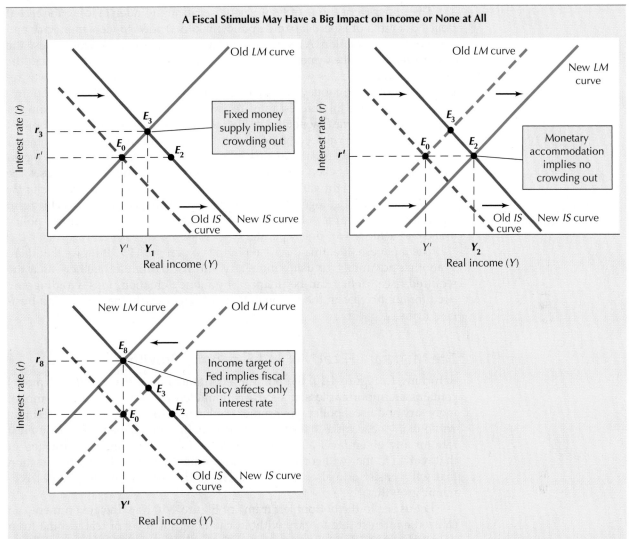

Figure 4-10 The Effect on Real Income of a Fiscal Stimulus with Three Alternative Monetary Policies

In the top left frame, the real money supply is held constant and the stimulus of fiscal policy on real income is partly crowded out (as in Figure 4-6). In the top right frame, the Fed maintains a fixed interest rate, which eliminates the crowding out effect (as in the top frame of Figure 4-9). In the bottom left frame, the Fed attempts to maintain a constant level of real income by shifting LM to the left whenever IS shifts to the right, implying complete crowding out; in this case, fiscal policy influences only the interest rate, not real income.

the fiscal stimulus is now the same as the Chapter 3 multiplier (k), which ignored the money market and the impact of interest rate changes. The economy goes from E_0 to E_2, the same as the new equilibrium position in the top frame of Figure 4-9. When trying to stabilize the interest rate and allowing the money supply to respond passively to any change in the IS curve, the Fed is said to "accommodate" fiscal policy. In effect, the east side of Washington has taken control of the west side.

The upper right frame of Figure 4-10 is critical in understanding the recent policy dilemma of Japan. Japanese policymakers tended to view monetary and fiscal policy in isolation. A fiscal stimulus had the defect that it would raise the interest rate, as in the upper left frame of Figure 4-10. Monetary policy had the defect that interest rates were already very low, and the Bank of Japan was reluctant to boost the money supply in the belief that it was difficult, if not impossible, to reduce the interest rate. Yet, as shown in the upper right frame of Figure 4-10, a *combined* monetary and fiscal policy stimulus could avoid both of these drawbacks. When combined with a fiscal stimulus that causes the *IS* curve to shift rightward, a monetary stimulus *does not require a decline in the interest rate*. Similarly, when combined with a monetary stimulus that causes the *LM* curve to shift rightward, a fiscal stimulus *does not require an increase in the interest rate*. Working together, monetary and fiscal policy could achieve in Japan (or elsewhere) a policy stimulus much more potent than either policy tool could achieve working separately.

The Japanese dilemma discussed in the box on pp. 118–19 shows that there is another advantage to using monetary and fiscal stimuli together—that the required fiscal deficit can be financed by money creation, thus avoiding any need for an increase in the national debt held by households, banks, and business firms.

The Monetary-Fiscal Mix and Economic Growth

Returning to Figure 4-10, the bottom left frame shows that the *IS-LM* model contains an important lesson about economic growth. By changing the mix of monetary and fiscal policy, government policymakers can alter the interest rate without any need for a change in real income. In general, the lower the interest rate for any given level of real income or real GDP, the larger the fraction of that real GDP that will consist of real investment and the smaller the fraction that will consist of real consumption. Higher investment tends to boost economic growth.

Let us see in the bottom left frame of Figure 4-10 how the government can cause the interest rate to vary without changing the level of real income from its initial level Y'. If the Fed wants to maintain income at Y', it can respond to a fiscal stimulus *by moving the* LM *curve in the opposite direction from the movement in the* IS *curve*. Thus, if government spending is increased, the Fed must reduce the money supply. In the bottom left frame of Figure 4-10, the economy moves from E_0 to E_8 (the same position shown in the bottom frame of Figure 4-9). When the Fed behaves this way, fiscal policy no longer has any control over the level of income and affects only the interest rate. The effect of fiscal policy is to raise the interest rate from r' to r_8, because the Fed has reduced the money supply by enough to maintain the initial level of income Y'.

This illustrates an important point about monetary and fiscal policy. Once the government has decided on the desirable level of income, say Y', it can achieve that level of income with many different interest rates, of which r' and r_8 are only two examples. We can assume that points E_0 and E_8 share not only the same level of output, but also the same unemployment rate. What are the differences?

Point E_8 offsets the fiscal policy stimulus, assumed to be a higher level of government spending, by reducing the money supply. In contrast, point E_0 has a higher real money supply (shown by the fact that the *LM* curve is farther to the right) but a tighter fiscal policy (shown by the fact that the *IS* curve is farther to the left). The higher interest rate at E_8 crowds out planned investment and autonomous consumption below that at point E_0, in order to make room for a higher level of government spending.

The two points E_0 and E_8 are said to differ in the mix of monetary and fiscal policy. Point E_0 has a **policy mix** of "easy money, tight fiscal," while point E_8 has the opposite policy mix of "tight money, easy fiscal." Which mix should society prefer? At E_0, investment is higher; thus the economy is building for the future, and its future level of productivity growth will be higher. At E_8, government spending is higher than at E_0, and investment is lower. Should society prefer the faster output growth of point E_0 or the higher level of public services of point E_8?

This is a central question of macroeconomics to which we return in Chapters 10–12. Its solution depends on whether the government spending consists largely of government consumption (national defense, police, and fire protection) or government investment (highways and school buildings). If the extra government spending at point E_8 consists of government consumption, then the choice between points E_8 and E_0 depends on society's taste for present consumption of goods and services (at E_8) versus future consumption, since a high investment strategy at E_0 yields higher consumption only in the future. If the extra government spending at E_8 consists of government investment, then the choice depends on whether there is a higher payoff for society from government investment (of which there is more at E_8) as compared with private investment (of which there is more at E_0). The same criteria are relevant if the fiscal stimulus takes the form of a tax cut that can stimulate either private investment or consumption, depending on the types of taxes that are cut.

The **policy mix** refers to the combination of monetary and fiscal policy in effect in a given situation. A mix of tight monetary and easy fiscal policy leads to high interest rates, while a mix of easy monetary and tight fiscal policy leads to low interest rates.

Infrastructure, Minneapolis, and the Monetary-Fiscal Policy Mix

On August 1, 2007, the I-35W highway bridge carrying traffic between Minneapolis and St. Paul, Minnesota, over the Mississippi River suddenly collapsed. Cars and even a school bus plunged down with the pavement, some into the river, and by a miracle of the construction of the bridge itself and the heroic local rescue efforts, only 13 people died. The event shocked the nation and led to concerns that many other bridges were deteriorating or of faulty design. That one Minneapolis event shifted public opinion toward more government investment in **infrastructure,** which includes all the physical entities—such as highways, airports, railways, telephone networks, and electricity grids—that are paid for by a mix of government and private investment.

If the public desires more investment in infrastructure, such as major projects to repair highway bridges, a monetary-fiscal policy mix with higher government investment spending and a smaller money supply, as at point E_8 in the lower left frame of Figure 4-10, would be preferred. This mix of tight monetary and easy fiscal policy would release more economic resources for government-financed infrastructure investment.

Infrastructure consists of types of capital that benefit society as a whole, including highways, airports, trains, waterways, ports, telephone networks, and electricity grids.

Summary of Monetary-Fiscal Interactions

By working together, monetary and fiscal policy can be more effective than if they are operated independently. A fiscal stimulus accompanied by a monetary expansion is more effective than a fiscal stimulus carried out in the presence of a fixed or shrinking money supply. This can be seen in the difference between the upper left and upper right frames of Figure 4-10, where the crowding out

International Perspective

Monetary and Fiscal Policy Paralysis in Japan's "Lost Decade"

The decade-long economic slump in Japan from 1991 to 2002 is one of the most remarkable macroeconomic phenomena of the postwar era. As shown in the graph, economic growth in Japan in the 1980s was so rapid that per-capita real GDP in Japan grew from 74 percent of the U.S. level in 1980 to 86 percent in 1991. But then the great slump began just as the U.S. economy began to take off. Between 1991 and 2002, growth in per-capita real GDP in Japan was a mere 0.6 percent per year, contrasted with 2.0 percent per year in the United States. Per-capita real GDP in Japan fell from 86 percent of the U.S. level in 1991 to 74 percent in 2008.

How could an economy that had been so successful suddenly cease its growth? The key to understanding the Japanese situation is to recognize the paralysis of monetary and fiscal policymakers. Monetary policymakers believed that there was nothing left for them to do, because interest rates were close to zero. Fiscal policymakers believed that there was nothing left for them to do, because the public debt in Japan is excessive, well over 100 percent of GDP, and to cut taxes or boost spending would cause a further increase in the already-excessive debt.

Interest Rates: Japan in the 1990s and the United States in the 1930s

The low level of interest rates in Japan has a historical precedent in the low level of U.S. interest rates in the 1930s. This similarity is shown in the pair of graphs on the opposite page. The Japanese short-term interest rate fell below 1 percent after 1995 and was less than 0.1 percent in 2001–05. In the United States, the short-term interest rate fell below 1 percent after 1931 and was less than 0.05 percent in 1938–40.

The economist Paul Krugman of Princeton has called attention to the similarity between these episodes. Krugman claims that the Japanese situation exhibits a liquidity trap, a situation (as defined on p. 112) in which the nominal interest rate is near zero, and monetary policy is rendered ineffective because it loses its power to reduce the interest rate further.

A liquidity trap is a situation in which, because the nominal interest rate obtainable on short-term assets other than money is close to zero, investors are indifferent whether they hold money or these short-term assets. As a result of this indifference, the interest responsiveness of the demand for money is infinite, and the *LM*

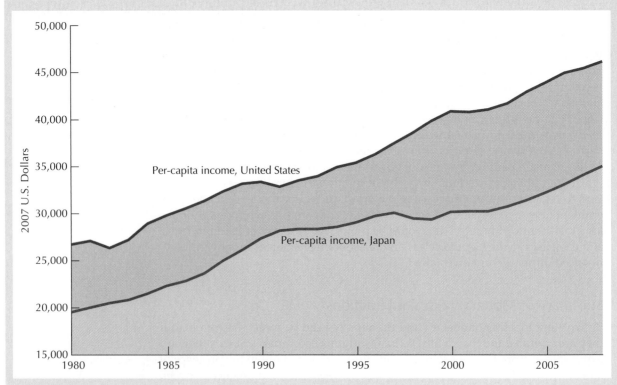

Source: Groningen Growth and Development Center, *Total Economy Database*. Details in Appendix C-4.

curve is a horizontal line like that depicted in the top frame of Figure 4-9, except that this horizontal line would be plotted very close to the horizontal axis.

If monetary policy is impotent because it cannot reduce the interest rate any further, a fiscal stimulus is required to end the slump and bring real GDP back to its desired level. This fiscal stimulus occurred in the United States in 1940–41 as exports and military expenditures increased.

The Japanese Policy Dilemma and the *IS-LM* Model

The low level of the Japanese interest rate created a policy dilemma in Japan. Monetary policy could not push interest rates appreciably lower, yet fiscal policymakers felt constrained in achieving a large fiscal stimulus by the high existing level of the fiscal deficit in Japan and by the fact that the public debt in Japan had exceeded 100 percent of real GDP.

However, the *IS-LM* model suggests a way out of the Japanese policy dilemma. As shown in the top right frame of Figure 4-10 on p. 115, a *combined* monetary and fiscal policy stimulus that shifts the *LM* and *IS* curves rightward by the same amount can boost real GDP without any need for a decline in interest rates. Also, with such a combined policy there is no need for a further increase in the national debt held by the public, since to achieve its monetary expansion, the central bank can buy the government bonds issued as a result of the increased fiscal deficit.

Despite the implication of the *IS-LM* model that monetary and fiscal expansion should be undertaken together, it took until 2003–04 for Japanese policymakers to realize that this was an option. Why did the bank of Japan resist what seemed to be the obvious solution, which was that the bank buy up the government bonds

issued as a result of the fiscal stimulus? This solution, sometimes called "monetizing the debt," would be the real-world equivalent of shifting the *LM* curve rightward along with the *IS* curve.

The traditional reason for the reluctance of central bankers to monetize the debt and conduct a simultaneous monetary and fiscal expansion has been fear of inflation. Yet Japan's problem was deflation, not inflation. In fact, Krugman's solution for the Japanese dilemma was that the Bank of Japan should buy up so much Japanese government debt that it would convince the public that there would be a steady inflation in the foreseeable future. Further, monetization of the debt would tend to depreciate the foreign exchange rate of the Japanese yen, which would stimulate Japanese net exports.

Only after 2002 did Japan begin to recover from its decade-long slump. Between 2002 and 2008 its real GDP per capita grew at the respectable rate of 2.0 percent, slightly faster than that in the United States. While the prescription of the *IS-LM* model in favor of a combined monetary-fiscal expansion seemed clear, implementing this policy recommendation was blocked by the reluctance of the Bank of Japan to give up its historic commitment to maintaining price stability, for example, zero inflation. As Princeton economist Kenneth Rogoff concluded, "The real problem is that the Bank of Japan does not have the big picture right. It does not realize that a good conservative central bank should be willing to let the price level rise on a rainy day—and Japan is experiencing a typhoon."[a]

---

[a] The best source is Charles Y. Horioka, "The Causes of Japan's Lost Decade: The Role of Household Consumption," *Japan and the World Economy*, vol. 18, no. 4, pp. 378–400. Also available as NBER Working Paper 12142.

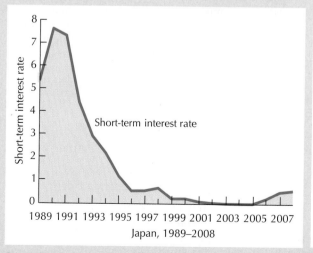

Japan, 1989–2008

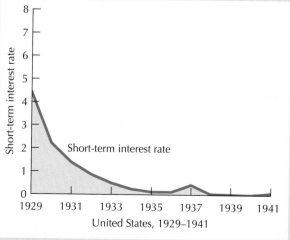

United States, 1929–1941

Source: Board of Governors of the Federal Reserve System *Banking and Monetary Statistics 1914–1941* and *OECD Economic Outlook no. 82*.

evident on the left is eliminated on the right by the increase in the money supply. Stagnation in Japan over the decade 1992–2002 (discussed in the box on pp. 118–19) is ample evidence that both monetary and fiscal policy can be paralyzed when they ignore the possibility of working together.

Further, by working together, monetary and fiscal policy can keep real GDP at the desirable natural level of real GDP, while choosing the level of the interest rate. Policies that lead to a government deficit and promote consumption imply a high interest rate, while policies that lead to a government surplus and promote private saving imply a low real interest rate that encourages domestic investment and reduces foreign borrowing.

Summary

1. The main functions of money are its use as a medium of exchange, a store of value, and a unit of account.
2. The real quantity of money that people demand depends both on real income and on the interest rate. Equilibrium in the money market requires that the real supply of money equal the demand for real money balances.
3. The *LM* curve represents all the combinations of real income and of the interest rate where the money market is in equilibrium.
4. An increase in the money supply raises real income and reduces the interest rate when the *IS* curve has its normal negative slope and the *LM* curve has its normal positive slope.
5. A fiscal expansion raises real income and the interest rate, causing crowding out if the money supply is held constant and both the *IS* and *LM* curves have their normal slopes.
6. Monetary policy has a relatively strong effect on real income when the interest responsiveness of the demand for money is relatively low (steep *LM* curve). Monetary policy is weak when the interest responsiveness of the demand for money is very high (flat *LM* curve), or when the interest responsiveness of autonomous planned spending is very low (steep *IS* curve).
7. The normal effect of a fiscal policy stimulus, consisting either of an increase in government spending or a reduction in tax rates, is to raise both real income and the interest rate. The fiscal multiplier is lower than the Chapter 3 multiplier (k) due to partial crowding out of planned investment and autonomous consumption.

8. A fiscal stimulus has a relatively strong effect on real income when the interest responsiveness of the demand for money is relatively high (flat *LM* curve) or the interest responsiveness of autonomous spending is relatively low (steep *IS* curve). A fiscal stimulus has a relatively weak effect with the opposite pattern of interest responsiveness (steep *LM* curve or flat *IS* curve).
9. The effect of a fiscal stimulus on income (fiscal multiplier) is greatest, and there is no crowding out effect, if the Fed is attempting to stabilize interest rates, since this requires that the money supply passively accommodate the fiscal stimulus (the *LM* curve must move to the right by exactly the same distance as the *IS* curve).
10. An intermediate fiscal multiplier, with partial crowding out, occurs when the Fed maintains a constant real money supply, the original case of Figure 4-6.
11. The fiscal multiplier is zero when the Fed stabilizes real income, moving the *LM* curve in the opposite direction from the *IS* curve.
12. By varying the monetary-fiscal mix, government policymakers can maintain a given level of real income with many different interest rates. An "easy money, tight fiscal" mix yields a low interest rate and stimulates private investment. A "tight money, easy fiscal" mix yields a higher interest rate, less private investment, and some combination of additional government consumption, government investment, or private consumption, depending on the particular fiscal policy chosen.

Note: Asterisks designate Concepts, Questions, and Problems that require the Appendix to Chapter 4.

Concepts

money supply
medium of exchange
store of value
unit of account
real money balances

LM curve
general equilibrium
expansionary monetary policy
contractionary monetary policy

crowding out effect
liquidity trap
policy mix
infrastructure

Questions

1. Explain how the determinants of the demand for money, income, and the interest rate are related to the uses of money as a medium of exchange and a store of value.

2. Describe the automatic adjustment that will take place in the economy when the current position of the economy is off the *IS* curve.

3. Describe the automatic adjustment that will take place in the economy when the current position of the economy is off the *LM* curve.

4. Why is the distinction between autonomous expenditure and induced expenditure crucial to an understanding of the crowding out effect?

5. Under what circumstances could government spending (federal, state, and local) be crowded out? Do you think this is likely to be the case?

6. What happens to the velocity of money (defined in the box on p. 101) when the economy moves along a given *LM* curve? Why does velocity behave this way?

7. Use Figure 4-4 to identify a point where each of the following situations occurs and how the economy will adjust:
   (a) planned spending exceeds income and there is an excess supply of money
   (b) unintended inventory investment is positive and the real demand for money is less than the real supply of money
   (c) unintended inventory investment is negative and there is an excess demand for money
   (d) planned spending is less than income and the real demand for money exceeds the real supply of money

8. Why did housing construction rise so much between 2001 and 2005? Why did housing construction fall so much between 2005 and 2007? (See the box on pp. 104–105.)

9. A change in which of the following would cause the *LM* curve to shift? To rotate? To both shift and rotate? Which do not affect the position or slope of the *LM* curve? (See the box on p. 101.)
   (a) nominal money supply (M^s)
   (b) responsiveness of the demand for money to the interest rate
   (c) responsiveness of the demand for money to income
   (d) business and consumer confidence
   (e) interest rate (r)
   (f) price level (P)
   (g) In 2001, many countries in Europe switched from their own currencies to the euro. In each country, the prices of goods and services and nominal amounts in checking accounts were adjusted in proportion to the amount a unit of each currency could be converted into the euro.

(h) People switch from using checks to using debit cards to buy goods and services.
(i) People switch from using checks to using credit cards to buy goods and services.

10. During the 1980s, the size of the federal government debt became so large that servicing the interest payments became a significant portion of total federal expenditure. In response, many representatives and senators felt that the federal deficit needed to be reduced. If government spending (G) becomes negatively sensitive to changes in the interest rate, what effect does this have on the amount of autonomous consumption and planned investment that is crowded out? If autonomous taxes (T_a) become positively sensitive to changes in the interest rate, what effect does this have on the amount of autonomous consumption and planned investment that is crowded out?

11. Suppose that private sector spending is highly sensitive to a change in the interest rate. Compare the effectiveness of monetary and fiscal policy in terms of raising and lowering real GDP.

12. Suppose that the demand for money is highly insensitive to a change in the interest rate. Compare the effectiveness of monetary and fiscal policy in terms of raising and lowering real GDP.

13. Suppose Congress raises autonomous taxes. How will this tax increase affect real income? The interest rate? Consumption? Planned investment?

14. The "Great Moderation" since 1985 could be due either to smaller demand shocks when compared to the period prior to 1985 or to a better response by monetary policymakers since 1985 to the same demand shocks that occurred prior to 1985. Evidence to determine which of these arguments is correct may be found by examining the behavior of the interest rate since 1985. If the Great Moderation is due to smaller demand shocks, then less variation in real GDP has been accompanied by less variation in the interest rate as well. On the other hand, if the Great Moderation is due to better response by monetary policymakers to the same demand shocks as previously, then the decline in the variation of real GDP has been accompanied by an increase in the variation of the interest rate. Evaluate these arguments using the *IS-LM* model.

15. Suppose that the Fed is not worried about inflation, but is convinced that unemployment is too high. Use the *IS-LM* model to explain what actions the Fed is likely to take to ensure that very little private sector spending is crowded out by a tax cut aimed at reducing unemployment.

16. You learned in Chapter 1 that inflation speeds up when actual real GDP exceeds natural real GDP. Suppose that policymakers believe actual real GDP exceeds natural real GDP and fear that inflation will

rise. Compare the effects on private sector spending of the following two policies: (a) only monetary policymakers are able to take actions to bring actual and natural real GDP in line with one another; (b) monetary and fiscal policymakers are able to jointly adopt a "tight money, tight fiscal" policy mix in an effort to reduce actual real GDP relative to natural real GDP.

17. Assume that the Federal Reserve Board has decided to maintain the level of real GDP at the current level. If Congress passes a $50 billion decrease in personal taxes, what action, if any, would the Fed have to take?

Describe the effect of the actions of Congress and the Fed on:
(a) the interest rate
(b) the composition of output
(c) the future growth rate of the GDP

18. Evaluate the following argument using the *IS-LM* model: When consumer and business confidence are high and the economy is booming, the interest rate is high. Therefore, during a recession the Fed could promote a higher level of income if it used monetary policy to raise the interest rate.

Problems

1. You are given the following equation for the real demand for money: $(M/P)^d = .25Y - 50r$.
   (a) Compute the demand for money for each of the following interest rates when income is equal to $11,940, $12,000, $12,060, $12,120, and $12,180:

   $$r = 4.4 \quad r = 4.7 \quad r = 5.0 \quad r = 5.3$$
   $$r = 5.6 \quad r = 5.9 \quad r = 6.2$$

   (b) Given your answers to part a, graph the demand for money curves when income equals $11,940 and income equals $12,180.
   (c) Suppose the real money supply, M^s/P, equals $2,750. Given your answers to part a, find the interest rates and levels of real income at which the money market is in equilibrium. Use these combinations of the interest rate and real income to graph the *LM* curve, given that the real money supply equals $2,750. Label this curve LM_0.
   (d) Suppose the real money supply increases to $2,780. Given your answers to part a, find the new combinations of the interest rates and real income at which the money market is in equilibrium. Use these combinations to graph the new *LM* curve, given that the real money supply now equals $2,780. Label this curve LM_1.
   (e) Suppose the real money supply decreases to $2,720. Given your answers to part a, find the new combinations of the interest rates and real income at which the money market is in equilibrium. Use these combinations to graph the new *LM* curve, given that the real money supply now equals $2,720. Label this curve LM_2.

2. You are given the following information for the commodity market, in which taxes, planned investment, government spending on goods and services, and net exports are autonomous, but consumption and planned investment change as the interest rate changes:

   $$C_a = 2,180 - 20r \quad c = 0.6 \quad I_p = 2,400 - 60r$$
   $$G = 2,000 \quad NX = -300 \quad T = 1,800$$

   The money market is described in problem 1.
   (a) Compute the values of the marginal propensity to save, s, and the multiplier, k.
   (b) Derive the equation for the autonomous planned spending A_p.
   (c) Derive the equation for the *IS* curve, $Y = kA_p$, and graph the *IS* curve when the interest rate equals 4.7, 5.0, 5.3, 5.6, and 5.9.
   (d) Using your answers to part c of problem 1 and part c of this problem, explain at what interest rate and at which level of real income the commodity and money markets are both in equilibrium.
   (e) In the first half of 2003, the Fed changed monetary policy because unemployment was too high and it feared any additional decline in the rate of inflation would result in deflation. Suppose that natural real GDP equals $12,060 and the equilibrium in part c is similar to economic conditions in the first half of 2003. Using your answers to parts d or e of problem 1 and part c of this problem, explain how the Fed should change the real money supply in order to move real income to natural real GDP in an effort to reduce unemployment and avoid a further reduction in the inflation rate.

3. The money and commodity markets are as described in problems 1 and 2 and the real money supply equals $2,750, so that the economy's equilibrium is initially the same as in part d of problem 2.
   (a) During the presidential campaign of 2008, Party A proposes to increase government spending on health care by $120 billion and to pay for that spending by raising taxes by that amount. If Party A's proposal were to be enacted, derive what the new equations for autonomous planned spending, A_p, and the *IS* curve, $Y = kA_p$, would be. Graph that new *IS* curve when the interest rate equals 4.7, 5.0, 5.3, 5.6, and 5.9.
   (b) Using your answer to part a, explain at what interest rate and at which level of real income the

commodity and money markets would both be in equilibrium under Party A's proposal.

(c) During the same campaign of 2008, Party B proposes to cut taxes by $80 billion and not change government spending. If Party B's proposal were to be enacted, derive what the new equations for the autonomous planned spending, A_p, and the IS curve, $Y = kA_p$, would be. Graph that new IS curve when the interest rate equals 4.7, 5.0, 5.3, 5.6, and 5.9.

(d) Using your answer to part c, explain at what interest rate and at which level of real income the commodity and money markets would both be in equilibrium under Party B's proposal.

(e) Explain how the economy would be similar and different under the proposals of Parties A and B.

4. The money and commodity markets are as described in problems 1 and 2 and the real money supply equals $2,750, so that the economy's equilibrium is initially the same as in part d of problem 2.

(a) Suppose that as a result of the bridge collapse in Minnesota on August 1, 2007, fiscal policymakers decide to increase government spending on infrastructure by $48 billion. Derive the new equations for the autonomous planned spending, A_p, and the IS curve, $Y = kA_p$, given the increase in infrastructure spending. Graph that new IS curve when the interest rate equals 4.7, 5.0, 5.3, 5.6, and 5.9.

(b) Using your answer to part a, explain at what interest rate and at which level of real income the commodity and money markets are both in equilibrium, given the increase in infrastructure spending.

(c) Using your graph of the new IS curve and your answer to part b, compute how much real income is crowded out by the increase in infrastructure spending. Using your equation for autonomous planned spending, compute how much autonomous private sector spending is crowded out by the increase in infrastructure spending.

(d) Suppose that the Fed wants to prevent any crowding out from the increase in infrastructure spending. Using your answer to either part d or e of problem 1, explain how the Fed should change the real money supply in order to avoid the crowding out effect. For the Fed to be willing to do this without risking a rise in the inflation rate, explain what the smallest level of natural real GDP could be.

(e) Suppose that natural real GDP equals $12,000 and that the Fed does not want the increase in infrastructure spending to cause a rise in the inflation rate. Using your answer to either part d or e of problem 1, explain how the Fed should change the real money supply in order to avoid a rise in the inflation rate.

*5. Assume the following equations summarize the structure of an economy.

$$C = C_a + 0.85(Y - T)$$
$$C_a = 260 - 10r$$
$$T = 200 + 0.2Y$$
$$(M/P)^d = 0.25Y - 25r$$
$$M^s/P = 2{,}125$$
$$I_p = 1{,}500 - 30r$$
$$G = 1{,}700$$
$$NX = 500 - 0.08Y$$

(a) Compute the value of the multiplier.

(b) Derive the equation for the autonomous planned spending schedule, A_p.

(c) Derive the equation for the IS curve.

(d) Calculate the slope of the IS curve, $\Delta r/\Delta Y$. (Hint: Use the equation of the IS curve to compute $\Delta Y/\Delta r$. Then use the fact that the slope of the IS curve, $\Delta r/\Delta Y$, equals the inverse of $\Delta Y/\Delta r$.)

(e) Derive the equation for the LM curve.

(f) Calculate the slope of the LM curve, $\Delta r/\Delta Y$. (To do this, use the same hint as in part d.)

(g) Compute the equilibrium interest rate (r).

(h) Compute the equilibrium real output (Y).

*6. Using the information given in problem 5, compute the new equilibrium real output and interest rate

(a) if government spending increases by 160. What is the amount of autonomous spending that is crowded out by this expansionary fiscal policy?

(b) if G equals 1,700 but the real money supply increases by 100.

*7. Using the information given in problem 5, compute by how much the Fed must increase the money supply if it wants to avoid the crowding out of the expansionary fiscal policy described in part a of problem 6. What will be the new value of real GDP?

*8. Suppose that the real demand for money in the economy changes to $(M/P)^d = 0.2Y - 75r$ and the real money supply changes to $M^s/P = 1{,}431.9$ but the structure of the commodity market is the same as in problem 5.

(a) Derive the equation for the new LM curve and verify that the equilibrium interest rate and real output are the same as you computed in parts 5g and 5h, respectively.

(b) Calculate the slope of the new LM curve, $\Delta r/\Delta Y$.

(c) Compared to the money demand curve given in problem 5, has money demand become more or less responsive to a change to the interest rate? Is the LM curve steeper or flatter as a result? How does this change in the interest responsiveness of money demand alter the amount by which real output will change following an expansionary change in fiscal or monetary policy?

(d) Compute the new equilibrium interest rate and real output if government spending increases by 160.

(e) Compute the new equilibrium interest rate and real output if G equals 1,700 but the real money supply increases by 100.

(f) How and why do the answers in parts d and e differ from problem 6a and 6b, respectively? Is your prediction in part c confirmed?

*9. Suppose that autonomous consumption and planned investment in the economy described in problem 5 change to $C_a = 470 - 15r$ and $I_p = 1,700 - 60r$. All other aspects of the structure of the commodity and the money markets are as described in problem 5.

(a) Derive the equation for the new *IS* curve and verify that the equilibrium interest rate and real output are the same as you computed in parts 5g and 5h, respectively.

(b) Calculate the slope of the new *IS* curve, $\Delta r / \Delta Y$.

(c) Compared to problem 5, have autonomous consumption and planned investment become more or less responsive to a change in the interest rate? Is the *IS* curve steeper or flatter as a result? How does this change in the interest responsiveness of autonomous spending alter the amount by which real output will change following an expansionary change in fiscal or monetary policy?

(d) Compute the new equilibrium interest rate and real output if government spending increases by 160.

(e) Compute the new equilibrium interest rate and real output if G equals 1,700 but the real money supply increases by 100.

(f) How and why do the answers in parts d and e differ from problem 6a and 6b, respectively? Is your prediction in part c confirmed?

*10. Assume the following equations summarize the structure of an economy.

$$C = C_a + 0.8(Y - T)$$
$$C_a = 260 - 10r$$
$$T = 200 + 0.2Y$$
$$(M/P)^d = 0.25Y - 25r$$
$$M^s/P = 2,000$$
$$I_p = 1,900 - 40r$$
$$G = 1,800$$
$$NX = 700 - 0.14Y$$

(a) Derive the equation for the *IS* curve.

(b) Derive the equation for the *LM* curve.

(c) Compute the equilibrium interest rate (r) and real output (Y).

(d) Suppose consumer and business confidence decline, resulting in decreases in the amounts of autonomous consumption and planned investment by 40 and 60, respectively. Derive the new equation for the *IS* curve and compute the new equilibrium interest rate (r) and real output (Y).

(e) Suppose that natural real GDP equals the amount of real output that you computed in part c. Compute the amount of a cut in autonomous taxes that would be necessary in order to overcome the declines in consumer and business confidence and restore real output to natural real GDP.

(f) Suppose that instead of fiscal policy, monetary policy is used to restore real output to natural real GDP. Compute by how much the Fed would have to increase the money supply in order to do so.

(g) Compute the amounts of autonomous consumption and planned investment associated with each of the policies described in parts e and f. Explain which policy is likely to result in a higher rate of growth in real output over the long run.

 SELF-TEST ANSWERS

p. 97 (1) The levels of income (Y) and the interest rate on assets other than money (r) are the two determinants of the real demand for money, $(M/P)^d$. (2) An increase in Y raises the real demand for money, and an increase in the interest rate reduces the real demand for money. (3) Neither determinant shifts the *IS* curve, because the axes of the *IS* curve diagram are these very determinants, Y and r.

p. 102 (1) In going from D to F, the interest rate rises from 5 to 10 percent, and the demand for money decreases by the interest responsiveness (200) times the change in the interest rate (5)—that is, by 1,000. (2) In going from D to G, the level of real income falls from 8,000 to 6,000. The

demand for money decreases by the income responsiveness (0.5) times the change in real income (2,000)—that is, by 1,000. (3) This is the reverse of Part (2); the demand for money increases by 1,000. (4) This is the reverse of Part (1). The demand for money increases by 1,000.

p. 112 (1) If the demand for money is independent of the interest rate (the variable on the vertical axis), then the *LM* curve is vertical. (2) An increase in the money supply has strong effects when the *LM* curve is steeper than normal, as occurs in the bottom frame of Figure 4-7. (3) An increase in the money supply has weak effects when the *LM* curve is flatter than normal, as occurs in the bottom frame of Figure 4-8.

p. 114 (1) Zero crowding out, because the increase in the interest rate caused by a fiscal policy expansion does not have any effect in reducing planned investment or autonomous consumption; (2) complete crowding out, the case shown in the bottom frame of Figure 4-9; (3) zero crowding out, the case shown in the top frame of Figure 4-9.

For additional practice and exploration, exercises that require the use of Excel are available at www.aw-bc.com/gordon.

Appendix to Chapter 4

The Elementary Algebra of the *IS-LM* Model

When you see an *IS* curve crossing an *LM* curve, as in Chapter 4, you know that the equilibrium level of income (Y) and the interest rate (r) occurs at the point of crossing, as at point E_0 in Figure 4-4. But how can the equilibrium level of income and the interest rate be calculated numerically without going to the trouble of making careful drawings of the *IS* and *LM* curves? Wherever you see two lines crossing to determine the values of two variables such as Y and r, exactly the same solution can be obtained by solving together the two equations describing the two lines.

In the Appendix to Chapter 3, we found that equilibrium income is equal to autonomous planned spending (A_p) divided by the marginal leakage rate, so that the autonomous spending multiplier (k) is equal to the inverse of the marginal leakage rate ($k = 1/\text{MLR}$).

$$\text{multiplier} = k = \frac{1}{\text{marginal leakage rate}} = \frac{1}{\text{MLR}} \tag{1}$$

In this appendix we shall continue using the same example as in the graphs of Chapters 3 and 4, namely $k = 4.0$.

Once we have determined the multiplier from equation (1) above, we can write real income simply as:

General Linear Form	Numerical Example	
$Y = kA_p$	$Y = 4.0A_p$	(2)

In Section 3-7, the assumption was introduced that autonomous planned spending A_p declines when there is an increase in the interest rate (r). If the amount of A_p at a zero interest rate is written as (A_p'), then the value of A_p can be written:

General Linear Form	Numerical Example	
$A_p = A_p' - br$	$A_p = A_p' - 100r$	(3)

Here b is the interest responsiveness of A_p; in our example there is a \$100 billion decline in A_p per one percentage point increase in the interest rate. Substituting (3) into (2), we obtain the equation for the *IS* schedule:

General Linear Form	Numerical Example	
$Y = k(A_p' - br)$	$Y = 4.0(A_p' - 100r)$	(4)

Thus if A_p' is 2,500 and $r = 0$, the IS_0 curve intersects the horizontal axis at 10,000.

The *LM* curve shows all combinations of income (Y) and the interest rate (r) where the real money supply (M^s/P) equals the real demand for money ($M/P)^d$, which in turn depends on Y and r. This situation of equilibrium in the money market was previously written as equation 4.1 in the text:

General Linear Form	Numerical Example	
$\left(\dfrac{M^s}{P}\right) = \left(\dfrac{M}{P}\right)^d = hY - fr$	$\left(\dfrac{M^s}{P}\right) = 0.5Y - 200r$	(5)

In this example, where h is the responsiveness of real money demand to higher real income, 0.5 here, and f is the interest responsiveness of real money demand, there is a \$200 billion decline in real money demand per one percentage point increase in the interest rate. Adding fr (or $200r$) to both sides of (5), and then dividing by h (or 0.5), we obtain the equation for the *LM* schedule when M^s/P is 2,000:

General Linear Form   Numerical Example

$$Y = \frac{\dfrac{M^s}{P} + fr}{h}$$ $$Y = \frac{2{,}000 + 200r}{0.5} \qquad (6)$$

We are assured that the commodity market is in equilibrium whenever Y is related to r by equation (4) and that the money market is in equilibrium whenever Y is related to r by equation (6). To make sure that both markets are in equilibrium, both equations must be satisfied at once.

Equations (4) and (6) together constitute an *economic model*. Finding the value of two unknown variables in economics is very much like baking a cake. One starts with a list of ingredients, the *parameters* (or knowns) of the model: A_p, M^s/P, b, f, h, and k. Then one stirs the ingredients together using the recipe instructions, in this case equations (4) and (6). The outcome is the value of the unknown variables, Y and r. The main rule in economic cake-baking is that the number of equations (the recipe instructions) must be equal to the number of unknowns to be determined. In this example, there are two equations and two unknowns (Y and r). There is no limit on the parameters, the number of ingredients known in advance. Here we have six parameters, but we could have seven, ten, or any number.

To convert the two equations of the model into one equation specifying the value of unknown Y in terms of the six known parameters, we simply substitute (6) into (4). To do this, we rearrange (6) to place the interest rate on the left side of the equation, and then we substitute the resulting expression for r in (4). First, rearrange (6) to move r to the left side:[1]

$$r = \frac{hY - \dfrac{M^s}{P}}{f} \qquad (6a)$$

Second, substitute the right side of (6a) for r in (4):

$$Y = k(A_0 - br) = k\left[A_p' - \frac{bhY}{f} + \frac{b}{f}\left(\frac{M^s}{P}\right) \right] \qquad (7)$$

Now (7) can be solved for Y by adding $kbhY/f$ to both sides and dividing both sides by k:

$$Y\left(\frac{1}{k} + \frac{bh}{f}\right) = A_p' + \frac{b}{f}\left(\frac{M^s}{P}\right)$$

---

[1] First multiply both sides of (6) by h:

$$hY = \frac{M^s}{P} + fr$$

then subtract M^s/P from both sides:

$$hY - \frac{M^s}{P} = fr$$

Now divide both sides by f:

$$\frac{hY - \dfrac{M^s}{P}}{f} = r$$

Equation (6a) is then obtained by reversing the two sides of this equation.

Finally, both sides are divided by the left term in parentheses:

$$Y = \frac{A'_p + \frac{b}{f}\left(\frac{M^s}{P}\right)}{\frac{1}{k} + \frac{bh}{f}} \tag{8}$$

Equation (8) is our master general equilibrium income equation and combines all the information in the *IS* and *LM* curves together; when (8) is satisfied, both the commodity market and money market are in equilibrium. It can be used in any situation to calculate the level of real income by simply substituting into (8) the particular values of the six known right-hand parameters in order to calculate unknown income.[2]

Because we are interested primarily in the effect on income of a change in A'_p or M^s/P, we can simplify (8):

$$Y = k_1 A'_p + k_2\left(\frac{M^s}{P}\right) \tag{9}$$

All we have done in converting (8) into (9) is to give new names, k_1 and k_2, to the multiplier effects of A'_p and M^s/P on income. The definitions and numerical values of k_1 and k_2 are:

<table>
<tr><td align="center">General Linear Form</td><td align="center">Numerical Example</td><td></td></tr>
<tr><td align="center">$$k_1 = \frac{1}{\frac{1}{k} + \frac{bh}{f}}$$</td><td align="center">$$k_1 = \frac{1}{\frac{1}{4.0} + \frac{100(0.5)}{200}} = 2.0$$</td><td align="right">(10)</td></tr>
<tr><td align="center">$$k_2 = \frac{b/f}{\frac{1}{k} + \frac{bh}{f}} = \left(\frac{b}{f}\right)k_1$$</td><td align="center">$$k_2 = \frac{100(2.0)}{200} = 1.0$$</td><td align="right">(11)</td></tr>
</table>

Using the numerical values in (10) and (11), the simplified equation (9) can be used to calculate the value of real income:

$$Y = k_1 A'_p + k_2\left(\frac{M^s}{P}\right) \tag{12}$$

$$= 2.0(2,500) + 1.0(2,000)$$

$$= 7,000$$

This is an example of how the value of income can be calculated for a specific numerical example. With this equation it is extremely easy to calculate the new value of Y when there is a change in A'_p caused by government fiscal policy or by a change in business and consumer confidence, and when there is a change in M^s/P caused by a change in the nominal money supply. Remember, however, that the definitions of k_1 and k_2 in (10) and (11) do depend on particular assumptions about the value of parameters $b, f, h,$ and k.

The main point of Sections 4-8 and 4-9 is that changes in fiscal and monetary policy may have either strong or weak effects on income, depending on the answers to these questions.

---

[2] A parameter is taken as given or known within a given exercise. Parameters include not just the small letters denoting the multiplier (k), and the interest and income responsiveness of planned autonomous expenditures and money demand ($b, h,$ and f), but also autonomous planned expenditures at a zero interest rate (A'_p) and the real money supply (M^s/P). Most exercises involve examining the effects of a change in a single parameter, as in A'_p or in M^s/P.

1. How does the effect of a change in A_p' on income, the multiplier k_1, depend on the values of b and f (the interest responsiveness of the demand for commodities and money)?

2. How does the effect of a change in M^s on income, the multiplier k_2, depend on the values of b and f?

You should work through these sections to see if you can derive each of the diagrammatic results by substituting the appropriate definition of k_1 and k_2 into the simplified general equilibrium equation (9).

Example: The top frame of Figure 4-7 shows the effects of raising the money supply. In our example let us raise M^s/P from 2,000 to 3,000. We know, using (10), that the value of k_1 is 2.0. Using (11), the value of k_2 is 1.0. Thus using equation (9), income in the new situation at point E_1 in the top frame of Figure 4-7 is

$$Y = k_1 A_p' + k_2 \left(\frac{M^s}{P} \right)$$
$$= 2.0(2,500) + 1(3,000)$$
$$= 8,000$$

Using equation (6a), we learn that the interest rate in the new situation is

$$r = \frac{[(0.5)(8,000) - 3,000]}{200} = 5.0$$

In the bottom frame, $f = 0$, and so

$$k_1 = \frac{1}{\dfrac{1}{k} + \dfrac{bh}{f}} = \frac{1}{\dfrac{1}{4} + \dfrac{100(0.5)}{0}} = 0$$

$$k_2 = \frac{h}{\dfrac{f}{k} + bh} = \frac{100}{\dfrac{0}{4} + 100(0.5)} = 2.0$$

Thus in the bottom frame of Figure 4-7, the new equilibrium situation at point E_4 is as follows when the real money supply rises from 3,500 along the old *LM* line to 4,500 along the new *LM* line:

$$Y = k_1 A_p' + k_2 \left(\frac{M^s}{P} \right) = 0(2,500) + 2.0(4,500) = 9,000$$

We cannot solve for the interest rate using (6a), since the denominator (f) is zero. Instead, we can use equation (4) to solve for the interest rate along the *IS* curve. When (4) is solved for the interest rate, we obtain the general expression:

$$r = \frac{A_p' - Y/k}{b} = \frac{2,500 - 9,000/4}{100} = \frac{250}{100} = 2.5$$

This lower interest rate is depicted by point E_4 in the lower frame of Figure 4-7.

The Government Budget, Foreign Borrowing, and the Twin Deficits

Any jackass can draw up a balanced budget on paper.
—Lane Kirkland, 1980

5-1 Introduction

We have now learned how to use the *IS-LM* model to determine the value of both real income (GDP) and the interest rate. We have also learned that there is a desirable level of real GDP, which we call "natural real GDP." When the economy is operating with actual real GDP equal to natural real GDP, there is no need for monetary or fiscal policy actions to boost or restrain the level of actual real GDP.[1] But sometimes actual real GDP may not be at its desired level, most notably in the U.S. Great Depression of the 1930s or Japan's slump of its "lost decade," and actions by monetary and fiscal policymakers are needed to stimulate the economy.

The U. S. economy slumped into recession in 2001 as a result of the collapse of the late 1990s' boom in the stock market and in high-tech investment, and a strong response by stimulative monetary and fiscal policy offset most of the decline in real GDP that otherwise would have occurred. We have already reviewed on pp. 104–05 the strong stimulative impact of monetary policy, which by sharply reducing interest rates in 2001–03 boosted interest-sensitive spending, particularly auto and home sales. And on the same pages we have questioned the wisdom of the Fed's low interest rate policy after 2001, which led to a boom in housing followed by a housing bust in 2006–08 as home buyers lost their bet that housing prices would rise forever, and as low initial rates on some home mortgages were readjusted upward to rates that some households could not afford.

We have learned that in certain conditions monetary or fiscal policy may be ineffective. However, the conditions that make monetary policy ineffective tend to make fiscal policy effective, and vice versa. Thus the two types of policy should be coordinated rather than used separately. We also learned at the end of the last chapter that the use of monetary and fiscal policy can be coordinated in order to obtain the desired or "natural" level of real GDP together with a wide range of possible interest rates, either high or low, depending on the importance of stimulating private investment with low interest rates.

In this chapter we take a closer look at fiscal policy and its interaction with the perennial U.S. deficit in international trade. We learn that changes in the government budget surplus or deficit reflect not just the decisions of policy-

---

[1] *Review:* "Natural" real GDP and the "natural" rate of unemployment are defined in Section 1-3 on pp. 7–8.

makers, but feedback from the economy itself in raising or reducing tax revenues. The budget influences real GDP, but real GDP also influences the budget. For instance, economic prosperity in the late 1990s explains part of the shift from a budget deficit to surplus, and the 2001 recession and its aftermath explain part of the shift back from surplus to deficit after 2001. We examine the role of the weak economy and of the Bush administration tax cuts and spending increases as explanations of this turnaround from the government budget surplus into deep deficits.

A second major theme in this chapter is the interaction of the government budget with net exports and foreign lending or borrowing. When net exports (*NX*) are positive, the nation lends to foreigners, whereas negative *NX* implies borrowing from foreigners. We learn how the government budget and foreign borrowing are interconnected through the magic equation initially introduced in Chapter 2. This states that national saving (the sum of the government budget surplus and private saving) must be equal to the sum of domestic and foreign investment. Thus when the government budget shifts from surplus to deficit, one way to balance the magic equation is for foreign investment to become more negative, that is, for borrowing from foreigners to increase, causing the government budget deficit to be joined by a foreign trade deficit, the so-called twin deficits.

But other outcomes are possible as well, including an increase in private saving and/or a decline in domestic investment. A simple theoretical graph displaying the government surplus, private saving, domestic investment, and foreign borrowing helps us to understand which combination of these alternative outcomes will occur. Finally, we ask how long the twin deficits can continue and what their likely long-run effects are on interest rates and economic growth.

As part of our linkage of the government budget and foreign deficits in this chapter, we learn about several concepts in international macroeconomics. What is the difference between the trade deficit and the current account deficit? How does a negative current account deficit lead to an increase in American indebtedness to foreigners? And why in some years is the current account negative yet international indebtedness does not increase?

5-2 The Pervasive Effects of the Government Budget

In this section we examine several adverse effects of persistent deficits that in the early 1990s eventually created the political will to end the deficits and push the government budget into surplus. However, this political will to convert the government budget deficit into a surplus, as was achieved in 1998–2001, was short-lived. The recession of 2001 and a political philosophy that favored tax cuts and increases in government spending brought a return of persistent budget deficits in 2002–08 that mirrored the deficits of 1980–1997.

Crowding Out of Net Exports

The *IS-LM* model in Chapter 4 emphasized that a fiscal expansion, taking the form of an increase in government spending or a reduction in tax rates, is likely to crowd out domestic private investment. But, in addition, a fiscal expansion may crowd out net exports. We can review the magic equation (2.6) in Chapter 2 on p. 35 (here renumbered as equation (5.1)) to see why one or the other type of crowding out must occur:

$$T - G \equiv (I + NX) - S \tag{5.1}$$

On the left-hand side of this definition is the government budget surplus $(T - G)$. On the right-hand side is the excess of total investment, both domestic (I) and foreign (NX), over private saving (S). This means that a government surplus is available to finance an excess of domestic investment over private saving $(I - S)$ or to lend to foreigners (positive NX).

When the quantity on the left-hand side is negative (T smaller than G), the government is running a deficit. Then equation (5.1) indicates that there are only three ways for the government deficit to be financed. First, private saving can go up. Second, domestic private investment can go down; this is the crowding out effect that we examined in Figure 4-6 on p. 107. Third, foreign investment can go down, and if it drops far enough and becomes negative, we call it foreign borrowing.

Impact on Future Generations

Persistent government budget deficits have another implication as well. A deficit raises the public (or national) debt, while a surplus reduces the public debt. Future generations, including current college students reading this book, will be obliged to pay higher taxes than otherwise would be necessary so the government can pay interest on its debt incurred as a result of the deficits incurred in 1980–97 and 2002–08.

Clearly, a persistent budget deficit has pervasive consequences on domestic investment, foreign investment or borrowing, and the wealth of citizens in the future. A persistent surplus reverses these effects. However, it will take many years of surpluses to offset fully the impact of the deficits that have already occurred. This is ample motivation to study closely the causes and effects of the budget deficit.

5-3 Case Study

The Government Budget in Historical Perspective

Throughout history the largest government budget deficits have been incurred as a result of wars, when government expenditures increased more than government tax revenues. Governments choose not to pay the full cost of wars through taxation for fear that heavy taxes will demoralize citizens when their utmost efforts are needed for war production.

The top frame of Figure 5-1 plots U.S. government real expenditures (including transfer payments) and revenues as a percentage of natural real GDP, for the century between 1900 and 2008. The difference between expenditures and revenues is shaded: red shading indicates a government budget deficit and green shading indicates a government budget surplus. Included is not just the federal government budget but also the budgets of the state and local governments.

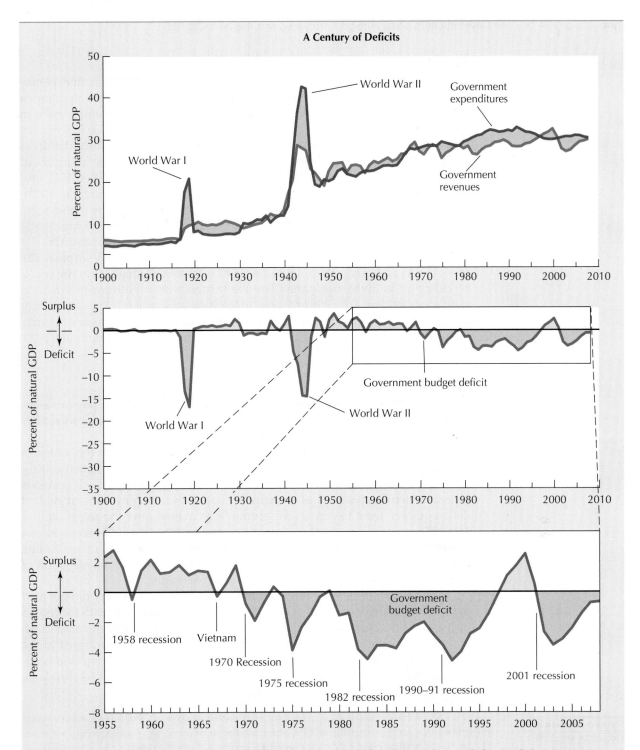

Figure 5-1 Real Government Expenditures, Real Government Revenues, and the Real Government Budget Deficit, 1900–2008

The top frame compares real government expenditures and revenues (for federal, state, and local government) as a share of natural GDP, and shows the dramatic effects of wars and also the gradual increase in the expenditure share in the 1970s and 1980s and its decline in the 1990s, followed by the temporary bulge of revenue in 1999–2000 and its collapse in 2002–04. The middle frame shows the government budget surplus and deficit for the century, and the bottom frame is a blowup of the experience of the 1955–2008 period, calling attention to the unusual 1980–97 and 2002–08 deficits.

Source: Bureau of Economic Analysis, Historical Statistics of the United States: Millennial Edition. Details in Appendix C-4.

Wars and the Increasing Size of Government

Five facts stand out in the top frame of Figure 5-1. First, government expenditures exhibit a marked spike in war years, with World War II having a much greater impact than World War I. Second, tax revenues also exhibit a spike in wartime, but a smaller spike than expenditures, so deficits increase in wartime. Third, the size of government has increased in the years since World War II, as compared with the years before 1940, with real expenditures averaging about 26 percent of GDP between 1950 and 1980 and 31 percent between 1981 and 2007. Fourth, expenditures increased more than revenues during the 1980s, leading to a persistent budget deficit except for 1998–2001. Fifth, revenues were stable at 28 to 30 percent during the 1980s and 1990s before briefly soaring to 33 percent in 2000 and then declining back to 27 to 30 percent in 2002 to 2008.

The middle frame shows the government budget deficit and surplus. The areas in red and green shading in the middle frame are identical to the corresponding areas in the top frame. Here the tendency of wars to create deficits is even more evident. The 1980–97 and 2002–08 deficits pale in comparison with the gigantic deficits of World War I and World War II. To compare more clearly the recent deficits, the period 1955–2008 is magnified in the bottom frame.

The Effect of Recessions

During a recession, government revenues decline and transfer payments increase. Notice in the bottom frame how deficits occurred during or soon after the recessions of 1958, 1970, 1975, 1982, 1990–91, and 2001.

If government deficits had frequently been associated with recessions in the past, why did the deficits of 1980–97 and 2002–08 create so much controversy? The answer is visible in the bottom frame of Figure 5-1. Each previous recession deficit episode has a sharp V shape, and the government budget deficit quickly went to zero as the economy recovered after the recession. But 1980–97 was different. As the economy recovered after the 1982 recession, the *government budget deficit did not disappear but remained large.* The major budget deficits after 1982 occurred in peacetime, not in wartime, and in a situation of economic recovery and expansion rather than recession.

Similarly, after the 2001 recession the recovery of the economy did not lead to the elimination of the budget deficit. In the next section we turn to the causes of the growing deficits during 2002–04 and the shrinking deficits after 2004. How much of the increase in the government budget can be attributed to the Bush administration tax cuts, how much to the Iraq war and homeland security, and how much to other factors? And what caused the post-2004 shrinkage in the government budget deficit? ●

The **cyclical deficit** is the amount by which the actual government budget deficit exceeds the **structural deficit,** which in turn is defined as what the deficit *would be* if the economy were operating at natural real GDP. The **cyclical surplus** and **structural surplus** are the same as the deficit concepts with the signs reversed.

5-4 The Structural Budget

In this section we distinguish between two types of change in the government budget deficit. The first type, called the **cyclical surplus** or **cyclical deficit,** occurs *automatically* as a result of the business cycle. Recessions cause government revenues to shrink and the cyclical deficit to grow; this condition is followed by recoveries and expansions that cause government revenues to grow and the cyclical deficit to shrink. The second type is called the **structural surplus** or **structural deficit;** this is the surplus or deficit that remains after the effect of the business cycle is separated out. The structural surplus or deficit is calculated by assuming that current levels of government spending and tax rates remain in effect, but that the economy is operating at natural real GDP rather than the actual observed level of real GDP.

Automatic Stabilization

Recall from Chapters 2 and 3 that the symbol T stands for "net" tax revenues, that is, total tax revenues minus government transfer payments. It net tax revenues (T) rise when income is high and fall when income is low, we can express net tax revenue as equal to the average net tax rate (t) times real income (Y):[2]

$$T = tY \qquad (5.2)$$

This implies that the government budget can be written as

$$\text{budget surplus} = T - G = tY - G \qquad (5.3)$$

The government budget deficit is simply a negative value of the surplus, as defined in (5.3). The purpose of writing the government budget surplus or deficit in this way is to distinguish two main sources of change in the surplus or deficit: (1) **automatic stabilization** through changes in Y, and (2) **discretionary fiscal policy** through changes in G and t.

When real GDP increases in an economic expansion, the government surplus automatically rises as more net tax revenues are generated (that is, gross tax revenues rise and transfer payments such as unemployment benefits fall). The higher surplus (or lower deficit) helps to stabilize the economy, since the extra net tax revenues that are generated by rising incomes leak out of the spending stream and help restrain the expansion. Similarly, tax revenues drop and transfers rise in a recession, cutting the leakages out of the spending stream and helping dampen the recession.

The automatic stabilization effect of real income or GDP (Y) on the government surplus or deficit is illustrated in Figure 5-2. The horizontal axis is real

Automatic stabilization occurs because government tax revenues depend on income, causing the economy to be stabilized by the leakage of tax revenues from the spending stream when income rises or falls.

Discretionary fiscal policy alters tax rates and/or government expenditures in a deliberate attempt to influence real output and the unemployment rate.

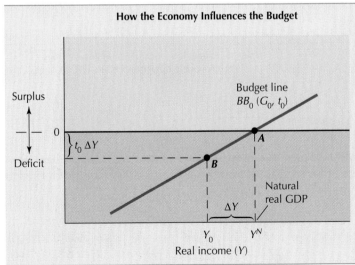

How the Economy Influences the Budget

Figure 5-2 The Relation Between the Government Budget Surplus or Deficit and Real Income

In the green area, the government budget is in surplus, while in the red area, the government budget is in deficit. The budget line BB_0 shows all the levels of the government budget surplus or deficit that are compatible with a given level of government expenditures (G_0) and tax rates (t_0). The BB line slopes upward to the right, because as we move rightward from B to A, the higher real income (Y) raises tax revenues (t_0Y), thus increasing the surplus or reducing the deficit by the amount $t\Delta Y$.

---

[2] Note that t is now the average ratio of total tax revenue to GDP, whereas in the Appendix to Chapter 3 the same symbol t was used for the marginal income tax rate.

income and the vertical axis is the government budget surplus and deficit. In the green area above the zero level on the vertical axis, the government runs a surplus, with tax revenues exceeding expenditures. In the red area below zero, the government runs a deficit, with expenditures exceeding tax revenues. Along the horizontal black line separating the green and red areas, the government budget is balanced, with expenditures exactly equal to tax revenues.

The **budget line** shows the government budget surplus or deficit at different levels of real income.

The purple upward-sloping BB_0 schedule is the **budget line,** which illustrates the automatic stabilization relationship between the government budget and real income when other determinants of the budget in equation (5.3) are constant, that is, at the assumed values G_0 and t_0. The budget line BB_0 has a slope equal to the tax rate t_0. In Figure 5-2 the budget line BB_0 is drawn so that the government runs a balanced budget at point A, when real income is equal to natural real GDP (Y^N). If real income were to fall from Y^N to Y_0, the economy would move from point A to point B, where the government is running a deficit because its tax revenues have fallen by $t_0\Delta Y$.

Discretionary Fiscal Policy

The second source of change in the government budget deficit comes from alterations in government spending (G) and in the tax rate (t). It is evident from equation (5.3) that a decline in government spending (G) reduces the budget deficit, while a decrease in the tax rate (t) raises the deficit. How do such discretionary changes affect the budget line? Figure 5-3 copies the budget line BB_0 from Figure 5-2. The initial budget line BB_0 is drawn on the assumption that government spending is G_0. An increase in government spending from G_0 to G_1 shifts the purple budget line downward for any given level of real income, since at a given level of income the government spends more and has a higher deficit at G_1 compared with the original spending level G_0. The new budget line is shown in the position BB_1.

Find point C along the new budget line BB_1. This shows that at the new higher level of government spending (G_1), the budget would have a large deficit at a real income level of Y_0. There are three ways to reduce the deficit. One way, shown by a movement from C to D, would be to increase real income

Figure 5-3 Effect on the Budget Line of an Increase in Government Expenditures

The upper budget line BB_0 is copied from Figure 5-2 and assumes a value for government spending of G_0. The lower budget line BB_1 assumes that the level of government spending has increased to G_1, thus reducing the government budget surplus or increasing the government budget deficit at every level of real income.

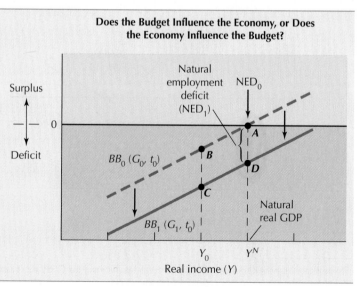

Does the Budget Influence the Economy, or Does the Economy Influence the Budget?

to Y^N through an expansionary monetary policy. The second way, shown by a movement from C to B, would be to reduce government spending. A third way, not shown separately, would be to increase the tax rate (t_0), which would also shift the budget line upward.[3]

Figures 5-2 and 5-3 show that "the budget can affect the economy" and the "economy can affect the budget." An increase in government spending or a reduction in tax rates move the *IS* curve of Chapter 4, altering real GDP. These same changes move the economy in Figures 5-2 and 5-3 to the right, altering real GDP, while also shifting downward the *BB* line.

The reverse effect, the impact of the economy on the budget, is shown by *the slope* of a given *BB* curve. When real GDP increases for some reason not related to fiscal policy (such as a change in monetary policy or consumer confidence), the economy moves northeast along a given *BB* curve. When real GDP decreases for some reason not related to fiscal policy, the economy moves southwest along a given *BB* curve.

The Natural Employment Surplus or Deficit

Since the actual budget surplus or deficit cannot identify discretionary fiscal policy changes, how can we summarize the effect of fiscal policy on the economy? In Figure 5-3 the more expansionary budget line BB_1 has a *lower* vertical position than the original budget line BB_0. Thus its expansionary effect can be summarized by describing the vertical position of the budget line at some standard agreed-upon level of real income, for instance, when real income is equal to natural real GDP (Y^N).

The budget surplus or deficit at the natural level of real GDP is called the **natural employment surplus (NES)** or the **natural employment deficit (NED).** It is defined as the government budget deficit that *would occur if* actual real GDP (Y) were equal to natural real GDP (Y^N). If we substitute natural real GDP (Y^N) for actual real GDP in equation (5.3), we can define the natural employment surplus as:

$$\text{natural employment surplus} = tY^N - G \qquad (5.4)$$

The natural employment deficit is simply a negative value of the surplus in (5.4) and changes when there is a change in government spending (G), the tax rate (t), or natural real GDP (Y^N) itself. Our terminology "natural employment deficit" helps us to remember that *this is the government budget deficit when the economy is operating at natural real GDP.* (You can review the concept of natural real GDP, and its relationship with inflation and the natural rate of unemployment, by looking back at pp. 5–8.)

In Figure 5-3 there is a different natural employment surplus or deficit for each of the two budget lines shown. For the original budget line BB_0, the natural employment deficit is abbreviated NED_0. The value of NED_0 is zero, since along BB_0 the government budget is in balance at Y^N. For the new budget line BB_1, the natural employment deficit is NED_1 and is shown by the distance AD, since along BB_1 the government deficit is the amount AD when the economy is operating at Y^N.

The **natural employment surplus** or **deficit** is government expenditures minus a hypothetical figure for government revenue, calculated by applying current tax rates to natural real GDP rather than actual real GDP.

[handwritten margin note: gov't budget deficit when the economy is operating at natural real GDP]

---

[3] An increase in the tax rate *rotates* the budget line about its fixed vertical intercept, shifting it upward while making it steeper. A reduction in the tax rate rotates the budget line down, making it flatter.

We can now review the major budget concepts with the help of Figure 5-3. The actual budget deficit is shown by the economy's actual vertical position along the appropriate *BB* line in the figure, for instance at points like *B* or *C*. The natural employment deficit is the deficit along each budget line measured at the natural level of real GDP, as at points like *A* and *D*. *Structural deficit* is another name for the natural employment deficit.[4] The cyclical deficit is the difference between the actual deficit and the natural employment deficit, the vertical distance between *A* and *B* along budget line BB_0, and the vertical distance between *D* and *C* along budget line BB_1. Automatic stabilization is represented by the slope of the budget line, since higher tax revenues and lower transfer payments cause a greater amount of real income to leak out of the spending stream whenever real income expands.

SELF-TEST

How would the following be shown in Figure 5-3 and what effect would each of these have on the natural employment deficit?

1. More spending for highway repair?
2. An increase in the Social Security tax rate?
3. An increase in Social Security benefits?
4. A recession that increases the unemployment rate from 5 to 10 percent?

The Actual and Natural Employment Deficits: Historical Behavior

How have actual and natural employment deficits differed since 1960? The purple line in Figure 5-4 displays the actual government budget outcome, copied from Figure 5-1 above. The natural employment surplus or deficit is shown by the orange line.

The orange line isolates the structural component of the budget deficit. The distance between the purple and orange lines represents the cyclical component of the deficit. When the purple line is underneath the orange line, as in 1975–77, 1980–85, 1991–95, and 2002–05, the economy is weak, as shown by the blue shading. When the purple line is above the orange line, the economy is prosperous, with actual real GDP greater than natural real GDP, as shown by the pink shading.

The orange line in Figure 5-4 shows that the government ran a natural employment deficit (NED) in every year between 1970 and 2007 except the four years 1998–2001. The brief disappearance of the NED in 1998–2001 was the result of a booming economy, a temporary upsurge of stock market prices that generated unprecedented government revenue from the capital gains tax, and an increase of income tax rates. The return of the NED after 2001 was due to a reversal of economic conditions and policies of the late 1990s. A collapse of the stock market between 2000 and 2002 greatly reduced government revenue from the capital gains tax, and income tax rates were cut in 2001 and again in 2003. And a new event, the war in Iraq, raised government spending by almost 1 percent of GDP per year starting in 2003.

---

[4] The Congressional Budget Office uses the term "standardized budget deficit" for the same concept as the "natural employment" or "structural" budget deficit.

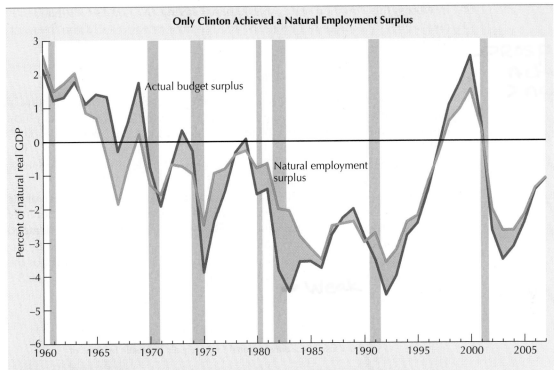

Figure 5-4 A Comparison of the Actual Budget and the Natural Employment Budget, 1960–2007

The orange "natural employment surplus" line lies above the purple "actual surplus" line in years when the economy is weak and lies below when the economy is strong. A natural employment deficit occurred in all years except in 1998–2001.

Source: Bureau of Economic Analysis and Congressional Budget Office. Details in Appendix C-4.

5-5 National Saving and the Consequences of the Government Budget

We have now learned that there is a distinction between the actual budget surplus or deficit and the structural budget surplus or deficit that corrects for the impact of the business cycle on government revenues and expenditures. In this section we study the impact of the government budget on the nation's total saving, which determines its ability to finance total investment.

Fiscal Policy and National Saving

In order to invest, a nation must save. Its total saving is called **national saving (NS)** and consists of private saving (S) plus government saving, which is the same thing as the actual government budget surplus ($T - G$). A government budget deficit reduces national saving. In turn, national saving is the amount available to finance domestic investment (I) and net foreign investment, which is the same as net exports (NX). The relation between national saving and the two types of investment is summarized in the following equation, which is a simple rearrangement of the magic equation (5.1) on p. 132.

$$S + (T - G) \equiv I + NX, \text{ or } NS \equiv I + NX \qquad (5.5)$$

National saving is the sum of private saving (by both households and business firms) and government saving. In turn, government saving is the government budget surplus; a government budget deficit subtracts from national saving.

In words, this equation states that national saving (NS) on the left-hand side must equal the sum of domestic and foreign investment (I + NX) on the right-hand side.

Crowding Out in a Closed Economy

We have learned that an increase in government spending (G) or a reduction in taxes (T) reduces national saving (NS). Figure 5-5 provides a simple graphical representation of the working of the magic equation in a "closed economy" that has no exports or imports, that is, where $NX = 0$. Subsequently we will use the same graph to interpret the effects of fiscal policy in an open economy that exports to and imports from the rest of the world.

In Figure 5-5, the vertical axis is the interest rate, just as in the graphs of the *IS-LM* model in Chapter 4. However, the horizontal axis is now the amount of investment (I) and of national saving (NS). As in the *IS-LM* model, the demand for investment (I^d) depends negatively on the interest rate, as indicated by the red downward sloping I^d line. This represents the same negative effect of the interest rate on investment spending as we have already studied in Figure 3-6 on p. 79.

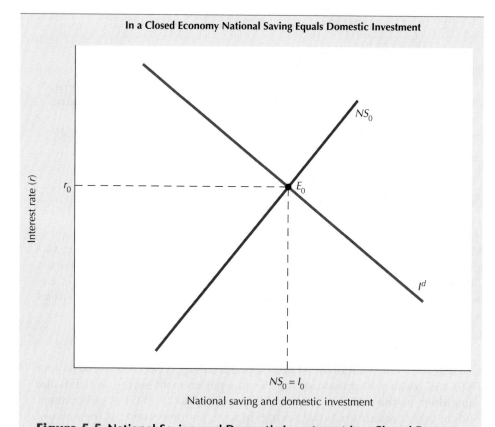

In a Closed Economy National Saving Equals Domestic Investment

Interest rate (r)

NS_0

r_0 E_0

I^d

$NS_0 = I_0$

National saving and domestic investment

Figure 5-5 National Saving and Domestic Investment in a Closed Economy
The downward sloping investment demand (I^d) line reflects the negative effect of higher interest rates on investment, just as in Figure 3-6. The upward sloping national saving (NS) line reflects the positive effect of higher interest rates on private saving, a component of national saving. The economy's equilibrium is at point E_0.

National saving (*NS*), as in equation (5.4), consists of two components, private saving (*S*) and the government budget surplus ($T - G$). The government component of national saving does not depend on the interest rate. But the private component of saving does depend on the interest rate. As we learned in Figure 3-6 on p. 79, autonomous consumption (C_a) depends negatively on the interest rate, just as does investment. But if autonomous consumption falls when the interest rate increases, then for any given amount of disposable income, private saving (which is disposable income minus consumption) must *rise* when the interest rate increases. The sum of government saving (which does not depend on the interest rate) and private saving (which depends positively on the interest rate) is national saving, and the *NS* line in Figure 5-5 is a positively sloped line reflecting the positive dependence of private saving on the interest rate. The economy's equilibrium is at point E_0 where the red I^d line crosses the blue *NS* line.

What happens when government spending is increased by an amount ΔG? As shown in Figure 5-6, this causes the national saving line to shift leftward from NS_0 to NS_1; the amount of the leftward shift is shown by the distance between points *A* and E_0. The new equilibrium is at point E_1, and the decline of

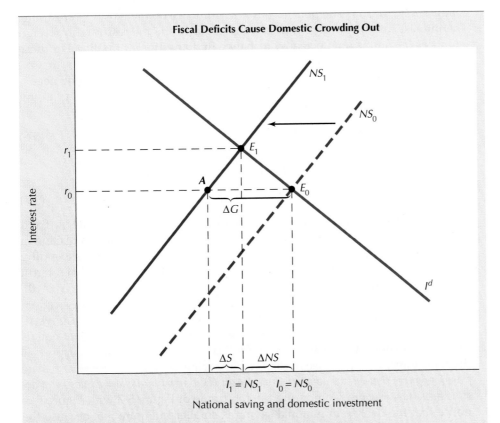

Fiscal Deficits Cause Domestic Crowding Out

Figure 5-6 Effect of a Fiscal Expansion in a Closed Economy
The downward sloping investment demand (I^d) line and upward sloping national saving (*NS*) lines are the same as in Figure 5-5. An increase in government spending (or a reduction in tax revenue) shifts the NS_0 line leftward to NS_1 and the equilibrium point northwest from E_0 to E_1.

investment between I_0 and I_1 demonstrates again the crowding out effect of a fiscal policy expansion. This is the same crowding out effect as was previously displayed in Figure 4-6 on p. 107; the only difference is that in that graph we plotted the impact of the fiscal policy expansion on real GDP, whereas here we plot the decline of investment that accompanies the fiscal expansion. The increase in the interest rate that occurs in the two diagrams is the same.[5]

Notice that the decline in national saving between points E_0 and E_1 (which is also indicated by ΔNS along the horizontal axis) is less than the increase in government spending. This is the result of the positive slope of the NS line; the increase in the interest rate not only crowds out private investment but also stimulates additional private saving (ΔS), shown by the horizontal distance between points A and E_1. The change in national saving is equal to the change in private saving minus the change in government spending ($\Delta NS = \Delta S - \Delta G$).[6]

Fiscal Policy in a Small Open Economy

An **open economy** sells exports to other nations, buys imports, and experiences capital flows consisting of purchases and sales of foreign assets by domestic residents and purchases and sales of domestic assets by foreign residents.

Now we relax the restriction in the previous section that the economy is closed, with no foreign trade. But in reality every country is an **open economy** that sells exports to and buys imports from foreign countries, and experiences inflows and outflows of capital to and from other nations. Many economies (Belgium or Costa Rica, for example) are called small open economies because changes in their domestic policies have no influence on the world interest rate. The interest rate in these countries (r) is equal to the interest rate in foreign countries (r^f) and is unaffected by a change in domestic fiscal policy. For these countries, an increase in government spending or decrease in tax rates that reduces national saving has no effect on the interest rate or on investment; net exports decline by the exact amount of the decrease in national saving. Using equation (5.4) we can write the change in national saving as:

$$\Delta NS = \Delta I + \Delta NX \tag{5.6}$$

and when there is a change in national saving in a small open economy with a fixed interest rate, we can solve for the change in net exports as

$$\Delta NX = \Delta NS \tag{5.7}$$

where the change of investment is zero because the interest rate is fixed ($\Delta I = 0$). The top frame of Figure 5-7 illustrates the adjustment to a decline in national saving (ΔNS) caused by the same increase in government spending that occurred in Figure 5-6. Now the interest rate is fixed at the foreign interest rate ($r = r^f$), and thus there is no crowding out of domestic investment ($\Delta I = 0$). The economy's new equilibrium point E_1 is at the same point as the original equilibrium point E_0 and investment is unchanged. The increase in government spending is exactly balanced by a decline in national saving that equals the decline in net exports ($\Delta G = -\Delta NS = -\Delta NX$). The decline in net exports is the same thing as an increase in foreign borrowing, so intuitively *it is borrowing from foreigners that allows domestic investment (I) to remain unchanged despite a decline in national saving.* Comparing the top frame of Figure 5-7 with Figure 5-6, notice that the decline in national saving is smaller in Figure 5-6, because the increase in the interest rate between the initial equilibrium at E_0 and the new

---

[5] In Figure 5-6 we simplify the analysis by ignoring the effect of changes in real GDP on private saving.

[6] As before, we simplify the analysis by ignoring the effect of changes in real GDP on private saving, and we also assume that all tax revenue is autonomous, not depending on income.

A Fiscal Deficit Causes Foreign Borrowing in a Small Open Economy

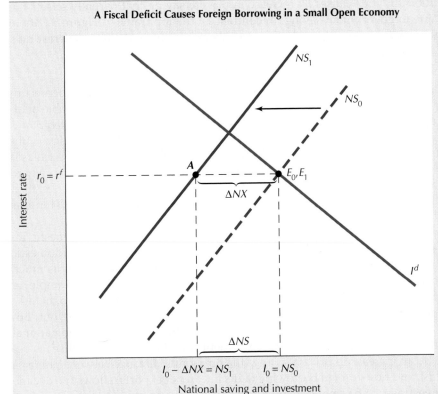

A Fiscal Deficit Causes Both Foreign Borrowing and
Crowding Out in a Large Open Economy

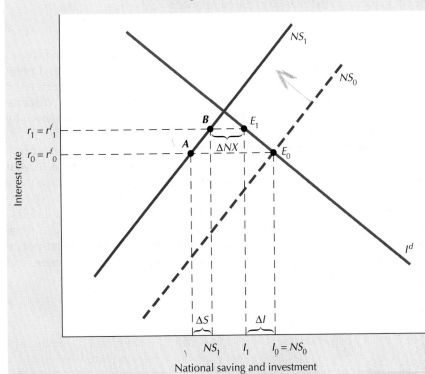

Figure 5-7 Effect of a
Fiscal Expansion in an Open
Economy

The downward sloping
investment demand (I^d) line
and upward sloping national
saving (NS) lines are the same
as in Figure 5-6. An increase in
government spending (or a
reduction in tax revenue) shifts
the NS_0 line leftward to NS_1.
The top frame depicts the
adjustment for a small open
economy in which the interest
rate is fixed at the level of the
foreign interest rate ($r = r^f$).
Because the interest rate does
not increase, there is no
crowding out of investment,
and the funds to maintain
domestic investment
unchanged at I_0 are provided
by borrowing from foreigners
(that is, a decline in net
exports). The bottom frame
depicts the adjustment in a
large open economy where
changes in domestic policy
influence the world interest
rate. The interest rate is shown
as increasing by half the
amount as in Figure 5-6. The
fiscal policy stimulus causes
three changes. There is a
decline in investment, as
shown by the horizontal
distance between point E_0 and
point E_1. There is a decline in
net exports (increase in foreign
borrowing), as shown by the
horizontal distance between
point E_1 and point B. And there
is an increase in private saving,
as shown by the horizontal
distance between point A and
point B.

equilibrium at E_1 causes an increase in private saving that partially offsets the decline in government saving. In contrast, in the top frame in Figure 5-7 there is no increase in private saving because there is no increase in the interest rate.

Fiscal Policy in a Large Open Economy

A large open economy like the United States differs from a small open economy because changes in domestic monetary and fiscal policy are capable of altering the foreign interest rate (r^f). A fiscal policy stimulus in the United States will put upward pressure on the foreign interest rate, but if fiscal policy is unchanged in other countries, then the interest rate will not increase as much as if the United States were a closed economy. For instance, in a simple case where the world consisted half of the United States and half of foreign countries, then the interest rate would increase by half as much following a U.S. fiscal stimulus as it would in a closed economy.

The bottom frame of Figure 5-7 continues to assume that the domestic interest rate equals the foreign interest rate ($r = r^f$). Now, however, a domestic fiscal stimulus causes an increase in the foreign interest rate by half as much following a domestic fiscal stimulus as in the closed-economy example of Figure 5-6. The economy moves from its initial equilibrium point E_0 to the new point E_1 and investment falls from I_0 to I_1. There is partial crowding out, but not as much as in the closed economy case of Figure 5-6. The decline in national saving caused by the increase in government spending is partially offset as before by an increase in private saving (the horizontal distance between points A and B), and now foreign borrowing (a decline in net exports) allows the decline of investment to be smaller than the decline in national saving.

To summarize this analysis, we can return to the first line of equation (5.5), the magic equation, and rewrite it (as in equation (2.6) on p. 35) with the government surplus on the left and its other components on the right, but now we include the Δ symbol to focus on the change in the components of the magic equation:

$$\Delta(T - G) \equiv \Delta I + \Delta NX - \Delta S \qquad (5.8)$$

In the bottom frame of Figure 5-7, an increase in government spending causes the government surplus to decline by the distance between point E_0 and point A. The decline in investment is shown by the horizontal distance between point E_0 and point E_1. The decline in net exports is shown by the horizontal distance between point E_1 and point B. And the increase in private saving is shown by the horizontal distance between point A and point B.

In general, a fiscal policy stimulus causes a combination of three events: a decline in domestic investment, a decline in net exports (increase in foreign borrowing), and an increase in private saving. The balance between these three outcomes depends on the responsiveness of private saving and domestic investment to a higher interest rate, and the responsiveness of the world interest rate to events within a large open economy like the United States. These three outcomes work in reverse when there is a restrictive change in fiscal policy caused by a decline in government spending or an increase in tax revenue.

> ## ▶ SELF-TEST
>
> 1. In a small open economy following a *decline* in government spending, is there an increase or decrease in net exports? In foreign borrowing? In private saving? In domestic investment?

> 2. In a large open economy following a *decline* in government spending, is there an increase or decrease in net exports? In foreign borrowing? In private saving? In domestic investment?

5-6 Case Study

How the Deficits Rejoined to Become "Twins"

In this decade, widespread attention has focused on the large government budget deficit and the large foreign trade deficit (i.e., negative net exports), and as indicated at the beginning of this chapter, these are often called the twin deficits. As is clear from Figure 5-7 and from the magic equation itself, there is no reason why a government budget deficit should be accompanied by a foreign trade deficit of the same size. Rearranging equation (5.5), we can express the relationship between the government deficit $(G - T)$ and the foreign trade deficit $(-NX)$:

$$G - T \equiv -NX + (S - I) \tag{5.9}$$

Thus the government budget deficit $(G - T)$ is equal to the foreign trade deficit $(-NX)$ only if private domestic saving is equal to domestic investment $(S = I)$. Yet there is no reason why this should be true, and in most periods private domestic saving is not equal to domestic investment. In fact, in the late 1990s domestic investment was so much larger than private domestic saving that a foreign trade deficit was accompanied by a government budget surplus rather than a government budget deficit.

The history of the components of equation (5.9) is shown in Figure 5-8 for the period 1960–2007. All data are expressed as a percentage of GDP, and a horizontal black line is drawn at zero. The distance between the horizontal line and the purple line at the bottom of the graph is the government budget deficit plotted as a negative number $(T - G)$, and this is the same as the government budget number shown by the purple lines in Figures 5-1 and 5-4. The red line plots domestic investment (I) and the blue line plots national saving $(NS = S + T - G)$. The orange shaded difference between the I and NS lines represents negative net exports (foreign borrowing), since we can rearrange the magic equation (5.9) to solve for foreign borrowing $(-NX)$:

$$-NX \equiv I - (S + T - G) \equiv I - NS \tag{5.10}$$

Stated another way, the sum of foreign borrowing and national saving $(-NX + NS)$ represents the amount available to finance domestic investment. Finally, the blue-shaded distance between national saving (NS) and the government surplus $(T - G)$ equals private saving (S). For instance, in the year 2000 the blue NS line is plotted at 5.9 percent of GDP, which represents the sum of the government surplus of 2.4 percent and private saving of 3.5 percent. A different situation is shown in the year 2006, when the blue NS line is plotted at a much lower 1.9 percent of GDP, representing the sum of the government surplus of −1.5 percent and private saving of 3.4 percent. While private saving remained relatively constant during 2000–06, the shrinking blue shaded area shows that private saving has fallen by almost half since before 1995. The average ratio to GDP of private saving was 9.5 percent in 1960–92 but fell to only 3.9 percent during 2000–06.

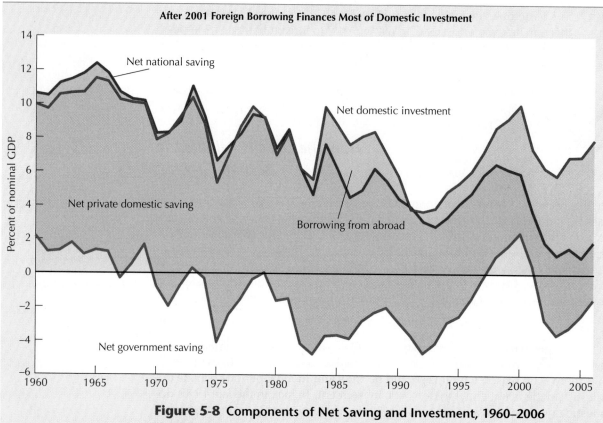

Figure 5-8 Components of Net Saving and Investment, 1960–2006

The bottom purple line is the government budget surplus and is the same as the purple line in Figure 5-1. The blue line is national saving, and the blue-shaded area between those lines is domestic private saving. The red line represents domestic private investment and the orange-shaded area represents foreign borrowing. Thus the chart shows how in 1982–2006 domestic private investment was partly financed by national saving and partly by foreign borrowing. Before 1980 both private and national saving were higher. The gray area shows foreign investment. In 1997–98, a shift toward budget surplus was accompanied by an increase in domestic investment, while borrowing from abroad increased as well, and after 2001 the government budget shifted to a deficit, national saving and domestic investment fell, and foreign borrowing increased further.

Source: See Appendix C-4.

To summarize, the government budget deficit and the foreign deficit were "twins" over the period 1983–97. After a brief period of government budget surplus in 1998–2001, the twin deficits were rejoined after 2001. ●

5-7 The Current Account and the Balance of Payments

Thus far in this book the only connection between the domestic economy and the rest of the world has been net exports. We have seen in the previous section that negative net exports is synonymous with foreign borrowing, and that the

United States in this decade has had a larger ratio of foreign borrowing to GDP than ever before, reaching 6.1 percent of GDP in 2006. Where does the money come from to finance such a large excess of U.S. imports over U.S. exports, that is, such a large negative amount of net exports?

In this section we look more closely at several key concepts of international macroeconomics, including the balance of payments and international indebtedness. We learn that the counterpart of the flows of goods and services counted as exports and imports are offsetting capital flows.

Just as government expenditures include not just goods and services but also interest and transfer payments, so U.S. international transactions include not just flows of goods and services but also flows of income and transfer payments. The all-inclusive measure of a nation's international transactions is called its **current account,** which includes net exports as well as two additional components that are not part of GDP, net income from abroad and net unilateral transfer payments.

The **current account** records the nation's current international transactions, including exports and imports of goods and services, net income from abroad, and net unilateral transfer payments.

Net exports.   We first learned in Chapter 2 that net exports—the difference between exports and imports—is included among the expenditures in GDP, along with consumption, investment, and government spending on goods and services. We usually think of exports and imports as goods that are loaded on ships and planes and sent to and received from foreign countries, such as U.S. exports of corn or Boeing aircraft, and U.S. imports of Japanese cars and Australian wine.

But net exports also include services. U.S. exports of services include the expenditure of a Japanese family on vacation in Hawaii, including their airfare if they fly on a U.S. airline. Fees earned by an American management consultant on assignment in Spain is also considered a U.S. export of services. Likewise, expenditures by an American family vacationing in Europe is an import of services, as is the use by American companies of call centers and computer programmers in India.

Net income from abroad.   Income receipts flowing into the United States include earnings of Americans working in other countries plus investment income (interest, dividends, and royalties) earned on assets abroad that are owned by Americans. Earnings from American-owned companies operating abroad include a Ford plant in Germany, a Procter & Gamble plant making Tide in France, or a McDonald's restaurant in China. Income payments flowing out of the United States include interest paid on a New York bank account owned by a resident of Sweden and profits sent back to Japan that are earned by the Toyota factory in Georgetown, Kentucky. Net income from abroad is the sum of income receipts from abroad minus income payments to foreigners.

Net unilateral transfers.   Just as Social Security benefits are a transfer payment because they do not represent a payment for labor, so international transfer payments are gifts that do not correspond to the purchase of any good, service, or asset. The most important type of unilateral transfer is the gift of money by Americans to their relatives who live in Mexico and other countries that are the source of American immigration.

While net exports are included in GDP, net income from abroad and net unilateral transfers are not included in GDP. Net income from abroad is included in an alternative concept called gross national product or GNP (this concept was introduced on pp. 29–30). Net unilateral transfers are excluded from both GDP and GNP, just like any other type of transfer payment.

Throughout the past two decades, the U.S. current account has been negative and since 2001 has grown to become an ever-larger share of GDP. To balance the perpetually negative current account, the United States must borrow from foreign firms and households, foreign governments, or both. Foreign borrowing builds up the total indebtedness of the United States to foreign nations and implies that some part of U.S. economic growth in the future is mortgaged to pay the interest payments on this debt.

The Current Account and the Capital Account

The **balance of payments** is the record of a nation's international transactions, and includes both credits (which arise from sales of exports and sales of assets) and debits (which arise from purchases of imports and purchases of assets).

The **capital account** is the part of the balance of payments that records capital flows, which consist of purchases and sales of foreign assets by domestic residents, and purchases and sales of domestic assets by foreign residents.

The foreign trade surplus or deficit is part of the official data on the international transactions of the United States. Like any nation, the United States has a balance of payments that records these transactions. The **balance of payments** is divided into two main parts.

1. The first part is the current account, which records the types of flows that matter for current income and output. The main components of the current account are exports and imports of goods and services, net income from abroad, and net unilateral transfer payments. Just as purchases and sales of assets are excluded from GDP, so too are they excluded from the current account.

2. The second part of the balance of payments is the **capital account,** which records purchases and sales of foreign assets by U.S. residents and purchases and sales of American assets by foreign residents.

Any category of the balance of payments can generate a *credit* or a *debit*. To keep these terms straight, think of flows of money. Any international transaction that creates a payment of money to a U.S. resident is a credit. Included are exports of goods and services, investment income on U.S. assets held in foreign countries, transfers to U.S. residents, and purchases of U.S. assets by foreigners. Debits are the opposite of credits and result from payments of money to foreigners by U.S. residents. Debits are created by imports of goods and services, investment income paid on foreign holdings of assets within the United States, transfer payments by U.S. residents to foreigners, and purchases of foreign assets by U.S. residents.

The Balance of Payments Outcome

When total credits are greater than total debits, the United States is said to run a balance of payments surplus. When this occurs, we receive more foreign money from the credits than the sum of dollars we pay out for the debits. The opposite situation, when we pay out more dollars for the debits, is called a balance of payments deficit. The overall balance of payments surplus or deficit is the sum of the balance for the current account and the capital account.

$$\text{Current account balance} + \text{capital account balance} = \text{balance of payments outcome} \tag{5.11}$$

Since the early 1980s, the United States has run a persistent current account deficit, because it has consistently run a deficit on its trade in goods and services and a deficit on its transfer payments as well. In the same time period, the United States has also run a persistent capital account surplus that has partly offset the current account deficit. When a nation runs a capital account surplus,

Table 5-1 The U.S. Balance of Payments, Selected Years

	1970	1980	1990	2000	2006
1. Current Account	2.3	2.3	−79.0	−417.4	−811.5
a. Trade in goods and services	2.3	−19.4	−80.9	−379.8	−758.5
b. Net income from abroad	6.2	30.1	28.6	21.1	36.6
c. Net unilateral transfer payments	−6.2	−8.3	−26.7	−58.6	−89.6
2. Capital Account	−5.9	−24.8	42.9	374.4	373.6
3. Balance of Payments (row 1+ row 2)	−3.6	−22.5	−36.1	−43.0	−437.9

Note: Balance on current account given in source. Balance of payments is the sum of the increase in foreign official assets minus the increase in U.S. official reserve assets. The capital account on line 2 is then calculated as line 3 minus line 1.

Source: www.bea.gov, U.S. International Transactions, Table 1.

households, firms, and the government *are engaged in net borrowing from foreigners* (borrowing from foreign central banks is counted not in the capital account but in the overall balance of payments surplus or deficit).

The U.S. balance of payments outcome for five different years (1970, 1980, 1990, 2000, and 2006) is presented in Table 5-1. In both 1970 and 1980, the current account was in surplus, but the capital account was in deficit by a greater amount, so the overall balance was negative. In 1990, 2000, and 2006, there was a large current account deficit that was only partly covered by a capital account surplus. As a result, the balance of payments was negative in all three of these years. The balance of payments in the most recent year, 2006, is particularly interesting, because the capital account surplus covered less than one-half of the current account deficit. The rest of the current account deficit was financed by massive borrowing from foreign governments, as reflected in the balance of payments outcome. Several Asian countries, particularly China and Japan, increased their foreign official reserves at a very rapid rate in order to keep their currencies from strengthening against the dollar. In effect, China and Japan willingly lent hundreds of billions of dollars to the United States to allow it to import much more than it exported in 2006.

How is the balance of payments related to the foreign trade concepts introduced earlier, namely, net exports (*NX*) and the current account deficit? Net exports are the same as the balance of trade in goods and services, shown on line 1a of Table 5-1. The additional items on lines 1b and 1c make the current account deficit differ somewhat from net exports. The items on lines 2 and 3 show how the current account deficit was financed, mainly by a massive inflow of capital from foreigners. Part of this inflow came from the private sector of foreign countries—that is, foreign households and business firms—and is counted as the capital account surplus on line 2. The remaining inflow involved foreign central banks and is counted on line 3 as the financing that allowed the United States to run a balance of payments deficit in all years shown.

 SELF-TEST

How much is the United States borrowing from (or lending to) foreign central banks in the following three situations?

1. Current account deficit of 100 and capital account surplus of 70.

2. Current account surplus of 100 and capital account deficit of 70.

3. Current account surplus of 70 and capital account deficit of 100.

Foreign Borrowing and International Indebtedness

A current account deficit must be financed either by net borrowing from foreign firms, households, and governments (counted as a capital account surplus), or from foreign central banks (counted as a balance of payments deficit). Either way, a country experiencing a current account deficit *automatically* must increase its indebtedness to foreigners in the private sector, to foreign governments, or to foreign central banks. Similarly, a current account surplus implies a reduction in foreign indebtedness or an increase in a country's net investment surplus. This relationship can be expressed in the following simple equation:

$$\text{Change in net international investment position} = \tag{5.12}$$
$$\text{current account balance} + \text{net revaluations}$$

There is an extra effect on the net international investment position called *net revaluations.* This breaks the tight link between the current account and the change in the net international investment position and is essential to understanding the evolution of U.S. international indebtedness during this decade.

The value of U.S. assets abroad minus foreign-owned assets in the United States, that is, the net international investment position, can change not just as a result of the current account balance but also if the value of the assets rises or falls. For instance, if the stock market in China goes up, then the value of American stock holdings in China increases, reducing American net international indebtedness. Similarly, if the American stock market goes down, there is a decline in foreign asset holdings in the United States, again reducing American net international indebtedness.

An important factor determining the dollar value of U.S. foreign assets is the exchange rate of the dollar (which we study in the next chapter). If an American owns one share of stock on the French stock market worth 100 euros, then it is worth $100 when the exchange rate of the dollar is 1.0 dollars per euro. But if the exchange rate changes to 1.5 dollars per euro, then the same share of stock is worth $150, thus raising American assets held abroad. The same change in the exchange rate of the dollar will also make U.S. factories and other assets in foreign countries more valuable.

A nation's **net international investment position** is the difference between all foreign assets owned by a nation's citizens and domestic assets owned by foreign citizens.

Figure 5-9 illustrates the workings of equation (5.12) for the United States during the period since 1975. The top frame displays the U.S. current account, showing its shift into large deficits during 1982–87, its recovery back to balance in 1991, and then its steady descent into unparalleled deficits exceeding −6 percent of GDP by 2006.[7] The bottom frame displays the U.S. **net international investment position.** This shows a shift in the net investment position from surplus during 1975–85 to a deficit equal to about 20 percent of GDP between 2001 and 2006.

---

[7] The current account was only briefly balanced in 1991, in contrast to persistent deficits during every other year in the interval 1983–2006. Why? Three reasons have been suggested: (1) Most important, foreign governments made large contributions to pay for the 1991 Gulf War, converting the transfer payment item in Table 5–1, line 1c, into a temporary positive item instead of the usual negative item, (2) the United States was in a recession in 1991, which reduced imports and made net exports less negative than usual, and (3) the 1990–91 reunification of Germany created a temporary economic boom in Europe that boosted U.S. exports.

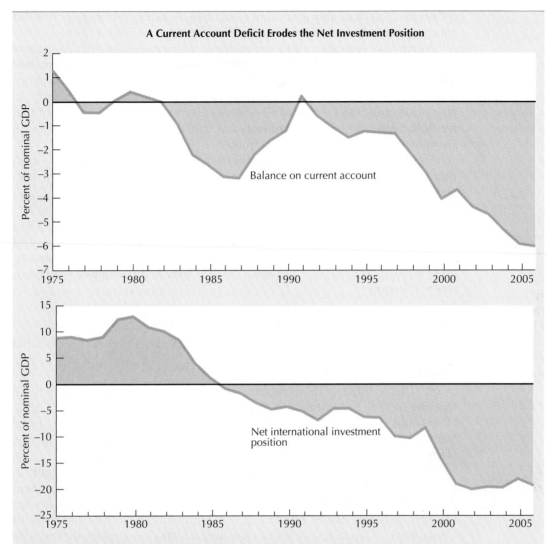

Figure 5-9 The U.S. Current Account Balance and Its Net International Investment Position, 1975–2006

The top frame shows the persistent U.S. deficit on current account after 1981. The bottom frame shows that the net investment position fell in most years after 1982. Overall, the net investment position fell by about 30 percent of GDP (more than $4 trillion in today's economy) between 1982 and 2006.

Source: Bureau of Economic Analysis *NIPA* tables.

Why the Large Current Account Deficit Did Not Erode the Net International Investment Position in 2002–06

The role of the net revaluation term in equation (5.12) is evident in comparing the top and bottom frames of Figure 5-9. During the six years 2001–2006, the U.S. current account deficit added up to −30.0 percent of GDP, implying that the net international investment position should have become 30 percent more negative. Instead, the investment position hardly changed at all, from −19.0 percent in 2001 to −19.2 percent in 2006. This implies that there must have been net revaluations amounting to 30 percent of GDP during this same period, an amazing amount.

As we have seen above with the example of an American owning a share of stock on the French stock market, the United States benefits from asset revaluations when the dollar loses value—in the example of a change in the exchange rate from 1.0 to 1.5 euros per dollar, the amount of euros that 1.0 dollars can buy falls from 1.0 to 1.0/1.5, or 67 cents. In the next chapter we will learn that the dollar *depreciates* when it becomes less valuable, as in this example, and it *appreciates* when it becomes more valuable.

Figure 5-9 becomes easier to understand when we learn, as in the next chapter, that the dollar appreciated, or become more valuable, between 1995 and 2002, and then it depreciated, or became less valuable, between 2002 and 2006. Thus the net revaluation term in equation 5.12 helps explain why the U.S. net international investment position became more negative between 1995 and 2001 as the dollar became stronger (making U.S. foreign assets worth less). And it helps explain why the net international investment position did *not* become more negative in 2002–06 as the dollar became weaker (making U.S. foreign assets worth more).

Why Is U.S. Income from Abroad Still Positive?

It would be natural to assume that the change from a positive U.S. international investment position in 1975–85 to the large negative position in this decade would have caused net income from abroad (the component of the current account in Table 5-1, line 1b) to become ever more negative. Yet Table 5-1 shows that net income from abroad was a positive number ($36.6 billion) in 2006. How could this occur? There is only one answer to this question: *The United States must earn a much higher rate of return on the assets that U.S. residents own abroad than foreigners earn on their assets owned in the United States.*

Why does the United States earn a higher return? The most straightforward answer is that about half of the negative U.S. international investment position shown in the bottom frame of Figure 5-9 is accounted for by foreign holdings of international reserves. These are the amounts that the Bank of China, Bank of Japan, and other foreign central banks hold in U.S. dollars with the intention of stabilizing their own exchange rates. Typically, these amounts are held in very short-term U.S. government debt or in U.S. bank accounts. In contrast, the U.S. government holds virtually no assets in foreign countries.

The relatively high rate of return on U.S. assets held in foreign countries also can be explained by the greater propensity of U.S. investors to build factories in foreign countries and buy foreign corporations, as when Dell and Intel built factories in Ireland. While foreigners also buy U.S. factories and U.S. corporations (as when British Petroleum bought the major Chicago-based oil company Amoco), a relatively greater share of foreign investment in the United States takes the form of relatively low-yielding bonds and stocks. Overall, most economists are surprised that the −20 percent international investment position of the United States shown in the bottom frame of Figure 5-9 has not yet implied large negative net income entries into line 1b of Table 5-1.

The International Investment Position and the U.S. Standard of Living

Even though the United States earns higher returns on its assets held in foreign countries than foreigners earn on their assets held in the United States, the inexorable arithmetic of continuing current account deficits implies a future effect on the U.S. standard of living. If the current account were to continue at the 2006 ratio of 6 percent of GDP, then with no further revaluations the international investment position of the United States would deteriorate by another 60 percent of GDP over the next decade. Even if the United States were to pay an interest rate to foreigners of only 5 percent on this extra 60 percent of indebtedness, that would imply that fully 3 percent (0.05×60 percent) of U.S. GDP would need to be diverted to foreign countries over that decade. If the growth rate of the U.S. standard of living would otherwise be 2.0 percent per year, then 0.25 percent per year of that would be unavailable for Americans to enjoy. The decline in the U.S. international investment position over the next decade would reduce the growth rate in the U.S. standard of living from 2.0 to 1.75 percent per year. Continuing large U.S. current account deficits (as shown in Figure 5-9) must inevitably impair the ability of Americans to enjoy the fruits of their economic growth.

SELF-TEST

The economy of a small country called Importia has net exports of negative $10 billion and its net income from abroad is zero while its net unilateral transfers are zero. Which of the following statements is true?

1. Its current account deficit is negative $10 billion.
2. The sum of its capital account balance minus its balance of payments outcome is positive $10 billion.
3. The net acquisition of Importia's assets by foreigners is positive $10 billion.
4. Importia's foreign borrowing is positive $10 billion.

5-8 Conclusion: Solutions to the National Saving Squeeze

The unifying theme of this chapter has been to study the consequences of sustained deficits in the government budget, such as have occurred since 1980 in the United States except for the brief interval 1998–2001. In a closed economy or a large open economy, a reduction of either government or private saving reduces national saving, raises the interest rate, and crowds out private investment. In turn, the decline in private investment reduces future economic growth and is bad news to future generations of Americans, including today's college students.

After 2001, the drop in domestic private investment (as shown in Figure 5-8 on p. 146) was smaller than the decline in national saving, because foreign borrowing expanded substantially. But foreign borrowing and its counterpart of a current account deficit are not a panacea. Foreigners do not send investment funds to the United States as a gift. Instead, they expect to receive interest and dividends on their investment. To the extent that the after-tax return on domestic private investment is just sufficient to pay interest and dividends to foreigners, domestic residents do not benefit from this investment (except to the extent that the government collects sales, Social Security, and corporate profits taxes from the foreign firms that make the investment).

International Perspective

Saving, Investment, and Government Budgets Around the World

We have seen that the U.S. government budget was in persistent deficit from 1980 to 1997 and again after 2001. How was the government able to finance this deficit? Do other major industrial nations run budget deficits, and how do they finance theirs?

The figure covers the period since 1980. It shows the workings of the magic equation (5.9), which states that the government budget deficit equals private saving minus total investment (domestic and foreign). When the government runs a deficit, total investment $(I + NX)$ must be smaller than private saving (S). For the United States in the top frame, saving $(S$, the blue line) exceeded total investment $(I + NX$, the red line) in all years but 1998–2000. The shaded red area between the two lines represents the government budget deficit. In the bottom frame, the European Union also ran persistent budget deficits, except in the year 2000. Japan had a budget surplus between 1987 and 1992 but a budget deficit before and after.

How were budget deficits financed? In the United States, saving (S) declined slowly and thus did not help finance the pre-1998 budget deficits at all. Instead, total investment declined. Domestic investment (I) and foreign investment (NX), while not shown separately in the figure, are listed separately in the table for three periods: 1980, before the large budget deficits began; and two more recent periods, 1988–90 and 2004–06.

In all three periods, the United States ran a government budget deficit, but the method of financing it was different. In 1980, private saving was higher than domestic investment by just enough to finance the government deficit without any need for foreign borrowing. In 1988–90, the excess of saving over investment financed

about half of the budget deficit with the rest financed by foreign borrowing. In the final period, the government budget deficit was much smaller than foreign borrowing, reflecting the low level of private saving.

For Japan each period is different. Notice that both domestic investment and private saving were much higher than for the United States or Europe in each period. In the first period, a large budget deficit was financed mainly by an excess of private saving over domestic investment. In the middle period, a government budget surplus was balanced by foreign lending, as private saving was roughly equal to domestic investment. In the final period, investment was a full 10 percent of GDP lower than private saving. The saving that was left over after financing the huge government budget deficit was sent abroad as foreign lending.

In Europe the story is simpler. In all three periods there were government deficits and negligible foreign investment, financed by a relatively small excess of private saving over domestic investment.

The figure and table reveal several similarities and differences among the regions. In Japan, a collapse of private investment in the third period along with strong private saving were the counterparts of a large budget deficit—both weak investment and the budget deficit were the counterparts of Japan's "lost decade" discussed on pp. 118–19. In Europe, both investment and saving declined slightly, and in the final period both the government budget deficit and foreign borrowing were relatively small. The United States had the lowest level of private saving in all three periods, but in the third period it had a higher rate of private investment than in Europe and a much larger foreign deficit than either Europe or Japan.

How the Government Budget Deficit Was Financed in the United States, Japan, and the European Union, Selected Intervals (all figures are expressed as percentages of GDP)

		$T-G$	=	$(I$	+	$NX)$	−	S
U.S.	1980	−3.0	=	19.6	+	0.1	−	22.7
	1988–1990	−3.7	=	19.0	+	−1.9	−	20.8
	2004–2006	−0.9	=	20.4	+	−4.2	−	17.1
Japan	1980	−4.6	=	32.6	+	−1.0	−	36.2
	1988–1990	1.5	=	32.1	+	2.2	−	32.8
	2004–2006	−7.3	=	24.4	+	2.5	−	34.3
EU	1980	−3.1	=	20.8	+	−1.2	−	22.7
	1988–1990	−2.9	=	20.8	+	−0.3	−	23.4
	2004–2006	−0.9	=	19.0	+	−0.2	−	19.7

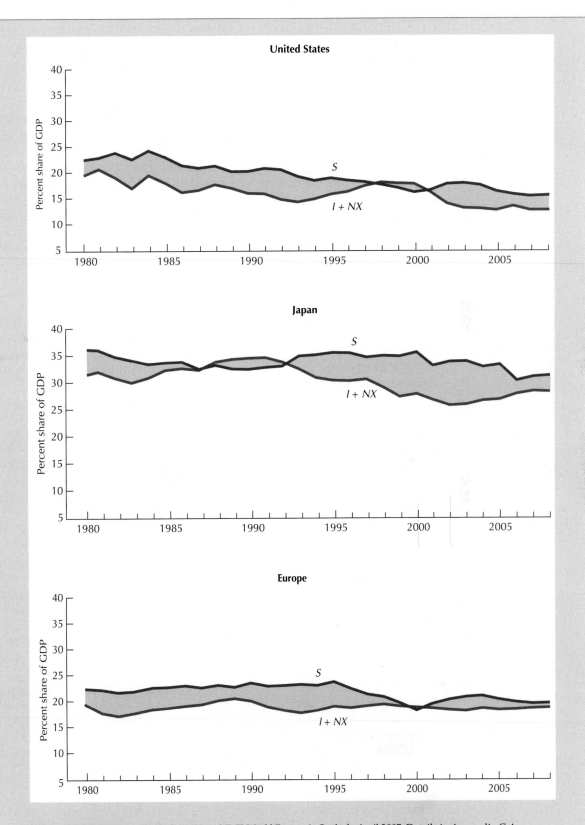

Sources: OECD *Economic Outlook no. 81* and IMF *World Economic Outlook, April 2007*. Details in Appendix C-4.

Since foreign borrowing is no solution, what other options remain to increase national saving in order to stimulate domestic investment and long-run economic growth? The two obvious solutions are (1) to increase private saving, and (2) to increase government saving.

Raise the private saving rate.   Many economists believe that the low U.S. household saving rate is unsustainable. To them, Americans are behaving irrationally, living beyond their means. They believe that as households realize how much debt they are in, they will reduce their spending and raise their saving. But these economists neglect an important fact. The U.S. household saving rate is low because households have enjoyed rapid appreciation of real estate and financial assets for the past 25 years. (Figure 15-8 on p. 512 shows the ratio of household wealth to disposable income.) The official measure of personal saving does not include increases in wealth due to capital gains on the stock market and on houses, but these gains can make people feel wealthy enough so they believe that they have no need to save.

Raise the government saving rate.   The basic solution to the inadequate national saving rate in the United States is to raise the government saving rate. This requires some combination of a decrease in government spending and an increase in tax rates, exactly the opposite policies from those pursued by the Bush administration in 2001–07.

While the Bush tax cuts were supported as necessary to stimulate the economy, we have seen (pp. 104–05) that monetary policy moved very quickly to reduce interest rates. These interest rate reductions stimulated spending on automobiles, housing, and other forms of consumption. Households that refinanced mortgages at lower interest rates were able to reduce their monthly payments and/or increase the principal value of their mortgage (receiving "cash back" in the amount of the new mortgage balance minus the old mortgage balance).

Because of the strong effects of monetary policy in 2001–04, some critics argued that the Bush tax cuts were not necessary and reduced national saving when there was no reason to do so. Other critics focused explicitly on the distributional impact of the tax cuts. In the year 2004, the tax cuts gave a boost in disposable income of $90 billion to the bottom 80 percent of the income distribution, $90 billion to households in the top 2 to 20 percent of the income distribution, and another $90 billion to households in the top 1 percent of the income distribution. Evidence shows that the marginal propensity to consume is much lower in the top 1 percent of the income distribution than in the bottom 80 percent.

Thus, if the goal of the tax cuts was to create a multiplier stimulus of real GDP, as in the *IS-LM* model, then all of the tax cuts should have gone to the bottom 80 or 90 percent of the income distribution, where households spend most of each extra dollar of disposable income. From the point of view of economic stimulus, the $90 billion provided to the top 1 percent of households was wasted, since they spent little on extra consumption.

Subsequent chapters.   We return in subsequent chapters to issues related to the effect of fiscal policy on national saving, domestic investment, and foreign borrowing. In Chapter 6, we take a closer look at international economic relationships. In Chapter 12, we return to the long-run consequences of fiscal deficits and the related problems of large future anticipated deficits in funding Social Security and Medicare.

Summary

1. An increase in the government budget deficit can crowd out domestic private investment and/or require foreign borrowing to maintain the initial level of domestic private investment.

2. Over the past century, the government has run a budget deficit in most years, primarily because of wars and recessions. The budget deficits of 1983–97 and 2002–07 were unusual because they were not caused by wars or recessions.

3. The actual budget surplus or deficit is what actually occurs. The natural employment surplus or deficit is the hypothetical level of the budget surplus if the economy were operating at its natural level of output. The natural employment surplus changes whenever there is a change in government spending and/or tax rates, and these changes are called discretionary fiscal policy.

4. For any given level of government spending and tax rates, the government budget surplus rises if GDP is high and falls if GDP is low. Thus the economy changes the budget surplus or deficit, just as discretionary fiscal policy can change the economy through the multiplier effect of Chapters 3 and 4.

5. A closed economy is one without foreign trade, lending, or borrowing. In such an economy, a fiscal policy stimulus raises the interest rate, crowds out investment, and raises private saving. The decline in national saving is less than the decline in the fiscal surplus (or increase in the fiscal deficit), due to the positive response of private saving to a higher interest rate.

6. A small open economy cannot influence its interest rate, which is set equal to the interest rate in the rest of the world. In such an economy, a fiscal policy stimulus does not crowd out investment but rather causes a reduction in foreign lending or an increase in foreign borrowing.

7. A large open economy can partially influence its interest rate. The most likely result of a fiscal policy stimulus is an increase in private saving, an increase in foreign borrowing, and a reduction in domestic investment.

8. In the 1960s and 1970s, domestic investment was mainly financed by private saving. In the 1980s and 1990s, domestic investment was financed by a combination of private saving and foreign borrowing, and a persistent fiscal deficit required additional foreign borrowing. After a brief respite when the government budget was in surplus in 1998–2001, during 2002–07 domestic investment was limited by sharply lower national saving, because the government budget went from surplus to deficit and because private saving remained low.

9. The current account includes net exports, net income from abroad, and net unilateral transfers. A current account deficit is balanced by some combination of private capital inflows and borrowing from foreign central banks. The balance of payments is negative, as for the United States, if the current account is a larger negative number than positive value of the capital account.

10. A nation has a negative net international investment position when its assets in foreign countries are smaller than the assets of foreigners in its country. The change in the international investment position equals the current account balance plus the net revaluation term, reflecting primarily the impact of changes in exchange rates and stock market prices on the values of assets held in foreign countries.

Concepts

cyclical surplus	discretionary fiscal policy	open economy
cyclical deficit	budget line	current account
structural surplus	natural employment surplus (NES)	balance of payments
structural deficit	natural employment deficit (NED)	capital account
automatic stabilization	national saving (NS)	net international investment position

Questions

1. You have heard that the actual government deficit for the current year is going to be $30 billion greater than in the past year. Based on this projection, what conclusions can you make regarding the government's fiscal policy?

2. Explain the distinction among the following concepts:
   (a) cyclical deficit
   (b) structural deficit
   (c) natural employment deficit
   (d) actual deficit

3. Government deficits and surpluses are expressed throughout this chapter as percents of natural real GDP. Explain why it is necessary to express government deficits and surpluses in this manner in order to compare them over time.

4. Respond to the following statements about an economy where the government budget deficit has increased during a recession.
   (a) The increase in the budget deficit indicates that policymakers have implemented expansionary fiscal policies to bring the economy out of recession.
   (b) The increase in the budget deficit indicates that fiscal policymakers have been irresponsible. They should enact restrictive policies, such as tax hikes or spending cuts, to reduce the deficit.

5. Explain whether each of the following results in a change in the cyclical deficit, or a change in the natural employment deficit, or both.
   (a) A cut in the tax rate aimed at reducing unemployment.
   (b) The rise in taxes that occurs during an expansion.
   (c) The higher defense spending associated with the Iraq war.
   (d) The increase in unemployment compensation due to a rise in the unemployment rate.

6. During the 1983–95 period and again in 2002–05, the behavior of the government budget deficit was quite different from that of other recent post-recession periods. Explain in what way the budget deficit differed and why this difference occurred.

7. Explain why you would expect the actual government deficit to be larger than the natural employment deficit when the economy is weak.

8. The combination of tax increases, tighter spending controls, and a very strong economy helped move the U.S. government budget from deficit to surplus by the end of the 1990s. Explain how these events led from budget deficit to surplus and relate them to the concepts of discretionary fiscal policy, automatic stabilization, budget line, cyclical deficit, and natural employment deficit.

9. Compare and contrast the effect of a tax increase on private saving, domestic investment, net exports, and foreign borrowing in (a) a closed economy, (b) a small open economy, and (c) a large open economy.

10. If expansionary fiscal policy is enacted during a recession, fiscal policy should turn contractionary as the economy expands. Evaluate this statement. In addition, discuss the political difficulties associated with changing fiscal policy from being expansionary to contractionary.

11. Explain the difference between a credit and a debit in the balance of payments.

12. Distinguish between the current account and the capital account in the balance of payments.

13. Four international transactions are listed below. For each, determine whether it is a credit or a debit in the U.S. balance of payments, whether it is a current account or capital account transaction, and whether it increases or decreases the size of the U.S. balance of payments deficit.
   (a) Japan buys rice from the United States.
   (b) Ford Motor Company builds an automobile plant in Russia.
   (c) A German insurance company buys U.S. government bonds.
   (d) U.S. residents vacation in Asia.

14. Suppose that the current account deficit equals $600 billion. Explain if the change in net foreign investment position will be larger or smaller than $600 billion in each of the following cases.
   (a) Initially, the value of U.S-owned assets overseas is $3 trillion and of foreign-owned assets overseas in the United States is $4 trillion. The value of U.S-owned assets overseas rises by 10 percent, but the value of foreign-owned assets in the United States increases by only 5 percent.
   (b) The number of yen required to buy a dollar increases from 110 to 115.

15. Explain why the net international investment position of the United States changed from only −19.0 percent of GDP in 2001 to −19.2 percent of GDP in 2006 despite rather large current account deficits during each of those years.

16. Figure 5-9 shows that the U.S. net international borrowing has become a larger percentage of GDP since 1990. Yet net investment income from the rest of the world has remained a positive, though declining, share of output. Explain how this is possible.

17. Compare and contrast how the United States, Japan, and the European Union have financed government budget deficits since 1980.

Problems

1. Assume $Y^N = 11,600$, $t = 0.2$, and $G = 2,610$.
   (a) Compute the amount of taxes at natural real GDP.
   (b) Explain why there is a natural employment deficit. Compute the amount of the natural employment deficit in terms of both billions of dollars and as a percent of natural real GDP.
   (c) Suppose that the goal of fiscal policymakers is to reduce the size of the natural employment deficit to 1 percent of natural real GDP. Compute what the size of the natural employment deficit must be in terms of billions of dollars in order for fiscal policymakers to achieve their goal.
   (d) Given no change in the tax rate, compute by how much fiscal policymakers must cut government spending in order to accomplish their goal.
   (e) Given no change in government spending, compute by how much fiscal policymakers must increase the tax rate in order to accomplish their goal.
   (f) Given the objective of fiscal policymakers, explain what action monetary policymakers must take for the actions of fiscal policymakers to have no effect on real income.
   (g) Suppose that private saving increases as the interest rate increases. Given the fiscal-monetary policy mix described in parts c–f, explain whether national saving increases by an amount that is larger than, equal to, or less than the decrease in the natural employment deficit.

2. Assume $Y^N = 10,900$, $Y = 10,600$, $t = 0.16$, and $G = 1,890$.
   (a) Compute the amount of taxes at natural real GDP and actual real GDP.
   (b) Compute the amount of the natural employment deficit.
   (c) Compute the amount of the actual deficit. Is there a cyclical surplus or deficit? How large is it?
   (d) Suppose that fiscal policy is used to increase actual real GDP to natural real GDP. This fiscal expansion requires the average tax rate to be cut to 0.14. Compute the new amount of taxes at natural real GDP.
   (e) Compute the new amount of the natural employment deficit. Why are the natural employment deficit and actual deficit now equal? Why is there neither a cyclical surplus nor a cyclical deficit?
   (f) Suppose that instead of fiscal policy, monetary policy is used to increase actual real GDP to natural real GDP. What are the actual and natural employment deficits? Why are these answers different from part e?

3. You are given the following information for the equations for investment demand, private saving, the government's budget deficit, and natural real GDP:
   $I^d = 2,400 - 125r$, $S = 1,760 + 75r$, $T - G = -360$,

   and $Y^N = 12,000$. Suppose that this is a closed economy. The equilibrium interest rate is the one at which national saving and investment demand are equal.
   (a) Derive the equation for national saving. Compute the government's budget deficit as a percent of natural real GDP.
   (b) Compute the equilibrium interest rate. Compute the amounts of investment demand, private saving, and national saving at the equilibrium interest rate.
   (c) Suppose that fiscal policymakers cut the government's budget deficit to 1 percent of natural real GDP. Calculate the new amount of the government's budget deficit. Derive the new equation for national saving. Compute the new equilibrium interest rate. Compute the amounts of investment demand, private saving, and national saving at the new equilibrium interest rate.
   (d) Compare and contrast the answers to parts b and c and explain what effect the cut in the government's budget deficit has on future economic growth.

4. Given the information at the beginning of problem 3, assume a small open economy and that the foreign interest rate is 4.6 percent.
   (a) Compute the amounts of investment demand, private saving, national saving, net exports, and net foreign borrowing at the foreign interest rate.
   (b) Suppose that fiscal policymakers cut the government's budget deficit to 1 percent of natural real GDP. Calculate the new amount of the government's budget deficit. Compute the new amounts of investment demand, private saving, national saving, and net exports. Is the economy now borrowing from the rest of the world or lending to the rest of the world?
   (c) Suppose that instead of a small open economy, we have a large open economy, and that initially the domestic and foreign interest rate is 4.6 percent. Again, fiscal policymakers cut the government's budget deficit to 1 percent of natural real GDP. As a result, the domestic and foreign interest rates decline to 4.2 percent. Compute the new amounts of investment demand, private saving, the government's budget deficit, national saving, net exports, and either foreign borrowing or foreign lending at the new domestic and foreign interest rates.
   (d) Explain why your answers to b and c differ.

5. Suppose a country has net exports of 40, transfer payments of 20, net investment income of –15, and a balance of payments surplus of 10. Find this country's current account balance and capital account balance.

6. You are given the following information:

Year	Current Account Balance	Change in the Net International Investment Position	Change in Foreign-owned Assets in U.S.	Change in U.S.-owned Assets Overseas
1	−500	−360	110	
2		−360	160	350
3	−380		−375	−150
4	−640	−670		−30

(a) Compute the amount of net revaluations in each of the four years.

(b) Compute the change in U.S.-owned assets overseas in year 1.

(c) Compute the current account balance in year 2.

(d) Compute the change in the net international investment position in year 3.

(e) Compute the change in foreign-owned assets in the United States in year 4.

 SELF-TEST ANSWERS

p. 138 (1) More spending for highway repair shifts the budget line *BB* down (raises the natural employment deficit, NED). (2) An increase in the Social Security tax rate moves *BB* up (reduces NED). (3) An increase in Social Security benefits moves *BB* down (raises NED). (4) A recession moves the economy leftward down a fixed *BB* schedule (no change in NED).

pp. 144–45 (1) Increase in net exports; decrease in foreign borrowing; no change in private saving; no change in domestic investment. (2) Increase in net exports; decrease in foreign borrowing; decrease in private saving; increase in domestic investment.

pp. 149–50 (1) Balance of payments deficit of 30, which requires borrowing 30 from foreign central banks; (2) balance of payments surplus of 30, which requires lending 30; (3) same as (1).

p. 153 All of the statements are true. They all are different ways of describing the same situation.

For additional practice and exploration, exercises that require the use of Excel are available at www.aw-bc.com/gordon.

International Trade, Exchange Rates, and Macroeconomic Policy

Trade is the mother of money.
—Thomas Draxe, 1605

6-1   Introduction

Throughout this book we have treated the economy as "open" to trade in goods and services, as well as capital flows. We learned in Chapter 2 that foreign trade contributes to overall economic activity. GDP includes exports minus imports, which we call net exports. When net exports rise, GDP increases. When net exports decline, GDP decreases.

We then learned in Chapter 5 that a country with positive net exports must lend to foreigners, while a country like the United States with negative net exports must borrow from foreigners. We learned about the interrelation of net exports and foreign borrowing through balance of payments accounting in Table 5-1. When the United States runs a negative current account deficit (equal to net exports plus net income from abroad plus net unilateral transfers), then it must borrow from foreigners.

Who lends to the United States to balance its large current account deficit? We learned in section 5-7 that in a recent year the voluntary capital flows to the United States amounted to less than half of the current account deficit. The job of financing the rest of the U.S. current account deficit falls to foreign central banks. The huge multibillion-dollar inflows from foreign central banks are treated as a balance of payments deficit by the United States, but the capital inflows from foreign central banks are just as valuable as from foreign private lenders in achieving balance in the U.S. international accounts.

What We Learn in This Chapter

We already have learned about the U.S. current account, the U.S. capital account, and the balance of payments in section 5-7. In this chapter, we begin by learning about the role of the foreign exchange rates and about the causes of changes in foreign exchange rates. Just as the price of wheat moves up or down to balance the supply and demand for wheat, so the foreign exchange rate moves up or down to balance the supply and demand for foreign exchange.

The foreign exchange rate of the dollar responds to imbalances in flows of exports, imports, and capital movements. We shall study the determinants of the foreign exchange rate and its interrelationship with monetary policy and interest rates. Later in the chapter we shall apply Chapter 4's *IS-LM* model to the analysis of the open economy. We shall learn that the effects of monetary and fiscal policy differ greatly, depending on whether the foreign exchange rate is fixed or flexible.

The "Trilemma"

The **trilemma** is the impossibility for any nation of maintaining simultaneously (1) independent control of domestic monetary policy, (2) fixed exchange rates, and (3) free flows of capital with other nations.

A unifying theme of this chapter is the international "**trilemma**"—that it is impossible for any nation to maintain simultaneously (1) independent control of domestic monetary policy, (2) fixed exchange rates, and (3) free flows of capital with other nations ("perfect capital mobility"). Thus fixed exchange rates and capital mobility create a new reason why domestic monetary policy may be impotent beyond those factors that we studied in Chapter 4. For instance, Europe's common currency (the euro) has stripped member nations of their ability to conduct an independent domestic monetary policy and has led to a persistent economic slump in some European nations, particularly Germany.

How is the United States affected by the trilemma? By adopting flexible exchange rates, the United States is free to pursue an active domestic monetary policy despite keeping its borders open to perfect capital mobility. But, while the United States may want to keep its exchange rate flexible, it cannot prevent foreign nations, particularly China and Japan, from keeping their exchange rates relatively or totally fixed to the dollar. Ordinarily, the tendency of the United States to run a large foreign trade deficit would cause the U.S. dollar to depreciate, but this tendency for the dollar to become weaker can be prevented when a foreign central bank, like that of China, buys up dollars to prevent the dollar from depreciating and to prevent the Chinese currency from appreciating.

In this decade, the United States has been running extraordinarily large foreign trade deficits, financed in part by the desire of China, Japan, and other countries to keep their currencies from strengthening against the dollar. Another main theme of this chapter is to ask whether the United States can continue to live beyond its means, borrowing more and more from foreign private companies, households, and governments. Why are these foreign countries accumulating so many dollars, can this situation last forever, and will foreigners, particularly Asians, soon change their behavior and cause the dollar to crash?

6-2 Exchange Rates

Nations trade goods and services within their own borders using a particular currency. Within the United States, of course, the U.S. dollar is used for transactions. Canada uses the Canadian dollar, the United Kingdom uses the pound, Japan uses the yen, Germany and France use the euro, and so on for all the other countries of the world. When an American wants to purchase a Japanese car, he or she wants to pay in dollars but the Japanese producer wants to be paid in yen.

How Exchange Rates Are Quoted

The **foreign exchange rate** for a nation's currency is the amount of one nation's money that can be obtained in exchange for a unit of another nation's money.

To make the preceding transaction possible, there must be a price of yen in terms of dollars, and a price of dollars in terms of yen. This price is called the **foreign exchange rate.** The foreign exchange rate of the dollar is quoted separately for every currency in the world, and these quotes are reported every day in many newspapers, as shown in Table 6-1.

To take an example, look at the first column at the line labeled Japan (yen). The foreign exchange rate of the yen is shown two ways, first as dollars per yen and second as yen per dollar. The first listing shows that the price of one yen is

that can cause major appreciations and depreciations in the exchange rate without altering the inflation differential. Some of these factors are:

1. A nation may invent new products that other countries want to import, such as the Internet software developed by U.S. firms in the 1990s. Such inventions may cause the dollar to appreciate without any change in the inflation differential.

2. A nation may discover new deposits of raw materials that it can sell to other nations, thus raising the demand for its currency. For instance, in the late 1970s the British began producing oil from the North Sea, causing the exchange rate of the pound to appreciate.

3. The exchange rate depends not just on exports and imports but on the demand for a currency by foreigners. Customers from all over the world send funds to Switzerland and other countries for deposit in banks and other financial institutions, often to avoid taxes or to hide the proceeds from criminal activity. The higher demand for the Swiss franc and other such currencies causes them to appreciate.

4. The theory of PPP is based on the comparison of the exchange rate with an economywide price index in two countries, but that price index may include types of economic activity that are not traded (for example, building construction and retail services). There is no mechanism that forces prices of nontraded goods and services to be the same across countries.

5. For any given inflation differential, government policy can cause a currency to depreciate when the government makes large foreign transfers. Governments can also interfere with free trade by subsidizing exports or taxing imports. Finally, a government may try to prevent its currency from appreciating by buying foreign currency, as did Japan and China in this decade (see pp. 176–79).

As we shall see later in Figure 6-3, the U.S. real exchange rate has not remained constant, as assumed in the PPP equation (6.2), which suggests that PPP is not a good description of U.S. exchange rate behavior.

6-5 Exchange Rate Systems

A balance of payments deficit like the one experienced by the United States in 2006 means that more dollars are flowing abroad as a result of the current account deficit than are coming back in the form of capital inflows from foreign private investors. As a result, there is a net outflow of dollars. Two basic systems have been developed to handle a surplus or deficit in the balance of payments, like the deficit that the United States ran in 2006 (Table 5-1, p. 149, line 3). The difference between these systems lies in whether the foreign exchange rate of the dollar is allowed, month after month, year after year, to change freely (say, from 0.75 euros per dollar this month to 0.65 euros per dollar next month) or is held fixed (at, say, 0.75 euros per dollar).

Flexible vs. Fixed Exchange Rates

Flexible exchange rate system. Under a "pure" version of the **flexible exchange rate system,** an outflow of dollars would act just like an excess supply

In a **flexible exchange rate system** the foreign exchange rate is free to change every day in order to establish an equilibrium between the quantities supplied and demanded of a nation's currency.

International Perspective

Big Mac Meets PPP

If PPP worked perfectly, goods would cost the same in all countries after conversion into a common currency. An interesting test of PPP has been constructed by the *Economist* magazine, which for many years has collected data on the prices of Big Mac hamburgers in the United States and in numerous foreign countries. In the month covered by the table, the Big Mac cost an average of $3.41 in four American cities. According to PPP, the cost in other countries should be $3.41 times the exchange rate of the other currency per dollar. To understand this table taken from *The Economist,* we will take the example of a single country, Sweden. The *actual* exchange rate of the Swedish kroner was 6.79 kroner per dollar. Multiplying the American cost of $3.41 by the actual exchange rate of $6.79, a Big Mac in Sweden should have cost 23.3 kroner. However, the actual cost in Sweden was 33 kroner, not 23.3 kroner.

Stated another way, if the relative prices of Big Macs in Sweden and the United States were representative of all goods, a dollar has the purchasing power of 9.68 kroner (Big Mac Swedish price of 33 kroner divided by U.S. price of $3.41), not the 6.79 kroner available on the foreign exchange market. The foreign exchange market appears to overvalue the kroner against the dollar by 42 percent (9.68 – 6.79)/6.79.

As shown in the right-hand column of the table, there are ten countries including Sweden that have currencies that are overvalued (+) against the dollar. These countries include the relatively rich countries of western Europe, including the euro zone, Britain, Denmark, Sweden, Switzerland, and a few others. American college students can anticipate that visits to these countries will be very expensive compared to the prices they would pay for restaurant meals in the United States. However, twenty other countries have currencies that are undervalued (−) against the dollar. In China, Hong Kong, and Malaysia, a Big Mac costs less than half the $3.41 U.S. price.

When other currencies are overvalued against the dollar, like those in Europe, the dollar is undervalued against them. The extent of over- or undervaluation of the U.S. dollar changes through time. As shown in Figures 6-1 and 6-3, the dollar appreciated from 1995 to 2001 against most currencies and then depreciated between 2002 and 2007. When the dollar was at its peak in 2001 it was overvalued relative to the euro area, in contrast to its undervaluation against the euro in 2007 as shown in the table. We explore reasons for the 1995–2001 appreciation of the dollar and its 2002–07 depreciation in subsequent sections of this chapter.

of any commodity—the price would go down until an equilibrium price is established. The balance of payments deficit would be eliminated by a decline in the foreign exchange rate of the dollar sufficient to raise exports and cut imports, as occurred in the United States following the huge 1985–87 decline in the value of the dollar. In addition, for reasons explained later, a decline in the exchange rate tends to stimulate larger private capital inflows. Although the exchange rates have varied widely since 1973, the current system of flexible exchange rates still is not a pure one. If it were, the United States could not run a balance of payments deficit as it did in 2007, as shown in Table 5-1. Instead, today's system is a mixture of flexible and fixed exchange rates.

Fixed exchange rate system.   During the post–World War II era prior to 1973, most major countries maintained a **fixed exchange rate system.** Under this system, central banks agreed in advance to finance any surplus or deficit in the balance of payments. To do this, central banks maintained foreign exchange reserves, mainly in gold and dollars. The banks stood ready to buy or sell dollars as needed to maintain the foreign exchange rate of their currencies.

In a **fixed exchange rate system,** the foreign exchange rate is fixed for long periods of time.

Cash and Carry: The Hamburger Standard

	Big Mac Prices		Implied PPP[a] of the dollar	Actual dollar exchange rate July 2nd	Under (−)/over (+) valuation against the dollar, %
	in local currency	in dollars			
United States[b]	$3.41	3.41			
Argentina	Peso 8.25	2.67	2.42	3.09	−22
Australia	A$3.45	2.95	1.01	1.17	−14
Brazil	Real 6.90	3.61	2.02	1.91	+6
Britain	£1.99	4.01	1.71[d]	2.01[d]	+18
Canada	C$3.88	3.68	1.14	1.05	+8
Chile	Peso 1,565	2.97	459	527	−13
China	Yuan 11.0	1.45	3.23	7.60	−58
Czech Rep	Koruna 52.9	2.51	15.5	21.1	−27
Denmark	Dkr 27.75	5.08	8.14	5.46	+49
Egypt	Pound 9.54	1.68	2.80	5.69	−51
Euro Area[c]	€3.06	4.17	1.12[e]	1.36[e]	+22
Hong Kong	HK$12.0	1.54	3.52	7.82	−55
Hungary	Forint 600	3.33	176	180	−2
Indonesia	Rupiah 15,900	1.76	4,663	9,015	−48
Japan	¥280	2.29	82.1	122	−33
Malaysia	Ringgit 5.50	1.6	1.61	3.43	−53
Mexico	Peso 29.0	2.69	8.5	10.8	−21
New Zealand	NZ$4.60	3.59	1.35	1.28	+5
Peru	New Sol 9.50	3	2.79	3.17	−12
Philippines	Peso 85.0	1.85	24.9	45.9	−46
Poland	Zloty 6.90	2.51	2.02	2.75	−26
Russia	Rouble 52.0	2.03	15.2	25.6	−41
Singapore	S$3.95	2.59	1.16	1.52	−24
South Africa	Rand 15.5	2.22	4.55	6.97	−35
South Korea	Won 2,900	3.14	850	923	−8
Sweden	Skr33.0	4.86	9.68	6.79	+42
Switzerland	SFr6.30	5.2	1.85	1.21	+53
Taiwan	NT$75.0	2.29	22.0	32.8	−33
Thailand	Baht 62.0	1.8	18.2	34.5	−47
Turkey	Lire 4.75	3.66	1.39	1.30	+7
Venezuela	Bolivar 7,400	3.45	2,170	2,147	+1

[a] Purchasing-power parity; local price divided by price in United States
[b] Average of New York, Chicago, Atlanta, and San Francisco
[c] Weighted average of prices in euro area
[d] Dollars per pound
[e] Dollars per euro

Sources: McDonald's; *The Economist*, July 5, 2007. More recent versions of the Big Mac Index can be found at www.economist.com/markets/bigmac/.

Workings of the Fixed Exchange Rate System

In the 1950s and 1960s, the German central bank (Bundesbank) maintained a rate of 4.0 marks per dollar. If an excess supply of dollars entered Germany (due, for instance, to higher U.S. imports of Volkswagens) and threatened to put downward pressure on the rate to, say, 3.5 marks per dollar, the Bundesbank could intervene by purchasing the excess dollars and adding them to its **foreign exchange reserves.** Similarly, if an excess demand for dollars (due, for instance, to exports of Boeing jet planes to Lufthansa, the German airline) put upward pressure on the rate to, say, 4.5 marks per dollar, the Bundesbank could intervene by selling dollars from its reserves, thus satisfying the excess demand for dollars.

Clearly, there is a flaw in this system. What if a country were to keep increasing its imports, paying for them by drawing down its reserves? Eventually it would run out of reserves, like a family whose bank balance has fallen to zero. Under the fixed exchange rate system, such an event would cause a crisis, and the country would be forced to reduce, or **devalue,** its exchange rate. An example occurred in 1994, when Mexico was forced to devalue the peso, thus making it less valuable in relation to the dollar. By doing so, Mexico intended to make Mexican exports less expensive and more attractive to foreign purchasers, thus increasing the demand for the peso. An example in the opposite direction occurred in 1969 when Germany's reserves of dollars were growing rapidly, and it decided to **revalue** the mark (that is, increase the value of the mark) by 5 percent.

Characteristics of the Flexible Exchange Rate System

Under the old, fixed exchange rate system, changes in the exchange rate were very infrequent. The word *devaluation* was used for a decline in the value of a country's currency and the word *revaluation* was used for an increase in the value of a country's currency. In today's flexible exchange rate system, different terms are used. A *depreciation* of the foreign exchange rate occurs when a country's currency decreases in value in terms of other currencies. An *appreciation* in the foreign exchange rate occurs when a country's currency increases in value in terms of other currencies.

The current system is not a pure flexible exchange rate system because the Fed and foreign central banks do not allow the dollar to fluctuate with complete freedom. The system is not pure because central banks have practiced **intervention.** Foreign central banks, particularly those of China and Japan, have "propped up" the value of the dollar by buying massive amounts of it, thus artificially inflating the demand for dollars and keeping the dollar's foreign exchange rate higher than it otherwise would have been. In the period 1986–2007, foreign central banks increased their dollar reserves by more than $1 trillion as a result of their intervention.

Other terms are used to describe flexible exchange rate systems. A "clean" system is one that is pure, without any intervention by central banks. A "dirty," or "managed," flexible exchange rate system is one with frequent intervention by central banks. Why is the current system so dirty? Central banks in China and Japan fear a possible collapse of the dollar, which would make American exports more competitive and reduce the American demand for imports. Such circumstances would create layoffs and factory closings in foreign countries, something governments want to avoid.

Foreign exchange reserves are government holdings of foreign money used under a fixed exchange rate system to respond to changes in the foreign demand for and supply of a particular nation's money. Such reserves are also used for intervention under a flexible exchange rate system.

Under the fixed exchange rate system, a nation **devalues,** or reduces the value of its money in terms of foreign money, when it runs out of foreign exchange reserves. A nation **revalues,** or raises the value of its money, when its foreign exchange reserves become so excessive that they cause domestic inflation.

Intervention occurs under the flexible exchange rate system when domestic or foreign central banks buy or sell a nation's money in order to prevent unwanted variations in the foreign exchange rate.

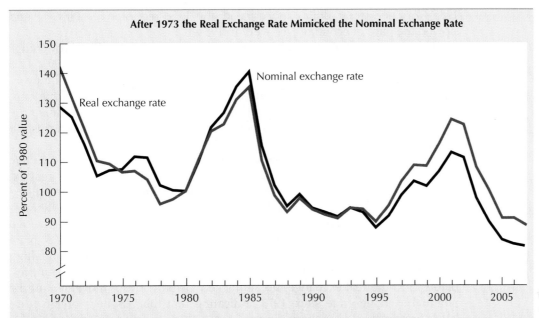

Figure 6-3 **Nominal and Real Effective Exchange Rates of the Dollar, 1970–2007**

Except for a minor difference after 1995, the real and nominal exchange rates for the United States followed essentially the same path. This means that the inflation differential between the United States and other nations was very small compared to the highly variable ups and downs of the nominal exchange rate. This implies that the real exchange rate should have mimicked the movements of the nominal exchange rate, which it did. By far the most dramatic movement of both the nominal and real exchange rates was the sharp appreciation of 1980–85, the equally sharp depreciation of 1985–87, the more recent appreciation of 1995–2001, and the subsequent depreciation of 2002–07.

Source: Federal Reserve Board of Governors *H.10 Foreign Exchange Rates.*

The Exchange Rate of the Dollar Since 1970

Since the flexible exchange rate system began in 1973, the dollar has experienced substantial volatility. Figure 6-3 shows the changes in both the nominal and real exchange rates of the dollar since 1970. Displayed is the effective exchange rate of the dollar, which weights the dollar's exchange rate against an average of the euro, British pound, Japanese yen, and other currencies, with each country weighted in proportion to its importance in American foreign trade. The base year for the effective exchange rate is 1980, so any period (such as 1985) with an exchange rate greater than 100 indicates that the dollar was stronger than in 1980. Any period with an exchange rate less than 100 (such as 1995) indicates that the dollar was weaker than in 1980.

Let us first examine the nominal exchange rate of the dollar, the black line in Figure 6-3. The transition to the flexible exchange rate system in 1971–73 involved a substantial depreciation of the dollar, and the dollar took another dip in 1977–80. Then, from 1980 to 1988, international economics was dominated by the effect of the enormous appreciation of the dollar, which peaked in February 1985, and the depreciation of equal magnitude that followed in

1985–87. The strong dollar exacerbated the U.S. recession of 1981–82 and slowed the pace of economic recovery in 1984–85.

From 1988 to 1995, the dollar fluctuated within a relatively narrow range but then began a sharp appreciation against most currencies after 1995. This strength of the dollar was the counterpart of the weakness of several currencies, particularly in Asia during the late 1990s and the weakness of the euro from its inception in early 1999 until early 2002. Then, in 2002–04, the dollar depreciated again and by 2007 was below its 1995 level in nominal terms, although not in real terms.

Has the real exchange rate behaved differently than the nominal effective exchange rate? As shown in Figure 6-3, between 1995 and 2001 the real exchange rate appreciated somewhat more rapidly than did the nominal exchange rate. And then between 2002 and 2007 the real exchange rate depreciated somewhat less than the nominal exchange rates. The gap between the two lines in Figure 6-3 indicates that during the period after 1995 the U.S. price level increased more than the foreign price level. This in turn reflected a falling price level in Japan and relatively low inflation in some European countries. Before 1995 the real exchange rate mimicked virtually every movement of the nominal exchange rate since 1973, indicating that the U.S. and foreign price levels have increased at about the same rate.

SELF-TEST

1. As a college student planning a trip to Europe this summer, do you hope for an appreciation or a depreciation of the dollar?

2. Looking at the plot of the real exchange rate in Figure 6-3, would you have preferred to travel to Europe in 1995 or 2001?

3. If a German student had the same choice, when would he or she have preferred to travel to the United States?

6-6   Case Study

Asia Intervenes with Buckets to Buy Dollars and Finance the U.S. Current Account Deficit—How Long Can This Continue?

The United States escapes the ironclad logic of the trilemma that no nation can simultaneously operate an independent domestic monetary policy while maintaining fixed exchange rates and allowing perfectly mobile international capital movements. The United States escapes this logic by maintaining flexible exchange rates with its trading partners, including the euro area, Britain, Japan, and many other nations. But the U.S. cannot *force* other nations to maintain flexible exchange rates between their currencies and the dollar. Instead, other nations can subvert the U.S. intention to maintain flexible exchange rates *by taking actions to fix the value of their currencies to the dollar*.

China is the world's leading example of a country that can unilaterally convert the dollar's flexible exchange rate into a virtually fixed exchange rate. During the decade between 1995 and 2005, the Chinese maintained an absolutely fixed exchange rate. The dollar exchange rate of the Chinese yuan during that decade was never higher than 8.33 or lower than 8.27. However, after 2005 the Chinese allowed their currency to appreciate and the dollar to depreciate; over the two years between mid-2005 and mid-2007, the dollar depreciated from 8.27 to 7.56 yuan, a depreciation of about 9 percent. Nevertheless, the equilibrium exchange rate is far lower than 7.56.

How do we know that the equilibrium exchange rate is far lower? This is because the situation of China versus the United States is just like the situation depicted in Figure 6-2 by the distance *AB* in which the central bank buys up billions of dollars to keep the dollar from depreciating from 1.0 to 0.75 euros per dollar. The new element after 2005 was that the Bank of China slightly decreased its purchases of dollars from the amount needed to keep the yuan absolutely fixed at 8.27 yuan per dollar, to smaller purchases that allowed the yuan to appreciate slowly, and the dollar to depreciate slowly, from 8.27 to 7.56 yuan per dollar.

Why does China pursue this policy? By fighting against an appreciation of the yuan, China receives all the benefits of any currency that has a relatively low exchange rate (as we saw on p. 173, a Big Mac in China costs 58 percent less than in the United States). With a low exchange rate, Chinese exporters can sell their goods at cheaper prices in the U.S. market, and higher volumes of exported goods allow Chinese business firms to employ more workers, helping to propel the remarkable economic growth of China that we examine in Chapter 11. Hong Kong is an even more extreme example, having fixed its exchange rate against the dollar at 7.8 Hong Kong dollars per U.S. dollar for more than two decades. Several other Asian nations also purchase dollars to keep their exchange rates from appreciating, particularly Japan, which has succeeded in keeping its exchange rate within the range of 105 to 122 yen per dollar between 2005 and 2007 (see Figure 6-1 on p. 165).

A remarkable aspect of this situation is that the United States is uniquely positioned to take advantage of the willingness of other nations to finance its current account deficit. The United States has been called "the country in the center" due to the attractiveness of U.S. dollars as the currency in which most nations prefer to hold their international reserves. Despite the depreciation of the dollar and appreciation of the euro in 2002–07, Asian nations continue to keep most of their international reserves in dollars. Thus, in essence, the United States can "print money" that Asians willingly hold in order to finance its U.S. current account deficit. Ironically, it was this same ability to print international money in the 1960s under the former Bretton Woods system that led to the breakdown in 1971 of fixed exchange rates. Many commentators are worried that the current system is equally unsustainable and must inevitably lead to a collapse of the U.S. dollar exchange rate at some point in the future—the near future according to pessimists and the far future according to optimists.

How Large Are the Reserves and Which Countries Hold Them?

Figure 6-4 displays foreign official holdings of dollars as a percent of U.S. GDP. These are the dollar reserves of nations such as China, Japan, and other countries (mainly in Asia).[4] As of 1995, these reserves were little more than 5 percent

---

[4] These data show the increase in the official balances that finance the U.S. balance of payments deficit. They take foreign official holdings of dollar assets and subtract U.S. holdings of official international reserves.

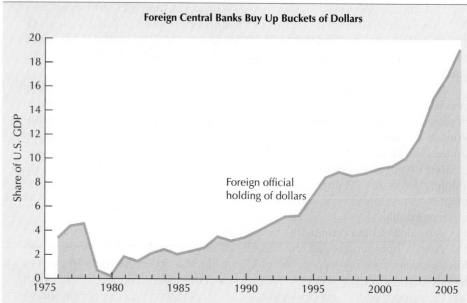

Figure 6-4 Foreign Official Holdings of Dollar Reserves as a Percent of U.S. GDP

Shown is the percentage ratio of foreign official holdings of dollar reserves to U.S. GDP. The rapid growth of these reserves since 1995 is the counterpart of the decline in the U.S. international investment position shown in the bottom frame of Figure 5-9. Almost half of the U.S. negative investment position is accounted for by foreign official holdings of dollar reserves.

Source: Department of Commerce. See Appendix C-4.

of U.S. GDP, little more than in 1978. But then the dollar reserves began to explode, soaring to almost 8 percent in 1998 and then to almost 20 percent in 2006.

The dollar reserves are held primarily by Asian central banks. In December 2006, the top four Asian central banks held $2.6 trillion of dollar reserves, almost double the figure only three years earlier. In order, the top four holdings of dollars among Asian central banks were China with $1,202 billion, Japan with $909 billion, Taiwan with $267 billion, and South Korea with $239 billion. With a population of only 23 million, Taiwan held more than $10,000 in dollar reserves for every Taiwanese resident! The only non-Asian country with such large holdings of dollar reserves in late 2006 was, surprisingly, Russia, with $339 billion, due largely to the high price of oil and Russia's large level of oil production.

Why Do the Asians Subject Themselves to Disastrous Capital Losses?

The U.S. government views this buildup of Asian dollar reserves with an attitude of "benign neglect." Why not, since the huge purchases of dollar securities, much of which is U.S. government debt, helps to support the U.S. stock and bond markets and allows the U.S. federal government to support tax cuts and expenditure increases without the sharp increase in domestic U.S. interest rates that would otherwise occur. But for Asian countries this is a raw deal, because the hundreds of billions of dollars that the Asians are spending of their own currencies to buy dollars could be used to raise the living standards of millions of their own inhabitants through investment in their domestic economies.

The Asian central banks are pouring their own funds into a currency, the dollar, on which they make capital losses. While China can buy enough dollars to keep its yuan/dollar exchange rate fixed, it cannot prevent the flexible exchange rate between the dollar and other currencies (such as the euro, the British pound, and the Swiss franc) from depreciating. Thus the buying power of Chinese and Japanese dollar reserves in the world economy sinks each year that the dollar depreciates, as it did between 2002 and 2007.

The Asian strategy of stabilizing their currencies against the dollar creates an economic dilemma for the European nations in the euro area. Since early 2002, the euro has appreciated by more than 60 percent against the dollar, making European exports more expensive. But the Asian policies make the European dilemma worse. If China keeps its currency pegged to the dollar, and the euro appreciates by 60 percent against the dollar, then *automatically* the euro appreciates by 60 percent against the Chinese yuan. Cheap Chinese exports flood not only the United States but also Europe, costing not just American but also European jobs. The willingness of the Bank of China to allow the yuan to appreciate by 9 percent between 2005 and 2007 takes a bit of pressure off the Europeans, but not much. The yuan would have to appreciate far more to reach its equilibrium exchange rate against the dollar and the euro.

Is There an Exit Strategy for the Asians?

The Asians keep buying dollars because they need to keep their own currencies low and the dollar strong in order to create jobs in China and Japan and avoid domestic unrest and unemployment. Policies of the U.S. government adopted during 2002–04 surprised the Asians by boosting the U.S. government budget deficit and increasing the amount that Asians had to finance. As one Japanese policymaker stated, "The U.S. government's procurement of funds for the Iraq war, and a huge tax cut, resulted in a sharp rise in U.S. debt, so if Japan cuts purchases of U.S. government bonds, the U.S. must raise interest rates, which could seriously harm world markets." Thus, from the Japanese point of view, the United States seems to be able to force Japan to finance its own government budget deficit.

Can this situation continue? The Asian nations and the United States both seem to be trapped in a symbiotic relationship. One journalist drew an analogy with a small shopkeeper:

> This is an absurd situation, like a shopkeeper lending ever larger amounts of money to an important customer who is also a profligate spender, so that he can maintain consumption. The customer signs ever-increasing amounts of IOUs, and the shopkeeper has decreasing faith in these. But he cannot sell them so long as he retains his dependence on keeping the customer happy.[5] ●

---

[5] Quotes in this section are from Kathy Wolfe, "Asia Ponders Exit Strategy from the Dollar," *Executive Intelligence Review*, February 20, 2004.

6-7 Determinants of Net Exports

Now we are ready to fit the foreign exchange rate into the *IS-LM* model of income determination developed in Chapters 3–5. The analysis proceeds in two steps. First, we allow net exports, previously assumed to be exogenous, to depend both on income and on the exchange rate. Second, we allow the exchange rate to depend on the interest rate. The combined effect of these two steps is to introduce an additional channel by which interest rates affect total expenditures.

Net exports (*NX*), as we learned in Chapter 2, is an aggregate that equals exports minus imports, and it is a component of total expenditure in GDP, along with consumption (*C*), investment (*I*), and government spending (*G*):

$$E = C + I + G + NX \tag{6.5}$$

A $200 billion increase in net exports provides just as much of a stimulus to income and employment as a $200 billion increase in consumption, investment, or government spending. A $200 billion decrease in net exports can offset much of the stimulus to expenditures provided by expansionary monetary and fiscal policy.

Net Exports and the Foreign Exchange Rate

Clearly, fluctuations of net exports play an important role in the fluctuations of total real expenditures. Determining the ups and downs of net exports are real income and the foreign exchange rate.

Effect of real income.   We can indicate the dependence of net exports (*NX*) on income as

$$NX = NX_a - nxY \tag{6.6}$$

Here, NX_a is the autonomous component of net exports (determined mainly by foreign income), nx is the fraction of a change in income that is spent on imports, and Y is real income.[6] If we ignored changes in the foreign exchange rate, then equation (6.6) would adequately explain net exports. For the given level of foreign income that determines the autonomous component (NX_a), net exports would be low in economic expansions when income is high, causing a large volume of imports, and net exports would be high in recessions when income is low, causing a small volume of imports.

Effect of the foreign exchange rate.   When the exchange rate appreciates against foreign currencies, U.S. exports become more expensive in terms of foreign currencies, so exports tend to decline. Also, the lower dollar prices of imports attract American customers, and the quantity of goods imported into the United States rises. With exports down and imports up, the appreciation of the foreign exchange rate causes a drop in net exports. This is just what happened in the United States during 1995–2001. The appreciation of the dollar and the collapse of net exports are shown in Figure 6-5.

The striking fact that stands out in Figure 6-5 is the strong negative relationship between net exports and the real exchange rate. When the real exchange rate was low in the late 1970s, U.S. net exports rose, peaking in 1980.

---

[6] This equation is identical to equation (10) in the Appendix to Chapter 3, p. 92.

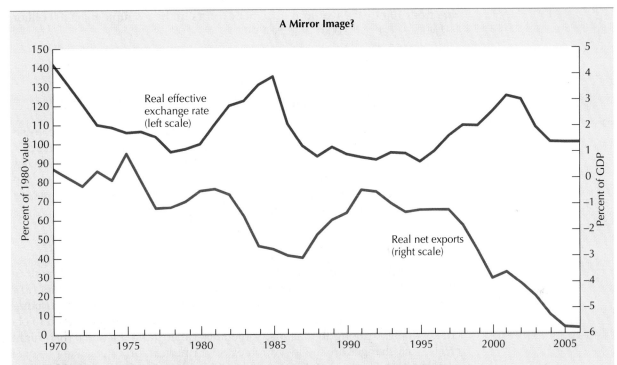

Figure 6-5 **U.S. Real Net Exports and the Real Exchange Rate of the Dollar, 1970–2007**

The two lines display a striking mirror-image relationship, indicating that an appreciating dollar tends to reduce net exports, and vice versa. The period 2003–07 is an important exception.

Sources: Bureau of Economic Analysis *NIPA Tables* and Federal Reserve Board *H.10 Foreign Exchange Rates.*

The rise in the real exchange rate between 1980 and 1985 was accompanied by a continuous decline in net exports. The 1985–88 depreciation of the dollar led to a sharp jump in net exports after 1987, and the 1996–2001 appreciation contributed to the collapse of net exports in 1998–2001. The failure of U.S. net exports to rise in 2003–07 in response to the dollar's depreciation is an important but rare exception.

To reflect this negative relationship, we amend equation (6.6) to allow net exports (NX) to depend not just on income but also on the real exchange rate (e), which is expressed as a percentage of a base year (for instance, 1980 = 100).

$$\text{General Linear Form} \qquad \text{Numerical Example}$$
$$NX = NX_a - nxY - ue \qquad NX = 1{,}400 - 0.1Y - 2e \qquad (6.7)$$

This equation states in words that net exports are equal to autonomous net exports (NX_a), minus a parameter (nx) times real income (Y), minus another parameter (u) times the real exchange rate (e). For any given level of income, an appreciation of the real exchange rate (as happened in the United States between 1995 and 2001) reduces net exports. For instance, if the economy is operating with actual real income at the natural real GDP level of $12,000 billion, and the real exchange rate is 100, then net exports are zero [$=1{,}400 - (0.1 \times 12{,}000) - (2 \times 100)$]. An appreciation in the real exchange rate from 100 to 150 would reduce net exports in the example to −$100 billion [=1,400 − (0.1 × 12,000) − (2 × 150)].

6-8 The Real Exchange Rate and Interest Rate

The foreign exchange rate is set in the foreign exchange market, which consists of bank employees all over the world buying and selling different currencies, primarily using online computer networks. When the demand for a currency like the dollar rises relative to the supply of dollars, these bank employees (foreign exchange traders) bid up the value of the dollar, causing it to appreciate. When the demand for dollars falls, its value falls, or depreciates.

The Demand for Dollars and the "Fundamentals"

The demand for dollars stems from two sources: the desire to buy American products and the desire to buy financial assets denominated in dollars (like bank deposits, U.S. government bonds, and the bonds issued by U.S. corporations). Changes in the worldwide desire to buy American products tend to occur gradually. Among the factors, sometimes called fundamentals, that might create such changes are the invention of new American products, like personal computers. A fundamental factor that could *reduce* the desire to hold dollars might be the development of new products in other countries, like Japanese-made Canon or Nikon digital cameras. Higher expected inflation in the United States than in other countries would also reduce the desire to hold dollars.

Because the fundamental factors tend to change slowly, they cannot account for much of the highly volatile movements evident in Figure 6-5 in the dollar's real exchange rate. Instead, these sharp up and down movements can be attributed to the second main source of the demand for dollars, the desire by foreigners to buy securities denominated in dollars. When U.S. securities become more attractive, the demand for dollars increases and the foreign exchange traders bid up the dollar's value. Similarly, when foreign securities become more attractive to Americans, U.S. residents supply extra dollars to the foreign exchange traders to obtain the foreign currencies they need to buy foreign securities and the dollar's value goes down.

The **interest rate differential** is the average U.S. interest rate minus the average foreign interest rate.

The relative attractiveness of U.S. and foreign securities depends on the **interest rate differential,** defined as the average U.S. interest rate minus the average foreign interest rate. When the U.S. interest rate increases and the foreign interest rate remains unchanged, the interest rate differential increases. Foreigners find U.S. securities attractive; they demand additional dollars to buy them, and the foreign exchange rate of the dollar is bid up by the foreign exchange traders.

This section has suggested that an increase in the U.S. interest rate should cause an appreciation of the dollar, and a decrease in the U.S. interest rate should cause a depreciation of the dollar. The relationship between the U.S. interest rate and the value of the dollar is demonstrated in Figure 6-6, which plots the two together for the period since 1970. The real exchange rate of the dollar is copied from Figure 6-5. The periods in the 1970s of the lowest real interest rates coincided with periods when the dollar was low. The period of high interest rates after 1980 was accompanied by an appreciation of the dollar. The 1984 peak in the real interest rate came shortly before the 1985 peak in the real ex-

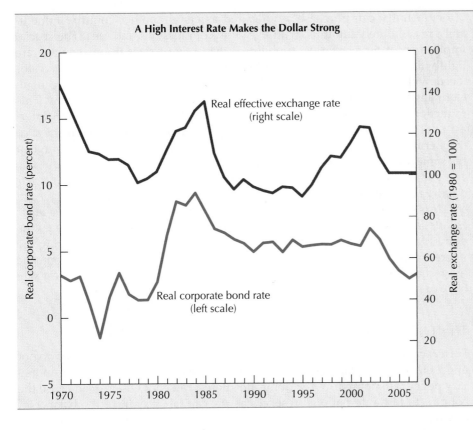

Figure 6-6 The U.S. Real Corporate Bond Rate and the Real Exchange Rate of the Dollar, 1970–2007

The real exchange rate is copied from Figure 6-5. A positive relationship between the two lines is evident, with movements in the interest rate appearing to occur prior to movements in the exchange rate. The relationship changed after 1995 as discussed in the text.

Sources: Moody's and Federal Reserve Board of Governors. See Appendix C-4.

change rate. The decline in the real interest rate during 1984–89 coincided with the decline in the real exchange rate from 1985 to 1989.

The positive relationship between the real interest rate and the real exchange rate appears to have broken down after 1995. The real exchange rate appreciated by almost as much as it did in 1980–85, but the real interest rate was virtually unchanged. This new relationship reflects the role of the late 1990s U.S. stock market boom in attracting foreign capital inflows, which pushed up the value of the dollar, even though the real interest rate did not rise. After 2002, the real effective exchange rate depreciated and the real interest rate fell at the same time, repeating the experience of 1985–88.

 SELF-TEST

Assume that you are an American student traveling to Europe next summer. Which would you prefer?

1. A boom in the U.S. stock market?
2. A collapse in the U.S. stock market?

Interest Rates and Capital Mobility

The mechanism by which interest rates affect the exchange rate involves flows of capital between countries. **Perfect capital mobility** occurs when a resident

Perfect capital mobility occurs when investors regard foreign financial assets as a perfect substitute for domestic assets, and when investors respond instantaneously to an interest rate differential between domestic and foreign assets by moving sufficient assets to eliminate that differential.

of one country can purchase any desired assets in another country immediately, in unlimited amounts, with very low commissions and fees. The crucial implication of perfect capital mobility is that interest rates in one country are tightly linked to interest rates in other countries. Why? An American investor faced with a choice of a return of 6.0 percent at home and 6.6 percent in Germany would immediately choose to buy financial assets in Germany. This reduction in the supply of funds in the United States would raise the U.S. interest rate, and the increase in the demand for German securities would reduce the German interest rate. Interest rates in the two countries would converge at the same level, say 6.3 percent.

The implication of perfect capital mobility is profound. *Any event in one country that tends to change its interest rate (r) relative to the interest rate in foreign countries (r^f) will generate huge capital movements that will soon eliminate the interest rate differential (r − r^f).* As an example, a monetary expansion that reduces the domestic interest rate will generate a huge capital outflow that will bring the interest rate back to its original level. A fiscal expansion that raises the domestic interest rate will generate a huge capital inflow that will bring the interest rate back to its original level.

The Two Adjustment Mechanisms: Fixed and Flexible Rates

Perfect capital mobility implies that domestic monetary and fiscal policy do not affect the domestic interest rate. With fixed exchange rates, a stimulative monetary policy will not reduce the domestic interest rate, but will instead cause the country to lose international reserves as the capital account in the balance of payments is thrown into deficit. In a pure flexible exchange rate system (in which there are no international reserves), the monetary policy stimulus generates an excess supply of dollars, and the exchange rate of the dollar drops until supply and demand are once again in balance.

In short, perfect capital mobility implies that both monetary and fiscal policy lose control over the interest rate. With fixed exchange rates, a monetary stimulus causes a loss of reserves and a fiscal stimulus causes an increase in reserves. With flexible exchange rates, a monetary stimulus causes a depreciation of the exchange rate and a fiscal stimulus causes an appreciation of the exchange rate. The reverse events occur with a monetary policy contraction or a fiscal policy contraction.

Is Perfect Capital Mobility Relevant for the United States?

A **small open economy** with perfect capital mobility has no power to set its domestic interest rate at a level that differs from foreign interest rates.

A **large open economy** can influence its domestic interest rate. A high domestic interest rate generates a steady stream of capital inflows that are not great enough to eliminate an interest rate differential between the domestic and foreign interest rate; a low domestic interest rate generates a steady stream of capital outflows.

As an analytical tool, perfect capital mobility is most relevant for a **small open economy,** too small to influence the world level of interest rates (r^f). In such an economy, because of perfect capital mobility, the small domestic capital market is swamped by capital inflows whenever there is even a minor increase in the domestic interest rate above the world interest rate (and capital outflows for even a minor decrease in the domestic interest rate).

The United States is too large to be considered a small open economy, and even under perfect capital mobility its own domestic capital market is too large for capital movements to bring its domestic interest rate into perfect equality with the foreign interest rate. We examine the case of the **large open economy** after first studying how monetary and fiscal policy work in a small open economy with perfect capital mobility. We already have had a preview of the effects of fiscal deficits in open economies on pp. 142–44.

6-9 Effects of Monetary and Fiscal Policy with Fixed and Flexible Exchange Rates

The assumption of perfect capital mobility introduces a new element into the *IS-LM* model of income determination. This is the assumption that the differential between domestic and foreign interest rates $(r - r^f)$ must remain at zero. Any small change in the domestic interest rate caused by shifts in monetary and fiscal policy (or in shifts in the *IS* curve due to different levels of consumer and business optimism) will generate capital flows that will quickly bring the domestic interest rate back into line with the unchanged foreign interest rate.

The Analysis with Fixed Exchange Rates

Now we will examine the effects of a monetary and then a fiscal expansion in a small open economy with fixed exchange rates. Throughout, we will assume that the price level is fixed. These results remain valid, even if the price level is allowed to change, as long as changes in the price level occur more slowly than the speed at which capital flows in and out of the small open economy.

Monetary expansion. As we learned in Chapter 4, a domestic monetary expansion occurs when the central bank (the Federal Reserve or "Fed" in the United States) raises the money supply, thus shifting the *LM* curve to the right. This normally reduces the interest rate and stimulates spending. But in a small open economy with perfect capital mobility, the interest rate is fixed at the level of the world interest rate. When the central bank increases the money supply, there immediately are huge capital outflows and losses of international reserves. Thus, as stated by the *trilemma* introduced at the beginning of this chapter, the Fed or any central bank loses control of the money supply when the exchange rate is fixed and capital is perfectly mobile. Thus monetary policy becomes completely impotent with fixed exchange rates.

Fiscal policy. As usual, fiscal policy works in the opposite way from monetary policy. As we learned in Chapter 4, when monetary policy is weak, fiscal policy is strong, and vice versa. This works in the same way in a small open economy. A fiscal policy stimulus works by shifting the *IS* curve to the right, just as in Chapter 4. But this tends to raise the interest rate relative to the world interest rate and attract inflows of capital, swamping the central bank with reserves. Under a fixed exchange rate system, the central bank must respond by allowing the money supply to rise until the interest rate returns to its initial level. Thus *both* the *IS* and *LM* curves move to the right, as in the top right frame of Figure 4-10 on p. 115. Perfect capital mobility clearly makes fiscal policy very effective, since it gives fiscal policy control over the money supply, forcing the *LM* curve to amplify any movement in the *IS* curve. *Perfect capital mobility with fixed exchange rates forces monetary policy to be accommodative; in effect, fiscal policy gains control over monetary policy.*

The Analysis with Flexible Exchange Rates

In the previous section we learned that a fixed exchange rate system makes monetary policy impotent and fiscal policy very effective in changing the level of real income. In this section we learn that the opposite is true with flexible exchange rates. Monetary policy becomes extremely effective, whereas fiscal policy becomes ineffective.

When exchange rates are flexible, the central bank does nothing to prevent an exchange rate appreciation or depreciation. Thus any event that reduces the domestic interest rate will cause a capital outflow, raising the supply of domestic currency on the foreign exchange market and causing the exchange rate to depreciate. The exchange rate depreciates whenever monetary policy reduces the interest rate and appreciates whenever monetary policy raises the interest rate.

The new ingredient in the *IS-LM* model implied by flexible exchange rates was introduced in equation (6.7). An exchange rate appreciation reduces net exports and hence shifts the *IS* curve to the left (since net exports are a component of autonomous planned spending, and any change in autonomous planned spending shifts the *IS* curve). Similarly, an exchange rate depreciation raises net exports and shifts the *IS* curve to the right.

Monetary expansion. When the central bank increases the money supply with flexible exchange rates, interest rates decline, the exchange rate depreciates, and net exports rise, thus shifting the *IS* curve to the right. Hence, in a small open economy, monetary policy is very powerful since monetary policy gains control of the *IS* curve and forces it to move in the same direction as the *LM* curve.

However, as also shown in equation (6.7) on p. 181, higher income boosts imports. As a result, when the economy arrives at its new equilibrium level of output, the boost to net exports from the depreciated exchange rate is offset exactly by the reduction in net exports caused by higher income. The current account is in balance and, because the domestic interest rate is equal to the foreign interest rate, the capital account is also in balance.

We learned in Chapter 4 that the normal effect of a fiscal expansion in a closed economy is to shift rightward the *IS* curve and raise the interest rate. But now, with flexible exchange rates, the fiscal expansion and higher interest rate causes the exchange rate to appreciate. Domestic exports are made more expensive, and domestic residents start buying more imported goods. Net exports fall, and this continues until the *IS* curve shifts back to its initial position. In this situation the *LM* curve does not shift.

Domestic crowding out is replaced by international crowding out, and international crowding out is complete. The domestic interest rate and income are the same as they were initially; thus, so are domestic investment and saving. The increase in the fiscal deficit caused by the higher level of government spending is exactly offset by the decline in net exports, and the higher fiscal deficit is totally financed by foreign borrowing. *The twin deficits are identical*, and the cause of the foreign trade deficit is the fiscal deficit. To summarize these different cases:

1. With fixed exchange rates, fiscal policy is highly effective and the central bank is forced to accommodate fiscal policy actions. Monetary policy is impotent, since any increase in the money supply immediately flows abroad and fails to stimulate the domestic economy.

2. With flexible exchange rates, monetary policy is highly effective. The central bank can control the money supply and can stimulate the economy by

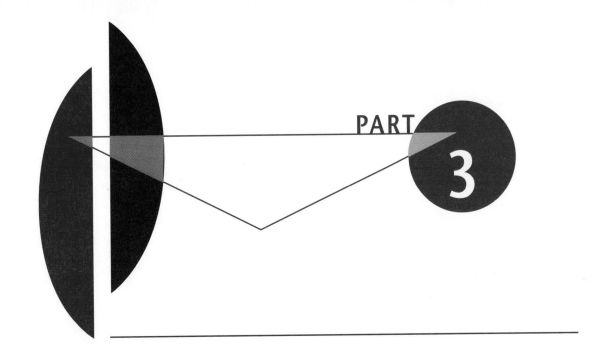

Aggregate Demand, Aggregate Supply, Unemployment, and Inflation

Aggregate Demand, Aggregate Supply, and the Self-Correcting Economy

The price of commodities in the market is formed by means of a certain struggle which takes place between the buyers and the sellers.
—Henry Thornton, 1802

We have now completed Part Two of the book, composed of Chapters 3–6. We have studied the determinants of aggregate demand, and we have seen that changes in any of these determinants create demand shocks.[1] Among the demand shocks introduced in Chapter 3 were changes in autonomous consumption, planned investment, net exports, and fiscal policy (i.e., changes in government spending and tax rates). We learned that changes in consumer confidence, in stock market prices, and in housing prices can alter autonomous consumption, and that changes in business optimism and expectations of future profits can alter planned investment. Added in Chapter 4 as a source of demand shocks was the money supply, which induces changes in interest rates that lead to changes in such interest-sensitive components of spending as autonomous consumption and planned investment. Then in Chapter 6 we learned that changes in the exchange rate constitute yet another source of demand shocks. All demand shocks can create multiplier effects of response in the total economy, and the size of the multiplier depends on the fraction of an extra dollar of income that leaks out of spending into saving, income taxes, and imports.

The economy's chief line of defense against demand shocks is monetary and fiscal policy. We have learned that these policies under some conditions can have strong or weak effects, and we have learned that their impact is quite different when exchange rates are fixed than when exchange rates are flexible.

7-1 Combining Aggregate Demand with Aggregate Supply

In principle, shocks to aggregate demand can change either real GDP, the price level (GDP deflator), or both. Up until now, in order to focus on changes in aggregate demand, we have made a bold but useful simplifying assumption: *that the price level is fixed in the short run*. This has implied that all changes in aggregate demand automatically cause changes in real GDP by the same amount in the same direction. Repeating from equation (3.1) on p. 59:

$$\text{Changes in Real GDP} = \frac{\text{Changes in Aggregate Demand}}{\text{Fixed Price Level}} \qquad (7.1)$$

---

[1] *Review:* The concepts "aggregate demand" and "demand shocks" were first defined in Chapter 3 on p. 58, and these definitions are also found in the glossary in the back of the book.

Now it is time to drop the unrealistic assumption that the price level is fixed. Recall that the price level is measured by an aggregate price index like the GDP deflator. When the prices of most goods are rising, the aggregate deflator (P) increases, and we have inflation. When the prices of most goods are falling, P decreases, and we have deflation. How can we determine whether changes in aggregate demand create changes in real GDP, the price level, or both?

This chapter introduces two new elements to answer that question. First, we introduce a negatively sloped schedule relating real GDP to the price level, called the **aggregate demand (AD) curve.** We have already learned in Chapters 3–6 all the reasons why the AD curve shifts its position; here the only new element is the curve has a negative slope, reflecting the fact that a higher price level reduces the real money supply and hence reduces aggregate demand.

But the AD curve by itself cannot determine two unknowns, real GDP and the price level. The needed extra relationship is the **short-run aggregate supply (SAS) curve,** a positively sloped relationship between real GDP and the price level. Whereas the AD curve shows how much people want to buy, the SAS curve shows how much business firms are willing to sell at each price level. When the price level increases, while the costs of labor and other inputs remain stable, then business profits will increase and firms will produce more real GDP. Both real GDP and the price level are determined at the point where the AD and SAS curves intersect. We shall learn that the reason for the positive slope of the SAS is inherently temporary, that prices adjust while labor costs (the nominal wage) do not. Once the nominal wage rate is free to adjust in proportion to the price level, the **long-run aggregate supply (LAS) curve** becomes vertical.

This chapter begins by deriving the AD and SAS curves, explaining why they are sloped as they are, and what causes them to shift their position. Subsequently, we use both curves to examine differing views of economists regarding the causes of business cycles and the effectiveness of monetary and fiscal policy. We use the distinction between aggregate demand and supply to examine the causes of the Great Depression, which involve the causes of the leftward shift in the AD curve, the slope of the SAS curve, and the determinants of shifts in the SAS curve.

> The **aggregate demand (AD) curve** shows different combinations of the price level and real output at which the money and commodity markets are both in equilibrium.

> The **short-run aggregate supply (SAS) curve** shows the amount of output that business firms are willing to produce at different price levels, holding constant the nominal wage rate.

> The **long-run aggregate supply (LAS) curve** shows the amount that business firms are willing to produce when the nominal wage rate has fully adjusted to any changes in the price level.

7-2 Flexible Prices and the *AD* Curve

In this section we develop the AD curve, which summarizes the effect of changing prices on the level of real GDP. The AD curve summarizes the *IS-LM* model of Chapter 4; the only new element is that the price level is now allowed to change instead of being fixed as in Chapters 3–6.

Effect of Changing Prices on the *LM* Curve

We already know that the LM curve shifts its position whenever there is a change in the *real* money supply. Until now, every LM shift has resulted from a change in the *nominal* money supply, while the price level has been fixed. The price level has been treated as a parameter, or a known variable, allowing us to concentrate on the determination of the two unknowns, real income (Y) and the interest rate (r).

However, the LM curve can shift *in exactly the same way* when a change in the real money supply M^s/P is caused by a change in the price level P, while the

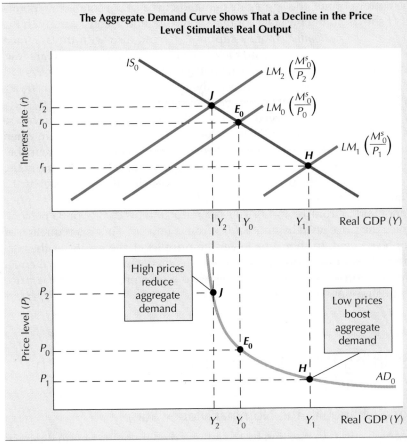

The Aggregate Demand Curve Shows That a Decline in the Price Level Stimulates Real Output

Figure 7-1 Effect on Real Income of Different Values of the Price Level

In the top frame, three different *LM* curves are drawn for three different hypothetical values of the price level. Corresponding to the three levels of the price level are three positions of equilibrium, *J*, E_0, and *H*. These three points are drawn again in the lower frame with the same horizontal axis (real income), but with the price level for the vertical axis. A drop in the price index from point *J* to E_0, and then to *H*, raises the *real* money supply and stimulates real output along the aggregate demand curve AD_0.

nominal money supply M^s remains fixed at a single value, say M_0^s. The top frame of Figure 7-1 illustrates three *LM* curves drawn for three values of *P* and M^s/P, each assuming the same nominal money supply, M_0^s. Initially the economy is at point E_0, where the *IS* curve crosses the LM_0 curve, drawn for the initial assumed price level P_0. The economy is in equilibrium with income level Y_0 and interest rate r_0. So far, everything is the same as in Chapter 4.

Now we consider something new, a change in the price level. If the price level were *lower* than P_0, say P_1, the real money supply would be *larger* (M_0^s/P_1). To maintain equilibrium in the money market, the interest rate would have to fall to r_1. This change would boost planned expenditures and cause real GDP to grow to the larger amount Y_1, so that the economy's equilibrium position would move from E_0 to point *H*. The reverse is true as well. A higher price level, say P_2, would reduce the real money supply and cause real GDP to shrink to the lower level Y_2, and the economy's equilibrium position would move to point *J*.

The bottom frame of Figure 7-1 presents the relationship between equilibrium real GDP (*Y*) and the assumed price level. The horizontal axis (real GDP) is the same as that in the top frame, but the vertical axis in the bottom frame plots the price level. Points *J*, E_0, and *H* in the bottom frame plot the three different assumed price levels and the corresponding level of real GDP from the top frame. In this example, price level P_2 is twice as high as P_0, and P_0 is twice as high as P_1.

In the bottom frame, the aggregate demand curve (AD_0) connecting points J, E_0, and H shows all the possible combinations of P and Y consistent with the assumed level of the *nominal* money supply (M_0^s) and also with the assumed IS_0 curve. If the price level is higher, then real spending and real GDP are low, and vice versa. Because the level of real GDP along the AD curve is always at a point where the IS and LM curves cross in the upper frame, *everywhere along the AD curve both the commodity and money markets are in equilibrium.*

Why is the AD curve a curved line instead of a straight line? Its curvature indicates that a given decline in the price level will boost real GDP more when the price level is low than when the price level is high. This in turn occurs because a given decline in the price level creates a greater *percentage* decline in the price level, the lower is the price level. Consider reducing the price level by 0.5 from 2.0 to 1.5. This is a reduction of 0.5/2.0, or 25 percent. Reduce the price level by another 0.5 from 1.5 to 1.0. This is a reduction of 0.5/1.5, or 33 percent. Then reduce the price level by another 0.5 from 1.0 to 0.5. This is a reduction of 0.5/1.0, or 50 percent. In short, the lower the price level, the greater is the percentage reduction in the price level, and hence percentage increase in the real money supply and in real GDP, in response to a given reduction in the price level by a set amount such as 0.5.

7-3 Shifting the Aggregate Demand Curve with Monetary and Fiscal Policy

Effects of a Change in the Nominal Money Supply

The AD curve is fixed in position by the assumed value of the nominal money supply and the assumed position of the IS curve, which in turn depends on consumer and business confidence, fiscal policy, and net exports. A change in any of these assumed conditions will shift the position of the AD curve and thus change the amount of spending and real GDP at any given price level.

To understand the factors that shift the AD curve, we begin with a doubling of the nominal money supply, from M_0^s to M_1^s. The economy starts out at point E_0 in the top frame of Figure 7-2, the same position as in Figure 7-1. Doubling the money supply shifts the LM curve rightward to the new position LM_1. Since the price level has not changed, in the bottom frame the economy remains at the same vertical position as at point E_0 but moves horizontally to point H', which lies directly below point H' in the upper frame. The economy's real GDP is exactly the same at point H and H'.

But, since we drew the initial AD_0 curve on the assumption that price level P_1 is half of P_0, it follows that the price level at H' is double its value at H in the bottom frame. Similarly, every point along the new, higher AD_1 curve is twice as high as along the original AD_0 curve. *The general rule is that an increase in the nominal money supply by a given percentage shifts the* AD *curve vertically by the same percentage.*[2] Why? The price level must shift upward by the same percent as the nominal money supply in order to leave the real money supply unchanged, and the position of the LM curve depends on the real money supply.

---

[2] The proportional vertical movement in the AD schedule requires that all forms of real wealth double when the nominal money supply doubles.

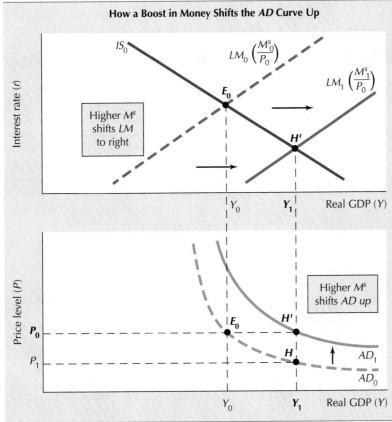

How a Boost in Money Shifts the AD Curve Up

Figure 7-2 The Effect on the *AD* Curve of a Doubling of the Nominal Money Supply

In the top frame, a doubling of the nominal money supply from M_0^s to M_1^s moves the *LM* curve rightward from LM_0 to LM_1 and moves the economy's general equilibrium (where *IS* crosses *LM*) from point E_0 to point H'. In the lower frame, we remain at a vertical distance of P_0, since nothing has happened to the price level. The higher money supply raises real income and causes the economy's equilibrium position in the bottom frame to be at point H' rather than at point E_0. Notice that the new AD_1 curve running through point H' lies everywhere twice as high as the old AD_0 curve.

 SELF-TEST

1. Would a steeper *IS* curve make the *AD* curve steeper or flatter?
2. Would a steeper *LM* curve make the *AD* curve steeper or flatter?

Effects of a Change in Autonomous Spending

In the last section, the *IS* curve remained fixed at its original position but an increase in the nominal money supply shifted the *LM* and *AD* curves. Now we reverse what is fixed and what changes. We hold fixed the nominal money supply but allow a drop in planned spending to shift the *IS* curve to the left. This change might occur because of a decline in consumer or business confidence, a decline in government spending, an increase in tax rates, an increase in autonomous net taxes, or a drop in the autonomous component of net exports.

When the *IS* curve shifts leftward in the top frame of Figure 7-3, the economy's equilibrium position shifts southwest from point E_0 to point F, at the crossing point of the new *IS* curve and the unchanged *LM* curve, drawn for the unchanged nominal money supply (M_0^s) and a given price level (P_0). In the bottom frame, if the price level remains at P_0, the economy shifts from point E_0 to point F. Real GDP falls from Y_0 to Y_3. The drop in planned spending creates a leftward shift in the *AD* curve.

Comparing the bottom frames of Figures 7-2 and 7-3, we note that the shifts in the *AD* curve are different. A change in the nominal money supply, as in Figure 7-2, shifts the *AD* curve up or down *vertically*. However, a change in

Learning About Diagrams: The *AD* Curve

The aggregate demand (*AD*) curve, as drawn in the bottom frames of Figures 7-1 to 7-3, summarizes everything we have already learned about the *IS-LM* model and adds a single new ingredient, the ability of the price level to change instead of remaining fixed (as in Chapters 3–6).

Diagram Elements and Reasons for Slope

The vertical axis is the price level and the horizontal axis is the level of real GDP.

The *AD* curve shows all the possible crossing points of a single *IS* commodity-market equilibrium curve with the various *LM* money-market equilibrium curves drawn for each possible price level. Everywhere along the *AD* curve *both* the commodity (*IS*) and money (*LM*) markets are in equilibrium (as shown in Figure 7-1).

The *AD* curve slopes downward because a lower price level (*P*) raises the real money supply, thereby lowering the interest rate and stimulating planned expenditures. This stimulus requires an increase in actual real GDP (*Y*) to keep the commodity market in equilibrium. The steeper the *IS* curve, the steeper the *AD* curve.

What Shifts the *AD* Curve?

The *AD* curve is drawn for a fixed nominal supply of money (M^s) and a fixed set of determinants of the *IS* curve (business and consumer confidence, government spending, tax rates, autonomous net taxes, and the autonomous component of net exports).

A given percentage increase in the nominal money supply will shift the *AD* curve *vertically* upward by a similar percentage.

Anything that shifts the *IS* curve creates a parallel *horizontal* shift in the *AD* curve in the same direction. The *amount* of the horizontal shift of the *AD* curve is usually less than that of the *IS* curve, because of the crowding out effect.[a]

The following is a list of factors that will shift the *AD* curve to the right. The opposite changes will shift the *AD* curve to the left.

An increase in autonomous consumption due to
  An increase in consumer optimism
  An increase in stock market or housing wealth
  A decrease in the interest rate due to a reduction in the demand for money caused, for instance, by the invention of credit cards
An increase in government spending
A reduction in either autonomous taxes or the income tax rate
An increase in the marginal propensity to consume
An increase in foreign income that raises exports
A reduction in the share of GDP spent on imports
A depreciation of the exchange rate that boosts net exports

What Is True of Points That Are Off the *AD* Curve?

The entire area to the right of the *AD* curve has an excess supply of commodities; too much is being produced relative to the demand for goods and services at that price level.

The entire area to the left of the *AD* curve has an excess demand for commodities; too little is being produced relative to the demand for goods and services at that price level.

At any point off the *AD* curve, there is pressure for change. For instance, at a point with excess production to the right of the *AD* curve, there is unplanned inventory accumulation, which places downward pressure on production. There is also downward pressure on prices as firms attempt to boost sales with lower prices.[b]

---

[a] For details, see equation (10) in the Appendix to Chapter 4. For any given change in, say, government spending, the *IS* curve shifts in the same direction by the multiplier k, while the *AD* curve shifts in the same direction by the multiplier k_1, defined in equation (10).

[b] The equation of the *AD* curve is the income equation (9) in the Appendix to Chapter 4.

$$Y = k_1 A_p' + k_2 \frac{M^s}{P}$$

---

autonomous spending in Figure 7-3 shifts the *AD* curve to the left or right *horizontally*. The decline in real GDP in the bottom frame that results from a given leftward shift in the *IS* curve is exactly the same, no matter whether the initial price level is low or high.

Will the reduction in planned spending reduce real income and leave the price level unchanged? Or will the reduction in planned spending reduce the

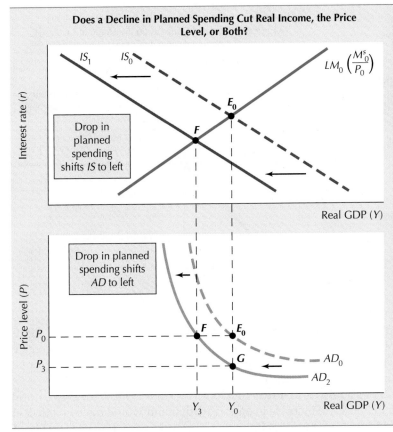

Does a Decline in Planned Spending Cut Real Income, the Price Level, or Both?

Figure 7-3 The Effect on the *AD* Curve of a Decline in Planned Autonomous Spending

Any event that reduces planned autonomous spending by shifting the *IS* curve leftward also creates a parallel leftward shift in the *AD* curve. If the price level remains stable at P_0, the economy shifts leftward to point *F* and real income drops to Y_3. Another possibility is that the price level could drop to P_3, moving the economy down to point *G* and allowing real income to remain at the original Y_0. A drop in the price level to P_3 would increase the real money supply and shift the *LM* curve to the right in the top frame to a position that intersects the IS_1 line directly above Y_0.

price level and leave real income unchanged? Which outcome will occur? Figure 7-3 cannot tell us, because the *AD* curve by itself does not contain enough information to pin down both the price level and real income. To ascertain where the economy will come to rest along the numerous possible positions along the *AD* curve, we must find another schedule to intersect the *AD* curve. This is the *SAS* curve initially defined on pp. 206–07.

7-4 Alternative Shapes of the Short-Run Aggregate Supply Curve

The short-run aggregate supply schedule shows how much business firms are willing to produce at different hypothetical price levels. Such a schedule of business firms' behavior can have several possible shapes. Depending on the shape, the implications of a shift in the *AD* curve are quite different. In Figure 7-4 we show a rightward shift in the *AD* curve from AD_0 to AD_1.

How will the increase in aggregate demand be divided between a higher level of real GDP and a higher price level? Three hypothetical answers, corresponding to three hypothetical aggregate supply curves, are shown in Figure 7-4. In Chapters 3–6 we assumed that the price level always remains fixed; thus

Figure 7-4 Effect of a Rightward Shift in the *AD* Curve with Three Alternative Short-Run Aggregate Supply Curves

The horizontal supply curve at the price level P_0 reflects the "fixed price" assumption of Chapters 3–6. An increase in aggregate demand that shifts the AD_0 curve to AD_1 will move the economy from its initial position E_0 to new position E_1. In contrast, if the supply curve is vertical, higher aggregate demand pushes the economy from point E_0 to E_3. An intermediate possibility is that both output and prices rise *in the short run* to a point such as E_2, and that *in the long run* the *boost* in real GDP gradually disappears until we arrive at E_3

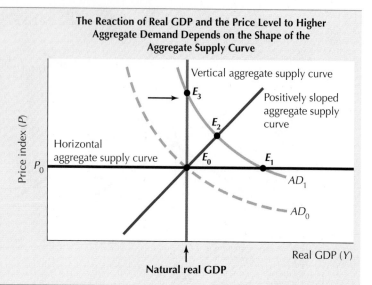

The Reaction of Real GDP and the Price Level to Higher Aggregate Demand Depends on the Shape of the Aggregate Supply Curve

we assumed that the economy moved from its initial position E_0 directly right-ward to a higher level of real GDP at point E_1 along the horizontal aggregate supply curve. Thus throughout Chapters 3–6 we were assuming a horizontal aggregate supply curve like that shown in Figure 7-4.

A second possibility is that real GDP is always fixed at the level of natural real GDP. If so, the same increase in aggregate demand would have no effect at all on real GDP. Instead, business firms would simply raise the price level from P_0 to a higher price level at point E_3 along the vertical aggregate supply curve in Figure 7-4, leaving their level of production (Y) unchanged. As we shall see, natural real GDP is the only output level consistent with equilibrium in the la-bor market.

A third possibility is shown by the line labeled "positively sloped aggre-gate supply curve." If this curve were valid, then the rightward shift in the AD curve would cause business firms to raise *both* their prices and their level of production, moving the economy to a point like E_2. As we shall see, a point like E_2 is likely to be achieved only temporarily.

The choice among the three shapes of the aggregate supply curve in Figure 7-4 has created decades of controversy in macroeconomics. The horizontal sup-ply curve that was assumed in our fixed-price analysis of Chapters 3–6 is very convenient but unrealistic, since it cannot explain why the inflation rate is not always zero. The vertical supply curve is a convenient shortcut for analyzing periods of very rapid inflation, since it implies that changes in the money sup-ply mainly or entirely affect the inflation rate with minor or negligible effects on real output. The third, positively sloping alternative seems more realistic, at least for the short run.

In the next section, we shall see that the positively sloped line in Figure 7-4 is the short-run aggregate supply (*SAS*) curve introduced at the beginning of this chapter. It is valid only in the short run, a period short enough for the price level to adjust but during which the nominal wage rate temporarily remains fixed. Also in the next section, we shall learn that the vertical line in Figure 7-4 is the long-run aggregate supply (*LAS*) curve that applies after nominal wage rates have fully adjusted to any changes in the price level.

7-5 The Short-Run Aggregate Supply (*SAS*) Curve When the Nominal Wage Rate Is Constant

We are now ready to learn why aggregate demand shocks, taking the form of changes in the nominal money supply or in any of the factors that can shift the *IS* curve, will change *both* real GDP and the price level. Will a demand shock change the price level more than it changes real GDP, or will the demand shock change real GDP more than the price level? The answer depends on the slope of the *SAS* curve.

In this section we show how the upward-sloping *SAS* curve can be derived from the behavior of firms in the labor market. We assume that the nominal wage rate is fixed and postpone until the next section the question of how long the wage rate is fixed and what factors cause it to change.

The Labor Demand Curve

Distinguishing the nominal and real wage rates. We first encountered the distinction between nominal and real variables in Chapter 2, where we introduced nominal and real GDP. The nominal wage rate is simply the actual wage rate paid (W). Initially, the nominal wage rate is assumed to be fixed at a particular amount (W_0), say \$15 per hour. The real wage rate (W/P) is the nominal wage rate (W) divided by an aggregate price index, such as the GDP deflator.

The left-hand frame of Figure 7-5 plots the real wage (W/P) on the vertical axis and the level of employment (N) on the horizontal axis. Since the real wage

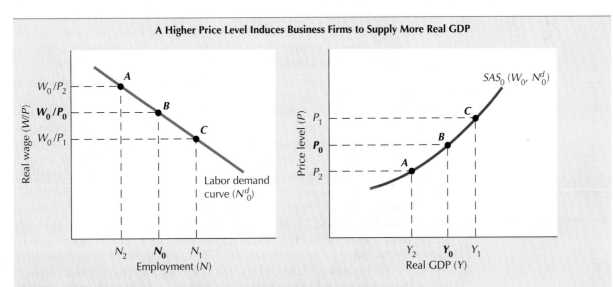

A Higher Price Level Induces Business Firms to Supply More Real GDP

Figure 7-5 The Labor Demand Curve and the Short-Run Aggregate Supply Curve

The left-hand frame displays the labor demand curve, which shows that a decline in the real wage induces firms to hire additional workers. The right-hand frame shows that a higher price level (by reducing the real wage and inducing firms to hire additional workers) raises real GDP.

is the price that firms pay to hire workers, the downward-sloping labor demand curve (N_0^d) states that a decrease in the real wage will induce firms to hire more workers, and vice versa. Any given labor demand curve holds constant other inputs that work together with labor, for example, land, capital, technology, materials, and energy. The vertical position of the labor demand curve represents the marginal product of labor; the labor demand curve slopes downward because the marginal product of labor declines as additional workers are hired to work with a fixed quantity of land, capital, technology, materials, and energy.[3] An increase in any of these nonlabor inputs will shift the N^d curve upward.

Firms hire workers up to the point that the real wage equals their marginal product. For instance, at point B in the left-hand frame of Figure 7-5, a real wage of W_0/P_0 induces firms to hire N_0 workers. To hire workers beyond that point, say to hire N_1 workers at point C, would mean hiring workers having a marginal product of labor less than the assumed real wage of W_0/P_0, causing firms to lose money on those extra workers.

The Short-Run Aggregate Supply (SAS) Curve

Now we can examine the relationship between employment and real GDP at different price levels. For instance, point B in the left frame of Figure 7-5 shows that N_0 workers will be hired if the price level is P_0 and the real wage is W_0/P_0. Looking directly to the right, we see that at point B the same price level (P_0) will induce a production level of Y_0, the amount that N_0 workers can produce.

The line connecting points A, B, and C in the right frame is the *SAS* curve. It slopes upward because a higher price level reduces the real wage and induces firms to hire more workers, which in turn raises real GDP. Notice that all three points in both the left and right frames—A, B, and C—share exactly the same nominal wage rate (W_0). For this reason, the *SAS* curve is labeled with the wage rate assumed in drawing it, W_0. Only the price level differs among the three points. Because a change in the price level also changes the real wage, it changes employment and real GDP.

For instance, at point C in the right frame of Figure 7-5, the price level is at P_1, a higher level than P_0. Since the nominal wage rate is assumed to be fixed at W_0, the real wage at point C in the left frame is W_0/P_1, a lower value of the real wage that induces firms to higher number of workers N_1 who can produce the higher value of output Y_1 at point C in the right frame. Similarly, point A shows that a lower price level P_2 in the right frame implies a higher real wage at point A in the left frame, and a lower level of employment N_2 and lower level of output Y_2.

The slope of the *SAS* curve determines how much real GDP responds to a demand shock, and how much the price level responds. As drawn in Figure 7-5, the response of real GDP and of the price level to a demand shock will be in roughly the same proportion. For the *SAS* curve to be much steeper than shown, the labor demand curve in the left frame of Figure 7-5 would have to have a steep downward slope, indicating that the addition of extra workers

---

[3] The decline in the marginal product as one factor of production is added while the quantity of other factors remains fixed is called the law of diminishing returns, and is introduced in every elementary economics textbook.

Learning About Diagrams: The *SAS* Curve

The short-run aggregate supply curve, abbreviated *SAS*, depicts the amount of output that business firms are willing to produce at different alternative price levels.

Diagram Elements and Reasons for Slope

The *SAS* curve is plotted with the same vertical and horizontal axes as the *AD* curve; the aggregate price level is on the vertical axis and real GDP is on the horizontal axis. Examples are shown in the right frame of Figures 7-5 and 7-6 on p. 205 and p. 208.

The *SAS* curve slopes up because, with a fixed nominal wage rate, a higher price level makes it profitable for business firms to increase output. Since increasing output requires adding more workers, each of whom is less productive than the last, the real wage must decline for firms to be willing to produce more output, and hence the price level must increase.

The greater the decline in worker productivity as additional workers are added, the steeper is the *SAS* curve.

What Shifts the *SAS* Curve?

The *SAS* curve is drawn for a fixed nominal wage rate and a fixed set of determinants of the labor demand curve. These are the inputs other than labor—land, capital, technology, materials, and energy.

A given percentage change in the nominal wage rate will shift the *SAS* curve upward by the same percentage. When the nominal wage rate and the price level (drawn on the vertical axis) increase by the same percentage, the real wage is fixed, employment and output are fixed, and we remain at the same horizontal position in the diagram.

Larger inputs of capital, technology, materials, or energy will shift the production function up and the *SAS* curve to the right, allowing more output to be produced at a given price level. The reverse is also true; an event like a sharp increase in oil prices can reduce nonlabor inputs like energy, shifting the *SAS* curve to the left.

What Is True of Points That Are Off the *SAS* Curve?

Since the *SAS* curve shows the different combinations of output and the price level consistent with profit maximization by business firms, any point off the *SAS* curve would not be chosen by these firms.

A point to the right of the *SAS* curve indicates that firms are producing too much, hiring workers whose marginal product is below their real wage. Firms could boost profits by reducing output.

A point to the left of the *SAS* curve indicates that firms are producing too little, since additional workers could be hired who produce more than their real wage. Firms could boost profits by raising output.

causes a sharp decline in the productivity of workers. Similarly, for the *SAS* curve to be relatively flat, the labor demand curve would also need to be relatively flat.

SELF-TEST

Which of the following causes a movement *along* the short-run aggregate supply (*SAS*) curve, and which causes a shift in the curve? If the curve shifts, does it shift up or down?

1. A union concession that reduces the wage rate to help a firm survive foreign competition.

2. A discovery of a giant oil field in Missouri that reduces the price of oil.

3. An increase in the money supply.

4. An increase in the GDP deflator.

7-6 How the Wage Rate Is Set

So far we have seen that the aggregate supply curve slopes upward for any *given* nominal wage rate. But surely the wage rate will not stay at the same level forever. If the wage rate increases, the *SAS* curve will shift up, and its intersection point with the economy's aggregate demand curve (*AD*) will shift as well. *Thus the determinants of the actual wage rate paid have a crucial effect on the nature of the economy's response to a change in aggregate demand.*

The Equilibrium Real Wage Rate

In Figure 7-5 we can see in operation the distinction between the nominal and real wage rates. As long as the labor demand curve is at the fixed position N_0^d, an increase in employment from N_0 to N_1 requires a decrease in the real wage rate from W_0/P_0 to W_0/P_1. Since the nominal wage rate W_0 remains fixed, then this required decline in the real wage rate *must* be accomplished by an increase in the price level. When P increases and W remains fixed, employment increases to N_1 in the left frame of Figure 7-6 and output increases to Y_1 in the right frame.

But the nominal wage rate is unlikely to stay fixed forever. If it shifts up to W_1, then the aggregate supply curve will shift up from SAS_0 to SAS_1. In Figure 7-6 we assume that W_1 exceeds W_0 by the same percentage as P_1 exceeds P_0, so

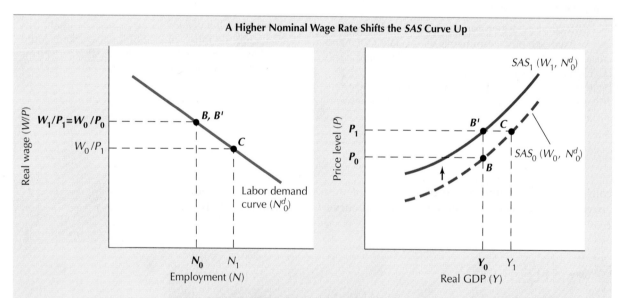

A Higher Nominal Wage Rate Shifts the SAS Curve Up

Figure 7-6 The Short-Run Aggregate Supply Curve for Two Different Values of the Wage Rate, W_0 and W_1

The labor demand curve and aggregate supply curve SAS_0 are identical to those drawn in Figure 7-5. So also are points B and C, the quantities N_0 and Y_0, and the price levels P_0 and P_1. The new ingredient here is a higher wage rate W_1, which shifts the aggregate supply curve up from SAS_0 to SAS_1. The higher wage rate shifts the *SAS* curve because at a given price level, workers are more costly, and so firms hire fewer workers and produce less output. Points B and B' in the left frame are identical, because we assume that the percentage difference between W_1 and W_0 is the same as between P_1 and P_0. Thus point B' lies directly above point B in the right frame.

$$\frac{W_1}{P_1} = \frac{W_0}{P_0}$$

Thus the real wage rate W_1/P_1 at point B' along the new SAS_1 line is exactly the same as the real wage rate W_0/P_0 at point B. Hence, the level of employment and real GDP (N_0 and Y_0) must be identical at points B and B', since the level of employment and real GDP depends only on the real wage. Indeed we see in the left frame of Figure 7-6 that points B and B' coincide because the real wage rate is identical at points B and B' in both the left and right frames of Figure 7-6.

Determinants of the equilibrium real wage rate.   Equilibrium is a situation in which there is no pressure for change. The key insight into understanding aggregate supply behavior is the concept of the **equilibrium real wage rate,** which is determined by the intersection of labor demand and supply curves. In Figure 7-7 we have copied our previous labor demand curve (N_0^d), which shows the marginal product of additional labor input.

The supply of labor is also assumed to depend on the real wage, and in Figure 7-7 labor supply is represented by a labor supply curve that slopes upward. This indicates that a higher real wage rate would induce a higher quantity of labor supplied. For instance, a higher real wage rate might induce homemakers to take outside jobs by increasing their willingness to put up with the inconvenience of commuting and arranging day care for their children. A higher real wage rate might also make people more willing to moonlight, sacrificing leisure and sleep to take second jobs.

The position of the labor supply curve can shift if anything occurs that makes people more or less willing to take jobs at a given real wage rate. For instance, an increase in the working-age population, due to immigration or a high birth rate, will tend to shift the labor supply curve to the right. Factors that make jobs less attractive—for instance, the availability of generous unemployment or welfare benefits for those not working—will tend to shift the labor supply curve to the left.

The **equilibrium real wage rate** is the real wage rate for the point at which the labor supply and demand curves intersect, so there is no pressure for change in the real wage.

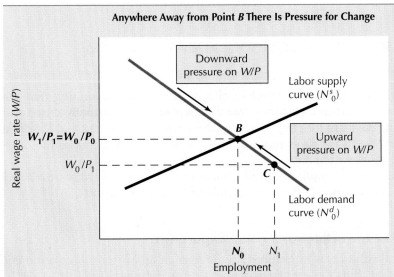

Anywhere Away from Point B There Is Pressure for Change

Figure 7-7 Determination of the Equilibrium Real Wage Rate

Here the labor demand curve (N_0^d) is the same as in Figures 7-5 and 7-6. But now we add a labor supply curve (N_0^s). This slopes upward, indicating that more people will be willing to take jobs at a higher real wage rate. Whenever an event pushes the economy away from point B, there is pressure for the real wage rate to change, as shown by the arrows.

The equilibrium real wage rate is the real wage rate located where the labor demand curve crosses the labor supply curve. Such an intersection occurs at point B in Figure 7-7, with an equilibrium level of employment (N_0) and an equilibrium real wage (W_0/P_0). The diagram poses a dilemma for firms, however. If firms are to raise employment from N_0 to N_1, the real wage rate must be reduced, as shown at point C. But point C does not lie on the labor supply curve.

Employers need to find some factor that will make workers willing to provide more work than shown by their labor supply curve. Otherwise, we would never observe changes in employment, nor changes in real GDP, over the business cycle.

Labor contracts and wage bargaining. Labor contracts are one factor that would explain the fixity of the nominal wage in the short run. Labor unions negotiate contracts with business firms, and often these contracts set the wage rate for as long as three years, or even longer. Unions and firms agree to such contracts as a way of minimizing time spent on negotiating and arguing and to reduce the disruption caused by strikes that may occur when the two sides to the wage negotiation fail to agree. Many workers do not belong to labor unions but have their wages or salaries set for one year at a time. For instance, most college professors earn a fixed salary during the academic year from September to August of the next year, and sometime in the spring they learn what their salary increase will be for the following academic year.

When the economy operates with an employment and output level above the levels of N_0 and Y_0 that are consistent with labor-market equilibrium, firms and workers know that the real wage is reduced below the equilibrium amount W_0/P_0 only temporarily. When the next wage change occurs, perhaps a year or even three years later, there will be upward pressure on the nominal wage rate to restore the equilibrium real wage rate. Similarly, in periods of weak aggregate demand when the economy is operating below the equilibrium levels of employment and output (N_0 and Y_0), the real wage is temporarily above the equilibrium amount W_0/P_0, and there will be downward pressure on the nominal wage rate to restore the equilibrium real wage rate.

7-7 Fiscal and Monetary Expansion in the Short and Long Run

In Chapter 4 we examined the effect of a fiscal stimulus, assuming that the price level was fixed, and we found that the fiscal stimulus normally raised real output. Now we learn that the fiscal stimulus causes both output and the price level to increase in the short run, but in the long run only increases the price level without increasing output.

In Figure 7-8, we begin in equilibrium at point B, with an actual price level equal to P_0. This is exactly the same as point B in Figures 7-5 and 7-6.

Initial Short-Run Effect of a Fiscal Expansion

Now a fiscal stimulus is introduced, in the form of an increase in government purchases that shifts the aggregate demand curve rightward from AD_0 to AD_1.

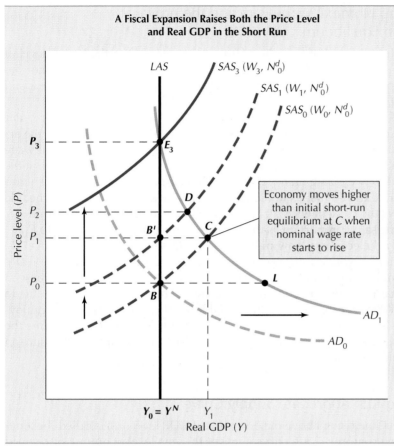

A Fiscal Expansion Raises Both the Price Level and Real GDP in the Short Run

Economy moves higher than initial short-run equilibrium at C when nominal wage rate starts to rise

Figure 7-8 **Effects on the Price Level and Real Income of an Increase in Planned Autonomous Spending from AD_0 to AD_1**

Higher planned autonomous spending shifts the economy's equilibrium position from the initial point B to point C, where both the price level and the real output have increased. Point C is not a sustainable position, however, because the real wage rate has fallen below the equilibrium real wage rate. Only at point E_3 does the actual real wage rate return to its initial equilibrium value.

Where do we find the new equilibrium levels of output and the price index? If the price level were to remain constant, we would move straight to the right from point B to point L. But the price level cannot remain fixed, because firms will insist on an increase in the price level in order to reduce the real wage and induce an increase in employment sufficient to raise the level of real GDP. In short, point L is not a point at which firms will be willing to produce.

Point C is at the intersection of the new AD_1 schedule and the SAS_0 schedule. The increase in government purchases has simultaneously raised the price level to P_1 and increased output to Y_1. This shift has occurred because higher aggregate demand has raised prices, stimulating business firms to produce more, at least as long as the wage rate fails to adjust.

Note that output has not increased by the full Chapter 4 multiplier based on a fixed price level, the horizontal distance between B and L. Instead, point C lies northwest of the constant price point L, because the higher price level at C reduces the real money supply and hence the demand for commodities. The situation illustrated in Figure 7-8 at point C would result from any stimulative factor that raises aggregate demand, as summarized in the box on p. 202. As long as the SAS curve slopes upward to the right, any of these changes will shift the AD curve rightward and simultaneously raise both output and prices to point C.

The Rising Nominal Wage Rate and the Arrival at Long-Run Equilibrium

Point C is not the end of the adjustment of the economy to the higher level of government purchases. Business firms are satisfied but workers are not because the price level has risen from P_0 to P_1, while the nominal wage rate is still stuck at W_0. The real wage rate has decreased to W_0/P_1.

Each SAS curve assumes that the nominal wage rate is fixed at a particular value, which is W_0 for the supply curve SAS_0. Once workers learn that the actual price level has risen, they will discover to their dismay that the real wage rate has fallen. To achieve a return of their real wage to the original level, at the next round of wage bargaining, workers will insist on an increase in the nominal wage rate to W_1. Just as in Figure 7-6, the new aggregate supply schedule SAS_1 shows the consequences of an increase in the nominal wage rate from W_0 to W_1, in the same proportion as the increase of the price level from P_0 to P_1.

Clearly the economy now moves to point D, with a higher price level P_2. But at point D workers are upset once again. The real wage rate is W_1/P_2, lower than the equilibrium real wage rate. Again they insist on an increase in the nominal wage rate. Eventually the economy must slide up the AD_1 line to point E_3. Why? Because only at the initial level of real GDP (Y_0) and employment (N_0) is the real wage rate at its equilibrium value (W_0/P_0). Any time the economy is operating in the area to the right of Y_0, there is upward pressure on the nominal wage rate, and SAS will shift up.

The Long-Run Aggregate Supply Curve

The vertical line rising above the original real GDP level (Y_0) is called the long-run aggregate supply (LAS) curve. Only at this one level of output, also called natural real GDP (Y^N), is the labor market in equilibrium at the original real wage (W_0/P_0). This is the only level of output where there is no pressure for change in the real wage, since this is the only level of output (and employment) where business firms are willing to produce and where workers are content with the real wage rate. This point of equilibrium in the labor market is where the labor supply and demand curves cross (in Figure 7-7). *Thus, only at the natural level of real GDP (Y^N) is the actual real wage rate equal to the equilibrium real wage rate. The vertical LAS line shows all the possible combinations of the price level (P) and natural real GDP (Y^N).* It was initially defined on p. 198.

Short-Run and Long-Run Equilibrium

Short-run equilibrium occurs at the point where the aggregate demand curve crosses the short-run aggregate supply curve.

The economy is in **short-run equilibrium** when two conditions are satisfied. First, the level of output produced must be enough to balance the demand for commodities. This first condition is satisfied at any point along the appropriate AD curve. Second, the price level P must be sufficient to make firms both able and willing to produce the level of output specified along the AD curve. This can happen only along a short-run supply (SAS) curve specified for a particular nominal wage rate (W_0).

Long-run equilibrium is a situation in which labor input is the amount voluntarily supplied and demanded at the equilibrium real wage rate.

The economy is in **long-run equilibrium** only when all the conditions for a short-run equilibrium are satisfied, and, in addition, the real wage rate is at its equilibrium value. In Figure 7-8, long-run equilibrium occurs only where all three schedules—AD, SAS, and LAS—intersect. The reason why the economy does not move immediately to its new long-run equilibrium following an AD

Monetary Impotence and the Failure of Self-Correction in Extreme Cases

We can use the aggregate demand and supply curves to illustrate Keynes's analysis of the high unemployment that bedeviled the world's economy in the 1930s. For Keynes, the economic problem could be divided into two categories: one concerning demand and one concerning supply. The demand problem was the possibility of **monetary impotence,** while the supply problem was that of **rigid wages.**

Monetary impotence is the failure of real GDP to respond to an increase in the real money supply.

Rigid wages refers to the failure of the nominal wage rate to adjust by the amount needed to maintain equilibrium in the labor market.

Unresponsive expenditures: The vertical *IS* curve. As we learned in Section 4-8 on pp. 109–12, increases in the real money supply (M^s/P) can have either strong or weak effects, depending on the shapes of the *IS* and *LM* curves. One case of monetary impotence occurs when the *IS* curve is vertical. Any change in the nominal money supply shifts the *LM* curve up and down along the vertical *IS* curve, leaving real GDP unaffected. Just as important, any decline in the price level (P) that raises the real money supply (M^s/P) leaves real GDP unaffected.

We examined a vertical *IS* curve in Figure 4-7; now, in Figure 7-10, we observe its implications for the aggregate demand curve. If *IS* is vertical at an income level like Y', then a decline in P has no power to raise real GDP above Y', so the aggregate demand curve is the vertical line AD' in Figure 7-10. Shown for contrast in Figure 7-10 is a normally sloped AD_0 curve, copied from Figure 7-8.

The liquidity trap: A horizontal *LM* curve. The same problem of a vertical AD' curve may occur if there is a horizontal *LM* curve and *if the* IS *curve intersects this horizontal* LM *curve to the left of* Y^N (a nearly horizontal *LM* curve was illustrated in the bottom frame of Figure 4-8). In this case, an increase in M^s/P does not shift the *LM* curve down. Real GDP is stuck at, for example, point Y', where the horizontal *LM* curve crosses the normally sloped *IS* curve. Again, the aggregate demand curve is vertical, as in Figure 7-10.

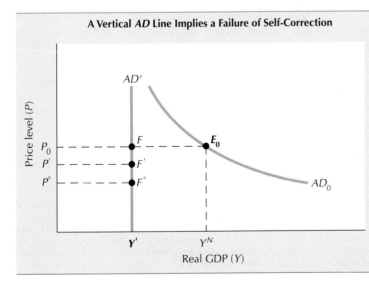

A Vertical *AD* Line Implies a Failure of Self-Correction

Figure 7-10 The Lack of Effect of a Drop in the Price Level When There Is a Failure of Self-Correction

The conditions of a failure of self-correction are either (1) a vertical *IS* curve that lies to the left of Y^N, or (2) a normal *IS* curve that intersects a horizontal *LM* curve to the left of Y^N. With a failure of self-correction, the aggregate demand schedule is a vertical line like AD', in contrast to the normally sloped AD_0 curve. Because of a failure of self-correction, the higher real money supply is unable to stimulate the economy; thus, a decline in the price level just moves the economy down from F to F' to F''.

Monetary impotence and a failure of self-correction arise when there is a vertical *IS* or horizontal *LM* curve.[5] In either case, the classical cure-all of deflation cannot remedy a cyclical recession or depression. In Figure 7-10, the price level can fall continuously, from P_0 to P' to P'', yet real GDP remains stuck at Y'. The economy just moves downward vertically from point F to F' to F'', without any rightward motion, as would be needed to return the economy from the depression level of real GDP (Y') to the desired level of real GDP (Y^N).

Fiscal Policy and the Real Balance Effect

The crucial problem that makes the *AD'* curve in Figure 7-10 lie to the left of natural real GDP (Y^N) is low business and consumer confidence. How can confidence be revived? All problems disappear if planned spending can be raised far enough to make the *IS* curve intersect *LM* at or to the right of Y^N. For this reason, Keynes believed that fiscal policy, which can shift the *IS* curve, is the obvious antidepression tool to use.

Stabilizing effects of falling prices. In theory at least, government action to shift the *AD* curve may not be necessary, because the *AD* curve may have a negative slope like the curve AD_0. There are two mechanisms by which lower prices raise aggregate demand, and so far we have discussed only one of them.

The **"Keynes Effect"** is a name given to the normal role of falling prices in raising the real money supply and boosting output. We have learned that the Keynes Effect can be made impotent by a horizontal *LM* curve, which in turn is one of the causes of the vertical *AD* curve in Figure 7-10.

The **Keynes Effect** is the stimulus to aggregate demand caused by a decline in the interest rate.

The **Pigou Effect** or **real balance effect** is the direct stimulus to aggregate demand caused by an increase in the real money supply and does not require a decline in the interest rate.

But the **Pigou Effect** or **real balance effect** can come to the rescue. The real money supply is part of household wealth, and we have seen in Chapter 3 that an increase in household wealth stimulates autonomous consumption and shifts the *IS* curve to the right. As prices fall and real money balances rise, consumers feel wealthier and spend more. This is a simple idea, that as the prices of goods from toothpaste to cars decline along with the overall price level, consumers with a given amount of money in their pockets and checking accounts can afford to buy more real goods and services.

So far we have learned that the Keynes Effect and Pigou Effect can stabilize the economy when prices fall. Unfortunately, there are two additional effects that can destabilize the economy. These are the destabilizing effects of falling prices.

Destabilizing effects of falling prices. Unfortunately, the stimulative effects of price deflation are not always favorable, even when the Pigou Effect or

---

[5] A more precise definition of the conditions necessary for monetary impotence and a failure of self-correction is as follows: There must be (1) no effect of a change in M^s/P on the *IS* curve, and (2) the interest rate along the *IS* curve, where actual real GDP equals natural real GDP (Y^N) and that we can call r^N, lies below the minimum attainable interest rate along the *LM* curve, which we can call r_{min}. When the *LM* curve is not horizontal, r_{min} is zero, and condition 2 is satisfied whenever r^N is negative or whenever *IS* is vertical and lies left of Y^N (as in the top frame of Figure 4-8). When there is a liquidity trap, the *LM* curve is horizontal at the level of r_{min} and condition 2 is satisfied even with a normally sloped *IS* curve, as long as r^N is less than r_{min}.

real balance effect is in operation. There are two major unfavorable effects of deflation:

- The **expectations effect.** When people expect prices to continue to fall, they tend to postpone purchases as much as possible to take advantage of lower prices in the future. This decline in the demand for commodities may be strong enough to offset the stimulus of the Pigou Effect.

- The **redistribution effect** may be more important than the expectations effect. It is caused by an *unexpected deflation* that causes a redistribution of income from debtors to creditors. Why? Debt repayments are usually fixed in dollar value so that a uniform deflation in all prices, which was not expected when the debts were incurred, causes an increase in the real value of mortgage and installment repayments from debtors to creditors (banks and, ultimately, savers).[6] This redistribution reduces aggregate demand, since creditors tend to spend only a relatively small share of their added income, while debtors have nothing to fall back on and are forced to reduce their consumption to meet their higher real interest payments.

> The **expectations effect** is the decline in aggregate demand caused by the postponement of purchases when consumers expect prices to decline in the future.

> The **redistribution effect** is the decline in aggregate demand caused by the effect of falling prices in redistributing income from high-spending debtors to low-spending savers.

During the Great Depression deflation of 1929–33, for instance, the GDP price deflator declined by 24 percent. Yet the interest income of creditors hardly fell at all, from \$4.7 to \$4.1 billion (current dollars). Farmers were hit worst by falling prices—their current-dollar income fell by two-thirds, from \$6.2 to \$2.6 billion—and many lost their farms through foreclosures as a result of this heavy debt burden. Although many factors were at work in the collapse of real autonomous spending during the Great Depression, it appears that the negative expectations and redistribution effects of the 1929–33 deflation dominated the stimulative Keynes and Pigou Effects. The International Perspective box on pp. 224–25 looks further into the puzzle of why the Great Depression was worse in the United States than in other nations.

The expectations and redistribution effects are not just ancient fossils relevant only to the 1930s. In the early and mid-1980s, falling prices of farm products, farmland, and oil reduced the income of farmers, oil producers, and employees of farms and oil companies. Many of these people were severely hurt by falling prices, especially because in the 1970s some (especially farmers) had incurred a heavy burden of debt to buy high-priced farmland.

 SELF-TEST

Not only do falling prices and a depressed economy affect aggregate demand, but so do rising prices and prosperity.

1. Explain whether the Pigou Effect (real balance effect) stabilizes or destabilizes the economy when aggregate demand is high.

2. How does this effect occur?

3. Similarly, explain whether the expectations and redistribution effects stabilize or destabilize the economy when prices are rising.

4. Describe how these effects occur.

---

[6] A concise discussion of the consequences of these effects on the economy's self-correcting mechanism is contained in James Tobin, "Keynesian Models of Recession and Depression," *American Economic Review* (May 1975), pp. 195–202. See also Axel Leijonhufvud, *On Keynesian Economics and the Economics of Keynes* (New York: Oxford University Press, 1968), pp. 315–31.

Nominal Wage Rigidity

Keynes attacked the classical economists on two fronts. As we have seen, his first line of attack was the possibility of a vertical AD' line that fails to intersect the LAS line, creating monetary impotence and a failure of self-correction. His second line of attack was simply that deflation would not occur in the necessary amount because of rigid nominal wages. And if little or no deflation occurred, *the debate about the relative potency of the Keynes, Pigou, expectations, and distribution effects would become irrelevant.*

Figure 7-11 shows the effects of rigid nominal wages. In the right-hand frame the two aggregate demand curves, AD_0 and AD_1, are copied from Figure 7-9. They have the normal negative slopes. AD_1 lies to the left of AD_0 because consumer and business pessimism lowers the assumed amount of planned spending. The short-run aggregate supply curve SAS_0 is fixed in position by the fixed nominal wage rate (W_0). Starting at point E_0, the leftward shift in aggregate demand moves the economy to point A, where the new AD_1 curve intersects the aggregate supply curve SAS_0.

Keynes pointed out that the economy would remain stuck at point A even with the normally sloped aggregate demand curve AD_1. Why? If the nominal wage is completely rigid and never changes from the value W_0, then the supply

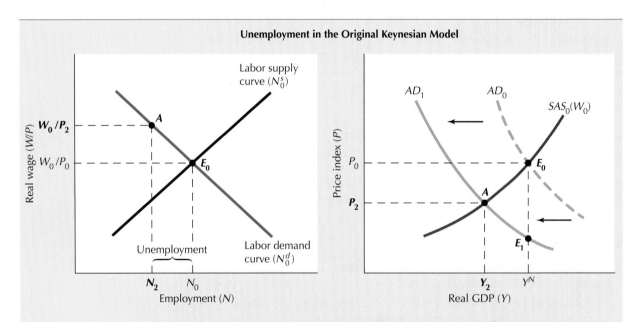

Unemployment in the Original Keynesian Model

Figure 7-11 Effect of a Decline in Planned Spending When the Nominal Rate Is Fixed at W_0

The short-run aggregate supply curve SAS_0 in the right frame is fixed in position by the assumption of a rigid nominal wage rate, W_0. The decline in planned spending shifts the aggregate demand curve in the right frame leftward from AD_0 to AD_1, and the economy moves southwest from point E_0 to point A. In the left frame, the reduction in the price level raises the real wage from the original W_0/P_0 to the new W_0/P_2, and the economy moves from point E_0 to point A. Unemployment is represented by the distance between N_2 and N_0.

curve is fixed as well at the position SAS_0. The price level would not fall below P_2. Hence the economy would not move from point A to point E_1, as required in the analysis of the classical economists.

Failure to attain equilibrium in the labor market.   Keynes's assumption of a rigid *nominal* wage differs from the description of the economy's adjustment toward long-run equilibrium in Sections 7-6 and 7-7, which assumed that there is an equilibrium *real* wage rate that equates demand and supply in the labor market.

Keynes's assumption of nominal wage rigidity fails to explain how or why the wage remains rigid. Its only virtue is that it provides an explanation of **persistent unemployment,** as at point A in the left frame of Figure 7-11, without requiring any special shape for the aggregate demand curve. But the arbitrariness of the assumption raises three important questions that will concern us in the next section as well as in Chapter 17.

> **Persistent unemployment** is a situation in which a high level of unemployment can last for many years, as in the United States from 1929 to 1941 and from 1980 to 1985.

1. Is the nominal wage rigidity assumption realistic? Did the aggregate supply curve in the Great Depression remain at a fixed position like SAS_0, or did it steadily shift downward and bring the economy to long-run equilibrium, as the classical economists would have predicted?

2. Is it possible to devise a convincing theory of business cycles without relying on either a vertical AD curve or rigid nominal wages? The Keynesian rigid nominal wage "story" raises a basic puzzle: Why do markets "fail to clear"? That is, why does the economy not operate continuously at the intersection of the labor supply and demand curves? Several prominent economists, particularly Milton Friedman, Robert Lucas, and Edward Prescott, have attempted to revive classical economics in a way that is consistent with observed business cycles yet allows for **market-clearing,** in contrast to the Keynesian tradition of **non–market-clearing.** We turn to these models in Chapter 17.

> The **market-clearing model** or theory holds that the economy is always in equilibrium at the intersection of the supply and demand curves, particularly in the labor market.

3. How do labor unions and current practices of wage negotiation relate to the Keynesian assumption of wage rigidity? Do they justify his assumption of non–market-clearing and support his explanation of persistent unemployment? This question is addressed in Chapter 17.

> The **non–market-clearing model** holds that the economy can be pushed off its supply and demand curves in the labor market and sometimes in other markets.

7-10   Case Study
What Caused the Great Depression?

This case study investigates several important aspects of the Great Depression years of 1929 to 1941. Three topics are given primary emphasis. First, why was aggregate demand so low? Is there evidence to support monetary impotence or a failure of self-correction? Second, did the economy's aggregate supply curve shift downward to provide self-correction, or did it remain stationary as it does in the right-hand frame of Figure 7-11 when the nominal wage is rigid? Third, was the nominal wage rigid, and did real wages fluctuate countercyclically?

Table 7-1 exhibits several important features of the period between 1929 and 1941. This twelve-year period is distinguished most by the unemployment

Table 7-1 Money, Output, Unemployment, Prices, and Wages in the Great Depression, 1929–41

Year	Money supply ($ billions)	Real money supply ($ billions, 1929 prices)	Real GDP	Real fixed investment	Output ratio (Y/ Y^N) (percent)	GDP deflator (1929 = 100)	Unemployment rate (percent)	Long-term interest rate	Average hourly earnings (dollars)	Average real hourly earnings (1929 dollars)
	(1)	(2)	(3)	(4)	(5)	(6)	(7)	(8)	(9)	(10)
1929	26.0	26.0	103.7	14.9	102.8	100.0	3.2	3.6	.563	.563
1930	25.2	26.1	94.8	11.4	90.8	96.3	8.9	3.3	.560	.581
1931	23.5	26.7	88.7	8.0	82.1	86.3	16.3	3.3	.532	.605
1932	20.6	25.5	77.2	4.5	69.0	76.2	24.1	3.7	.485	.600
1933	19.4	24.4	76.1	3.9	65.7	74.1	25.2	3.3	.457	.575
1934	21.4	26.0	84.3	5.2	70.4	78.3	22.0	3.1	.512	.623
1935	25.3	30.4	91.9	6.7	74.1	79.8	20.3	2.8	.524	.630
1936	28.8	34.4	103.7	8.9	80.8	80.7	17.0	2.7	.534	.637
1937	30.2	35.0	109.2	11.0	82.2	84.2	14.3	2.7	.566	.656
1938	29.8	35.3	105.4	9.1	76.7	81.7	19.1	2.6	.576	.681
1939	33.4	39.8	114.0	10.9	80.1	80.7	17.2	2.4	.583	.695
1940	38.8	45.8	123.7	13.2	84.0	81.9	14.6	2.2	.597	.705
1941	45.4	51.1	144.9	15.5	95.0	87.4	9.9	2.0	.655	.737

Sources: See Appendix A. The interest rate is series B-72 in *Long-Term Economic Growth* (U.S. Department of Commerce, 1970). Average hourly earnings are from Martin N. Baily, "The Labor Market in the 1930s," in James Tobin, ed., *Macroeconomics, Prices, and Quantities* (Brookings Institution, 1983), Table 1, p. 23.

figures shown in column 7, especially by the extraordinarily high level reached by the unemployment rate (25.2 percent in 1933), and the long duration of high unemployment (ten straight years, 1931–40, with unemployment above 10 percent). An obvious puzzle is why the economy was so weak, especially between 1934 and 1939. In 1939, *the real money supply (column 2) was 48 percent higher than in 1929.* Yet in 1939 real GDP (column 3) *was only 10 percent higher than in 1929.* In 1939 the unemployment rate was still 17.2 percent because real GDP barely kept up with growth in the working-age population.

Explanations of Weak Aggregate Demand

The Keynesian interpretation that the *IS* curve shifted far to the left is supported in Table 7-1 by column 4, which shows the collapse of real fixed investment from $14.9 billion in 1929 prices in 1929 to $3.9 billion in 1933, *a decline of 74 percent.* Also shown is the incomplete recovery of real fixed investment, with a value in 1939 that was still 27 percent below the 1929 level. The failure of in-

1940, even though Y/Y^N remained at or below 86 percent throughout that five-year interval.

Despite the absence of perfect price flexibility, the price level was not rigid during the Great Depression and did drop 26 percent between 1929 and 1933. The path from northeast to southwest to northeast reflects a regularity, as if the AD curve were following a well-marked highway. The bottom frame of Figure 7-12 represents a hypothetical interpretation of what happened. The AD curve in 1929 was close to the vertical LAS schedule, but by 1933 it had moved well to the left as business and consumer confidence collapsed. The actual location of the economy in 1933 suggests that the economy's aggregate supply schedule looks like SAS_0 of Figure 7-11, and so we have drawn in a positively sloped SAS_0 curve in the bottom frame of Figure 7-12.

Behavior of nominal and real wage rates.   The interpretation of the Great Depression contained in Figure 7-12 raises an obvious question: Why did the aggregate supply curve fail to shift downward to bring the economy to its long-run equilibrium level of output along the vertical LAS line at a lower price level? A fixed SAS curve requires a rigid nominal wage rate. Data on the nominal wage rate are included in Table 7-1, column 9.

By 1937, the nominal wage rate was back to the 1929 level, despite an unemployment rate of 14 percent. Thus, it is an exaggeration for the Keynesian model to treat the nominal wage rate as absolutely rigid. A decline did occur in 1931–33. But the nominal wage rate did not exhibit the continued decline after 1933 that would have been necessary to bring the economy back to natural real GDP through the classical mechanism of self-correction.

Policy failures after 1932.   As we have seen, there was a profound failure of monetary policy in 1929–33, as banks were allowed to fail and as the nominal money supply was allowed to decline. And, as shown in the box, the failure to devalue the dollar in response to the British devaluation of 1931 prolonged the U.S. depression, in constrast to the rapid recovery of the British economy.

But policy failures did not stop with the inauguration of President Franklin D. Roosevelt in 1933. The government could have pursued an aggressive fiscal expansion but did not. It failed to understand the difference between actual and structural budget deficits, as explained in Figures 5-2 and 5-3 on pp. 135–36. It was inhibited in raising government spending and cutting taxes by its fear of budget deficits, yet these deficits were caused by the weakness of the economy, not by fiscal expansion.

Just as serious an error was the failure to understand the role of falling wages and prices in promoting a recovery; the SAS curve needed to shift down but instead the government tried to push the SAS curve up. During 1934 and 1935 the National Industrial Recovery Act (NIRA) explicitly attempted to raise wages and prices. Although the NIRA was declared unconstitutional in 1935, it was succeeded in the next several years by alternative legislation aimed at boosting prices and particularly wages. ●

Summary

1. The aggregate demand curve shows the different combinations of real output and the price level that are consistent with equilibrium in the commodity and money markets. The position of the aggregate demand curve depends on planned spending and on the money supply.

2. A shift in aggregate demand may change the level of real output, the price level, or both. With a horizontal aggregate supply curve, only real output changes. With a vertical aggregate supply curve, only the price level changes. With a positively sloped aggregate supply curve, both real output and the price level change.

3. The short-run aggregate supply curve slopes upward because a higher price level reduces the real wage. This induces firms to hire more workers, and the resulting increase in output raises real GDP.

4. The equilibrium real wage rate is located where the labor supply and demand curves cross. If a shift in demand changes the price level, and hence pushes the real wage rate away from the equilibrium real wage rate, there is pressure for change in the nominal wage rate.

5. The position of the short-run aggregate supply curve for the economy depends on the nominal wage rate. When changing demand conditions raise the nominal wage rate, the short-run aggregate supply curve shifts up.

6. In the short run, a fiscal or monetary expansion raises both real output and the price level. However, the short-run change in real output puts pressure for change on the nominal wage rate and causes the short-run aggregate supply curve to shift. This pressure for change is eliminated only when real output returns to the value that occurred prior to the fiscal or monetary expansion.

7. The economy is in long-run equilibrium only at a single level of natural real GDP, where there is no upward or downward pressure on the nominal wage rate. In the long run, any change in aggregate demand changes the price level without causing a change in real GDP.

8. Classical economists believed that cycles in aggregate demand mainly affected the price level, not real output. The economy's self-correcting forces of price flexibility protected real output from fluctuations.

9. Keynes criticized the classical economists on two grounds. The first was that the aggregate demand curve might be vertical rather than negatively sloped, due to a failure of planned spending to respond to the interest rate (vertical *IS* curve), or to a failure of a higher real money supply to lower the interest rate (horizontal *LM* curve), or both. Pigou countered that falling prices raise wealth and spending, guaranteeing a negatively sloped aggregate demand curve.

10. Keynes also criticized the classical economists because he believed that nominal wages were rigid, preventing prices from adjusting sufficiently to return real GDP to the level of natural real GDP.

Concepts

aggregate demand curve
short-run aggregate supply curve
long-run aggregate supply curve
equilibrium real wage rate
short-run equilibrium
long-run equilibrium

countercyclical variable
self-correcting forces
quantity theory of money
monetary impotence
rigid wages
Keynes Effect

Pigou Effect or real balance effect
expectations effect
redistribution effect
persistent unemployment
market-clearing model
non–market-clearing model

Questions

1. Explain the difference between the aggregate demand curve developed in this chapter and the demand curve for a product (for example, movies) used in microeconomics.
2. How will the *AD* curve be affected if, all other things remaining equal, (a) the interest responsiveness of the demand for money becomes larger? (b) the income responsiveness of the demand for money becomes larger?
3. All other things remaining equal, which of the following changes would cause the *AD* curve to shift to the right? To the left? Make it flatter? Make it steeper? Leave it unchanged (that is, cause a movement along the *AD* curve)? (*Hint:* Explain how each change affects the *IS* or *LM* curves that lie behind the *AD* curve.)
   (a) an increase in the nominal money supply
   (b) an increase in foreign income
   (c) an increase in the income tax rate
   (d) an increase in the marginal propensity to consume
   (e) a decrease in the responsiveness of investment to changes in the interest rate
   (f) an increase in the price level
   (g) an increase in government spending
   (h) a decrease in the exchange rate
   (i) a decrease in consumer confidence
4. Explain the importance of the assumption of fixed *nominal* wages in the determination of the short-run aggregate supply curve.
5. Each point along the short-run aggregate supply (*SAS*) curve corresponds to a point on the labor demand curve. Using the *SAS* and Figure 7-7, explain whether workers are working more or less than they would like at points along the *SAS* where (a) actual real GDP is less than natural real GDP and (b) actual real GDP is greater than natural real GDP.
6. Describe whether the following variables increase or decrease when real GDP (*Y*) increases above Y_0 in Figure 7-5.
   (a) the price level
   (b) the nominal wage rate
   (c) the real wage rate
   (d) the level of employment
   (e) the demand for labor
   (f) the quantity of labor demanded
7. Explain whether the labor demand curve or labor supply curve shifts and how the equilibrium real wage rate changes for each of the following:
   (a) Concerns over homeland security reduce the amount of immigration by workers willing to work for less than present American workers.
   (b) Improvements in education raise labor productivity.
   (c) Higher oil prices force companies to switch to equipment and structures that save energy but simultaneously reduce labor productivity.
   (d) The government cuts unemployment benefits in order to reduce its budget deficit.
8. Explain with words and diagrams how each of the following events affects the *SAS* curve.
   (a) technology improves
   (b) the nominal wage rate decreases
   (c) the quantity of nonlabor inputs declines
9. Explain why relatively flat, as opposed to relatively steep, labor demand and short-run aggregate supply curves are more consistent with the empirical observation that there are relatively minor changes in the real wage rate over the course of the business cycle.
10. Assume that the aggregate demand curve shifts to the right through increased government spending. Assuming that the position of the *AD* curve changes, how does this event affect the government budget deficit and the foreign trade deficit?
11. Predict, with the aid of the *IS-LM* and the *SAS-AD* models, the short-run and long-run results of each of the following:
    (a) a decrease in the nominal money supply
    (b) an increase in net exports that results from a depreciation of the dollar.
    (*Hint:* Both models measure real GDP on the horizontal axis, so aligning the diagrams vertically will help you to see how they are related. Assume the economy is initially in long-run equilibrium at the natural real GDP [Y^N]. Also, remember that changes in the price level shift the *LM* curve.)
12. Is sustainable long-run equilibrium always reached when the *AD* and *SAS* curves intersect? Why or why not?
13. According to the view of the classical economists, there should have been a movement down the *AD* curve during the 1930s. Explain why this type of movement would require a shifting *SAS* curve. Did the *SAS* curve shift during the Great Depression in the way expected by the classical economists?
14. What is meant by the term *monetary impotence*? According to Keynes, what two conditions could lead to monetary impotence? Were either of these conditions present during the Great Depression?
15. Use the *AD-SAS* model to explain how differences in exchange rate policy, fiscal policy, and policy toward wages and prices made the Great Depression worse in the United States than it was in the United Kingdom or Germany.

16. Explain the role played by the interest rate in the Pigou Effect.

17. Why does the existence of a potent Pigou Effect guarantee a negatively sloped AD curve?

18. If policymakers were trying to decrease output in a period of continuing inflation, would the existence of the Pigou Effect have any impact? Can you explain, under these circumstances, how the redistribution effect and the expectations effect might affect the economy?

19. Given the existence of a Pigou Effect, or real balance effect, what do you predict will happen to the IS and AD curves if the economy experiences an unexpected increase in autonomous exports? (Assume that the economy begins in a long-run equilibrium position where AD crosses LAS.)

20. The whole controversy regarding the location of the IS curve and the potency of the real balance effect becomes irrelevant if nominal wages are rigid downward. Why is this so? Use the AD-SAS model to explain your answer.

Problems

*Indicates that the problem requires the Appendix to Chapter 4.

1. You are given the following equations for the aggregate demand (AD) and short-run aggregate supply (SAS) curves:

$$AD: Y = 1.25A_p' + 2.5M^s/P$$

$$SAS: Y = 11,250 - 20W + 1,000P$$

where Y is real GDP, A_p' is the amount of autonomous planned spending that is independent of the interest rate, M^s is the nominal money supply, P is the price level, and W is the nominal wage rate. Assume that A_p' equals 5,000, M^s equals 2,000, W equals 50, and natural real GDP, Y^N, equals 11,250.

(a) Use the values for the amounts of autonomous planned spending that is independent of the interest rate and the nominal money supply to derive the equation for the aggregate demand curve. Compute the amount of aggregate demand when the price level equals 2.0, 1.25, 1.0, 0.8, and 0.5. Graph the aggregate demand curve.

(b) Derive the equation for the short-run aggregate supply curve, given that the nominal wage rate equals 50. Compute the amount of short-run aggregate supply when the price level equals 2.0, 1.25, 1.0, 0.8, and 0.5. Graph the short-run aggregate supply curve.

(c) Given your answers to parts a and b, explain what the short-run and long-run equilibrium levels of real GDP and the price level are.

(d) Given your answers to part c, explain what the equilibrium real wage rate is.

(e) Suppose that autonomous planned spending increases by 800 billion so that $A_p' = 5,800$. Explain if this increase is the result of a fall in the exchange rate or a collapse in the housing market, which reduces household wealth and housing construction. Derive the new equation for the aggregate demand curve. Compute the new amount of aggregate demand when the price level equals 2.0, 1.25, 1.0, 0.8, and 0.5. Graph the new aggregate demand curve.

(f) Given your graphs in parts b and e, explain what the new short-run equilibrium values of real GDP and the price level approximately are. (Note: You can find the exact equilibrium values of the real GDP and price level by setting the equation for the new aggregate demand curve equal to the equation for the short-run aggregate supply curve and solve for the price level. Solving for the price level requires that you find the roots of a quadratic equation.)

(g) Explain what the new long-run equilibrium real GDP and equilibrium price level are, given the increase in aggregate demand. Explain how the short-run aggregate supply curve shifts as the economy adjusts to the new long-run equilibrium. Compute the new nominal wage rate at the new long-run equilibrium price level and derive the new short-run aggregate supply curve, given the new nominal wage rate.

(h) Suppose policymakers want to prevent a rise in the price level that would otherwise result from the increase in planned spending. Explain by how much fiscal policymakers would have to reduce planned spending in order to prevent a rise in the price level. Explain by how much monetary policymakers would have to decrease the nominal money supply in order to prevent a rise in the price level.

2. Use the information given at the start of problem 1.

(a) Suppose that autonomous planned spending decreases by 1,000 billion so that $A_p' = 4,000$. Explain if this decrease is the result of a fall in the exchange rate or a collapse in the housing market, which reduces household wealth and housing construction. Derive the new equation for the aggregate demand curve. Compute the new amount of aggregate demand when the price level equals 2.0, 1.25, 1.0, 0.8, and 0.5. Graph the new aggregate demand curve.

(b) Given your graphs in part a of this problem and part b of problem 1, explain what the new short-run equilibrium values of real GDP and the price level approximately are. (*Note*: Again you can find the exact equilibrium values of the real GDP and price level by proceeding as you did for part f of problem 1.)

(c) Explain what the new long-run equilibrium real GDP and equilibrium price level are, given the decrease in aggregate demand. Explain how the short-run aggregate supply curve shifts as the economy adjusts to the new long-run equilibrium. Compute the new nominal wage rate at the new long-run equilibrium price level and derive the new short-run aggregate supply curve, given the new nominal wage rate.

(d) Suppose policymakers want to prevent a rise in unemployment that would otherwise result from the drop in planned spending. Explain by how much fiscal policymakers would have to increase planned spending in order to prevent a rise in unemployment. Explain by how much monetary policymakers would have to increase the nominal money supply in order to prevent a rise in unemployment.

3. You are given the following labor demand and labor supply curves for the economy.

$$N^d = 250 - 2(W/P)$$
$$N^s = 3(W/P)$$

(a) Calculate the equilibrium real wage rate and the equilibrium quantity of labor.

(b) Suppose that the nominal wage rate equals 60. In the short-run, aggregate demand and aggregate supply are equal at a price level of 1.0. Compute the real wage rate. Explain where actual real output is relative to natural real output. Suppose that policymakers change aggregate demand so that in long-run equilibrium, the nominal wage rate stays at 60. What is the long-run equilibrium price level? Explain whether policymakers took actions that increased or decreased aggregate demand.

(c) Suppose that the nominal wage rate equals 56. In the short-run, aggregate demand and aggregate supply are equal at a price level of 1.4. Calculate the real wage rate. Where is actual real output relative to natural real output? Given the aggregate demand curve, suppose that in long-run equilibrium the price level equals 1.6. Calculate the value of the nominal wage rate that equates the demand for and supply of labor. How does the nominal

wage rate change and the *SAS* curve shift as the economy adjusts from its current short-run equilibrium to the new long-run equilibrium?

*4. The *IS* and *LM* curves for the economy have the following equations:

$$IS: Y = k(A_p' - 200r)$$
$$LM: Y = 5(M^s/P) + 500r$$

where $k = 2.5$, $A_p' = 5,200$, $M^s = 1,800$, and $P = 1.0$.

(a) Find the equilibrium level of output and the equilibrium interest rate.

(b) What are the equilibrium real output and equilibrium interest rate when the price level equals 0.8? When it is 1.2? When it is 2.0? Plot the aggregate demand curve based on these answers.

(c) Suppose that natural real output $[Y^N]$ equals 11,000. Given the aggregate demand curve from part b, determine long-run equilibrium real output, the interest rate, and the price level.

(d) Suppose that autonomous spending increases by 600 billion so that $A_p' = 5,800$. What are the equilibrium levels of real output and the interest rate when the price level equals 0.8, 1.0, 1.2, and 2.0? Plot the new aggregate demand curve.

(e) Assume an upward-sloping *SAS* curve that intersects the original *AD* curve at $Y = 11,000$ and $P = 1.0$. What will happen in the short-run to actual real output, the price level, and the real wage rate as a result of the increase in aggregate demand?

(f) Given the increase in aggregate demand, determine the new long-run equilibrium real output, equilibrium interest rate, and equilibrium price level. Explain what will happen to the nominal wage rate and the *SAS* curve as the economy adjusts to the new long-run equilibrium.

*5. A Pigou Effect is introduced into an economy similar to problem 4 by allowing A_p' to become price-dependent. We now have:

$$IS: Y = k(A_p' - 200r)$$
$$LM: Y = 5(M^s/P) + 500r$$

where $k = 2.5$, $A_p' = 4,600 + 600/P$, $M^s = 1,800$, and $P = 1.0$. As with parts a and b of problem 4, this problem aims to derive the *AD* curve.

(a) Find the equilibrium level of output and the equilibrium interest rate.

(b) What are the equilibrium real output and equilibrium interest rate when the price level equals 0.8? When it is 1.2? When it is 2.0? Plot the aggregate demand curve based on these answers.

(c) Is the *AD* curve flatter or steeper than the *AD* curve of part b of problem 4?

SELF-TEST ANSWERS

p. 201 (1) When the *IS* curve is steep, an increase in the real money supply causes output to increase less than when the *IS* curve is flat, implying a steeper *AD* curve. (2) When the *LM* curve is steep, an increase in the real money supply causes output to increase more than when the *LM* curve is flat (compare the top and bottom frames of Figure 4-7). Thus, when the *LM* curve is steep, a given price reduction (which raises the real money supply) leads to a greater output increase and a *flatter* *AD* curve than when the *LM* curve is flat.

p. 207 (1) A union concession shifts the *SAS* curve down. (2) A discovery of a giant oil field shifts the *SAS* curve down. (3) An increase in the money supply shifts the aggregate demand *(AD)* curve upward and thus causes a movement *along* the *SAS* curve. (4) An increase in the price level causes movement *along* the *SAS* curve.

p. 213 (1)–(3) All these events cause an upward shift in the aggregate demand *(AD)* curve. In long-run equilibrium, the price level and nominal wage level must increase by the same percentage, while the level of real GDP does not change. (4) This causes a rightward shift in both the *LAS* and *SAS* downward along the fixed *AD* curve, reducing the long-run equilibrium price level and raising real output.

p. 219 (1) The Pigou Effect stabilizes the economy when demand is high. (2) Rising prices reduce the value of real balances and real wealth, which in turn reduce consumption. (3) The expectations and redistribution effects destabilize the economy. (4) The expectations effect causes people to spend sooner, since they expect future prices to be higher. This boosts demand when demand is already high. Similarly, the redistribution effect causes income to be redistributed from savers who spend little to borrowers who spend much, thus boosting demand when demand is already high.

For additional practice and exploration, exercises that require the use of Excel are available at www.aw-bc.com/gordon.

Inflation: Its Causes and Cures

Why is our money ever less valuable? Perhaps it is simply that we have inflation because we expect inflation, and we expect inflation because we've had it.

—Robert M. Solow[1]

8-1 Introduction

Explaining the Inflation Rate: The Central Target of Monetary Policy

Throughout Chapters 3–6 the price level was assumed to be fixed, implying that the inflation rate was zero. In Chapter 7 for the first time the price level was allowed to rise or fall, responding to shifts in the aggregate demand (*AD*) curve and in the short-run aggregate supply (*SAS*) curve. The *AD-SAS* model implies that any event that causes a *single upward shift* in the economy's *AD* curve will cause a *single upward jump* in the price level. But **inflation** is a continuous increase in the price level, not a single jump. Thus sustained inflation requires a *continuous increase* in aggregate demand. To focus on the causes of a sustained inflation, in this chapter we will alter our *AD-SAS* model to explain the inflation rate (designated as lowercase *p*), instead of explaining the price level (designed as uppercase *P*) as in Chapter 7.

Inflation is a sustained upward movement in the aggregate price level that is shared by most products.

Inflation is important because if it continues at apparently small annual rates of change for a long time, it can cause the price level to double or triple. For instance, an annual inflation rate of 7 percent causes the price level to double in ten years and an annual inflation rate of 14 percent causes the price level to double in only five years. Rapid inflation erodes the purchasing power of the amounts parents have saved to send their children to college and of the amounts families have saved up for their retirement. Because of its insidious effects, which we investigate further in Chapter 9, a central goal of all central banks, including the U.S. Federal Reserve, is to control inflation by raising the interest rate when the inflation rate rises. Since the inflation rate is at the core of monetary policy goals, it is important that in this chapter we understand the causes of inflation and the constraints that the central bank faces in its attempt to control inflation.

We learn that an acceleration or deceleration of inflation can be caused either by shifts in aggregate demand ("demand shocks") or in aggregate supply ("supply shocks"). When supply shocks are absent, shifts in aggregate demand are the main cause of swings in real GDP and in the rate of inflation. Any attempt to sustain a level of real GDP above the natural level of real GDP will cause continuously accelerating inflation. The unfortunate corollary is that a reduction of inflation requires a transition period of recession in which actual

---

[1] *Technology Review* (December/January 1979), p. 31.

real GDP falls below natural real GDP. It is a central goal of the Fed to restrain inflation, and on repeated occasions during the postwar era, the Fed has been sufficiently concerned about accelerating inflation to institute restrictive policies that raise interest rates, in order deliberately to create a recession as needed to reduce the inflation rate. The impact of higher aggregate demand in creating inflation forces the Fed into a constant state of vigilance, to make sure that aggregate demand does not become excessive and to always be prepared to move to a restrictive monetary policy when needed.

The Volatile History of the Inflation Rate

The price level (P) is measured by the GDP deflator. The rate of inflation (p) is measured by the *percentage rate of change* of the GDP deflator, and this is plotted in the top frame of Figure 8-1. There we see that the inflation rate in the United States since 1960 has ranged from low values of around 1 percent per year in the early 1960s and again briefly in 1998, to high values of 10 percent per year in 1975 and again in 1982. How can these volatile ups and downs in the inflation rate be explained? One promising hypothesis is suggested by Chapter 7, where we learned that an increase in aggregate demand raises the price level permanently, and it also raises actual real GDP temporarily above natural real GDP. We begin our search for the causes of inflation in this chapter by examining the relationship between the inflation rate and the ratio of actual real GDP to natural real GDP.

How Is Inflation Related to the Output Ratio?

The **output ratio** is the ratio of actual real GDP to natural real GDP. In the absence of supply shocks, the inflation rate remains constant when the output ratio is 100 percent, accelerates when the output ratio is above 100 percent, and decelerates when the output ratio is below 100 percent.

The central theme of this chapter is that there is no unique relationship between inflation and the **output ratio,** that is, the ratio of actual real GDP to natural real GDP. The output ratio exceeds 100 percent when actual real GDP exceeds natural real GDP. The output ratio falls short of 100 percent when actual real GDP is less than natural real GDP.

The volatile history of the output ratio is plotted in the bottom frame of Figure 8-1. There we see five periods when the output ratio soared above 100 percent (that is, the percentage amount by which actual real GDP exceeded natural real GDP). The longest period with the highest output ratio was the Vietnam-era expansion of 1966–69, and the output ratio reached its second-highest peak at the end of the economic boom of the late 1990s. Smaller values of the output ratio above 100 percent are observed in 1972–73, 1978–79, and 1988–90. Sustained periods when the output ratio was below 100 percent are observed in the early 1960s, 1974–75, and especially 1982–83. The output ratio barely dipped below 100 percent in the recession period of 2001.

Demand Shocks and Supply Shocks

A **demand shock** is a sustained acceleration or deceleration in aggregate demand, measured most directly as a sustained acceleration or deceleration in the growth rate of nominal GDP.

Sometimes inflation and the output ratio rise or fall together. The economy's response to an upward shift in aggregate demand has already been examined in Figure 7-8; an increase in aggregate demand raises the price level and also raises the output ratio above 100 percent, but only temporarily. Soon the nominal wage rate begins to increase, and the output ratio gradually declines back to 100 percent, ending its temporary increase.

In this chapter we are interested in changes in the growth rate of aggregate demand, which we will call a **demand shock.**[2] When a positive demand shock

---

[2] The term "demand shock" was previously defined in Section 3-1 on p. 58.

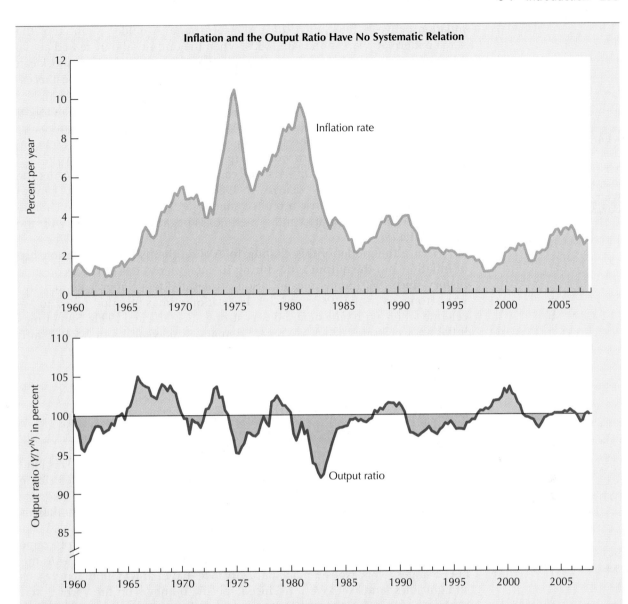

Figure 8-1 The Inflation Rate and the Output Ratio, 1960–2007

The top frame displays the inflation rate, measured as the percentage rate of change of the GDP deflator over the previous four quarters. The bottom frame displays the output ratio, that is, the percentage ratio of actual real GDP to natural real GDP. The high output ratio of 1965–69 caused inflation to accelerate during the late 1960s, and the same pattern is evident in the late 1980s. The low output ratio observed in the 1982–83 period explains part of the sharp drop in the inflation rate between 1981 and 1984. But sometimes the inflation rate and output ratio moved in opposite directions, as in 1974–75, 1979–81, and 1995–98.

Sources: Bureau of Economic Analysis *NIPA Tables* and research by Robert J. Gordon. Details in Appendix C-4.

occurs, inflation increases and the output ratio rises temporarily. The most important of these demand shocks occurred in the late 1960s, due primarily to Vietnam War spending, and in the bottom frame of Figure 8-1 we can clearly see the effect of the sustained high ratio in causing a steady acceleration of inflation between 1965 and 1970 in the top frame. A milder example of the same pattern appears in the late 1980s, when the output ratio increased above 100 percent, causing an acceleration of inflation. A negative demand shock can cause the inflation rate to fall, most notably in 1982–83 when the deepest recession of the postwar era caused a sharp reduction of the inflation rate.

A **supply shock** is caused by a sharp change in the price of an important commodity (e.g., oil) that causes the inflation rate to rise or fall in the absence of demand shocks.

We learn in this chapter that there is a second reason why inflation might be accompanied by a decline, rather than an increase, in the output ratio. An adverse **supply shock** can boost inflation while causing the output ratio to decline, as occurred when there were sharp jumps in the price of oil in 1974–75 and 1979–81. A beneficial supply shock can reduce inflation while causing the output ratio to increase, as occurred in 1986 and in the late 1990s. The central goal of this chapter is to use a unified model to explain why inflation sometimes is positively correlated and sometimes is negatively correlated with the output ratio.

We use the model of this chapter to explain the real-world relationship of inflation and the output ratio during the major episodes of U.S. economic history since 1960. Sometimes inflation accelerated when aggregate demand was strong, as in the 1960s and late 1980s. Sometimes inflation failed to accelerate when aggregate demand was strong, as in the late 1990s. Sometimes inflation accelerated when aggregate demand was weak, as in 1974–75 and 1980–81.

8-2 Real GDP, the Inflation Rate, and the Short-Run Phillips Curve

A *continuous* increase in demand pulls the price level up *continuously*. This kind of inflationary process is sometimes called demand-pull inflation, describing the role of rising aggregate demand as the factor "pulling up" on the price level. This type of inflation can be caused by large government budget deficits and excessive rates of growth of the money supply.

We see how demand-pull inflation works in Figure 8-2. Here the top frame repeats the aggregate demand and supply schedules from Chapter 7, with minor changes: For expositional simplicity, we have drawn both curves as straight lines, and we have introduced specific numbers on the vertical and horizontal axes. The horizontal axis now plots the output ratio, that is, the ratio of actual to natural real GDP. When the output ratio is 100 percent, actual and natural real GDP are equal. The economy initially is assumed to be at point E_0, where the AD_0 and SAS_0 curves cross. The initial values of the price index (P_0) and an index of the nominal wage rate (W_0) are both 1.0. The real wage rate (W_0/P_0) is initially at its equilibrium value of 1.0. The output ratio is 100 percent.

The short-run aggregate supply (SAS) curve has a positive slope, meaning that a higher level of output raises the price level. Each SAS curve is drawn for a particular nominal wage rate, shifting upward when the nominal wage rate increases, just as in Chapter 7. The long-run aggregate supply (LAS) curve is a vertical line at the point when the output ratio is 100 percent. As we learned in Chapter 7, there is upward pressure for an increase in the wage rate (and thus for an upward shift in the SAS curve), whenever the output ratio exceeds 100 percent. This occurs whenever the economy operates to the right of the vertical LAS curve.

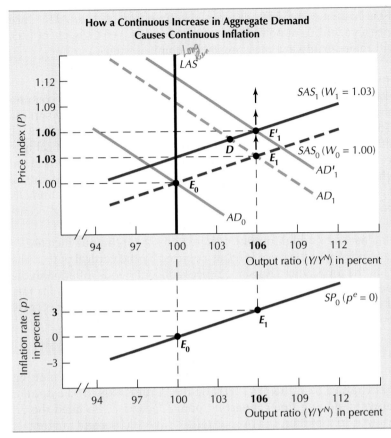

How a Continuous Increase in Aggregate Demand Causes Continuous Inflation

Figure 8-2 Relationship of the Short-Run Aggregate Supply (SAS) Curve to the Short-Run Phillips (SP) Curve

In the top frame, the economy starts in long-run equilibrium at point E_0. When aggregate demand shifts up from the AD_0 curve to the AD_1 curve, the price level moves to point E_1. The economy can stay to the right of the LAS line only if aggregate demand shifts up continuously from AD_1 to AD_1' to even higher levels of aggregate demand. The nominal wage rate adjusts upward whenever the economy is in the area to the right of LAS. Aggregate demand must keep ahead of the upward adjustment of the nominal wage rate, shown by the vertical path marked by black arrows. This continuous inflation of 3 percent per period is represented directly below in the lower frame at point E_1.

Effects of an Increase in Aggregate Demand

An increase in aggregate demand shifts the AD curve upward from AD_0 to AD_1 in Figure 8-2. The economy moves initially to point E_1, where the price level is 1.03. The higher price level puts upward pressure on the nominal wage rate to rise. Everywhere to the right of the LAS curve, including point E_1, there is upward pressure on the nominal wage rate, so gradually the SAS curve will shift up. When this occurs, we move to the new SAS_1 curve, which assumes that the nominal wage rate is 3 percent higher than it was along the original SAS_0 curve.

How Continuous Inflation Occurs

What happens to the output ratio and the price level as the result of the upward shift from SAS_0 to SAS_1? There are two possibilities, both illustrated in the top frame of Figure 8-2.

A one-shot increase in aggregate demand.   The first possibility is that aggregate demand remains at the level indicated by the AD_1 schedule. Then the upward shift of the supply curve to SAS_1 shifts the economy from E_1 northwest to point D. What must happen to prevent the output ratio from declining? The aggregate demand schedule AD must shift upward by exactly the same amount as the supply schedule SAS. Thus if the nominal wage rate increases from 1.00 to 1.03, shifting supply up from SAS_0 to SAS_1, output can remain fixed *only if the demand curve shifts up* again, this time from AD_1 to AD_1'. Once again the price level of 1.06 at point E_1' has raced ahead of the wage rate of 1.03, and there will again be upward pressure on the nominal wage rate.

A continuous increase in aggregate demand. To keep the output ratio from declining, aggregate demand must increase continuously; the economy will move straight upward along the path depicted by the black arrows in the top frame. The bottom frame shows the same process in a much simpler way. The horizontal axis is the same as in the top frame, but now the vertical axis measures not the price level but its rate of change, the inflation rate. Thus in the top frame when the price level is fixed in long-run equilibrium, as at point E_0, the percentage rate of change of prices (or inflation rate) in the bottom frame is zero, as at point E_0. The vertical axis measures the zero rate of inflation occurring at point E_0 as $p = 0$.

The maintenance of a high output ratio requires a continuous increase in aggregate demand and in the price level, as depicted by the vertical path of the black arrows in the top frame. This same process of continuous inflation in the bottom frame is illustrated by *the single point E_1*, where in each period the rate of change of the price level is 3 percent (just as in the top frame the price level rises by 3 percent between points E_1 and E_1').

The *SP* Curve

The bottom frame of Figure 8-2 differs from the top frame only by plotting the *inflation rate* rather than the price *level* on the vertical axis. In the bottom frame, the upward-sloping line connecting points E_0 and E_1 is called the *SP* line. It shows that to maintain the output ratio above 100 percent, aggregate demand must be raised *continuously* to create a *continuous* inflation (3 percent at point E_1).

Thus point E_1 in the lower frame and indeed all points with an output ratio above 100 percent share the characteristic that the economy is not in a long-run equilibrium, because the price level is constantly racing ahead of the nominal wage rate. The reason for the continuous upward pressure for higher wages is that labor contracts fail to *anticipate further inflation, and, as a result, they fail to specify in advance the wage increases needed to keep up with inflation.* Such wage contracts are said to have an **expected rate of inflation** of zero. This is abbreviated $p^e = 0$ and is included as a label on the *SP* line.

The term *SP curve* is used as an abbreviation for the term **short-run Phillips (SP) Curve,** which is named after A. W. H. Phillips, who first discovered the statistical relationship between real GDP and the inflation rate.[3] The *SP* curve slopes upward for the same reason that the *SAS* curve slopes up in Chapter 7. There are additional reasons for the upward slope of the *SP* curve. As output increases, the economywide inflation rate tends to rise, due to the

The **expected rate of inflation** is the rate of inflation that is expected to occur in the future.

The schedule relating real GDP to the inflation rate achievable given a fixed expected rate of inflation is the **short-run Phillips (SP) Curve.**

---

[3] Phillips showed that over 100 years of British history, the rate of change of wage rates was related to the level of unemployment. Because the change in wage rates, in turn, is related to inflation, and unemployment is related to real GDP, the research of Phillips popularized the idea, depicted by the *SP* curve in Figure 8-2, that a high level of output is associated with a high inflation rate. See A. W. H. Phillips, "The Relation Between Unemployment and the Rate of Change of Money Wage Rates in the United Kingdom, 1861–1957," *Economica* (November 1958), pp. 283–299. The curve should actually be called the Fisher Curve, since the relationship between the unemployment and inflation rates had been pointed out much earlier in Irving Fisher, "A Statistical Relation Between Unemployment and Price Changes," *International Labour Review* (June 1926), pp. 785–792, reprinted in *Journal of Political Economy* (March/April 1973), pp. 596–602.

sensitivity of raw materials prices to higher aggregate demand, and due to the tendency of business firms to boost prices more rapidly when aggregate demand is high.

The position of the SP curve is fixed by the rate of inflation that was expected at the time current wage contracts were negotiated (p^e), assumed in Figure 8-2 to be zero. Because the position of the SP curve depends on expectations, it is sometimes called the **expectations-augmented Phillips Curve**.

> The **expectations-augmented Phillips Curve** (another name for the SP curve) shifts its position whenever there is a change in the expected rate of inflation.

> ### ▶ SELF-TEST
>
> From what you have learned so far, try to generalize about the accuracy of the expected rate of inflation in the bottom frame of Figure 8-2.
>
> 1. In what area is actual inflation greater than expected inflation?
>
> 2. In what area is actual inflation less than expected inflation?
>
> 3. Where in the diagram does the expected rate of inflation turn out to be exactly right?

8-3 The Adjustment of Expectations

The remarkable thing about the inflation process illustrated in Figure 8-2 is that it presupposes that people never learn to *anticipate* inflation when they negotiate their labor contracts. Each period, the price level races ahead of the nominal wage rate along the path shown by the upward-pointing arrows, but people fail to build this inflation into their labor contracts *ahead of time*.

Changing Inflation Expectations Shift the SP Curve

Once negotiators anticipate inflation in advance, the short-run Phillips Curve shifts upward, as illustrated in Figure 8-3. There the lower SP_0 short-run Phillips Curve is copied directly from the bottom frame of Figure 8-2. Everywhere along the SP_0 curve, no inflation is expected. At point E_0 the actual inflation rate is just what is expected—zero—and the economy is in a long-run equilibrium position with the price level completely fixed. At point E_1, no inflation is expected ($p^e = 0$) either, but the actual inflation rate turns out to be 3 percent.

When an expected 3 percent inflation occurs ($p = p^e = 3$), the long-run equilibrium position occurs at point E_2. The entire short-run Phillips Curve has shifted upward by exactly 3 percent, the degree of adjustment of the expected inflation rate. The rise of the output ratio above 100 percent has led firms to raise their prices, and workers have obtained larger wage increases in newly negotiated contracts. Now an output ratio above 100 percent cannot be achieved along the new SP_1 schedule unless the actual inflation rate exceeds 3 percent, in which case the actual inflation rate would again exceed the expected inflation rate.

The economy is in long-run equilibrium only when there is no pressure for change. Point E_1 certainly does not qualify, because the actual inflation rate of 3 percent at point E_1 exceeds the zero inflation rate expected along the SP_0 curve. There is pressure for people to adjust their erroneous expectation ($p^e = 0$) to

Figure 8-3 Effect on the Short-Run Phillips Curve of an Increase in the Expected Inflation Rate (p^e) from Zero to 3 Percent

The lower SP_0 curve is copied directly from the bottom frame of Figure 8-2 and shows the relation between output and inflation when no inflation is expected ($p^e = 0$). But when people begin fully to expect the 3 percent inflation, the 3 percent actual inflation yields only the level of real GDP at E_2. The short-run Phillips Curve has shifted upward by exactly 3 percent, the amount by which people have raised their expected inflation rate. The vertical LP line running through points E_0 and E_2 shows all the possible positions of long-run equilibrium where the actual and expected inflation rates are equal ($p^e = p$).

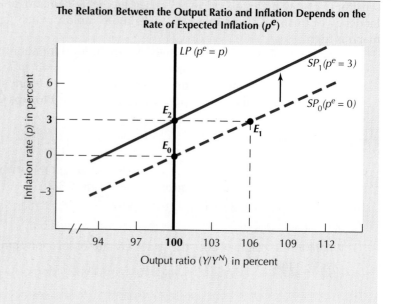

The Relation Between the Output Ratio and Inflation Depends on the Rate of Expected Inflation (p^e)

take account of the continuing inflation. At point E_2, the pressure for change ceases, because expected inflation has been boosted enough ($p^e = 3$). Wage agreements allow *in advance* for a 3 percent inflation. This keeps employment and output unaffected by inflation.

Thus point E_2 qualifies as a point of long-run equilibrium, because expectations turn out to be correct, just as does point E_0. The only difference between points E_0 and E_2 is the inflation rate that is correctly expected, zero at E_0 versus 3 percent at E_2. Otherwise the two points share the correctness of expectations and the same output ratio of 100 percent.

The *LP* "Correct Expectations" Line

The black vertical LP line connects E_0 and E_2 and shows all possible points where the expected inflation rate turns out to be correct. The term *LP line* stands for Long-run Phillips Curve and can be thought of as the "correct expectations" line. Everywhere to the right of the LP line, inflation turns out to be higher than expected, and the expected inflation rate will be raised. Everywhere to the left, inflation turns out to be lower than expected, and the expected inflation rate will be reduced. The vertical LP line showing all possible positions of long-run equilibrium is analogous to the vertical LAS long-run supply schedule of Chapter 7. Its message is the same: Real GDP (Y) cannot be pushed permanently away from its long-run natural level (Y^N), and the output ratio cannot be permanently raised above 100 percent.

What important message does the vertical LP line send to policymakers? It tells them that the best way to stabilize the economy is to adopt policies to keep the output ratio equal to 100 percent. If the output ratio is too high, inflation is likely to accelerate (as between points E_0 and E_1 in Figure 8-3). The appropriate response is that policymakers adopt restrictive policies that reduce back to 100

Learning About Diagrams: The Short-Run (*SP*) and Long-Run (*LP*) Phillips Curves

The Phillips Curve depicts the relationship between inflation and the output ratio.

Diagram Elements and Reasons for Slope

Both the *SP* curve and *LP* curve are plotted with the output ratio on the horizontal axis and with the inflation rate on the vertical axis.

The *SP* curve slopes upward because higher output boosts inflation through the same mechanisms that cause the short-run aggregate supply curve to slope upward in Chapter 7.

The *LP* curve shows the level of output when inflation is accurately anticipated ($p^e = p$). The *LP* curve is a vertical line, because accurate anticipations can occur only when the output ratio is 100 percent, that is, when actual and natural real GDP are equal ($Y = Y^N$).

What Shifts the *SP* Curve and *LP* Curve?

The crossing point of the *SP* curve with the *LP* curve shows the rate of anticipated inflation (p^e). An increase in p^e will shift the *SP* curve up, and a decrease in p^e will shift the *SP* curve down.

The *LP* curve does not shift its position. If there is an increase in natural real GDP, then actual real GDP must increase by the same amount for the output ratio to remain at 100 percent.

What Is True at Points Off the Curves?

A point below the *SP* curve represents an inflation rate below that anticipated by firms and workers. A point above the *SP* curve represents the opposite.

A point to the right of the *LP* curve but on the *SP* curve represents a situation in which actual inflation exceeds expected inflation. In such a situation, there is upward pressure on the expected rate of inflation. A point to the left of the *LP* curve but on the *SP* curve represents a situation in which actual inflation is less than expected inflation, putting downward pressure on expected inflation.

What Is True at a Short-run Equilibrium?

The economy is at a short-run equilibrium when it is operating on its *SP* curve.

What Is True at a Long-run Equilibrium?

The economy is at a long-run equilibrium when three conditions are met. First, it must be operating on its *SP* curve. Second, the inflation rate (p) must be equal to the growth rate of nominal GDP (x), which is required for real GDP growth to be zero. Third, the economy must be on its *LP* line along which expected inflation (p^e) is equal to the actual inflation rate (p).

percent. Similarly, if the output ratio is to the left of the *LP* line, then output is needlessly being wasted and jobs are being destroyed, and policymakers should adopt stimulative policies to spur a recovery in the output ratio that pushes the economy rightward, back to the *LP* line.

SELF-TEST

Assume that the economy is initially at point E_2 in Figure 8-3. There is a decline in aggregate demand, and the output ratio declines from 100 to 94 percent.

1. What happens subsequently to the expected inflation rate?

2. What happens to the position of the *SP* curve?

3. What happens to the position of the *LP* curve?

8-4   Nominal GDP Growth and Inflation

Once we have determined the value of p^e, the expected inflation rate at the time contracts were negotiated, we know which *SP* curve applies to today's economy. But we still have a major question remaining if we are to understand the determination of the output ratio and the inflation rate: *Where will the economy's position be along the current SP curve?* For instance, along SP_0, will the economy be at point E_0, point E_1, or some other point?

The *SP* curve is a single relationship between the inflation rate and the output ratio. We need to find an additional relationship, because two separate relations between inflation and the output ratio are needed to pin down the values of these two unknown variables.

Our model of inflation in this chapter uses a single variable to represent the growth rate of aggregate demand, and this is the growth rate of nominal GDP. First we review the relationship between the *levels* of nominal GDP, real GDP, and the GDP deflator. Then we introduce the relationship between the *growth rates* of nominal GDP, real GDP, and the GDP deflator (the growth rate of the GDP deflator is the same thing as the inflation rate).

Starting with the *levels* of these variables, we recall from Chapter 2 that nominal GDP (X) is defined as the price level (P) times real GDP (Y):

$$X = PY \qquad (8.1)$$

Just as real GDP is determined in the *IS-LM* model of Chapter 4 by such factors as real government spending and the real money supply, so nominal GDP is determined by nominal government spending and the nominal money supply. In addition, nominal GDP is determined by any other *shock* to aggregate demand discussed in the preceding chapters, including changes in tax rates, autonomous net taxes, the autonomous component of net exports, real wealth, and shifts in business and consumer optimism.

In this chapter we are interested in the *growth rate* of the price level, that is, the rate of inflation, and its relation to the *growth rate* of nominal GDP. The growth rate of any product of two numbers, such as P times Y in equation (8.1), is equal to the sum of the separate growth rates of the two numbers.[4] Writing the growth rates of variables in equation (8.1) as, respectively, x, p, and y, implies

$$x = p + y \qquad (8.2)$$

In words, this equation says that the growth rate of nominal GDP (x) equals the inflation rate (p) plus the growth rate of real GDP (y).

If the level of nominal GDP starts out at 100, as in period 0 in Table 8-1, then a growth rate of 6 percent will bring the level to 106 in period 1. As shown in Table 8-1, several different combinations of inflation and real GDP growth are compatible with a 6 percent growth rate for nominal GDP ($x = 6$). The lesson we learn from Table 8-1 is that for any given growth rate of nominal GDP, the rate of real GDP growth will vary inversely with the inflation rate.

For instance, alternative B shows that if inflation is 6 percent, higher prices will absorb all of the 6 percent growth of nominal GDP so that nothing will remain for real GDP growth. Real GDP remains constant, then, at its initial level of 100. Inflation "uses up" all of nominal GDP growth.

---

[4] The formal way to show this is to take the logarithm of the product of two terms, such as PY:

$$\log X = \log P + \log Y$$

Then the derivative of both sides is taken with respect to time:

$$\frac{d \log X}{dt} = \frac{d \log P}{dt} + \frac{d \log Y}{dt}$$

This is the same as the equality in equation (8.2), since x is defined as $(d \log X)/dt$ and likewise for p and y.

Table 8-1 Alternative Divisions of 6 Percent Nominal GDP Growth Between Inflation and Real GDP Growth

	Period	Level of variable			Growth rate of variable between periods 0 and 1		
		Nominal GDP (X)	Real GDP (Y)	GDP deflator (P)	Nominal GDP (x)	Real GDP (y)	GDP deflator (p)
Alternative A: Inflation at 9 percent	0	100	100	1.00	6	−3	9
	1	106	97	1.09			
Alternative B: Inflation at 6 percent	0	100	100	1.00	6	0	6
	1	106	100	1.06			
Alternative C: Inflation at 3 percent	0	100	100	1.00	6	3	3
	1	106	103	1.03			

In contrast, alternative C shows that if inflation is only 3 percent, then half of the 6 percent growth in nominal GDP will remain for real GDP to grow by 3 percent, from 100 initially to 103 in period 1. Here inflation uses up only half of nominal GDP growth.

Finally, alternative A on the top line of Table 8-1 shows that if inflation is 9 percent, then nominal GDP growth of 6 percent will not be sufficient to maintain real GDP constant at 100. Real GDP growth must be *minus* 3 percent, forcing the level of real GDP to fall from 100 in period 0 to 97 in period 1. Here inflation uses up more than the available rate of nominal GDP, forcing real GDP to fall.

Example: When inflation is less than the growth rate of nominal GDP, real GDP must rise, just as in alternative C. When inflation is greater than the growth rate of nominal GDP, real GDP must fall, just as in alternative A.

		x	$=$	p	$+$	y
Years like Alternative C	1977	10.7	=	6.2	+	4.5
	1984	10.6	=	3.7	+	6.9
	2007	4.9	=	2.7	+	2.2
Years like Alternative A	1974	8.1	=	8.6	+	−0.5
	1982	4.0	=	5.9	+	−1.9
	1991	3.3	=	3.4	+	−0.1

8-5 Effects of an Acceleration in Nominal GDP Growth

The basic theme of this chapter is that the inflation rate can be either positively or negatively correlated with the output ratio, depending on the evolution of demand shocks and supply shocks. The role of supply shocks is examined later

Figure 8-4 The Adjustment Path of Inflation and the Output Ratio to an Acceleration of Nominal GDP Growth from Zero to 6 Percent When Expectations Fail to Adjust

The economy initially is at point E_0 with actual and expected inflation of 0 percent. A 6 percent acceleration in nominal GDP growth moves the economy in the first period to point F. If the expected rate of inflation ($p^e = 0$) fails to respond to faster actual inflation (an unrealistic assumption), the economy eventually arrives at point E_3. Once we allow expectations to adjust, the economy will move to point E_4, which is both on the LP line and allows inflation to be equal to nominal GDP growth.

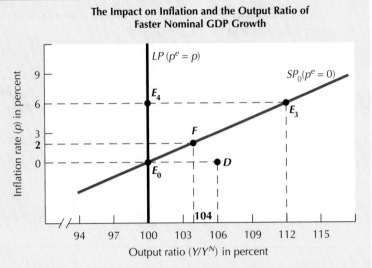

The Impact on Inflation and the Output Ratio of Faster Nominal GDP Growth

in this chapter. Now we are concerned with the role of demand shocks. As in the previous section, we measure demand shocks by a single variable, that is, changes in the growth rate of nominal GDP (x).

How do changes in nominal GDP growth (x) affect real GDP (Y) and the inflation rate (p)? We shall assume that initially the economy is in a long-run equilibrium in Figure 8-4 at point E_0. The actual and expected inflation rates are both zero ($p = p^e = 0$). Thus the SP curve that applies is SP_0, which assumes $p^e = 0$, and is copied from Figure 8-3.

If nominal GDP growth is also zero ($x = 0$), then the economy can stay at point E_0, since $x = p$. Why? As we can see by subtracting p from both sides of equation (8.2), when $x = p$, the growth rate of real GDP (y) must be zero:

$$y = x - p \tag{8.3}$$

$$0 = 0 - 0 \text{ (the specific values at point } E_0)$$

As long as $x = 0$, point E_0 is a long-run equilibrium, meeting the three conditions (1) that the economy is on the SP curve, (2) that $x = p$ (so $y = 0$), and (3) that expectations are accurate ($p^e = p$).[5] These are the same three conditions listed in the box on p. 241.

Now let us assume that nominal GDP growth (x) accelerates permanently from 0 to 6 percent. What happens? The economy can no longer stay at E_0, because it is no longer true that $x = p$. Instead, the 6 percent value of x exceeds the 0 percent initial value of p, and real GDP must grow. Equation (8.3) teaches us the following key rule about the adjustment of real GDP and inflation: *Real GDP must grow; that is, the growth rate of real GDP is positive (y > 0), whenever nominal GDP growth exceeds the inflation rate (x > p).*

Starting from E_0, an acceleration in nominal GDP growth from zero to 6 percent will slide the economy up the fixed positively sloped schedule SP_0,

---

[5] In order to link equation (8.3) to Figure 8-4, we need to assume that the growth rate of natural real GDP is zero ($y^N = 0$). The Appendix to Chapter 8 loosens this assumption that the growth rate of natural real GDP is zero and allows for any rate of change of natural real GDP.

since people initially expect an inflation rate of zero ($p^e = 0$). This extra 6 percent of nominal GDP growth is divided between inflation and output growth, according to equation (8.3). In this example, two percentage points of the total six percentage point acceleration in x are devoted to higher inflation at point F, and the remaining four percentage points are devoted to output growth, that is, raising the output ratio from 100 to 104. Point F is a position of *short-run equilibrium*, since it is on the SP_0 curve and it also satisfies equation (8.3).

The continuing adjustment.   What happens next? The economy cannot stay at point F, because F *is not a position of long-run equilibrium*. It violates two of the three requirements stated earlier for long-run equilibrium: that $x = p$ and that expectations be accurate.

Let us deal with the first of these issues. Real GDP grows whenever nominal GDP growth exceeds the inflation rate. This means that *real GDP must keep growing until inflation "uses up" all of nominal GDP growth*, that is, until inflation rises until it reaches 6 percent, the assumed permanent growth rate of nominal GDP.

While point E_3 plots 6 percent inflation, it is not satisfactory, because it fails to satisfy the second condition for long-run equilibrium—that expectations be accurate. The economy cannot stay at E_3 because this point has inflation racing along at 6 percent, while expectations of inflation (p^e) remain at zero. It is inevitable that labor contract negotiations will take the ongoing 6 percent inflation into account. As the rate of wage increase is raised to take account of the unfortunate reality of 6 percent inflation, the SP curve will shift upward.

The SP curve will stop shifting upward only when the economy reaches a long-run equilibrium, satisfying the three requirements that (1) the economy is on the SP curve, (2) $x = p$ (so the output ratio stops growing), and (3) expectations are accurate ($p^e = p$). While the first two conditions are met at point E_3, the third is satisfied only along the vertical LP line. Given the assumed growth rate of nominal GDP ($x = 6$), this occurs only at point E_4, where $x = p = 6$. Why? Only when $x = p$ does the output ratio stop growing, with $y = 0$.

To summarize this section, when the growth rate of nominal GDP accelerates (from zero to 6 percent in this example), the inflation rate must accelerate by the same amount, from zero to 6 percent. But the inflation rate does not respond instantly, because it takes time for workers and firms to raise their expected rate of inflation. During the time period when the workers and firms are gradually raising their expected rate of inflation (p^e), there is a temporary increase in the output ratio.

8-6 Expectations and the Inflation Cycle

Forward-Looking, Backward-Looking, and Adaptive Expectations

How high can real GDP be pushed by the acceleration in nominal GDP growth, and for how long? Everything depends on the speed at which p^e (the average rate of inflation expected when current wage and price contracts were negotiated) responds to higher inflation. This speed of adjustment depends on several factors.

Forward-looking expectations.   First, are expectations forward-looking or backward-looking? **Forward-looking expectations** attempt to predict the future behavior of an economic variable, like the inflation rate, using an economic

Forward-looking expectations attempt to predict the future behavior of an economic variable, using an economic model that specifies the interrelationship of that variable with other variables.

model. Contract negotiators with forward-looking expectations might reason, for instance, that an acceleration of nominal GDP growth from zero to 6 percent implies 6 percent inflation in the long run, and immediately raise the expected rate of inflation to 6 percent. The growth rate of the nominal wage rate would speed up by 6 percent, and this would shift the SP curve directly upward by 6 percent. The economy would move *immediately* from point E_0 to point E_4, without any interval at all with the output ratio greater than 100 percent.

Backward-looking expectations use only information on the past behavior of economic variables.

The rationality of backward-looking expectations. Another alternative, **backward-looking expectations,** does not attempt to calculate the implications of economic disturbances *in advance,* but simply adjusts to what has *already* happened. For instance, the backward-looking approach bases expectations of inflation on the past behavior of inflation, without any attempt to guess the future path of nominal GDP growth or its implications. There are two important reasons why rational workers and firms may form their expectations by looking backward rather than forward:

1. People may have no reason to believe that an acceleration in nominal GDP growth will be permanent. Nominal GDP growth has fluctuated up and down before, making individuals reluctant to leap to the conclusion that the change is permanent. They may prefer just to wait and see what happens.

2. Even if the acceleration of nominal GDP growth were permanent, the existence of long-term wage and price contracts and agreements, both formal and informal, would prevent *actual* inflation from responding immediately. Since people know about these contracts and agreements, they know that changes in wages and prices will adjust *gradually* to the acceleration in nominal GDP. The exact speed of adjustment cannot be predicted in advance, since it depends on many factors, including the average length of wage and price contracts and agreements. Further, *one* set of contract negotiators may have no idea whether *other* negotiators expect future nominal GDP growth to be 6 percent, 0 percent, or some other number.

Adaptive expectations base expectations for next period's values on an average of actual values during previous periods.

The most popular form of backward-looking expectations, and one that has been widely studied and verified, is called **adaptive expectations.**[6] The idea is simply that when people find that actual events do not turn out as they were expected to, they adjust their expectations to bring them closer to reality. Here is a particularly simple example of adaptive expectations. Assume that the expected inflation rate is always set equal to what actually happened last period. In Figure 8-4, the acceleration of nominal GDP growth from zero to 6 percent, which raises actual inflation from zero to 2 percent as the economy moves from point E_0 to point F, would cause the next period's expected inflation rate to rise by the same amount, to 2 percent. Here is the simple relation to remember: *This period's expected inflation rate equals last period's actual inflation rate, or $p^e = p_{-1}$.*

---

[6] The idea of adaptive expectations was first used in macroeconomics in a classic paper, Phillip Cagan, "The Monetary Dynamics of Hyperinflation," in Milton Friedman, ed., *Studies in the Quantity Theory of Money* (Chicago: University of Chicago Press, 1956), pp. 25–117.

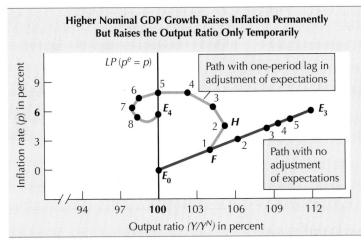

Higher Nominal GDP Growth Raises Inflation Permanently But Raises the Output Ratio Only Temporarily

Figure 8-5 Effect on Inflation and Real GDP of an Acceleration of Demand Growth from Zero to 6 Percent

When expectations do not adjust at all, the economy follows the blue path northeast from E_0 to E_3, exactly as in Figure 8-4. When expectations adjust fully to last period's actual inflation, the economy moves upward along the orange path going northwest from point H toward the long-run equilibrium at point E_4.

Adjustment Loops

The economy's response to higher demand growth depends on the adjustment of expectations. In Figure 8-5, two responses are plotted. The blue line moving straight northeast from point E_0 through point F to E_3 duplicates Figure 8-4. Expectations do not adjust at all, and the economy remains on its original SP_0 curve. As before, point E_3 is not a long-run equilibrium because it is not on the LP line.

The orange line shows full adjustment with a one-period lag. In each period the SP curve shifts upward by exactly the previous period's increase in actual inflation. Because actual inflation increases by two percentage points in going from E_0 to point F, then in the next period the SP curve shifts upward by two percentage points and takes the economy northward from F to H. But then expectations adjust upward again, because at H inflation has risen above the 2 percent people expected. Eventually, after looping around the long-run equilibrium point E_4, the economy arrives there. (The appendix to this chapter shows how to calculate the exact location of the economy in every time period along this path.)

The orange path exhibits several basic characteristics of the inflation process:

1. An acceleration of demand growth (as in Figures 8-4 and 8-5) raises the inflation rate and the output ratio in the short run.

2. In the long run, the inflation rate (p) rises by exactly the same amount as x, and any increase in the output ratio along the way is only temporary. The economy eventually arrives at point E_4.

3. Following a permanent increase in nominal GDP growth (x), inflation (p) always experiences a temporary period when it overshoots the new growth rate of nominal GDP. For instance, in Figure 8-5, x increases from 0 to 6, and eventually inflation settles down to 6 percent at point E_4. But along the adjustment path, actual inflation temporarily exceeds the final equilibrium value of 6 percent inflation. Along the orange path, for instance, inflation reaches 8 percent in periods 4 and 5. Overshooting occurs along this path because the economy initially arrives at its long-run inflation rate ($p = 6$) in period 3 before expected inflation has caught up with actual inflation. The subsequent points that lie above 6 percent reflect the

combined influence on inflation of (1) the upward adjustment of expectations and (2) the continued upward demand pressure that raises actual inflation above expected inflation whenever the economy is to the right of its *LP* line.

SELF-TEST

Look at the orange adjustment loop in Figure 8-5. Why is the line from point 1 to point 2 steeper than from E_0 to point 1?

8-7 Recession as a Cure for Inflation

How to Achieve Disinflation

Disinflation is a marked deceleration in the inflation rate.

In the theoretical model summarized in Figure 8-5, an increase in nominal GDP growth causes an acceleration of inflation. Now we need to find out how to achieve **disinflation**, that is, a marked deceleration in the inflation rate. It seems obvious that the most straightforward way of eliminating inflation would be *to set in reverse* the process that created the inflation. By causing demand growth (x) to slow down, the government can cause inflation to decelerate.

The "Cold Turkey" Remedy for Inflation

The **cold turkey** approach to disinflation operates by implementing a sudden and permanent slowdown in nominal GDP growth.

The response of inflation to a slowdown in nominal GDP growth is explored in Figure 8-6. This figure is identical to Figure 8-4, except that here we begin with 10 percent inflation. On the horizontal axis, we plot the output ratio. Expected inflation is assumed to be 10 percent along the SP_2 line, and the economy is initially at point E_5.

In this diagram, we assume that the government introduces a policy, sometimes called **cold turkey,** that suddenly reduces demand growth (x) from 10 to 4 percent. If people expect inflation of 10 percent because inflation last

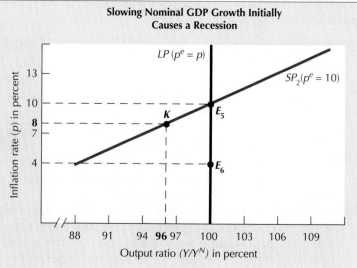

Figure 8-6 Initial Effect on Inflation and Real GDP of a Slowdown in Nominal GDP Growth from 10 Percent to 4 Percent

Initially the economy is in a long-run equilibrium at point E_5 with expected inflation (p^e) equal to the actual inflation rate (p) of 10 percent. When nominal GDP growth slows down suddenly and permanently from 10 percent to 4 percent, the economy initially moves to point K in the first period. Eventually the economy will reach long-run equilibrium at point E_6.

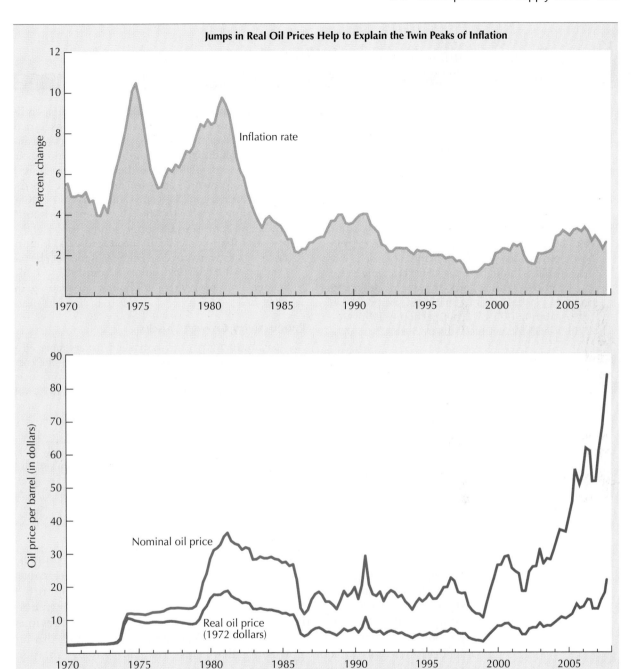

Figure 8-8 **Four-Quarter Growth Rate of the GDP Deflator and the Level of Nominal and Real Oil Prices, 1970–2007**

The top frame displays the inflation rate since 1970; this is the same series as was plotted in Figure 8-1. In the bottom frame, the nominal price of oil is compared with the real price of oil, using 1972 as a base year. Notice the upsurge in inflation in the top frame at the times of the two oil shocks in the bottom frame, that is, in 1974 and 1979–80. Notice also the low point of inflation in 1986 when oil prices tumbled, and also the low level of inflation and oil prices in 1998. The gradual rise in the real oil price during 2003–07 caused only a modest increase in the inflation rate plotted in the top frame.

Sources: Top frame: Bureau of Economic Analysis *NIPA Tables*. Details in Appendix C-4. Bottom frame: Energy Information Administration *Monthly Energy Review*. Details in Appendix C-4.

Types of Supply Shocks and When They Mattered

This box summarizes the four types of supply shocks and when they mattered. When they were adverse they pushed the inflation rate higher. When they were beneficial they pushed the inflation rate lower.

Oil Shocks

Since 1970, the price of oil per barrel has ranged from $2 to $100. Oil shocks matter because oil prices affect all energy prices, including gasoline, heating oil, natural gas, and coal, and because past increases in oil prices have been sudden. Oil prices matter because a sharp increase filters through the rest of the economy by raising the prices of airline fares, trucking prices, and the prices of plastics and raw materials. Oil prices were adverse during 1973–81, beneficial during 1981–86 and again in 1995–99, and then adverse during 2003–07.

Farm Price Shocks

The prices of farm products doubled between 1972 and 1974, helping to set off the rapid inflation of the 1970s. More recently in 2005–2008, farm prices have begun to rise due to the increased demand for corn as a key ingredient in ethanol, an alternative to imported petroleum.

Import Price Shocks

When the dollar depreciates, the price of imported products rise, and this raises the price of consumer products, since so much of U.S. consumer expenditure is on imported products. Imports are excluded from GDP (because although they are part of consumer expenditures, they are not part of domestic production or GDP), nevertheless higher import prices put upward pressure on domestic prices. When Volkswagen, Mercedes, and BMW raise their prices of imported cars, this gives General Motors, Ford, and Chrysler the opportunity to raise the prices of their domestically produced cars. Import price shocks were adverse from 1970 to 1980, beneficial from 1980 to 1985, adverse from 1985 to 1987, beneficial from 1995 to 2002, and adverse again since 2002.

Productivity Growth Shocks

Faster productivity growth makes workers more efficient and, for any given wage rate, reduces the cost of hiring them in terms of the output they produce. The productivity growth effect on inflation does not happen month-to-month or year-to-year but over long time spans of five to ten years. Productivity growth shocks were adverse from 1965 to 1980, modestly beneficial in the early 1980s, strongly positive from 1995 to 2004, and have been mildly adverse since 2004.

imports is found on pp. 168–71). This then allows domestic producers competing with imports to raise the prices. Thus a depreciating dollar can cause higher inflation and an appreciating dollar can cause lower inflation. Figure 8-8 shows that most recently, inflation was held down during 1995–2002 by a dollar appreciation and pushed up in 2003–07 by a dollar depreciation. Previous periods with major depreciations were 1970–80 and 1985–87, and during 1980–85 there was a major appreciation that helps to explain why the inflation rate declined so much during that period in Figure 8-8.

Productivity growth shocks. When productivity growth is rapid, the amount each worker can produce grows rapidly, and it becomes cheaper to hire workers per unit that they produce. The effect of productivity growth on inflation does not come from year-to-year movements but from changes in productivity growth over longer periods of five to ten years, often labeled the "productivity growth trend." This trend slowed down from 1965 to 1980, helping to explain the high inflation of the 1980s. The trend gradually recovered after 1980, helping to explain the rapid decrease of inflation during 1980–85, but surged in 1995–2004, helping explain why inflation was so low in the late 1990s (a graph of the productivity trend for the United States is in Figure 11-5 on p. 372).

Adverse and Beneficial Supply Shocks

Supply shocks can be either *adverse* or *beneficial*. An adverse supply shock is one that makes inflation worse while causing real GDP to fall, as in the case of sharp increases in oil in the 1970s. A beneficial supply shock is one that reduces inflation while causing real GDP to rise, as in the case of the sharp decline in oil prices in 1986.

Whether adverse or beneficial, supply shocks pose a difficult challenge for the makers of monetary and fiscal policy. Adverse supply shocks impose unpleasant choices on policymakers, who can avoid extra inflation only at the cost of lower real GDP, or vice versa. But even beneficial supply shocks may require policymakers to make choices.

Supply Shocks, the "Twin Peaks," and the "Valleys"

If demand shocks were the only cause of inflation, then we would observe periods after an acceleration of nominal GDP growth during which the output ratio would rise and the inflation rate would rise. Yet in other periods, the relationship between inflation and the output ratio would not be positive but rather negative. In the next section, we will learn to understand the source of this negative correlation as due to supply shocks that cause inflation to move sharply higher or lower, followed by a subsequent movement of the output ratio in the opposite direction. This explains the "twin peaks" of inflation in the periods 1974–75 and 1979–81. It also explains the "valleys" of low inflation in 1986 and 1997–98, both periods when the output ratio was rising.

Overall, we have seen that there are four types of supply shocks: oil, farm prices, import prices, and productivity growth. Each can be adverse or beneficial. An important reason that inflation was so high in the 1970s and early 1980s was that all four shocks were adverse during this period. Then inflation fell very rapidly after 1980, and this was due not just to tight monetary policy but to the fact that the oil, import price, and productivity growth shocks all turned from adverse to beneficial around 1980. Similarly, inflation was low despite a prosperous economy with a high output ratio between 1995 and 2000. In 2004–07, the oil price, import price, and productivity growth shocks were adverse, but inflation responded less to these shocks than in the 1970s.

8-9 The Response of Inflation and the Output Ratio to a Supply Shock

In Figure 8-8 we examined the relationship between oil price shocks and the U.S. inflation rate. There we saw that increases in the *level* of the real price of oil caused a change in the aggregate *rate of inflation*. How can this response of the rate of inflation be explained in terms of the *SP* diagram?

Supply Shocks and the Short-Run Phillips (*SP*) Curve

To see how supply shocks can shift the *SP* curve, we use Figure 8-9. The SP_2 curve in Figure 8-9 assumes that the expected rate of inflation is 6 percent. The vertical axis plots the aggregate rate of inflation, while the horizontal axis plots the output ratio.

Figure 8-9 The Effect on the Inflation Rate and the Output Ratio of an Adverse Supply Shock That Shifts the *SP* Curve Upward by 3 Percent

The economy is initially at point E_4, with an output ratio of 100 percent and both actual and expected inflation rates of 6 percent. The supply shock shifts the *SP* curve upward to SP_3. The movement of the economy depends on the policy response. With an accommodating policy, the economy moves from E_4 to point N, with a neutral policy to point L, and with an extinguishing policy to point M.

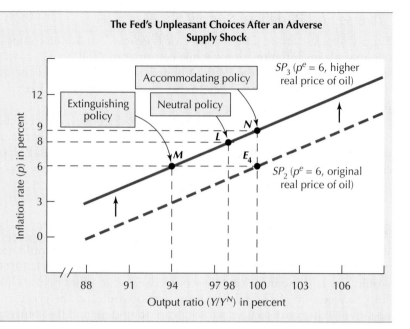

The Fed's Unpleasant Choices After an Adverse Supply Shock

Supply shocks shift the *SP* schedule.

As long as the real price of oil remains constant, the only factor that could make the *SP* curve shift would be a change in the expected rate of inflation (p^e). But if a supply shock changes the real price of oil, then we have a second reason why the *SP* curve might shift up.

Point E_4 in Figure 8-9 depicts a situation of long-run equilibrium. Actual inflation is 6 percent, and initially the rate of nominal GDP growth is assumed to be 6 percent. Since SP_2 assumes that expected inflation (p^e) is 6 percent, the condition $p^e = p$, required for long-run equilibrium, is satisfied.

Now let us assume that oil producers suddenly double the price of oil over the course of a year, as occurred in 1979, and let us assume that its action is sufficient *to add three extra percentage points to the inflation rate at any given level of the output ratio.* The three extra points of inflation are reflected in the upward shift of the *SP* schedule from SP_2 to SP_3. Where will the economy move along the new SP_3?

Policy Responses to Supply Shocks

The response of the economy to the adverse permanent supply shock depicted in Figure 8-9 *depends on the response of nominal GDP growth.* The government can implement policy measures to alter nominal GDP growth. These policy actions determine where the economy moves along the new SP_3 schedule.

Following a supply shock, a **neutral policy** maintains nominal GDP growth so as to allow a decline in the output ratio equal to the increase of the inflation rate.

Neutral, accommodating, and extinguishing policy responses.

There are three possible policy responses. The first is called a **neutral policy.** Such a policy would attempt to keep nominal GDP growth unchanged from the original rate (6 percent). This is shown by point L in Figure 8-9. Since real GDP growth, by definition, must be equal to nominal GDP growth minus the inflation rate ($y = x - p$), *a neutral policy makes the output ratio decline by the same amount as inflation increases.* Thus, at point L, the output ratio falls by 2 percent (from 100 to 98) and inflation rises by 2 percentage points (from 6 to 8 percent).[7] The sum of -2 and $+2$ is precisely zero, the assumed zero change in the growth rate of nominal GDP.

Does the government have any way to escape the simultaneous worsening of inflation and decline in the output ratio shown at point L? It can keep the output ratio fixed only if it is willing to accept more inflation. Or, it can keep inflation from accelerating above 6 percent only if it is willing to accept a greater decline in the output ratio.

An **accommodating policy** attempts to maintain the output ratio intact at point N. To do this, inflation must be allowed to rise by the full extent of the vertical shift in SP, so that inflation jumps from 6 to 9 percent per year. This acceleration of inflation requires an acceleration of nominal GDP growth from 6 to 9 percent per year.

An **extinguishing policy** attempts to eliminate entirely the extra inflation caused by the supply shock. This requires cutting nominal GDP growth by 6 percent to zero, which is enough to take the economy to point M, where the inflation rate is 6 percent, but the output ratio has fallen from 100 to 94 percent (instead of to 98 percent at point L). Why is the extra four-point decline in the output ratio necessary? To extinguish the extra two percentage points of inflation that occur at L compared to M, the output ratio must be cut by four percentage points, since the slope of the SP curve is assumed to be $1/2$ (two units in a vertical direction for each four units in the horizontal direction).

Following a supply shock, an **accommodating policy** raises nominal GDP growth so as to maintain the original output ratio.

Following a supply shock, an **extinguishing policy** reduces nominal GDP growth so as to maintain the original inflation rate.

What Happens in Subsequent Periods

If the hypothetical supply shock occurs for just one period, then in Figure 8-9 the SP curve shifts down to its original position (SP_2) after one period at position SP_3. The economy would then be free to return to the original output ratio and the original inflation rate. The indirect effect on the output ratio (Y/Y^N) and on the rate of inflation would last for just one period.

But the SP curve returns to position SP_2 only if *the expected inflation rate remains at 6 percent*. The expected inflation rate must not respond to the increase in the actual inflation rate that occurs at points L and N in Figure 8-9. Is this plausible? The response of the expected inflation rate depends on whether people view the supply shock as temporary or permanent and on whether labor contracts incorporate cost-of-living agreements (COLAs) that automatically boost wages by a percentage that is related to the inflation rate.

Why are COLAs crucial? Without COLAs, contract negotiators will recognize that it is possible for the economy to return to its original position (point E_4 in Figure 8-9) after the one-period effect of the supply shock. But with COLAs, the one-period increase of inflation (to point L or N) will be incorporated automatically into a faster growth of nominal wage rates *next period*. Contract negotiators in subsequent periods will see that COLAs have raised the rate of change of the nominal wage and will realize that this makes it impossible for the economy to return to point E_4. Their expected rate of inflation

---

[7] The text discussion of the graphical example in Figure 8-9 ignores the decline in Y^N that is likely to occur. The precise definition of a neutral policy is one involving no change in the excess of nominal GDP growth over the growth rate of natural real GDP from its initial value, assumed to be 6 percent ($x - y^N = 6$). This more precise definition is developed in the appendix to this chapter.

will shift up above the original 6 percent, and the *SP* curve will shift to a position above the original SP_2 in subsequent periods.

The policy dilemma. Thus we see that COLAs create a dilemma for the makers of monetary policy. COLAs imply that a permanent supply shock will permanently raise the inflation rate *unless an extinguishing policy response to the initial impact of the supply shock prevents any increase at all of inflation and thus prevents any increase at all in the rate of change of nominal wage rates.*

What should the Fed do when presented with this dilemma? It faces the classic trade-off between inflation and lost output. With even partial COLA protection for workers, a permanent adverse supply shock will permanently raise the inflation rate in the absence of an extinguishing policy. But this does not mean that the Fed should actually pursue such an extinguishing policy. The social costs of the loss in output may be severe, as Y/Y^N declines to point M in Figure 8-9, while the social costs of permanently higher inflation following a neutral or accommodating policy response may be relatively small. We examine those social costs in the next chapter.[8]

Why Beneficial Supply Shocks Help Us Understand the 1990s

The great macroeconomic puzzle about U.S. economic performance in the 1990s, especially in 1996–2000, is why the economy performed so well. By early 2000, the unemployment rate had reached a lower level than in any calendar quarter since 1969, while in 1997–98 the inflation rate was lower than at any time since 1961. How could both unemployment and inflation be so low at the same time? Our analysis of supply shocks provides the answer.

The policy options in response to beneficial supply shocks like those in the late 1990s are the same as for adverse supply shocks like those of the 1970s and early 1980s. A neutral policy maintains constant nominal GDP growth, thus causing the benefits of the supply shock to be split between lower inflation and higher real GDP. An accommodating policy requires a reduction in nominal GDP growth, so that the entire impact of the beneficial shock reduces the inflation rate and none spills over to boost the output ratio. In contrast, the third policy option, an extinguishing policy, would keep the inflation rate constant and allow the full impact of the shock to boost the output ratio.

Preview: A Graphical Summary of the Role of Supply Shocks

The evolution of the U.S. economy was dominated by the effects of supply shocks in 1974–75, 1979–81, 1986, and again in 1996–2000. In the first two episodes, the supply shocks operated in an adverse direction, primarily due to sharp jumps in oil prices but also due to increases in non-oil import prices in response to a decline in the foreign exchange rate of the dollar. Accordingly, the main response of the economy was for inflation to increase and for the output ratio to decline, as shown by the arrow marked "1970s" in Figure 8-10.

---

[8] The analysis of supply shocks in this chapter was introduced in two papers. See Robert J. Gordon, "Alternative Responses of Policy to External Supply Shocks," *Brookings Papers on Economic Activity*, vol. 6, no. 1 (1975), pp. 183–206, and Edmund S. Phelps, "Commodity Supply Shocks and Full-Employment Monetary Policy," *Journal of Money, Credit, and Banking*, vol. 10 (May 1978), pp. 206–21. The separate models in these two papers were merged and summarized in Robert J. Gordon, "Supply Shocks and Monetary Policy Revisited," *American Economic Review Papers and Proceedings*, vol. 74 (May 1984), pp. 38–43.

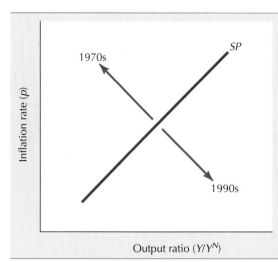

Figure 8-10 Effect of Adverse Supply Shocks in the 1970s and Beneficial Supply Shocks in the 1990s

The blue *SP* line shows the relationship between the inflation rate and the output ratio if there are no supply shocks. Adverse supply shocks, primarily increases in the real price of oil, moved the economy in an undesirable direction in the 1970s, with an acceleration of inflation and decline in the output ratio. Beneficial supply shocks, as discussed in the text, moved the economy in a desirable direction in the late 1990s, with a deceleration of inflation and an increase in the output ratio.

As we have seen, several supply shocks operated in the opposite (beneficial) direction during the late 1990s. These were oil prizes, import prices, and productivity growth. As a result, the main response of the economy was for inflation to decrease and for the output ratio to increase, as shown by the arrow marked "1990s" in Figure 8-10.

 SELF-TEST

Imagine that the real price of oil falls by half within a single year and exhibits no change thereafter.

1. With what policy response will the inflation rate be reduced by this event in the year of the change?

2. With what policy response will the output ratio increase in the year of the change?

3. With what policy response will there be no change in the inflation rate? No change in the output ratio?

8-10 Case Study

Why Did Inflation Creep Up After 2003?

Given how prosperous was the economy of the late 1990s, with a high output ratio (shown in Figure 8-1 on p. 235) and low unemployment rate (shown in Figure 8-13 on p. 267), it seems amazing that inflation was so low. The average inflation rate of the GDP deflator in 1996–2000 was a mere 1.64 percent per year, a full percentage point lower than in the much less prosperous period of 1990–95 when the average inflation rate was 2.65 percent per year. The full history of the inflation rate of the GDP deflator has already been shown twice in this chapter, in Figure 8-1 on p. 235 and in Figure 8-8 on p. 253.

Why Was Inflation So Low in the Late 1990s?

Shouldn't the demand shocks of the late 1990s, which pushed up the output ratio, pushed down unemployment, and created a boom in the stock market, have created extra inflation as a counterpart? Why did inflation fall rather than rise? We have seen in the last section that this resulted from the fact that three of the four types of supply shocks had turned in a beneficial direction, especially during 1995–99. The nominal price of oil fell to only $9.50 in late 1998, from as high as $36.77 in mid-1981. The price of imports was declining due to the appreciation of the dollar, and the economy was enjoying an unexpected revival in productivity growth that helped to hold down inflation.

But the good times came to an end. The economy fell into a mild recession during 2001, and the stock market (as measured by the S&P 500 index) fell by almost half between early 2000 and late 2002. Unemployment rose from below 4 percent to above 6 percent. But inflation was actually slightly higher during the 2001–03 period of weak employment and output than in the 1996–2000 period of strong employment and output, with respective inflation rates of 2.07 and 1.64 percent.

The Turning Point Toward Higher Inflation After 2003

The turning point for inflation came after 2003, when the average inflation rate increased from 2.1 percent per year in 2001–03 to a full percentage point higher, 3.0 percent per year in 2004–07. Yet, as shown in Figure 8-1 on p. 235, the output ratio remained between 99 and 100 percent, putting no upward pressure on inflation. What happened?

The answer again shows us how important it is to pay attention to supply shocks. Oil prices rose from an average of $26 per barrel during the year 2003 to a whopping $95 per barrel in December 2007. The exchange rate of the dollar depreciated by about 15 percent between early 2002 and late 2007, putting upward pressure on import prices and hence overall inflation. Finally, productivity growth, which had been extremely strong through mid-2004, fell by at least half in 2005–07. All of these shifts of supply shocks from the beneficial direction of the late 1990s to the adverse direction after 2003 and 2004 put upward pressure on inflation.

The Fed's Dilemma

The Fed reacted to the upward creep of inflation in 2004–07 by raising its short-term target interest rate from 1.0 percent in June 2004 to 5.25 percent in June 2006. But it refused to raise interest rates any further to foster its goal of restraining the inflation rate to roughly 2.0 percent. Why? In a controversial choice, the Fed decided to base its inflation goal on an alternative inflation rate *excluding the prices of food and energy*, the so-called **core inflation rate**.[9] Thus, the extent to which the increase of inflation after 2003 was due to higher energy prices was ignored by the Fed.

The Fed has been criticized by some economists, including the governor of the Bank of England, for paying so much attention to core inflation rather than

The **core inflation rate** is the inflation rate for all products and services other than food and energy. The core inflation rate attracts attention because roughly a 2 percent annual rate of core inflation appears to be the inflation goal of the Federal Reserve.

_____

[9] The Fed relates its inflation goal to the core (excluding food and energy prices) inflation rate for the deflator of personal consumption expenditures (PCE), which is about two-thirds of GDP. Differences between GDP and PCE inflation tend to be minor over periods from two to five years, although in the period 2001–07 the GDP deflator rose slightly faster than the PCE deflator.

total inflation, which is sometimes called "headline" inflation. Ignoring changes in food and energy prices, as is implied by a goal of core inflation, suggests that all changes in food and energy prices are temporary. On the contrary, oil prices exhibited a sustained rise from 2003 to 2007, and this may continue into the future. Many products included in the index of core inflation, such as airline fares and products made of plastic, are directly affected when the real price of energy rises permanently. ●

8-11 Inflation and Output Fluctuations: Recapitulation of Causes and Cures

In this chapter, we have learned that an acceleration of inflation can be caused by excessive nominal GDP growth and by adverse supply shocks. Supply inflation and demand inflation are interrelated because the extent and duration of the acceleration of inflation following a supply shock depends on the response of nominal GDP growth, which is controlled in part by policymakers.

A Summary of Inflation and Output Responses

Figure 8-11 provides a highly simplified summary of our analysis in this chapter. The figure presents four cases corresponding to (a) demand shifts alone, (b) supply shifts alone, (c) demand and supply shifts in the same vertical direction, and (d) demand and supply shifts in opposite directions. In our discussion we identify examples from U.S. history that illustrate the four cases.

Case A: Demand shifts alone. When we observe a marked increase in the output ratio with a modest or small increase in the rate of inflation, we can infer that there has been an increase in nominal aggregate demand growth with little if any shift in the SP curve. Expectations of inflation (p^e) remain roughly constant, and there are no supply shocks. The economy exhibited this type of response during 1963–66, when tax cuts and the beginning of Vietnam War spending, supported by monetary accommodation, boosted nominal GDP growth. A similar movement to the northeast occurred in 1987–89. Examples of a shift in a southwestern direction, with a deceleration of nominal GDP growth, occurred in the first few quarters of the 1981–82 recession, when there was a sharp decline in the output ratio with little downward response of the inflation rate, and a milder repeat of this episode in 1990–91 and 2001–02.

Case B: Supply shifts alone. The United States experienced a straight northwestward movement in 1973–74, when food and energy supply shocks, together with rising import prices and slowing productivity growth, sharply boosted the inflation rate, with a relatively small change in the rate of nominal GDP growth. As a result, the inflation rate and the output ratio moved in opposite directions and by about the same amount. In 1979 and 1980, a second supply shock had roughly the same impact. The most important examples of a southeast movement were caused by the 1986 collapse in the price of oil and by the beneficial supply shocks of 1996–2000 reviewed in the previous section.

A Summary of Inflation and Output Responses

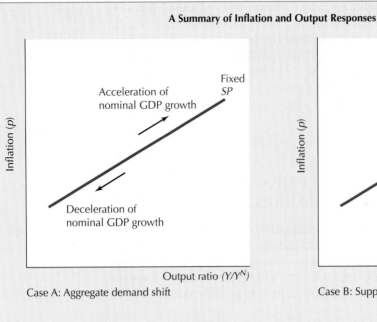

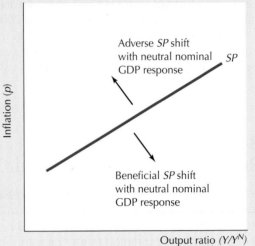

Case A: Aggregate demand shift

Case B: Supply shock

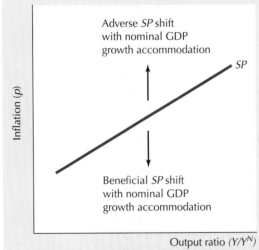

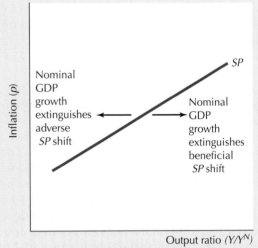

Case C: Simultaneous demand and supply
shifts in same direction

Case D: Simultaneous demand and supply
shifts in opposite direction

Figure 8-11 Responses of the Inflation Rate (p) and the Output Ratio (Y/Y^N) to Shifts in Nominal GDP Growth and in the SP Curve

In Case A, an aggregate demand shift moves the economy to the southwest, or to the northeast if there is no supply shift. In Case B, a supply shift moves the economy to the northwest, or to the southeast when nominal GDP growth is unchanged (a neutral policy response). Case C illustrates the northward or southward movement that occurs with an accommodative policy response to a supply shift. Case D illustrates the westward or eastward movement that accompanies a supply shift with an extinguishing supply response.

Case C: Demand and supply shifts in the same vertical direction. When we observe the economy move straight north on the diagram, with an acceleration of inflation but little change in the output ratio, we can infer that there is a simultaneous demand and supply shift. For instance, between 1967 and 1969 nominal GDP growth accelerated while the *SP* curve shifted upward in response to accelerating inflationary expectations. As a result of this, inflation accelerated while the output ratio remained constant.

Case D: Demand and supply shifts in opposite directions. The economy can move straight to the right when nominal GDP growth accelerates and cancels out the effect of a downward *SP* shift. This occurred in 1984, when the effect of falling inflation expectations in holding down the inflation rate was offset by rapid nominal GDP growth. A leftward movement can occur when nominal GDP growth decelerates while the *SP* curve is shifting upward. This occurred during the 1969–70 recession, when nominal GDP growth slowed while the *SP* curve was shifting upward as the expected inflation rate (p^e) continued its slow and delayed adjustment to the acceleration of actual inflation during 1966–69. This interpretation helps us understand why inflation in early 1971 was still as rapid as in 1969 despite an intervening decline in the output ratio. The same pattern was repeated in 1989–90.

 SELF-TEST

In Figure 8-11, which plots the inflation rate against the output ratio, it is possible for the economy to move in any direction. Can you explain why the economy would move in each possible direction:

1. North?	5. South?
2. Northeast?	6. Southwest?
3. East?	7. West?
4. Southeast?	8. Northwest?

Cures for Inflation

Just as excessive nominal GDP growth and adverse supply shocks are the fundamental causes of inflation, the basic cure for inflation is to turn these causes on their head. The reverse of fast nominal GDP growth is obviously slow nominal GDP growth. A decision to reduce the inflation rate by restricting the growth rate of nominal GDP can be both effective and costly, as in 1981–82 or, to a lesser extent, in 1990–92. Inflation can be cut markedly, but only at the cost of a substantial and prolonged slump in the output ratio and a substantial increase in the number of jobless workers.

But government policy against inflation is not limited to creating a deceleration of nominal GDP growth. Whether there are adverse supply shocks or not, the government can attempt to create beneficial supply shocks by eliminating or weakening price-raising or cost-raising legislation, and by creative tax and subsidy policy.

Sometimes government policymakers are just plain lucky, as when a beneficial supply shock occurs. The decline in oil prices in 1986 was one example of such a beneficial shock, and so was the role of several beneficial supply shocks in 1996–2000. In these episodes, it is important for policymakers to recognize their good luck and to prepare for a possible reversal in the sources of the beneficial shocks by not allowing the economy to become overstimulated. For instance, some observers think that the Fed should have raised interest rates sooner in 1998–2000 because the output ratio was too high and the stock market boom was unsustainable.

8-12 How Is the Unemployment Rate Related to the Inflation Rate?

Economists frequently discuss the "tradeoff between unemployment and inflation." Is there such a tradeoff? In this section we learn that there is a strong negative correlation between the unemployment rate and the *output ratio*, and so: *Everything we have learned in this chapter about the relationship between the output ratio and the inflation rate is true in the reverse direction for the relationship between the unemployment rate and the inflation rate. Since the relationship between the output ratio and the inflation rate can be positive, negative, vertical, or horizontal, the same is true for the relationship between the unemployment rate and the inflation rate. In short, there is no systematic negative relationship between the unemployment rate and the inflation rate.*

Changes in the Unemployment Rate Are the Mirror Image of Changes in Real GDP

At the beginning of this book, we learned that the unemployment rate and inflation rate are two of the most important concepts in macroeconomics. What have we learned thus far about the unemployment rate? Beginning in Chapter 1 (see Figure 1-2 on p. 7) we learned that the unemployment rate is *inversely related* to real GDP, or more precisely, to the *output ratio* (the ratio of actual real GDP to natural real GDP). Thus we can discuss the economy's prosperity as described either by *low* unemployment or a *high* output ratio. We can describe the opposite conditions of weak aggregate demand, recessions, and job loss either by *high* unemployment or a *low* output ratio.

Throughout Chapters 3–6 of this book, we focused on explaining business cycles in real GDP, caused primarily by the ups and downs in aggregate demand. *We have not required a separate theory to explain unemployment, simply because unemployment is inversely related to the output ratio.* Any factor that raises aggregate demand—whether events in the private sector of the economy such as business and consumer optimism or an increase in foreign income that raises net exports, or an event in the government sector such as higher government spending, lower tax rates, or a higher money supply—all of these both boost the output ratio and reduce unemployment. In this section, we will take a closer look at the mirror image relationship between the unemployment rate and the output ratio.

The Unemployment Rate, the Output Ratio, and Okun's Law

The close relationship between the unemployment rate and the output ratio is illustrated in Figure 8-12. The unemployment rate is plotted on the vertical axis, and the average unemployment rate since 1965 is indicated at a vertical

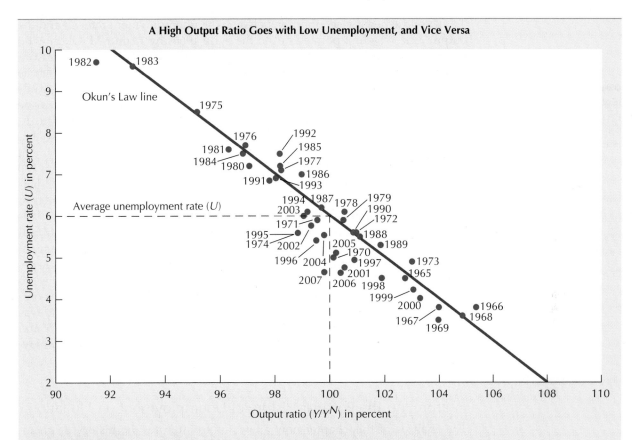

Figure 8-12 The U.S. Ratio of Actual to Natural Real GDP (Y/Y^N) and the Unemployment Rate, 1965–2007

This diagram illustrates that unemployment (U) moves inversely with the output ratio (Y/Y^N). In prosperous years, such as 1965–69 and 1999–2000, the observations are in the lower right corner, with a high output ratio and low unemployment. The opposite extreme occurred in 1982, with the observation plotted at the upper left corner. A recession occurred, the output ratio fell, and workers were laid off. The negatively sloped blue line expresses the relationship between U and Y/Y^N, sometimes called Okun's Law.

Sources: Appendix Table A-1. Bureau of Labor Statistics, Bureau of Economic Analysis, and research by Robert J. Gordon. Details in Appendix C-4.

level of 6.0 percent. The output ratio is plotted on the horizontal axis, and the long-run equilibrium value of the output ratio is marked at 100 percent.

In Figure 8-12 we notice the cluster of prosperous years, 1965–69 and 1999–2000, in the lower right corner, with values of the output ratio well above 100 percent and unusually low unemployment rates. The contrasting situation in the upper left corner occurred in the recession years 1975, 1982, and 1983, when massive layoffs caused the output ratio to fall and unemployment to rise. The negative slope of the blue line going through the points in Figure 8-12 just reflects common sense. When sales slump, workers are laid off and the jobless rate rises. But when sales boom and the output ratio is high, some of the jobless are hired and the unemployment rate declines.

The close negative connection between the unemployment rate (U) and the output ratio was first pointed out in the early 1960s by Arthur M. Okun, who was chairman of the Council of Economic Advisers in the Johnson administration. Because this theory has held up so well, the relationship is known as **Okun's Law.** U tends to follow the major movements in the output ratio; in addition, the percentage-point change in the unemployment rate tends to be roughly 0.5 times the percentage change in the output ratio, in the opposite direction. For instance, the downward-sloping Okun's Law line is drawn so that an output ratio of 100 percent corresponds to an average actual unemployment rate of 6.0 percent. A drop in the output ratio by 4 percentage points, from 100 to 96, would correspond to an increase in the unemployment rate of 2.0 percentage points, as indicated by the Okun's Law line going through 8.0 percent unemployment on the vertical axis and 96 percent on the horizontal axis.

Recall that the output ratio is defined as the ratio of actual to natural real GDP. When the output ratio is equal to 100 percent, the actual unemployment rate is equal to the natural rate of unemployment. Throughout much of the period plotted in Figure 8-12, the natural unemployment rate was very close to the average unemployment rate of 6.0 percent. In periods like 1965–69, the output ratio was well above 100 percent and the actual unemployment rate was well below the natural rate of unemployment. In periods like 1975 and 1982–83, the output ratio was well below 100 percent and the actual unemployment rate was well above the natural rate of unemployment.[10]

Interpreting the Postwar History of Unemployment and Inflation

The analysis of this chapter now allows us to interpret the history of unemployment and inflation since 1960, as displayed in Figure 8-13. We have already learned that when supply shocks are absent, an increase in aggregate demand boosts the output ratio and the inflation rate. Because unemployment declines when the output ratio rises, an increase in aggregate demand creates a *negative tradeoff* between unemployment and inflation. It is this negative tradeoff that restrains the Fed from allowing aggregate demand to increase so much that the unemployment rate is pushed substantially below the natural rate of unemployment.

When is the unemployment rate too low? This occurs whenever the output ratio rises above 100 percent, implying that the actual unemployment rate falls substantially below the natural rate of unemployment. As shown in Figure 8-13 by the blue line, the unemployment rate fell to its lowest level of the entire period during 1965–69, and the orange line shows the acceleration of inflation that occurred between 1965 and 1970. This was the classic period of the negative tradeoff between unemployment and inflation, but once inflation expectations and wages began to ratchet upward in response to accelerating inflation, the Fed introduced restrictive policies that reduced aggregate demand, and the unemployment rate shot up in 1970–71.

A similar and milder episode of relatively low unemployment in 1988–89 also pushed up the inflation rate in 1988–90 and again elicited a restrictive response by the Fed that reduced aggregate demand and led to the recession of

---

[10] *Review:* Natural real GDP and the natural rate of unemployment are both defined as a situation consistent with a constant inflation rate. See Section 1-3, pp. 5–8.

The Peaks and the Valleys

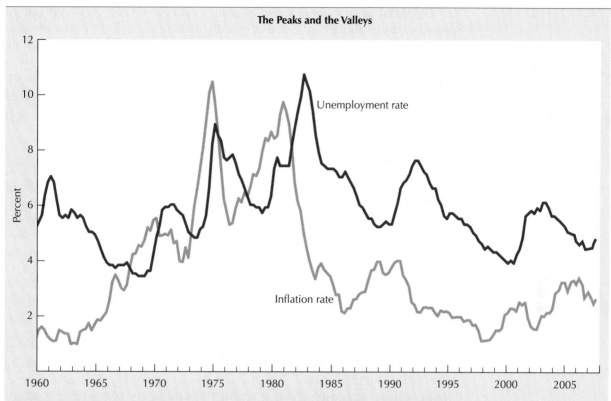

Figure 8-13 **The Unemployment Rate and the Inflation Rate, 1960–2007**

During 1963–70 and 1986–90, the inflation–unemployment relation was negative, as falling unemployment indicated a positive demand shock that boosted inflation. But in 1973–75, 1979–81, and 1997–98, the unemployment–inflation relation was positive, as an autonomous upward or downward movement of the inflation rate caused by supply shocks was followed by a movement of the unemployment rate in the same direction.

Source: Bureau of Labor Statistics and Bureau of Economic Analysis *NIPA Tables.* Details in Appendix C-4.

1990–91. The negative tradeoff between unemployment and inflation is also evident in the periods when high unemployment brought the inflation rate down, as in 1975–76, 1982–83, 1991–92, and 2001–02.

A central theme of this chapter has been that demand shocks and supply shocks have opposing effects on the relationship between the output ratio and inflation—demand shocks create a positive relation and supply shocks create a negative relationship. The same thing is true of the relationship between unemployment and inflation, but in reverse. There is a *negative tradeoff* between unemployment and inflation created by demand shocks, and a *positive relation* between unemployment and inflation created by supply shocks. This is evident in the 1970s, when sharp increases in oil prices in 1974–75 and 1979–81 created the "twin peaks" of unemployment and inflation. In each case, inflation soared first, which pushed the economy into recession. In 1975, the peak of unemployment came about six months after the peak of inflation; in 1982, the peak of unemployment came about 18 months after the peak of inflation. Thus inflation created these recessions, just as in the theoretical model of Figure 8-9 on p. 256.

Beneficial supply shocks also created a positive relation between unemployment and inflation in the late 1990s. By making possible a decline of inflation in 1997–98 despite high aggregate demand, supply shocks made it possible for the Fed to keep interest rates relatively stable, and as a result unemployment declined steadily from 1992 to 1999. These beneficial supply shocks were reversed in 2002–03, and inflation after 2003 was almost twice as high as in the late 1990s.

Implications of the Unemployment–Inflation Tradeoff

As we can see from Figure 8-13, unemployment is sometimes negatively related to inflation because of demand shocks and sometimes positively related because of supply shocks. In the absence of supply shocks, however, the negative unemployment–inflation tradeoff is the primary constraint that prevents the Fed from allowing aggregate demand to grow without limit. When the unemployment rate falls below the natural rate of unemployment, the Fed must raise interest rates in order to restrain the growth of aggregate demand and prevent an acceleration of inflation. Often the Fed's restrictive policies create a recession, as in 1969–70, 1981–82, and 1990–91, and the recession raises the unemployment rate and reverses the acceleration of inflation, working through the negative unemployment–inflation tradeoff.

The unemployment–inflation tradeoff suggests that the unemployment rate cannot be maintained below the natural rate of unemployment for any substantial length of time. To achieve a lower unemployment rate permanently, something must happen to reduce the natural rate of unemployment itself. Indeed, in the 1990s the natural rate of unemployment fell from roughly 6 percent to roughly 5 percent. In the next chapter, we will learn about both the costs of inflation and the determinants of the natural rate of unemployment, and about some of the factors that reduced the natural rate of unemployment after 1990.

Summary

1. The fundamental cause of demand inflation is excessive growth in nominal GDP. In long-run equilibrium, when actual inflation turns out to be exactly what people expected when they negotiated their labor contracts, the pace of that inflation depends only on the growth rate of nominal GDP.

2. In the short run, actual inflation may be higher or lower than expected, and real GDP can differ from long-run equilibrium natural real GDP. An acceleration of nominal GDP growth in the short run goes partially into an acceleration of inflation, but also partly into an increase in the output ratio, that is, the ratio of actual to natural real GDP. When expectations of inflation catch up to actual inflation, the economy will return to its level of natural real GDP.

3. The response of inflation to an acceleration in demand growth depends on the slope of the short-run Phillips Curve (SP) and the speed with which expectations of inflation respond to changes in the actual inflation rate. The flatter is the SP curve, the longer it takes for inflation to respond to faster nominal GDP growth, and the longer the temporary expansion of the output ratio.

4. A permanent end to inflation requires that nominal GDP growth drop to the growth rate of natural real GDP, assumed in the text to be zero. But this will cause a temporary recession in actual real GDP, the length and intensity of which will depend on the slope of the SP curve.

5. The highly variable inflation experience of the United States since the 1960s cannot be explained solely as the consequence of previous fluctuations in the growth rate of nominal GDP. Instead, supply shocks caused inflation to accelerate and decelerate independently of the influence of nominal GDP growth.

6. The main effect of an adverse supply shock is the impact on the inflation rate and on the output ratio. Policymakers cannot avoid a worsening of inflation, a

decline in the output ratio, or both. An accommodating policy keeps real GDP at its previous level, but causes inflation to accelerate by the full impact of the supply shock; an extinguishing policy attempts to cancel out the acceleration of inflation, but at the cost of a reduction in real GDP.

7. There are four types of supply shocks, each of which can be adverse or beneficial. An increase in the real price of oil, the real price of farm products, the real price of imports, and a decrease in the long-term trend in productivity growth are adverse supply shocks. The reverse changes are beneficial supply shocks.

8. Accommodation would be an attractive policy if the upward shift in the *SP* curve were expected to be temporary, and if expectations of inflation did not respond to the temporary jump in the inflation rate. But accommodation may cause a permanent increase of inflation if wage contracts have cost-of-living adjustment clauses that incorporate the supply shock into wage growth.

9. The low inflation rate experienced by the United States in the late 1990s reflected in part the role of beneficial supply shocks, created by favorable developments in the medical care and computer industries, as well as the falling real prices of energy and imports.

10. Demand shocks create a negative tradeoff between unemployment and inflation, and supply shocks create a positive relation between unemployment and inflation. The negative tradeoff created by demand shocks explains why the Fed has used restrictive policy in several episodes to create recessions in order to control inflation.

Concepts

inflation
output ratio
demand shock
supply shock
expected rate of inflation
short-run Phillips Curve
expectations-augmented Phillips
    Curve

forward-looking expectations
backward-looking expectations
adaptive expectations
disinflation
cold turkey
sacrifice ratio
demand inflation
supply inflation

neutral policy
accommodating policy
extinguishing policy
core inflation rate
Okun's Law

Questions

1. Use Figure 8-1 to discuss when, since 1960, the output ratio and the inflation rate moved in the same direction and when they moved in opposite directions.

2. In what ways are the *SAS* curve and the *SP* curve similar? In what ways do they differ?

3. Explain whether each of the following events causes a movement up or down along the *SP* curve or an upward or downward shift of the *SP* curve.
   (a) an increase in the rate of money supply growth
   (b) an increase in the inflation rate expected by workers and business firms
   (c) a decrease in production costs resulting from technological improvements
   (d) a decrease in nominal GDP growth

4. If the equilibrium real wage remains constant, what happens to the nominal wage when the actual inflation rate exceeds the expected inflation rate?

5. What are the three conditions for long-run equilibrium? What happens if each of the conditions is violated?

6. In Figure 8-4, why can't the economy move from point E_0 to point D when the level of real GDP increases?

7. Distinguish between forward-looking and backward-looking expectations. Which type of expectations would rational workers and firms be most likely to use? Explain why.

8. Suppose that when nominal GDP growth changes, workers and firms immediately adjust their inflation expectations so that $p^e = x$. Is this an example of forward-looking or backward-looking expectations? How does it alter the adjustment loops in Figures 8-5 and 8-7? How does it affect the output cost of disinflation?

9. Suppose that workers and business firms believe that the Fed will take action to prevent demand shocks from causing a permanent change in the inflation rate.
   (a) Will the short-run Phillips Curve shift when a change in the output ratio changes the inflation rate?
   (b) For workers and business firms to continue to hold these expectations, explain what actions the Fed must take when there is a positive demand shock and when there is a negative demand shock.

10. Assume that the output ratio initially equals 100 and that natural real GDP grows by 3 percent per year. If p^e remains constant and actual real GDP rises, what happens to the rate of inflation?

11. Explain what the four types of supply shocks are and when each type had an adverse or beneficial impact on the economy.
12. What differentiates accommodating, extinguishing, and neutral policy responses to an adverse supply shock? What happens to the rate of inflation and the output ratio in each of the three cases?
13. Under what conditions would a permanent supply shock cause a temporary increase in the inflation rate? If these conditions exist, are there any permanent effects of the supply shock on the economy?
14. Explain why inflation was so low in the late 1990s and why it rose after 2003.
15. Identify the combination of changes in nominal GDP growth and supply shocks that could account for each of the following observed changes in inflation and the output ratio.

(a) Inflation and the output ratio both increase.
(b) Inflation increases and the output ratio decreases.
(c) Inflation is constant and the output ratio decreases.
(d) Inflation decreases and the output ratio is constant.

16. Explain why the correlation between the unemployment and inflation rates can be positive, zero, or negative.
17. In each of the following cases, explain whether the policymakers' response to a beneficial supply shock was accommodating, extinguishing, or neutral.
    (a) The inflation rate fell, but the unemployment rate did not change.
    (b) The inflation and the unemployment rates both fell.
    (c) The unemployment rate fell, but the inflation rate did not change.

Problems

1. Suppose that natural real GDP is constant. For every 1 percent increase in the rate of inflation above its expected level, firms are willing to increase real GDP by 4 percent. The purpose of this problem is to learn how to draw the short-run Phillips Curve and to understand how either a change in the expected rate of inflation or a supply shock causes it to shift.
   (a) Given that the output ratio is initially 100 and the expected inflation rate equals 3.2 percent, calculate the rate of inflation if real GDP grows by 3.2 percent.
   (b) Given that the output ratio is initially 100 and the expected inflation rate equals 3.2 percent, calculate the rate of inflation if real GDP grows by 5.6 percent.
   (c) Given that the output ratio is initially 100 and the expected inflation rate equals 3.2 percent, calculate the rate of inflation if real GDP declines by 2.4 percent.
   (d) Given that the output ratio is initially 100 and the expected inflation rate equals 3.2 percent, calculate the rate of inflation if real GDP declines by 4.4 percent.
   (e) Use your answers to parts a–d to draw the short-run Phillips Curve, given that the expected inflation rate equals 3.2 percent.
   (f) Given that the output ratio is initially 100 and the expected inflation rate equals 1.4 percent, calculate the rate of inflation if real GDP grows by 2.8 percent.
   (g) Given that the output ratio is initially 100 and the expected inflation rate equals 1.4 percent, calculate the rate of inflation if real GDP grows by 5.2 percent.
   (h) Given that the output ratio is initially 100 and the expected inflation rate equals 1.4 percent, calcu-

late the rate of inflation if real GDP declines by 1.6 percent.
   (i) Given that the output ratio is initially 100 and the expected inflation rate equals 1.4 percent, calculate the rate of inflation if real GDP declines by 6.4 percent.
   (j) Use your answers to parts f–i to draw the short-run Phillips Curve, given that the expected inflation rate equals 1.4 percent.
   (k) Suppose that a beneficial supply shock lowers the inflation rate by 1.2 percentage points at any output ratio. Use your answers to parts f–i to draw the short-run Phillips Curve, given the beneficial supply shock.

2. Suppose that natural real GDP is constant. For every 1 percent increase in the rate of inflation above its expected level, firms are willing to increase real GDP by 1 percent. The expected rate of inflation in the current period equals the actual rate of inflation in the previous period. Initially the output ratio is 100 and the actual and expected inflation rates equal 2 percent.
   (a) Compute points on the short-run Phillips Curve when the inflation rate equals 0, 1, 2, 3, 4, and 5. Graph the short-run Phillips Curve.
   (b) What is the growth rate of nominal GDP in the economy?

   Suppose that due to baby boomers becoming eligible for Medicare, there is a permanent increase in the growth rate of the federal government's spending. That increase causes the growth rate of nominal GDP to accelerate to 4 percent.
   (c) Use the short-run Phillips Curve to explain what the rate of inflation and the output ratio are in the first period after the increase in the growth rate of nominal GDP.

(d) Explain what the inflation rate is in the long run, given the increase in the growth rate of nominal GDP, and describe how the economy adjusts to the long-run equilibrium.

3. Use the information contained in problem 2 to answer this problem. Suppose that monetary policymakers do not want to see a permanent rise in the inflation rate result from the increase in government spending. So following the increase in government spending, they take actions to reduce the growth rate of nominal GDP.

(a) What is the expected inflation rate in the second period? Compute points on the new short-run Phillips Curve for the second period when the inflation rate equals 0, 1, 2, 3, 4, and 5, given the expected inflation rate in the second period. Graph the short-run Phillips Curve for the second period.

(b) If monetary policymakers wish to reduce the rate of inflation to 2 percent in the second period, what must they reduce the growth rate of the nominal GDP to in the second period and what is the output ratio at the end of the second period, given the monetary contraction?

(c) What is the expected inflation rate in the third period? Compute points on the new short-run Phillips Curve for the third period when the inflation rate equals 0, 1, 2, 3, 4, and 5, given the expected inflation rate in the third period. Graph the short-run Phillips Curve for the third period. In order to maintain an inflation rate of 2 percent in the third period, explain why the growth rate in nominal GDP would have to be greater than 2 percent in the third period. What would the growth rate of nominal GDP have to be the long run in order to maintain an inflation rate equal to 2 percent?

Suppose that monetary policymakers have been able to establish a record of maintaining inflation at 2 percent. As a result, workers and employers expect that any increase or decrease in the inflation rate is only temporary because monetary policymakers take steps to change the growth rate of nominal GDP so as to quickly restore inflation to its long-run equilibrium level of 2 percent.

(d) Given the expectation that any increase or decrease in the inflation rate is only temporary, does the short-run Phillips Curve shift up or down when the actual inflation rate deviates from the expected inflation rate?

(e) Given your answer to part d, what must monetary policymakers reduce the growth rate of the nominal GDP to in the second period in order to reduce the inflation rate to 2 percent and what is the output ratio at the end of the second period, given the monetary contraction? What would the growth rate of nominal GDP have to be in the third period in order to maintain an inflation rate of 2 percent?

(f) Explain why your answers to parts b, c, and e are different.

4. The purpose of this problem is to study the sacrifice ratio. Suppose that initially actual and natural real GDP both equal 11,000 and that the rate of inflation is 3.5 percent. Natural real GDP grows by 3 percent per year over the next five years. Actual real GDP decreases by 2 percent in the first year, but then grows by 4 percent in the second year, 5.5 percent in the third year, 4.2 percent in the fourth year, and 3.5 percent in the fifth year. Inflation in years 1–5 equals 3.1 percent, 2.2 percent, 1.6 percent, 1.3 percent, and 1.1 percent, respectively.

(a) Calculate natural real GDP for years 1–5.
(b) Calculate actual real GDP for years 1–5.
(c) Calculate the output ratio for years 1–5.
(d) Calculate the cumulative loss of output for years 1–5.
(e) Calculate the sacrifice ratio.

5. Suppose that natural real GDP is constant. For every 1 percent increase in the rate of inflation above its expected level, firms are willing to increase real GDP by 2 percent. The output ratio is initially 100 and the inflation rate equals 2 percent.

(a) Based upon the preceding information, draw the short-run Phillips Curve.
(b) What is the growth rate of nominal GDP in the economy?

An adverse supply shock raises the inflation rate associated with every output ratio by 3 percentage points.

(c) Draw the new short-run Phillips Curve.
(d) The government chooses to follow a neutral policy in response to this shock. What will be the growth rate of nominal GDP? What will be the new rate of inflation? What will be the output ratio?
(e) If the government chooses to follow an accommodating policy, what would be the new inflation rate? The output ratio? The growth rate of nominal GDP?
(f) If the government chooses to follow an extinguishing policy, what would be the new inflation rate? The output ratio? The growth rate of nominal GDP?

SELF-TEST ANSWERS

p. 239 (1) Everywhere to the right of 100 percent actual inflation is greater than expected inflation (for instance, actual inflation of 3 percent at E_1 is greater than expected inflation of $p^e = 0$ along the SP_0 line). (2) Everywhere to the left of 100 percent actual inflation is less than expected inflation. (3) Only at 100 percent is expected inflation correct.

p. 241 (1) A decline in aggregate demand moves the economy to the left of point E_3, down along the SP_1 curve. (2) When real GDP declines from 100 to 94, the actual inflation rate drops to zero, and is now below the 3 percent inflation rate expected everywhere along the SP_1 curve. Eventually the expected inflation rate will decline as well, shifting the SP curve downward. (3) The LP curve remains fixed.

p. 248 Why in Figure 8-5 is the orange line from point 1 to 2 steeper than the blue line from E_0 to point 1? The line is steeper because inflation is higher at point 2 than at point 1, because the expected rate of inflation (p^e) has shifted up in response to the actual inflation that occurred at point 1. And, since nominal GDP growth (x) is the same at point 1 and point 2, but inflation (p) is higher, the growth of real GDP ($y = x - p$) must be less from 1 to 2 than from E_0 to point 1. Similarly, since inflation is even higher at point 3, real GDP growth must be even lower, and in fact is negative, going from point 2 to point 3.

p. 250 (1) The slope of the SP curve determines how a slowdown in nominal GDP growth is divided between a decline in the inflation rate (p) and a decline in real GDP growth (y). The flatter the SP curve, the larger is the decline in real GDP and the smaller is the decline in actual inflation. With backward-looking (adaptive) expectations, a smaller decline in the actual inflation rate produces a smaller decline in the next period's expected inflation rate. Smaller declines in expected inflation make the economy's adjustment path longer: It takes more time for the economy to return to long-run equilibrium. (2) Conversely, the economy's adjustment path is shorter the steeper the SP curve and the faster the decline in actual and, hence, in expected inflation.

p. 259 (1) The inflation rate will fall in the year of the decline in the relative price of oil, except in the case of an extinguishing policy that raises nominal GDP growth sufficiently to cancel out the oil price effect. And, if the inflation rate declines in the first year, it will also decline in subsequent years if the expected rate of inflation declines and/or if COLA agreements cause lower inflation in the first year to cause lower wage changes in subsequent years. (2) The output ratio will increase unless there is an accommodating policy that cuts nominal GDP growth by the amount of the supply stock. (3) An extinguishing policy response will prevent a change in the inflation rate. An accommodating policy response will prevent a change in the output ratio.

p. 263 *North:* an adverse supply shock accommodated by an increase in nominal GDP growth. *Northeast:* an acceleration of nominal GDP growth, causing inflation during the period prior to the adjustment of expectations. *East:* a beneficial supply shock extinguished by an increase in nominal GDP growth. *Southeast:* a beneficial supply shock accompanied by an unchanged rate of nominal GDP growth. *South:* a beneficial supply shock accommodated by a reduction in nominal GDP growth. *Southwest:* a deceleration of nominal GDP growth, causing disinflation prior to the adjustment of expectations. *West:* an adverse supply shock extinguished by a reduction in nominal GDP growth. *Northwest:* an adverse supply shock accompanied by an unchanged rate of nominal GDP growth.

For additional practice and exploration, exercises that require the use of Excel are available at www.aw-bc.com/gordon.

Appendix to Chapter 8

The Elementary Algebra of the SP-DG Model

Throughout Chapter 8, we have located the short-run equilibrium rate of inflation and level of real GDP along an SP curve, as at point E_4 of Figure 8-9. Now we learn how to draw a second line—the DG line—which shows where the economy will operate along the SP schedule. We also learn how to calculate the inflation rate and level of real GDP without going to the trouble of making drawings of the SP and DG lines. We do this by solving together the equations that describe the SP and DG lines, just as we did in the Appendix to Chapter 4, where we learned the equivalent in algebra to the IS and LM curves. We use SP-DG diagrams to show that either the algebraic or graphical method leads to the same answer.

The centerpiece of our model in this appendix is the deviation of the output ratio from 100 percent. One way to write this deviation is:

$$100(Y/Y^N) - 100$$

This deviation is zero when the output ratio (Y/Y^N) equals 1.0, which occurs when actual output (Y) equals natural output (Y^N).

Calculations in the model are more accurate and straightforward when we use natural logarithms. Since the natural logarithm of 1.0 is zero, the natural log of the output ratio is zero when the output ratio is unity. Thus a second way of expressing the deviation of the output ratio from 100 percent is the "log output ratio" expressed as a percentage.

$$\hat{Y} = 100[LN(Y/Y^N)]$$

The following table shows that $\hat{Y}$ is very close in value to the deviation $100(Y/Y^N) - 100$:

Y/Y^N	$100(Y/Y^N) - 100$	$\hat{Y}$
0.90	−10	−10.5
1.00	0	0.0
1.05	5	4.9

In the rest of this appendix, a value of $\hat{Y}$ of zero corresponds to 100 on the horizontal axis of those diagrams in Chapter 8 that plot the output ratio against the inflation rate.

Equation for the SP Curve

The SP curve can be written as a relationship between the actual inflation rate (p), the expected inflation rate (p^e), and the log output ratio $(\hat{Y})$.

General Linear Form	Numerical Example	
$p = p^e + g\hat{Y} + z$	$p = p^e + 0.5\hat{Y}$	(1)

Here the z designates the contribution of supply shocks to inflation, and initially in the numerical example we assume that the element of supply shocks is absent $(z = 0)$, so that we can concentrate on demand inflation. The numerical example also assumes that the slope of the SP, designated g in the general linear form, is 0.5 in the numerical example. Thus $g = 0.5$ indicates that the SP line slopes up by one percentage point in extra inflation for each two percentage points of extra real GDP relative to natural real GDP. We also note that when $\hat{Y} = 0$, the economy is on its vertical LP line where actual and expected inflation are equal $(p = p^e)$.

In order to understand what makes the *SP* curve shift, we assume the expectations of inflation (p^e) are formed adaptively as a weighted average of last period's actual inflation rate (p_{-1}) and last period's expected inflation rate (p^e_{-1}), where *j* is the weight on last period's actual inflation rate (*j* must be between 0 and 1).

General Linear Form   Numerical Example

$$p^e = jp_{-1} + (1 - j)p^e_{-1} \qquad\qquad p^e = p_{-1} \qquad\qquad (2)$$

The numerical example assumes that $j = 1$; that is, that expected inflation depends simply on what the inflation rate actually turned out to be last period, with the subscript -1 indicating "last period." This was also assumed in drawing Figures 8-5 and 8-7.

When we substitute (2) into (1), we obtain a new expression for the *SP* line that depends on two current-period variables ($\hat{Y}$ and z) and two variables from last period (p_{-1} and p^e_{-1}):

General Linear Form   Numerical Example

$$p = jp_{-1} + (1 - j)p^e_{-1} + g\hat{Y} + z \qquad\qquad p = p_{-1} + 0.5\hat{Y} \qquad\qquad (3)$$

Equation for the *DG* Line

But we need more information than that contained in (3) to find both current inflation (p) and the current log output ratio ($\hat{Y}$). In other words, we have two unknown variables and one equation to determine their equilibrium values. What is the missing equation? This is the *DG* line and is based on the definition that nominal GDP growth (x) equals the inflation rate (p) plus real GDP growth (y), all expressed as percentages:

$$x \equiv p + y \qquad\qquad (4)$$

In the theoretical diagrams of Chapter 8, the natural level of real GDP (Y^N) is constant. But now we want to be more general and allow Y^N to grow, as it does in the real world. We subtract the growth rate of natural real GDP (y^N) from each side of equation (4):

$$x - y^N \equiv p + y - y^N \qquad\qquad (5)$$

Let us give a new name, "excess nominal GDP growth" ($\hat{x}$), to the excess of nominal GDP growth over the growth rate of natural real GDP ($\hat{x} = x - y^N$). We can also replace the excess of actual over natural real GDP growth ($y - y^N$) with the change in the log output ratio ($\hat{Y}$) from its value last period ($\hat{Y}_{-1}$).[1]

When these replacements are combined, (5) becomes

$$\hat{x} \equiv p + \hat{Y} - \hat{Y}_{-1} \qquad\qquad (6)$$

Combining the *SP* and *DG* Equations

Now we are ready to combine our equations for the *SP* line (3) and *DG* line (6). When (6) is solved for the log output ratio $\hat{Y}$, we obtain the following equation for the *DG* line:

$$\hat{Y} \equiv \hat{Y}_{-1} + \hat{x} - p \qquad\qquad (7)$$

This says that the *DG* relation between $\hat{Y}$ and p has a slope of -1 and that the relation shifts when there is any change in $\hat{Y}_{-1}$ or $\hat{x}$. Now (7) can be substituted into the *SP* equation (3) to obtain:

---

[1] This replacement relies on the definition of a growth rate from one period to another as the change in logs (here we omit the "100" that changes decimals to percents):

$$y = \log(Y) - \log(Y_{-1})$$
$$y^N = \log(Y^N) - \log(Y^N_{-1})$$

Subtracting the second line from the first, we have

$$y - y^N = \log(Y) - \log(Y^N) - [\log(Y_{-1}) - \log(Y^N_{-1})] = \hat{Y} - \hat{Y}_{-1}$$

The Goals of Stabilization Policy: Low Inflation and Low Unemployment

The government fighting inflation is like the Mafia fighting crime.
—Laurence J. Peter

This book began by introducing three major concepts of macroeconomics—unemployment, inflation, and growth in per person output—that are linked to the three major goals of macroeconomic policy, namely, to achieve low unemployment, low inflation, and rapid growth in per person output. In Chapter 1 we learned why growth in output per person is desirable. Simply put, economic growth produces more goods and services, and more is better, allowing society to have everything it now produces and more, without the need to sacrifice something currently produced.

Now we inquire into the two other major goals of economic policy, beginning with low inflation in the first part of this chapter and ending with low unemployment in the last part. As we learned in Chapter 8, in order to achieve a lower inflation rate by restrictive monetary or fiscal policies, policymakers must be willing to accept a transition period during which the output ratio is lower and the unemployment rate is higher. Is the goal of achieving lower inflation worth the cost of lost jobs in the period during which inflation is reduced? This depends on the costs of inflation—just what is it that society loses if inflation proceeds at a rate of 5 percent per year instead of 2 percent?

In the last part of the chapter we inquire into the costs of unemployment. Is unemployment of a teenager seeking a part-time job as costly to individuals and society as unemployment of an adult head of household? Why can't the unemployment rate be pushed down to zero percent? Why are some people unemployed even in a prosperous economy?

9-1 The Costs and Causes of Inflation

Inflation is widely viewed as a social evil, although the degree of its seriousness is debated. At one extreme, inflation is considered as serious a problem as unemployment. This view was popularized by Arthur Okun, who defined the "misery index" as the sum of the inflation and unemployment rates. This index implies that the social value of a reduction of inflation by one percentage point (say from 3 to 2 percent) exactly offsets the social cost of an increase in the unemployment rate by one percentage point (say from 6 to 7 percent), leaving the economy with an unchanged level of "misery."

Others think that the harm done by inflation is minimal. James Tobin has written that "inflation is greatly exaggerated as a social evil." Many economists like Tobin do not regard the benefits of lower inflation as worth the sacrifice of lost output and jobs necessary to achieve it.

In Chapter 8 we learned that the basic cause of inflation is excessive growth in nominal GDP. In this chapter we ask why governments inflate; that is, why do they allow excessive nominal GDP growth to occur? We then examine the costs of inflation, asking whether they are serious enough to warrant stopping inflation, even though doing so may require policies that cut output and cause millions to lose their jobs.

Hyperinflation is a very rapid inflation, sometimes defined as a rate of more than 22 percent per month, or 1,000 percent per year, experienced over a year or more.

Any debate about the costs of inflation must distinguish between moderate (crawling) inflation and extreme inflation, usually called **hyperinflation.** One traditional definition of hyperinflation is an inflation rate of 50 percent per month, or 12,975 percent per year.[1] We shall use as our definition an inflation rate of 1,000 percent per year or above; a rate of 1,000 percent per year (or 22 percent per month) afflicts a society with all the problems usually associated with hyperinflation. Argentina, Brazil, Nicaragua, Peru, and Poland all suffered from inflation rates of over 1,000 percent per year for one or more years in the late 1980s or 1990s.[2] The African country of Zimbabwe experienced a hyperinflation of 5,000 or more percent per year in 2006–07.

Everyone agrees that hyperinflation is a severe plague, and we will learn how economic policymakers have managed to stop hyperinflations in several specific cases. Before turning to hyperinflation, we will examine the social costs of moderate inflation, such as that experienced by the United States. We will see that there are quite different costs associated with an inflation that is fully anticipated (crawling along at roughly the same rate year after year) and an inflation that is a "surprise," changing in an unpredictable way.

9-2 Money and Inflation

In Chapter 8 our model of inflation showed that a permanent increase in the growth rate of nominal GDP would lead to a permanent increase in the inflation rate. Since nominal GDP growth is so important in determining the inflation rate, we need to understand its determinants.

Definitions Linking Money, Velocity, Inflation, and Output

A convenient starting point for understanding the determinants of inflation is provided by the quantity equation of Section 7-8:

$$M^s V \equiv X \equiv PY \qquad (9.1)$$

This equation is familiar; it duplicates equation (7.2) on p. 214. The right side of the equation states that nominal GDP (X), by definition, is equal to the price in-

---

[1] Why is a 50 percent monthly inflation equivalent to an annual rate of 12,975 percent? This occurs because of compounding. Starting at 100, after one month prices are up to 150, after two months they are at 225, after three months they are at 338, and after twelve months they are at 12,975. Although these simple geometric changes are widely cited in the literature, they become increasingly misleading at high rates of inflation; a better measure is the logarithmic price change, which in this example is 40.5 percent per month, or 487 percent per year. See problems 1 and 2 at the end of the chapter.

[2] The 1,000 percent cutoff for episodes of "extreme" inflation is suggested in R. Dornbusch et al., "Extreme Inflation: Dynamics and Stabilization," *Brookings Papers on Economic Activity*, 1990, no. 2, pp. 1–84.

dex, or the GDP deflator (P), multiplied by real GDP (Y). The left side states that nominal GDP is also equal, by definition, to the money supply (M^s) multiplied by velocity (V).[3] Thus nominal GDP must rise if there is an increase in either the money supply or in velocity.

Equation (9.1) is a good beginning, but it concerns the price *level*. How can we convert equation (9.1) into a relationship that shows the determinants of the rate of *inflation*, that is, the rate of change of the price level? As we learned in Chapter 8, the growth rate of any product of two numbers, such as P times Y in equation (9.1), is equal to the sum of the separate growth rates of the two numbers. This allows us to take equation (9.1), a relationship among *levels* (written as uppercase letters), and restate it as a relationship among *growth rates* (written as lowercase letters):

$$m^s + v \equiv x \equiv p + y \qquad (9.2)$$

In words, this states that the growth rate of the money supply (m^s) plus the growth in velocity (v) equals the growth rate of nominal GDP (x), which in turn equals the sum of the inflation rate (p) and the growth rate of real GDP (y). The formula immediately allows us to classify the determinants of inflation, when we rewrite equation (9.2) with inflation on the left side:

$$p \equiv x - y \equiv m^s + v - y \qquad (9.3)$$

If we are interested in the long-run determinants of inflation, we can assume that the growth rate of real output (y) is fairly constant, roughly fixed by the growth rate of the population and of productivity. This leads to the same conclusion that we reached in Chapter 8: *In the long run, the inflation rate equals the excess growth rate of nominal GDP, that is, the difference between nominal GDP growth and the long-run growth rate of real GDP.*

The right-hand terms in equation (9.3) provide additional insight into the causes of inflation. In the long run, the inflation rate must equal the excess growth rate of money plus velocity, relative to the long-run growth rate of real GDP.[4]

Thus, to understand the determinants of inflation, we need to know what determines the excess growth of money plus velocity. The growth rate of the money supply is controlled by the central bank (in the United States by the Federal Reserve, in Canada by the Bank of Canada, and by similar institutions in other countries). Velocity changes whenever there is a change in real GDP relative to the real money supply (M^s/P). In Chapter 4 we learned that anything that shifts the *IS* curve will change velocity, including changes in business and consumer confidence, government spending, tax rates, autonomous net taxes, autonomous net exports, or the foreign exchange rate. Further, if the demand for money changes for reasons independent of changes in income, then velocity will change. For in-

---

[3] Why is the left side true by definition? As we learned in Chapter 4 in the box on p. 101, velocity is defined as $V \equiv PY/M^s$, or $V \equiv Y/(M^s/P)$. This definition is repeated in Chapter 7 on p. 214.

[4] In the Appendix to Chapter 8, we subtracted the long-run growth rate of natural real GDP (y^N) explicitly from both nominal and real GDP growth. Applying the same subtraction to equation (9.3), we have

$$p \equiv (x - y^N) - (y - y^N) \equiv (m^s + v - y^N) - (y - y^N)$$

This states that in the long run when $y - y^N$ is zero, inflation equals the excess growth of nominal GDP relative to that of natural real GDP, and inflation also equals the excess growth of money plus velocity relative to that of natural real GDP.

stance, velocity would increase following the introduction of credit cards that allow households to economize on their holdings of money.

While the growth rate of velocity can be highly volatile in the short run, over the long run velocity growth tends to be quite stable. For the United States, the average annual growth rate of velocity has been almost exactly zero over the past five decades.[5] Thus if we assume $v = 0$ in equation (9.3), the determinants of inflation become extremely simple: *In the long run, the inflation rate equals the excess growth rate of the money supply, that is, the difference between the growth rate of the money supply and the long-run growth rate of real GDP. If the central bank allows the money supply to grow rapidly, rapid inflation will result. The key to attaining zero inflation is for the central bank to allow the money supply to grow no faster than the long-run growth rate of real output.*

 SELF-TEST

Assume that over a decade the growth rate of the money supply is constant at 5 percent per year, and the growth rate of velocity is constant at 3 percent per year. In the first half of the decade, the growth rate of output is 4 percent per year; then, because of a slowdown in productivity growth, it is only 2 percent for the last half of the decade. The growth in money and in velocity are not affected by the productivity growth slowdown.

1. What is the inflation rate in the first half of the decade?
2. What is the inflation rate in the last half of the decade?
3. What is the nominal GDP growth rate in the first half of the decade?
4. What is the nominal GDP growth rate in the last half of the decade?

Why Do Central Banks Allow Excessive Monetary Growth?

The previous section identified excessive monetary growth as the fundamental cause of inflation *in the long run*. If the growth rate of velocity is zero in the long run, then excessive nominal GDP growth and excessive monetary growth are identical. Why do governments and central banks allow excessive monetary growth to occur?

Four basic factors examined below can lead to excessive nominal GDP and monetary growth. As shown in Chapter 8, a permanent increase in nominal GDP growth leads to a- *temporary* increase in output along with a *permanent* increase in the inflation rate. A permanent decrease in nominal GDP growth leads to a *temporary* decrease in output along with a *permanent* decrease of the inflation rate. This analysis underlies the first reason governments cause inflation.

Reason 1: Temptation of demand stimulation. Governments and central banks may set off inflation when they attempt to raise output and reduce unemployment. While Chapter 8 indicated that such policies can boost inflation with only a temporary benefit to output, governments may think (erroneously) that the benefits of higher output will last forever or (perhaps cor-

---

[5] The velocity of the money supply concept M2 (defined in Chapter 13) was 1.73 in 1960 and 1.91 in 2007, for an average annual growth rate of 0.2 percent.

International Perspective

Money Growth and Inflation

Equation (9.3) in the text ($p \equiv m^s + v - y$) states that the inflation rate (p) is equal to the rate of monetary growth (m^s) plus the difference between velocity growth and real GDP growth ($v - y$). If this difference is positive, then inflation exceeds the rate of monetary growth, and vice versa.

The graph plots the inflation rate over the period 1990–2006 against the rate of monetary growth for 15 countries. The diagonal 45-degree line shows all the points with equal rates of inflation and monetary growth, that is, with $v = y$. In most of the low-inflation countries, the plotted points lie below the 45-degree line, indicating that velocity growth was less than real GDP growth. For instance, in the United States, velocity growth was roughly zero, less than output growth of about 3.3 percent per year. These plotted points illustrate that the relationship between inflation and monetary growth is relatively close, supporting the theme of the text that the key to understanding inflation is to understand why some governments choose much higher rates of monetary growth than others.

Compared to previous decades, the incidence of very rapid inflation in the period shown in the graph, 1990–2006, was substantially less than in previous decades. For instance, Brazil had an inflation rate of more than 400 percent per year from 1990 to 1998, but then inflation suddenly came to almost a halt, with Brazil's inflation rate of only about 8 percent from 1999 to 2006. The average inflation rate from 1990 to 2006 shown in the graph is about 100 percent, an average of very fast inflation before 1998 and much slower inflation after 1998. Why did inflation subside after the 1990s? Clearly, Brazil and other formerly high-inflation countries have learned to manage the growth of their money supplies and have cut back the fiscal deficits that previously made rapid monetary expansion necessary.

Inflation vs. Money Growth, 1990–2006

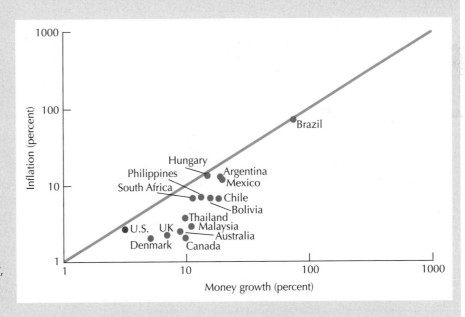

Sources: International Monetary Fund World Economic Report, April 2007, and International Financial Statistics database.

rectly) at least long enough to benefit the government at the next election. In some countries, the central bank is controlled directly or indirectly by the government. Even in the United States, with its relatively independent central bank, it is widely believed that the Fed boosted monetary growth in 1972 to help reelect President Nixon.

Reason 2: Fear of recession and job loss. The corollary to the first reason is the fact that stopping inflation usually causes a temporary drop in output and loss of jobs. Thus an implication of the first reason for higher inflation is that governments are reluctant to stop inflation once it gets started: An economy must sacrifice a substantial amount of lost output in order to reduce the inflation rate permanently. The size of this output sacrifice is highly controversial and differs among countries. One estimate for the United States is that a permanent decrease in the inflation rate of one percentage point would require a one-time loss of 4.7 percent of a year's GDP, or about $650 billion. The sacrifice required in some countries may be higher, in others lower. Politicians and central banks may be reluctant to impose this sacrifice on citizens, and as a result inflation tends to persist year after year.

Reason 3: Adverse supply shocks. Chapter 8 also introduced adverse supply shocks as a cause of higher inflation. When higher food or oil prices raise business costs, the inflation rate rises unless the central bank introduces an extinguishing policy that offsets the extra inflation with a massive recession. Any sharp increase in the price of oil, such as those that occurred in 1973–74 and 1979–80, poses a distasteful choice for central banks. An extinguishing policy reaction can offset extra inflation only at the cost of extra unemployment. An accommodative policy calls for the central bank to "print the extra money to pay for the inflation," and this is likely to create a permanent upsurge of inflation following an adverse supply shock. Even a neutral policy, which leaves the growth rate of nominal GDP and the money supply unchanged, will cause a temporary upsurge of inflation. This issue returned to center stage in 2007 when both food and oil prices reached new heights.

Reason 4: Financing government deficits by printing money. In our analysis of the *IS-LM* model of Chapter 4, we learned that governments can run deficits (by boosting expenditures or cutting taxes) in two ways. First, they can hold the real money supply steady and issue bonds to pay for the deficit, which usually requires an increase in the interest rate. Or they can hold the interest rate steady by raising the money supply sufficiently, a policy previously described as monetary accommodation of a fiscal stimulus. However, many countries lack markets in which the government can sell bonds; in such countries virtually the only source of finance for government deficits is an increase in the money supply (often called financing deficits by "printing money"). Thus governments with excessive spending or insufficient tax revenues can cause inflation (p), according to equation (9.3), by boosting the growth rate of the money supply (m^s).

In summary, we have learned that the basic reasons why central banks allow excessive monetary growth are the temptation of demand stimulation together with the related fear of recession and output loss, the partial or complete accommodation of adverse supply shocks, and the effect of government deficits in boosting monetary growth.

9-3 Why Inflation Is Not Harmless

If a temporary period of lost output and higher unemployment must be experienced in order to reduce inflation, then policymakers need to be convinced that inflation is harmful. At first glance, worry about inflation may appear misplaced. When inflation is zero, wages may increase at 2 percent a year. When inflation

The Indexed Bond (TIPS) Protects Investors from Inflation

Following the lead of Canada, the United Kingdom, and other countries, the U.S. Treasury introduced inflation-indexed bonds to investors in 1997. These bonds protect the savings of investors from being eroded by unanticipated increases in the inflation rate. The indexed bond introduced in the United States is called TIPS, for Treasury Inflation-Protected Securities.

Unlike a conventional bond, an indexed bond promises to pay its holder a fixed real rate of return. An indexed bond maintains its promised real rate of return even if inflation suddenly accelerates by 5, 10, or even 20 percent relative to the inflation rate that was expected when the saver purchased the bond.

For the U.S. Treasury's 10-year indexed bond, semiannual interest payments are calculated by adjusting the principal for inflation (using the Consumer Price Index or CPI) and applying the fixed real interest rate (determined at the auction at which the bonds were first issued) to the inflation-adjusted principal.

The benefits for the U.S. Treasury are several. Indexed bonds can reduce the risk premium that the government must pay to savers who fear that their returns on bonds will be eroded by future unanticipated inflation. By eliminating the risk of loss from future unanticipated inflation, the Treasury can reduce its average borrowing costs, thus reducing the interest component of the federal government deficit. An additional benefit is that the process of issuing indexed bonds provides information about the inflation expectations of investors, measured as the difference in market-determined interest rates on conventional and indexed bonds of the same maturities.

The figure in this box plots the 10-year Treasury bond (which is not inflation-protected) and the 10-year TIPS. The green shading shows the real interest rate based on the expectations of those who buy TIPS, and the orange shading shows the inflation rate expected by those investors. Between 2002 and 2004 there was a decline in the expected real interest rate from more than 3 percent to an average of 2 percent from 2004 to 2007. There was a corresponding increase in the implied expected inflation rate from an average of 1.7 percent in 2001–03 to an average of 2.5 percent in 2004–07. TIPS investors naturally became more pessimistic about future inflation because actual inflation began to rise, as we learned on pp. 259–61, because of declining unemployment, higher oil prices, the depreciation of the dollar, and slowing productivity growth.

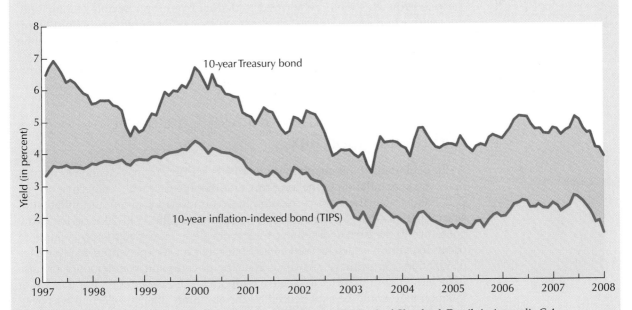

Sources: Federal Reserve Board, *Selected Interest Rates,* and Federal Reserve Bank of Cleveland. Details in Appendix C-4.

recommended that the government issue an indexed bond that would fully protect savers against any unexpected movements in the inflation rate. Finally, in 1997, the U.S. government responded to these recommendations by issuing an indexed bond, called *TIPS*, which stands for "Treasury Inflation-Protected Securities."

An **indexed bond** pays a fixed real interest rate; its nominal interest rate is equal to this real interest rate plus the actual inflation rate.

An **indexed bond** protects savers from unexpected movements in the inflation rate by paying a fixed real interest rate (r_0) plus the actual inflation rate (p). Thus the saver's nominal interest rate would be

General Form	Numerical Example
$i = r_0 + p$	(a) $3 = 3 + 0$
	(b) $13 = 3 + 10$

In numerical example (a), savers would receive a 3 percent return if the inflation rate were zero. If inflation suddenly accelerated to 10 percent, as in example (b), savers would find that the nominal return (*i*) rose to 13 percent, and they would be just as well off as if there had been no inflation. The box on p. 295 discusses the performance of TIPS since they were introduced in 1997.

Indexed Tax System

Another important reform made effective in 1985 is the partial indexation of the personal income tax system. This now raises the dollar amounts of tax credits, exemptions, standard deductions, and tax rate brackets each year by the amount of inflation that has been experienced. Without an indexed tax system, inflation would raise individual incomes and push taxpayers into higher tax brackets.

But the government must do more to achieve a fully inflation-neutral tax system. It must end present rules that discriminate against savers and favor borrowers and instead tax real rather than nominal interest and capital gains. Just as savers should be taxed only on real interest income and real capital gains, borrowers should be allowed to deduct from their taxable income only the real portion of the interest they pay on loans. These reforms would eliminate the present effect of inflation in the U.S. tax system of discouraging saving and encouraging borrowing and spending.

9-5 The Government Budget Constraint and the Inflation Tax

At the beginning of this chapter we identified excessive money creation as the primary cause of inflation in the long run, and the International Perspective box on p. 285 illustrated the close correlation between money creation and inflation in several nations that experienced rapid inflation over the 1990–2006 period. Now we return to the puzzle of why governments allow excessive money creation to occur. In countries such as the United States that have experienced modest rates of inflation, the primary answer is that the government was tempted to raise monetary growth in order to create a temporary increase in output at the cost of inflation that would be experienced by the electorate after the election was over. Also, the government was reluctant to stop an inflation, once started, for fear of the temporary period of high unemployment that would be a by-product of the effort to stop inflation, as occurred during 1982–83.

But in countries that have experienced rapid inflation or hyperinflation, the reason for excessive money creation is almost always large government deficits. By definition, government spending must be financed by some combination of tax revenues, bond creation, or money creation. When there are political obstacles to raising sufficient tax revenue, and in countries that do not have active bond markets, the government has no option other than money creation, that is, turning on the printing press.

A household must withdraw its savings or borrow if its expenditures exceed its income; the same is true of the government. The options open to the government for financing its expenditures are summarized in the **government budget constraint.** This divides government spending into two parts, spending on goods and services (G) and spending on interest payments (iB), where i is the nominal interest rate on government bonds and B is the dollar amount of government bonds outstanding. Government revenue sources are tax revenue net of transfer payments (T), the issuance of additional bonds (ΔB), and the issuance of additional government monetary liabilities (ΔH). Government monetary liabilities, which consist of currency held by the public and bank reserves, are often called high-powered money and are abbreviated H. Both B and H are part of the government debt; the only difference is that bonds pay interest and high-powered money does not.

The **government budget constraint** relates government spending to the three sources available to finance that spending: tax revenue, creation of bonds, and creation of money.

The Government Budget Constraint Equation

The government budget constraint can be expressed in a simple formula:

$$\underbrace{G - T}_{\text{basic deficit}} + \frac{iB}{P} = \frac{\Delta B}{P} + \frac{\Delta H}{P} \qquad (9.8)$$

In words, this equation states that the government's basic deficit ($G - T$) plus its real interest expense (iB/P) equals the real increase in bonds ($\Delta B/P$) plus the real increase in high-powered money ($\Delta H/P$). Why are three of the terms in equation (9.8) divided by P but $G - T$ is not divided by P? This is because G and T have been defined as real inflation-adjusted variables through this book going back to Chapter 2, whereas B and H are *nominal* variables that must be divided by P to express them in real terms.

Over the past several decades in the United States, the federal government has run both a basic deficit and a basic surplus. Compare the following four situations. In the first, the federal government ran a basic deficit. In the second, it ran a basic surplus, that is, a negative basic deficit, but a positive total deficit. In the third, it ran a basic and a total surplus, that is, a negative basic deficit and a negative total deficit. In the fourth, it returned to the 1992 situation by running both a basic and total deficit, although the basic deficit was quite small. As in equation (9.8), the data are expressed in real terms (in billions of dollars at 2000 prices):

	Basic Deficit	+	Interest Cost	=	Total Deficit
1992	105.3	+	230.7	=	336.1
1996	−142.5	+	256.9	=	114.4
2000	−459.1	+	222.9	=	−236.2
2006	18.5	+	194.4	=	212.9

Stated another way, the basic deficit in 2006 was less than 10 percent of the total deficit; almost all of the total deficit was accounted for by the interest cost.

Bond Creation Versus Money Creation

Despite the fact that the U.S. federal government moved into surplus between 1998 and 2001, it moved back into deficit after 2001; for many years before 1998, it ran a deficit. Most other industrialized countries have run a government budget deficit rather than a surplus throughout the past two decades, without the interruption of a surplus as the United States enjoyed in 1998–2001. How are governments able to finance these deficits? There are two methods. These are the issuance of additional government bonds, represented by ΔB, and the issuance of additional high-powered money, represented by ΔH. When the government raises H, the total nominal money supply (M) increases.

An increase in H raises aggregate demand more than an increase in B, because a higher H raises the money supply and eliminates the crowding out effect of Chapter 4. Because a deficit financed by H is more stimulative to the economy, the government may want to finance its budget deficit by issuing more H when the economy is weak and by issuing more B when the economy is strong.

In the United States, the size of the government deficit is determined by the administration and Congress, while the choice between bond and money creation is made by the Federal Reserve. Since the Fed controls ΔH, and since there is a large, well-organized market for government bonds, the Fed can respond to a larger government deficit by raising ΔH, reducing ΔH, or leaving ΔH unchanged. However, not every nation is able to choose between bond and monetary finance of government deficits. Developed nations such as the United States, Japan, Canada, and the more prosperous European nations have sophisticated capital markets where the government can sell bonds. But less developed nations lack these markets, so their governments have little latitude to finance their government deficits by selling bonds. As a result, in many countries a higher government deficit *automatically* requires raising ΔH, which boosts the growth rate of the money supply and (according to equation (9.3) on p. 283) the rate of inflation.

Effects of Inflation

Inflation may seem to aggravate the government's problem of financing its basic deficit, since according to the Fisher Effect, inflation raises the nominal interest rate (i) that appears on the left-hand side of equation (9.8). However, inflation also eases the government's problem. This is not evident in equation (9.8), where the inflation rate (p) does not appear. However, we can slightly rearrange equation (9.8) by multiplying the first term on the right-hand side by B/B and the second term by H/H. This converts (9.8) into:

$$G - T + \frac{iB}{P} = \left(\frac{\Delta B}{B}\right)\frac{B}{P} + \left(\frac{\Delta H}{H}\right)\frac{H}{P} \tag{9.9}$$

The term $\Delta BB/BP$ is the percentage change in bonds ($\Delta B/B$) times the amount of real bonds outstanding (B/P), and ($\Delta HH/HP$) is the percentage change in high-powered money ($\Delta H/H$) times the amount of real high-powered money (H/P) outstanding. Clearly, if B/P and H/P are to remain stable, then the percentage growth rate of B, represented by a lowercase b, and the growth rate of H, designated by a lowercase h, will each have to equal the inflation rate (p):

$$\Delta B/B = b = \Delta H/H = h = p \tag{9.10}$$

This equation says simply that the growth rate of bonds (b) and the growth rate of high-powered money (h) equal the rate of inflation. If that is true, then the real value of bonds (B/P) and the real value of high-powered money (H/P) will remain fixed. That is, the numerator of each ratio (B/P and H/P) will grow at the same rate as the denominator when $b = h = p$.

Why Inflation Is Tempting to Governments

Our aim is to determine the nature of the government's budget constraint that would keep the real value of bonds and high-powered money fixed. Since equation (9.10) gives the condition ($b = h = p$) that will allow this situation to persist, we need to substitute the inflation rate (p) into equation (9.9), replacing the term there for the growth rate of bonds ($\Delta B/B$) and also replacing the term for the growth rate of high-powered money ($\Delta H/H$). In arriving at this final statement of the government budget constraint, we also move the term representing real interest payments (iB/P) from the left-hand side of equation (9.9) to the right-hand side of equation (9.11):

$$G - T \quad = \quad \frac{pH}{P} \quad - \quad \frac{(i - p)B}{P} \qquad (9.11)$$

$$\text{basic deficit} \quad = \quad \begin{array}{c} \text{seignorage} \\ \text{or} \\ \text{inflation tax} \end{array} \quad - \quad \begin{array}{c} \text{real interest} \\ \text{on bonds} \end{array}$$

The first term on the right-hand side of equation (9.11), namely (pH/P), represents the inflation rate times real high-powered money, that is, the revenue that the government receives when it creates just enough H to maintain fixed the real quantity of high-powered money (H/P). This revenue that the government gets from inflation is called **seignorage.** Think of this simply as the revenue the government receives when it prints money. From the point of view of private households and firms that must add to their nominal quantity of H enough to keep real H/P constant, this same revenue is called the **inflation tax.**

Stated simply, if pH/P were the only term on the right-hand side of equation (9.11), it would indicate the amount of the deficit that the government could run by creating the right amount of nominal high-powered money (H) that would be consistent with keeping the real quantity of high-powered money constant. If the inflation rate is not zero, then this amount is not zero, and the government can run a deficit and still maintain real high-powered money constant. Subsequently we will see that the inflation tax is a cost of inflation to households, the exact counterpart of the benefit that inflation provides to the government.

Inflation does not eliminate the government's obligation to pay interest on its outstanding bonds held by private households and firms. But the second right-hand term [$(i - p)B/P$] in equation (9.11) illustrates that the government only has to worry about paying the *real* interest expense of servicing the bonds. While it pays bond holders the nominal interest rate (i), bond holders have to give part of i back to the government to purchase sufficient additional bonds to keep their real bond holdings (B/P) constant.

Seignorage is the revenue the government receives from inflation and is equal to the inflation rate times real high-powered money.

The **inflation tax** is the revenue the government receives from inflation and is the same as seignorage, but viewed from the perspective of households.

An Example Showing That the Government Gains

To see how this works in an example, imagine that we start with $100 of bonds, a 5 percent inflation rate per year, an 8 percent nominal interest rate, and a 3 percent real interest rate. The government must pay $8 in interest. But, to keep the real quantity of bonds (B/P) constant, the government sells $5 in new bonds to the public, raising the value of outstanding bonds to $105. The government's net interest expense is just $3 (the real interest rate of 3 percent times the original $100 of bonds). Why? Because the government *pays* $8 in interest but *receives* $5 as a payment by the public for the new bonds.[11]

Thus the government benefits from inflation in two ways. First, it obtains an extra source of revenue, called seignorage or the inflation tax. The government can then lower ordinary taxes or increase spending more than it could otherwise. Second, the government may gain if inflation raises the nominal interest rate by less than inflation itself. Sharp increases of inflation, particularly such as those during the oil shock periods of the 1970s, are often accompanied by an increase in the nominal interest rate of less than one-for-one, thus reducing the real interest rate. And, as shown in equation (9.11), it is the real interest rate that matters for government finance.

 SELF-TEST

Assume that after centuries of a zero budget deficit and a zero debt, the nation of Abstinia runs a one-year deficit equal to 1 percent of GDP, which it finances by creating H/P equal to 1 percent of GDP.

1. If inflation over the next decade occurs at 5 percent per year, what must be true of the basic deficit and the level of H for Abstinia to end the decade with the same level of H/P equal to 1 percent of GDP?

2. What is the answer to the same question if the inflation rate over the next decade is 10 percent per year?

9-6   Starting and Stopping a Hyperinflation

We have already defined hyperinflation as an inflation rate of 1,000 percent or more per year. If an inflation of 1,000 percent per year were to occur in the United States, a Big Mac would increase in price from around $2.50 to $2,500![12] Clearly, such an inflation rate would be disruptive if wages and salaries did not grow as rapidly, and if interest rates on savings accounts were less than the inflation rate.

---

[11] To simplify the presentation, both equation (9.11) and the numerical example in this paragraph neglect the taxation of interest earnings, which further reduces the government's net real interest expense.

[12] The text oversimplifies to state that a 1,000 percent per year inflation will raise the price of a Big Mac over one year from $2.50 to $2,500. Using the natural logarithm formula in the growth rate box in Chapter 2 on p. 41, we can calculate the amount by which a $1 price would rise after one year of 1,000 percent annual inflation. First we convert the 1,000 percent inflation back from a percent value to a decimal value $(1000/100 = 10)$. The price by the end of the year can be calculated as $P_1 = e^{(1000/100)} = 22026$. This can be checked with the growth rate formula in the box on p. 41, where the annual growth rate between an initial value of 1.0 and a final value of 22026 over one year is $x = 100 \times LN(22046/1)/1 = 1,000$. Thus with 1,000 percent per year continuous inflation, the price of the Big Mac would rise from $2.50 to $55,065.

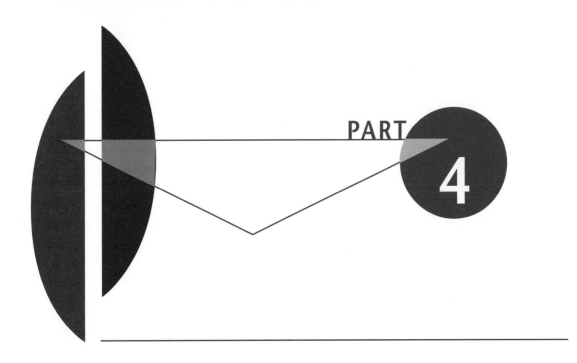

Macroeconomics in the Long Run: Growth and Public Finance

CHAPTER 10 **The Theory of Economic Growth**

CHAPTER 11 **The Big Questions of Economic Growth**

CHAPTER 12 **The Government Budget,
the Public Debt, and Social Security**

CHAPTER

The Theory of Economic Growth

In essence the question of growth is nothing new but a new disguise for an age-old issue, one which has always intrigued and preoccupied economics: the present versus the future.

—James Tobin[1]

10-1 The Importance of Economic Growth

As we learned in Chapter 1, a fundamental task of macroeconomics is to determine the sources of economic growth. By economic growth we usually mean the growth rate of real GDP per person (or per capita). The achievement of rapid economic growth is one of the most (if not *the* most) important distinguishing features of a successful economy. The fact that the U.S. economy grew more rapidly than those of the industrialized nations of Europe during the century between 1850 and 1950 allowed Americans to enjoy a higher standard of living than most residents of Europe throughout the postwar era.

Welfare Gains from Growth

The profound importance of growth comes from the power of compound arithmetic. Even apparently small differences in growth rates make a huge difference in the standard of living over, say, a period of fifty years. Consider an average income of $45,000 in 2007. At a growth rate of 2 percent, that income would grow over fifty years to $122,300 in the year 2057. At a growth rate of 2.5 percent, that income would grow to $157,100 in 2057, a difference of $34,800, or more than three-quarters of the initial income level!

Thus the welfare gains resulting from even minor increases in the rate of economic growth are enormous. In the oft-quoted words of Nobel Prize–winning University of Chicago economist Robert E. Lucas, Jr., "the consequences for human welfare are simply staggering. Once one starts thinking about them, it is hard to think of anything else."[2] This is true because small differences in the rate of economic growth can make a huge difference in the welfare of the average citizen when compounded over 50 or 100 years.

The newly industrializing countries of Asia (China, India, Korea, Taiwan, Hong Kong, and Singapore) are widely admired for their success in achieving very rapid economic growth over the past forty years. Although Korea had about the same level of real income per capita as the Philippines in 1965, by

---

[1] "Economic Growth as an Objective of Government Policy," *American Economic Review*, vol. 54 (May 1964), p. 1.

[2] Robert E. Lucas, Jr., "On the Mechanics of Economic Development," *Journal of Monetary Economics*, vol. 22 (July 1988), p. 5.

2007 (thanks to its stunning achievement of rapid economic growth), Korea's real income per capita was *six times* that of the Philippines.[3]

The Great Questions of Economic Growth

By far the most important reason to study economic growth is the great and growing chasm between standards of living in the world's rich and poor countries. By "rich" we mean North America, much of Europe, Japan, some of the successful Asian countries, and Australasia. By "poor" we mean many of the rest. In between, there are middle-income countries like most former members of the Soviet Bloc, which are neither rich nor poor. As is illustrated by the contrast between Korea and the Philippines, only a few decades of fast growth were necessary for Korea to leave the ranks of the poor and join the rich nations, while the Philippines remains mired in poverty. What secrets did the Koreans discover? What kept the Philippines from benefiting from the same methods? After we learn about the theory of growth in this chapter, we turn in the next chapter to the puzzle of rich versus poor.

A less cosmic question, but one of great interest to citizens of a single nation like the United States, is what explains the ebb and flow of economic growth? American growth in productivity, or output per hour, was much slower during 1972–95 than before 1972 or since 1995. The average American is roughly one-quarter poorer today because growth was so slow in 1972–95. What explains that dismal period of slow productivity growth? Why did productivity growth accelerate after 1995, and was that revival of more rapid growth a temporary event or is it likely to continue through the next decade? This topic, which is of great importance for the future American standard of living as well as for the country's ability to sustain the Social Security system and provide improved medical care, is also treated in the next chapter.

The Next Three Chapters

Economic growth has always been a central topic in macroeconomics. We now begin a three-chapter discussion of economic growth and other issues related to the long-run evolution of the economy. In this chapter we examine the simple theory of economic growth and its relation to growth in population and in the capital stock. To address puzzles that the simple theory cannot explain, we broaden the approach to include other types of investments that tend to favor growth, including education, research, and development.

Chapter 11 begins by taking a closer look at the success of rich nations and the failure of poor nations. Simple growth theory suggests that poor nations should grow more rapidly, yet some succeed while others fail. Why? We introduce the role of political and other noneconomic factors that may promote or retard growth, including crime, corruption, absence of property rights and a reliable legal system, and the geographical disadvantages suffered by some nations. We also examine the past century of U.S. economic growth and ask whether the unusually rapid productivity growth of the 1995–2004 period can be sustained in the future, in light of the sharp slowdown in U.S. productivity growth that occurred after 2004.

A key source of growth is saving and investment; the total amount of investment is boosted when the government runs a budget surplus and is re-

---

[3] See Figure 1-9 on p. 18.

2. The figure is plotted on a logarithmic scale. This means that the slope of each line indicates the economic growth rate; a steep line means fast growth and a flat line indicates slow growth. For all countries, 1955–73 was the period of fastest growth, and all countries have experienced a growth slowdown since 1973.

3. Differing growth rates among countries have led to changes in relative positions. Japan had the most rapid growth, particularly between 1955 and 1973, when it reached the incredible rate of 7.9 percent per annum. Japan overtook Italy in 1970 and the United Kingdom in 1980.

4. The United Kingdom's loss of relative position has been continuous over the entire century. From 1870 to 1973, the United Kingdom had a growth rate at the bottom of the group. The United Kingdom was overtaken by the United States in 1916, by France and Germany in 1960, and by Japan in 1980.

5. The United States is something of a "has-been" in the growth race, owing its high living standard to its superior growth performance before 1950. In particular, the United States gained an advantage in its freedom from wartime destruction as compared to some European nations.

Types of Economic Change

The figure displays not only the process of economic growth that raises the standard of living decade after decade, but two types of shorter-term movements. The first of these is wartime destruction, which is clearly visible in the sharp drop in the living standards of Germany and Japan from 1940 to 1950. Making up for wartime destruction explains much of the rapid economic growth in these two countries in the 1950s and early 1960s.

The second type of short-term economic change is the business cycle. The data for each country are annual, so the alternation of business recessions and expansions is visible, most notably during the depression years of the 1930s. The figure also highlights the unique nature of the Great Depression in the United States and Canada, where per person real GDP declined much more than in the other countries, as discussed in the box on pp. 224–25.

Level and Growth Rate of per Capita Real GDP in 2006 Dollars for Seven Countries, 1870–2007

	Level in 2006 U.S. dollars		Average annual growth rate in percent				
	1870	2007	1870–2008	1870–1913	1913–1955	1955–1973	1973–2007
United States	2,933	44,791	1.98	1.80	2.14	2.36	1.82
Canada	2,427	35,742	1.96	2.24	1.46	2.91	1.74
United Kingdom	4,706	34,587	1.46	1.01	1.12	2.36	1.97
Japan	1,059	33,640	2.53	1.47	1.65	7.87	2.12
France	2,733	33,550	1.83	1.44	1.41	4.06	1.66
Germany	2,713	30,754	1.77	1.59	1.10	4.03	1.64
Italy	2,254	30,023	1.89	1.25	1.43	4.57	1.85

Sources: OECD Development Center, *The World Economy: Historical Statistics,* and Groningen Growth and Development Center, *Total Economy Database.* Details in Appendix C-4.

10-3 The Production Function and Economic Growth

The traditional theory of economic growth (often called the "neoclassical" theory) has filled many academic journals with highly mathematical articles. Yet the basic ideas are very simple. The theory divides output growth into two categories: (1) growth of **factor inputs,** such as labor and capital, and (2) growth in

The economic elements that directly produce real GDP are **factor inputs**.

output relative to growth in factor inputs. Thus the theory converts the question of how to achieve faster output growth into two subquestions: how to achieve faster growth in factor inputs, and how to achieve faster growth in output relative to inputs.

Throughout most of this book we have examined the causes and consequences of changes in the ratio of actual real GDP to natural real GDP, which we have called the output ratio (Y/Y^N). But now we are interested in changes in economic conditions over long periods during which the output ratio may be expected to be roughly constant. Thus our theory of economic growth refers to the growth of natural real GDP.

The Production Function

How much real GDP (Y) can be produced at any given time? This depends on the total available quantity of the two main factor inputs, capital (K) and labor (N), and also the behavior of output per average available factor input, which the neoclassical theory calls A (for the "autonomous" growth factor).[5]

The **production function** states the relationship between Y, A, K, and N:

$$Y = AF(K, N) \tag{10.1}$$

The **production function**, a relationship usually written algebraically, shows how much output can be produced by a given quantity of factor inputs.

In words, real GDP (Y) equals an autonomous growth factor (A), expressed as an index, multiplied by a function of an index of capital input (K) and labor input (N). The appendix to this chapter provides background information on the general functional form used in equation (10.1) and a popular numerical example often used to illustrate the workings of the production function.

Output per person and the capital-labor ratio. We need to isolate those factors that determine the increase in per person real GDP, which can be written as follows when the production function is divided through by the amount of labor input (N).[6]

$$\frac{Y}{N} = Af\left(\frac{K}{N}\right) \tag{10.2}$$

This important relationship states that there are just two sources of growth in the standard of living, or real GDP per person (Y/N). These are the autonomous growth factor (A), and the ratio of capital to labor input (K/N), or "capital per person." (In this chapter we simplify by treating "persons" and "employment" as synonyms, ignoring changes in the ratio of employment to the population.)

---

[5] The use of the symbol A in this context and the decomposition of real GDP growth into growth in labor, capital, and the "residual" A date back to the seminal paper by Robert M. Solow, "Technical Change and the Aggregate Production Function," *Review of Economics and Statistics*, vol. 39 (August 1957), pp. 312–20. The symbol A stands for autonomous growth factor and should not be confused with A_p, the symbol for autonomous planned spending in Chapters 3–7.

[6] How can equation (10.2) be derived from equation (10.1)? There are two intermediate steps. First, we multiply and divide K by N in equation (10.1):

$$Y = AF(NK/N, N) \tag{10.1'}$$

If the function F displays constant returns to scale (see appendix to this chapter), then there is a unit elasticity of Y with respect to a given percentage increase in both N and K. This fact allows us to factor out the N term and rewrite equation (10.1') as follows:

$$Y = ANf(K/N, 1) \tag{10.1''}$$

Notice here that we have given a new name (f) to the function. Equation (10.2) in the text is obtained by dividing through both sides of (10.1'') by N.

Equation (10.2) is the per person version of the production function. It is illustrated in Figure 10-1. This production function is drawn by assuming that the autonomous growth factor is fixed at A_0. Like the production functions presented in Chapter 7, which plotted output against labor input, this one exhibits diminishing returns. Thus each successive addition to the per person stock of capital (K/N) yields less and less of an increase in per person output (Y/N). In the diagram, point B represents one possible level of production, with capital input per person $(K/N)_0$ producing output per person $(Y/N)_0$.

SELF-TEST

1. Why is the production function a curved line instead of a straight line?
2. What happens to the ratio of output to capital (Y/K) as more capital per person is accumulated?
3. What happens to Y/K if the level of capital per person declines?

The production function in Figure 10-1 is just a start toward an adequate theory of economic growth. So far our analysis tells us simply that the main sources of growth in the standard of living are an autonomous factor (A) and growth in capital per person (K/N). But this does not explain why these two sources of growth differ among countries or among historical eras. We do not yet know why the autonomous growth factor in Figure 10-1 is A_0 rather than some other amount, nor do we know what determines the level of K/N.

Our study of what determines the autonomous growth factor is deferred until later. Here, we focus on the determinants of growth of capital per person (K/N). We begin by reviewing the basic relationships between investment, the growth in capital, and saving.

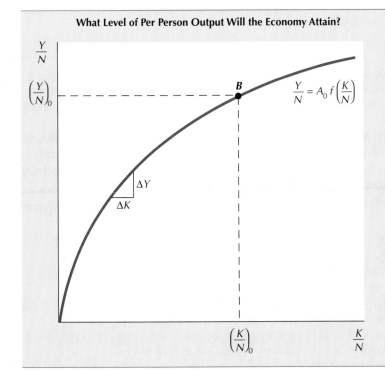

What Level of Per Person Output Will the Economy Attain?

$$\frac{Y}{N} = A_0 f\left(\frac{K}{N}\right)$$

Figure 10-1 A Production Function Relating per Person Output to per Person Capital Input

The production function shows how much output per person can be produced by different amounts of capital per person. One possible position for the economy is point B, but other positions are possible as well. We cannot tell from this diagram how large the economy's per person capital stock will be. The slope of the production function is the marginal product of capital ($\Delta Y/\Delta K$), showing the extra amount produced by raising capital, when the amount of labor is held constant.

Saving and Investment in the Steady State

How is K/N related to total national saving? This relationship is important, since it represents the link between the government's fiscal policy, private saving decisions, and the long-run growth of output per person.

We will first study an economy that has no technical change, implying that the autonomous growth factor (A in equation 10.2) is constant, so that the economy stands still at a point like B in Figure 10-1. The economy is at a fixed vertical position at point B when Y and K grow at the same rate, implying that the ratio Y/K is fixed. This situation is called a **steady state.** When we add the additional assumption that there is no technical change, then the growth rates of Y and K are also equal to the growth rate of labor input (N), implying that the ratio K/N is fixed.

As in previous chapters, we use lowercase letters to designate growth rates, including the growth rate of output ($y = \Delta Y/Y$), the growth rate of capital ($k = \Delta K/K$), and the growth rate of labor input ($n = \Delta N/N$). Thus the condition for a steady state with no technical change in which capital per person (K/N) is constant, can be written as

$$k = n \qquad (10.3)$$

In commonsense terms, equation (10.3) states the condition necessary for the economy to stand still at a point like B in Figure 10-1, since equal growth rates of k and n imply that the ratio K/N is fixed. The growth rate of capital can also be written as the change in capital (ΔK) divided by capital itself (K):

$$\frac{\Delta K}{K} = k = n \qquad (10.4)$$

Now we link the growth rate of capital to the two types of investment (I), net investment that causes the capital stock to increase (ΔK), replacement investment that replaces old capital that becomes worn out or obsolete (dK) where d is the fraction of the capital stock (say 0.10) that is replaced each year due to wear and tear and obsolescence.

$$I = \Delta K + dK = \left(\frac{\Delta K}{K} + d\right)K = (n + d)K \qquad (10.5)$$

Here we obtain the third term by dividing and multiplying the second term by K, and then we obtain the fourth term using equation (10.4) to replace $\Delta K/K$ by n.

Now we are ready to relate investment to total national saving, and here we will use the symbol S to represent national saving (in contrast to Chapters 3–5 where the symbol S represented private saving). If we assume that net exports are zero, total *national* saving (S) equals private investment (I).[7]

$$S = I \qquad (10.6)$$

---

[7] We can repeat here a version of the magic equation, equation (5.5) on p. 139, which shows the relation of national saving ($S + T - G$) to private investment (I) and net exports (NX):

$$S + (T - G) = I + NX$$

When S is redefined to include both private saving and government saving, we have:

$$S = I + NX$$

This is the same as equation (10.6) in the text, where NX is set equal to zero.

A **steady state** is a situation in which output and capital input grow at the same rate, implying a fixed ratio of output to capital input.

When we define a lowercase s as the ratio of saving to GDP ($s = S/Y$), then we can replace the left side of equation (10.6) by sY and replace investment on the right side by equation (10.5), yielding

$$sY = (n + d)K \qquad (10.7)$$

Our last step is to divide both sides of equation (10.7) by the amount of labor (N), and we now have our central relationship that links the vertical axis (Y/N) of Figure 10-1 to the horizontal axis (K/N).

$$\frac{sY}{N} = (n + d)\frac{K}{N} \qquad (10.8)$$

In words, equation (10.8) states that total national saving per person equals capital per person times the growth rate of capital plus the fraction of capital that must occur as replacement investment.

SELF-TEST

There are five components of equation (10.8): s, Y/N, K/N, n, and d.

1. Which of these components changes its value as we move to the left or right along the production function in Figure 10-1?

2. For those components that do not change, suggest at least one factor that determines the value of that component.

10-4 Solow's Theory of Economic Growth

Can an increase in the ratio of national saving to output (s) create a permanent increase in the growth rate of output? The answer is no. This was the most surprising result of the "neoclassical" theory of economic growth originally developed in the 1950s by MIT's Robert M. Solow,[8] a theory for which he was awarded the Nobel Prize in 1987. We have already developed the major building blocks of Solow's theory. These are the per person production function of equation (10.2) and Figure 10-1, and the relationship between saving and steady-state investment in equation (10.8).

Solow's Insight

The algebra of equation (10.8) had been worked out in the 1940s by Sir Roy Harrod, an English economist, and Evsey Domar, who later taught at MIT. In their Harrod-Domar model of economic growth, all of the elements of equation (10.8) are constant. But then, why does the left side of equation (10.8) equal the right side? This equality seems an unlikely coincidence, since the elements of equation (10.8) depend on totally unrelated factors. The ratio of national saving to output (s) on the left-hand side of the equation is determined by the saving decisions of households, business firms, and the government. And the growth rate of labor input (n) and depreciation rate (d) on the right-hand side of equation (10.8) are determined by totally different considerations—birth rates, death rates, immigration, and the rate at which old capital wears out or becomes obsolete.

Robert M. Solow (1924–)

Solow, 1987 Nobel Prize winner, invented both the modern theory of economic growth and the standard method for empirically distinguishing the roles of capital and technological change in the growth process.

[8] Robert M. Solow, "A Contribution to the Theory of Economic Growth," *Quarterly Journal of Economics*, vol. 70 (February 1956), pp. 65–94.

What Solow did was to marry the per person production function of equation (10.2) to the saving-investment relation in equation (10.8). Once again, on the left-hand side of equation (10.8), we have total national saving per person, which is the national saving rate (s) times output per person (Y/N), and this, in turn, is given by the per person production function of equation (10.2). On the right-hand side of equation (10.8), we have the amount of steady-state investment per person, that is, the amount of investment needed to equip each new population member with the same capital per person as the existing population, and to replace worn-out or obsolete capital.

The Solow Model in Pictures

The two sides of equation (10.8) can be plotted separately, as in Figure 10-2. In the left frame, the upper red line is a copy of the per person production function from Figure 10-1, plotting the output-labor ratio (Y/N) as a function of the capital-labor ratio (K/N). When we multiply this line by the fixed saving rate (s), we obtain the blue line, national saving per person (sY/N). The distance between the two lines indicates consumption per person. The right-hand frame plots steady-state investment per person, which rises steadily to the right, since a larger K/N raises the amount of investment needed to equip new population members and replace worn-out and obsolete capital.

Now in Figure 10-3 we put together the two parts of Figure 10-2, omitting for clarity the per person production function. The steady state occurs at point

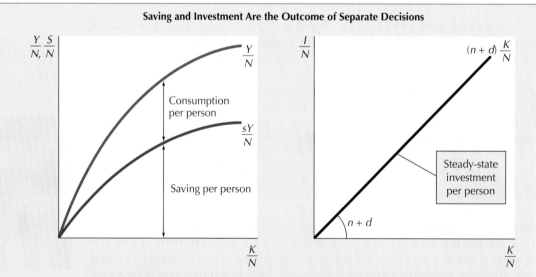

Saving and Investment Are the Outcome of Separate Decisions

Figure 10-2 Output, Saving, and Steady-State Investment per Person
The upper curved red line in the left frame copies the per person production function from Figure 10-1. Multiplying it by the saving rate (s) produces the lower curved blue line showing per person saving. Consumption per person is the distance between the two lines. The right frame shows steady-state investment per person, the amount needed to replace old capital and equip new workers for each capital-labor ratio (K/N).

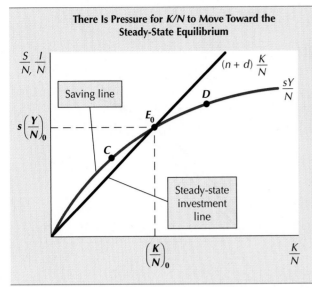

There Is Pressure for K/N to Move Toward the Steady-State Equilibrium

Figure 10-3 Equilibrium of Saving and Investment in the Solow Growth Model

This figure superimposes the two frames of Figure 10-2. The saving line crosses the steady-state investment line at point E_0. At any point to the left, like C, saving and actual investment exceed steady-state investment (the amount needed to keep K/N constant), and accordingly K/N grows until the economy reaches point E_0. At any point to the right, like D, saving and actual investment are less than steady-state investment and K/N shrinks back to E_0. Only at E_0 is per person saving just the right amount to equip new members of the population with $(K/N)_0$ and replace worn-out and obsolete capital.

E_0, where the capital-labor ratio is $(K/N)_0$. Why is this a steady state? At any point to the left of E_0, say point C, saving and investment are higher than the investment required to maintain (K/N) at a fixed level. This extra investment makes (K/N) grow, moving the economy rightward from point C to the steady-state equilibrium E_0. Similarly, starting at point D, saving and investment are below the required amount, meaning that not enough is being invested to equip new members of the population and replace worn-out and obsolete capital. Hence starting from point D, the economy moves leftward back down the blue line to the steady-state equilibrium at point E_0.

Effects of a Higher Saving Rate

To understand the startling implication of the Solow growth model that a change in the ratio of national saving to output does not create a permanent change in the growth rate of output, let us see how an increase in the saving rate affects the economy. In Figure 10-4 we begin by copying the steady-state investment line (which remains unchanged in the examples of Figures 10-2, 10-3, and 10-4, but could change as in the self-test on p. 327) and the "old saving line" directly from Figure 10-3. The economy's initial position is at point E_0, just as it was in that figure.

Now in Figure 10-4 we introduce a sudden increase in the saving rate from s_0 to s_1, which shifts the blue saving line up. The distance between point F along the new blue saving line and point E_0 along the old blue saving line represents *additional saving available to fuel growth in capital per person*. The economy moves to the right up the new saving line, since there is extra saving available to equip new members of the population with a higher capital-labor ratio, and as well to provide for the added depreciation of old capital at that higher ratio. Eventually the economy arrives at point E_1 along the new saving line. But once at E_1, the capital-labor ratio is fixed at the new higher ratio, per person saving and output are fixed, and the growth in output is once again equal to the growth rate of labor input (at E_1 as at E_0, $y = k = n$).

Figure 10-4 The Effect of a Higher Saving Rate on Capital and Income per Person

The lower "old saving line" is copied from Figure 10-3. A higher saving rate implies the higher "new saving line." The economy's position immediately jumps from E_0 to F. Now saving and actual investment are above steady-state investment, and so K/N grows until the economy reaches point E_1.

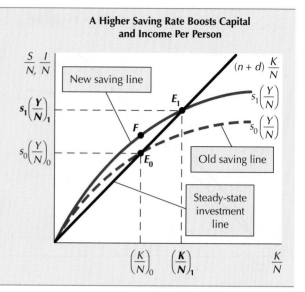

A Higher Saving Rate Boosts Capital and Income Per Person

Thus the saving rate matters, but not as people had believed prior to the development of Solow's model. An increase in the saving rate raises the standard of living, since the higher capital-labor ratio at E_1 produces a higher output-labor ratio. To achieve this higher standard of living, the growth rate of output is *temporarily* raised above the growth rate of N. But the higher saving rate does not create a permanently higher growth rate of output, which depends only on population growth. In the steady state Y/N is fixed, so that Y and N must grow at the same rate. Intuitively, the extra saving finances only a higher *level* of the capital stock per person (K/N), not continuing *growth* in the capital stock per person. The extra saving is "eaten up" by the extra replacement investment implied by the higher capital stock, and the extra net investment required to equip each worker with the higher level of capital stock per person.

 SELF-TEST

Explain the effect of a reduction in the rate of population growth (*n*) on the following:

1. The growth rate of output.
2. The capital-output (K/Y) ratio.
3. The capital-labor (K/N) ratio.

One aspect of this theory may seem puzzling. We learned in Chapter 3 that an increase in the saving rate (*s*) depresses the economy by reducing consumption spending. How can we be so sure here that an increase in the saving rate will stimulate the growth of per person capital? The answer is that *the Solow model is intended for long-run analysis* (decades, not months or years) *and assumes continuous full employment and flexible prices.* Thus, when the saving rate rises in this model, consumption and the price level both decline. The interest rate falls by enough to stimulate sufficient investment to guarantee that saving and investment will remain equal along the economy's path between E_0 and E_1.

Clearly, in addition to responding to a change in the saving rate (s), the economy must also adjust to the other parameters in equation (10.8), namely the rate of population growth (n) and the depreciation rate (d). An increase in either the rate of population growth or the depreciation rate will make the black line rotate up and to the left around the origin of the diagram, moving the economy's equilibrium down and to the left. Faster population growth reduces the economy's standard of living (Y/N) and its capital-labor ratio (K/N). In the new steady state, Y/N and K/N are lower and remain constant, but the growth rates of y and k are more rapid, reflecting the new higher population growth rate. A higher depreciation rate causes the same decline in Y/N and K/N without any change in the growth rates y and k, which remain equal to unchanged population growth.

10-5   Technology in Theory and Practice

At first glance, the Solow growth model seems to contain a major flaw. As presented thus far, the model implies that the permanent growth rate of output should be the same as the growth rate of the population, and that the standard of living (Y/N) should be fixed. How, then, does the theory explain the sharp increase in the standard of living shown in the box on pp. 322–23 that has occurred over the past century in each of the major industrialized nations?

Two Types of Technological Change

Solow used two methods to make the model consistent with history. Both methods introduce an added element into the story: growth in technology in all its forms, including better schooling, improved organization, better health care, and all the fruits of innovation and research. The two methods for introducing technological change into the Solow growth model are to assume (1) that technology makes each worker more efficient, and (2) that technology shifts the production function relating per person output to per person capital.

Labor-augmenting technological change.   This approach leaves our previous discussion of the Solow growth model, including the diagrams, completely intact. We simply need to adopt a broad definition of growth in "labor input." Instead of just counting the number of bodies at work, we count effective labor input, taking into account improved education and the storehouse of technology that makes today's workers more efficient than workers a century ago. We now interpret N as effective labor input, and n as the growth rate of effective labor input. In the steady state, output can grow at 3 percent ($y = 3$) if effective labor input grows at 3 percent ($n = 3$), leaving the ratio of output to effective labor input (Y/N) fixed. Now K/N remains fixed if the capital stock grows at 3 percent. Effective labor input growth of 3 percent exceeds population growth of, say, 1 percent, allowing the standard of living (Y per person) to grow at 2 percent.[9]

---

[9] Labor-augmenting technical change can be introduced into our original production function from equation (10.1) by defining effective labor input as a technological factor (A) times the population:

$$Y = F(K, AN)$$

When A enters in this form, it is sometimes called "Harrod-neutral" technical change.

Neutral technological change. One problem with the first approach is that it assumes that technology only makes workers more efficient, with no impact on capital input. A more realistic assumption is that technology makes *both* labor and capital input more efficient. This "neutral" type of technological change simply means that the autonomous growth factor (A) in equations (10.1) and (10.2) grows over time. Here we copy equation (10.2) and renumber it for convenience:

$$\frac{Y}{N} = Af\left(\frac{K}{N}\right) \tag{10.9}$$

If education, innovations, and research raise the value of A every year, then per person GDP can increase steadily. The growth rate of per person GDP ($y - n$) is

General Form	Numerical Example	
$y - n = a + b(k - n)$	$y - n = a + 0.25(k - n)$	(10.10)

Here a is the growth rate of the autonomous growth factor, and b is the elasticity of output with respect to capital input, assumed to be 0.25 in the numerical example. An economy might, for instance, have values of $a = 1.5$ and $k - n = 2$, which would be consistent with a steady state in which

$$y - n = a + b(k - n) = 1.5 + 0.25(2) = 2.0$$

In this example, there is a steady state, because per person output and per person capital are growing at the same rate, allowing Y/K to remain fixed. After introducing neutral technological change into the diagrams of the Solow growth model, the production function shifts upward steadily, thus shifting the saving line up and to the right along a fixed steady-state investment line. Y/N and K/N rise in the steady state, but at the same rate.

 SELF-TEST

Calculate the percentage growth rate of real GDP per person ($y - n$) from the numerical example of equation (10.9), assuming that b always equals 0.25, for the following combinations of the rates a, k, and n:

a	k	n	$y - n$
0	0	4	____
0	4	4	____
4	0	0	____
4	4	4	____

The "Solow Residual"

Soon after Solow developed his theory of growth, he applied the theory to the measurement of the autonomous growth factor (a) in equation (10.10). His idea was to turn equation (10.9) around so that a could be calculated from the other components:

$$a = (y - n) - b(k - n) \tag{10.11}$$

Since data were available on the growth rates of output (y) and of both capital and labor input (k and n), the only trick in determining the value of a was to identify the elasticity b. Here Solow's idea was to apply the theory of profit maximization in a competitive firm. Solow pointed out that such firms would also set the return on capital equal to the marginal product of capital, which implies that the elasticity *b* can be measured by the share of capital income in total GDP.[10]

Solow's finding was controversial. Fully seven-eighths of the growth in output per hour of work $(y - n)$ over the period he studied (1909–57) was attributed to "technical change in the broadest sense," including education, research, innovations, and other improvements, while only the remaining one-eighth was attributed to growth in the capital stock per hour of work $(k - n)$. But this is not a very satisfactory outcome. Knowing that some mysterious *a* factor was important in the growth process does not tell us, for instance, what caused *a* to grow more slowly during 1973–95 or more rapidly after 1995.

Some skeptics believe that *a* should not be given a name like "technological change," which implies we know precisely what determines *a*. They suggest that we call *a* instead the **residual** or, more frankly, "the measure of our ignorance." Government agencies like the U.S. Bureau of Labor Statistics, which now routinely calculate *a*, describe *a* as the growth in **multifactor productivity**, or **total factor productivity**. In recent years macroeconomists have come to describe *a* as **Solow's residual.**

The simplified version of Solow's growth model summarized in the previous section (Figures 10-2, 10-3, and 10-4) illustrated one key implication of his model, that a change in the saving rate would cause only a temporary, rather than a permanent, increase in the growth rate of output per unit of labor input. That simplified version could not explain steady growth of output—a defect that we have remedied in this section by introducing technological change. And we have seen that Solow's own empirical research identified technological change (broadly defined) as a much more important source of economic growth than increases in capital input per unit of labor input. However, the Solow growth model has received substantial criticism. In the next section we identify several puzzles that his model cannot explain, and in the following section, we learn about recent developments in growth theory.

> The **residual** is the amount that remains after subtracting from the rate of real GDP growth all of the identifiable sources of economic growth.

> The growth in **multifactor productivity**, or **total factor productivity**, is the growth rate of output per hour of work, minus the contribution to output of the growth in the quantity of other factors of production per hour of work, notably capital but sometimes including energy, raw materials, or other factors of production.

> **Solow's residual** is the same as growth in multifactor productivity.

10-6   Puzzles That Solow's Theory Cannot Explain

In recent years economists have become increasingly dissatisfied with Solow's neoclassical theory of economic growth, for two primary reasons. First, the theory makes economic growth depend primarily on "Solow's residual," which remains unexplained. Thus we are left with very little understanding of why the world's standard of living stagnated until the industrial revolution that occurred around the year 1800, why it grew rapidly from then until the early 1970s, and why in some countries like the United States the standard of living grew slowly in the 1970s and 1980s but then accelerated after 1995. Second, we are left with little understanding of differences among nations—why some are rich and some remain poor, and why some grow rapidly while others stagnate.

---

[10] Let *r* be the rate of return to capital. Then competitive firms will set *r* equal to the marginal product of capital (*MPK*). The share of capital in GDP is rK/Y, which competitive firms will set equal to $(MPK)(K/Y)$, which is equal to the elasticity of output with respect to capital, $(dY/dK)(K/Y) = (dY/Y)(dK/K)$.

The critics of neoclassical growth theory go beyond claiming that the theory provides an inadequate explanation of growth. They point to widely observed phenomena in the world that *conflict* with the predictions of the theory. In this section we review these conflicts.

Conflict 1: Income per Capita Varies Too Much Across Countries

Real income per capita in a rich country like the United States is more than ten times as high as in a poor country like India or Bangladesh. Yet this fact conflicts with the neoclassical theory. Why? The theory states that there are only two reasons for differences in per capita income. One reason could be a difference in saving rates, since, as shown in Figure 10-4, an increase in the saving rate raises income per capita (Y/N). Another could be a difference in the slope of the steady-state investment line ($n + d$). However, even very large differences in the saving rate or rate of population growth cause only small variations in per capita income, not the large variations observed in the world. To take one example, quadrupling the saving rate and reducing the rate of population growth by two-thirds would boost per capita income only from 1.0 to 1.7, whereas in the real world we observe countries differing in per capita income by magnitudes on the order of 1.0 to 10.0.[11]

A flaw in the neoclassical theory is to assume that all countries have the same production function (equation (10.9). Poor countries are assumed to operate at the same level of technology and knowledge as rich countries. To see that the production function is at fault, consider a specific version of equation (10.9) called the Cobb-Douglas production function (see the appendix to this chapter).

General Form   Numerical Example

$$Y/N = (K/N)^b \qquad Y/N = (K/N)^{0.25} \qquad (10.12)$$

Here we set the autonomous growth factor (A) equal to unity to simplify the exposition.

To see what difference in K/N would be needed to explain a ten-fold difference in per capita income, we can solve for K/N:

General Form   Numerical Example

$$K/N = (Y/N)^{1/b} \qquad K/N = (Y/N)^{1/0.25} \qquad (10.13)$$

---

[11] To see this, let us combine equation (10.8) with the Cobb-Douglas production function (explained in the appendix to this chapter):

$$s\left(\frac{Y}{N}\right) = (n + d)\left(\frac{K}{N}\right) \qquad \text{(i)}$$

$$\left(\frac{Y}{N}\right) = \left(\frac{K}{N}\right)^b \qquad \text{(ii)}$$

By solving equation (ii) for (K/N), substituting into equation (i), and simplifying, we obtain:

$$\left(\frac{Y}{N}\right) = \left(\frac{s}{n + d}\right)^{\frac{b}{1-b}} \qquad \text{(iii)}$$

Using as examples $s = 0.1$, $n = 0.03$, $d = 0.07$, and $b/(1 - b) = 1/3$, we can calculate that $Y/N = 1^{1/3} = 1$. Quadrupling the saving rate to 0.4 would raise Y/N from 1 to $4^{1/3} = 1.59$. Reducing the rate of population growth from 0.03 to 0.01 (assuming the saving rate remains at 0.4) would raise Y/N further from 1.59 to $(0.4/0.08)^{1/3} = 1.7$.

Let us take the value of Y/N for the poor nation to be 1 and the value of Y/N for the rich nation to be 10. Substituting 10 for the rich nation's Y/N in the numerical example, we see that the rich nation's K/N must be equal to $(Y/N)^{1/0.25}$ or 10^4, which is 10,000. Yet there is no evidence of such huge differences among nations in K/N. In fact, a regular feature of real-world economies is a roughly constant ratio of K/N, not ratios of K/N that are hugely greater in rich countries than poor countries (by 10,000/10 or 1,000 times greater in the example).

Conflict 2: Poor Countries Do Not Have a Higher Rate of Return on Capital

The neoclassical theory describes the difference in per capita income between poor countries and rich countries simply as a result of differing levels of per capita capital, which in turn result from differences in the three parameters that appear in equation (10.8)—the saving rate (s), population growth rate (n), and depreciation rate (d). As shown in Figure 10-5 a poor country is at a position like point P, with a low capital-labor ratio $(K/N)_P$, while a rich country is at a position like point R, with a high capital-labor ratio $(K/N)_R$.

But this leads to an unrealistic implication. The slope of the per person production function in Figure 10-5 is the marginal product of capital ($\Delta Y/\Delta K$), and this is much higher on the left side of the diagram for the poor country than on the right side of the diagram for the rich country. A simple numerical example shows that the marginal product of capital should be as much as 4,000 times higher in a poor country as in a rich country when per capita income is ten

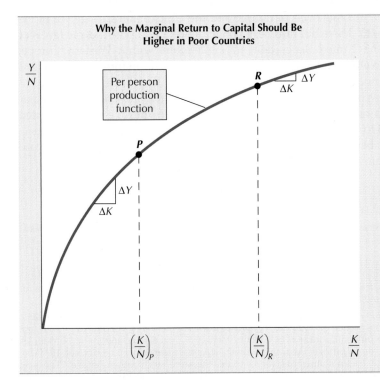

Why the Marginal Return to Capital Should Be Higher in Poor Countries

Figure 10-5 A Production Function Relating per Person Output to per Person Capital Input

The per person production function is the same as in Figures 10-1 and 10-2. The poor country has a capital-labor ratio of $(K/N)_P$ and produces at point P. The rich country has a capital-labor ratio of $(K/N)_R$ and produces at point R. The marginal product of capital is given by the slope of the production function, $\Delta Y/\Delta K$. Because of the curvature of the per person production function, this slope is clearly larger for the poor country than for the rich country. The text discusses reasons why this diagram makes the erroneous prediction that the marginal return to capital is higher in poor countries than in rich countries.

times as high.[12] The implied high marginal product of capital in the poor country implies that the rate of return on capital in poor countries should be much higher than in rich countries, *and that there should be massive flows of capital from rich countries to poor countries to earn this higher rate of return.* Yet we do not observe high rates of return on capital, or massive capital inflows, in many of the poorest countries of the world. Some less-developed countries enjoy substantial inflows, but others do not.

How can we explain why the rate of return on capital in very poor countries is not substantially higher than in rich countries? The poor countries may not be operating on the same production function as the rich countries, unlike the single production function drawn in Figure 10-5.

Conflict 3: Convergence Has Not Been Uniform

The neoclassical model predicts that poor nations should "converge" to the income levels of the rich. That is, nations that are initially poor should have faster growth rates than nations that are initially rich. This occurs for three reasons. First, nations that are below their steady-state growth paths (for instance, at point F in Figure 10-4) will grow faster until they reach the steady state (at point E_1 in Figure 10-4). Second, as noted, the neoclassical model predicts that the rate of return is much higher in poor countries, causing capital to flow from rich to poor countries and thus boosting the capital stocks of poor countries. Third, whatever the barriers that prevent poor countries from fully utilizing the production technology, the passage of time should allow poor countries to learn how to use the productive techniques of the rich countries.

Economists have devoted much attention in recent years to the issue of convergence, and the subject is controversial.[13] There has been convergence among the major industrialized countries; for example, Japan has caught up substantially to the per capita income levels of Europe and the United States, as shown in the box on pp. 322–23. There has also been convergence among the income levels of states within the United States and among regions within Western Europe. However, in the world at large, convergence has not been uniform. Many nations of Africa and some of the poorer nations of Asia have fallen further behind the advanced countries over the past fifty years, and the relative income levels of major Latin American nations have fallen relative to Western Europe and the United States. We need to go beyond neoclassical growth theory to understand the persistent differences between rich and poor nations. We return to the facts about convergence in the next chapter (see pp. 355–58).

---

[12] With the Cobb-Douglas production function, the marginal product of capital (*MPK*) is

General Form	Numerical Example
$MPK = b(K/N)^{b-1}$	$MPK = 0.25(K/N)^{-0.75}$
$= b(Y/N)^{(b-1)/b}$	$MPK = 0.25(Y/N)^{-3.0}$

Thus, if Y/N is ten times greater in a rich country, the marginal product of capital in the numerical example would be 0.25 times 10^{-3} or 1/4,000 times smaller.

[13] A pioneering study of cross-country differences in growth rates is Robert J. Barro, "Economic Growth in a Cross Section of Countries," *Quarterly Journal of Economics*, vol. 106 (May 1991), pp. 407–33. Another influential study is N. Gregory Mankiw, David Romer, and David N. Weil, "A Contribution to the Empirics of Economic Growth," *Quarterly Journal of Economics*, vol. 107 (May 1992), pp. 407–37. For an illuminating survey of this literature, see Jonathan Temple, "The New Growth Evidence," *Journal of Economic Literature*, vol. 37 (March 1999), pp. 112–56. A less technical introduction is contained in Robert J. Barro, *Determinants of Economic Growth: A Cross-Country Empirical Study* (Cambridge, Mass.: MIT Press, 1997), Chapter 1.

10-7 Human Capital, Immigration, and the Solow Puzzles

If the neoclassical model cannot explain differences in per capita income by observed differences in capital per person, then what explanation remains? One of the most promising is to recognize that most of the income that labor receives in the rich countries is not a reward to "pure" labor (that is, just the fact that someone is alive) but rather to the education that people have acquired. Education makes a tremendous difference in the incomes that people receive. Management consultants with an MBA degree are typically paid double the salary earned by those with no more than an undergraduate degree, who in turn receive double or more the typical earnings of high-school graduates, who in turn earn substantially more than high-school drop-outs.

What Is Human Capital?

Economists use the term **human capital** to refer to the value over one's lifetime of the extra earnings made possible by education. A 20-year-old planning to work for 45 years might be able to make $6 million in the future with an MBA degree, but someone of that age might be limited to a lifetime income of only $600,000 if he or she drops out of school with only an elementary-school education, thus limiting the available job options to menial jobs like digging ditches and washing dishes. The difference between $6 million and $600,000, or $5.4 million, is said to be the "human capital" that the MBA degree-holder has accumulated. Another person who stops his or her education with an undergraduate degree might be expected to make $3 million in the future and to acquire $2.4 million in human capital (the difference versus the alternative of a mere elementary-school education). For society as a whole, the value of human capital is the sum of the human capital of each inhabitant.

> **Human capital** is the value, for a person or for society as a whole, of the extra future earnings made possible by education.

The name "human capital" was given to the value of education in order to reflect the parallels between investing in education and investing in physical capital, that is, structures and equipment like computers and forklifts. Investment in physical capital requires that money be spent in order to earn a future return, in the form of the extra profits that can be made after the structure is built or the equipment is purchased. Similarly, investment in human capital requires an expenditure of money on education and the sacrifice of income that could otherwise be earned by working instead of going to school. This expenditure is made in order to earn a higher income in the future, and the rate of return on the cost of education can be stated on a percentage basis in just the same way as the rate of return on the cost for a firm of buying a new computer.

How Does Human Capital Raise Total Output?

An economy like the United States that contains many educated people can produce more output and a higher standard of living than an economy like many in Africa where most inhabitants have had little education. Thus human capital (H) becomes a factor of production, just like physical capital (K), and the production function, instead of using equation (10.1), can be written as:

$$Y = A\,F(K, H, N) \qquad (10.14)$$

In words, this states that real GDP (Y) equals an autonomous growth factor (A), expressed as an index, multiplied by a function of an index of physical capital (K), human capital (H), and labor (N). Now labor is interpreted as the productive capability of the population *if* everyone had dropped out of school after elementary school (sometimes called "brute force" labor, capable only of digging ditches), while all the extra earnings of the population above that educational level are included in human capital input (H).

Human Capital and the Solow Puzzles

The inclusion of human capital goes a long way toward repairing the inability of the Solow neoclassical model to explain differences between the rich and poor countries. Let us write the per person production function in the Cobb-Douglas form of equation (10.12), making only a single change, namely, to add human capital per person (H/N) as an extra determinant of output per person (Y/N):

General Form	Numerical Example
$$Y/N = (K/N)^b (H/N)^c$$	$$Y/N = (K/N)^{0.25} (H/N)^{0.65}$$

This states that output per person equals physical capital per person (K/N) raised to the power b, which is 0.25 as before, and human capital raised to the power c, which is assumed to be 0.65. Instead of labor making a contribution to output of $(1 - b)$ or 0.75, the contribution of uneducated labor (N) is now $1 - b - c$, or only 0.10 (which equals 1.0 minus 0.25 minus 0.65).

As we saw in the preceding discussion of equations (10.12) and (10.13), the basic reason that the Solow neoclassical model cannot explain observed differences between rich and poor nations is that the exponent on capital ($b = 0.25$) is so small. If capital is so unimportant, then why should poor countries lag so far behind rich countries? But now we have introduced human capital as an additional difference between rich and poor countries, and the sum of the exponents on the two types of capital ($b + c$) is now 0.9, not 0.25. If we replace 1/0.25 in equation (10.13) by 1/0.9, we find that a rich nation having 10 times the per person income (Y/N) as a poor nation needs to have only $10^{1/0.9}$ or about 12.6 times as much combined physical and human capital as the poor nation. This is much more plausible than the implication of equation (10.13) in the model without human capital that the rich nation needed to have 10,000 times as much physical capital as the poor nation.[14] In the same way, if the exponent on total capital is 0.9 rather than 0.25, it is no longer necessary for the rate of return on investment in capital (both physical and human) to be much lower in rich countries than in poor countries (this was the second conflict discussed in this section).[15]

The Immigration Puzzle

Thus the addition of human capital to the Solow neoclassical growth theory goes a long way toward explaining the conflicts introduced in the previous section. Rich countries differ from poor countries not just because they have many more structures and lots more equipment, but because their inhabitants are much better educated than those in poor countries. Yet the human capital explanation runs into a problem when we consider the immigration of an unskilled person from a

---

[14] This insight is one of the contributions of the article by Mankiw, Romer, and Weil cited in the previous footnote.

[15] Go back to footnote 12 on p. 336 and substitute $b = 0.9$ in place of $b = 0.25$. The bottom line of the numerical example becomes:

$$MPK = 0.9(Y/N)^{-0.1/0.9}$$

If Y/N in the rich country is 10 times higher, then the marginal product of capital in the rich country should be 0.9/1.29 or about 0.7 times that in the poor country, not 1/4,000 as in the example of footnote 12 based on $b = 0.25$.

poor country to a rich country. To be specific, let us consider a poorly educated Guatemalan who crosses the Rio Grande and soon finds a job in the United States paying, say, $10 per hour in contrast to the $1 per hour that he earned in Guatemala. Yet the first day on the job, there has been no change in the former Guatemalan's human capital. What is it about the process of production in a rich country that allows a recent immigrant to have a much higher marginal product and earn a much higher wage than was previously possible in Guatemala?

Let us say that the Guatemalan's new job is with a landscaping service that mows the lawns of well-to-do Americans. The task of mowing the lawn (using physical capital consisting of a gas-powered lawn mower) takes virtually no education. What enables the Guatemalan to earn $10 per hour is that there are Americans who themselves are rich enough to be able to afford to pay to have their lawn mowed instead of mowing it themselves. Thus the immigration puzzle comes down to this: *every factor* that makes the United States a richer country than Guatemala contributes to the ability of the new immigrant to earn much more. As we will see in the next chapter, there are many factors not included in a production function like equation (10.14) that help to explain the immigration puzzle—differences between rich and poor countries include additional factors beyond physical and human capital, among them cultural attitudes toward work, climate and geography, how well the legal system protects property rights, the presence or absence of crime and corruption, and infrastructure in the form of highways, airports, and a well-functioning electricity supply and telephone system.

10-8 Endogenous Growth Theory: How Is Technological Change Produced?

Ever since the development of Solow's neoclassical growth model in the 1950s, economists have been uneasy about several of its implications. We have now reviewed several implications of the model that conflict with important facts about the real world. As we have seen, a primary problem is that technical change (*a*, the autonomous growth factor) is *exogenous*, dropping from the sky totally unexplained. Thus a nation desiring to boost its growth rate of output gains no insight into how to achieve a higher level and growth rate of *A*.

Since the late 1980s there has been an explosion of activity in what is now called "endogenous growth theory," so named because it attempts to explain technical change as the outcome of market activity in response to economic incentives rather than just assuming that technical change drops exogenously from the sky. The chief inventors of endogenous growth theory are Paul Romer of Stanford University and his Ph.D. thesis adviser at the University of Chicago, Robert E. Lucas, Jr. (also the inventor of the new classical macroeconomics and pictured in Chapter 17). Much of the writing on endogenous growth theory is highly technical; here we summarize some of the main ideas at a nontechnical level.[16] As the early ideas of Romer and Lucas continue to be subjected to critical reviews and reconsidered, the theory is still evolving.

---

[16] Frequently cited academic papers include Paul M. Romer, "Increasing Returns and Long-Run Growth," *Journal of Political Economy*, vol. 94 (1986), pp. 1002–37; the same author's "Endogenous Technological Change," *Journal of Political Economy*, vol. 98 (1990), pp. S71–103; and Robert E. Lucas, Jr., "On the Mechanics of Economic Development," *Journal of Monetary Economics*, vol. 22 (1988), pp. 3–42. The summary in this section is partly based on Paul M. Romer, "Increasing Returns and New Developments in the Theory of Growth," in W. A. Barnett, et al., eds., *Equilibrium Theory and Applications* (Cambridge University Press, 1991), pp. 83–100.

The Production of Ideas

Endogenous growth theory begins from the awkward fact that, as we have seen, the standard of living in many advanced countries is as much as ten times higher than that in many less-developed countries. But if technical change is freely available to all nations, then *all* of this huge superiority in standards of living must be attributable to a capital-labor ratio that is higher by a factor of 10,000. This would imply very little capital in less-developed countries and a huge rate of return to additional investment, since this would be guaranteed to bring these countries up toward the level of advanced nations. As a consequence, we should observe massive flows of capital from advanced countries to poor countries, but in fact we do not.

As we have seen, one solution to this puzzle is to introduce human capital as a key source of difference between rich and poor nations. But consideration of immigration leads to basic problems for the human capital approach, as it does for the concept of "effective labor" in the neoclassical model. Both of these models imply that immigrants to a rich country from a poor country with, say, 1/10 the output per person and 1/10 the human capital per person, upon arrival in the rich country should earn only 1/10 as much as native citizens. But many immigrants to the United States and other rich countries soon achieve the same high average standard of living as native residents.

Endogenous growth theorists thus have been led to focus on what are the characteristics of a rich society that not only make its native residents rich but also seem automatically to equip immigrants from poor countries with much higher incomes than they earned before. They have built models in which the key to growth is the development of ideas for new goods. To solve the incentive problem of how these ideas get produced, the models rely on monopoly power that is reinforced by patents and copyrights. International trade also plays an important role, since each country can concentrate on developing the ideas to produce a few new goods and then trade them with other countries, so that consumers can enjoy all of the new goods produced anywhere in the world. For instance, American households enjoying DVD movies are benefiting from early research that took place in Europe and the United States, together with product development in Japan and Korea that made the DVD player inexpensive to buy and relatively repair-free.

When the concept of ideas is applied broadly, it helps explain not only the introduction of new goods but also the development of better production techniques and higher quality in older goods like automobiles and household appliances. Rich countries use ideas and techniques that produce more and better goods per person. Furthermore, most of these ideas won't work without associated investment in physical capital and human capital. Even if a poor country like Bangladesh obtained piles of instruction manuals for making automobiles and personal computers, these manuals would be useless without educated people, factories, and equipment. This approach simultaneously explains why poor people clamor to migrate to rich countries, and also why poor nations are so eager for foreign investment by companies from rich countries, companies that can bring with them the required equipment and educated engineers and managers.

Empirical Studies and Policy Implications

As endogenous growth theory has developed, so has research on a wide variety of rich and poor countries, looking for correlations between growth rates and other variables. The conclusion is that faster growth is associated with a

Appendix to Chapter 10

General Functional Forms and the Production Function

Until this point, we have used only "specific linear" forms for the behavioral equations. For instance, the demand for money in the Appendix to Chapter 4 on p. 126 was written as:

$$\left(\frac{M}{P}\right)^d = hY - fr$$

This equation can be stated in words as: The real demand for money $(M/P)^d$ is equal to a positive number (h), times real GDP (Y), minus another number (f), times the interest rate (r). The equation tells specifically how the real demand for money depends on real GDP and the interest rate.

The production function can also be written in a specific form called the Cobb-Douglas production function.[1]

General Linear Form	Numerical Example
$Y = AK^bN^{1-b}$	$Y = AK^{0.25}N^{0.75}$

In words, this states that real GDP (Y) is equal to an autonomous growth factor (A), multiplied by a geometric weighted average of an index of capital (K) and of labor (N). The weights, b and $1 - b$, represent the elasticity (or percentage response) of real GDP to an increase in either factor.[2] For instance, in our numerical example if all variables are indexes initially at 1.0, a 4 percent increase in labor input will cause a 3 percent increase in real GDP. Initially:

$$1.0 = 1.0(1.0^{0.25}\ 1.0^{0.75})$$

After a 4 percent increase in labor input:

$$1.03 = 1.0(1.0^{0.25}\ 1.04^{0.75})$$

Thus the elasticity of real GDP with respect to a change in labor input is 0.75 (= 3/4).

Several other characteristics of the production function are evident. First, an equal percentage increase in both factors, capital and labor, raises real GDP by the same percentage. This characteristic, called *constant returns to scale*, occurs because the sum of the weights (b and $1 - b$) is unity. When both factor inputs increase by 4 percent, we have

$$1.04 = 1.0(1.04^{0.25}\ 1.04^{0.75})$$

after a 4 percent increase in both K and N.

A second characteristic is the direct one-for-one response of real GDP to the autonomous growth factor A. If A increases by four percentage points, while capital and labor input remain fixed at 1.0, real GDP increases by the same four percentage points

$$1.04 = 1.04(1.0^{0.25}\ 1.0^{0.75})$$

after a 4 percent increase in A.

The Cobb-Douglas production function is only one of many ways in which real GDP might be related to A, K, and N. Often in economics we want to make the simple

---

[1] The function is named after an Amherst mathematics professor, Charles W. Cobb, and a University of Chicago economics professor (later U.S. senator), Paul H. Douglas, and is described in a book by the latter, *The Theory of Wages* (New York: Macmillan, 1934), especially Chapter V.

[2] *Elasticity* is a term introduced in most elementary economics courses and refers to the percentage change in one variable in response to a 1 percent change in another variable.

statement that "Y is related to A, K, and N," but without restricting the particular form of the relationship. To accomplish this, we sometimes use a *general functional form*. An example of such a general form for the production function is:

$$Y = F(A, K, N)$$

In words, this states simply that real GDP (Y) depends on an autonomous growth factor (A), an index of capital input (K) and an index of labor input (N). The capital letter F and the parentheses mean *depends on*, and any alphabetical letter can be used.

Why is it interesting to know simply that one variable depends on others? By writing an alternative equation, one could state the *alternative hypothesis* that there is no role for an autonomous growth factor:

$$Y = F(K, N)$$

This states that real GDP depends *only on* capital and labor input.

Sometimes it is desirable to make a specific assumption about the form in which one variable enters, but not the others. This occurs in equation (10.1) on p. 324 in the text, which states that the elasticity of real GDP with respect to the autonomous growth factor is unity, but does not restrict the form of the relationship between real GDP and the other inputs, capital and labor:

$$Y = A \, F(K, N)$$

Without further information one cannot look at these general functional forms and learn whether the assumed relationship is positive or negative. The positive relationship between real GDP and both capital and labor inputs can be written in either of two ways:

$$\text{Method 1: } Y = A \, F(K, N)$$
$$(+)(+)$$

$$\text{Method 2: } Y = A \, F(K, N); \ F_K > 0, F_N > 0$$

The terms to the right of the semicolon in method 2 can be put into these words: The response of real GDP to a change in capital input (F_K) and in labor input (F_N) is positive (>0).

Exercise: Consider a general functional form for the demand for money:

$$\left(\frac{M}{P}\right)^d = L(Y, r)$$

State in words what this function states about the relationship between the real demand for money ($(M/P)^d$) and real GDP (Y) and the interest rate (r). Use both methods 1 and 2 to write down the facts that the real demand for money depends positively on real GDP and negatively on the interest rate.

The Big Questions of Economic Growth

Few problems are more fascinating, more important, or more neglected than the rates at which development proceeds in successive generations in different countries.
—Wesley Mitchell, 1927

11-1   Answering the Big Questions

More than half of the world's population lives on less than $3,200 per year, well below one-tenth of the $45,000 average level of per-person income in the United States. This startling level of inequality of the average income level across countries is much greater than the degree of inequality within a single country like the United States. Many theoretical models, like the Solow neo-classical growth model examined in the last chapter, predict that poor countries would steadily *converge* to the income levels of the rich countries. But this has not happened; the ratio of income per person in the richest countries to that of the poor countries has barely changed in the past 40 years.

Why Are We So Rich and They So Poor?

There is no more important question in economics than understanding the success of some countries in becoming relatively rich and the failure of other countries that have remained so poor. As expressed by Harvard economist David Landes, "Why Are We So Rich and They So Poor?"[1] Some countries, like the United States, Britain, and France, have remained at or near the frontier of income per person throughout the past half-century. Some other countries, like Asia's "Four Tigers" (Korea, Taiwan, Hong Kong, and Singapore), have achieved very rapid growth and within only one generation have transformed themselves from a group of poor nations to a group of rich nations, achieving the convergence predicted by the Solow growth model. The "BRIC" countries (Brazil, Russia, India, China) are also growing rapidly. But a third group of countries, including Pakistan, Bangladesh, and numerous countries in Africa and Latin America, have failed to converge. In many cases, their income per-person was below 10 percent of the U.S. level in 1960 and remains there today.

The Solow growth model of Chapter 10 provides a partial answer to the first basic question about economic growth. Countries with a higher level of income per person have a higher level of capital per person, which they achieve by saving and investing. The weakness of the Solow model is that it predicts differences between rich and poor nations in both capital per person and the rate of return on capital that are several orders of magnitude greater than is true in the data. This weakness is partially remedied, as we have seen on pp. 337–39, by including human capital as well as physical capital in the analysis and by

---

[1] David S. Landes, "Why Are We So Rich and They So Poor?" *American Economic Review Papers and Proceedings* (May 1990), pp. 1–13.

assuming that much of the income earned by labor is actually a reward to human capital rather than pure physical exertion. Yet even then we are left with questions, starting with the need to explain why an immigrant from a poor country to a rich country is able to achieve such a big jump in income without any immediate change in his human capital (i.e., educational attainment).

A bigger question is why some countries are so much more productive than others in using the capital that they have. In this chapter we broaden our investigation of the sources of economic growth in several directions. We will see that people will not start businesses or invest in those businesses if they cannot earn a decent return on their investment. Economic growth requires a political environment that creates incentives for investment, requiring a legal system that protects property rights and protection of ordinary citizens against corruption, bribery, theft, and confiscation of the returns on their investments. Even in a crime-free environment, political decisions can influence the incentives to invest and the productivity of those investments, including regulations on the trading of securities, on the protection of ideas through patent rights, and on the costs and difficulty of hiring and firing workers. Growth also requires investment in **infrastructure,** including some types of capital that benefit society as a whole and are often provided by government investment, including highways, airports, telephone systems, and electricity supply.

Infrastructure consists of types of capital that benefit society as a whole, including highways, airports, trains, waterways, ports, telephone networks, and electricity grids.

What Creates a Growth Miracle?

We have divided nations into the rich, the poor that have remained poor, and an intermediate group of countries, including Asia's Four Tigers, that have sprinted ahead from the ranks of the poor to the ranks of the rich. The experience of such countries that have sustained growth rates of 5 percent or more for several decades—often called a "growth miracle"—is illustrated by the comparison of Korea versus the Philippines on pp. 17–18. Such sustained rates of growth create unbelievable changes in the standard of living of ordinary citizens; for instance, a 5 percent growth rate sustained for four decades is sufficient to boost per-capita real income by a factor of 7.4, from $2,500 to $18,500.

The Solow theory suggests that all nations should eventually converge to the level of the world's technological leader, which for most of the past century has been the United States. The achievements of the fast-growing miracle economies could simply be dismissed as an automatic process if it were not for the fact that their achievements are so unusual; in fact, many other countries that started out poor 40 years ago are still just as poor, with income levels less than one-tenth of the United States. We can learn a great deal by studying the experience of the miracle nations as well as those countries that failed, especially by contrasting them as in this chapter.

The Mechanism of Growth

In addition to questions about the success or failure of poor countries in catching up to the technological frontier established by the rich countries, there is the separate question of the frontier itself. What determines the rate at which the frontier advances? Is it saving and investment, technological change, education, or other factors? As we shall see, growth would grind to a halt without a continuing stream of new inventions, and maintaining the flow of inventions and new ideas requires incentives to inventors to make the large, up-front investments needed to create new computer chips, software, medical technology, drugs, and other novel products.

What Caused the Worldwide Growth Slowdown and Subsequent Revival?

Growth at the frontier, that is, the level of per-capita income enjoyed by the leading rich country, is not smooth or steady. Much of this book has been devoted to understanding the business cycles that cause periods of prosperity to alternate with shorter periods of recession and high unemployment. But even disregarding the recessions and averaging over the entire business cycle, growth proceeds at an uneven pace. The period of most rapid growth in the United States was the entire half-century between 1913 and 1973; in Europe and Japan the period of rapid growth was compressed into the shorter interval between 1948 and 1973, part of which consisted of making up for wartime destruction.

The last sections of this chapter examine the pace of economic growth in the rich countries, particularly the United States, over the past century. Why was growth fastest in the middle of the twentieth century, and why did it slow down after 1973? A new event to examine is the revival of productivity growth in the United States after 1995. Why did this revival occur, and what made it occur in the United States but not, at least so far, in Europe or Japan? Does the return of rapid U.S. productivity growth in 1995–2007 at rates similar to 1913–73 indicate that the slowdown period of 1973–95 is a historical oddity, never to be repeated? Or is the post-1995 revival itself an oddity that may already have fizzled out?

11-2 The Standard of Living and Concepts of Productivity

In Chapter 10 we used the concepts of "output per person," "productivity," and "output per hour" interchangeably, using the symbol Y/N. As before, the growth rate of a ratio is the difference between the growth rates of the numerator and denominator, so the growth rate of these concepts was designated as $y - n$.

Distinguishing the Standard of Living from Labor Productivity

However, it is possible for the growth rate of the population to differ from the growth rate of labor input. To maintain intact our previous development of the Solow growth model, we will continue to use the symbol N (growing at rate n) for labor input or hours of work, and we will introduce the new symbol q for the rate of population growth. Factors that could cause work hours to grow faster than the population ($n > q$) include a movement of women into the labor force, as happened in the 1970s and 1980s, or a decline in the birthrate that initially reduces growth in the number of children and only later reduces growth in the workforce, defined as those aged 16 and older. Factors that could cause work hours to grow more slowly than the population ($n < q$) include a move to

The **standard of living** is real GDP per member of the population, or "real output per capita."

Labor productivity is real GDP per hour of work, or "real output per hour."

an earlier age of retirement and to longer vacations, as well as factors causing higher unemployment or a lower labor-force participation rate.[2]

Economic growth refers to an improvement in the **standard of living,** defined as output per capita or member of the population (Y/Q). **Labor productivity** is defined as output per hour of work (Y/N), using the same definition of output. The growth rate of the standard of living is $y - q$, while the growth rate of labor productivity is $y - n$. Thus the difference between the growth rate of the standard of living and that of labor productivity is

$$y - q - (y - n) = n - q \qquad (11.1)$$

Therefore, whenever hours grow faster than the population $(n > q)$, the standard of living grows faster than labor productivity, and vice versa.

The distinction between q and n is worth making when examining differences between the United States and other countries. As shown in the figure on p. 322, European countries still lag well behind the United States in their output per capita, but several of the leading European nations have caught up to the United States in their level of labor productivity, or output per hour. The reason that productivity in Europe has grown faster than the standard of living is clear from equation (11.1)—hours of work in Europe have grown more slowly than the population. Over the past few decades, Europeans have chosen to take longer vacations than are typical in the United States, their average unemployment rate has risen, and their labor-force participation rate has declined. Europeans retire at earlier ages than Americans. These events prevent the European standard of living from catching up to the United States even as the productivity gap has vanished for some European nations. We return to contrasts between Europe and the United States in the last section of this chapter.

Multifactor Productivity (Solow's Residual)

A second concept of productivity is important in the study of economic growth. Already defined in Chapter 10, this is multifactor productivity (MFP), which is sometimes called "Solow's residual" after Robert M. Solow, the Nobel-prize winning inventor of neoclassical growth theory. The concept of MFP differs from labor productivity in that it expresses the amount of output produced relative to *both* labor and capital inputs; in contrast, labor productivity expresses the amount of output produced relative to labor input only. The contribution that capital makes to output is measured by the elasticity of output to capital (b), which we will continue, as in Chapter 10, to assume is 0.25 in our numerical examples. The elasticity of output to capital and labor input together is unity (1.0), and so the elasticity of output to labor is the remaining amount not attributable to capital $(1 - b)$, or 0.75 in the numerical example.

The growth rate of MFP (for which we use, as before, the symbol a) can be written as the growth rate of output (y) minus the contribution of capital (bk) minus the contribution of labor hours $[(1 - b)n]$:

$$a = y - bk - (1 - b)n \qquad (11.2)$$

---

[2] The labor force, defined on p. 43, is the sum of employment plus unemployment. The labor-force participation rate is the ratio of the labor force to the working-age population, aged 16 and older. The labor-force participation rate in the United States in December 2007 was 66.0 percent.

Thus, to measure the growth rate of multifactor productivity, we need to know four facts: the growth rates of output, capital, and labor (y, k, and n), and the elasticity of output with respect to capital (b). As Robert Solow showed in the 1950s in part of the work that earned him the Nobel Prize in economics, this elasticity can be measured by the share of capital in national income, including corporate profits, depreciation, rent, interest, and the portion of the income of the self-employed that is attributable to capital.[3]

How are the growth rates of multifactor productivity (a) and labor productivity ($y - n$) related to each other? Equation (11.2) can be rearranged to show their relationship.[4]

General Form   Numerical Example

$$a = (y - n) - b(k - n) \qquad 2.25 = (4 - 1) - 0.25(4 - 1) \qquad (11.3)$$

In words, the growth rate of multifactor productivity is equal to the growth rate of labor productivity minus b times the growth in the ratio of capital input to labor input.[5] Since growth in the ratio is almost always positive, the growth of MFP is almost always slower than that of labor productivity.

 SELF-TEST

The definition of MFP growth in equation (11.3) has five elements: y, a, k, n, and b.

1. Assuming that b always equals 0.25, any of the four remaining elements can be calculated if the other three are known. Fill in the blanks:

y	a	k	n
—	4	4	1
4	3	4	—
3	0	—	1

2. For each example in the table above, which is higher: labor productivity growth or MFP growth? Why should this be the case?

How the Real Wage Is Related to Productivity

If labor productivity (Y/N) grows slowly, the real wage (W/P) tends to grow slowly. We have already learned in equation (11.2) that an ingredient in the measurement of multifactor productivity (MFP) is labor's share in national income ($1 - b$). This central concept, called labor's share, can be defined in a way that connects labor productivity with the real wage:

$$\text{Labor's share} = 1 - b = \frac{WN}{PY} = \frac{W/P}{Y/N} \qquad (11.4)$$

The first expression states that labor's share is equal to the total compensation of labor [the nominal wage rate (W), times the quantity of labor input (N)], divided by total income in nominal terms (PY). The second expression states that this is exactly the same as the real wage divided by labor productivity.

---

[3] Solow's idea of linking the elasticity of output to capital with capital's share in national income is explained in Chapter 10, footnote 10, on p. 333.

[4] Equation (11.3) is identical to equation (10.11) on p. 332.

[5] The growth of the ratio of capital input to labor input is often called "capital deepening."

Equation (11.4) helps us see that if labor's share in national income is constant, then the real wage must grow at the same rate as labor productivity. As usual, we employ lowercase symbols to represent growth rates, and we can use the familiar relationship that the growth rate of any ratio equals the growth rate of the numerator minus the growth rate of the denominator. This implies that the growth rate of labor's share equals the growth rate of the real wage $(w - p)$, minus the growth rate of labor productivity $(y - n)$:

$$\text{Growth rate of labor's share} = (w - p) - (y - n) \qquad (11.5)$$

This leads us to a very important conclusion about the growth rate of the real wage. If labor's share is constant (so that the growth rate of labor's share is zero), then *the growth rate of the real wage must be exactly equal to the growth rate of productivity.*

Condition if the growth rate of labor's share is zero

$$w - p = y - n \qquad (11.6)$$

Labor's share of national income in the United States has been virtually constant for the past 30 years. As a result, the real wage has grown at the same rate as labor productivity.

11-3 The Failure of Convergence

If half of the world's population still lives in countries with output per capita that is less than one-tenth the level of the United States, then this implies that these countries have failed to converge to the U.S. standard of living. Yet convergence is just what is predicted to occur by the Solow neoclassical growth model studied in the last chapter. First, let us review why the Solow model predicts convergence; then we will look at the facts.

The Theoretical Prediction of Convergence

The simple Solow model with no technical change does not actually explain economic growth. It predicts that a country with a given per-person production function and given saving rate (s) will have a fixed level of labor productivity (Y/N) and capital per worker (K/N). For instance, in Figure 11-1 we have copied the equilibrium in the Solow model from Figure 10-3, where the economy operates at point E_0 with a capital stock per hour of $(K/N)_0$ and a level of saving equal to $s(Y/N)_0$. How does the Solow model explain how a poor nation might be operating at point P with a much lower level of capital per hour $(K/N)_P$ and level of saving $s(Y/N)_P$?

Clearly, such an economy must not be in its long-run equilibrium, because its level of saving per person at point P exceeds its investment requirements shown at point A, that is, the amount of investment $(n + d)(K/N)_P$ needed to provide for population growth and depreciation. Since actual investment equals saving and is in excess of investment requirements, the capital-labor ratio will grow steadily until the economy reaches long-run equilibrium at point E_0. According to the Solow model, the only difference between rich nations and poor nations is that the poor nations have a lower capital-labor ratio K/N. Since there is no difference in the per-person production function between rich and poor nations, the process of saving in excess of investment requirements

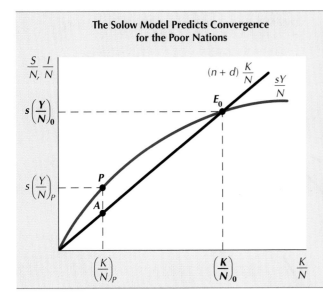

The Solow Model Predicts Convergence for the Poor Nations

Figure 11-1 Saving, Investment, and Capital per Hour in Long-Run Equilibrium for a Poor Nation

The blue saving line and black investment requirements line are copied from Figure 10-3. The long-run equilibrium point is shown at E_0. The only reason given by the Solow growth model for the low output per hour $(Y/N)_P$ of poor nations is their low level of capital per hour $(K/N)_P$, and their economies operate at the point labeled P. Because their saving and investment per hour at P exceed their investment requirements for population growth and depreciation, shown at A, there is sufficient excess investment to boost the K/N ratio up to the equilibrium value $(K/N)_0$.

will automatically cause the poor nations to converge to the same equilibrium point E_0 as the rich nations.

Does technological change alter the convergence prediction of the Solow model? No, because technology is assumed to be freely available to all countries. Thus the model continues to assume that the only reason for nations to be poor is that they start at a level of the capital-labor ratio (K/N) that is well below the equilibrium value. As shown in Figure 11-2, the equilibrium level of labor productivity (Y/N) can steadily increase, but the Solow model predicts that rich countries and poor countries alike will eventually converge to the same equilibrium value. The rich countries reach the equilibrium value earlier because they started with a higher capital-labor ratio and thus required a shorter period of saving and investment.

A key empirical prediction of the Solow model is that the poorer the nation, that is, the lower its labor productivity (Y/N) in an initial period of time, the faster the growth of its labor productivity. We can see this in Figure 11-2, where the arrow labeled "Poor nations" rises at a steeper slope than the arrow labeled "Rich nations." Thus the Solow model would predict that there would be a *negative* relationship between a nation's initial level of Y/N and its subsequent growth rate $(y - n)$. In short, poor nations should uniformly exhibit faster growth rates of labor productivity and per-capita output than rich nations. After rich and poor nations converge to the long-run equilibrium path, their growth rates should be identical.

Facts About Convergence

Data on rich and poor countries refer to output per person. Extensive research has been carried out by Robert Summers and Alan Heston of the University of Pennsylvania to improve the comparability of real output data across countries. The Summers-Heston data measure real output per person at a common set of prices for all nations, and this tends to improve the standing of poor

Figure 11-2 Output per Hour of Rich and Poor Nations During the Period of Convergence

Both the rich and poor nations are assumed to start off with an equilibrium level of capital per hour (K/N) that is below equilibrium, but the poor nations begin much below the rich nations. Because all nations initially have investment in excess of requirements for population growth and depreciation, they all grow faster than the equilibrium path until they catch up. Since the poor nations start further back, it takes them more time to converge to the equilibrium path, and their growth rates are faster during this time period.

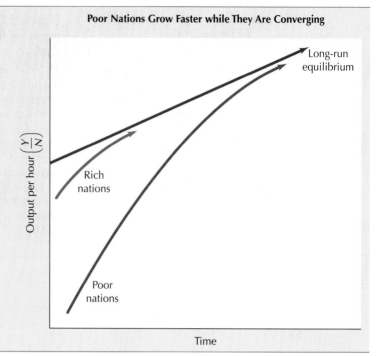

Poor Nations Grow Faster while They Are Converging

nations markedly compared to the crude alternative of comparing GDP across nations using foreign exchange rates.[6]

Despite these corrections for common prices, many nations remain very poor. This is shown in Figure 11-3, which has one dot for each of 97 nations. The horizontal position of each dot represents real output per worker in 1960 as a percentage of the United States, and the vertical position represents the growth rate of real output per worker from 1960 to 2004. The extent of world-wide poverty in 1960 is shown by the number of dots to the left of 10 percent on the horizontal axis; in each of these nations (31 of the 97), real output per worker in 1960 was less than 10 percent of the U.S. level. Among these poor countries, those that grew slower than the U.S. after 1960 are shown by red dots. *These are the poor countries that failed to converge.*

Recall that the Solow model predicts faster growth in poor nations than in rich nations, indicating that the slope of the dots in Figure 11-3 should be nega-tive, slanting downward from left to right. Indeed, there are green dots at the upper left corner of the diagram; among the fast growing nations that started out relatively poor in 1960 are China, Korea, Hong Kong, and Taiwan. These four nations all registered growth rates in the vertical direction of 5.0 percent or higher. The next group of nations with growth rates around 4.0 to 4.5 percent include Malaysia, Thailand, and Singapore.

However, the overall correlation of the dots in Figure 11-3 is zero. There are far more countries having growth rates below the U.S. rate, shown by the red

---

[6] Robert Summers and Alan Heston, "The Penn World Table (Mark 5): An Expanded Set of International Comparisons, 1950–1988," *Quarterly Journal of Economics*, vol. 106 (May 1991), pp. 327–68. The latest data are available at pwt.econ.upenn.edu/php_site/pwt62/pwt62_form.php.

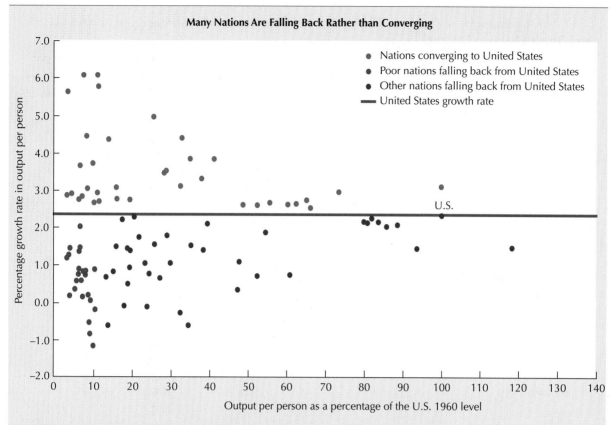

Many Nations Are Falling Back Rather than Converging

- Nations converging to United States
- Poor nations falling back from United States
- Other nations falling back from United States
- United States growth rate

y-axis: Percentage growth rate in output per person

x-axis: Output per person as a percentage of the U.S. 1960 level

Figure 11-3 **Output per Worker Relative to the United States in 1960 and the Growth of Output per Person, 1960–2004**

The convergence hypothesis suggests that the poorest nations, those on the left of the diagram, will have the fastest rates of growth. The dots should slope downward to the right and all dots should be above the horizontal line, which represents the growth rate of the United States. The low correlation of the growth rates and levels and the substantial number of red dots, showing poor countries with growth rates below that of the United States, are evidence contradicting the convergence hypothesis.

Source: Alan Heston, Robert Summers, and Bettina Aten, Penn World Table Version 6.2, Center for International Comparisons of Production, Income, and Prices at the University of Pennsylvania, September 2006. See pwt.econ.upenn.edu/php_site/pwt62/pwt62_form.php.

and blue dots, than having growth rates above the U.S. rate, shown by the green dots. There are even a few rich nations that failed to converge. Among these, shown in the second section of Table 11-1, are New Zealand, Venezuela, and Argentina. The next section of the table lists China, Hong Kong, and South Korea, nations that were initially poor but converged rapidly. Poor nations that slipped back, the opposite direction of convergence, included Bolivia in Latin America, as well as Cameroon and Mali in sub-Saharan Africa. Any country with an average growth rate below the U.S. growth rate of 2.3 percent per year wound up with an average level of output per person relative to the United States that was *worse* in 2004 than in 1960, the opposite of convergence. About

Table 11-1 Examples of Countries Displaying Convergence, Anti-Convergence, or Neither (Levels and Growth Rates in Percent)

Country	Output per person relative to the United States		Growth rate of output per person, 1960–2004	
	2004	1960	Actual	Relative to U.S.
Rich countries that converged				
Austria	78	65	2.7	0.4
Italy	64	56	2.7	0.3
France	72	66	2.5	0.2
Rich countries that failed to converge				
New Zealand	63	94	1.4	−0.9
Venezuela	20	47	0.3	−2.0
Argentina	30	61	0.8	−1.6
Poor countries that converged				
China	15	3	5.6	3.3
Hong Kong	82	26	5.0	2.6
South Korea	51	11	5.8	3.4
Poor countries that fell back				
Bolivia	8	19	0.5	−1.8
Cameroon	8	15	0.8	−1.5
Mali	3	6	0.9	−1.4
Poor countries that made no progress				
Syria	6	6	2.0	−0.3
Pakistan	7	6	2.8	0.4

Source: Alan Heston, Robert Summers, and Bettina Aten, Penn World Table Version 6.2, Center for International Comparisons of Production, Income, and Prices at the University of Pennsylvania, September 2006. The latest data are available at pwt.econ.upenn.edu/php_site/pwt62/pwt62.form_php.

two-thirds of the nations plotted in Figure 11-3 experienced the opposite of convergence. Some others, including the examples shown in the bottom section of Table 11-1, made no progress, exhibiting roughly the same growth rates as the United States over the 1960–2004 period.

While the prediction of convergence seems to be a failure of the Solow model, this verdict needs to be qualified. Among the rich nations, the required negative correlation between the initial income level and subsequent growth rate was quite strong, with few exceptions. This verdict is valid either for the 1960–2004 period examined in Figure 11-3 or the longer 1885–2004 period.[7] What seems to go wrong with the prediction of convergence refers to the poor countries. When the poor countries are included, as in Figure 11-3, the negative correlation disappears, and there appears to be no systematic relationship between the initial 1960 level of real GDP relative to the United States and the subsequent growth rate.

---

[7] See Charles I. Jones, *Introduction to Economic Growth*, 2d ed. (New York: Norton, 2001), Chapter 3.

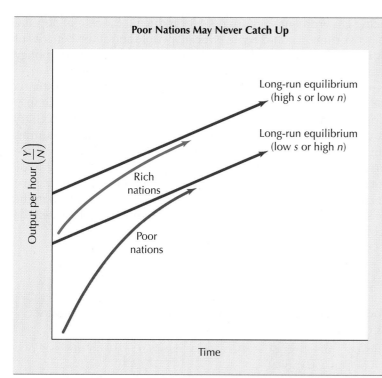

Poor Nations May Never Catch Up

Long-run equilibrium (high *s* or low *n*)

Long-run equilibrium (low *s* or high *n*)

Rich nations

Poor nations

Output per hour $\left(\frac{Y}{N}\right)$

Time

Figure 11-4 The Effect of a Low Saving Rate or High Rate of Population Growth on Output per Person

The upper blue line shows the long-run equilibrium growth path for the rich nations. Two factors could cause the long-run path to be lower for the poor nations—either a lower saving rate (*s*) or a faster rate of population growth (*n*).

Solutions Suggested by the Solow Model

The reason the Solow model suggests convergence is that it assumes unrealistically that all nations have the same per-person production function, saving rate, growth rate of the population, and depreciation rate. We have already seen in Figure 10-4 on p. 330 the Solow model's prediction that an increase in the saving rate can temporarily *raise* the growth rate of output and capital per person. In the same diagram, an increase in the rate of population growth (*n*) would *reduce* the growth rate of output and capital per person.[8] Thus one valid explanation for the failure of poor countries to converge is that, with either a lower saving rate (low *s*) or higher rate of population growth (high *n*), their equilibrium growth path is not the single path depicted by the blue line in Figure 11-2 but rather is a lower path as shown by the lower blue line in Figure 11-4. Thus the puzzle of why some poor countries do not fully converge to the output per person level of the rich nations can be explained by any combination of lower saving rates or faster rates of population growth.

What government policies can achieve a higher saving rate or a lower rate of population growth? The first method to increase saving is to reduce the taxation of saving, for instance by shifting from a progressive income tax to a progressive consumption tax that exempts saving from taxation. Most studies suggest that such policies have only a small impact on saving. A more effective method of raising national saving is for the government to switch from a budget deficit to a budget surplus by some combination of raising

---

[8] Turn back to Figure 10-4 on p. 330. Imagine tilting the black investment requirements line labeled $(n + d)(K/N)$ upward. This will cause the equilibrium point E_0 to move downward and to the left, reducing the equilibrium levels of Y/N and K/N. Thus an increase in the rate of population growth (*n*) will reduce the equilibrium levels of Y/N and K/N, just as an increase in the saving rate (*s*) will have the opposite effect.

taxes and reducing government spending. As for reducing the rate of population growth, the government could try to educate people about the benefits of birth control. An extreme example of such a policy was the "one-child" policy of China that was enforced by the political dictatorship of that country.

Does the empirical evidence support the Solow model's prediction that a higher investment rate allows nations to achieve a higher standard of living? The relationship between the investment rate (the share of investment in GDP) and the standard of living across many nations is very weak. Poor countries have investment ratios ranging all the way from 2 percent to 25 percent relative to GDP. Similarly, rich countries have investment rates ranging from 12 to 30 percent. Thus the Solow model ultimately cannot explain the failure of at least half of the poor countries to converge over the past few decades. We turn in the next two sections to alternative explanations of the continuing gap between the rich and poor countries.

 SELF-TEST

The Solow growth model makes predictions both about the level of per-person output and its growth rate.

1. What is the long-run effect of an increase in the saving rate on the level of per-person output and capital?

2. What is the long-run effect of an increase in the saving rate on the growth rate of output per capita?

3. What is the long-run effect of an increase in the rate of population growth on the level of per-person output and capital?

4. What is the long-run effect of an increase in the rate of population growth on the growth rate of output per capita?

11-4 Human Capital and Technology

The Solow model as developed in Chapter 10 cannot explain the relationship between the levels and growth rates of output per capita, as displayed in Figure 11-3. While the Solow model, as in Figure 11-4, can allow the saving rate and population growth rate to differ, thus yielding a lower equilibrium level of output per capita for poor nations, it seems to assume much more likeness between poor and rich nations than is true in fact. In particular, its assumptions that the per-person production function and the rate of technological change are identical across poor and rich countries seem dubious. Also, the Solow model as treated so far in this chapter neglects the role of human capital, previously introduced in Section 10-7 on pp. 337–39.

Human Capital and Economic Growth

Perhaps the most basic flaw in the simple Solow model is to assume that labor input is identical across rich and poor countries. In fact, educational attainment (the number of years of education achieved by an average member of the population) is vastly different between rich and poor countries. Studies of economic growth usually find that poor nations fall short in every measure of factors that tend to promote growth, including insufficient physical capital, human capital, and saving rates, as well as excessive rates of population growth. But, to use an old phrase, "correlation does not imply causation." Perhaps the sources of low growth are themselves *endogenous*, that is, caused by low growth itself. Poor countries simply cannot afford to engage in high levels of investment in physical and human capital. Further, for poor countries to achieve the lower fertility rates needed to achieve lower rates of population growth may require education, the crucial growth factor that poor nations cannot afford.

Does Technological Change Require Human Capital?

The Solow model assumes that the rate of technological change is the same in every country, *and that the best available technology is freely available to all countries*. This explains why in Figure 11-2 we have drawn the upper blue long-run equilibrium line as the same for rich and poor countries alike. The different levels for rich and poor countries of the blue long-run equilibrium lines in Figure 11-4 are caused solely by different saving rates and rates of population growth, not different growth rates of technological change.

Yet this is surely an unrealistic assumption in the Solow model. Modern technology often requires modern equipment and software. Thus both investment and technological change require educated workers, that is, a previous investment in human capital. If workers are illiterate, how can they use personal computers and the Internet as fruitfully as in countries where all workers can read and write, and where most workers are familiar with personal computers? As a skeptic suggested, "If you unloaded a pile of Dell computers and Microsoft software on a pier in Bangladesh, would that create the long-awaited convergence of the Bangladeshi standard of living to the level of the United States?" Bangladesh and many other poor countries do not have sufficient numbers of educated workers who know how to use modern computers and software, rendering modern technology inaccessible, in contrast to the assumption of the Solow model that it is freely available everywhere.

Importing Technological Change Through Foreign Investment

Most research and development takes place in the rich countries, especially in the United States, western Europe, and Japan. Poor countries are unable to afford large investments in research and development activities, so what can they do to acquire the technical knowledge being developed by the rich nations? Three main methods are available. First, engineers in poor countries may try to copy modern products made in rich countries. However, this is very difficult and often impossible for the most advanced products, including computer chips. A second method is to purchase imported machinery that embodies the latest technology. Developing nations have been importing the latest technology since the early nineteenth century, when American firms imported British steam engines. A third method is to obtain investment by foreign firms, which open factories in the poor country based on the latest technology. Mexican economic growth has been spurred in the past decade by American investment, and Singapore's inclusion as one of Asia's four fast-growing "tigers" has been heavily dependent on foreign investment, mainly by Japanese and American companies. More recently, rapid economic growth in China has been propelled by foreign investment, not just from Japan and the United States, but from neighboring Hong Kong and Taiwan.

"Not so fast," economics ministers in many poor countries might respond if shown this list of three channels by which they might obtain modern technology. "Our people are not sufficiently educated to copy the latest techniques, we cannot afford to pay for imported modern machinery, and our countries are not attractive as locations for foreign investment." This hypothetical comment from the poor countries brings us to the heart of the development problem that they face. Everything depends on everything else, and some countries are in a "vicious" circle in which they are too poor to improve the educational level of their citizens or to obtain modern technology, two prerequisites to growth.

The view that "everything is endogenous" and that some poor countries are caught in a "poverty trap" makes the prospects for growth seem hopeless for many poor countries. Yet this ignores the fact that many other poor nations have succeeded in launching themselves on the path to convergence, as shown by the many green dots in Figure 11-3 on p. 357. Perhaps not every growth-inducing factor is endogenous, and there are some other factors that governments can influence, that is, convert into an exogenous growth-promoting influence. The next section discusses two important factors that governments can influence, the political/legal environment and infrastructure investment, and one that they cannot influence, the geographical location of their countries.

11-5 Political Capital, Infrastructure, and Geography

Recently economists have made substantial progress toward identifying fundamental, underlying sources of growth that help us understand why some countries "take off" on a path toward convergence, while other countries remain mired at extremely low levels of income. The most basic of these sources is the legal and political environment. The free market system requires that entrepreneurs who are taking risks by starting a new business have a high probability of making a decent profit to reward them for their effort and for the risk they are taking that their business may fail. The legal system must protect the right to own property and must protect it from thieves; the tax system must be fairly administered; and the opportunity to start a business must be open, not limited to relatives or cronies of corrupt dictators. The second major factor that involves government decisions is infrastructure investment in such crucial factors of production as highways, airports, ports, telephone networks, and electricity systems. Unfortunately, a third factor, geography, impairs the growth opportunities of some nations but cannot usually be influenced by government policy.[9]

Political and Legal Determinants of Costs and Returns

In most countries, permits must be purchased in order to start a business and construct a building. In advanced countries like the United States, these permits are easily obtained, and their price is only a small fraction of the overall

---

[9] Parts of this section are based on Charles I. Jones, *Introduction to Economic Growth*, 2d ed. (New York: Norton, 2001), Chapter 7. See also Robert E. Hall and Charles I. Jones, "Why Do Some Countries Produce So Much More Output per Worker than Others?" *Quarterly Journal of Economics*, vol. 114 (February 1999), pp. 83–116.

International Perspective

A Symptom of Poverty:
Urban Slums in the Poor Cities

College students may find it hard to believe that billions of people, as shown in Figure 11-3 on p. 357, had a standard of living in 1960 below 10 percent of the U.S. level and were even further behind in 2004. How can people survive when the GDP per person in their country is so low? Many of the world's poor live in rural villages in primitive homes with no electricity or running water, similar to American farm families in 1875 but with much less land per person. More interesting are the conditions of life of poor people in poor countries who have chosen to move from their rural villages to the city.

In most poor countries, the large cities are surrounded by urban slums, occupied by thousands and even millions of people. Sometimes the slums are in the middle of the cities as in the case of Kibera, an area of about one square mile located in the middle of Nairobi, Kenya, populated by between 600,000 and 1 million people (nobody knows for sure). In 1960, Kenya, a former British colony, had an income per person of 9 percent of the U.S. level; by 2004, this had fallen back to 3 percent, due to the fact that Kenya registered a growth rate of per-person income of *exactly zero* between 1960 and 2004.

Kibera is an "informal" settlement, meaning that legally it does not exist. The government provides nothing. There are no basic services, no schools, no hospitals, no running water, no lavatories. Many people make money by privately providing such services to the inhabitants, often extracting bribe money. Residents must use privately owned latrines, paying the equivalent of about four American cents for the privilege. Permission to put up a shack costs about $70—but provides no legal deed or other printed document proving ownership. Most shacks are owned by an elite group that rents them out, but the renters have no security of tenure and can be kicked out on a landlord's any whim.

Shacks are packed so densely that many can be reached only on foot, because there is no room for roads. There is dust in the dry season and mud in the wet season. Low-hanging roofs of jagged corrugated iron can wound people who accidentally collide with them. Litter is everywhere, including the "flying toilet," plastic bags thrown out from their doorways. The stench is ever-present.

The uneducated and unskilled people of Kibera have no choice but to provide cheap labor—which is conve-

nient for the upper-income inhabitants of the surrounding Nairobi. Those lucky enough to have jobs must walk to them.

The misery of slums is pervasive in poor countries. In gigantic Mumbai (formerly Bombay), India, perhaps half of the 16 million residents live in slums. Less than half of the slum dwellers have running water and some of that is contaminated. Housing units have no lavatories, and hundreds of people have to use a single outdoor lavatory. Everywhere there is the stench of sewage. But India is making economic progress more rapidly than such tropical African countries as Kenya. India's urban slum dwellers are starting to earn enough money to rent apartments and buy TV sets and mobile phones. Still, life is hard. Because Mumbai is so large, most workers have to commute to work on overcrowded roads and trains, with sometimes 700 passengers crammed into (or holding onto) train cars intended for 100 passengers.

Why do urban residents endure such conditions? What else can they do? In India, the agricultural economy grows very slowly while the urban economies grow rapidly, allowing India to reach economic growth rates in recent years of close to 8 percent. Many agricultural laborers are essentially slaves, so deeply in debt that they have to do the bidding of the landowner; cities with their slums may seem to offer more opportunities.

Anyone who has experienced the slums of Kenya, India, or other poor countries and knows the United States finds the contrast incredible. American dwelling units have twice as much interior space and four times the outdoor space as typical dwelling units even in Europe's rich countries. Cities in rich countries have problems, but they are of a different magnitude than those of cities in poor countries. Most people would agree, for instance, that New York City's traffic congestion and Los Angeles's underdeveloped and underfunded public transportation system are issues that pale in comparison to Kibera's absolute lack of basic human services and Mumbai's poor sanitation system.[a]

---

[a] For more on urban slums, see a special survey in the *Economist*, May 5, 2007.

cost of starting the business. But in other countries, the permits may be very expensive, there may be long delays in obtaining them, and, more important, officials may expect bribes. In Russia some investors have reported that as many as ten different agencies each expected a bribe in order to grant permission for new projects. In another example, the cost of starting a small business in Peru was estimated to be 32 times the monthly minimum wage, an impossible sum for an average worker or even a relatively well-off citizen. Not surprisingly, Peru is one of the growth failures shown in Figure 11-3 that barely registered positive growth in output per person during 1960–2004, and its output per person fell back from 24 percent of the U.S. level in 1960 to 12 percent in 2004. Over the entire period from 1975 to 2004, output per person in Peru registered a negative growth rate.

There are a wider variety of factors that can influence the expected returns from starting a business. First, the country must have relatively free trade so that products manufactured in that country can be exported. Governments obtain access for their exports to other countries by having relatively low barriers to trade for imports into their countries.

Second, those who develop new ideas must be protected by a strong patent system, such as that in the United States that protects inventors for a substantial period of time from having their new ideas copied by imitators. Patents are essential to give potential inventors the incentive to develop new products and techniques. Just as important is what has been called "diversion," which includes the problem of theft (both "outside" robberies and theft by managers or workers), very high levels of taxation levied by governments, or "protection money" like that paid to the Mafia in gangster movies. Any kind of diversion reduces the expected profits on a business investment both directly and indirectly, by forcing business firms to invest in such anti-diversion activities as security systems.

Overall, even if there is no diversion at all, it still is difficult for most people in poor countries to start their own businesses. Typically in poor countries, inequality is high, with most of the income earned by a small number of rich people. The remaining people find it difficult to start a business because they are poor, lack education about how to run a business, and often do not qualify for credit.

The amount of diversion in a country is determined by government policy and the type of legal system that is provided by a country's constitution. Sometimes the diversion is created by the government itself, as when dictators in Indonesia and some African countries give lucrative contracts to businesses owned by a dictator's relatives. Not only must diversion be minimized, but government policies must also be *predictable*. Countries with reputations for frequent changes in government, whether by political coups or constitutional changes, will have low expected returns to investment due to the high risks of locating a business there.

An interesting aspect of economic development is the colonial origins of a particular country's legal system. Former colonies of the United Kingdom, such as the United States, Canada, Australia, India, and Singapore, have a legal system based on common law dating back to medieval England. Former colonies of France and Spain, including most of Latin America, have a legal system dating back to the Napoleonic Codes. Studies have found that legal protections for shareholders and creditors are stronger in the English-based legal systems than in the French-based systems. As a result, countries with

English-based legal systems tend to have better developed capital markets in which it is easier for new small companies to finance investment projects and develop their businesses.[10]

Why Do Governments Tolerate and Even Engage in Diversion?

It seems obvious that theft and corruption would impede economic growth by reducing the expected returns to investment, both by domestic citizens and foreign firms, which can choose from a wide variety of countries for the location of investment projects. Why then do governments tolerate these forms of diversion, and why do some governments engage directly in diversion through bribe taking and corruption? Douglass North, the 1993 Nobel prizewinner in economics, points out that government officials may want to maximize their own power and their own monetary incomes rather than being "benevolent social planners" who attempt to maximize the welfare of everyone in society. North's notion takes one step further the conventional economic precept that individuals try to maximize utility and firms try to maximize profits. Government bureaucrats may deliberately take bribes and tolerate theft by Mafia-type organizations in order to maximize income and power or minimize the nuisance of trying to get rid of offenders.[11]

MIT economist Daron Acemoglu and Berkeley economist James Robinson attempt to go further and determine the political environment that encourages or discourages government activities that minimize diversion:

> Political elites may block technological and institutional development, because of a political replacement effect. Innovations often erode elites' incumbency advantage, increasing the likelihood that they will be replaced. Fearing replacement, political elites are unwilling to initiate change, and may even block economic development.... It is only when political competition is limited and also their power is threatened that elites will block development.[12]

Empirically, the presence or absence of diversion helps explain not only economic growth but also the values of other determinants of growth like investment rates and education.[13] Just as education is often called "human capital," as in the analysis of Chapter 10, in the same way we can refer to a healthy political and legal environment that discourages diversion as "political capital." Since it is a key ingredient both in growth and in fostering other growth-inducing factors like investment in physical capital and human capital, the presence of political capital may be the key to understanding why some countries succeed and others fail at achieving economic growth.[14]

---

[10] See Rafael La Porta, Florencio Lopez-de-Silanes, Andrei Shleifer, and Robert Vishny, "Law and Finance," *Journal of Political Economy*, vol. 106, 1998, pp. 1113–55.

[11] Douglass C. North, *Structure and Change in Economic History* (New York: Norton, 1991).

[12] Daron Acemoglu and James A. Robinson, "Economic Backwardness in Political Perspective," *American Political Science Review*, February 2006, vol. 100, pp. 115–31. See also Daron Acemoglu, Simon Johnson, and James Robinson, "Institutions as the Fundamental Cause of Long-run Growth," in P. Aghion and S. Durlauf eds., *Handbook of Economic Growth* (Elsevier, 2005).

[13] See the article by Hall and Jones cited in footnote 9. See also Jeffrey D. Sachs and Andrew Warner, "Economic Reform and the Process of Global Integration," *Brookings Papers on Economic Activity*, 1995, vol. 26, no. 1, pp. 1–95.

[14] A comprehensive introduction to the problem of low economic growth in poor countries is William Easterly, *The Elusive Quest for Growth* (Cambridge, MA: MIT Press, 2002).

International Perspective

Institutions Matter: South Korea Versus North Korea

There is no better example of the power of institutions as a critical determinant of economic growth than the example of North Korea and South Korea. As we have seen in Figure 1-9 on p. 18, South Korea has experienced remarkable growth since 1960 and in that graph has left the Philippines "in the dust." The success of South Korea is also evident in Table 11-1

on p. 358, where South Korea achieved a growth rate between 1960 and 2004 of 5.8 percent per year, leaping from 11 percent to 51 percent of the level of U.S. income per person. Correspondingly, South Korea is one of the four green dots in the upper left corner of Figure 11-1, representing the countries that started furthest behind the United States that have grown the fastest since 1960 (the others are China, Hong Kong, and Taiwan).

The two Koreas make an excellent case study. A unified Korea had been a colony of Japan since 1910, and both north and south portions were in identical conditions of economic poverty when World War II ended. After the Korean War ended in a stalemate in 1953, the Korean peninsula was divided into two countries, South Korea and North Korea. Following the divide, the southern half of the peninsula prospered and became an economic powerhouse, competing with Japan in many industries. Among the South Korean products familiar to Americans are Samsung mobile telephones and Hyundai and Kia automobiles. South Korea achieved its success by a combination of emphasis on education, particularly in math and science, and a government policy of encouraging exports and fostering large corporations such as Samsung and Hyundai that became dominant in their industries by producing technologically advanced products at relatively low prices.

The contrast with North Korea could not be greater. In the north, a rigid version of Soviet-style

Physical Infrastructure

The capital of Costa Rica, a country in Central America, is San Jose, which is located in the center of the country. To reach either the Atlantic or Pacific Ocean from San Jose, it is necessary to drive on two-lane winding roads, and it often takes three hours or more to drive 60 miles. American tourists sometimes return from Costa Rica by changing planes at the Dallas–Fort Worth International Airport, where outside their airplane window they see seven runways and many miles of taxiways and surrounding multilane expressways. In the immediate vicinity of this airport, there are probably more cubic yards of concrete than in all of Costa Rica.

Infrastructure is any type of capital not owned by the individual business firm that makes the firm's production more efficient. Good highways allow truck-

communism that continues today was imposed: All property is owned by the government and there is no incentive for individual initiative or effort other than coercion. North Korea started out in 1953 at the same economic level as South Korea, with the same level of education and per-person income. Also, both were culturally and racially homogeneous.

In the 1960s and 1970s, North Korea did experience significant economic growth, occurring mainly in state-owned manufacturing and bolstered by aid from its communist allies China and the Soviet Union. But per capita income began to decline in the 1980s, then fell precipitously through the 1990s to a current level of around $1,000 per person, perhaps 4 or 5 percent of the level of South Korea.

Floods, droughts, and economic mismanagement resulted in a famine in North Korea during the mid-1990s, with deaths estimated at between 300,000 and 800,000 people per year. A 2006 survey estimated that one out of three North Koreans was malnourished and anemic because of the famine's lingering effects. Matters have been made worse by an enforced "personality cult" and the nuclear weapons mania of the dictator Kim Jong Il, the son of the first dictator, Kim Il Sung.

Foreign estimates suggest that, under Kim Jong Il, North Korea may spend as much as one-quarter of its low level of GDP on its military, further reducing resources for other economic development and needed human services. Recently, several countries, including China and the United States, have tried to use food aid as a bargaining chip to persuade North Korea to end its program of developing nuclear weapons. It is unclear if such efforts will change the North Korean dictator's policies.

Source: http://en.wikipedia.org/wiki/North_Korea

ing firms to produce more output with the same number of trucks; airports with multiple runways allow airlines to minimize delays; fast railways provide a better transport option than airplanes over distances shorter than 200 miles; ports with many docks help shipping firms to avoid waiting time; well-functioning telephone networks help people communicate easily without waiting for dial tones or having their phone calls interrupted; and a grid providing ample amounts of electricity avoids the inefficiency created by blackouts and brownouts.

Countries differ in how much of their infrastructure is financed by the government. In France, the highways, airports, ports, railroads, telephone network, and electricity grid are all entirely or partly owned by the government. In the United States, infrastructure is owned by a mix of private companies and governmental organizations.

How is physical infrastructure related to growth? In some poor countries, the value of a business investment is reduced by poor highways and airports, by the absence of railroads, by telephone systems in which it takes months for a telephone to be installed and in which dial tones may be delayed, and by electricity systems that have inadequate capacity. Like political capital, physical infrastructure is crucial for growth, and its quantity can be influenced by government decisions.

Geography

If income per capita is plotted on a map of the world, it quickly becomes apparent that rich countries lie in temperate zones and many poor countries lie in tropical zones. Of the 30 economies classified as high income, only two (Hong Kong and Singapore) lie in the tropical zone, and these two small countries have only 1 percent of the total population of the rich countries. Otherwise, all of the rich countries, including those in North America, Western Europe, Northeast Asia, the Southern Cone of Latin America, and Australasia, are located outside the tropics. In addition to being located in the tropics, another predictor of poverty is lack of access to sea-based trade. Countries that are both tropical and landlocked, including Cameroon and Mali in Africa (Mali appears as a nonconverging country in Table 11-1 on p. 358), are among the very poorest in the world.

The leading scholar of the role of geography in economic development is Jeffrey Sachs of Columbia University. Sachs proposes four hypotheses regarding the role of geography in the growth performance of poor countries.[15]

1. Technologies developed in the temperate zones may not be applicable to tropical areas, where insects may transmit different diseases than are common in the temperate zones, and where the soil and weather are not suitable for agricultural techniques common in rich countries.

2. Technological innovation in any region often involves high development costs and low production costs, as in the case of Microsoft Windows, where hundreds of millions may be spent in development, but producing each copy costs only a few cents. Thus the bigger the market, the quicker the initial investment will be recouped and the higher the total profits will be. Small economies in tropical regions may be too small to justify any significant investment in technological innovation.

3. Poor productivity in rural agriculture in tropical countries and the prevalence of tropical diseases directly affect population growth—recall in the Solow model that a lower rate of population growth boosts the standard of living and stimulates a transition to a higher capital-labor ratio. As rich countries developed, the rapid growth of agricultural productivity produced a surplus of food and encouraged families to move from farm to city, where the cost of raising children was higher. This encouraged a "demographic transition" to lower birth rates, lower death rates, and a lower rate of population growth.

4. Most tropical countries were conquered and included in the empires of temperate-zone countries like Britain, France, Germany, and Belgium. Colonial domination impeded the process of economic growth by neglecting the

---

[15] This section is based on Jeffrey D. Sachs, "Tropical Underdevelopment," NBER Working Paper 8819 (February 2001). His five hypotheses regarding tropical underdevelopment have been reduced to four to simplify the exposition.

substantial period of years, much less than the rate of close to 3 percent achieved in the early 1960s.

Yet, as shown by the green line in Figure 11-5, good news began to arrive, as actual productivity growth moved solidly above 2 percent in the late 1990s through 2004. Our discussion in this section is divided into two main topics: what caused the dismal years of slow productivity growth between 1974 and 1995 and what caused the revival in productivity growth after 1995.

Causes of the 1973–95 Productivity Growth Slowdown

In assessing alternative hypotheses, we need to remember that the productivity growth slowdown lasted for two decades, and it was concentrated outside of the manufacturing sector. The growth rate of labor productivity in manufacturing did not experience a slowdown and indeed was somewhat faster during 1973–95 than before 1973. Here we review some of the leading explanations, starting with those that center on slower growth in inputs. Then we turn to hypotheses that try to explain the slowdown in MFP, the Solow residual, represented by the lowercase letter a in equations (11.2) and (11.3) above.

1. **Measured capital per labor hour.** The growth of measured capital per labor hour slowed in the United States after 1973, both because the growth of the capital stock slowed down and because the growth of labor hours increased. Labor was relatively cheap in the United States after 1973, so lots of workers were hired for unskilled jobs, and productivity growth fell.

2. **Raw materials and energy.** The late Michael Bruno of Hebrew University in Jerusalem and Jeffrey Sachs of Columbia University stressed the direct effect of the higher relative prices of energy and raw materials, together with restrictive macroeconomic policies that were introduced in response to those increases in relative prices.[17] More recent research by William Nordhaus of Yale University identifies particular energy-dependent industries that bore the brunt of the slowdown, including oil and gas extraction, motor vehicles, electricity generation, pipelines, and air transportation.[18]

3. **Decline in labor quality.** The role of labor quality in the productivity slowdown is still debated. The percentage of teenagers and adult women in the labor force rose after 1973, yet their average wages were lower than those of adult men. Consequently, analysts who measured the relative productivity of groups of workers by their relative wages concluded that the quality of the workforce declined as its age-gender composition shifted toward a greater share of adult female workers and teenagers of both genders. However, other economists believed that the low relative wages of women reflected, at least in part, the effects of discrimination rather than lower productivity.

4. **Infrastructure.** Section 11-5 and equation (11.8) on p. 370 included infrastructure capital as an important source of growth. Rich nations differ from poor nations by spending more on education, sewers, highways, railroads, airports, and other types of infrastructure investment. Inadequate public investment in infrastructure has been cited as a major cause of the 1973–95

---

[17] Michael Bruno and Jeffrey Sachs, *Economics of Worldwide Stagnation* (Cambridge, MA: Harvard University Press, 1985).

[18] William D. Nordhaus, "Retrospective on the 1970s Productivity Slowdown," NBER Working Paper 10950 (December 2004).

productivity slowdown in the United States.[19] However, this conclusion is controversial, and another study over a longer historical time period and comparing a number of industrialized nations finds little systematic relationship between productivity growth and the share of output devoted to infrastructure investment.[20]

5. **Problems of particular industries.** Several industries experienced slower productivity growth during 1973–95 for reasons going beyond the high price of energy in the 1970s and early 1980s. The oil-producing industry suffered because its old oil wells were drying up faster than new ones could be discovered. The electric utility industry suffered because government antipollution regulations required it to add new smoke-reducing equipment to its generating plants, requiring more employees per unit of electricity to install and maintain the cleaning devices. Finally, the construction industry experienced slow productivity growth for reasons that are not well understood.

Running Out of Resources and Ideas

Because the 1973–95 productivity growth slowdown was so pervasive and long-lasting, some economists believed that the fundamental cause went beyond slower growth in factor inputs. William Nordhaus helped popularize the depletion hypothesis, which is a much more pessimistic approach than those reviewed earlier in this section.[21] One aspect is the depletion of natural resources, in particular the decline in the rate of finding new productive oil wells in the United States, already discussed above.

Perhaps the more rapid productivity growth prior to 1973, dating back to the early twentieth century, was the direct effect of ideas developed back in the late nineteenth century. These great inventions included the electric motor, motor transport, air transport, radio, television, plastics, and other petrochemicals. This was the era that saw the emergence of the suburb, the supermarket, and the superhighway, not to mention indoor plumbing and central heating. Perhaps the economy had finished exploiting most of the benefits of the great inventions and was short on new ideas to replace them.

Overall, there is no simple answer to the puzzle posed by the productivity growth slowdown. There is probably an element of truth to several of the ideas that have just been explored, including the role of energy prices, the depletion hypothesis, and the problems experienced by specific industries. The absence of a single simple answer to the puzzle is perplexing to policymakers, because the lack of a single explanation makes it hard to devise government policies to boost productivity growth.

The Post-1995 Revival of Productivity Growth

The historical record in Figure 11-5 on p. 372 shows how productivity growth revived after 1995. Gradually economists abandoned the pessimism of the

---

[19] See David A. Aschauer, "Is Public Expenditure Productive?" *Journal of Monetary Economics,* vol. 23 (March 1989), pp. 177–200.

[20] See Robert Ford and Pierre Poret, "Infrastructure and Private-Sector Productivity," *OECD Economic Studies,* no. 17 (Autumn 1991), pp. 63–89.

[21] The Nordhaus approach is set out in William D. Nordhaus, "Economic Policy in the Face of Declining Productivity Growth," *European Economic Review,* vol. 18 (May/June 1982), pp. 131–58.

1973–95 slowdown period and began to debate the causes of the revival. In this section, we ask what caused the revival and whether it will continue.

As recently as 1997–98, economists had been struggling to explain "Solow's paradox" as set forth a decade earlier by Robert M. Solow (the inventor of the Solow growth model): "We can see the computer age everywhere except in the productivity statistics." But by 1999 and 2000, economists suddenly looked up from their word processors to discover that before they had satisfactorily explained Solow's paradox, it had been rendered obsolete by the post-1995 productivity revival. Suddenly the economy was awash not only in computers, but also in productivity growth.

The New Economy and the Delay Hypothesis

Commentators universally adopted the phrase "New Economy" to describe what appeared to be a new era in macroeconomics. Since the period of the productivity revival coincided with the spread of the Internet and cellular phones as well as the invention of the World Wide Web (WWW) and e-commerce, it was natural to suppose that the basic cause of the productivity growth revival was both the production and use of high-tech equipment. A widespread consensus emerged that the New Economy represented a fundamental transformation in macroeconomics.

The sudden revival of productivity growth, after years in which Solow's paradox accurately captured the lack of productivity payoff from computers, appeared to vindicate Stanford economist Paul David, who had predicted that the benefits of computers were being delayed, but after some period would finally begin to boost economywide productivity. His "delay hypothesis" was based on the historical example of electricity, which was invented in the 1880s but had its big productivity payoff four decades later in the 1920s. Enthusiasts treated the New Economy as a fundamental industrial revolution as great or greater in importance than the concurrence of inventions, particularly electricity and the internal combustion engine, that transformed the world at the turn of the last century.

Causes of the Productivity Growth Revival

Analysts were unanimous in their belief that the production and use of high-tech equipment was a fundamental cause of the productivity revival.[22] Starting in 1995, as shown in Figure 16-5 on p. 541, there was an acceleration in the rate at which the prices of computers were declining, from a decline of roughly 15 percent per year to more than 30 percent per year. Real investment in computer equipment accelerated from an annual growth rate of 20 percent to 40 percent, and this directly translated into faster growth in output per hour of those employees making the computers, since it took only a few extra employees to make the additional computers.

Initially it appeared that most of the productivity growth revival could be explained by the production of computers and other high-tech equipment, but by 1999–2000 the productivity revival had continued long enough and was big enough to require additional explanations. It appeared that productivity growth had increased not just in firms *producing* the high-tech equipment but

---

[22] A separate analysis of the New Economy investment boom and bust appears in Section 16-9. The major papers analyzing the causes of the productivity revival are listed in Chapter 16, footnote 14, on p. 543.

also in several sectors of the economy that were heavy *users* of the equipment, including the securities industry (where daily trading totals of four billion shares per day became commonplace) as well as wholesale and retail trade.

Why Did Productivity Growth Explode after the High-Tech Investment Boom Collapsed?

The post-1995 period can be divided into three parts. From 1995 to 2000, the stock market boomed and high-tech investment grew rapidly to an unusually high level relative to total GDP. Those who had attributed most of the explanation of the post-1995 productivity revival to New Economy high-tech investment predicted that productivity growth would decline once the investment boom ended. Indeed, the stock market collapsed starting in early 2000, many new "dot.com" Internet companies went out of business, and growth in high-tech investment turned from strongly positive to strongly negative. What was the response of productivity growth?

The answer is given in Figure 11-5 on p. 372. Actual productivity growth soared in 2002–04, and the green line showing the productivity growth trend rose to 2.3 percent, higher than at any time since the 1960s. How could productivity growth explode upward while high-tech investment was collapsing? Economists searching for answers pointed to several unusual aspects of the 2001–04 period.[23]

1. The 2001 recession was characterized by a much steeper decline in profits than in the previous mild recession of 1990–91. Also, the decline in the stock market was much steeper than a decade earlier. Part of the reason for the sharp decline in both profits and stock prices was a string of accounting and corruption scandals involving corporations such as Enron, Tyco, and Worldcom that had significantly overstated their profits. Because of the sharp downward pressure on profits, business firms embarked on an unprecedented attack on their costs, laying off millions of employees.[24] The resulting "jobless recovery" had as its counterpart sharply rising productivity, as firms learned that they could produce the same amount of output with many fewer employees. We previously introduced the jobless recovery in Figure 2-5 on p. 45, where the "payroll survey" measure of employment (this is the measure used in computing the productivity statistics) exhibits a decline until the end of 2003, fully two years after the end of the recession in output.

2. But how did business firms succeed in producing more output with so many fewer employees? In addition to the profit squeeze and associated cost cutting, another hypothesis centers on *intangible capital,* types of investment that are not included in the measured totals of fixed investment in the GDP data. According to this hypothesis, the investment boom of the late 1990s produced unmeasured intangible capital in the form of improvements of business practices and training of employees to understand and use computers and the Internet. When the high-tech investment boom was over, the intangi-

---

[23] This section summarizes part of Robert J. Gordon, "Exploding Productivity Growth: Context, Causes, and Implications," *Brookings Papers on Economic Activity,* no. 2 (2003) pp. 207–98.

[24] The hypothesis that declining profits led to both the slump of employment and the boom of productivity growth has recently been supported in a cross-industry empirical study. See Stephen D. Oliner, Daniel E. Sichel, and Kevin J. Stiroh, "Explaining a Productive Decade," *Brookings Papers on Economic Activity,* 2007, no. 1, pp. 81–152.

ble capital remained, and the improved business practices and better understanding of what computers and the Internet could do explain how business firms could produce more output with fewer employees.[25]

Between the middle of 2004 and the end of 2007, the growth rate of productivity slowed down, both the actual numbers shown by the red line in Figure 11-5 and the trend shown by the green line. Was this a temporary hiatus in the post-1995 productivity growth revival or an ominous cloud on the horizon, suggesting that the U.S. was about to return to the slow productivity growth rates typical of 1973–95?

Over the years 2005–2007, economists became more pessimistic about future productivity growth. A series of downward revisions in the data reduced the actual growth rate of productivity below previous estimates, and the newly emerging data for 2005–07 were relatively poor. Some productivity experts suggested that the post-1995 revival had come to an end and had been created by two "one-shot" events that were inherently temporary. One was the mid-1990s marriage of the personal computer and communication, resulting in the Internet and the World Wide Web. This clearly stimulated productivity growth in the late 1990s, but the Internet could only be invented once and its benefits for productivity growth appeared to be dissipating after 2004. Most of the new products, such as flat-screen TVs, game-players, and smart phones, were beneficial for consumers without raising the productivity of business firms.

It also appeared that much of the boom in productivity growth between 2001 and 2004 also had temporary causes. As discussed above, two of these were the profit squeeze, which temporarily boosted productivity while cutting employment, and the intangible capital idea that many of the benefits of the New Economy operated with long lags. By 2007, it appeared that most of those benefits on productivity growth had already occurred.

SELF-TEST

Explain how each of the following contributed to the 1973–95 slowdown in labor productivity growth:

1. The increase in women's labor force participation rate.
2. The increase in energy prices during the 1970s.
3. The construction of the interstate highway system in the 1958–85 period.

11-7   Labor Supply Shifts as a Source of Faster or Slower Productivity Growth

We are interested in productivity growth because it is the fundamental cause of increases in the standard of living and of real wages over long periods of time. It is frequently assumed that the problem of slow real wage growth in the United States during the 1973–95 period must have been caused by slow productivity growth during the same period. Indeed, we can use the standard

---

[25] See Susanto Basu et al., "The Case of the Missing Productivity Growth, or Does Information Technology Explain Why Productivity Accelerated in the United States but not in the United Kingdom?" *NBER Macroeconomics Annual 2003*, pp. 9–63.

labor market diagram, first introduced in Figure 7-7 on p. 209, to illustrate this assumption.

An Adverse Productivity Shock Reduces the Real Wage, Hours, or Both

The top frame of Figure 11-6 plots the real wage on the vertical axis and the level of labor input (measured in hours) on the horizontal axis. The initial labor demand curve is shown as the dashed line (N_0^d) and slopes downward,

Figure 11-6 The Effect on the Labor Market of an Adverse Productivity Shock and a Downward Shift in Labor Supply

In the top frame, the economy is initially at point B. An adverse productivity shock shifts the labor demand curve downward. If the amount of labor input remains unchanged, the economy moves to point Z, where the real wage is lower than at point B. Another possibility is that the real wage is held fixed, possibly by union contracts, in which case the economy goes to point X, and labor input falls to point N_1. In the bottom frame, a downward shift in the labor supply curve, for reasons suggested in the text, would move the economy from point B to point C along a fixed labor demand curve. Labor input would rise from N_0 to N_2, while the real wage would fall from $(W/P)_0$ to $(W/P)_1$. The marginal product of labor is lower at point C than at point B, implying that average labor productivity is lower as well.

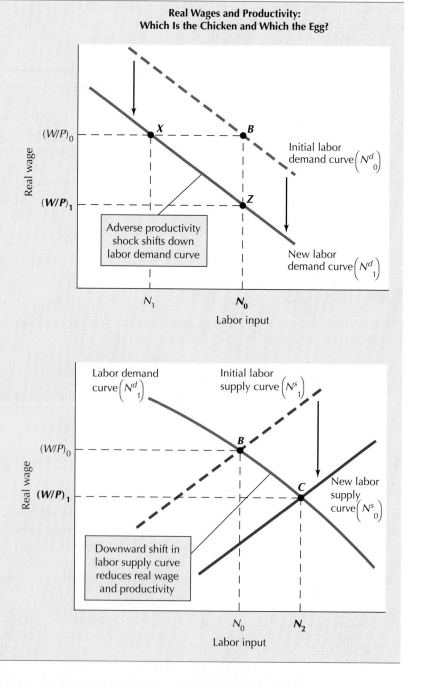

Real Wages and Productivity: Which Is the Chicken and Which the Egg?

reflecting the decline in the marginal product of labor that occurs when more labor input is added while the quantity of other factors of production (not just capital, but also energy and imported materials) remains constant.

Instead of staying in its initial position, two events could cause the labor demand curve to shift downward to a position like N_1^d. First, this shift could occur if the quantity of the other factors of production (in addition to labor) were to decline instead of staying constant. Second, such a downward shift could occur even if the quantity of these other factors of production remained constant— for example, if MFP were to decline (that is, if less output were produced by a given quantity of factors of production). In either case, the new lower labor demand curve is shown by the solid line in the top frame of Figure 11-6. The original level of employment (N_0) could be maintained only at point Z, where the real wage is shown to fall in the same proportion as the vertical downward shift in the labor demand curve.

Is there any escape from the logic that an autonomous decline in labor productivity must cause an equiproportionate decline in the real wage rate, as occurs at point Z? If for some reason the real wage were completely rigid, as at point X, employment could not be maintained at point N_0 but instead would decline to point N_1. Some analysts believe that this outcome occurred in Europe during the 1970s and early 1980s at the time of the adverse supply shocks, and that this helps to explain why unemployment increased so much in Europe relative to the United States during that period.

The Possibility of Feedback from Low Real Wages to Low Productivity

The top frame of Figure 11-6, as we have seen, shows how an adverse shock to labor productivity can cause a decline in the real wage. However, the relation can work in reverse. The bottom frame of Figure 11-6 shows a fixed labor demand curve, which assumes a fixed quantity of factors of production (other than labor) and a fixed level of MFP. Now let us assume that there is an outward shift in the labor supply curve.

What factors might cause such a downward shift? This could be caused by any event that increases the supply of labor, such as a larger workforce caused by more immigration. Another factor causing such a shift would be any event that reduces the wage at which a given quantity of labor input is willing to work, including a reduction in the power of unions or a reduction in the real minimum wage (which may tend to depress wages for unskilled workers). Increased anxiety among workers about job security might also cause such a shift.

If the labor supply curve shifts downward along the labor demand curve, the real wage will decline, but so also will labor productivity.[26] The economy will shift from point B to point C, and the decline in both the real wage and productivity will have been caused by a shift in the labor supply curve rather than a shift in the labor demand curve.

While Figure 11-6 shows why a downward shift in the *levels* of labor productivity and the real wage are related, caused either by a downward shift in labor supply or labor demand, the same logic applies to the growth rates of

---

[26] The labor demand curve is drawn on the assumption that the real wage equals the marginal product of labor. When the marginal product of labor declines, as from point B to point C in the bottom frame of Figure 11-6, the average product of labor (Y/N) declines as well. In the special case of the Cobb-Douglas production function, the change in the average product of labor is proportional to that of the marginal product.

labor productivity and the real wage. For instance, growth in labor productivity and the real wage could be held down by inadequate growth in capital input, whether that takes the form of slow growth in physical capital, in forms of human capital such as education and training, or in government-financed infrastructure such as highways and airports.

Similarly, any event that stimulates the *growth* of labor supply can hold down the growth rates of labor productivity and the real wage, including steady growth in the labor force caused by immigration, or a shift in labor's bargaining position resulting from a decline in the strength of labor unions. Some observers interpret the steady increase in foreign trade, sometimes called the globalization of the world economy, as having the effect of creating competition between foreign workers and domestic U.S. workers, thus weakening the position of U.S. workers. This would directly slow the growth of the real wage and indirectly, as in the bottom frame of Figure 11-6, slow the growth rate of productivity.

SELF-TEST

For each of the following events, indicate whether it shifts the labor demand curve or the labor supply curve, and whether the shift is to the left or right. In addition, how does each event affect labor productivity and real wages?

1. College tuition becomes more expensive, causing some students to drop out and look for work.
2. Tighter rules prevent immigration of unskilled workers.
3. The real price of oil declines.
4. A tax on equipment investment makes it more expensive to purchase equipment.

 Case Study

The Productivity Growth Contrast
Between Europe and the United States

American travelers to several of the more prosperous European countries, including France, Germany, and Sweden, notice interesting differences. For instance, it is much less common in Europe for supermarkets to employ baggers in addition to checkout cashiers. Parking lots are more likely to be fully automated than to employ attendants. Valet parking services are nowhere to be seen. The bus boy occupation—clearing and setting tables—that is so prevalent in American restaurants at the middle-price and high-price level is largely absent in similar restaurants in these European countries.

These observations are symptoms of a broader set of differences in the evolution of the economies of the United States and leading European nations over the past two decades. While the United States lagged behind Europe in the growth of real wages and in productivity during the 1973–95 period, the United States had a much superior record in achieving growth in jobs and maintaining a relatively low unemployment rate.

Europe Catches Up, Then Falls Back

Figure 11-7 displays the *level* of productivity in Europe and in the United States. During the long period when American productivity was growing slowly, Europe caught up from 69 percent of the American level in 1973 to 93 percent in 1995. During this period, as we learn in this section, Europeans emphasized policies that made labor expensive to employ, as shown along the initial labor supply curve in the bottom frame of Figure 11-6. As a result, in Europe employment grew slowly but productivity grew rapidly as firms tried to minimize their use of labor input to avoid its high cost. The United States during this period was operating along the new labor supply curve in the bottom frame of Figure 11-6, pursuing policies that made it cheap for firms to hire unskilled labor, leading to many low-wage jobs but also leading to the slow productivity growth.

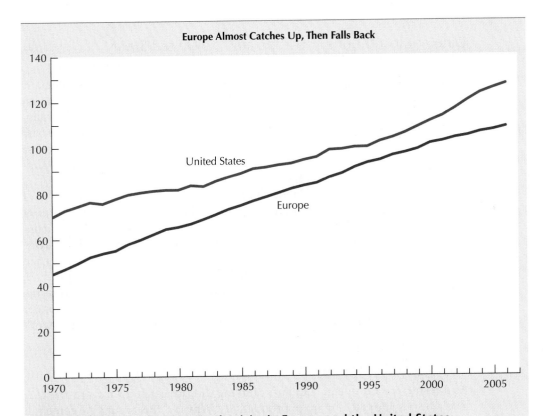

Figure 11-7 **Level of Labor Productivity in Europe and the United States, 1970–2006**

The level of productivity in the United States is displayed as an index number with 1995 = 100. The level of productivity in the 15 members of the pre-2004 European Union is displayed as an index number with 1995 = 93, based on evidence that in 1995 European productivity was roughly 7 percent below that of the United States. The level of productivity of Europe had almost caught up to that in the United States by 1995, but after 2001 the level of productivity in Europe slipped back relative to the United States to a ratio of 85 percent.

Source: Groningen Growth and Development Center, *Total Economy Database.* Details in Appendix C-4.

After 1995, productivity growth in the United Stated revived, as we learned in Section 11-6. This occurred not because the United States changed its labor market policies, and indeed immigration increased steadily throughout the 1990s. What changed in the United States was an upward shift in the labor demand curve, due to the productivity enhancing effects of high-tech investment in computer and telecommunications hardware and software. Despite the influence of this New Economy investment, Europe's level of productivity grew at the same rate, and so in 2001 Europe still achieved a productivity level equal to 93 percent of that of the United States.

However, during 2001–06, productivity growth in the United States was much faster than in Europe, and so the level of European productivity in Figure 11-7 fell back from 93 to 85 percent. Europe did not experience the drastic decline in profits and in the stock market, or the collapse of high-tech investment, that occurred in the United States. The jobless recovery of the U.S. economy, which combined rising output with falling employment, did not occur to the same extent in Europe.

Different Institutions in Europe and the United States

The long period during 1973–95 of slow productivity growth and rapid employment growth in the United States compared to Europe reflected systematic differences in institutions and policies. The United States has relatively weak labor unions, a relatively low and declining real minimum wage, and substantial competition for low-skilled jobs from legal and illegal immigrants. In some countries like France it is very expensive to hire low-skilled workers, because of a high minimum wage and high payroll taxes that finance government-supported medical care and old-age pensions.

As these differences in labor market policies fostered a catching up of European productivity toward the U.S. level in 1973–95, Europe suffered from the lack of employment growth that was the counterpart of a strong productivity performance. Employment stagnated, unemployment was high, the average duration of unemployment was much longer than in the United States, job prospects for young people were bleak, labor force participation languished, and many workers were encouraged to retire at young ages compared to the United States. Europeans also reacted to the scarcity of jobs by taking longer vacations than in the United States, in effect spreading the available work among more people.

How Could Europe Be So Productive Yet So Poor?

As a result, the European standard of living did not catch up toward the U.S. level, despite the catching up of productivity. Why did this occur? We come full circle back to the first equation in this chapter, repeated here for convenience:

$$y - q - (y - n) = n - q. \tag{11.1}$$

Here the growth rate of output is y, the growth rate of labor hours is n, and the growth rate of the population is q. The reason that the European standard of living ($y - q$) grew more slowly than labor productivity ($y - n$) is that labor hours per member of the population ($n - q$) experienced negative growth. Long vacations, high unemployment, low labor force participation, and early retirement meant that Europeans worked many fewer hours per member of the population than occurred in the United States.

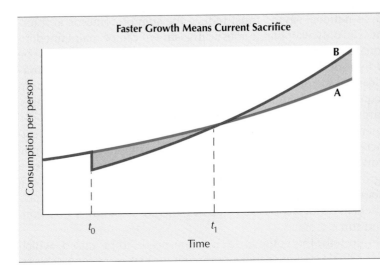

Faster Growth Means Current Sacrifice

Figure 12-1 Two Alternative Paths of Consumption per Person

Before time t_0, both paths involve exactly the same consumption per person. Along path A, consumption per person continues to grow at the same steady rate after time t_0. But along path B, a policy decision is made to consume less in order to save and invest more. At first, between time t_0 and t_1, consumption along path B drops below path A by an amount shown by the blue shading. Then, after t_1 (and forever thereafter), consumption along path B exceeds that along path A, as shown by the red shading.

return higher than the rate of time preference (sometimes called the rate at which individuals "discount" future consumption), society should save more and consume less, as along path B. This principle can be stated as follows: *The United States saves too little if the rate at which individuals discount future consumption is less than the rate of return on private investment.*

In recent years the real rate of return on private investment in the corporate sector has been about 12 percent, and the rate of time preference of individuals is less than that. How much less? The *real* interest rate on corporate bonds was roughly 4 percent in 2008. Many individuals have been willing to save despite the relatively low real interest rates available to them. Thus it is accurate to say that the United States now saves too little, because a dollar diverted from present consumption to present saving could earn a real return of about 12 percent, more than the real return after taxes now earned by most savers. People would want to save more than they save now if they were offered a real return of 12 percent instead of a real return of 4 percent or less.

National Saving, Economic Growth, and the Government Budget Deficit

To boost the growth rate of output and productivity, fiscal policy must raise the rate of national saving, which in turn would boost the growth rate of output. By definition, **national saving** is the sum of private saving and government saving. A government budget surplus is the same as government saving, while a government budget deficit is treated as *negative* government saving. Thus at any given amount of private saving, the larger the government budget deficit, *the more is subtracted from private saving—that is, the lower is the national saving rate.*

National saving is the sum of private saving and government saving.

We have already learned to express national saving in the magic equation, originally introduced in Chapter 2 and used in equation (5.5) on p. 139 to examine national saving (*NS*). Using the familiar symbols:

$$S + (T - G) \equiv I + NX \qquad (12.1)$$

$$NS \equiv I + NX$$

In words, this states that national saving on the left-hand side must be equal to the sum of domestic and foreign investment ($I + NX$) on the right-hand side.

A reduction in national saving must reduce the sum of domestic and foreign investment. The only way that domestic investment can be maintained intact when national saving decreases is for the decline in national saving to be *completely offset* by a decline in foreign investment or increase in foreign borrowing. As we learned in Figure 5-7 on p. 143, this complete offset may occur in a small open economy but not in a large open economy like the United States. Instead, in a large open economy a decline in national saving caused by a higher government budget deficit must cause *both* a decline in domestic investment and an increase in foreign borrowing. Such an event will reduce the rate of economic growth for two reasons. First, less domestic investment implies a slower future growth rate (Path A instead of Path B in Figure 12-1). Second, higher foreign borrowing requires the nation's residents to make interest payments to foreigners in future years, thus reducing the growth of their own consumption expenditures.

To stimulate growth, the national saving rate needs to be raised, which means either that private saving or the government budget surplus must be increased. In choosing methods to raise the government budget surplus, policymakers should take care that the larger surplus is not accompanied by a reduction in private saving. For instance, attempting to raise the surplus by raising income tax rates will reduce the after-tax return to private saving. The beneficial boost to national saving caused by the higher budget surplus will be partly offset by a decline in private saving. To achieve an increase in national saving, a preferable method would be to raise taxes on consumption (rather than income) or reduce government expenditures in order to boost the government budget surplus.

The ultimate aim of policies to boost the rate of national saving is to increase the ratio of investment to real GDP. However, the types of investment that contribute to growth include not just private expenditures on machines and structures but also government investment, for instance on education, research, and highways. Thus policymakers attempting to boost growth should either boost taxes on consumption or cut expenditures on government consumption rather than cutting government investment.

SELF-TEST

Would the following events raise or lower national saving as a percent of GDP?

1. An increase in federal spending on military aircraft without any change in tax rates.
2. An increase in sales taxes on food.
3. A reduction in income taxes.
4. An increase in the amount that can be contributed to tax-free retirement plans.

12-3   The Future Burden of the Government Debt

We have already learned that a higher government budget surplus raises national saving, holding other factors constant. Similarly, a higher government budget deficit reduces national saving, holding other factors constant. Each extra dollar of government deficit requires the government to issue one more dollar of government debt. We ask in this section whether the additional dollars of government debt are harmful. How do we assess the impact on the well-being of future generations implied by these extra dollars of government debt?

Government investment projects, such as the construction of highways, schools, and public universities, generate a future return, consisting of the benefits to future generations created by the project. Whether or not the government debt is a burden depends partly on whether the extra dollars of government debt pay for government expenditures on investment goods or for consumption goods. There is no burden if the government deficit finances productive government investment projects. In this case, the government acts just like a private corporation, say Dell Computers, which pays for much of its new plant and equipment by selling bonds to the public.

But there is a burden if the extra dollars of government debt pay for consumption goods that yield no future benefits. Such expenditures would include, for instance, ammunition fired at target practice by soldiers or groceries purchased by recipients of Social Security benefits. These consumption expenditures have value for their recipients at the current time but not in the future.

True Burdens of the Debt

The true burden on future generations is created by government spending that is financed by deficits rather than tax revenues and pays for goods that yield no future benefits, or benefits less than their social opportunity cost—for example, meals currently consumed by members of the armed forces. Nothing is generated in the future as a rate of return; all benefits accrue in the present. The government must pay interest to keep bondholders happy, just as Dell must pay interest, yet in current government deficit-financed consumption there is no future benefit or income to pay the interest. Future taxpayers are forced to hand over extra payments to the government to cover the interest cost on the debt, and the taxpayers receive no benefit in return. Similarly, investment projects such as highways may impose a burden if their benefits are less than their social opportunity costs, such as for a little-used highway or the famous Alaska "bridge to nowhere" proposed in Congress in 2006.

12-4   Will the Government Remain Solvent?

How can we tell if a government budget deficit in the United States or in some other country is too high? In this section we take a different approach to answer this question. What matters, according to this approach, is not whether the deficit is zero, but rather the criterion of stabilizing the ratio of the outstanding nominal federal debt (D) to nominal GDP (PY). The federal deficit can be quite large, yet the D/PY ratio can nevertheless remain stable instead of rise.

This paradox seems less mysterious when we recognize that the nominal government budget deficit is equal to the change in the debt (ΔD). How large can the deficit be and keep the debt-GDP ratio, D/PY, constant? It will remain constant as long as the *growth rate* of the debt-GDP ratio is zero.

Thus, our task is to determine what size deficit will keep the growth rate of the debt-GDP ratio equal to zero. We begin by noting that the growth rate of the debt-GDP ratio (D/PY) is the difference between the growth rate in debt (d) and the growth rate in nominal GDP $(p + y)$:

$$\text{Growth Rate of } \frac{D}{PY} = d - (p + y) \tag{12.2}$$

For stability in the debt-GDP ratio, we need the growth rate of debt (d) equal to the growth rate of nominal GDP $(p + y)$:

$$d = p + y \tag{12.3}$$

When we multiply both sides of equation (12.3) by the size of the debt (D), we obtain the allowable deficit (that is, addition to debt) that is consistent with keeping the debt-GDP ratio constant:

<table>
<tr><td>General Form</td><td>Numerical Example</td></tr>
<tr><td>$dD = (p + y)D$</td><td>$(0.05)(\$4{,}500 \text{ billion}) = \$225 \text{ billion}$</td><td>(12.4)</td></tr>
</table>

This simple expression (12.4) leads to a surprising conclusion: *The debt-GDP ratio remains constant if the deficit equals the outstanding debt times the growth rate of nominal GDP.* In the numerical example, federal government debt in the year 2008 is about $4,500 billion; that times an assumed growth rate of nominal GDP in 2008 of about 5 percent equals an "allowable deficit" of $225 billion.[1] Because the actual deficit was so close to the allowable deficit, it is not surprising in Figure 12-2 (p. 397) to find that the debt-GDP ratio was stable during 2005–08. The 2008 deficit was about $200 billion—somewhat below the allowable amount of $225 billion.[2]

But what is the optimum debt-GDP ratio? Should the ratio be stable, as it was during 2005–08?

The Solvency Condition

Surely there is a limit to the size of the government debt, expressed as a percentage of GDP. The government must pay interest on the debt held by the public in the form of bonds. Some observers have pointed out that it is possible for the government to pay the interest on its outstanding debt by issuing more bonds. A typical bondholder holding $100,000 in bonds, let us call her Claudia R. Asset, would expect to earn $5,000 in interest each year when the overall economywide interest rate is 5 percent. Surely the government could simply issue $5,000 in extra bonds to meet its interest obligations without needing to levy taxes on future generations to pay this interest bill.

The government can meet its interest bill forever by issuing more bonds without increasing the debt-GDP ratio *only if the economy's real growth rate of output equals or exceeds its real interest rate.* Let us assume that the real growth rate is 3 percent and the real interest rate is 3 percent. Then each year the government could issue 3 percent additional debt, raising Claudia's holdings from $100,000 to $103,000 without raising the ratio of outstanding debt to GDP

Gov't consumption provides current benefits

---

[1] The assumed 5.0 percent growth rate of nominal GDP $(p + y)$ in this example is the sum of the rate of inflation (p) that seemed likely to occur in the 2008–09 period, assumed to be 2.0 percent, plus the growth rate of natural real GDP (y^N) of 3.0 percent. The debt of $4,500 billion in 2008 refers to the debt held by the public (excluding debt held by the Federal Reserve and government trust funds).

[2] Data in this chapter on the total debt refer to the federal government, but data on deficits in this book refer to the combined federal, state, and local governments.

International Perspective

The Debt-GDP Ratio: How Does the United States Compare?

As shown in the accompanying figure, the debt-GDP ratio almost doubled in the United States between the mid-1970s and mid-1990s before it began to decline. How does this experience compare with other countries? The figure displays debt-GDP ratios for two European countries, Germany and Italy. The ratio for Germany became larger than in the United States after 1999.

In Italy, the ratio is much higher than in the United States. The rapidly growing ratio between 1970 and 1998 reflected persistent government deficits that were at least twice as large as those in the United States at that time. One reason for the large deficits in Italy is the political system; political support is splintered among numerous parties. Under the parliamentary system it is possible to form a government only through a coalition among several parties. The necessary political compromises tend to prevent tough action to raise taxes or cut spending.

Nevertheless, the high debt-GDP ratio in Italy is not as serious a problem as it might appear. Italy offsets its government deficit with a very high private saving rate, so that its national saving rate is more than double that in the United States. As a result, high private saving creates a large demand for the bonds that the government must constantly issue to cover its deficit.

A notable fact about Italy's debt-GDP ratio is that it increased rapidly from 1980 to 1998 but then turned around, falling after 1998. Like several other European nations, Italy sharply tightened its fiscal policy in order to reduce its deficit-GDP and debt-GDP ratios to meet the conditions to enter the euro single-currency block in early 1999 (see pp. 478–79).

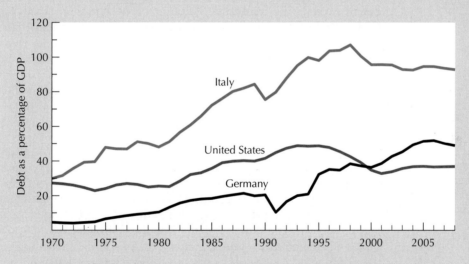

Sources: Economic Report of the President and OECD *Economic Outlook*. Details in Appendix C-4.

(which also has grown 3 percent by assumption). In this case, Claudia would receive the $3,000 payment that she expects, but the government would not have to levy additional taxes.

Clearly, if the real growth rate of output is less than the real interest rate, this method of financing the government debt is not available. To finance this interest obligation by printing more debt, the government will further raise the ratio of debt to GDP. Eventually, the ratio of debt to GDP will grow and grow, approaching infinity. The growth rate of real output was close to the real interest rate in 2008, but in some previous eras this has not been true.

SELF-TEST

Calculate the allowable deficit that maintains a fixed debt to GDP ratio for the following situations:

		Real growth rate	Inflation rate	Existing debt
	1.	0.01	0.10	$4,000 billion
	2.	0.03	0.00	$4,000 billion
	3.	0.03	0.00	$1,000 billion
	4.	0.01	0.10	$1,000 billion

12-5   Case Study

Historical Behavior of the Debt-GDP Ratio Since 1790

We have now learned that the debt-GDP ratio increases when the government deficit exceeds the borderline value given by equation (12.4). And the debt-GDP ratio decreases when the government deficit is smaller than that borderline value. In the history of the United States, which events were responsible for causing the debt-GDP ratio to rise, and under which circumstances did the debt-GDP ratio decline?

Figure 12-2 exhibits the debt-GDP ratio of the U.S. federal government (excluding government bonds held by the Federal Reserve and other government agencies) since 1790. From this figure we can draw several significant generalizations.

Wars and Depressions

The most consistent feature of the historical record is the tendency of the debt ratio to jump during wars and to shrink during succeeding years until the next war breaks out. The Revolutionary War, the Civil War, World War I, and World War II all created major jumps in the debt ratio, while in most other periods the debt ratio fell. Less visible, but also important, is the effect of economic recessions and depressions in raising the public debt through the effect of automatic stabilization (which reduces government revenue automatically as the output ratio Y/Y^N falls, requiring an increase in the public debt to finance ongoing government expenditures). The most important example of this was the decade of the Great Depression, when the debt ratio rose from 16 percent in 1929 to 44 percent in 1939.

1980–2008: The Ratio Rises and Then Declines

The bottom frame of Figure 12-2 magnifies the period since 1960 in order to exhibit the debt ratio more clearly over the past five decades. Until 1974 the debt ratio fell. From 1974 to 1976 the ratio rose, but then leveled off at about 25–27 percent until 1981. From 1981 to 1992 the ratio rose, indicating that the federal budget deficits were sizable enough to make the government debt grow much faster than nominal GDP.

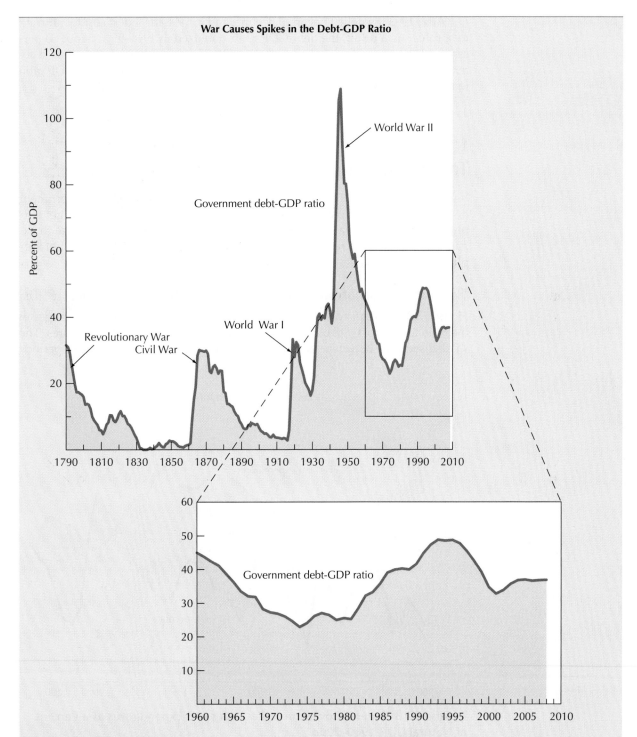

Figure 12-2 **The Ratio of U.S. Government Debt to GDP, 1790–2008**

The ratio of debt to GDP has ranged widely throughout U.S. history, rising during wartime and falling between wars. During peacetime periods, the debt-GDP ratio increased during the Great Depression decade of the 1930s and during the high-deficit period of 1981–93. The shift of the federal budget from deficit to surplus caused the debt-GDP ratio to decline sharply after 1995, but then a shift back to deficits caused the ratio to rise briefly and by a small percentage between 2001–04, after which the ratio stabilized.

Sources: Historical Statistics of the United States Millennial Edition and Economic Report of the President 2008. Details in Appendix C-4.

After 1993 the deficit began to decline, and in 1998 the federal budget turned to surplus. As a result, the debt-GDP ratio stabilized in 1994–95 at about 50 percent and then fell sharply during 1998–2001. The fiscal deficits after 2001 were relatively small compared to the growth of nominal GDP, and the debt-GDP ratio increased by only a small amount after 2001 and then stabilized after 2004. ●

12-6 Why the Budget Deficit Disappeared Temporarily and Then Reappeared

Viewed from the context of the 1980–2008 period of consistent government deficits, what was unusual about the brief period of government budget surpluses during 1998–2001? Were the persistent deficits due to an increase in expenditures, a drop in revenues, or both? Did the brief 1998–2001 period of surpluses reflect a surge in revenue, a cut in expenditures, or both?

The Budget Turnaround from Deficit to Surplus in the Late 1990s

Figure 12-3 allows us to identify periods when there were significant changes in the ratio to natural GDP of federal government revenues and expenditures. The shaded red area between the expenditure and revenue lines identifies periods

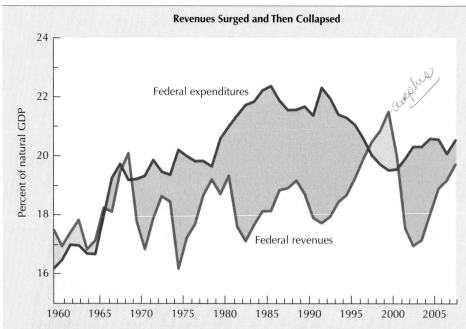

Figure 12-3 Federal Government Revenues and Expenditures as a Percent of Natural GDP, 1960–2008

The federal revenue share in GDP was amazingly stable at about 18 percent until 1995–2000, when it jumped rapidly to 21 percent, and then collapsed to 17 percent before recovering. The expenditure share gradually increased until 1992, when it reached 22 percent. Then the expenditure share dropped back to between 19.5 and 20.5 percent between 1999 and 2008.

Sources: Bureau of Economic Analysis *NIPA Tables* and Congressional Budget Office. Details in Appendix C-4.

when the federal government was running a deficit, and the shaded green area identifies periods of a federal budget surplus. The interval 1998–2001 clearly was unusual, representing the first period of federal government budget surpluses since 1970. What caused this turnaround?

Before 1980, large federal budget deficits were caused primarily by recessions, as in 1971 and 1975. But beginning around 1980, deficits persisted year after year and did not come close to disappearing, as they had in 1973–74 and 1979. We can identify the source of the persistent post-1980 deficits by looking at averages of revenues and expenditures as a percentage share of natural GDP.

	1968–80	1981–96	1997–2001	2002–07
Expenditures	19.8	21.7	19.9	20.3
Revenues	18.3	18.4	20.6	17.7
Deficit	1.5	3.3	−0.7	2.6

Thus the shift into persistent deficits after 1980 was almost entirely due to a higher share of expenditures in GDP. Despite the Reagan-era tax cuts, revenues as a share of GDP were almost as high in 1981–96 as in 1968–80.

The line for federal revenues in Figure 12-3 prior to 1995 exhibits a zigzag pattern in which revenues creep up over the years, then fall sharply, then creep up again. This reflects "bracket creep," caused by an elasticity of tax revenues to increases of nominal GDP that is greater than unity. When bracket creep causes the share of government revenues in GDP to reach a relatively high level, Congress and the administration tend to institute periodic tax cuts that offset the creep, as in 1964, 1970–71, 1975, and 1982–84. The fact that the ratio of revenues to GDP remained so long in the range of 18 percent of natural GDP may reflect the "revealed preference" of the political process.

The unusual nature of the late 1990s federal government budget is shown both by the green surplus area and by the table, which shows that in 1997–2001 expenditures fell from 21.7 to 19.9 percent of natural GDP while revenues rose from 18.4 to 20.6 percent. After 2001, federal revenues collapsed while expenditures remained stable, resulting in an average deficit in 2002–07 almost as large as in 1981–96 but with both expenditures and revenues slightly smaller.

Tax Revenues: The Explosion of the Late 1990s, Collapse in 2000–03, and Subsequent Recovery

The collapse of federal tax revenues after 2000 reflected the reversal of all the factors that had boosted revenues in the late 1990s. In contrast to the higher tax rates introduced by the Clinton administration in 1993, the Bush administration cut tax rates in 2001 and again in 2003, not just on ordinary income but also on dividends and capital gains. The Bush tax cuts disproportionately benefited higher income individuals and, in fact, fully one-third of the tax reductions went to those in the top 1 percent of the income distribution. Another cause of the decline in federal tax revenue was the decline in stock market prices from 2000 to 2003, in contrast to the boom in the stock market that had poured revenue from capital gains taxes into the federal coffers during the late 1990s. Once stock prices began to recover in 2004–07, federal revenue began to recover, as shown in Figure 12-3.

In summary, the temporary movement of the federal budget from deficit to surplus in 1998–2001 reflected in roughly equal parts an increase in the revenue share and a decrease in the expenditure share of about the same amount. But the return to deficits after 2001 was entirely due to a drop in the revenue share, with no further change in the expenditure share. The deficit was reduced from

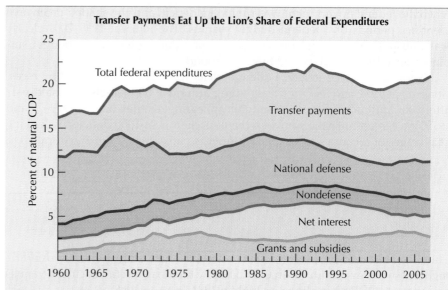

Figure 12-4 Components of Federal Government Expenditures as a Percent of Natural GDP, 1960–2007

The diagram has five "slices" corresponding to the shares in GDP of the five major types of federal government spending. The sum of the five slices is the share of total federal government spending in GDP. The increase in the share of federal government spending in GDP is mainly accounted for by transfer payments throughout the period and by net interest payments in the 1980s. The share of national defense declined until 2000 and then rose in 2001–04. Grants and subsidies rose until 1978 and then declined. Net interest declined after 1995 as the debt-GDP ratio began to decline, and it declined further in 2001–04 in response to low interest rates.

Source: Bureau of Economic Analysis *NIPA Tables*. Details in Appendix C-4.

2004 to 2007 by a gradual recovery of federal revenues partly offset by a small upcreep in federal expenditures.

Categories of Spending

What caused the upward drift and then downturn in the percentage of expenditures in GDP? As illustrated in Figure 12-4, virtually all of the increased share of government spending in GDP can be attributed to transfer payments, mainly Social Security and Medicare, which went from 4.4 percent of GDP in 1960 to 9.2 percent in 2006. "Non-defense plus grants and subsidies programs" were the same 5.1 percent in both 1980 and 2006, while the share of defense spending fell from 7.7 percent in 1960 to 4.1 percent on average in 2004–06. Also, the share of net interest declined from 4.1 percent in 1991 to 2.1 percent in 2006.

12-7 Alternative Views of Fiscal Policy: Supply-Side Economics

The period of persistent deficits began in the early 1980s with President Ronald Reagan's tax reductions enacted in 1981–83. This was the most dramatic shift in fiscal policy of the postwar era not related to the financing of wars. We have seen in this chapter that the period between 1980 and 1993 witnessed the most rapid increase in the debt-GDP ratio of the postwar period.

Supply-Side Argument for Reagan Tax Cuts

The Reagan program differed from previous episodes of fiscal policy stimulus, because its primary motive was *not* a belief that the economy was so weak, or unemployment so high, or monetary policy so impotent that the government needed to apply a fiscal stimulus. Instead, the Reagan administration believed that tax rates were simply too high and that the government sector was too large. According to the doctrine called **supply-side economics** embraced by the Reagan administration, high tax rates stifled individual initiative and saving.

The supply-side theory makes one uncontroversial statement and two controversial claims:

1. Income taxes reduce the after-tax reward to work and saving.

2. An increase in the after-tax reward to work and saving creates a *significant increase in the amount of work and saving*.

3. The resulting increase in work and saving is so significant that after the tax cuts, the federal government would collect more revenue than before the tax cuts.

Response of work effort and saving.   The first statement is uncontroversial, because everyone agrees that taxes reduce the after-tax reward to work and saving. In the second statement, the supply-siders argued that reductions in personal income taxes would lead people to work longer hours, would encourage more people to take second ("moonlighting") jobs, and would allow and encourage people to save more. Many economists were skeptical of these claims. At the time of the original 1981 debate about supply-side economics, Charles Schultze quipped that "There's nothing wrong with supply-side economics that division by ten couldn't cure."

As it turned out, even Schultze's skeptical assessment may have been too optimistic. When we compare the economy before the Reagan tax cuts to the economy after the tax cuts, we find that the amount of work effort, as measured by the labor-force participation rate, grew more slowly after 1981 than before, and the personal saving rate fell after rising during 1977–81. The only bit of support for supply-side doctrines is that hours per employee fell more slowly after 1981 than before.

Response of productivity growth.   Some supply-side advocates also predicted a rebound in productivity growth. Everyone agreed in 1981 that the U.S. productivity growth record had been dismal since 1972—a slowdown that no one fully understood. If the supply-side advocates were correct, we would expect productivity growth to have been substantially more rapid after 1981 than before. But productivity growth was only moderately faster after 1981 in contrast to the larger acceleration that occurred after tax rates were raised in 1993.

> **Supply-side economics**
> predicts that a reduction in marginal income tax rates will create an increase in the supply of output, that is, in natural real GDP.

	1948–72	1972–80	1980–93	1993–2007
Private nonfarm output per hour (annual growth rate in percent)	2.7	1.2	1.6	2.4

Figure 12-5 The Laffer Curve

The curve shows that total government tax revenue depends on the tax rate. With either a zero or 100 percent tax rate, the government collects no revenue. Maximum revenue occurs at point C. If tax rates are cut starting from point B, government revenue declines, but if tax rates are cut starting from point D, government revenue increases.

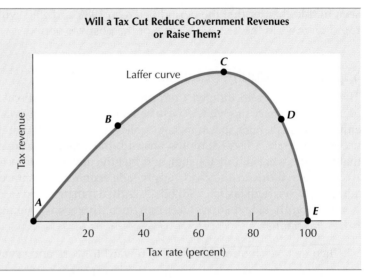

Will a Tax Cut Reduce Government Revenues or Raise Them?

The Laffer curve. The third supply-side claim, that tax cuts raise government revenue, is even more controversial than the second. This claim was widely touted in 1981 during the debate about the Reagan tax cuts, because critics had claimed that such large tax cuts would create unprecedented government budget deficits. Supply-side proponents argued that the tax cuts would "pay for themselves."

The proponents' argument was illustrated by the famous Laffer curve, which Arthur Laffer (now a private business consultant) had drawn on a napkin in a Washington restaurant in an inspired moment in 1974. The Laffer curve, reproduced in Figure 12-5, starts from the obvious point that the government will raise no tax revenue at all if tax rates are zero, as at point A, and if tax rates are 100 percent, as at point E. In between, as the tax rate rises from zero to 100 percent, tax revenues will first rise and then fall. If the government introduces a tax cut (like the 1981 Reagan package) starting from point B, the economy would move leftward along the Laffer curve and government revenue would fall. But a tax cut starting from point D would cause a leftward movement that would raise government revenue.

Was the economy at point B or point D in 1981? Clearly, one can draw a Laffer curve with its peak at any tax rate—20, 50, or 80 percent. The peak at 70 percent in Figure 12-5 is completely arbitrary. The fact that the United States entered an era of persistent deficits after the Reagan tax cuts suggests that it moved from a point like C to B in the 1980s, not from D to C.

 SELF-TEST

1. Looking at the Laffer curve in Figure 12-5 and assuming that government spending is fixed, does a reduction in tax rates starting from point B raise or lower the government budget deficit? Starting from point D?

2. Which point, B or D, was believed to describe the position of the U.S. economy in 1981 by the following: Arthur Laffer? President Reagan? Critics of supply-side economics?

12-8   Alternative Views of Fiscal Policy: The Barro-Ricardo Equivalence Theorem

We have seen in the previous section that supply-siders depart from the traditional Keynesian analysis of fiscal policy by predicting a large effect on supply (Y^N), not just on demand. Another attack on the traditional Keynesian analysis of fiscal policy was launched in 1974 by Robert J. Barro of Harvard University.[3] Because Barro's approach echoed a theme originally proposed by the classical economist David Ricardo in the early nineteenth century, his point has become known as the "Barro-Ricardo equivalence theorem."

Barro's theory denies the efficacy of discretionary fiscal policy that takes the form of tax changes, because tax cuts are balanced by an increase in saving rather than an increase in consumption. Why? Barro points out that any tax cut is financed by deficit spending, which requires future tax payments to meet the interest on the public debt. People who see their taxes cut will tell themselves, "This just means lower taxes today and higher taxes in the future when the government needs to pay the interest on the debt; I'll save today in order to build up a savings account that will be needed to meet those future taxes."

Robert J. Barro (1944–)

Barro's fame stems from his theory of fiscal policy, the Keynesian non-market-clearing model (Chapter 17), and his recent research on new models of economic growth (Section 10-7).

Bequests Imply Concern About Children

While economists had recognized that taxpayers might perceive their future obligation to meet government interest payments, most had not taken seriously the possibility that people would view higher future taxes as *completely equivalent* to lower current taxes (hence the name "equivalence theorem"). Economists had previously pointed out that much of the future interest burden of the higher public debt would occur after today's taxpayers are dead. Barro's contribution was to argue that people leave bequests to their children, implying that they care about their children and hence, indirectly, about the tax burden that they will face. His striking deduction was that *today's taxpayers, reacting to a tax cut today, would raise their saving so as to increase their bequests to their children in order to pay for future taxes levied by the government.*

In other words, today's holdings of government bonds do not represent net wealth. When the government prints an additional one-dollar bond to pay for a tax cut, bondholders feel richer by one dollar, but taxpayers feel poorer by the same dollar, since they recognize that one dollar's worth of future taxes will have to be levied to pay the interest on the bonds.

Criticism of the Equivalence Proposition

Barro's ingenious argument let loose a torrent of criticism. The link between bequests and concern for children was doubted. Decision horizons of private individuals are often quite short. Some parents do not care about their descendants. Perhaps more important, the absence of "perfect" rental markets for consumer housing and household possessions means that almost every homeowner is likely to die with a significant positive net worth in the form of housing and furnishings, which will be bequeathed to charity or to some heir even if the deceased does not care about the exact standard of living that the heir achieves.

---

[3] Robert J. Barro, "Are Government Bonds Net Wealth?" *Journal of Political Economy*, vol. 82 (November/December 1974), pp. 1095–1117.

A separate criticism pointed out that most individuals pay a substantially higher interest rate to borrow than does the government (for example, 18 percent on credit cards compared to a long-term government bond rate in early 2008 below 4 percent). This means that people apply a much higher discount rate to future government tax levies than the interest rate the government has to pay on its bonds. This point applies with special force when it is recognized that the typical adult consumer has an expected life span of about 35 years. If the government cuts taxes by raising the public debt, most of the burden of servicing or repaying the debt will be borne within that 35-year lifetime. Only a very small portion of the debt burden will be passed on to future generations, making moot the debate about the motives for bequests.

Going beyond the interest rate on credit cards, some households cannot borrow at all. They live from paycheck to paycheck because low ability and/or bad luck has limited their incomes, and because they may have high expenses due to large families or unavoidable medical expenses. For these households, consumption depends on current income, not lifetime income. Tax cuts increase their current disposable income and their opportunities to consume, and they do not care about future consequences.

Evidence from the 1981 Tax Cuts

Most of the skepticism about the Barro-Ricardo equivalence theorem emerged immediately after the 1974 publication of Barro's article and was based on general principles. However, saving behavior after the 1981–83 tax cuts provided additional reason for doubt. If consumers had behaved in the forward-looking way postulated by the Barro proposition, consumption would have remained unaffected while saving would have jumped to pay for the future tax burden created by the extra federal debt. However, the personal saving rate *fell* after 1981, from 10.9 percent of disposable personal income in 1981 to an average of 9.6 percent in 1982–86. To set aside sufficient saving to pay for the future tax burden of the extra debt, households should have raised their saving rate from 10.9 percent in 1981 to roughly 14 percent in 1986, but *actual behavior went in the opposite direction*.

The same question can be asked about the behavior of saving after the Bush tax cuts of 2001 and 2003. Again, the Barro theory would have predicted a jump in household saving. Instead, household saving dropped from an already-low 2.3 percent of disposable income to an average of 0.6 percent in 2005–07. Thus it does not appear that consumers raise saving and cut consumption to offset tax cuts, and thus the original Keynesian analysis of fiscal policy (introduced in Chapters 3 and 4) remains valid.

12-9 The Great Debate over Social Security

The reemergence of persistent government budget deficits after 2001 led to concerns about the immediate impact of the deficits. As shown earlier in equation (12.1) on p. 391, a shift of the government budget from surplus to deficit must reduce national saving and in turn this will cause a reduction in domestic investment and an increase in foreign borrowing. Immediate concerns, as we have learned in Chapter 6, focused on whether an increase in foreign borrowing was feasible and sustainable, and whether the indirect effect of

ductivity growth both by crowding out private investment and requiring that interest and dividends be paid out to foreign investors as the result of foreign borrowing that is an inevitable result of low national saving (see equation (12.1) on p. 391). The U.S. dollar fell substantially from 2002 to 2007, raising the cost of imported goods and foreign travel for Americans and indirectly reducing their standard of living.

The solutions to the federal budget deficit are easy to suggest from the standpoint of economics but difficult to implement politically. The Bush tax cuts should be reversed, particularly on the very high-income individuals who benefited the most from the 2001–03 tax cuts. The extent that federal expenditures can be reduced depends in part on whether the wars in Iraq and Afghanistan can be ended, another political rather than economic decision. But one thing is sure from the economic analysis of the first sections of this chapter: Any expenditure reductions should avoid those government functions that contribute directly to growth and technological change, including support of education and research through such government programs as scholarship aid for college students and support for the National Science Foundation and the National Institutes of Health.

Summary

1. A budget surplus raises national saving and raises the rate of economic growth. A budget deficit reduces national saving and lowers the rate of economic growth.

2. The two methods for stimulating national saving and hence economic growth are for policymakers to create incentives that raise private saving or to run a larger government surplus (or smaller deficit).

3. Deficits that raise the future level of the public debt create a burden on future generations if the deficits finance government consumption expenditures that yield no future benefits to balance the burden of taxes required to pay the interest on the debt.

4. The government faces a solvency condition, which states that it cannot perpetually run a deficit in the long run if the real interest rate exceeds the economy's growth rate of real output.

5. The U.S. ratio of public debt to GDP fell throughout the postwar period until 1974, rose between 1974 and 1993, fell between 1993 and 2001, and rose again after 2001. The deficits in the 1980s and 1990s were due to a higher ratio of government spending to GDP, not to a lower ratio of tax revenue to GDP. The shift to surplus after 1997 was mainly due to rapid increases in receipts from the personal income tax, and the shift to deficits after 2001 was due primarily to cuts in personal income tax rates.

6. The Laffer curve predicts that if initial tax rates are high enough, a cut in tax rates raises government tax revenue. Supply-side economists predicted in the early 1980s that tax rate cuts would not only raise government tax revenues but would also stimulate saving and work effort. The predicted effects did not occur.

7. The Barro-Ricardo equivalence theorem states that deficit-financed tax cuts will stimulate saving rather than consumption, because individuals will try to build up their savings accounts to pay the future taxes required to service the higher government debt.

8. The Social Security trust fund is projected to run out of money in the year 2046. This forecast is based on unrealistically pessimistic projections for real GDP and population growth. More realistic projections put off the Social Security crisis for several more decades.

9. Reformers of Social Security agree that funds should be invested in the stock market, not just (as at present) in government bonds. But there is a political disagreement as to whether individuals should be allowed to invest funds in their own retirement accounts or whether the trust fund should invest directly in the stock market without the extra costs or complications of individual accounts.

Concepts

rate of time preference   national saving   supply-side economics

Questions

1. Economic policymakers are concerned with both economic growth and economic stabilization. Explain the distinction between them. Are different policies used for the two purposes? Give some examples.

2. What is national saving? Under what circumstances would it be appropriate to increase the level of national saving?

3. Explain why a country saves too much if its rate of time preference equals 10 percent per year and the rate of return on private investment is 8 percent.

4. If the level of real GDP is held fixed by monetary policy, which of the following will provide the greatest stimulus to saving?
   (a) An increase in the personal income tax rates paid by the rich.
   (b) An increase in the personal income tax rates paid by the poor.
   (c) The introduction of a federal retail sales tax.

5. "An increase in national saving will increase economic growth. It follows, then, that deep cuts in government spending should be adopted to boost economic growth." Evaluate this argument.

6. "Unnecessary fears of the rising government deficit have restricted desirable government spending." Explain.

7. Explain why in a large open economy an increase in government consumption expenditures that is not offset by an increase in taxes or private saving must result in lower consumption expenditures in the future. Suppose that the increase in government spending is for an investment project, and again that there is no offsetting increase in either taxes or private saving. What must be true in terms of the return on the government investment project if future consumption expenditures are to remain unchanged?

8. We rarely hear concern about the "burden" of privately held debt, yet many people share a concern about the public debt. Why is this so? Is the concern about the public debt reasonable?

9. Many people are less concerned with the absolute size of the government debt than they are about its size relative to GDP. Such people would not worry about the size of government deficits if the ratio of government debt to GDP remained equal to some "appropriate" level.
   (a) Should people who hold this view worry about the solvency of the government?
   (b) Explain the conditions under which it is possible for the debt-GDP ratio to be a constant.
   (c) Don't people who hold the view that has just been described have to worry about the future solvency of the government?

10. (a) Was it a decrease in spending or a rise in tax revenues or some combination of the two that resulted in the temporary disappearance of budget deficits during the late 1990s?
    (b) Was it an increase in spending or a fall in tax revenues or some combination of the two that resulted in the re-emergence of budget deficits after 2001?

11. The supply-side argument for tax cuts is based on one uncontroversial claim and two controversial claims. What are they? Is the empirical record consistent or inconsistent with the controversial claims? Explain.

12. When analyzing the effects of price changes, microeconomists consider how consumers' behavior will respond to changes in relative prices (the "substitution" effect) and to changes in real purchasing power (the "income" effect). Substitution and income effects also occur when tax rates change. Not only do tax changes affect disposable income, but they also change the relative "prices" of certain types of behavior.
    (a) What is the opportunity cost of leisure? What happens to leisure's opportunity cost (its "price") following a tax rate cut? Describe the substitution and income effects on people's decision to consume leisure. Do these effects reinforce or offset one another?
    (b) Do the proponents of supply-side economics see the substitution effect or the income effect having the dominant impact on decisions to consume leisure following a tax rate cut? Explain.

13. Just as income tax rates affect the opportunity cost of leisure, they also affect the relative price of current versus future consumption. Describe the substitution and income effects of the following two proposals for raising national saving in order to determine which is likely to have the larger impact.
    (a) A cut in income tax rates that is offset by a decrease in government consumption expenditures, leaving the budget deficit unchanged.
    (b) A cut in income tax rates that is accompanied by an expansion of the income tax base, leaving income tax revenues unchanged. (This type of cut in income tax rates is referred to as being revenue neutral.)

14. State and critique the Barro-Ricardo equivalence theorem.

15. Evaluate each of the following statements in terms of the Barro-Ricardo equivalence theorem's implications for saving.
    (a) "Retirement benefits promised by Social Security reduce workers' incentives to save and thus diminish private saving in the economy."
    (b) "Social Security is solvent now, but over the next 40 years it will likely go broke unless taxes are raised or benefits are reduced."

16. Projections that the Social Security system will run out of money sometime around 2046 have given rise to numerous proposals to reform Social Security.
    (a) How sensitive are the predictions of impending crisis in the Social Security system to projected

growth rates of the labor force, labor productivity, and real GDP?

(b) What are three proposals to "save" the Social Security system as a pay-as-you-go program? Do these proposals generate enough revenue and/or reduce benefits enough to do so?

(c) What are the arguments for and against investing Social Security funds in the stock market, either through private accounts or having the government invest the funds?

17. What were the positions of the "termites" and the "pussycats" in the 1980s and early 1990s concerning the effect of persistent federal budget deficits on economic growth? Which one of these positions is supported by the behavior of the economy over the last 25 years?

Problems

1. Congress passes and the president signs into law a bill authorizing the construction of two public recreational facilities, each of which costs $400,000 now and will last for ten years. Each project is financed by government borrowing at an interest rate of 5 percent. The benefits of the first project are $40,000 per year for the first five years, $60,000 per year for the next two years, and $80,000 per year for the last three years. The benefits of the second project are $70,000 per year for the first four years, $50,000 in the fifth year, $40,000 in the sixth year, and $30,000 per year for the last four years. Evaluate whether the spending on each of these projects adds to the burden of government debt over the next ten years.

2. In 2008 a country had real GDP of $10,000 billion, a government debt of $5,000 billion, and a real interest rate of 3 percent. The country's growth rate of real GDP is 3 percent.

(a) What is the value of the ratio of government debt to GDP for this country in 2008?

(b) What is the amount of interest paid on the country's debt in 2008? What is the interest payment as a percentage of real GDP in 2008?

(c) If the government issues new debt in 2009 to cover the interest charges on the 2008 debt, what is the new level of government debt in 2009? How much interest has to be paid in 2009 on the government debt, assuming the real interest rate is still 3 percent?

(d) What was the level of real GDP in 2009? Compare the percentage of real GDP going for interest payments in 2009 to that for 2008. Compare the ratio of government debt to real GDP for the two years. Is the ratio of government debt to real GDP equal in the two years? If so, why? If not, why not?

(e) Assume that the real interest rate was actually 5 percent, not 3 percent, for both years. How does this change affect your answers to b–d?

3. Suppose that nominal GDP equals $14,000 billion, the current budget deficit is $112 billion, and the government's debt-GDP ratio is 20 percent.

(a) Given that the government wishes to maintain the debt-GDP ratio at 20 percent, explain whether the government needs to decrease its budget deficit, maintain the current budget deficit, or can increase its budget deficit if over the next year, nominal GDP grow by: (i) 2 percent; (ii) 4 percent; and (iii) 6 percent.

(b) Suppose that the only differences between the three nominal GDP growth rates given in part a are the growth rates of real GDP. Given your answers to part a, do the fiscal policies imposed by the desire to maintain a constant debt-GDP ratio seem appropriate from the standpoint of stabilization policy?

(c) Do your answers to part b strengthen or weaken the argument that monetary policy should be the primary tool for smoothing the business cycle?

4. A country currently has a nominal GDP of $12 trillion and a debt of $4.8 trillion. The rate of inflation over the next thirty years will equal 2 percent per year and the growth rate of real GDP will equal 3 percent per year. For the last 2 decades of this period, the real government debt will grow by 4 percent per year due to the demands of an aging population. At the end of this thirty-year period, the country would like to have the same debt-GDP ratio that it has now.

(a) Calculate the country's nominal GDP at the end of ten and thirty years.

(b) Calculate the country's debt at the end of thirty years, given the country's desired debt-GDP ratio at the time.

(c) Calculate the country's debt at the end of ten years, given the country's desired debt-GDP ratio at the end of thirty years.

(d) For the country to achieve its desired debt-GDP ratio at the end of thirty years, calculate the annual growth rate of its debt over the next ten years.

5. The Laffer curve expresses tax revenue, T, as a function of the tax rate, t. The value of T clearly equals zero when t is 0 or 1. For at least one intermediate value of t, the value of T is positive. Hence, the Laffer curve must be an increasing function of t initially, and a decreasing function of t for higher values of t. Assume T is found by multiplying t and the tax base, T_B (taxable income):

$$T = tT_B.$$

The phenomenon of the Laffer curve arises because T_B is, by hypothesis, a decreasing function of the tax rate t. Assume:

$$T_B = 8,000 - 8,000t.$$

(a) For values of $t = 0.25, 0.4, 0.5, 0.6,$ and 0.75, find T and T_B.

(b) Note that for small changes, $\Delta T/T = (\Delta t/t) + (\Delta T_B/T_B)$. (This is analogous to the case of demand growth in Chapter 8—when $X = PY$,

percentage rates of change are given by $x = p + y$.) The tax-rate elasticity of any variable Z is defined to be $\eta = (\Delta Z/Z)/(\Delta t/t)$. Let η_1 be the tax-rate elasticity of tax revenue and η_2 be the tax-rate elasticity of the tax base. Find η_1 in terms of η_2.

(c) Find η_1 for the values of t in part a. On the basis of your calculations for this particular Laffer curve, over what range of t are tax revenues increasing in t? Decreasing in t?

 SELF-TEST ANSWERS

p. 392 By looking at the impact on national saving as a percent of GDP, we are able to ignore the multiplier effects of these fiscal policies. Since national saving is the sum of government saving and private saving, for each item we must determine the effect on each. (1) Government saving declines (deficit rises) with no impact on private saving, so national saving declines. (2) Government saving increases (deficit falls) while private saving may also increase due to the higher price of food, so national saving increases. (3) Government saving declines (deficit rises), while the increase in personal disposable income is split between higher private saving and higher consumption; thus national saving declines because government saving declines more than private saving increases. (4) Government tax revenue falls but private saving does not necessarily rise since money can be switched from taxable saving accounts to tax-free retirement accounts. National saving may rise or decline.

p. 396 (1) $440 billion; (2) $120 billion; (3) $30 billion; (4) $110 billion.

p. 402 (1) A reduction in tax rates moves the economy to the left in Figure 12-5, the Laffer curve diagram. Thus, starting from point B, tax revenues fall as we move to the left, raising the government deficit if government expenditures are fixed. Starting from point D, tax revenues rise and the government deficit declines. (2) Arthur Laffer and President Reagan believed that the 1981 economy was at point D, and critics of the supply-side economists believed that the 1981 economy was at point B.

For additional practice and exploration, exercises that require the use of Excel are available at www.aw-bc.com/gordon.

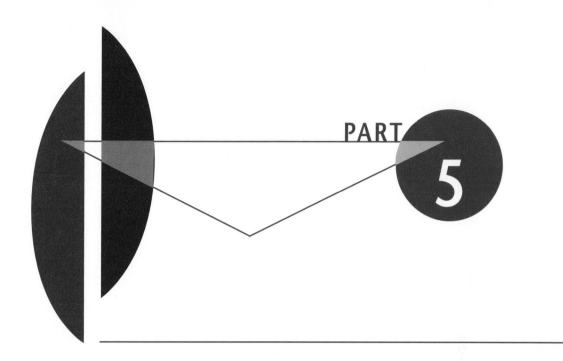

Stabilization Policy in an Open Economy

tal deposits to 190, consisting of the initial deposit of 100 and the new deposit of 90. Because the used-raft dealer has redeposited the 90 gold coins that were borrowed to pay for the raft, the bank again has the original 100 gold coins. At this point, the banker again decides to hold as reserves 10 percent of "total" deposits. Since the banker decides to hold only 10 percent of 190 for reserves, the remaining "excess" reserves of 81 gold coins can be loaned out.

The banker can continue making loans of excess reserves until total deposits equal 1,000. At that point, the banker's actual reserves (100) equal required reserves (100 = 10 percent of 1,000) and excess reserves equal zero. Thus the original deposit of 100 gold coins leads to the creation of 1,000 units of money, all in the form of bank deposits. The First Desert Island Bank has succeeded in creating an additional nine units of money for every gold coin that it initially received.

How has this magic occurred? Four conditions are necessary for the banker to turn 100 gold coins into a money supply of 1,000.

1. **Equivalence of coins and deposits.** Paper receipts representing ownership of bank deposits, that is, checks, must be accepted as a means of payment on a one-for-one basis. In other words, checks must be treated as equivalent to payment of gold coins.

2. **Redeposit of proceeds from loans.** Any consumer or business firm receiving a cash or check payment must deposit it into an account at the same bank. We assumed in the example that the used-raft dealer redeposited the 90 gold coins received as the proceeds of the first loan.

3. **Holding of cash reserves.** The bank must hold some fraction of its reserves in the form of cash (10 percent in gold coins in this example).

4. **Willing borrowers.** Someone must be willing to borrow from the bank at an interest rate that covers the bank's cost of operation. If the First Desert Island Bank stopped lending its excess reserves, the process of money creation would stop.

The Money-Creation Multiplier

When these four conditions are met, then the entire process of money creation can be summed up in a simple equation. We let the symbol H denote **high-powered money,** that is, the type of money that is held by banks as reserves. In the example, H consists of the 100 gold coins, which are high-powered because they generate the multiple expansion of money by the First Desert Island Bank. A synonym for high-powered money is the "monetary base."

High-powered money is the sum of currency held outside depository institutions and the reserves held inside them.

The symbol D represents the total bank deposits. The symbol e represents the fraction of deposits that banks hold as reserves. In equilibrium, the *demand* for high-powered money to be held as reserves (eD) equals the *supply* of high-powered money (H):

General Form   Numerical Example

$$eD = H \qquad\qquad 0.1(1,000) = 100 \qquad\qquad (13.1)$$

The same equation can be rearranged (dividing both sides by e) to determine the amount of deposits (D) relative to the quantity of high-powered money (H) and the bank reserve-holding ratio (e):

General Form   Numerical Example

$$D = \frac{H}{e} \qquad\qquad 1,000 = \frac{100}{0.1} \qquad\qquad (13.2)$$

Comparison with income-determination multiplier. The money-creation multiplier is $1/e$, or $1/0.1 = 10$ in the numerical example. This is the second usage of the word *multiplier* in this book. In Chapter 3 we examined the factors that determined the income-determination multiplier. In its simplest version, that multiplier in Chapter 3 was

$$\frac{\text{income-determination}}{\text{multipler } (k)} = \frac{1}{\text{marginal propensity to save } (s)}$$

An increase in autonomous planned spending (A_p) is "multiplied" because spending creates income, a fraction of which *leaks out* into saving and taxes and the remainder of which goes into additional spending. The multiplier process ends only when the total of extra induced leakages equals the original increase in A_p.

The intuition behind the money-creation multiplier is the same. An increase in high-powered money (H) is multiplied in equation (13.2) because the initial deposit of H becomes reserves, a fraction of which *leaks out* into required reserves and the remainder of which is lent out and comes back as additional deposits of the households and business firms that receive the loan proceeds. The money-creation multiplier process continues until the extra induced leakages into required reserves equal the original increase in H.

Comparison with real-world conditions. In reality, some of the four conditions required to obtain the simple money-creation multiplier may not hold.

Condition (2) required that any seller receiving a payment from the proceeds of a loan redeposit it into the bank. If not, the multiplier process of money creation cannot occur at that bank. If the cash is redeposited at another depository institution, then the second institution will find itself with excess reserves, allowing the multiplier process to proceed. Thus condition (2) can be revised to apply to, say, all the banks within the United States. As long as sellers who receive loan proceeds in the form of either cash or checks redeposit the funds in a U.S. bank, the money-creation multiplier in equation (13.2) remains valid for the U.S. banking system as a whole.

Cash holding. The money-creation multiplier is changed, however, if households or businesses want to hold not only checkable deposits but some pocket cash as well. Imagine that everyone wants to hold a fixed fraction (c) of his or her deposits, say 15 percent, in the form of cash.[1] This demand for currency adds an extra amount (cD) to the total demand for high-powered money. In a revised desert island example, the demand for gold coins, the only form of high-powered money, might be 10 percent of deposits for bank reserves ($eD = 0.1D$), plus 15 percent of deposits for pocket cash ($cD = 0.15D$).

In practice in the real world, high-powered money (H) is equal to the liabilities of the Federal Reserve, namely bank reserves and currency. The demand for bank reserves (eD) plus the demand for currency (cD) equals the total supply of high-powered money (H):

---

[1] The cash fraction c has nothing whatsoever to do with the marginal propensity to consume (c) of Chapter 3. Nor does the reserve holding ratio (e) have anything to do with the foreign exchange rate (e) of Chapter 5. At this stage we have run through the alphabet and are asking some letters to perform double duty. See the guide to symbols provided on the inside back cover.

General Form	Numerical Example
Demand = Supply	Demand = Supply
$eD + cD = H$	$0.1D + 0.15D = 100$

or

$$(e + c)D = H \qquad\qquad 0.25D = 100 \qquad\qquad (13.3)$$

Dividing both sides by $(e + c)$, we can solve for deposits:

$$D = \frac{H}{e + c} \qquad\qquad D = \frac{100}{0.25} = 400 \qquad\qquad (13.4)$$

In words, total deposits equal the supply of high-powered money (H) divided by the fraction of deposits that leaks into reserves (e) plus the fraction that leaks into cash (c).

Remember that the total money supply (M) includes not only deposits (D) but also currency:

$$M = D + cD = (1 + c)D \qquad\qquad (13.5)$$

Substituting for D in (13.5) from (13.4), we obtain

$$M = (1 + c)D = \frac{(1 + c)H}{e + c} = \frac{1.15(100)}{0.25} = 460 \qquad\qquad (13.6)$$

The ratio of the money supply (M) to high-powered money (H) is called the **money multiplier** (M/H). In equation (13.6), the money multiplier is equal to $(1 + c)/(e + c)$. In the next two sections we will learn that the money multiplier is volatile due to additional factors omitted from (13.6).

> The **money multiplier** is the ratio of the money supply to high-powered money, that is, M/H. There is a separate money multiplier for each definition of the money supply.

Gold Discoveries and Bank Panics

The supply of money depends only on the three terms that appear in equation (13.6): the supply of high-powered money (H), the cash-holding ratio (c), and the ratio of reserves to deposits (e). When only gold can serve as high-powered money (H), the total supply of money depends on the demand for and supply of gold. Because a sustained increase in monetary growth causes higher inflation in the long run, gold discoveries have caused some episodes of inflation. For instance, inflation was higher immediately following the gold discoveries in California in 1848 and in Alaska in 1898.

Before the establishment of the Federal Reserve in 1913 and the introduction of federal deposit insurance in 1934, the U.S. economy was at the mercy of capricious changes in the money supply, stemming not only from the influence of gold discoveries on the growth of H but also from episodes in which the cash-holding ratio (c) and the reserve ratio (e) fluctuated dramatically. During banking panics, which occurred about once a decade and culminated in the serious panic of 1907, depositors feared for the safety of their deposits and withdrew their deposits as cash. This raised the cash-holding ratio (c) and thereby lowered the money supply. To deal with the tide of withdrawals, banks began to bolster their reserves by raising the reserve ratio (e), which further reduced the money supply.[2] In the pre–Federal Reserve era, there was no way for the

---

[2] Notice in equation (13.6) that any increase in e reduces the quantity of money (M). Although c appears in both the numerator and denominator, an increase in c reduces the money supply as long as the reserve-holding ratio (e) is less than 1.0.

government to raise H to offset panic-induced increases in c and e. Panics caused a drop in the money supply and in aggregate demand, cutting both output and prices. It was the panic of 1907 that led directly to the formation of the Federal Reserve in 1914. The Fed was established to control directly two components of equation (13.6), namely high-powered money (H) and the reserves ratio (e) to offset both undesired changes in the cash-holding ratio (c) as well as any adverse events in the economy as a whole.

 SELF-TEST

Assume that high-powered money is 500, the fraction of deposits held as currency is 0.25, and the fraction of deposits held as reserves is 0.15. Answer the following:

1. Calculate the value of deposits and the money supply.

2. Calculate the new value of deposits and the money supply if the currency-holding fraction changes from 0.25 to 0.35.

3. Calculate the new value of deposits and the money supply if the reserve-holding fraction changes from 0.15 to 0.25 (while the currency-holding fraction remains at the original 0.25).

13-5   The Fed's Three Tools for Changing the Money Supply

Suppose the Federal Reserve wants the economy to have a given money supply M. The Fed must predict the public's desired cash-holding ratio (c), over which the Fed has no control. Then the Fed can adjust the two remaining variables in equation (13.6), high-powered money (H) and the reserve ratio (e), to make its desired M consistent with the public's chosen c. The Fed uses three tools to accomplish this task; the first two control H and the last influences e. This section helps us understand which real-world events change H and e.

The Fed's Balance Sheet

A commercial bank has two main kinds of assets, the bank reserves it holds on deposit at the Fed and the loans that it grants to households and business firms; these earn interest for the bank. The main liabilities of a commercial bank are the deposits that households and business firms entrust to the bank. By paying a lower interest rate on deposits than it receives on its loans, the bank has enough left over to pay its employees, cover its other expenses, and earn a profit.

Likewise, the Fed has a balance sheet, as illustrated in Table 13-3. The Fed's main asset consists of its holdings of government bonds. The Fed has two main types of liabilities. The first is the currency that it has printed and that it is obligated to redeem at any time, hence a liability. The second type of Fed liability is the total of bank reserves that it holds on deposit for the commercial banks. As shown in Table 13-3, in this example the Fed owns $850 billion of government bonds, and its liabilities consist of $800 billion of currency and $50 billion of bank reserves. The total of its liabilities is called "the monetary base," which is $850 billion in this example. The monetary base is the same as high-powered

Table 13-3	A Simplified Version of the Fed's Balance Sheet (all values in $ billions)		
Assets		**Liabilities**	
		Currency	800
Government Bonds	850	Bank Reserves	50
Total Assets	850	Total Liabilities = Monetary Base (High-Powered Money)	850

money, and we continue to use the symbol H to designate the sum of the Fed's liabilities, which is $850 billion in Table 13-3.

What Action by the Fed Will Raise the Money Supply?

The Fed's liabilities are not the same as the money supply. The money supply consists of currency ($800 billion in Table 13-3) and checking deposits at banks. Since the banks are required to hold 10 percent of their checking deposits as reserves at the Fed, we know that the $50 billion of bank reserves in Table 13-3 must be supporting $500 billion of checking deposits (in this simplified example we ignore saving deposits, certificates of deposits, and other types of bank deposits). Thus the total money supply is the total of $800 billion of currency and $500 billion of checking deposits, a total of $1,300 billion.

The money supply (M^s) is equal to the monetary base times the amount of high-powered money (H):

$$M^s = \text{money multiplier} \times H \qquad (13.7)$$

or, in this example

$$\$1{,}300 \text{ billion} = 1.53(\$850 \text{ billion}).$$

But the Fed may not always be satisfied with a money supply of $1,300 billion. Let us say that the Fed has decided that real GDP is too low, and to stimulate more planned spending, the Fed needs to raise the money supply. It has three tools to achieve the desired increase in the money supply.

First Tool: Open-Market Operations

The first tool is by far the most important. The Fed can change H by purchasing and selling government securities like Treasury bills. When it buys Treasury bills in the open market, the Fed (electronically) receives the Treasury bills from the seller and pays for them with high-powered money. The Fed pays for the Treasury bills it has bought simply by raising (electronically) the account balance of the seller at the seller's bank and the reserve balance of the seller's bank at the seller's bank's Federal Reserve Bank. This addition to H, brought about by the Fed's **open-market operations,** leads to an even larger increase in M through the money multiplier.

Federal Reserve monetary policy is decided by the Federal Open Market Committee at meetings scheduled eight times each year. The meetings of the FOMC are held in a large and imposing room at the Federal Reserve Board in Washington, D.C., and are attended by the seven governors of the Federal Reserve Board and the twelve presidents of the regional Federal Reserve

Open-market operations are purchases and sales of government securities made by the Federal Reserve in order to change high-powered money.

banks.[3] After its meetings, the FOMC often issues a statement indicating generally what policy it has decided to follow. The FOMC also issues a directive to the Fed's open-market manager at the Federal Reserve Bank of New York, a position held in 2008 by William Dudley.

H **is created out of thin air.** The Fed issues its instructions in terms of a target federal funds interest rate, the interest rate that banks charge each other to borrow overnight reserves. In the fall of 2007, this target rate was reduced from 5.25 percent, the Fed's target rate between June 2006 and September 2007, to 4.75 percent on September 18, 2007, and then to 4.50 percent on October 31, 2007. These federal funds loans are necessary because at the end of any day of business, banks may wind up with too many or too few reserves. If a bank is open until 5 p.m. and at 4:59 p.m. a depositor walks in with a deposit of $3 million and the reserve requirement is 10 percent, or $300,000, then the bank must quickly find $300,000 in extra reserves. The federal funds market allows the bank automatically, by a simple computer entry, to borrow federal funds from a bank that has a surplus, and the Fed's key federal funds interest rate is that set on these overnight loans between banks. Many other interest rates, including the prime rate that banks charge to large corporations and is the basis for most home equity loans, are pegged to the federal funds rate determined by the Fed.

Let us say that Mr. Dudley's directive from the FOMC calls for continued moderate growth in the money supply, and that he has decided that the time has come for a $100 million increase in high-powered money (*H*). All Mr. Dudley has to do is pick up the phone and buy $100 million in U.S. Treasury bills from a government bond dealer, say Goldman Sachs. *H* is created out of thin air when the Fed electronically gives a credit of $100 million to the reserve account at the bank, say Citibank, where Goldman Sachs has a checking account. At the same time, the Fed notifies Citibank that it should give a $100 million credit to the Goldman Sachs checking account.

This transaction has given Citibank an additional liability of $100 million of deposits and an additional asset of $100 million of reserves, which earn no interest. Suppose that Citibank chooses to hold $10 million of reserves against the additional $100 million deposit. It then has $90 million of excess reserves that it can use to make interest-bearing loans. Borrowers usually get loans so that they can spend the funds. When the proceeds of the loans are spent, some will be redeposited in a depository institution someplace. That institution will then have excess reserves that it can lend out, just as Citibank did. Note that depository institutions no longer have excess reserves once all the funds have been loaned out and they are withdrawn to be spent. Thus another way to view the money-creation process is that it continues until no depository institution has excess reserves it is willing to lend out.

By buying Treasury bills with electronic credits, Mr. Dudley has "created" more high-powered money, *H*. Goldman Sachs transferred Treasury bills to the Fed, but Fed regulations do not permit Treasury bills to be counted toward reserves. Thus, the transfer of Treasury bills did not lower *H* or reserves, but the Fed's paying for the Treasury bills did raise reserves. That is why the Fed's

---

[3] All twelve regional presidents attend, but only five may vote. The New York Fed president always has a vote and the other four votes are rotated. All governors are entitled to vote at every FOMC meeting.

open-market purchase produced an increase in H. Mr. Dudley also created a multiple increase in the money supply. The total money supply rises each time funds are deposited. As the money-creation multiplier showed us, the money supply is likely to rise by a multiple of the original value of Treasury bills purchased by the Fed on the open market.

Effect on interest rates.   Mr. Dudley's purchase influences not only the total supply of money but also the interest rate. When he buys $100 million of Treasury bills, the price of Treasury bills rises, thereby lowering the return, or interest rate, they pay.

Sometimes the Fed must engage in open-market operations even when it has no desire to raise or lower the money supply. For instance, during the Christmas shopping season, the public needs more cash for transactions and raises its desired cash-holding ratio (c). Without action by the Federal Reserve, this increase in the denominator of the money-supply equation (13.6) would reduce the money supply by a multiple of the public's cash withdrawals from deposit accounts. The Fed can prevent this decline in the money supply and the associated leftward shift of the LM curve by conducting a "defensive" open-market purchase of Treasury bills. To prevent a decline in the money supply, the Fed would raise H enough to offset the effect of the higher c.

Second Tool: Discount Rate   *control MB*

Depository institutions' incentives to borrow from the Fed increase when market interest rates rise relative to the **discount rate,** the interest rate that the Fed charges them when they borrow reserves. Depository institutions' so-called discount-window borrowings tend to be high when the interest rates they can earn on money market instruments, like Treasury bills, are substantially above the discount rate that the Fed has set.

> The **discount rate** is the interest rate the Federal Reserve charges depository institutions when they borrow reserves.

Because $100 million in Fed loans provides banks with the same $100 million in bank reserves as a $100 million open-market purchase, the Fed can control high-powered money (H) either by varying the discount rate or by conducting open-market operations. Monetary control can be achieved with either instrument and does not require both. The primary justification for allowing discount-window borrowing at the Fed is the need for immediate help by individual banks suffering from an unexpected rush of withdrawals. Such cases are rare and can be handled individually. Many economists have criticized the Fed for keeping the discount rate low enough to induce banks to borrow substantially. The unpredictability of this borrowing reduces the Fed's day-to-day control over H.

While the discount rate mechanism of the Fed had fallen into disuse in the past few decades, it jumped back into attention as the Fed responded to the subprime mortgage crisis of the summer of 2007. In between meetings of the Federal Open Market Committee, the Fed decided in August 2007 to reduce the discount rate and it actively invited banks that were having difficulties because of the subprime loan crisis to borrow from the Fed. Again in January 2008 the Fed cut the discount rate in between meetings, in that case to moderate a worldwide decline in stock prices.

Third Tool: Reserve Requirements   *- Reserve ratio*

Unlike the desert island, where the banker chose *voluntarily* to keep 10 percent of the bank's deposits on hand in the form of gold coin reserves, in the United

Required reserves are the reserves that Federal Reserve regulations require depository institutions to hold.

Reserve requirements are the rules that stipulate the minimum fraction of deposits that must be held as reserves.

States all depository institutions must hold reserves equal to 10 percent of transactions balances as **required reserves.** Reserves can be held in reserve accounts at the Fed or as vault cash (currency and coin).

Reserve requirements apply only to transactions accounts. In Table 13-2 on p. 423, we see that these are the portion of the money supply definition M1 other than currency. Reserve requirements previously applied to savings accounts and some other parts of the money supply definition M2, but over the past several decades the Fed has discontinued reserve requirements on any part of M2 other than the transactions accounts. The Fed rarely changes reserve requirements, and so this is the most infrequently used of the Fed's three tools.

The main reason that the Fed retains reserve requirements is that they help the Fed control the money supply. Even without reserve requirements, depository institutions would hold some reserves. Institutions hold vault cash because customers control the depositing and withdrawing of cash and their deposits and withdrawals are somewhat unpredictable. Because the 10 percent required reserve ratio is considerably higher than most depository institutions need to satisfy their customers' cash withdrawals, depository institutions typically hold no more reserves than they are required to hold. That is, depository institutions typically face a binding reserve ratio constraint and hold few, if any, excess reserves when the required reserve ratio is high. A high required reserve ratio then means that the reserve ratio, e, stays close to it. In the absence of binding reserve requirements, however, depository institutions would have lower and less predictable (excess) reserve ratios. As we can see from equation (13.6), low and unpredictable reserve ratios unpredictably change the money-creation multiplier and the money supply by sizable amounts.[4]

 SELF-TEST

Be sure you can answer the following questions without looking back at the preceding text:

1. If the Fed wants to reduce the money supply, does it conduct an open-market purchase of bonds or sale of bonds?

2. Why might lowering the discount rate lead to a larger money supply?

3. If the Fed wants to raise the money supply, does it raise or reduce the reserve requirement ratio (e)?

Why the Fed Can't Control the Money Supply Precisely

This chapter focuses on two problems faced by the Fed: Why it can't control the money supply precisely, and why an unstable demand for money can break the link between changes in the money supply and changes in nominal GDP. We have now learned that the Fed can use its three instruments—open-market operations, the discount rate, and changes in reserve requirements—to achieve control of the money supply (as in equation (13.6) on p. 427). Why, then, is its control imprecise?

---

[4] The Fed's control of reserve requirements was also useful during World War II. The Fed needed to expand H rapidly to buy up the huge federal government deficit caused by wartime expenditures, and in order to minimize the impact on the money supply, the Fed raised the reserve ratio e to offset some (but not all) of the increase in H.

"safe" or "riskless."[11] The prices of other financial assets, like those of stocks or long-term bonds, vary all the time and thus are "risky" assets. If investors dislike the risk that the prices of the assets they own will fluctuate, they will hold risky assets only when those assets are expected to provide higher returns than riskless assets do. Without this risk premium on risky assets, risk-averse investors would not hold them.

Faced with various safe and risky assets, with the former paying less interest than the latter, most investors compromise, diversifying their portfolios of assets. Holding only risky assets yields a high average interest return but exposes investors to much risk. Holding only safe assets eliminates risk completely but yields a low average return. A mixed, or diversified, portfolio is usually the best approach.

Although the Tobin approach gives a very appealing reason for diversifying portfolios, it does not explain why anyone holds currency or non-interest-bearing checking accounts when safe, interest-bearing assets are available. The major contribution of the portfolio approach is to explain why most households hold both safe, interest-bearing components of M1 and M2 and risky stocks and bonds.

Friedman's version.   At roughly the same time that Tobin was writing, Milton Friedman developed a similar approach to the demand for money.[12] Friedman's theory was a generalization of the older quantity theory of money, in which he treated money as one among several assets, including bonds, equities (stocks), and goods. Friedman emphasized that, in principle, any category of spending on GDP could be a substitute for money and might be stimulated by an expansion of the real money supply. Because he viewed a wider range of assets as being substitutes for money than did Tobin, Friedman viewed monetary policy as having more potent effects on spending.

The portfolio approach pioneered by both Tobin and Friedman makes the demand for money a function of both income and wealth, not just income. The response of the demand for money to wealth has an implication for the efficacy of fiscal policy. A stimulative fiscal policy financed by deficit spending raises real wealth if people treat government bonds as part of their wealth (see Chapter 12, pp. 403–04). The increase in wealth, in turn, raises the demand for money and shifts the *LM* curve to the left, reducing the fiscal policy multipliers below those we calculated in Chapter 4, where the wealth effect on the demand for money was ignored.[13]

---

[11] "Riskless" is placed in quotes because M1 is not free of risk when prices are flexible, since inflation reduces the real value of nominal holdings of M1. This is one of the costs of inflation emphasized in Chapter 9.

[12] Friedman's approach is explained in more detail in his "The Quantity Theory of Money—A Restatement," in Friedman, ed., *Studies in the Quantity Theory of Money* (Chicago: University of Chicago Press, 1956), pp. 3–21.

[13] A formal analysis of the wealth effect in the demand-for-money function is the subject of Alan S. Blinder and Robert M. Solow, "Analytical Foundations of Fiscal Policy," in *The Economics of Public Finance* (Washington, D.C.: Brookings Institution, 1974), pp. 45–57. See also Benjamin M. Friedman, "Crowding Out or Crowding In? Economic Consequences of Financing Government Deficits," *Brookings Papers on Economic Activity*, vol 9. (1978), pp. 593–641.

International Perspective

Plastic Replaces Cash, and the Cell Phone Replaces Plastic

In 2003, the United States passed a watershed. For the first time American households used plastic cards—both debit and credit—to pay for more retail goods and services than they used cash or checks. Much of the growth in plastic card use has been in debit cards, not credit cards. The share of debit cards in total retail transactions in 2005 was 33 percent, which when added to the 19 percent share held by credit cards and 4 percent for prepaid cards, totaled a 56 percent share for plastic. The remaining 44 percent share was made up of an 11 percent share for checks and a 33 percent share for cash.[a]

The explosion of card use occurred because more people carry cards and because more retail outlets accept them. The development of "affinity cards" that provide additional benefits such as airline miles or charitable contributions has also speeded the transition from cash and checks to card purchases. Why send checks to the local plumber and electrician if they accept cards that can earn you airline miles and eventual free trips?

A novel example of a completely cashless society is the aircraft carrier U.S.S. *Harry S Truman*, which eliminated cash transactions early in 2004. The Navy issued MasterCards to all 5,000 sailors aboard. Each card is loaded with a credit amount on a sailor's payday and then debited for transactions during the following month. Records show that sailors on the ship buy 250,000 soft drinks monthly. Allowing the sailors to purchase these drinks with plastic saves the effort of collecting half a ton of quarters from vending machines each month. Even contributions at Sunday chapel services can be made by swiping the card at the door of the chapel.

The aircraft carrier provides the example of a new type of plastic called the prepaid or "smart" card. An electronic credit is loaded onto the card and then purchases are deducted until the next deposit is made. Many college students are familiar with prepaid cards with which they can pay for bookstore expenses and meals at campus dining facilities. The author's prepaid card at Northwestern University is called a "Wildcard" after the school's football mascot, "Willie the Wildcat." The use of prepaid cards is proliferating at retail outlets such as the Gap and Starbucks.

The increasing use of debit cards relative to credit cards reflects the high interest rates charged on credit cards and the fear that many Americans rightly have of running up excessive debt on credit cards. Banks issuing credit cards make large profits from customers who "roll over balances" at high interest rates, and these customers in effect subsidize convenience and zero fees for the customers who pay their bills in full each month. While banks prefer that their customers use credit cards instead of debit cards, these banks nevertheless collect fees from merchants for every plastic transaction, whether made with a credit or debit card. The largest card issuer is Citigroup, parent company of Citibank, which issues 145 million cards and brings in $19 billion in revenue each year.

As the use of credit cards spreads, life gets harder for the 60 million Americans who do not have bank accounts, typically the poor and the young. It is difficult to rent a car or stay in a hotel without having a credit card, and the growing world of electronic-commerce has been built almost entirely around the ease of entering a credit card number on a computer hooked up to the Internet. Buying books from Amazon or computers from Dell over the Internet would be impossible if retailers had to wait a week or two for the checks to arrive by mail and be cleared.

The first credit card was issued in 1950 by Francis X. McNamara, who had been embarrassed to find that he lacked enough cash to pay the bill in a restaurant. Initially, he started a network of restaurant charge accounts in which customers identified themselves with a card. This network soon became Diners Club, the first credit card company. The mass use of credit cards began in 1958 with the BankAmericard, which became an association of many banks issuing cards with the same name. Its name was changed in 1976 to the familiar "Visa."

The gradual disappearance of cash has proceeded faster in some countries than others. Cash hangs on in Japan, which has almost $4,000 of currency per person, twice that of the United States. Cash is used in Japan for

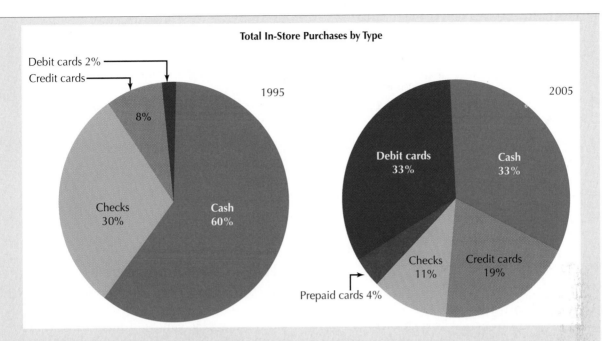

Total In-Store Purchases by Type

1995

Debit cards 2%
Credit cards
8%
Checks
30%
Cash
60%

2005

Debit cards
33%
Cash
33%
Credit cards
19%
Checks
11%
Prepaid cards 4%

many transactions that in the United States would be handled by checks or plastic cards. Because street crime is very low, Japanese housewives feel comfortable carrying large amounts of cash and routinely peel off 10,000 yen notes (about $87) to pay for their shopping. Utility bills and other invoices that Americans would handle over the Internet or by checks through the mail are paid by Japanese who go to local convenience stores and pay in cash.

The surprisingly large amount of U.S. currency outstanding, about $2,300 per U.S. resident, is not used mainly for legitimate retail transactions within U.S. borders. Some of it is used within U.S. borders by drug dealers and for cash transactions in the "underground economy" by people trying to avoid paying income taxes. And at least two-thirds of the cash in the United States is believed to be outside U.S. borders, used for transactions in many countries with a history of rapid inflation, now or in the past.

Credit cards facilitate transactions but are not considered to be "money" and are not part of any of the definitions of the money supply listed in Table 13-2 on p. 423. Credit cards are simply a very convenient and fast way of taking out a bank loan, even for $1.00 at a soft drink machine. To the extent that credit cards allow households to reduce their use of currency and checking accounts, credit cards increase the velocity of money, that is, the ratio of nominal GDP to the money supply.

Are debit cards money? With a debit card, your bank account is instantly debited when you make a transaction. In the old days you might start the month with $900 in cash, gradually spending down the $900 to $0

by the end of the month, as shown by the green triangle in the left frame of Figure 13-2 on p. 434. If all transactions can now be made with debit cards instead of cash, then you start the month with $900 in your checking account and gradually spend down the $900 to $0 through use of your debit card. In this example, the invention of debit cards has no effect at all on the demand for money. In contrast, credit cards reduce the demand for cash and also reduce the demand for checking accounts for those who choose not to pay their full balances each month.

The next wave of the cashless society is the use of cell phones to pay for almost everything. In Japan, the traditional haven of old-fashioned cash, the use of cell phones has advanced further than almost anywhere else. In Japan, everyday transactions, from buying railway tickets to picking up groceries, already take place with customers passing their handsets over a payment receiver. When the receiver accepts the payment, it responds with the sound of a bell like an old-fashioned cash register. Using cell phones as a payment method is more convenient than using cash or having to sign a credit card receipt. And cell phones are much smarter than credit cards, as they have screens to display balances and keyboards to enter information including PIN codes. Like prepaid cards, balances are added to the cell phones before purchases are made, so no credit checks are necessary.

---

[a] Data from American Bankers Association. Some of the details in this box come from Jathon Sapsford, "Paper Losses," *The Wall Street Journal*, July 23, 2004, p. A1; Katrina Brooker, "Just One Word: Plastic," *Fortune*, February 23, 2004, pp. 125–38; and "A Cash Call," *The Economist*, February 17, 2007, p. 71.

> ◤ SELF-TEST
>
> Answer the following questions according to the Tobin and Friedman versions of the portfolio theory:
>
> 1. Would an increase in the supply of M1 tend to raise or lower prices in the bond market?
> 2. Would an increase in the supply of M1 tend to raise or lower prices in the stock market?
> 3. Would an increase in stock market prices raise or reduce the demand for money?

13-7 Case Study

Why Interest Rates Were More Volatile in the 1980s and Less Volatile in the 1990s

This chapter began by introducing the wide variety of financial instruments that are available. We showed which assets are included in the major definitions of the money supply. It can be difficult to decide whether a particular type of asset should be included in M2, for example. Before the 1980s money market mutual funds were not included in M2. Now they are, because they are regarded as being close substitutes for other types of assets in M2, like money market deposit accounts and other interest-bearing checkable deposits. The definitions of the money supply can also change because deregulation and innovations alter the menu of assets that are available for households and businesses to hold. Next we show how the deregulation of financial markets can increase the volatility of interest rates.

Effects of regulations.   Until 1986 federal regulations put ceilings on the interest rates that could be paid on various categories of deposits at banks and thrift institutions. When interest rates on money market instruments, like Treasury bills, increased, either because of a rightward shift of the *IS* curve or a leftward shift of the *LM* curve, a substantial gap could open up between the interest rates on money market instruments and the deposit interest rates that were *held down by regulations*.

Large gaps between the interest rates on Treasury bills and on savings accounts caused massive withdrawals of funds from commercial banks and thrift institutions, each of which are depository institutions. The resulting reduction in loans made by thrifts had a disproportionately depressing effect on the housing market, because thrifts were required by law to hold almost all their assets in the form of mortgages. The supply of mortgage finance declined for purchasers of both new and used homes. The shift toward bonds, Treasury bills, and money market mutual funds and away from depository institutions was called **disintermediation.** An outflow of funds from the thrifts, a drop in mortgage finance, and a decline in housing expenditure occurred in every postwar episode of high interest rates before 1983.

Disintermediation was the withdrawal of funds from financial intermediaries like thrift institutions when market interest rates rose above the interest rate ceilings on savings and time deposit accounts.

Financial Deregulation and the *IS* Curve

Financial deregulation and innovation beginning in the late 1970s, including the introduction of new interest-sensitive deposits at the thrifts, the removal of deposit-rate and loan-rate ceilings, and the development of mortgage-backed securities, largely eliminated the incentive for disintermediation and its effects on mortgage finance. Another innovation was the **adjustable-rate mortgage** (ARM). Interest rates on ARMs tend to adjust to the interest rates in the open market, rising and falling about the same amount as interest rates on Treasury bills, for example.

> An **adjustable-rate mortgage** has an interest rate that can change frequently in response to changes in short-term interest rates, in contrast to a fixed-interest mortgage.

Prior to financial deregulation and innovation, purchases of new homes and of consumer durables declined sharply when interest rates in the open market rose. They declined because disintermediation reduced the funds that depository institutions had available to lend. At the same time, regulations prevented some loan and mortgage rates from rising as much as other rates rose. Thus construction of new houses declined dramatically even though mortgage rates rose relatively little when disintermediation reduced the funds that depository institutions had available to lend out. With the removal of virtually all ceilings on deposit and loan interest rates, depository institutions are free to raise deposit rates to prevent disintermediation and keep mortgage rates in line with other interest rates. Because disintermediation no longer stymies spending, larger increases in interest rates are now required to reduce spending by the same amount.

Recall that the *IS* curve displays all the combinations of real output (Y) and the market real interest rate (r) that are consistent with equilibrium in the commodity market. The slope of the *IS* curve indicates how much an increase in the interest rate reduces interest-sensitive spending, and thus reduces real output. Changes in financial markets made the *IS* curve steeper, shown in the left frame of Figure 13-3, because a larger increase in the interest rate on financial assets is required to reduce spending by the same amount.

Why the *LM* Curve Became Steeper

Chapter 4 showed that the *LM* curve normally slopes up because the demand for M1 responds to the interest rate paid on bonds and other nonmonetary assets. That interest rate (r) is plotted on the vertical axis in Figure 13-3. Our previous analysis, and the curve in Figure 13-3 labeled "old *LM* curve," assumed that the interest rate paid on M1 (r_m) was zero. Thus an increase in r raised $r - r_m$ by the same amount and increased the incentive for individuals to reduce their holdings of M1.

This analysis is still valid for holdings of currency, which pays no interest. But financial reforms have allowed banks to offer interest-bearing checking accounts. The interest rate on these accounts is variable, tending to rise and fall with the interest rate paid on nonmonetary assets (r). Thus r_m, which is an average of the zero interest rate on currency and the positive interest rate paid on some types of checking accounts, responds partially to changes in r. Thus the difference, $r - r_m$, now rises by less than the amount of any increase in r, providing less of an incentive than previously for individuals to reduce their checking account balances. As a result, the demand for money function, and thus the *LM* curve, has become steeper in the right frame of Figure 13-3.

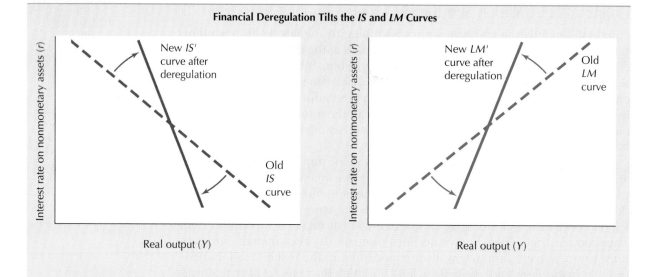

Figure 13-3 The Effect of Financial Deregulation in the Commodity and Money Markets

In the left frame, deregulation caused the *IS* curve to become the steeper line, *IS'*. This was the result not only of deregulation, but also of the introduction of new types of deposits at depository institutions with flexible interest rates, the development of mortgage-backed securities, and the introduction of adjustable-rate mortgages. In the right frame, the *LM* curve became the steeper line *LM'* because a given increase in the interest rate in financial markets does not cause as much of a reduction of the demand for M1 as previously, since depository institutions are now able to raise the rates they pay for deposits.

Effects on Interest Rates

Now we can put our analysis into action and learn why the main effect of deregulation is likely to be increased volatility of interest rates. In Figure 13-4 both frames show the *LM* curve shifting to the left by the same horizontal distance, as the result of a decision by the Fed to tighten monetary policy. The difference between the frames is that the left-hand frame shows the economy before deregulation, with the flatter "old *IS* curve" and "old *LM* curve" copied from Figure 13-3. The right-hand frame shows the economy after deregulation, with the new curves *IS'* and *LM'*, also copied from Figure 13-3. The economy moves from point *A* to *B* in the left frame and from point *A* to *B'* in the right frame, with a much greater increase in the interest rate under the new deregulated environment.

This analysis helps us to understand why the short-term interest rate was so volatile in the 1980s, as shown in Figure 14-4 on p. 465. Interest rates became less volatile in the 1990s, because the Fed placed a higher priority on maintaining stability in the interest rate. The Fed achieved this stability by active open-market operations to offset shifts in the *IS* and *LM* curves. The following section examines the conditions under which the Fed finds it desirable to stabilize interest rates.

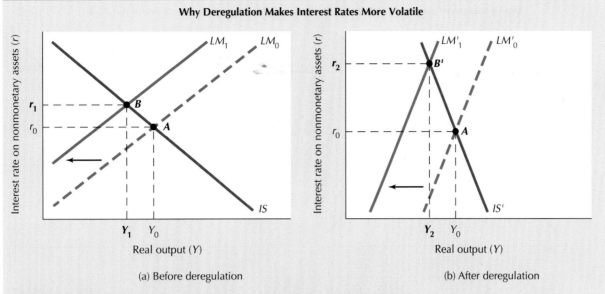

Figure 13-4 The Effect of a Lower Money Supply on Interest Rates and Output

Both frames show the effect of the same leftward horizontal shift in the *LM* curve as the result of a decision by the Fed to tighten monetary policy. In both frames, the *IS* curve remains fixed. The difference is that the left frame uses the flatter *IS* and *LM* curves from the period before deregulation of financial markets, copied from Figure 13-3. The right frame uses the new steeper *IS'* and *LM'* curves, also copied from Figure 13-3. As a result of the steeper curves, a given leftward shift in the *LM* curve creates a much larger increase in the interest rate in the right frame than in the left frame. We cannot tell whether output fell more in the right frame than in the left frame.

13-8   Why the Federal Reserve "Sets" Interest Rates

We have just seen how financial deregulation and innovation can alter the slopes of the *IS* and *LM* curves. The effects, and even the occurrence, of financial deregulation and innovation will not always be predictable. In addition, the *IS* and *LM* curves will sometimes shift unpredictably for reasons unrelated to financial deregulation and innovation.

Pervasive deregulation and innovation in financial markets were major contributors to the frequent instability of the demand for money after the mid-1970s. In this section we use the *IS-LM* model of Chapter 4 to explain why the unpredictability, or instability, of the demand for money led the Federal Reserve to shift its policies toward setting interest rates instead of trying to control the money supply. Reports in the media and announcements from the Fed that the FOMC has decided to change interest rates often give the (incorrect) impression that the Fed sets interest rates directly. It is important to remember that the Fed can only affect the nominal federal funds interest rate indirectly. When the Fed wants to raise short-term interest rates, it undertakes open-market sales of bonds, which reduce reserves and thus the money supply.

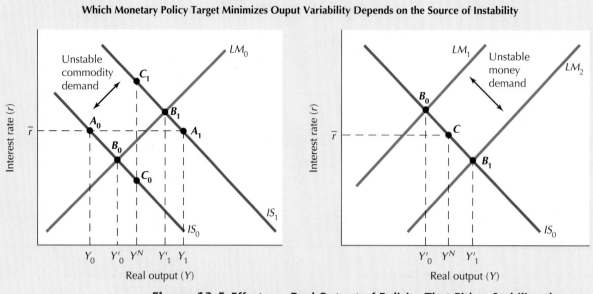

Which Monetary Policy Target Minimizes Ouput Variability Depends on the Source of Instability

Figure 13-5 **Effects on Real Output of Policies That Either Stabilize the Interest Rate or Stabilize the Real Money Supply When Either Commodity Demand or Money Demand Is Unstable**

In the left frame, the demand for commodities is unstable, fluctuating unpredictably between IS_0 and IS_1. A policy that maintains a fixed real money supply and a fixed LM_0 curve leads to smaller fluctuations of output than an alternative policy that stabilizes the interest rate at r by shifting LM. A third policy, which stabilizes real GDP at Y^N, causes interest rate instability between points C_0 and C_1. In the right frame, the demand for money is unstable. In this case, a policy of stabilizing the interest rate at $\bar{r}$ will stabilize real GDP. When the real money supply is held fixed, unstable money demand shifts the LM curve from LM_1 to LM_2 and causes output to fluctuate between Y'_0 and Y'_1

When the Fed sells the right amount of bonds, the LM curve shifts leftward and intersects the IS curve at the higher interest rate that the Fed seeks. The Fed does not care what value of the money supply is required to achieve its interest rate target.

As in Chapter 4, Figure 13-5 illustrates the working of the IS-LM model. We assume that the expected inflation rate is zero, so that the nominal and real interest rates are the same; both are labeled simply as the "interest rate" on the vertical axis. A constant price level is an acceptable assumption when wage and price contracts in the real world limit the flexibility of the price level in the short run. In such a case, the shifts in the IS or LM curves of Figure 13-5 mainly influence the level of real output in the first few months or quarters after the shift.

The position of the IS curve can be shifted by changes in business and consumer optimism, by changes in net exports, and by changes in government spending, autonomous net taxes, and tax rates. When *commodity demand is unstable* because of swings in optimism, net exports, or government policy, the IS curve shifts back and forth as shown in the left-hand frame of Figure 13-5. The position of the LM curve can be shifted by a change in the real money supply;

the LM_0 curve in the left-hand frame assumes that the real money supply is fixed.[14] The LM curve will also be shifted when the demand for money is unstable. A sudden increase in the demand for money brought on by a financial panic would shift the LM curve leftward.

Implications of unstable commodity demand.
William Poole, then of Brown University and in 2008 the president of the Federal Reserve Bank of St. Louis, first popularized the use of the IS-LM model to compare targeting of the money supply with the alternative of targeting the interest rate.[15] Unstable commodity demand, shown by the shifting IS curve in the left-hand frame of Figure 13-5, calls into question the wisdom of targeting the interest rate. When the real money supply is held constant and the LM curve remains fixed at LM_0, the economy moves back and forth between positions B_0 and B_1, and real output moves over the limited range between Y_0' and Y_1'.

With unstable commodity demand, fixing the LM curve by targeting the money supply is superior to a policy of maintaining stable interest rates. When commodity demand is high (as along IS_1), a stable interest rate policy means that the real money supply must be allowed to rise to prevent the interest rate from increasing. The Federal Reserve must increase the money supply to accommodate the additional demand for money that occurs when commodity demand is high. The stable interest rate policy causes the economy to fluctuate between points A_0 and A_1 and it allows real output to vary over the wide range between Y_0 and Y_1.

Instead of targeting interest rates or the money supply, an alternative approach for the Fed would be to target real GDP itself. The policy of targeting real output is illustrated in the left-hand frame of Figure 13-5 by the points C_0 and C_1. Fluctuations in commodity demand would have to be offset by fluctuations in the supply of money in the *opposite* direction. If the LM curve can be promptly moved in the opposite direction of the shift in the IS curve, then the economy could remain at its natural real GDP (Y^N). And, as we learned in Chapter 8, keeping the economy at Y^N is consistent with steady inflation in the absence of supply shocks.

The analysis with unstable money demand.
The right-hand frame of Figure 13-5 assumes that commodity demand is fixed, so that the IS curve remains fixed at IS_0. But here the demand for money is assumed to be unstable. When the real money supply is fixed, *an unstable demand for money causes the LM curve to move about unpredictably between* LM_1 *and* LM_2. A constant money supply policy leads to fluctuations in the economy between points B_0 and B_1, with output varying between Y_0' and Y_1'. A superior policy is to change the money supply in order to maintain a constant interest rate. When the demand for money rises, the interest rate is prevented from rising by raising the money supply. This constant interest rate policy keeps the economy pinned to point C, with a fixed interest rate $\bar{r}$ and a fixed output level Y^N. In this diagram, an interest rate target and a natural real GDP (Y^N) target amount to the same thing.

---

[14] A fixed real money supply (M/P) and a fixed LM curve can be achieved either with a constant nominal money supply (M) and a fixed price level (P), or with the money supply growing at the same rate as the price level ($m = p$).

[15] William Poole, "Optimal Choice of Monetary Policy Instruments in a Simple Stochastic Macro Model," *Quarterly Journal of Economics*, vol. 84 (May 1970), pp. 197–216. A little-known earlier reference is M. L. Burstein, *Economic Theory* (New York: Wiley, 1966), Chapter 13.

The Choice of Targets

In the left-hand frame of Figure 13-5, an unstable demand for commodities makes a real GDP target superior to a money supply target, which in turn is superior to an interest rate target. In the right-hand frame, with an unstable demand for money, a real GDP and interest rate target are the same, and both are superior to a money supply target. If, as is likely, there is instability in both commodity and money demand, a real GDP target is superior to an interest rate target.

 The Fed's decision since the early 1980s to target the interest rate reflects its view that instability in the demand for money is a more significant problem than instability in the demand for commodities. Eight times each year at meetings of the Federal Open Market Committee, it conducts a debate among the participants as to whether the current interest rate target should be maintained or should be changed up or down. In doing so, it considers the expected future behavior of its two goals, maintaining low inflation and minimizing the output gap, that is, keeping actual real GDP as close as possible to real GDP.

We will return in the next chapter to the Fed's monetary policy choices and to its two-goal approach based on trying to control inflation and the output gap at the same time. Thus, in contrast to having a single goal of controlling the money supply, the interest rate, or real GDP as in the above discussion of Figure 13-5, instead the Fed targets the interest rate in the short-run, with the further objective of achieving its longer-term inflation and output gap goals. This approach to characterizing the Fed's interest rate decisions having the double goals of achieving low inflation and a low output gap is called the *Taylor Rule*; we will see in the next chapter how it works.

 SELF-TEST

Using the *IS-LM* model analysis of Figure 13-5, which neglects both lags and inflation, rank three types of policies (money supply rule, interest rate rule, real GDP rule) under two sets of circumstances:

1. If commodity demand is unstable, take the three policies and rank first the policy that minimizes the fluctuations in real output, rank second the policy that is next best, and rank third the policy that is worst.

2. If the demand for money is unstable, take the three policies and rank first the policy that minimizes the fluctuations in real output, rank second the policy that is next best, and rank third the policy that is worst.

Summary

1. Surplus funds from savers are channeled to borrowers by way of financial intermediaries and financial markets. The main types of financial intermediaries are depository institutions, contractual savings institutions, and investment intermediaries. The main types of financial market instruments are money market and capital market instruments.

2. The United States has two major definitions of the money supply. M1 includes currency, balances in transactions accounts, and traveler's checks. M2 comprises M1 plus other assets, including savings deposits, small time deposits, and retail money market mutual funds.

3. A set of banks in a closed economy—one with no transfers of funds to the outside—can "create money" by a multiple of each dollar of cash that is initially received. This is true for a single bank on a desert island or for all banks in the United States taken together.

4. The deposit-creation multiplier is 1.0 divided by the fraction of the initial cash receipt that is held as

ing and tax rates. A given government deficit can be achieved with high spending and high tax rates or low spending and low tax rates. Thus another target of policy is the size of government spending and revenue relative to natural real GDP.

So far we are up to four instruments and four targets:

Instruments	Targets
Structural employment policy	Unemployment rate
High-powered money	Inflation rate
Government spending	Size of government
Tax rates	Long-run growth in real GDP per person

Figure 14-1 gives a more complete illustration of the principles of economic policy. The goal of economic policy is economic welfare, represented by the red box in the upper right corner. Economic welfare can be thought of simply as happiness, the things that individual members of society want—stable prices, full employment, and a high standard of living.

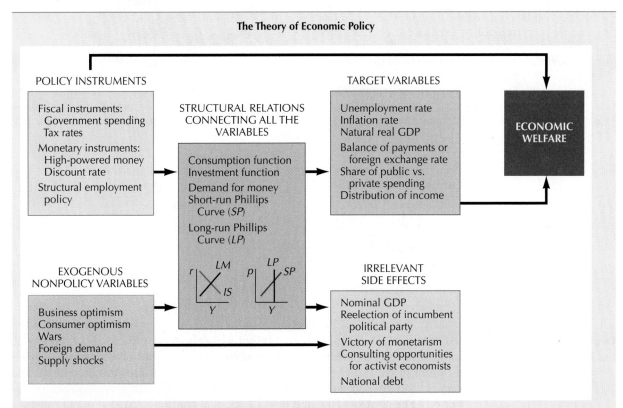

Figure 14-1 A Flowchart Showing the Relationship Between Policy Instruments, Policy Targets, and Economic Welfare

Both policy instruments and exogenous nonpolicy variables are fed into the structural relations that connect the exogenous (policy and nonpolicy) variables with the endogenous (target and nontarget) variables. Total economic welfare at the upper right depends on the achieved values of the target variables, and thus it depends on policymakers' decisions about the settings of policy instruments.

Rules Versus Activism in a Nutshell: The Optimism-Pessimism Grid

The table in this box sorts out a wide variety of issues in debate between the policy activists and rules advocates. Activists' beliefs are presented in the top line. Activists are relatively pessimistic about the stability of the private economy. This pessimism stems from their concern that the private (that is, nongovernment) economy is subject to substantial business fluctuation. Such fluctuations are sometimes the result of a wave of business and consumer pessimism, as in the 1930s, or of a collapse of housing investment, as in 2007–08. Business fluctuations may result also from government actions, as when military spending exploded during wartime.

While the activists are pessimistic about the stability of the private economy, they are optimistic about the feasibility of stabilizing the economy through government policy. This reflects their belief that the activists' paradise, while a caricature designed to exaggerate the conditions needed for successful policy activism, nevertheless contains a kernel of truth.

As shown in the table, the activists' position is disputed on both counts by policy rules advocates. This group optimistically views the private economy as inherently self-correcting, due in part to the belief that demand disturbances are partly or largely absorbed by changes in private saving. And policy rules advocates are pes-

simistic about stabilization policy, believing it can do more harm than good, due to lags, forecasting errors, uncertainty, and the other problems discussed in this chapter.

	Belief regarding automatic self-correcting properties of private economy?	Belief regarding efficacy of government stabilization policy?
Activists	Pessimistic	Optimistic
Rules advocates	Optimistic	Pessimistic

Targets, Instruments, and Structural Relations

Target variables are the economic aggregates whose values society cares most about—society's goals.

Directly to the left of the economic welfare box in Figure 14-1 we find a light red box that lists the main policy **target variables** that influence economic welfare. Some are more important than others. The distribution of income is quite different from the other targets; any policy shift that raises the income of one group at the expense of others (rich versus poor; creditors versus debtors) is bound to be controversial and lead to political conflict.

In the upper left corner of Figure 14-1 is a list of some of the policy instruments that the government can use to try to achieve its targets. Linking the green instrument box with the upper right red target box is the large blue central box, which contains the structural relations that link the variables. The *IS* and *LM* curves of Chapter 4 and *SP* and *LP* curves of Chapter 8 summarize the main relations that link money, taxes, and government spending to unemployment and inflation. But as shown in the lower left orange box, those curves can also be shifted by several exogenous factors not under the direct control of policymakers, such as a burst of business or consumer optimism or higher export sales (shifting the *IS* curve upward) or an adverse supply shock (shifting the *SP* curve upward).

When the values of the exogenous and instrument variables are fed into the structural economic relations in the middle box, they produce the values of the target variables—unemployment, inflation, and the others. Other variables, shown in the lower right purple box, are also affected, but these are called irrelevant variables because they are not major determinants of economic welfare.

As shown in the box on the opposite page, one easy way to think about the rules-versus-activism debate is to note the contrast between where the two groups place their optimism and pessimism. Policy activists are pessimistic about the self-correcting powers of the private economy and optimistic about the efficacy of stabilization policy. In contrast, rules advocates are optimistic about the underlying stability of the private economy but pessimistic about the efficacy of stabilization policy.

 SELF-TEST

Classify the following as policy instruments or target variables:

1. The inflation rate
2. The personal income tax rate
3. The Federal Reserve discount rate
4. The unemployment rate
5. High-powered money

14-3 Policy Rules

The great debate over policy rules primarily concerns monetary policy. In the 1930s, University of Chicago economist Henry Simons posed a stark contrast between a totally discretionary monetary policy and a fixed rule that takes away all discretion from the central bank.[2] In reality, there is a continuum in monetary policy between completely **discretionary policy** at one extreme and a **rigid rule** at the other extreme.

The most extreme form of a rigid rule would be for the Fed to carry out a specified set of open-market operations, for example, to buy exactly enough securities to make high-powered money (*H*, the sum of currency and reserves) grow by, say, 5 percent per year. However, as we learned in the last chapter (see equation (13.6) on p. 427), such an action would not lead to steady growth in the money supply, since the money supply depends not only on *H* but also on the reserve ratio and the public's currency-holding ratio. Even if growth in *H* is kept absolutely rigid, choices by the public to raise or lower its holdings of currency could lead to major swings in the money supply. Another form of a rigid rule would be for the Fed to conduct whatever open-market operations are required to maintain absolutely constant a short-term interest rate like the federal funds rate.

The best-known early proposal for a policy rule, a **constant growth rate rule (CGRR)** for the money supply, was made in the late 1950s by Milton

Discretionary policy treats each macroeconomic episode as a unique event, without any attempt to respond in the same way from one episode to another.

A **rigid rule** for policy sets a key policy instrument at a fixed value, as in a constant growth rate rule for the money supply.

A **constant growth rate rule (CGRR)** stipulates a fixed percentage growth rate for the money supply, in contrast to the variable growth rate recommended by policy activists.

---

[2] Henry C. Simons, *Economic Policy for a Free Society* (Chicago: University of Chicago Press, 1948). Simons originally wrote on rules versus discretion in the mid-1930s.

A **feedback rule** sets stabilization policy to respond in a systematic way to a macroeconomic event, such as an increase in unemployment or inflation.

Monetarism is a school of thought that opposes activist or discretionary monetary policy and instead favors a fixed rule for the growth rate of high-powered money or of the money supply.

Friedman, then at the University of Chicago. Just as maintaining a fixed growth rate for H does not ensure a fixed growth rate for the money supply, due to variations in the money multiplier (M/H), the reverse is true as well. Maintaining a CGRR for the money supply would require the Fed to manipulate H actively in order to offset changes in the money multiplier.

In addition to rules calling for a fixed growth rate of H or the money supply, many other types of rules have been proposed. Some involve not a monetary variable like H or the money supply, but rather a target variable like the price level or output. Other rules fall under the category of **feedback rules,** which systematically change monetary variables like the money supply or interest rates in response to actual or forecasted changes in target variables like inflation or unemployment. The leading example of such a feedback rule is called the Taylor Rule, discussed in section 14-7.

The early school of thought advocating a rule for monetary policy was called **monetarism.**[3] This approach combined the key elements in the box on p. 454—optimism regarding the stability of the private economy and pessimism regarding the efficacy of discretionary policy—with a specific policy proposal advocating a CGRR for the money supply.[4] Subsequently, monetarism faded in popularity and was replaced by advocacy of rules that target the inflation rate, so called "inflation targeting," and mixed feedback rules such as the Taylor Rule.

The Positive Case for Rules

The case for rules takes two forms. One is a positive case based on the advantages of rules themselves, and the other is a negative case based on the defects of a completely discretionary policy.

The main arguments for rules as set forth by Milton Friedman are three. First, a rule insulates the central bank from political pressure, which might, for instance, take the form of pushing the central bank to overstimulate the economy in the year before an election. Second, a rule allows the performance of the central bank to be judged by the government and the public. For instance, a central bank charged with a CGRR for the money supply would be judged to be a failure if in reality the money supply gyrated wildly or grew at an average rate different from the one specified in the rule. Third, a rule reduces uncertainty since firms, workers, and consumers are able to gauge accurately what the central bank will be doing over the next several years.

However, as suggested by Stanley Fischer, formerly of MIT and now the Governor of the Central Bank of Israel, there are weaknesses in each of these arguments.[5] First, it is not necessarily desirable for the central bank to operate independently of political pressure; a central bank, in its attempts to achieve or maintain low inflation, might be more willing to sacrifice jobs in the short run than the general public is. The merits of the second and third arguments fail as a general support for rules, since their validity depends on what variable the central bank chooses to target. For instance, the public has no reason to care directly about the quantity of high-powered money or the money supply, since

---

[3] The term *monetarism* was introduced in Karl Brunner, "The Role of Money and Monetary Policy," *Federal Reserve Bank of St. Louis Review,* no. 50 (1968), pp. 9–24.

[4] See Milton Friedman, *A Program for Monetary Stability* (New York: Fordham University Press, 1959).

[5] Stanley Fischer, "Rules versus Discretion in Monetary Policy," in Benjamin Friedman and Frank Hahn, eds., *Handbook of Monetary Economics,* vol. 2 (Amsterdam: Elsevier Science Publishers, 1990), pp. 1156–84.

the target variables that concern the public are inflation, unemployment, and productivity growth.

In short, it is hard to make a general case for rules without specifying the exact nature of the rule. As in the saying "there are many slips between cup and lip," there are many sources of slippage between the Fed's policy instruments, particularly open-market operations, and the most important target variables, that is, inflation, unemployment, and productivity growth. These slippages include money-multiplier shocks (Chapter 13), money demand shocks (Chapter 13), commodity demand shocks (anything discussed in Chapters 3 or 4 that can shift the *IS* curve), and supply shocks (Chapter 8).

The Negative Case for Rules

The negative case for rules consists of a criticism of activism. As shown in the box on p. 454, rules advocates are pessimistic about activist (discretionary) policy, believing that such measures can do more harm than good. Much of the rest of this chapter looks in detail at their case by examining the many reasons why the activists' optimism about policy is unrealistic—lags, uncertainty, forecasting errors, and other issues.

However, just as the merits of the positive case for rules depend on the particular type of rule being considered, so does the negative case for rules. For instance, lags and uncertainty may create so much slippage between the Fed's policy instruments and the economy's target variables that it becomes infeasible for the Fed to carry out a rule involving a target, such as the proposal that the Fed adhere to a fixed target for the inflation rate.

In recent years, the popularity of the Taylor Rule, which advocates that the central bank choose a mixed target of the inflation rate and output ratio, has caused the distinction between the rules advocates and activists to evaporate. All the obstacles to activism, such as the difficulty of controlling the money supply and the long lags between changes of interest rates and the response of both inflation and the output ratio, are equally applicable to Taylor's Rule as to old-fashioned activism. We now turn to the first obstacle to either activism or Taylor's Rule: the long lags between the effects of central bank actions and the ultimate response of the economy.

14-4   Policy Pitfalls: Lags and Uncertain Multipliers

The core of Milton Friedman's case against policy activism and in favor of a monetary rule has always been that there are what he called "long and variable" lags between changes in monetary policy instruments and the ultimate response of target variables like inflation and unemployment. As we have seen, Friedman's arguments against activism also represent significant obstacles to modern rules like inflation targeting or Taylor's Rule. In this section we distinguish five types of lags for monetary policy and attempt to estimate the length of these lags.

The Five Types of Lags

Lags prevent either monetary or fiscal policy from immediately offsetting an unexpected shift in the demand for commodities or in the demand for money or in the impact of a supply shock. There are five main types of lags. Some are common to both monetary and fiscal policy; others are more important for one policy than the other:

1. The data lag
2. The recognition lag
3. The legislative lag
4. The transmission lag
5. The effectiveness lag

To explain the meaning of each lag and to estimate its length, let us take as an example the end of the 2001 recession, the most recent recession that provides us with an example.

1. **The data lag.** Policymakers do not know what is going on in the economy the moment it happens. The index of industrial production exhibited its first significant increase during January 2002. But this news did not arrive until mid-February 2002. Typically, an economic change that starts at the beginning of one month, say January, is not fully evident in the data until the middle of the next month, so that the data lag is about 1.5 months.

2. **The recognition lag.** Policymakers do not pay much attention to changes in data that occur only for one month. The subsequent month might exhibit a reversal in the opposite direction, and frequently data are revised to change small increases into small decreases, or vice versa. Thus it was necessary to wait for the February data to confirm that industrial production had increased for two months in a row, and these data series were not released until March 2002.

3. **The legislative lag.** Although most changes in fiscal policy must be legislated by Congress, an important advantage of monetary policy is the short legislative lag. Once a majority of the Federal Open Market Committee (FOMC) decides that a monetary policy stimulus is needed, only a short wait is necessary, since the FOMC has eight regularly scheduled meetings annually and can meet by phone anytime. This brings us to April 2002.

4. **The transmission lag.** The transmission lag is the time interval between the policy decision and the subsequent change in policy instruments. Like the legislative lag, this lag is a more serious obstacle for fiscal policy. Once the FOMC has given its order for the open-market manager to make open-market purchases, the short-term (federal funds) interest rate declines immediately.

5. **The effectiveness lag.** Most of the controversy about the lags of monetary policy concerns the length of time required for an acceleration or deceleration in the money supply to influence real output. As we have seen, Milton Friedman has argued that the effectiveness lag is long and variable.

Evidence on the Effectiveness Lag

The most difficult lag to measure, as well as the longest, is the effectiveness lag between the change in monetary policy and the response of the economy. Estimates of this lag differ for numerous reasons, including the use of different measures of monetary policy (for example, money supply versus interest rates) and different indicators of the economy's response (for example, a monthly index of production or employment or a quarterly index of real GDP).

In determining the length of the effectiveness lag, it is useful to measure the monetary policy action by the change in short-term interest rates, since the Fed can change those interest rates almost immediately after a meeting of the FOMC (thus eliminating the transmission lag). One set of estimates of the effectiveness lag is presented in Figure 14-2. This figure plots for three alternative intervals the response of real GDP to a change in the short-term interest rate, specifically the Treasury bill rate.[6]

As shown by Figure 14-2, in all three intervals (1961–75, 1976–90, and 1991–2007) real GDP declined following an increase in the short-term interest

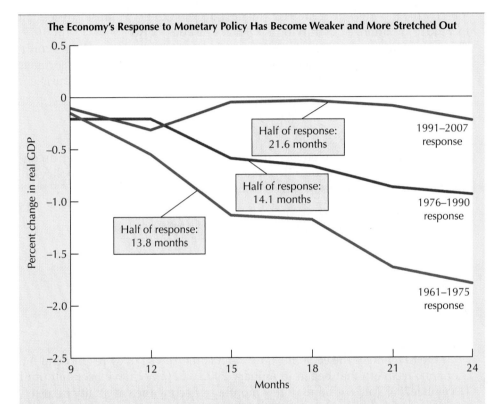

Figure 14-2 The Percent Change in Real GDP Following a 1 Percentage Point Change in the Treasury Bill Rate, Three Intervals, 1961–2007

Following a 1 percentage point change in the short-term (Treasury bill) interest rate, real GDP changes in the opposite direction by the percentages shown by the plotted lines drawn for each of three intervals, 1961–75, 1976–90, and 1991–2007. The lines show, for instance, that after 24 months real GDP would have dropped by about 1.8 percent during the 1961–75 period, by 0.9 percent during 1976–90, but by only 0.2 percent in the more recent 1991–2007 interval. The boxed labels show how many months were required for half of the ultimate impact on real GDP to occur.

Source: See Appendix C-4.

---

[6] For those readers trained in econometrics, the details lying behind Figure 14-2 are as follows: The annualized percentage change in quarterly real GDP over the indicated intervals was regressed on a constant and lags 3 through 8 of the quarterly changes in the nominal Treasury bill rate. Lag lengths of 9 quarters or greater were statistically insignificant and were omitted. The current change and the first and second lags were omitted because their coefficients are positive, indicating the presence of feedback from real GDP to the interest rate.

rate. But the change in GDP is very spread out over time, distributed over more than two years. Because the economy's response is so spread out, the best measure of the effectiveness lag is not obvious. One sensible measure of this lag is the length of time necessary for *half of the ultimate effect* to be felt. As shown by the small boxes in the figure, this lag was 13.8, 14.1, and 21.6 months respectively. Notable also is the fact that the total responses in the more recent intervals were much smaller than in the first; we explain this shift in a subsequent section.

Another measure of the policy lag, one that does not rely on interest rate data, can be extracted from earlier research by David and Christina Romer of the University of California, Berkeley. They read the minutes of the FOMC to identify the months when the Fed "made a decision to try to cause a recession to reduce inflation,"[7] identifying six such episodes between 1947 and 1979. They ran a statistical test similar to that in Figure 14-2 to examine the response of industrial production in the three years after the Fed's policy shift. For their six episodes, their estimated effectiveness lag averages 19 months, consistent with the lags of 14 to 21 months shown in Figure 14-2.[8]

Adding the Lags Together

To summarize this section on lags, let us add up the total delay between an unexpected economic event and the economy's reaction to a monetary policy action taken in response to such an economic event.

Type of lag	Estimated length (months)
1. Data	1.5
2. Recognition	2.0
3. Legislative	0.5
4. Transmission	0.0
5. Effectiveness	19.0
Total	23.0

Thus the first half of the economy's reaction to the Fed's policy response to the economic recovery that began in January 2002 would not have been felt until December 2003 (plus or minus a few months, reflecting the variability of the effectiveness lag).

Multiplier Uncertainty

Chapters 3 and 4 developed a set of multiplier formulas indicating the size of the change in real GDP that would result from a change in a policy instrument, such as tax rates, government spending, or the money supply. But the *IS-LM* model summarized in those chapters was very simple. This section shows that

---

[7] Christina D. Romer and David H. Romer, "Does Monetary Policy Matter? A New Test in the Spirit of Friedman and Schwartz," in O. J. Blanchard and S. Fischer, *NBER Macroeconomics Annual 1989* (Cambridge, MA: MIT Press), p. 152.

[8] Romer and Romer, ibid., Table 1, p. 153. The maximum effect of their monetary policy variable (defined as unity in one of the six months when the Fed changed policy and zero otherwise) is reached 32 months after the policy change. Half of the total effect occurs after 18.8 months. This estimate is approximate, as it omits the impact of the lagged dependent variable in their equation.

we do not know nearly as much about the values of the multipliers as the simple *IS-LM* model initially led us to believe.

Figure 14-2 illustrates **dynamic multipliers** that show the response of real GDP to a change in the interest rate over several intervals. We noted that the multipliers were much smaller in 1991–2007 than before 1991. Also, even for a given time period economists differ widely regarding the size of the monetary and fiscal multipliers. This **multiplier uncertainty** creates a dilemma for policymakers. Even if they could forecast perfectly that the economy needs a policy stimulus now to add 2.0 percent to real GDP four quarters from now, there remains the question as to what exact policy action should be taken. Should the interest rate be dropped today by 0.5, 1.0, or 2.0 percentage points? Any of these numbers might be correct, depending on the policy multiplier.[9]

Dynamic multipliers are the amount by which output is raised during each of several time periods after a given change in the policy instrument.

Multiplier uncertainty concerns the lack of firm knowledge regarding the change in output caused by a change in a policy instrument.

Why Have Monetary Policy Multipliers Changed?

Three aspects of Figure 14-2 make life especially difficult for policymakers—these are the length of the lag, the change in the lag, and the change in the multiplier (that is, the total effect of an interest rate change on real GDP). We have already noted the fact that the effectiveness lag is long, with half of the effect taking 21 months during 1991–2007. Why is this lag longer now than it was before 1991?

Three changes in the structure of the economy since the 1960s help explain why lags are now longer and multipliers are now smaller than they were in the 1960s. The first change concerns thrift institutions and housing. In earlier decades housing expenditures took the brunt of tight monetary policy, declining quickly in response to upward movements in interest rates. After the late 1970s this channel of influence on housing became less important, because deregulation lifted the ceilings on interest rates paid to depositors by thrifts. Also, other types of financial institutions that were not subject to interest rate ceilings began to participate more in mortgage markets, further insulating the housing sector from the impact of tightened monetary policy (see pp. 474–75).

The second major change is the reduced impact of changing interest rates on consumer spending. More consumer borrowing now occurs on credit cards, but interest rates on credit cards are very insensitive to monetary policy.

The third major change was the adoption of flexible exchange rates in 1973, previously examined in Chapter 6. This added a major channel of influence of monetary policy, as changing interest rates cause changes in the foreign exchange rate and, after a long lag, changes in net exports. It takes two years or more for net exports to respond fully to changes in the foreign exchange rate.

Summary: The effectiveness lag of monetary policy has become longer, and the multiplier of real GDP response to a change in interest rates has become smaller, because the prompt channel working through housing finance

---

[9] See William Brainard, "Uncertainty and the Effectiveness of Policy," *American Economic Review,* vol. 57 (May 1967), pp. 411–25. Brainard's formula suggests that the expected gap between actual and target GDP should be closed by only a fraction of the gap, but that fraction depends on correlations that we are most unlikely to know. An earlier analysis is Milton Friedman, "The Effects of a Full-Employment Policy on Economic Stability: A Formal Analysis," *Essays in Positive Economics* (Chicago: University of Chicago Press, 1953), pp. 117–32.

has become weaker, while the time-consuming channel working through exchange rates and net exports has become stronger.

 SELF-TEST

For each of the following statements, indicate whether it relates to multiplier uncertainty or lags, and if your answer is "lags," indicate which of the five types of lags is most closely related to the statement:

1. Congress debated President Johnson's proposal for an income tax surcharge for 18 months, from late 1966 to mid-1968.

2. Interest rate ceilings on savings accounts were eliminated by financial deregulation.

3. A record-setting snowstorm in Washington delays publication of the Consumer Price Index by two weeks.

4. Flexible exchange rates were adopted in 1973.

 14-5 Case Study

Was the Fed Responsible for the Great Moderation?

The U.S. economy has been considerably more stable since the mid-1980s than it was previously. This decline in macroeconomic volatility is frequently called "the Great Moderation." Our task in this section is to explain the apparently paradoxical stability of the economy in view of the difficulties of managing monetary policy. One possibility is that the performance of monetary policy has improved substantially; another complementary hypothesis is that the economy's stability has improved for reasons unrelated to monetary policy. Both explanations could be true at the same time.

One way to appreciate the improved stability of the economy is to examine Figure 14-3, which in the top frame plots the log output ratio (the log ratio of actual to natural output, Y/Y^N) since 1960.[10] Clearly visible are the large positive output ratios of the late 1960s and the large negative ratios created by the 1973–75 and 1981–82 recessions. In contrast, since 1982 the log output ratio has been much closer to its desired value of zero. Shown in the bottom frame of Figure 14-3 is one way of summarizing the decreased volatility of the ratio, a 20-quarter moving average of the absolute value of the ratio.[11] If the ratio was always either +2 or −2 percent, the moving average of its absolute value would be 2.0. If the ratio followed the pattern 2, 0, −2, 0, averaging those numbers together would give an average of 1.0. As shown in the bottom frame, this measure of volatility was 2.9 in 1970:Q1, fell and then rose to a peak of 3.9 in 1985:Q2, and then declined to values of 2.0 percent or below

---

[10] The log output ratio is zero when actual real GDP equals natural real GDP. This concept was introduced in the Appendix to Chapter 8, p. 273.

[11] The absolute value of any number is its actual value with any negative signs converted to positive.

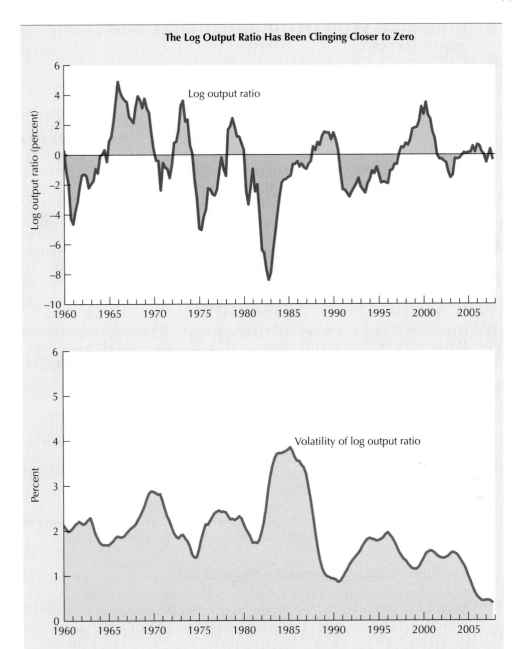

Figure 14-3 The Log Output Ratio and the Moving Average of its Absolute Value, 1960–2007

The top frame shows the log output ratio in percent, that is, the log of the ratio of actual to natural real GDP (Y/Y^N). After 1985 the ratio never exceeded 3 percent nor fell below −3 percent, in contrast to the period before 1985 when the range extended from +4.9 to −8.4 percent. This decrease in volatility is summarized by the 20-quarter moving average of the ratio's absolute value, as shown in the bottom frame. This moving average reached peaks of 2.9 in 1970 and 3.9 in 1985, in contrast to the period after 1989 when the moving average never exceeded 1.9 and fell as low as 0.4 in 2007.

Source: See Appendix C-4.

from 1988:Q2 to 2004. In 2005–2007 there was a further remarkable decline to below 1.0 percent.[12]

Causes of Decreased Volatility: Smaller Demand and Supply Shocks

One hypothesis is that demand and/or supply shocks became less important and less harmful after the mid-1980s. Three types of demand shocks contributed to this improvement. Most important was the smaller size of government military spending (measured as a share of GDP) and its reduced volatility. The Korean War (1950–53) and the Vietnam War (1965–75) caused sharp increases in military spending followed by sharp decreases. The second cause was financial regulation that made residential construction more volatile; these regulations were eliminated in the early 1980s (see pp. 440–43). Finally, computers and improvements in management practices reduced the volatility of inventory investment. All three of these sources of demand shocks made output more volatile in the 1950s, 1960s, and 1970s, followed by less volatility after the mid-1980s.

Subsequently as the Vietnam War was winding down in the 1970s, the economy was hit by several adverse supply shocks, consisting of the oil price shocks of 1974–75, farm price shocks in 1972–73, higher non-oil import prices in 1973–74 due to the depreciation of the U.S. dollar, and, finally, the termination of Nixon-era price controls in 1974–75. All these shocks caused inflation to shoot up, and a side effect (as we learned in Chapter 8 on pp. 255–59) was a sharp decline in the output ratio.

Comparing the periods 1950–83 and 1984–2007, it has been estimated that about two-thirds of the reduction in output volatility was achieved by the reduced amplitude of demand shocks, mainly military spending, residential construction, and inventory investment. The other one-third is due to the reduced volatility of supply shocks. During the 1950s and 1960s, demand shocks were important but supply shocks were not. From 1970 to 1983, both demand and supply shocks contributed high volatility. After 1984, both demand and supply shocks exhibited greater stability and contributed to the Great Moderation.[13]

The Role of the Fed Between 1983 and 2001

The reduced volatility of both demand and supply shocks after 1983 made life much easier for the Fed. When adverse supply shocks strike, as in 1974–75 and 1979–81, the Fed is forced to choose between faster inflation, lower output, or a

---

[12] A slightly different measure of decreased volatility is considered in Olivier Blanchard and John Simon, "The Long and Large Decline in U.S. Output Volatility," *Brookings Papers on Economic Activity*, vol. 32, no. 1 (2001), pp. 135–64. Volatility measures based on four-quarter changes of real GDP show an even more pronounced reduction in volatility; see Robert J. Gordon, "What Caused the Decline in U.S. Business Cycle Volatility?" NBER Working Paper 11777, November 2005.

[13] This paragraph is based on the author's NBER Working Paper cited in footnote 12. See also James H. Stock and Mark W. Watson, "Has the Business Cycle Changed? Evidence and Explanations," in *Monetary Policy and Uncertainty: Adapting to a Changing Economy*, Federal Reserve Bank of Kansas City, 2003, pp. 9–56. Another broad overview is S. Ahmed, A. Levin, and B. A. Wilson, "Recent U.S. Macroeconomic Stability: Good Policies, Good Practices, or Good Luck?" *The Review of Economics and Statistics*, vol. 86, no. 3, pp. 824–32. The role of financial deregulations and innovations is explored in K. E. Dynan, D. W. Elmendorf, and D. E. Sichel, "Can Financial Innovation Help to Explain the Reduced Volatility of Economic Activity?" *Journal of Monetary Economics*, vol. 53, January 2006, pp. 123–50.

combination of the two (see Figure 8-10 on p. 259). But with beneficial supply shocks the Fed has the pleasant task of choosing between lower inflation and higher output. Among the beneficial supply shocks that help to explain the Fed's improved choices and the improved outcome for the economy were a sharp decline in oil prices in 1986 and again in 1997–98, an appreciation of the dollar between 1995 and 2002, and a revival of productivity growth after 1995.

As shown in the left portion of Figure 14-4, the log output ratio first went above zero in 1988, and the Fed reacted almost immediately by raising the federal funds rate, with a delay of only about six months. Then when the output ratio fell below zero in late 1990, the Fed dropped the federal funds rate in a series of steps that lasted until early 1993. The Fed's actions in 1988–93 were prompt and represented movements in the right direction.

Perhaps trying to improve on its performance, the Fed took dramatic action to raise the federal funds rate in 1994, more than two years before the log

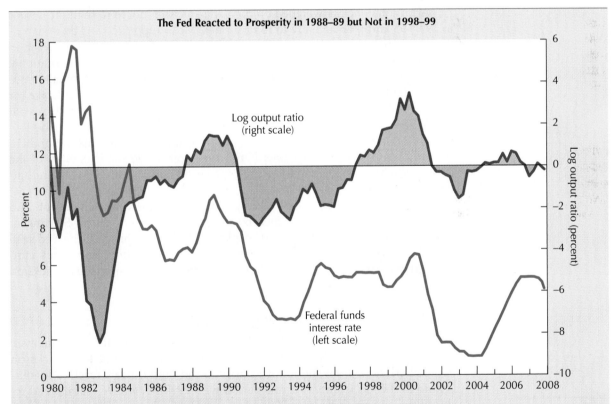

Figure 14-4 The Federal Funds Interest Rate and the Log Output Ratio, 1980–2007

Since the 1980s the Fed has tended to raise and lower interest rates in anticipation of the economy's overheating or stalling out. In the late 1980s the Fed began to raise interest rates when the log output ratio went above zero. When signals began to suggest in 1989 that the log output ratio would be falling appreciably below zero in the near future, the Fed began lowering interest rates. The Fed raised interest rates in 1994 as the log output ratio again seemed headed above zero. But after 1996 the Fed changed its behavior for reasons discussed in the text.

Source: See Appendix C-4.

466 Chapter 14 • Stabilization Policy in the Closed and Open Economy

output ratio rose above zero. This move, called at the time a "preemptive strike," reflected imperfect knowledge of the log output ratio, which was thought at the time to be higher than it actually was, due to an underestimate of the economy's natural output (Y^N). But then the Fed reversed its preemptive strike and left the federal funds rate virtually constant as the log output ratio inched up from zero to +3 percent in 1998–2000, actually *reducing* the federal funds rate in late 1998 and early 1999.

The Fed's failure to raise the federal funds rate in 1997–99 appears to be a radical departure from its past policies aimed at stabilizing the log output ratio. Why did the Fed avoid the monetary tightening that it had successfully pursued a decade earlier in 1988–89? By far the most important reason was the behavior of inflation. As we learned from Figure 8-13 on p. 267, the inflation rate did not accelerate in 1996–98 in response to the rising log output ratio and declining unemployment rate and instead decelerated. The reasons for this unusual behavior were explored on p. 259, and include low oil prices, an appreciating dollar, faster productivity growth, and also a temporary hiatus in rapid cost inflation of medical care prices.

Additional factors weighed on the Fed's decision not to raise interest rates in 1997–98 and then actually to reduce rates. Most important was the Asian financial crisis, which began in Thailand in July 1997 and spread to Russia in August 1998 and then to Latin America. To help stem the flow of international capital from these countries to the United States, the Fed reduced interest rates in the fall of 1998. Many observers think, in retrospect, that it was a mistake for the Fed to lower interest rates at this time when the log output ratio was well above zero. While inflation accelerated only modestly in 1999–2000, the low level of interest rates encouraged excess optimism in the stock market and excessive high-tech fixed investment and thus aggravated the instability of the economy when the stock market and high-tech fixed investment collapsed after mid-2000.

Only in early 2000 did the Fed respond to the excessively high output ratio by raising interest rates, and then by much less than in 1988–89. Starting in mid-2000, the output ratio began to plummet, and in this case the Fed also acted preemptively, reducing the federal funds rate before the output ratio reached zero (which occurred at about the same time as the terrorist attacks on the United States on September 11, 2001).

The Fed's Controversial Easing After 2000

As shown in Figure 14-4, the Fed began to reduce the federal funds rate even before the log output ratio reached zero around the time of the attacks on September 11, 2001. Further reductions occurred until the rate reached 1.0 percent in mid-2003. Comparing this period with 1990–93, we see that the Fed reduced the rate much faster in 2001–02 than in 1990–93.

Numerous observers have argued, particularly with hindsight, that the Fed reduced the rate too fast and by too much. The box on pp. 474–75 discusses the view that by keeping rates so low, the Fed poured fuel on the fire of a housing boom that reached the proportions of a speculative bubble. Just as the stock market and Internet investment booms of the late 1990s turned out to be bubbles, with a sharp collapse in both the stock market and investment in 2000–03, so the housing bubble of 2003–06 led to a collapse in 2007–08.

Is there any systematic way of describing the Fed's policy actions? Did it go too far toward easy money after 2000? Subsequently in Section 14-7 we will compare the Fed's actual policy with the Taylor Rule that calls for the Fed to raise interest rates whenever inflation speeds up or whenever the log output ratio rises above zero.   ●

14-6   Time Inconsistency, Credibility, and Reputation

We have already seen that one of the advantages that Milton Friedman claimed for policy rules was that firms, workers, and consumers would be able to form accurate expectations of future policy actions. Proponents of activism saw no merit in this claim, since any good rule could be adopted by a discretionary policymaker.

Time Inconsistency

In 1977, Finn Kydland of Carnegie-Mellon University and his colleague Edward Prescott (now at Arizona State University) introduced the concept of **time inconsistency**.[14] The basic idea is that discretionary policymakers decide on policy A because it is optimal at that time, and private decisionmakers make consumption, investment, and labor supply decisions based on that policy. However, once private decisionmakers have done so, it may be optimal for policymakers to shift to policy B, thus invalidating the expectations on which private decisionmakers acted.

Time inconsistency describes the temptations of policymakers to deviate from a policy after it is announced and private decisionmakers have reacted to it.

The simplest example arises in the classroom. Professors want their students to learn but hate to make up tests and grade them. Time inconsistency occurs when a professor announces that there will be a tough final exam. The students respond to policy A by studying hard, but then, just before the scheduled exam time, the professor announces policy B, that the exam has been canceled.

In macroeconomics the prominent example of time inconsistency involves the Phillips Curve trade-off between inflation and unemployment. For any given unemployment rate, the actual inflation rate will be low if expectations of future inflation are low. This gives the Fed an incentive to pursue policy A, vowing to achieve low inflation. But once inflation expectations have shifted down, the Fed is tempted to shift to policy B by a monetary stimulus that reduces unemployment, even though policy B will raise inflation and invalidate the low expectations of inflation held by workers and firms.

The implication of the time inconsistency argument is that economic performance may be better, on average, if private decisionmakers know that the central bank will adhere to a rigid rule to target the inflation rate. Knowing that there is no discretion and thus no chance of a surprise monetary stimulus (policy B), expectations of future inflation will subside, making possible a lower actual inflation rate for any given unemployment rate.

Credibility and Reputation

In order to achieve the best possible economic performance, with low or even zero inflation combined with unemployment at the natural rate (U^N), it may

---

[14] Kydland and Prescott won the Nobel Prize in economics in 2004. The original reference is Finn E. Kydland and Edward C. Prescott, "Rules Rather Than Discretion: The Inconsistency of Optimal Plans," *Journal of Political Economy*, vol. 85 (June 1977), pp. 473–92. The most influential subsequent article was Robert J. Barro and David B. Gordon, "A Positive Theory of Monetary Policy in a Natural Rate Model," *Journal of Political Economy*, vol. 91 (August 1983), pp. 589–610.

Policy credibility is the belief by the public that the policymakers will actually carry out an announced policy.

pay a central bank to invest in its reputation. If the central bank succeeds year after year in avoiding the temptation to boost monetary growth in order to reduce unemployment (policy B), it will convince private decisionmakers that a future upsurge of inflation is unlikely. Once the actions of policymakers create this type of reputation, they are said to gain **policy credibility.**[15]

Over the past decade economists have built sophisticated models of "reputational equilibrium."[16] These lead to the conclusion that *if* the policymaker has a long time horizon and *if* the policymaker has a low discount rate, then an equilibrium with zero inflation is possible. That is, the policymaker has an incentive to produce a time-consistent policy, and private decisionmakers adjust their expectations accordingly. However, such theoretical models are not very practical for real-world situations in which governments and central bankers do not last forever and in which governments face regular election campaigns.

In order to reduce the influence of the vagaries of government political motives, many nations like the United Kingdom have granted freedom to the central bank to operate independently of the elected economic officials of the government. And many central banks in foreign countries, but not the Federal Reserve in the United States, have used their independence to adopt rules that rigidly target the inflation rate without any concern for the performance of real output.[17]

Implications for Rules Versus Discretion

The debate over time inconsistency focuses on the process by which private decisionmakers form expectations concerning the inflation rate. Other target variables, such as the unemployment rate, are ignored on the assumption that the natural rate hypothesis is valid, so in the long run policymakers have no power to make the actual unemployment rate deviate from the natural rate.

Like many other aspects of the rules versus discretion debate, much of the literature on time inconsistency ignores the variety of different rules that are possible. It ignores as well the many slippages that occur between the policy instrument most directly under the Fed's control and the target variable of central concern in the debate, that is, the inflation rate.

Because of these slippages, no monetary policy based on rigid control of high-powered money is likely to produce a steady inflation rate. Only a policy rule that targets the inflation rate is likely to establish policy credibility, but all the problems with activism examined in this chapter apply as well to such a policy rule. We return to inflation targeting in Section 14-8 below.

 SELF-TEST

Are the following statements true, false, or uncertain?

1. For any given deceleration of nominal GDP growth created by a tight monetary policy, the recession will be shorter and less severe if the central bank possesses policy credibility with the public.

---

[15] A useful introduction is Benjamin M. Friedman, "The Use and Meaning of Words in Central Banking: Inflation Targeting, Credibility, and Transparency," NBER Working Paper 8972, June 2002.

[16] See Fischer, "Rules versus Discretion," pp. 1175–78.

[17] An important reference on the concept and implementation of inflation targeting, and a set of papers on the experience of several countries is Ben S. Bernanke et al., *Inflation Targeting: Lessons from the International Experience* (Princeton, NJ: Princeton University Press, 1999).

2. For any given deceleration of nominal GDP growth created by tight monetary policy, the recession will be shorter and less severe if the public believes that the central bank's policy is subject to time inconsistency.

3. Policy credibility increases the merits of a "cold turkey" disinflation as compared to a policy of "living with inflation."

4. The possibility of time inconsistency strengthens the case of discretionary policy against a policy rule that targets the growth rate of high-powered money.

14-7 Case Study

The Taylor Rule and the Changing Fed Attitude Toward Inflation and Output

No matter what type of rule the Fed attempts to achieve, its short-term instrument of control is the federal funds rate, plotted as the green line in Figure 14-4 on p. 465 and in Figure 14-5 in this section. If the Fed attempts to achieve a rule for growth in the money supply, then the federal funds rate must be raised when the money supply exceeds the desired growth rate. Similarly, if the Fed wants to target the inflation rate, the federal funds rate must rise when the inflation rate exceeds the desired inflation rate.

A problem with targeting the inflation rate is that there are very long lags between an increase in the federal funds rate and a subsequent reduction in the inflation rate. Continuing increases in the federal funds rate, while the Fed waits for inflation to subside, may cause economic activity to falter, the output ratio to decline, and the unemployment rate to increase. The Fed may prefer to pursue two objectives at the same time, responding to *both* excessive inflation and insufficient output.

John Taylor, of Stanford University and formerly undersecretary of the Treasury, has proposed a simple rule for the Fed (or any other central bank) to follow in setting the real federal funds rate (r^{FF}).[18] The Fed would raise the real interest rate above its desired long-term value whenever inflation exceeded the desired rate and also whenever actual output exceeded natural output:

$$r^{FF} = r^{FF*} + a(p - p^*) + b\hat{Y} \qquad (14.1)$$

The terms on the right-hand side are the desired real federal funds rate (r^{FF*}), a parameter (a) times the deviation of the actual rate of inflation from the desired rate of inflation ($p - p^*$), and another parameter (b) times the log output ratio ($\hat{Y}$).[19] The more the Fed cares about avoiding an acceleration of inflation, the higher would be the parameter a. The more the Fed cares about avoiding recessions and high unemployment, the higher would be the parameter b. If

---

[18] John B. Taylor, "How Should Monetary Policy Respond to Shocks While Maintaining Long-Term Price Stability? Conceptual Issues," in *Achieving Price Stability*, Federal Reserve Bank of Kansas City, 1996, pp. 181–95.

[19] *Review:* The symbol $\hat{Y}$ stands for the logarithm of the ratio of actual real GDP (Y) to natural real GDP (Y^N), expressed as a percent. Whenever $\hat{Y}$ equals zero, then actual real GDP is equal to natural real GDP. This notation was introduced at the beginning of the Appendix to Chapter 8; see p. 273.

The **Taylor Rule** calls for the central bank to move the real short-term interest rate away from its desired long-term value in response to any deviation of actual inflation from desired inflation and in response to any deviation of real GDP from natural real GDP.

the Fed cares equally about 1 percent of excess inflation and 1 percent of insufficient output, then it would set a and b equal to each other, for instance, $a = b = 0.5$. No matter what the values of a and b are, the formula written as equation (14.1) has become known as the **Taylor Rule.** The special case of a Taylor Rule with a zero weight on output ($b = 0$) is called an "inflation targeting rule."[20]

How closely did the Fed follow a Taylor Rule? To answer this question, we need to assume a value for the desired real interest rate (3.0 percent) and for the desired inflation rate (2 percent per year). Let us also assume that the Fed places equal weights on inflation and output and assign values of $a = b = 0.5$. Then we can calculate the nominal federal funds rate (the real rate plus the actual inflation rate) called for by the Taylor Rule. Figure 14-5 compares the actual federal funds rate as the green line with the calculated "fixed Taylor Rule" using fixed values of the parameters assumed in this paragraph.[21]

Compared with the green actual rate line, the blue fixed Taylor Rule line reveals interesting differences. First, the Fed did not cut the actual rate in 1981–86 by nearly as much as the Taylor Rule would have required, that is, the Fed did not care enough about the large negative output ratio that occurred in the early 1980s. The blue Taylor Rule line tracks the actual rate remarkably well in the late 1980s but does not decline enough in 1993–94 nor increase at all in 1994. Most interestingly, the blue line fails to decline nearly as much as the actual green line in 2001–04, although it is equal to the actual rate in late 2007.

The errors made by the blue line suggest that the Fed cared more about inflation and less about the output ratio during the disinflation period of the early 1980s. But the errors after 1990 suggest that the Fed cared more about low output in 1992–93 and 2001–04 than the Taylor Rule. To implement this idea, we can recalculate the Taylor Rule line *by assuming that the Fed changed its preferences, from caring so much about inflation to caring much more about output.* The red line in Figure 14-5 is calculated in just the same way as the blue line, but it assumes that the Fed's weight on inflation (a) is not 0.5 throughout, but rather changes from 1.0 to 0.0 after 1990. The red line also assumes that the Fed's weight on the output ratio (b) changes in the opposite direction from 0.0 before 1990 to 1.0 after 1990. The red line comes closer to the actual green line, especially in tracking the disinflation of 1981–84, the stimulative reduction of interest rates in 1992–93, and the reduction of interest rates in 2001–03.[22]

The differences between the actual green line and the alternative red "variable Taylor Rule" line highlights several periods when the Fed deviated from the Taylor Rule. The Fed's "preemptive" increase in interest rates in 1994 deviated from the Taylor Rule, because inflation was not accelerating and output was still below natural output. In this case the Fed was forecasting an ominous future of higher inflation that did not actually happen. The red Taylor Rule line

---

[20] On inflation targeting, see Lars E. O. Svensson, "Inflation Targeting: Should It be Modeled as an Instrument Rule or a Targeting Rule?" *European Economic Review,* vol. 46 (2002), pp. 771–80.

[21] The inflation rate is the percent change in the quarterly GDP deflator from one year earlier, the log output ratio is the same as that plotted in Figure 14-4, and the desired real interest rate is chosen to minimize the mean difference between the actual rate and the calculated fixed Taylor Rule rate. Note that there is no need for the parameters a and b to sum to 1.0.

[22] While the target real federal funds rate for the fixed Taylor Rule is 3.0 percent, it is 2.5 percent for the variable Taylor Rule in order to keep the average 1980–2007 value of the red and blue lines in Figure 14-5 equal to the average 1980–2007 value of the green line, the actual value of the federal funds rate.

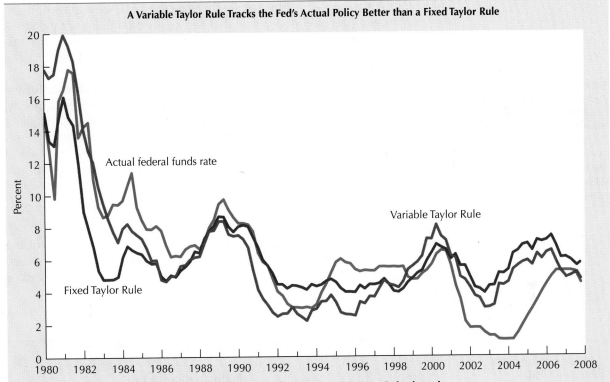

Figure 14-5 **The Actual Federal Funds Rate and Interest Rates Calculated by Two Versions of the Taylor Rule, 1980–2007**

The green line plots the actual federal funds rate. The blue line plots the interest rate forecast by a Taylor Rule with equal weights of 0.5 on inflation and output ($a = b = 0.5$). The red line plots the interest rate forecast by a Taylor Rule that shifts the weights toward less concern about inflation and more concern about output after 1990. Comparing the actual green line with the variable red line, the surprises in the Fed's behavior were keeping interest rates so high in 1984–86, raising them preemptively in 1994, increasing them so little in 1998–2000, and reducing them so much in 2001–04.

Source: See Appendix C-4.

indicates that the Fed should have raised interest rates more than it did in the late 1990s, a period when the Fed has been criticized for excessive monetary ease. Finally, neither of the Taylor Rule lines comes close to tracking the aggressiveness of the Fed's interest rate reductions in 2001–04. ⬤

14-8 Rules Versus Discretion: An Assessment

A central theme of this chapter is that money-multiplier shocks, money demand shocks, commodity demand shocks, and supply shocks loosen the links between the Fed's policy instruments and its targets for the economy. These shocks imply that a rigid rule for setting the growth rate of the supply of high-powered money (the only policy rule that the Fed is capable of achieving directly) may not achieve the nation's unemployment, inflation, and other targets. Similarly, these shocks may make a rule for a target variable like the inflation rate difficult to achieve.

A second theme is that some policy rules provide a **nominal anchor** for the economy. That is, these rules target a nominal variable (high-powered money, the money supply, nominal GDP, or the inflation rate) and thus automatically place a limit on the ability of inflation to accelerate. A nominal anchor is inherently desirable because it increases the chance that inflation expectations will turn out to be accurate, thus facilitating financial planning by households and firms.

> A **nominal anchor** is a rule that sets a limit on the growth rate of a nominal variable, for instance, high-powered money, the money supply, the price level, or nominal GDP. A nominal anchor prevents inflation from accelerating without limit.

Rules for Policy Instruments

Table 14-1 assesses seven policy rules. The first two rules set the values of the Fed's policy instruments, either high-powered money or the federal funds interest rate. A rule for high-powered money growth provides a nominal anchor

---

Table 14-1   Assessing Alternative Policy Rules

Variable to be fixed by policy rule	Main advantages	Main disadvantages
Growth rate of high-powered money	Feasible for Fed to achieve; provides nominal anchor	May lead to variable inflation and unemployment rates
Nominal interest rate	Feasible for Fed to achieve (in short run)	*IS* curve shocks or unstable commodity demand may lead to variable unemployment rate. Does not provide nominal anchor; hence inflation can increase without bound
Growth rate of the money supply (monetarist CGRR)	Provides nominal anchor	Money supply hard to control; money demand instability may lead to variable inflation and unemployment rates
Inflation rate or price level	Provides nominal anchor; if successful, most likely to stabilize inflation expectations and avoid time inconsistency	Hard to control; requires extinguishing reaction to supply shocks, creating highly variable unemployment rate
Unemployment rate or output ratio	Avoids welfare cost of variable unemployment; allows households and firms to carry through on plans without making mistakes	Hard to control; requires accommodating reaction to supply shocks, creating highly variable inflation rate; does not provide nominal anchor
Growth rate of nominal GDP	Provides nominal anchor; splits supply shock effect between output and inflation	Hard to control
Taylor Rule (combines inflation and output targeting)	Provides the advantages of inflation targeting and a nominal anchor while reducing the variance of output and unemployment	Hard to control

but allows shocks to carry the economy away from its target. A nominal interest rate target does not provide a nominal anchor, and either a fiscal stimulus or other positive *IS* shock, or a positive commodity demand shock, can lead to explosive inflation under a nominal interest rate rule.[23]

A Rule for the Money Supply

The money supply is neither directly under the control of the Fed nor is it a target variable. For this reason it is sometimes called an "intermediate variable." A money supply rule (like the monetarist CGRR) has only two advantages. In the first place, it provides a nominal anchor; in the second (as in Figure 13-5 on p. 444), it is superior to an interest rate rule when commodity demand is unstable but money demand is stable. Otherwise, it combines the weakness of rules for targets (they are difficult to control) with the weakness of a high-powered money rule.

Rules for Target Variables

The main target variables are inflation and unemployment. Unemployment moves inversely with the ratio of actual to natural output, so a rule that targets unemployment is similar to a rule that targets the output ratio.[24] Because inflation plus real GDP growth equals nominal GDP growth, a nominal GDP growth rule has some of the characteristics of other rules for target variables, even though nominal GDP itself is not a target variable.

Rules for target variables avoid slippage between the instruments and the targets. In particular, all target rules (if successful) prevent instability in either commodity or money demand from causing undesirable fluctuations in target variables. These rules also suffer from a common disadvantage: It is difficult to control target variables because of policy lags, forecasting errors, and multiplier uncertainty. As shown in Table 14-1, rules for target variables differ. Rules for nominal GDP growth or inflation provide a nominal anchor; rules for unemployment or the output ratio do not.

The main advantage of a nominal GDP rule is that it requires no policy response to a supply shock (defined in Chapter 8 as a "neutral policy" response). In contrast, an inflation rule requires that the effect of supply shocks on the price level be extinguished, which raises the variability of output; whereas a real GDP or unemployment rule requires that the effect of supply shocks be "accommodated," which raises the variability of inflation. Because a nominal GDP rule represents a compromise response to supply shocks and provides a nominal anchor, several economists have come to advocate that the Fed adopt such a rule.

---

[23] This defect of a nominal interest rate rule was a major theme of Milton Friedman's 1967 address to the American Economic Association. A positive commodity demand shift boosts the nominal interest rate; to maintain its target, the Fed must raise the money supply; this raises inflationary expectations and boosts the nominal interest rate again; again, the Fed must raise the money supply. Soon the Fed has caused a spiral of accelerating money growth and inflation. This phenomenon occurred when the Fed accommodated the fiscal stimulus of the Vietnam War during 1967–68.

[24] The negative "Okun's Law" line describing the close inverse relation of the unemployment rate and the output ratio is displayed in Figure 8-13 on p. 267.

How the Fed Reinvented Instability in Residential Construction

In discussing the Great Moderation on pp. 462–67, we listed three sources of reduced volatility of demand shocks: the smaller ups and downs of military spending, residential construction, and inventory change after 1984 than before 1984. This box is about residential construction, and the chart shows 1960–2007 housing starts (the number of new housing units on which construction begins in a given quarter, expressed as an annual rate). Clearly visible is the much higher volatility of housing starts before 1984 than after 1984, and volatility was at its highest between 1970 and 1984.

As discussed in the previous chapter (pp. 440–43), pre-1984 volatility in residential construction was created by financial regulations. Notice in the diagram that housing starts were much more stable after 1984, except for a short-lived dip in 1990–91. Financial deregulation eliminated interest rate ceilings, allowed many different financial institutions to issue mortgages, and allowed all institutions to sell and resell these mortgages to hedge funds and other types of relatively unregulated investors. From 1985 to 2001, residential construction was much more stable than prior to 1984.

But then along came the Fed. As is evident from Figure 14-5 on p. 471, during 2001–04 the Fed reduced the federal funds rate by far more than predicted by either a fixed-coefficient or variable-coefficient Taylor Rule. Because interest rates were so low, a whole new industry of mortgage brokers burst onto the scene. The brokers received fees from financial institutions such as the giants Countryside and Washington Mutual ("Wa Mu") to lure households into refinancing existing mortgages and to take out new mortgages. They talked their customers into adjustable-rate mortgages (ARMs) that initially had a low interest rate but then, after two to three years, would "reset" to a much higher interest rate. Unsuspecting customers signed contracts to borrow at low "teaser" rates, often unaware that their monthly payments might increase by a third or a half in the future.

Many of the customers lured by the mortgage brokers to take out teaser rates on ARMs were low-income families who rented houses and apartments and previously could never have dreamed of owning their own home. During 2001–06 the percentage of American families owning their own home rose from 65 to 69 percent as a result of low-interest rates and aggressive mortgage brokers. This would have been fine, except that many of these low-income households could not afford the higher monthly payments after the teaser rates expired.

As the ARMs reset in 2007 and 2008, the rate of foreclosures soared. In November 2007, foreclosures were occurring at an annual rate of more than two million per year. The phrase "subprime mortgage crisis" became ubiquitous in 2007–08.

The problem created by the subprime mortgage crisis spread into the broader financial markets. Unlike the pre-1984 regulated era, when each saving bank would hold the mortgages that it had granted, in the post-2001 world mortgage originators such as Countryside and Wa-Mu would sell mortgages to a wide variety of institutions attracted to them by their relatively high interest rates. But when the families who could not afford the reset mortgages began to default, the value of these assets declined, and large financial institutions found that the value they could obtain by selling the mortgages had declined to much less than what they had originally paid for them.

The real estate bubble of this decade involved most homeowners, not just those with low incomes. Because interest rates were so low, homeowners with existing high-interest mortgages could refinance at lower interest rates. More enticing was the chance to raise the amount of the mortgage as house prices shot up. A family with a house valued in 2003 at $300,000 with a $250,000 mortgage might find themselves with a house value in 2005 of $400,000. They could take out a new mortgage for $350,000, pay off the old mortgage, and "extract" $100,000 in cash to do anything they wanted—home improvements, vacations, new cars, or paying off credit card debt.

The lower chart shows the enormous value of these "equity extractions" displayed as a share of personal disposable income, more than doubling from less than 4 percent in 2000 to a peak of 9 percent in 2005–06, the equivalent of $850 billion of consumer borrowing against their homes. But this party had to come to an end. Builders constructed too many homes; too many buyers had purchased homes (particularly condominiums), not with the intention to live in them but with the intention to "flip" them, making a big profit on the sale. The inventory of unsold homes started to build up in 2006–07 and for the first time in decades, home prices began to decline. Many borrowers found that they owed more on their homes than the reduced value.

Then a vicious circle set in. Falling home values meant homeowners could no longer refinance. Because those who had bought condos for investment no longer could expect to make profits from rising prices, they tried to sell them, placing further downward pressure on home prices. Equity extraction plunged as shown on the lower chart, and housing starts collapsed as shown on the upper chart. Since equity extraction had propped up personal consumption expenditures for years, there was a danger that the economy would tumble into a recession because households could no longer maintain their high level of consumption by borrowing against their houses.

By keeping interest rates too low for too long, the Fed had contributed to the subprime crisis, also called the "mortgage meltdown," of 2007–08.[a] Critics of the Fed went further than citing the low interest rates of 2001–04. They claimed that the Fed had failed in its role of regulatory oversight of financial institutions and that it should have worked closely with other federal regulatory institutions to limit subprime mortgages before the foreclosure crisis spun out of control.

Overall it is ironic that, despite the financial reforms that ended the pre-1984 era of instability in residential construction, the failure of the Fed's actions to regulate the mortgage market had created a situation in 2007–08 in which housing starts fell by more than half, as in 1974–75 and 1979–82, and the economy teetered on the brink of a recession.

---

[a] For background on the subprime crisis and mortgage meltdown, see Martin Feldstein, "Liquidity Now!" *Wall Street Journal,* September 12, 2007.

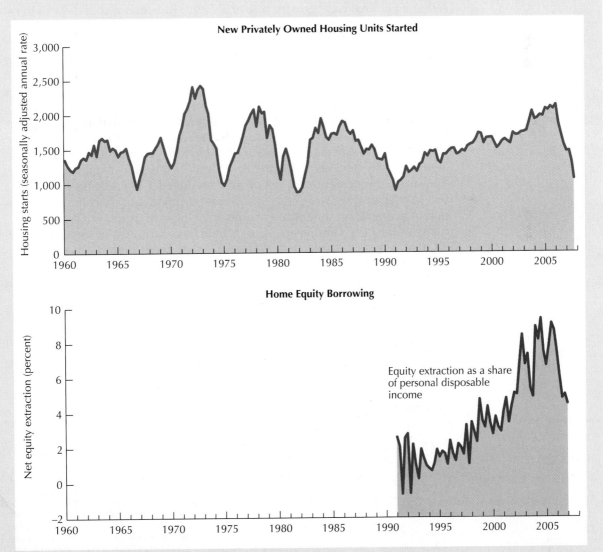

Sources: Upper frame: U.S. Census Bureau, *Manufacturing and Construction Division*. Bottom frame: Alan Greenspan and James Kennedy, "Sources and Uses of Equity Extracted from Homes." Details in Appendix C-4.

By placing weight both on inflation and output, a Taylor Rule (as examined on pp. 469–71) is similar to a nominal GDP rule. A nominal GDP rule is the same as a Taylor Rule that places equal weights on inflation and real GDP *growth* (relative to desired values), in contrast to the traditional Taylor Rule, which targets inflation and the *level* of real GDP relative to natural real GDP (that is, the output ratio). What is the difference? Consider a deep recession like that of 1981–82. The growth rate of real GDP was rapid after early 1983, but the previous recession had created a large negative output ratio that did not return to zero until 1987. In the intervening period of 1983–87, a Taylor Rule based on the output ratio would have caused a lower interest rate than a rule based on the growth rate of output and thus would have helped to make output less variable. *This distinction suggests that a traditional Taylor Rule is superior to a nominal GDP growth rule.*

Implementing a Nominal GDP Rule or a Taylor Rule

Either a nominal GDP growth rule or a Taylor Rule that responds both to excess inflation and insufficient output avoid some of the flaws of other rules listed in Table 14-1. But both approaches are still subject to the difficulties of forecasting and long lags between changes in the instruments controlled by the Fed and the ultimate response of inflation and output. One approach that attempts to circumvent the problem of long lags is for the central bank to target its best *forecast* of inflation and output. Thus, if the average lag between a monetary policy action and the response of inflation is two years, the central bank would respond to changes in its best forecast of inflation two years from now, rather than of inflation today.[25] Indeed, it is clear in analyzing Figure 14-5 on p. 471 that in at least two episodes the Fed relied on forecasts in implementing a policy that resembled a Taylor Rule. In 1994, the Fed's "preemptive strike" raised the federal funds rate sharply in anticipation of accelerating inflation and a positive log output ratio that did not actually occur for several years. And, in 2001, the sharpness of the Fed's interest rate reductions reflected its forecast that there would be a recession deeper than actually occurred.

In the end, we may conclude that the distinction between policy discretion and rules may have been exaggerated in the literature on macroeconomic policy. As it implements a policy that seems similar to a Taylor Rule, the Fed has shown that it can change the weights on inflation and output within that rule. And in order to implement that rule, it still must choose a desired long-term real interest rate, a desired inflation rate, and it must determine the current value of natural real GDP in order to calculate the output ratio. Even in implementing a rule, there is plenty of discretion for the Fed and other central banks in deciding exactly how to implement that rule.

---

[25] See Lars E. O. Svensson and Michael Woodford, "Implementing Optimal Policy through Inflation-Forecast Targeting," in Ben S. Bernanke and Michael Woodford, *The Inflation Targeting Debate* (Chicago and London: University of Chicago Press, 2005), pp. 19–83. The same book contains numerous other assessments and critiques of inflation targeting. A much earlier assessment of nominal GDP targeting and recommendation that is also based on targeting the forecast value is Robert J. Gordon, "The Conduct of Monetary Policy," in A. Ando, H. Eguchi, R. Farmer, and Y. Suzuki, eds., *Monetary Policy in Our Times* (Cambridge MA: MIT Press, 1985, pp. 45–81.)

Case Study

Should Monetary Policy Target the Exchange Rate?

In Chapter 6 we learned that when a country has flexible exchange rates, its central bank is free to set policy to attain its objectives for the domestic economy. The more expansionary the monetary policy is, the more the exchange rate is likely to depreciate. The weaker currency stimulates exports and restrains domestic purchases of imported goods and services. Thus the easier monetary policy is likely to raise that country's net exports, thereby shifting its *IS* curve to the right. By contrast, when a country chooses to fix its exchange rate in relation to some other currency or some other group of countries, its central bank surrenders the freedom to pursue domestic objectives; its central bank must use monetary policy to keep the exchange rate fixed. It cannot independently operate to attain other domestic objectives, like stimulating aggregate demand. This is a fundamental lesson of the Chapter 6 trilemma.

In the previous section we saw that a country's average inflation rate would be lower if the central bank were committed to a rigid rule for the inflation rate. One way for the central bank to convey its commitment to a rigid inflation rule is to fix the exchange rate. Fixing the exchange rate commits the central bank to keeping domestic interest rates in line with that of the country to which its currency is fixed, thereby precluding the possibility of the central bank adopting a more stimulative monetary policy.

Countries do not casually inflate their economies. More often they print money out of desperation. Hyperinflations have almost always occurred among the vanquished following an international or civil war or other major calamity (Germany, Hungary, the Soviet Union, China, Nicaragua). The very high inflations in Latin America (Brazil, Argentina, Bolivia) occurred after the prices of commodities they exported collapsed, and energy prices and the interest rates they paid to foreigners soared. The very high inflations in eastern Europe and the countries of the former Soviet Union occurred during the difficult transition to market economies, when their needs for public outlays were high and their ability to generate tax revenue was low (Poland, Russia). (For more on hyperinflation and rapid inflation, see Section 9-6 on pp. 300–303).

During the 1990s many of the countries of western Europe pledged to keep their exchange rates fixed relative to each other (but not relative to the United States or Japan). This system was the precursor to the ultimate fixed exchange rate system, a single currency (the euro), discussed in the International Perspective box on pp. 478–79. ●

International Perspective

The Debate About the Euro

Ever since the end of World War II, the nations of western Europe have been moving toward closer relations. The formation of the NATO security alliance in 1949 was followed by the formation of an economic alliance, the European Economic Community, in the 1950s. During the 1960s and 1970s, a "single market" was created to permit the unfettered movement across national borders of goods and services, financial capital, and people. During the 1980s, economic policies were coordinated even more when the European Monetary System was formed to stabilize the exchange rates of its member nations. The 1992 Maastricht Treaty called for much greater economic integration in its proposal for a monetary union that would replace each member nation's currency with a single European currency.

The Euro Arrives

Finally, on January 1, 1999, the euro was created, while the franc, mark, and nine other European currencies disappeared from the computer screens of currency traders. Euro coins and currency began to circulate in January 2002, and the colorful French franc, German mark, and other European currencies disappeared from the purses and wallets of citizens in twelve different European countries.

The euro is the third stage of the Economic and Monetary Union (EMU), which has been controversial. Interestingly, the most ardent group of supporters has been politicians. Politicians across Europe have sought greater economic cooperation because, in general, such cooperation seems to enhance the chances of having Europe remain prosperous and at peace. Economists as a group have been among the most vocal detractors of the EMU and the euro.

For the Euro

Some have argued that international trade within Europe would be enhanced by having a single currency, which would eliminate the costs and risks associated with exchange rates. The irony is that advances in financial markets now make it easier and cheaper than before for firms and financial institutions to manage risks associated with exchange rate fluctuations. In spite of that, it may still be expensive, especially for smaller firms and tourists, to deal with the numerous European currencies and the risks and uncertainties that they entail.

Since World War II, Germany has kept its inflation rate low. Some supported the EMU as a vehicle for other countries to "free-ride" on the German resolve and reputation for low inflation. The European Central Bank (ECB), seems to carry out monetary policy the way the German Bundesbank did, with a single goal of low inflation. Thus the euro is favored by some as a vehicle for achieving the low inflation rates that Germany achieved.

The euro is a common currency, but it may also provide fiscal discipline. Countries that have very high inflation rates sometimes adopt fixed exchange rates in order to discipline both their monetary and their fiscal policies. Among the criteria of the Maastricht Treaty for countries to qualify for inclusion in the euro were that government deficits not exceed 3 percent of GDP and that government debt not exceed 60 percent of GDP. Other entrance criteria stipulated that inflation and interest rates not diverge too widely from those of the other countries entering the euro.

The figure shows the ratio of fiscal deficits to GDP for several member countries of the euro, compared to the 3 percent goal. Countries such as Italy and Spain struggled to implement sharp fiscal contractions to achieve admission into the euro club.

Against the Euro

In Chapter 6 we learned about some of the important *economic* costs and benefits of a fixed exchange rate regime like the euro or its predecessor, the EMU. Recall that when a nation chooses to fix its exchange rate, it surrenders the independence of its central bank. Its central bank is committed to use its one policy instrument, the money supply, to achieve its one goal, the exchange rate. In the case of the euro, each member gives up its national currency and any independent monetary policy.

To the extent that the macroeconomic shocks that strike Europe have similar effects on all euro members

(f) Use the Taylor Rule as given by equation (14.1) to calculate the real federal funds rate for the given combinations of inflation and real GDP, when $a = 1$ and $b = 0$

(g) Use your answers to parts c–f to explain why the greater the weight the Fed places on output, the greater the variation in the real federal funds rate.

(h) Use your answers to part g and your knowledge of the monetary policy effectiveness lag to discuss how the weight the Fed places on inflation relative to output affects how long it takes for the economy's output to return to natural GDP after a demand shock, all other things being equal.

 SELF-TEST ANSWERS

p. 455 (1) target, (2) instrument, (3) instrument, (4) target, (5) instrument.

p. 462 (1) Legislative lag. (2) Multiplier uncertainty. (3) Data lag. (4) Both the effectiveness lag and multiplier uncertainty.

pp. 468–69 (1) True; the public will believe that the central bank will maintain low rates of growth of the money supply and the price level. (2) False; opposite of (1). (3) True; same as (1). (4) False; time inconsistency strengthens advocates of rules involving nominal variables such as the growth of high-powered money or the inflation rate.

> For additional practice and exploration, exercises that require the use of Excel are available at www.aw-bc.com/gordon.

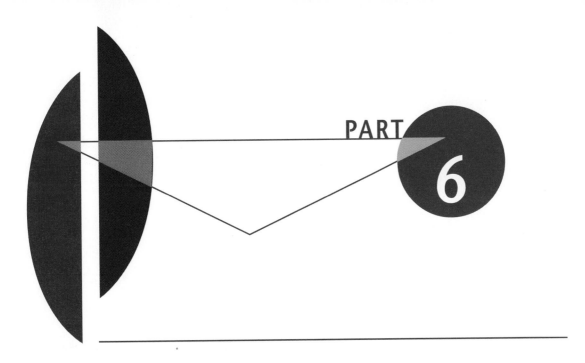

Stability and Instability in the Private Economy

The Economics of Consumption Behavior

Economists become upset when they learn that
we aren't spending money as they've planned for us.
—Eliot Marshall

15-1 Consumption and Economic Stability

In Part Five (Chapters 13–14), we studied the role of stabilization policy, which consists of monetary and fiscal policy. The most basic question about stabilization policy is whether "activist" policy intervention should be attempted or whether policy rules are preferable. If policy rules are preferable, what variable should be targeted by such rules? A central issue in making these choices is the set of shocks that can cause target variables to be unstable even if a policy instrument is successfully targeted by a rigid rule. These shocks include money multiplier and money demand shocks (Chapter 13), supply shocks (Chapter 8), and commodity demand shocks (Chapters 3 and 4).

We now return to the sources of commodity demand shocks in order to deepen our understanding of the behavior of consumption and investment spending. This chapter deals with the theory and actual behavior of personal consumption expenditures; Chapter 16 deals with the theory and actual behavior of investment expenditures.

We learned in the last chapter that advocates of activism were pessimistic about the self-correcting properties of the private economy, while advocates of rules were optimistic. Who is right? We learn that consumption and investment behavior is quite different. This chapter suggests that the optimistic rules advocates are right about consumption and wrong about investment.

Unlike the simple Keynesian consumption function of Chapter 3, in which consumption responds instantly to changes in disposable income, in reality consumption has only a small response to income changes that households believe to be temporary. This implies that consumption is a source of stability. In recessions, consumption declines much less than total GDP and in some recessions consumption does not decline at all. In contrast, investment is more volatile than real GDP and tends to respond to *changes* in real GDP.

Forward-Looking Theories of Consumer Behavior

The focus of this chapter is a theory of consumer behavior that incorporates more sophisticated and realistic behavior than the Keynesian consumption function of Chapter 3. This theory states that consumers have **forward-looking expectations.** Because consumers prefer stable as opposed to highly variable patterns of consumption, they assess whether changes in their incomes are likely to persist when deciding how much to change their consumption. Consumers behave quite differently in response to a change in disposable

Forward-looking expectations are estimates of the future values of economic variables. They are generally based on the current and past values of several variables and an economic model that accounts for their behavior.

income that is expected to be *temporary* than they do in response to a change in disposable income that is expected to be *permanent*. Consumers can maintain their consumption when income changes temporarily by drawing down their accumulated savings. By contrast, if income is reduced permanently, consumption will fall more dramatically.

Introducing the PIH and LCH. The hypothesis that consumption depends on forward-looking expectations was developed independently in the 1950s by two economists who later won the Nobel Prize, Milton Friedman and Franco Modigliani. Friedman's version is called the **permanent-income hypothesis (PIH).** It predicts that consumption responds only to permanent changes in income, not to transitory ones. The PIH suggests that temporary changes in income will have minor effects on permanent income and, therefore, on consumption. As a result, the multiplier effect of a temporary change in autonomous spending is much smaller than the effect calculated in Chapter 3. In that case, the shifts in the *IS* curve are also much smaller than suggested in Chapter 4. The resulting stability of consumption spending supports the view of those who advocate policy rules that the economy can be trusted to remain fairly close to natural output.

Modigliani's version, called the **life-cycle hypothesis (LCH),** holds that consumers attempt to smooth out their consumption spending over their lifetimes. This version also implies that transitory blips of income will cause only a small response in consumption. The LCH also implies that consumption spending depends not just on disposable income but on the real wealth of consumers as well. It implies, for instance, that major movements in stock market and housing prices affect consumption.

> The **permanent-income hypothesis (PIH)** holds that consumption spending depends on the long-run average (or permanent) income that people expect to receive.

> The **life-cycle hypothesis (LCH)** implies that households base their current consumption on their expected total lifetime incomes and their wealth.

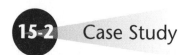

15-2   Case Study

Main Features of U.S. Consumption Data

Before we study these two forward-looking theories of consumption behavior, we will examine data on aggregate consumption in the United States. Plotted in Figure 15-1 are total real consumption expenditures over the period 1960–2007, as well as the behavior of the three main components of consumption: durable goods, nondurable goods, and services.

Note that the growth of total consumption spending, shown by the top line, has not been perfectly steady. Particularly sharp slowdowns in the growth of total consumption spending took place in 1974–75, 1980–82, and 1990–91. In contrast, consumption spending never declined for even a single quarter in the recession of 2001. As we will see, the forward-looking theories emphasize that because consumers consider their permanent or lifetime incomes, they react to temporary declines in income (such as occur in a recession) primarily by reducing saving rather than consumption. Clearly, some consumers cut their consumption during recessions. They may not, for example, have enough savings to absorb the blow of losing a job. Also, banks typically will not lend to unemployed people, even though they may have good prospects of regaining their jobs and making an impressive total lifetime income.

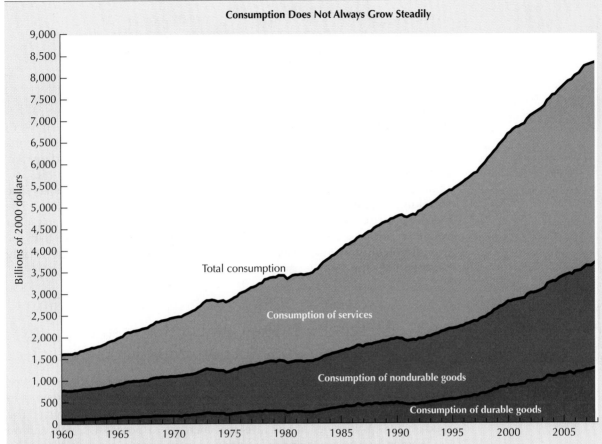

Figure 15-1 Real Consumer Expenditure and Its Three Components, 1960–2007

The top line plots consumer expenditure and shows a marked pause in growth in 1974–75, 1980–82, and 1990–91, but not in the recession of 2001. Consumption of durable goods is both the most volatile and fastest-growing component on average over this period. Consumption of services also has grown rapidly but is much less volatile than expenditures on durable goods. Consumption of nondurable goods is the slowest-growing component and has moderate volatility.

Source: Bureau of Economic Analysis, *NIPA Tables*.

Of the three components of consumption expenditures, spending on durable goods is by far the most volatile. Consumer durable expenditures, like the fixed-investment expenditures studied in the next chapter, are often made for big-ticket items that can be postponed. Many households buy new automobiles or TV sets simply because they want improved quality or new features; they can often postpone such purchases if income declines temporarily. Consumption of nondurable goods displays moderate cyclical volatility, while consumption of services tends to grow more smoothly. People still buy haircuts and car repair services in recessions.

Both durable goods and services spending grew much faster than spending on nondurable goods over the period shown in Figure 15-1. Percentages of total consumption for the three major categories of real consumption expenditures at the beginning and end of the period depicted are as follows:

	1960:Q1	2007:Q3
Durable goods	5.9	14.9
Nondurable goods	41.2	28.7
Services	52.9	56.4

The basic reason for the slow growth in nondurable goods purchases is that many such goods, particularly food and clothing, are necessities. Many types of durable goods (such as computers, DVD players, and cell phones) and services (airline trips to Florida) are luxuries, which experience disproportionately fast growth in demand when incomes rise.

Have these trends made total consumption more or less stable? The shrinking segment, nondurable goods, has moderate cyclical volatility. The increases in the shares of high-volatility durable goods spending and low-volatility services spending have roughly cancelled out, implying that the overall volatility of total consumption spending did not change appreciably between 1960 and 2007. ●

15-3 Background: The Conflict Between the Time-Series and Cross-Section Evidence

One of the major innovations in Keynes's *General Theory* was the multiplier, which followed directly from the assumptions that consumption responds to income and that the marginal propensity to consume is less than unity: "The fundamental psychological law ... is that men are disposed, as a rule and on the average, to increase their consumption as their income increases, but not by as much as the increase in their income."[1]

Keynes's second innovative idea was that there is a given amount, *a*, that individuals will consume no matter what their income, so that it is possible for saving to be negative if disposable income is very low. Denoting consumption

---

Figure 15-2 The Relation Between Disposable Income (Y_D), Consumption Spending (*C*), and the Ratio of Saving to Income (S/Y_D)

The top frame repeats the consumption function introduced in Chapter 3. At levels of disposable income below (to the left of) Y_{D0}, people consume more than their income and saving is negative, as shown by the shaded red area. To the right of Y_{D0} consumption is less than income, and the shaded blue area, which represents the difference between income and consumption, that is, the amount of saving, is a steadily growing fraction of disposable income. In the middle frame, the share of saving in disposable income is plotted as a negative fraction to the left of Y_{D0} and a positive and growing fraction to the right. The bottom frame plots actual data on the relation of saving to disposable income from a survey of consumers. Notice the close correspondence between the theoretical diagram in the middle frame and the actual data in the bottom frame.

---

[1] See John Maynard Keynes, *The General Theory of Employment, Interest and Money* (New York: Macmillan, 1936), Book III. The idea of the multiplier was first introduced by R. F. Kahn, "The Relation of Home Investment to Unemployment," *Economic Journal* (June 1931), but Keynes was the first to fit the multiplier into a general economic model of commodity and money markets.

People with Higher Incomes Have Higher Saving Rates

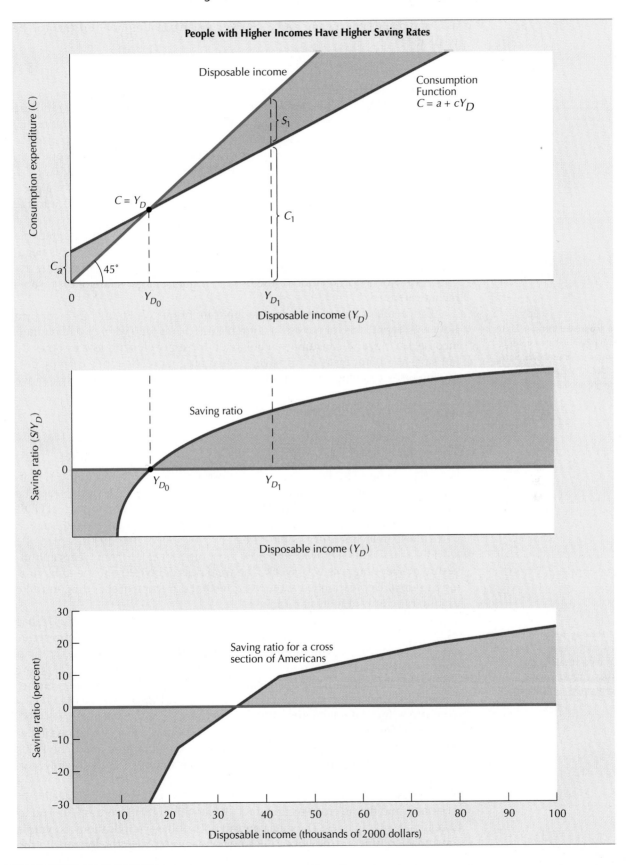

as C and disposable income as Y_D, the Keynesian consumption function can be written:

$$C = C_a + cY_D \qquad (15.1)$$

This is identical to equation (3.3) on p. 61.

The hypothetical Keynesian consumption function and saving ratio are plotted in the top two frames of Figure 15-2. In the top frame, consumption (C) rises less rapidly than disposable income (Y_D), since the marginal propensity to consume (c) is less than 1.0. Consumption starts out greater than Y_D, equals Y_D at the income level Y_{D0}, and then is less than Y_D. Everywhere to the right of Y_{D0} the shortfall of consumption below disposable income allows room for a positive amount of saving. For instance, the income level Y_{D1} is divided into the consumption level C_1 and the saving level S_1.

Moving down to the middle frame of Figure 15-2, we find plotted the saving/income ratio, S/Y_D. To the left of the income level Y_{D0}, saving is negative; to the right of Y_{D0}, saving is positive. As income rises, according to the hypothetical Keynesian relation in the middle frame, a larger share of disposable income is saved.

The actual data plotted in the bottom frame of Figure 15-2 confirm Keynes's hypothesis for a **cross section** of Americans who were polled on their income, saving, and consumption behavior. Most people with low incomes do not save at all, but instead "dissave," consuming more than they earn by borrowing or by drawing on accumulated assets in savings accounts. As we move rightward from the poor to the rich, we find that the saving/income ratio increases, just as in the hypothetical relationship of the middle frame.

A **cross section** consists of data for numerous units (for instance, households, firms, cities, or states) observed over a single period of time.

The Saving Rate: Short-Run Variability, Long-Run Constancy

Implicit in Figure 15-2 is a potentially serious problem for the economy. If individuals save more as their incomes rise, then consumption spending may be inadequate to maintain actual real GDP at the desired level of natural real GDP. Keynes's concern that the saving rate would rise as the years passed seemed particularly relevant during the Great Depression of the 1930s, when the world's actual real GDP was far below its natural level for many years and investment spending was very weak. The weakness of investment spending during the Great Depression led some to argue that government spending must be used to raise output to its natural level.

But, has the saving rate, in fact, risen over time as natural real GDP has risen? Look now at Figure 15-3, which plots the actual historical **time-series** data for the average saving ratio for each major business cycle of the twentieth century. Between 1894–1896, the first observation plotted, and 2001–2007, the last observation plotted, real income per person increased by a factor of ten. Yet there is little indication that the saving ratio trended upward over the twentieth century. Instead, the saving ratio did not change dramatically between 1895 and 1980 when it began a sharp decline. The main longer-term variations in the saving ratio were the low saving ratio during the Great Depression of the 1930s and the high saving ratio during World War II, and more recently the low saving ratio since 1980 that we discuss later in this chapter.

Keynes's consumption function implies that the saving ratio will decline in recessions and that in cross-section data, those with higher incomes will tend to have higher saving rates. The data confirm both of these implications. Keynes's consumption function, however, does not explain why over the longer run the

A **time series** consists of data covering a span of time for one or more measures (for instance, disposable income or consumption spending).

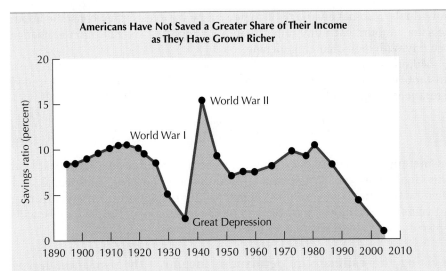

Figure 15-3 Ratio of Personal Saving to Disposable Personal Income (S/Y_D), Averages over Business Cycles, 1894–2007

The low level of saving during the Great Depression is consistent with our theory (compare Figure 3-3 on p. 65). The high level of saving during World War II was caused by the shortages of civilian goods and services. Leaving out these two extreme periods, the ratio of saving to disposable income was fairly constant until 1980, after which it declined almost to zero. Observations plotted are averages over complete business cycles.

Sources: For 1987–99: Paul David and John Scadding, "Private Savings: Ultrarationality, Aggregation, and 'Denison's Law,' " *Journal of Political Economy* (March/April 1974). For 1900–32: *Historical Statistics of the United States Millennial Edition. 1933–2007: National Income and Product Accounts*. Business cycle data from NBER *Business Cycle Expansions and Contractions*.

saving ratio is constant or even declining instead of rising as predicted. The two most important hypotheses about consumption (and thus about saving) that can account for the long-run near-constancy of the saving ratio, as well as the short-run variability and the cross-section pattern of saving, are Friedman's permanent-income hypothesis and Modigliani's life-cycle hypothesis.

15-4 Forward-Looking Behavior: The Permanent-Income Hypothesis

A Theory of Steady Consumption

Imagine that you have a job and receive your take-home pay of $1,000 on the first day of each month. Suppose you regard your income on the first day of each month as $1,000, and your income on each of the remaining days of the month as zero. If you spend based on the simple Keynesian consumption function with a high marginal propensity to consume and a small autonomous component, you will do almost all your consumption spending on the first day of the month and consume very little over the rest of the month!

Of course people consume more steadily than that, setting aside part of their pay to buy groceries and other items during the rest of the month.

Individuals who have variable income will be happier if they consume about the same amount each day rather than allowing their consumption to change each day with their changing income.

Milton Friedman first proposed the hypothesis that individuals consume a constant fraction (k) of their expected income, which Friedman called **permanent income** (Y^P).[2]

Permanent income is the annual average income that people expect to receive over a period of years in the future.

General Form	Numerical Example	
$C = kY^P$	$C = 0.9(\$10,000) = \$9,000$	(15.2)

The marginal propensity to consume out of permanent income (k) depends on individual tastes and on the variability of income (farmers, salespeople, and others with variable income need higher saving to support themselves during bad years). In addition, k may depend on the interest rate. People may be willing to save more (and spend less) when interest rates are higher.[3]

Revising the estimate of permanent income. The permanent-income hypothesis summarized in equation (15.2) does not say that individuals consume exactly the same amount year after year. Every year new events occur that are likely to change individuals' guesses about their permanent income. For instance, an individual might find that in good years income has increased. Gradually the individual will revise his or her estimate of average expected income upward and will increase his or her stable-consumption level.

Friedman's permanent-income hypothesis consists of the assumption in equation (15.2) that individuals consume a constant portion of their permanent income. But this is not enough, because an additional assumption is required to indicate how individuals estimate the size of their permanent income. Friedman proposed that individual estimates of permanent income for this year (Y^P) be revised from last year's estimate (Y^P_{-1}) by some fraction (j) of the amount by which actual income (Y) differs from (Y^P_{-1}):

General Form	Numerical Example	
$Y^P = Y^P_{-1} + j(Y - Y^P_{-1})$	$Y^P = 10,000 + 0.2(15,000 - 10,000)$	(15.3)
	$= 11,000$	

Adaptive expectations. The behavior described in equation (15.3) is sometimes called the "error-learning" or "adaptive" hypothesis of expectation formation. This hypothesis implies that individuals will allow their consumption to respond modestly to changes in actual income because consumption depends on permanent income, and in turn permanent income in equation (15.3) depends only in part on this period's actual income. When we substitute (15.3) into (15.2), we obtain the following relationship between an individual's current consumption (C), this period's actual income (Y), and last period's estimate of permanent income (Y^P_{-1}):

General Form	Numerical Example	
$C = kY^P_{-1} + kj(Y - Y^P_{-1})$	$C = 0.9Y^P_{-1} + 0.18(Y - Y^P_{-1})$	(15.4)

---

[2] Milton Friedman, *A Theory of the Consumption Function* (Princeton, NJ: Princeton University Press, 1957). Milton Friedman's photo appears on p. 554.

[3] Because of the limitations of the alphabet we are once again forced to duplicate the use of letters. The k here is completely unrelated to the k used in Chapters 3 and 4 to represent the multiplier.

Exactly the same hypothesis for the formation of expectations was introduced in the Appendix to Chapter 8 in the discussion of inflation expectations (see equation (2) on p. 274). Equation (15.3) can be rewritten in the form used there.

$$Y^P = jY + (1 - j)Y^P_{-1}$$

This says that permanent income in this period is a weighted average of actual income and last period's permanent income.

Two marginal propensities to consume. Equation (15.4) helps us see that Friedman's theory is based on a distinction between two concepts of the marginal propensity to consume (MPC). The *long-run* MPC is simply the coefficient (k) of permanent income in the original consumption function (15.2), and indeed k is the coefficient of the first term in (15.4). In our numerical example, the long-term MPC (k) is 0.9. The *short-run* MPC is the coefficient of a change in actual income, the coefficient kj (or $0.18 = 0.9$ times 0.2) in the second term in (15.4). When today's actual income (Y) increases, the second term in (15.4) shows that today's consumption goes up by the short-run MPC (kj, or 0.18).

The portion of today's income change that is not expected to be permanent is called **transitory income** in Friedman's theory. Transitory income (Y^t) is simply actual income minus permanent income:

Transitory income is the difference between actual and permanent income and is not expected to recur.

General Form	Numerical Example	
$Y^t = Y - Y^P$	$Y^t = Y - Y^P$	
$\quad = Y - Y^P_{-1} - j(Y - Y^P_{-1})$	$\quad = 0.8(Y - Y^P_{-1})$	(15.5)
$\quad = (1 - j)(Y - Y^P_{-1})$		

Friedman achieves his sharp distinction between the long-run and short-run MPC by assuming that the MPC out of transitory income is zero. Thus his consumption function (15.2) could be rewritten as:

$$C = 0Y^t + kY^P \qquad (15.6)$$

Reconciling the Conflict Between Cross-Section and Time-Series Data

The motivation for Friedman's PIH was the apparent conflict between the cross-section data in Figure 15-2, where high-income people were shown to have higher saving ratios than low-income people, and the long-run near-constancy of the saving ratio shown in Figure 15-3. The PIH contends that the high saving ratios of high-income people are due to their having atypically large, positive, transitory incomes (for example, executives who received large bonuses after a good year; movie stars after the release of unusually popular films; or professional athletes, who have short-lived, high-income careers). Similarly, the PIH contends that low-income people dissave or have low saving ratios (as in Figure 15-2) because they are more likely than the average person to have actual incomes that are temporarily below their permanent incomes. (Examples of people with negative transitory income include farmers whose crops were ruined by drought, floods, or disease; executives who have just been fired; and college students who believe that their incomes will be higher in the future.) Thus, the PIH explains how, even when the longer-run savings

Figure 15-4 The Permanent-Income Hypothesis of Consumption and Saving

The long-run schedule shows that consumption is a fixed fraction of income in the long run, when actual and permanent income are equal. But short-run gains in actual income, as at point *B*, are not fully incorporated into permanent income. Thus consumption increases only a small amount (compare points *B* and *A*), and at *B* most of the short-run increase in income is saved. When the same gain in income is maintained permanently, the short-run schedule shifts upward along the long-run schedule to point *F*.

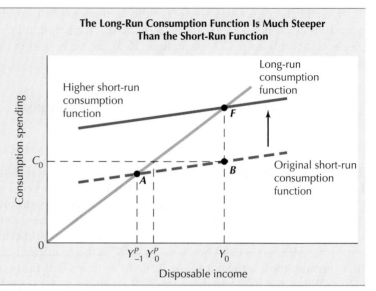

The Long-Run Consumption Function Is Much Steeper Than the Short-Run Function

ratio is constant across individuals and across time, cross-section data will record that high-income people have higher saving ratios.

The two consumption functions illustrated. Figure 15-4 illustrates the distinction between the long-run and short-run consumption functions. The solid orange line running through points *A* and *F* is the long-run consumption function; its slope is the long-run MPC (*k*, or 0.9 in our example). It is called the long-run consumption function because it indicates the level of consumption only when actual income has remained long enough at a particular level for individuals to fully adjust their estimated permanent income to the actual level.

What happens in the short run, when actual income can differ from permanent income? The flatter dashed red schedule running between *A* and *B* is the short-run schedule and plots equation (15.4). When current income (*Y*) is exactly equal to last period's permanent income Y^P_{-1}, the short-run schedule intersects the long-run schedule at point *A*. But during an unusually good year, when an individual's income is at the high level Y_0, the current estimate of permanent income (Y^P) rises above last period's estimate Y^P_{-1} by a fraction (*j*) of the excess of actual income over last period's estimate. And the higher value of Y^P raises consumption by *k* times the increase in permanent income.

Thus consumption at point *B* lies vertically above point *A* by the fraction *kj* (18 percent in the numerical example) times the horizontal distance between Y^P_{-1} and Y_0. With the short-run marginal propensity to consume (*kj*) so far below the long-run propensity (*k*), any short-run increase in income goes disproportionately into saving. If Y_0 comes to be regarded as permanent, the short-run consumption function will go through *F*.

To summarize, estimates of permanent income are continually raised as actual income outstrips previous levels, causing the relationship between consumption and income to follow the long-run schedule, as marked by the arrow in Figure 15-4. Thus in the long run the saving ratio is roughly constant. But in the short run a temporary increase in income raises the saving ratio and a temporary decrease in income reduces the saving ratio, because permanent income does not adjust completely to changes in actual income.

SELF-TEST

Determine whether actual income is above or below permanent income in each of the following situations and how consumption and saving compare to the values predicted by Friedman's theory if the income changes were permanent:

1. A stockbroker enjoying the best year of his or her career.
2. A North Dakota wheat farmer suffering from a severe drought.
3. The U.S. economy in a recession.
4. The U.S. economy in a period of unusually high real GDP, such as 1999–2000.

15-5 Forward-Looking Behavior: The Life-Cycle Hypothesis

About the same time that Friedman wrote his book on the permanent-income hypothesis, Franco Modigliani of MIT and collaborators devised a somewhat different way of reconciling the positive relation between the saving ratio and income observed in cross-section data and the constancy of the saving ratio observed over long periods in the historical time-series data.[4] Modigliani and Friedman both began with the perspective that individuals prefer to maintain a stable consumption pattern rather than allow consumption to rise or fall with every transitory oscillation of their income. But Modigliani carried the stable-consumption argument further than Friedman and suggested that people *would try to stabilize their consumption over their entire lifetimes.*

Because of its emphasis on the lifetime horizon of consumers, the Modigliani theory is called the life-cycle hypothesis (LCH). Since it stresses the way consumers smooth consumption over their lifetimes and save in preparation for their retirement years, the LCH falls into the category of theories based on *forward-looking expectations.* It shares with Friedman's theory the ability to reconcile a low short-run MPC with a high and stable long-run MPC. But the LCH adds a "lifetime budget constraint" to Friedman's theory, which is the condition that the consumption of households over their lifetimes equals their income plus their holdings of assets coming from sources other than work (for example, gifts from parents). This feature of the LCH provides a rigorous connection between consumption expenditures and the value of the assets held by

Franco Modigliani (1918–2003)

The 1985 Nobel Prize winner is best known for the life-cycle model of consumption behavior and for his articulate advocacy of policy activism.

---

[4] Franco Modigliani and R. E. Brumberg, "Utility Analysis and the Consumption Function," in K. K. Kurihara, ed., *Post-Keynesian Economics* (New Brunswick, NJ: Rutgers University Press, 1954). Also A. Ando and F. Modigliani, "The 'Life Cycle' Hypothesis of Saving: Aggregate Implications and Tests," *American Economic Review*, vol. 53 (March 1963), pp. 55–84.

consumers. As a result, the LCH *predicts that a stock market crash, like the one in 2000–02, will reduce consumption expenditures and a stock market boom, like that of the 1990s, will raise consumption expenditures.*

Lifetime Asset Holding: Modigliani's Asset Pyramid Illustrated

We now examine Figure 15-5, which shows how a simple version of Modigliani's theory predicts how income, consumption, saving, and asset accumulation will behave over the lifetime of the typical consumer. The horizontal axis shows various ages, with the age at retirement marked by R and the age at death marked by L. An individual is assumed to maintain a constant level of consumption (C_0) throughout life. Income, however, is earned only during the R working years. If there are no assets initially, as shown by the zero level of initial assets (A_0) in the bottom frame, then the only way individuals can manage to consume without any income during their retirement is to save during their working years. The amount saved, income minus consumption, is shown by the blue area during the period up to time R, and then the dissaving that occurs when consumption exceeds income during retirement is shown by the red area from time R through time L. In the bottom frame, the accumulation of assets occurs steadily during the working years through time R, when assets reach their maximum level A_R. Assets decline thereafter and are zero at time L.

Figure 15-5 The Behavior of Consumption, Saving, and Assets under the Life-Cycle Hypothesis

Under the life-cycle hypothesis particular attention is paid to the relation between the length of the lifetime (L) and an individual's age at retirement (R). The length of the retirement period is $L - R$. In the upper frame, a constant amount (C_0) is consumed every year of one's life, as indicated by the red line. A constant amount of income Y_0 is earned each year until retirement. During the working years until R, income exceeds consumption, as shown by the saving that occurs in the blue area. Then consumption exceeds the zero income during retirement and is financed by dissaving, as shown by the red area. In the bottom frame, the green line shows the growth of assets from the initial level (A_0) to the maximum level at retirement (A_R), followed by a decline in assets back to zero at death.

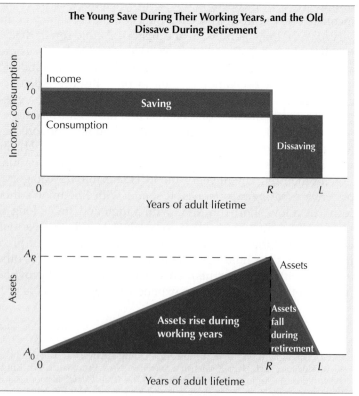

The Young Save During Their Working Years, and the Old Dissave During Retirement

No initial assets. How are consumption and income related when there are no initial assets? Total lifetime consumption of C_0 per year for L years is constrained to equal total income Y_0 per year for R years:

$$C_0 L = Y_0 R \quad \text{or} \quad C_0 = \left(\frac{R}{L}\right) Y_0 \tag{15.7}$$

As Figure 15-5 is drawn, R is four-fifths of L, so consumption per year is limited to four-fifths of Y_0.[5]

The simple version of the life-cycle hypothesis can explain the positive association of saving and income, since the upward trend in per capita, natural real GDP raises both the saving and income of those of working age relative to those who are retired. The long-run constancy of the saving ratio can be explained by the fact that if the population in each historical era is divided into the same proportions of working and retired people, and each age group has the same saving behavior in generation after generation, then the long-run saving ratio will be constant.

The life-cycle hypothesis shares with Friedman's permanent-income hypothesis the implication that the saving ratio should rise in economic boom years and fall in recession years. A temporary increase in income today will be consumed over one's entire lifetime. For instance, imagine a person who believes he has 40 years left to live and receives an unexpected increase in income this year of $4,000 that he does not expect to receive again. His total lifetime consumption goes up by the $4,000 and his actual consumption this year goes up by only 1/40 of that amount, a mere $100. In each succeeding year, an additional $100 would be spent, for a total of $4,000 over the remaining 40 years of life.

Thus, in an economic boom widely expected to be temporary, an unexpected bonus of $4,000 would lead to only $100 extra of current consumption and $3,900 extra of saving. The short-run propensity to consume would be just 0.025, or 100/4,000. By contrast, if the $4,000 income increase is expected to be maintained for each of the next 40 years, then $4,000 extra can be consumed this year and again in each of the next 39 years and the saving ratio will not rise.

The role of assets. The Modigliani theory provides an important role for assets as a determinant of consumption behavior. Let us assume that initially a person has an endowment of assets of A_1, but plans to use these assets to raise consumption through his or her lifetime rather than to leave the assets to heirs.

---

[5] There are several simplifications in Figure 15-5 and equation (15.7) involving the treatment of interest income. Assuming that interest is earned on asset holdings at the nominal interest rate i, then total income is equal to wage income in real terms (W/P) plus real interest income (rA), where r is the real interest rate. Then (15.7) becomes

$$C_0 L = (W/P)_0 R + \sum_{t=0}^{L} rA_t$$

Thus total income increases gradually through time R and then decreases to zero, but is nevertheless positive during the retirement period. To reflect the fact that consumption depends on total income, including both wage income and earnings from the holding of assets, the symbol Y (for total real income) rather than W/P is used in (15.7) in the text. The official definition of income overstates Y, since it includes the entire income from assets, including that portion of the nominal return $(i - r)$ needed to maintain intact the real value of assets.

Figure 15-6 Consumption, Saving, and Assets under the Life-Cycle Hypothesis When There Is an Initial Stock of Assets

This diagram is identical to Figure 15-5, but here there is an initial stock of assets, A_1, in contrast to the initial stock of zero in the previous diagram. If we continue to assume that dissaving during retirement runs the stock of assets down to zero, then the existence of A_1 makes more total consumption possible with a smaller amount of saving. This is shown by an upward shift from the previous level of consumption (C_0) to a new higher level (C_1). The blue saving area is now smaller, as is the blue area in the bottom frame, which shows the increase in assets due to saving.

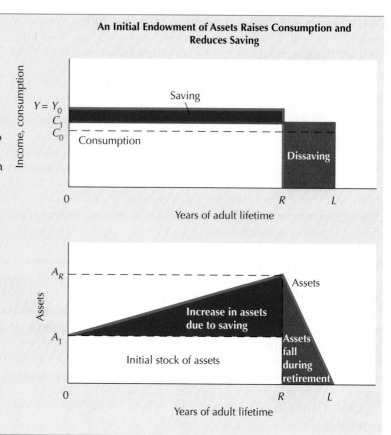

An Initial Endowment of Assets Raises Consumption and Reduces Saving

Then, as shown in Figure 15-6, consumption can be higher for a given level of income (Y_0), and saving can be lower, since the initial asset endowment provides more spending power. Now total lifetime consumption equals total lifetime income from work plus the available assets:

$$C_1 L = A_1 + Y_0 R$$

or

$$C_1 = \frac{A_1}{L} + \frac{R}{L} Y_0 \tag{15.8}$$

The right-hand expression shows that consumption per year (C_1) depends not just on income (Y_0); it also depends on the ratio of available assets per year of life.

Figure 15-6 is oversimplified because it assumes that the initial endowment of assets is received at the beginning of the working life. In reality, however, increases in the value of assets occur throughout one's life, so one would expect the response of annual consumption to a change in asset value to be larger than is assumed in equation (15.8). Modigliani's empirical research has estimated that a $1 increase in real asset values raised annual real consumption by about $0.06, which would indicate that people use a 15-year horizon over which to spend an increase in real assets.

In Chapter 7 we learned that the economy's self-correcting forces are enhanced when real consumption spending depends on real assets or real wealth.

If a drop in spending cuts the price level, the level of real wealth is raised, which helps arrest the decline in spending.[6] In the other direction, if an increase in spending raises the price level, the level of real wealth declines, which helps dampen the original stimulus to spending. We return to the relationship between real wealth and consumption behavior in Section 15-8.

Thus, ironically, Modigliani's life-cycle hypothesis supports the optimism of rules advocates regarding the stability of the private economy, even though Modigliani was a prominent critic of policy rules. Private spending is stabilized because transitory increases in disposable income, those that are not expected to last very long, have only a modest influence on current consumption. In addition, the real-asset effect stabilizes the economy because higher prices cut the real value of assets and dampen spending. Overall, life-cycle considerations reduce the current marginal propensity to consume, cut the multiplier, and insulate the economy from unexpected changes in investment, net exports, or other types of spending.

 SELF-TEST

Assume that an adult is making a consumption plan and anticipates a life of 40 more years, 30 of which will be spent in work and 10 in retirement.

1. If income during the working years is $50,000, and the endowment of initial assets is zero, what will annual consumption expenditures be during the working years? During the retirement years?

2. What will be the average propensity to consume (C/Y) during the working years?

3. Now, assume instead that initial assets are $200,000. What will annual consumption expenditures be during the working years? During the retirement years?

4. What will be the average propensity to consume during the working years?

15-6   Rational Expectations and Other Amendments to the Simple Forward-Looking Theories

In recent years consumption behavior has been one of the most active areas of research in macroeconomics. Much attention has been directed toward the implications of households using more sophisticated methods of forming their expectations about their future incomes than the simple adaptive expectations method shown in equation (15.3). The contrast between the predictions of the resulting theory and the actual cyclical behavior of consumption has highlighted the role of several additional factors that are not part of the pure PIH or LCH theories: liquidity constraints, consumer durables, bequests, and uncertainty.

Rational Expectations

Recall from equation (15.3) that in its original Friedman formulation, the PIH is combined with the adaptive or error-learning method of calculating permanent

---

[6] Review the Pigou, or real balance, effect discussed in Section 7-9 on pp. 218–19.

income. Thus when actual income increases, people only *gradually* revise upward their estimate of permanent income. Though it provides a simple and convenient approximation to how households might form their expectations about their future incomes, the adaptive expectations hypothesis may be too simple. Among its drawbacks are that it mechanically extrapolates the past and that it does not explicitly allow for the effects of variables other than income on expectations of future income.

The **rational expectations** hypothesis suggests that people use a more sophisticated method of forming their expectations about their future incomes. Rational expectations assume that expectations of future events are formed using *all* the information available. Thus rational expectations imply that all the information that can be gleaned from the past and even from credible announcements about the future, like tax cuts that have been enacted but that have not yet taken effect, will be used to form estimates of permanent income. As a result, only *new* information will change estimated permanent incomes, which implies that consumption will change only if *unanticipated* events occur. Previously expected events provide no news and therefore no revisions to permanent income and no change in consumption.

Rational expectations are forecasts of future economic magnitudes based on information currently available about the structure and past performance of the economy and future government policies.

Is consumption too volatile or too smooth?   A controversy has developed over the empirical implications of the rational expectations version of the PIH. Everything depends on how consumers view the nature of new information about income. If a change in current income provides no information about income in the future, then estimates of permanent income change very little, and the marginal propensity to consume out of this change in current income should be close to zero.[7] However, our case study (Section 15-2) showed that consumption displayed visible responses to the decline of income in the 1974–75, 1980–82, and 1990–91 recessions. This points toward the conclusion that actual consumption responds too strongly to changes in actual income, that is, it is *excessively volatile* relative to the prediction of the theory.[8]

However, another possibility is that changes in current income provide a good prediction of changes in future income. For instance, a person who loses a high-paying job may have very good reason to predict that future income will be lower, perhaps for many years. In the extreme case, if it were true that estimates of permanent income always responded by one dollar to any change in current income of one dollar (that is, $j = 1$ in equations (15.3) and (15.4)), then the marginal propensity to consume out of current income would be k (simply because the marginal propensity to consume out of permanent income is k). But the data show clearly that consumption is smoother than current income.

---

[7] In this case it can be shown in a specific mathematical model that the MPC would be $r/(1 + r)$, where r is the real rate of interest. Thus, depending on the asset used to measure r, the MPC would be between zero and 0.07. This result is developed in the excellent but mathematically advanced survey by Andrew B. Abel, "Consumption and Investment," in B. M. Friedman and F. Hahn, eds., *Handbook of Monetary Economics* (Amsterdam: Elsevier Science Publishers, 1990), pp. 725–78.

[8] The rational expectations approach to the study of consumption behavior was introduced in Robert E. Hall, "Stochastic Implications of the Life Cycle-Permanent Income Hypothesis: Theory and Evidence," *Journal of Political Economy*, vol. 86 (December 1978), pp. 971–87. The excess volatility argument is usually credited to Marjorie Flavin, "The Adjustment of Consumption to Changing Expectations about Future Income," *Journal of Political Economy*, vol. 89 (October 1981), pp. 974–1009. A collection of Hall's essays on consumption is Robert E. Hall, *The Rational Consumer* (MIT Press, 1990).

Did Households Spend or Save the 2001 Tax Rebate?

After a long period of disuse, the role of fiscal policy for stabilization purposes was revived on June 7, 2001, when President Bush signed the Economic Growth and Tax Relief Reconciliation Act of 2001. Under the bill, taxpayers were entitled to receive an immediate check in the mail as a credit on their 2001 taxes, up to $300 for single taxpayers and up to $600 for married couples. The checks themselves were mailed during the period between late July and late September. These payments were commonly referred to as "tax rebates."

The theories of consumer behavior examined in this chapter predict that households will spend more of a change in disposable income if it is expected in advance rather than unexpected, and if it is permanent rather than temporary. Since the tax rebate was a first installment on tax reductions that had been legislated to be in effect for at least ten years, and since they were well publicized in advance, they can be considered both "expected" and "permanent." Thus economic theory would have predicted that most of the rebates would have been spent, that is, that the marginal propensity to spend would have been almost unity.

To assess this prediction, Matthew Shapiro and Joel Slemrod of the University of Michigan conducted a survey to determine how the receipt of the rebate checks would change behavior.[a] Much to their surprise, they found that only 22 percent of those receiving the rebate reported that it would mainly lead them to increase spending. Of those who did not plan to spend the rebates, 59 percent said they would repay debt and 41 percent said they would save the rebate. The implication of this low propensity to spend the rebate is that this type of fiscal policy intervention has a much lower multiplier effect on aggregate demand in relation to its budgetary cost to the government.

How do the authors explain the low spending response? Most important, survey respondents did not believe that the legislated tax cuts would occur. The authors also found that it would not have helped to target

the tax rebate entirely at low-income households, since these households were no more likely to spend the rebates than high-income households. Skeptics might consider the authors' study flawed by its timing in the middle of the recession of 2001, for perhaps households were unusually likely to save the rebates (or pay off debts) because they feared they might lose their jobs in the recession. Perhaps other households were feeling financial pain from the decline in the stock market over the previous year and were anxious to rebuild their assets. However, these factors just amplify the bad news for fiscal policymakers that is implied by the survey, for if you choose not to introduce a stabilizing tax cut during a recession, at what other time would you want to implement it?

---

[a] Matthew D. Shapiro and Joel Slemrod, "Consumer Response to Tax Rebates," *American Economic Review*, vol. 93 (March 2003), pp. 381–96.

So by this contrasting approach, actual consumption is *too smooth* relative to the prediction of the theory.[9]

Thus far the debate over the cyclical behavior of consumption has not been settled. However, the initial conclusion that consumption was too volatile led to the realization that the simple versions of the PIH and LCH we have just

---

[9] See Angus Deaton, "Life-Cycle Models of Consumption: Is the Evidence Consistent with the Theory?" in T. F. Bewley, ed., *Advances in Econometrics Fifth World Congress* (New York: Cambridge University Press, 1987), pp. 121–48.

reviewed, as well as the rational expectations updating of these theories, omit several important aspects of consumption behavior. Until these issues are adequately integrated into the theory, it is unlikely that the question of whether consumption is too volatile or too smooth will be resolved.

Consumer Durables

Both the permanent-income hypothesis and the life-cycle hypothesis are based on the desirability of maintaining a roughly constant level of enjoyment over time from consumption goods and services. If there is an increase in permanent income, people will not only want to increase their expenditures on services and nondurable goods, but will also want to increase their enjoyment of the services of durable goods. For consumer services and nondurable goods, such as haircuts and doughnuts, the enjoyment and the consumer spending occur at about the same time. Consumer durable goods are different. A television set is purchased at a single instant in time but produces enjoyment for many years thereafter. Thus the PIH and LCH suggest that it is not purchases of consumer durable goods that are kept equal to a fixed fraction of permanent income, but rather the flow of services (enjoyment) received from consumer durables. Consumers can keep the service flow at the same fixed fraction of permanent income by keeping the *stock* of consumer durable goods at the same fixed fraction of permanent income.

The essence of a durable good is that it provides service for many periods. New cars, for example, have service lives of ten years or more. Like any long-term asset, a durable good costs far more to purchase than the service it provides each period. A new car that sells for $25,000, for example, may provide only $2,500 worth of service each year. Thus, when a household decides that its higher permanent income warrants its annually consuming another $2,500 of car services, expenditure initially rises by $25,000. As a result, expenditures for durables may surge temporarily as consumers raise their stocks of durables in proportion to the increase in their permanent incomes.

As a result of the upsurge in purchases of consumer durables, total consumption expenditures may *rise* as a fraction of income when actual income rises, even though the PIH and LCH predict that consumption should *fall* as a fraction of income when actual income rises. Both the PIH and LCH predict that the saving ratio *falls* with higher income when consumer durables are counted as consumption expenditure but *rises* with higher income when consumer durables are counted as saving. Realization of the procyclical nature of consumer durable expenditures limits research on the validity of the PIH and LCH to consumer expenditures *excluding* durables—that is, including just services (haircuts) and nondurables (doughnuts).

Behavior of consumer durable expenditures in recessions. Both the PIH and LCH predict that in a recession, when income exhibits a transitory decline, households should maintain their consumption expenditures *by cutting back on the ratio of saving to disposable income* (S/Y^D). Data for postwar recessions confirm that the saving ratio declined slightly between the peak quarter and the trough quarters in nine recessions between 1953–54 and 2001. This tendency of the saving rate to decline is augmented considerably when we take account of the procyclical nature of expenditures on consumer durables. In the following table, the household saving rate, the ratio of consumer durables expenditure to disposable income, and the ratio of the sum of saving and consumer durables expenditure to disposable income $[(S + C^D)/Y^D]$ all decline in recessions.

Averages for Nine Recessions, 1953–54 to 2001, in percent			
Ratio to disposable income	Peak	Trough	Peak to trough change
Personal saving	8.2	7.8	−0.4
Consumer durable expenditures	11.8	10.9	−0.9
Sum of personal saving and consumer durable expenditures	20.0	18.7	−1.3

Liquidity Constraints

The simple version of the LCH in Figure 15-5 assumes that consumption is constant over the lifetime and that labor income is constant until the date of retirement. Actually, however, labor income tends to rise with age, peaking a bit after age 50. To achieve a constant level of consumption throughout their lifetimes, young people would need to borrow during their low-income years and repay the loans later in high-income years. But banks generally will not allow young people to borrow all they would like, which implies that the consumption expenditures of young people are subject to a **liquidity constraint.** A liquidity constraint may afflict people of any age who are suffering from a transitory loss of income; for instance, banks may be unwilling to lend to a farmer who is close to bankruptcy after a year of poor growing weather, even though the weather can be expected to be better in the future.

A **liquidity constraint** prevents households from borrowing as much as they wish, even though there is sufficient expected future income to repay the loans.

People whose consumption can go no higher than their *current income* because of the unavailability of loans will have a much higher marginal propensity to consume in response to temporary changes in income than is predicted by the PIH or LCH theories. Economists have attempted to measure the importance of this so-called excess sensitivity of consumption to current changes in income. The consensus is that households whose consumption is subject to liquidity constraints account for about 15 percent of aggregate income. These households have MPCs out of transitory income of about 1. The remaining unconstrained households behave roughly as predicted by the LCH: They have negligible MPCs out of transitory income.[10] Thus liquidity constraints do not seem to be prevalent enough to seriously weaken the implication of the LCH (and PIH) that the short-run MPC will be much lower than the long-run MPC.

15-7 Bequests and Uncertainty

In both of our diagrams of the LCH (Figures 15-5 and 15-6), individuals are assumed *to consume all of their lifetime savings during retirement.* Their assets dwindle to zero on the date of death, and nothing is left in the form of bequests to heirs. In fact, however, people do leave bequests. It has been claimed that

---

[10] Estimates that the share of aggregate income accruing to liquidity-constrained households has been as high as 50 percent can be found in John Y. Campbell and N. Gregory Mankiw, "Consumption, Income, and Interest Rates: Reinterpreting the Time Series Evidence," *NBER Macroeconomics Annual 1989* (Cambridge, MA: The MIT Press), pp. 185–216.

International Perspective

Why Do Some Countries Save So Much?

While the world saving rate has remained relatively stable over the past few decades, saving rates differ by large amounts across countries and have fluctuated greatly within many countries. In general, saving rates in industrialized countries have been both lower and more stable than they have been in developing countries. National saving rates for industrialized countries have averaged about 20 percent since 1970, but they have averaged more than 25 percent in developing countries. In individual industrial countries, the national saving rate has typically fluctuated within a 10 percentage point range.

The Life-Cycle Model and Dependency Ratios

We have learned that consumption, and thus saving, responds to a number of factors: the stage of the life cycle, interest rates, wealth, and expectations about future income. The life-cycle model suggests that saving rates are lower for the young, who have recently embarked on their working lives, and for the retired, who have left the labor force. Workers, especially those near their peak earnings years, have considerably higher saving rates. That means that countries with higher dependency ratios, that is, with larger fractions of the population not working, would save less.

Over the next few decades, dependency ratios are expected to rise in developed countries (especially Japan), where the number of retired people will increase markedly as life expectancy continues to rise and the huge baby-boom generation retires. By contrast, dependency ratios are expected to fall in developing countries, which now have populations with low average ages. Over the next few decades, large numbers of young people in developing countries will move from being students to being workers, but relatively few people in those countries will attain retirement age.

Saving and Economic Growth

In Chapter 10 we learned that an increase in the private saving rate can increase the rate of economic growth temporarily. But much of the causality runs in the opposite direction, from growth to saving rather than from saving to growth. Sustained increases in growth are associated with permanent increases in the rate of saving; in fact, an increase in the growth rate of 1 percent per annum can raise the private saving rate by as much as 1 percent.

Why does a higher growth rate tend to raise the saving rate? Look back at the top frame of Figure 15-5 on p. 498, which shows the lifetime pattern for a household that saves during the working years and spends all that saving during retirement. If a country has no economic growth, then there is no difference between the income of working people, say aged 40 today, and the income that today's 70-year-old retired people earned 30 years ago when they were aged 40. But if a country is growing rapidly, as in the case of Korea, then today's 40-year-old workers have much higher incomes than today's retired people had 30 years ago, and so the saving by people of working age is much greater than the dissaving of today's retired people, who were saving out of much smaller incomes 30 years ago.

Government Deficits and Private Saving

Do increased government deficits lead to increased private saving? If the Barro-Ricardo equivalence theorem holds (see pp. 403–04), then an increase in the government deficit would generate an equal increase in private saving, which would offset the expected future tax burden associated with the increased deficit. The very low level of U.S. private saving in 2003–07 accompanying large government deficits provides evidence that deficits do not boost private saving.

Interest Rates and Consumer Credit

Higher interest rates may either raise saving by providing people with a higher income level (some of which will be saved) or may lower saving by making less saving necessary to achieve a target level of saving for purposes such as retirement. There is no consensus in the economic literature on which effect is stronger. In the United States, the saving rate was lower in the 1990s than in the 1980s, which may have been partly due to a decline in the real interest rate over that period. However, as we shall see later in the chapter, the biggest reason for the decline in the U.S. saving rate was the large capital gains earned by American households on their holdings of equities on the stock market and on their ownership stake in their homes.

Forward-looking consumers will raise their current spending, and thus reduce their saving out of current income, in response to an increase in their expected future incomes. One reason why consumers might raise their spending less than their permanent or life-cycle incomes justify, and thus may raise their saving by more, is the inability to borrow on the basis of expected future incomes. Today's college students are experts on this phenomenon. An economics major may expect a relatively high income after graduation, but few financial institutions will lend today's student more than just a small fraction of that expected future income. In the same way, the household saving rate will tend to be low in countries like the United States where consumer credit is relatively easy to obtain and high in countries like Italy where consumer credit is harder to obtain.

Cross-Country Differences in Saving

The bar chart displays the 2007 household saving rate for seven countries, ranging from 12.5 percent for France down to −1.7 percent for the United States. How can these differences be explained? In this chapter we explore several explanations of differences across nations in their household saving rates. The LCH suggests that countries with faster economic growth will save more, because they have more households in the high-saving working age groups and fewer retirees. Yet in the bar chart, Korea has a relatively low household saving rate despite achieving rapid economic growth.

The most notable aspect of the bar chart is the low saving rates of the United States, Canada, and Australia. The experience of these three countries supports the view that capital gains on the stock market and housing raise consumption and depress saving. These three nations have enjoyed substantial gains in stock market and housing wealth over the past decade, whereas in high-saving nations such as Italy and France, there has been much less accumulation of household wealth in the form of capital gains on stocks and housing equity, so Italian and French households need to save more by abstaining from consumption. We return subsequently in this chapter to discussing alternative measures of U.S. household saving that take account of wealth accumulation.

The relatively low saving rate of Japan, only 2.9 percent, is surprising in light of Japan's history as a high-saving country. Part of the decline in saving directly results from Japan's economic slump since the early 1990s (see pp. 118–19). As suggested by the permanent-income hypothesis, households reduce their saving in response to higher unemployment or lower incomes that they believe to be temporary. Young Japanese, unable to afford their own housing, are returning to live with their parents and are able to consume all of their income without the need to save up for their own houses. Formerly many Japanese received semiannual bonuses, which they put into savings accounts, but economic hard times have caused firms to cut these bonuses drastically. Finally, interest rates on saving accounts in Japan are in many cases below 1 percent, providing no incentive to save.

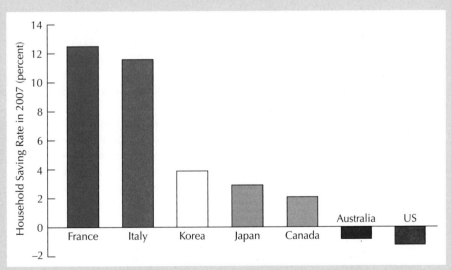

Source: OECD Economic Outlook 81, June 2007, Annex Table 23. Rates are predicted by OECD and may differ from actual outcomes.

about 80 percent of asset accumulation by U.S. households is transmitted to heirs rather than used for consumption during retirement.[11] This evidence seems to deny that the appropriate horizon to describe consumer behavior is the lifetime.

The Role of Bequests

As we learned in Section 12-8 on pp. 403–04, the existence of bequests has been interpreted as support for a striking theory of fiscal policy, often called the Barro-Ricardo equivalence theorem. People are expected to leave bequests because they care about their children. Any event that leaves their children worse off will lead members of the present generation to increase saving in order to leave a larger bequest to their children. A prime example of such an event would be a deficit-financed tax cut that raises the taxes that must be paid by future generations (to pay the interest and principal on the bonds issued to finance the debt). According to the Barro-Ricardo theorem, such a tax cut would not stimulate consumption because people would save all of the increase in their after-tax income in order to raise their bequests.

In Chapter 12 and in the International Perspective box, we reviewed some of the criticisms of the Barro-Ricardo theorem. Most important, the U.S. household saving rate did not increase at all following the Reagan tax cuts of the 1980s or the Bush tax cuts of 2001–03, as the theorem would have predicted. In fact, as we shall see in Figure 15-7 on p. 511, the saving rate in 2006–07 fell to its lowest level since the Great Depression. Thus it seems likely that the mere existence of bequests does not validate the kind of behavior postulated by the theorem—specifically the refusal of current households to raise their consumption in response to a tax cut.

Motives for Bequests

If parents do not adjust their bequests for every current event that changes their heirs' future tax liabilities, why does a large fraction of personal saving eventually flow to children in the form of bequests? Many think that the central issue is the uncertainty of the age of death. Benjamin Franklin's observation that "in this world nothing can be said to be certain, except death and taxes" omits the fact that the *timing* of death is quite uncertain. Contrary to the assumption of Figures 15-5 and 15-6, households cannot know the lengths of their lifetimes.

By this interpretation, *much saving is life cycle in nature, but only for a part of the lifetime and for medical care that does not occur for everyone.* Many people die before expensive nursing care treatment becomes necessary and thus have substantial wealth "left over" that goes as bequests to the children. By this interpretation, bequests are primarily involuntary and are made because par-

---

[11] Laurence J. Kotlikoff and Lawrence H. Summers, "The Role of Intergenerational Transfers in Aggregate Capital Accumulation," *Journal of Political Economy*, vol. 89 (August 1981), pp. 706–32. This finding is very controversial. A lengthy scholarly debate on the Kotlikoff-Summers findings is contained in Franco Modigliani, "The Role of Intergenerational Transfers and Life Cycle Saving in the Accumulation of Wealth," and Laurence J. Kotlikoff, "Intergenerational Transfers and Savings," both in *Journal of Economic Perspectives*, vol. 2 (Spring 1988), pp. 15–40 and 41–58, respectively.

ents do not want to lose control of their assets and their living conditions prior to death.

Implications for the LCH theory.   The interpretation of bequests as primarily involuntary leaves the main predictions of the LCH intact. The only adjustment to the LCH is that the relevant horizon for most households extends beyond the actual age of death (as assumed in Figures 15-5 and 15-6) to the *oldest conceivable age of death*. For instance, a 25-year-old may have a future life expectancy of 50 years, with 75 the most probable age of death, but may base consumption and saving decisions on the outside chance of living until age 90.

This amended version of the LCH would operate just like the version depicted in Figure 15-6, except the extended lifetime (L^*, say 90) replaces the most probable lifetime (L, say 75). Use of L^* instead of the lower L would imply an even lower MPC for temporary changes in income, and would imply that increases in wealth from the stock market would be consumed over the extended period until L^*. If parents are unwilling to move out of their homes (and are also unwilling to sell their homes to their children and pay them rent), then the gains parents make from higher housing prices may not be consumed over the lifetime but may be largely ignored and lead to a larger bequest.

Why Retirees Cut Their Consumption So Much

Looking back at Figure 15-5 on p. 498, the LCH predicts that consumption is maintained at a fixed level throughout a person's working life and retirement years. But a growing body of evidence suggests that retirees consume much less than working people who are otherwise the same in terms of income and family characteristics.

Why do people cut their consumption after they retire? First, many people react to retirement by moving, because they are no longer tied to the location of their job, and they often move into smaller dwellings. Second, many retirees have paid off the mortgages on their homes, even if they do not move. Third, retirees can eliminate consumption expenses previously required by work, including job-related clothing, automobile and fuel expenses required by commuting, and business-related meals eaten outside the home. Fourth—perhaps a minor factor—retirees have more leisure time and can spend more time searching for bargains, thus reducing the cost of everyday household necessities.[12]

Does the decline in consumption after retirement, in contrast to the steady retirement depicted in Figure 15-5, invalidate the LCH? Not at all, because all of the reasons for lower consumption after retirement are anticipated by households long in advance of retirement. All the predictions of the LCH, including the effect of higher stock market or housing wealth in raising consumption and reducing saving, and the lack of response of consumption by working-age households to temporary changes of income, are still valid for households that plan their retirement consumption in advance, no matter whether that consumption is planned to equal working-age consumption or whether it is planned in advance to be lower.

---

[12] Two papers provide an illuminating analysis of the drop in consumption after retirement. See Michael Hurd and Susann Rohwedder, "Some Answers to the Retirement-Consumption Puzzle," NBER working paper 12057, February 2006 and John Ameriks, Andrew Caplin, and John Leahy, "Retirement Consumption: Insights from a Survey," NBER working paper 8735, January 2002.

SELF-TEST

Imagine that, in order to reduce the federal budget deficit, the government institutes a $1,000 increase in the yearly personal income tax paid by every household. The tax increase is announced to be permanent. What would the following theories predict to be the effects on consumption?

1. Permanent-income hypothesis

2. Life-cycle hypothesis with certain lifetime

3. Life-cycle hypothesis that explains bequests as resulting from uncertain lifetimes

4. Barro-Ricardo equivalence theory

 Case Study

Did Soaring Household Assets Cause the Collapse in the Household Saving Rate?

Early in this book (Figure 3-3 on p. 65) we saw that since the late 1990s, household saving as a percentage of disposable income in the United States has been at its lowest level since the Great Depression of the 1930s. Figure 15-7 plots as a blue line the annual household saving rate since 1970. The rate was above 10 percent as recently as 1984 and was almost 8 percent in 1992, but since then has declined steadily to a record low rate of below 1.0 percent in 2007.

What do the theories of this chapter predict as possible causes of a low or negative saving rate? The prediction of the Friedman permanent-income hypothesis goes in the opposite direction of the late 1990s' outcome, that unusually rapid income growth should cause the saving rate to be well above normal, not below normal. The Modigliani life-cycle hypothesis is more successful in predicting a decline in the household saving rate in the late 1990s. As we learned on pp. 499–501, the Modigliani theory makes consumption depend not only on lifetime income but also on real assets. The extraordinary boom in the stock market that occurred in the late 1990s created huge gains in real household wealth and substantially boosted consumption relative to income, thus (by definition) depressing the percentage of disposable income saved by households.

The Household Wealth Explosion

The most relevant measure of wealth for explaining household consumption and saving behavior is a series on household net worth, compiled by government statisticians at the Fed.[13] Figure 15-7 shows the ratio of net worth to disposable income as the green line that is compared to the household saving rate shown as the blue line. There is a clear negative correlation between the two lines, with low wealth and a high saving rate between 1974 and 1985, followed by an initial upward jump in wealth and decline in the saving rate between 1985 and 1989, and then a second larger jump in wealth and decline in the saving rate between 1995 and 2000.

---

[13] The data can also be found at www.econstats.com/FOF/foftata.htm. The data displayed in Figures 15-7 and 15-8 are also found in table B.100 at this Web site. The data include not just households but also nonprofit institutions such as hospitals and universities.

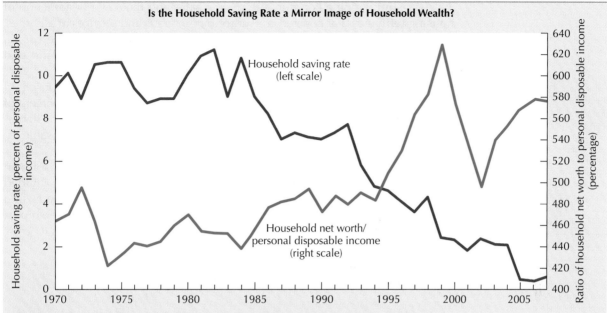

Figure 15-7 **The Household Saving Rate and the Ratio of Household Net Worth to Personal Disposable Income, 1970–2007**

Sources: Federal Reserve Board *Flow of Funds Accounts* and Bureau of Economic Analysis *NIPA Tables*. Details in Appendix C-4.

What triggered the two big jumps in household net worth? Clearly the cause was the behavior of the stock market, which enjoyed a long boom over almost twenty years starting in August 1982, at the depths of the 1981–82 period of high unemployment, high inflation, and very high interest rates, and ending in mid-2000. The S&P 500 index of stock prices more than doubled from 160 to 335 between 1984 and 1989, and then it tripled from 460 in 1994 to 1,427 in 2000.[14] As of November 2007, the S&P 500 index was at 1,450, little different from its value seven years earlier.

Up to 2000, the close negative relationship between household net worth and the household saving rate, as shown in Figure 15-7, supports the Modigliani LCH reviewed in Section 15-5. Households with a lifetime perspective react to capital gains on the stock market by consuming some of these gains and thus reducing their saving. However, after 2000 the relationship appears to break down. Stock prices plummeted from 2000 to 2002, accounting for the sharp drop in household wealth during those years. Then from 2003 to 2007 household wealth recovered. We would have expected the saving rate to rise appreciably in response to the decline in household wealth in 2000–02 and then fall again in response to the subsequent increase in wealth, but this did not happen. Why?

Capital Gains on Houses and Low Interest Rates Keep the Saving Rate Low

There are two answers to the failure of the saving rate to revive during 2000–02. First, as we learned in the box on pp. 104–05 and in Section 14-7 on pp. 469–71, the Fed pushed interest rates down rapidly to very low levels in

---

[14] S&P index values are averages of daily closing prices for each year.

2002–03, stimulating a boom in automobile sales and the new phenomenon of housing refinance that boosted consumption on goods and services of all types. A second factor driving consumption and reducing saving were the capital gains that people made on their houses, boosting their housing wealth and partly offsetting their stock market losses.

Household net worth as shown in Figure 15-7 consists of total household assets minus total household liabilities. In 2006, total assets were 719 percent of disposable income and total liabilities were 142 percent. Subtracting the liabilities from the assets yields the 577 percent ratio of net wealth to disposable income shown in Figure 15-7.

In order to understand what happened after the year 2000, we display in Figure 15-8 the ratio of total household assets to disposable income, divided between financial assets (including volatile stocks and stock mutual funds) and "tangible assets" consisting mainly of the value of household ownership of houses and condominiums. The red area representing tangible assets grew

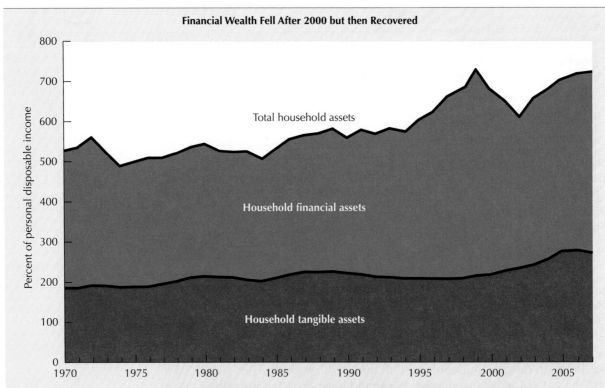

Figure 15-8 Components of Household Assets as a Ratio to Personal Disposable Income, 1970–2006, in Percent

The red section shows the ratio of household tangible assets, primarily consisting of the value of owner-occupied homes, to disposable income. This ratio rose in the late 1970s, in the late 1980s, and especially during 2000–06. The green section shows the ratio of household financial wealth, including direct holdings of stocks and stock mutual funds, to disposable income. This ratio rose in the late 1980s and especially during 1994–2000. The total ratio shown by the top of the green area fell sharply from 2000 to 2002 and recovered from 2002 to 2006.

Sources: Federal Reserve Board *Flow of Funds Accounts* and Bureau of Economic Analysis *NIPA Tables*. Details in Appendix C-4.

from 2000 to 2006, because this was a period of record-setting year-after-year increases in house prices. This partly offset the shrinkage in the green area representing financial assets such as stocks. By 2006 total household assets had returned to the peak ratio previously reached in the year 2000.

Besides the effects of low interest rates, what then explains the continued low household saving rate in 2002–06? An important hypothesis has been suggested by Karl Case of Wellesley College, John Quigley of the University of California–Berkeley, and Robert Shiller of Yale. Using data that vary across countries and across states within the United States, they find that the effect of housing wealth on consumption is much stronger than the effect of stock market wealth.[15] This result makes sense, since almost 70 percent of American households own their own homes and most of these have at least some equity in their houses, that is, the market value of the house or condominium is larger than the mortgage debt owed. While many households have stock mutual funds and retirement funds that are invested in stocks, more than 75 percent of the value of all stocks is owned by the top 10 percent of households, and the bottom 50 percent of households own virtually no stocks. Thus fewer people were affected by the decline of the stock market in 2000–02 than by the increase in house prices and home equity that occurred in 2000–06. This analysis helps us to understand why consumption spending was so strong during this period and why the household saving rate remained so low.   ●

15-9 Why the Official Household Saving Data Are Misleading

When we say the household saving rate was only 0.7 percent in 2007, as in Figure 15-7, we are referring to the measure of saving used in the national income and product accounts (NIPA, reviewed in Chapter 2), namely personal disposable income minus consumption expenditures minus personal interest payments. However, the NIPA measure understates the true household saving rate. The most notable feature of the NIPA saving concept is that capital gains on stocks, bonds, houses, and other assets are excluded because these gains do not reflect returns from the current production of goods and services.

A second flaw is that the NIPA saving measure does not include purchases of consumer durable goods, even though these goods provide a stream of benefits in the future, for example, the benefit of being able to use a large-screen color TV set or automobile over a number of years. A third flaw is that inflation influences the real significance of the household saving rate. Households receive nominal interest returns from corporations, and the nominal interest rate rises with the inflation rate. Thus when inflation is rapid, as in the period between 1974 and 1982, household saving is overstated by receipt of nominal interest earnings, which are simply a compensation for inflation, not real income. Conversely, when inflation declines as it has since 1990, household saving is understated because households receive lower nominal income but not lower real income.

---

[15] Karl E. Case, John M. Quigley, and Robert J. Shiller, "Home-Buyers, Housing, and the Macroeconomy," in Anthony Richards and Tim Robinson, eds., *Asset Prices and Monetary Policy* (Sydney: Reserve Bank of Australia, 2004), pp. 149–88.

Alternative Measures of Saving

Fortunately, alternative data sources are available to provide a more accurate impression of household saving behavior than the NIPA saving rate. Shown in Figure 15-9 is the NIPA series on the household saving rate compared with the equivalent saving rate from the "Flow of Fund Accounts" (FFA), which differ by including net investment in consumer durables. Here we see that in most years the FFA measure is substantially larger than the NIPA saving rate by an average of 3.8 percent over the full period 1960–2006. However, in 2005 and 2006, the FFA measure was virtually the same as the NIPA measure, and the FFA measure had declined even more from its pre-1990 values than had the NIPA measure. The decline in both measures is misleading, though, because the FFA measure like the NIPA measure excludes the effect of capital gains.

Figure 15-10 shows an alternative measure of saving defined in terms of increases in household wealth (including financial assets and housing equity) relative to total income including capital gains. Clearly the adjustment makes an enormous difference. First, the alternative "gains-inclusive saving rate" is much more volatile than either the FFA or NIPA measures; for instance, it jumped from 13.7 percent in 1994 to 34.4 percent in 1995, and it collapsed from 42.9 percent in 1999 to −26.0 percent in 2002. Second, the broader measure con-

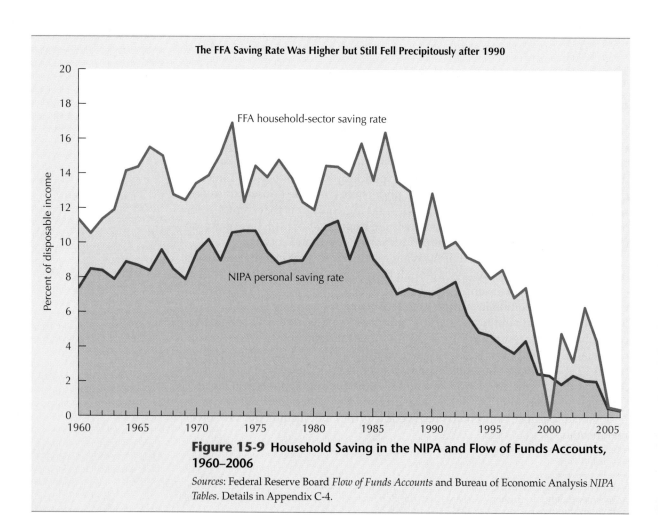

Figure 15-9 Household Saving in the NIPA and Flow of Funds Accounts, 1960–2006

Sources: Federal Reserve Board *Flow of Funds Accounts* and Bureau of Economic Analysis *NIPA Tables*. Details in Appendix C-4.

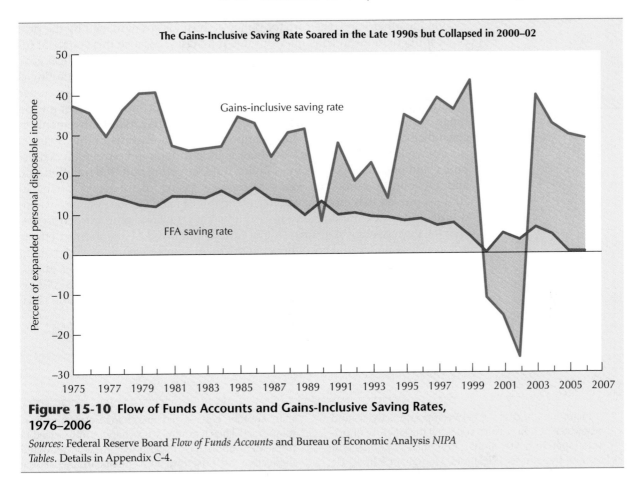

The Gains-Inclusive Saving Rate Soared in the Late 1990s but Collapsed in 2000–02

Figure 15-10 Flow of Funds Accounts and Gains-Inclusive Saving Rates, 1976–2006

Sources: Federal Reserve Board *Flow of Funds Accounts* and Bureau of Economic Analysis *NIPA Tables*. Details in Appendix C-4.

tradicts the implication of the NIPA that household saving nearly disappeared in recent years; its average value was 21.7 percent in 1995–2006, a substantial value albeit lower than the average value of 32.1 percent in 1976–85.[16]

15-10 Conclusion: Consumption and the Case For and Against Activism

If all consumption spending consisted of nondurable goods and services, the permanent-income hypothesis and life-cycle hypothesis both would strengthen the case of those who advocate policy rules and are optimistic that the private economy is basically stable if left alone by the government. Consumption would respond only partially to temporary bursts of nonconsumption spending, so that the economy's true short-run multipliers would be smaller than those calculated in Chapters 3 and 4.

---

[16] For a comprehensive analysis of differences in saving rate concepts, see Marshall B. Reinsdorf, "Alternative Measures of Personal Saving," *Survey of Current Business* (September 2004), pp. 17–27. This article can also be found at www.bea.gov/bea/ARTICLES/2004/09September/ PersonalSavingWEB.pdf.

On the other hand, the case for policy activism is strengthened by the pro-cyclical fluctuations in consumer durable purchases, because this source of instability in the private economy may need to be offset by countercyclical government policy. The importance of erratic fluctuations in consumer spending is summarized by movements in the ratio of personal saving plus consumer durable expenditures to personal income. This ratio has fluctuated over a wide range during the postwar years. Part of these swings may reflect movements in consumer confidence, which are an important source of shifts in the *IS* curve.

As we learned in Chapter 14, there is little difference between an activist policy and one that operates by a Taylor Rule, targeting both the inflation rate and the output ratio. The Fed's aggressive easing of monetary policy in 2001–04 proved that monetary policy is capable of stabilizing consumer expenditures and residential housing investment. And we have now learned in this chapter that consumption spending is further stabilized by the indirect effects of low interest rates that boost housing prices, raising household wealth held in the form of housing equity and reducing the household saving rate. The ability of the Fed to keep consumption from declining significantly during the 2001 recession helps to explain why the economy has been much more stable since 1984, as shown in Figure 14-3 on p. 463.

Summary

1. A major area of dispute between policy activists and advocates of policy rules concerns the stability of private spending decisions. Friedman's permanent-income hypothesis (PIH) and Modigliani's life-cycle hypothesis (LCH) are based on the assumption that individuals achieve a higher level of total utility (enjoyment) when they maintain a stable consumption pattern than when they allow consumption to rise or fall with every transitory fluctuation in their actual income. Individuals can achieve the desired stable consumption pattern by consuming a stable fraction of their permanent or lifetime income.

2. If all consumption consisted of nondurable goods and services, both the PIH and the LCH would strengthen the case of those who advocate policy rules, who claim that the private economy is basically stable if left alone by the government. Consumption would respond only partially to temporary fluctuations of nonconsumption spending, so that the economy's short-run multipliers would be smaller than the simple theoretical multipliers of Chapters 3 and 4.

3. Both the PIH and the LCH can reconcile the observed cross-section increase in the saving ratio for higher incomes with the observed long-run historical constancy of the aggregate saving ratio.

4. Both hypotheses have important implications for fiscal policy. For example, a tax change announced as permanent should cause a bigger change in permanent income, and hence in consumption expenditures, than another equal-sized tax change announced as temporary. Thus temporary tax changes introduced to implement an activist fiscal policy may be rendered ineffective by offsetting movements in the saving ratio.

5. Numerous criticisms of the PIH and LCH have emerged in recent years. A large share of saving seems to be used not for consumption during retirement, but for bequests to children. Households may save more than they need, because they are uncertain about the date of death. People cut their consumption spending when they retire, conflicting with the LCH assumption that consumption is stable over the lifetime. Liquidity constraints imply that perhaps 15 percent of income is earned by households for whom the short-run marginal propensity to consume is much higher than implied by the PIH or LCH.

6. An additional consideration in explaining observed consumption and saving behavior is that consumer durable expenditures should be treated as a form of saving, not as current consumption. Sharp increases in income tend to go mainly into saving, which means that consumer durable expenditures treated as a form of saving may be very responsive to transitory income changes. Thus the PIH and LCH may be valid, but consumer durable purchases are still a source of instability in the private economy.

7. The puzzle of the decline in the U.S. household saving rate during the 1992–2007 period can be traced partly to the stock market boom of this period, as well as

steady increases in housing prices. The National Income and Product Accounts concept of the saving rate excludes capital gains and adjustments for inflation and thus greatly understates increases in household wealth during the 1990s and most earlier decades.

Concepts

forward-looking expectations
permanent-income hypothesis (PIH)
life-cycle hypothesis (LCH)

cross section
time series
permanent income

transitory income
rational expectations
liquidity constraint

Questions

1. The saving ratio has been remarkably stable since 1900. When we examine cross-section data, however, we find that the saving ratio tends to rise as incomes rise. How can these two observations be reconciled?

2. Why is a distinction made between a short-run marginal propensity to consume and a long-run marginal propensity to consume in the permanent-income hypothesis (PIH)?

3. Is permanent income permanent? If not, what causes it to change?

4. Is it true that both the adaptive expectations and rational expectations forms of the PIH give identical predictions concerning the effect of the 2001 tax rebate on consumption?

5. How does the existence of assets affect consumption and income in the life-cycle hypothesis (LCH)?

6. What is likely to happen to the household saving rate in the United States and other industrialized economies as the proportion of the population that is retired rises? What are some ways that this effect on the saving rate could be reversed?

7. In each of the following cases, explain whether permanent income would change and if so, how much it would change initially if permanent income is calculated using adaptive expectations or rational expectations.
   (a) Due to increased health care costs, Food-2-Go reduces its work force by 10 percent. In order to maintain its output, it requires the employees it retains to work overtime on a regular basis. (Answer this question for both the workers retained and the workers let go by Food-2-Go. Assume that when workers let go by Food-2-Go get new jobs, they will earn less than they earned at Food-2-Go.)
   (b) An unusually snowy winter forces a ski resort to offer its help overtime pay in order to provide the extra services demanded by the extra skiers it has that season.
   (c) A person receives a promotion that she was expecting. However, the salary that she earns in her new job is much more than she was expecting.

8. Does the fact that many individuals leave bequests (i.e., do not consume their entire income over their lifetimes) invalidate the LCH?

9. Both the LCH and the PIH predict that the marginal propensity to consume out of transitory income is quite small (perhaps, even zero). Nevertheless, we observe many younger families spending a fairly large percentage of their transitory incomes. Is this observation consistent with the two hypotheses?

10. The PIH and LCH suggest that consumer durable expenditures should be considered separately from expenditures on nondurables and services. Why? How does this distinction alter the appearance of saving and consumption behavior? Why do some economists argue that consumer durable expenditures should be treated as saving rather than consumption?

11. Both the PIH and the LCH predict that consumers react differently to tax changes that are perceived to be permanent rather than temporary. Explain why this is so. Has the empirical record of the past twenty years supported this prediction?

12. Explain why a rapid increase in economic growth can cause an increase in the savings rate.

13. Use the LCH to explain how differences in capital gains from the stock market and housing can be used to explain the differences between the household saving rates of Italy and France compared to those of the United States, Canada, and Australia.

14. Does a decline in consumption by retirees invalidate the LCH? Explain why retirees can reduce their consumption when compared to groups that are similar in terms of income.

15. The national income and product accounts (NIPA) measure of the personal saving rate fell dramatically during the late 1990s to 0.8 percent in 2007. Why did this happen? Does it accurately portray actual household saving behavior during this time period?

16. Just like the FFA and NIPA measures of the saving rate, even the "gains-inclusive saving rate" eventually declined and turned negative in 2000–02. Is it true, therefore, that even the results of the "gains-inclusive

saving rate" support the predictions of the LCH by suggesting that the stock market boom of the late 1990s lowered the saving rate?

17. Explain why the household saving rate remained low during 2002–04 despite the fact that during those years, the stock market remained well below the peak it reached in 2000.

18. Do forward-looking theories of consumption such as the PIH and the LCH strengthen or weaken the case for the superiority of policy rules over activism?

Problems

1. Assume that consumption and permanent income are derived as shown in equations (15.2) and (15.3). In those equations, let $k = 0.8$ and $j = 0.5$. Assume that 2007 actual income of $30,000 equals permanent income.
   (a) What would be the permanent income for 2008, 2009, and 2010 if actual income for those three years were $36,000, $45,000, and $30,000, respectively?
   (b) What would be consumption spending in those three years?
   (c) What would be the short-run marginal propensity to consume in each of those three years?
   (d) Using the distinction between permanent income and transitory income, explain why the short-run marginal propensity to consume would differ from the long-run marginal propensity to consume in 2008.

2. You are given the following information concerning income, transitory income, and permanent consumption:

Income	Transitory income	Permanent consumption
6,000	0	4,500
6,880	−120	5,250
8,020	20	6,000
8,955	−45	6,750
10,200	200	7,500

   (a) Calculate the amount of permanent income at each level of income.
   (b) Calculate the long-run marginal propensity to consume, k.
   (c) Assuming that the marginal propensity to consume out of transitory income equals 0, compute the short-run marginal propensities to consume at income levels of $6,000, $6,880, $8,020, $8,955, and $10,200.
   (d) Explain how the short-run marginal propensities to consume differ from the long-run marginal propensity to consume.

3. The marginal propensity to consume out of permanent income equals 0.9 and the marginal propensity to consume out of transitory income equals 0.1. Suppose that there is an emergency increase in government spending of $200 billion to repair infrastructure. The spending takes place within a year. The spending increase is financed by a one-time increase in taxes. Prior to the increase in government spending, permanent income equals $9,600 billion and transitory income equals zero.
   (a) Compute the amounts of consumption expenditures and private saving prior to the tax increase.
   (b) Compute the amount of changes in consumption expenditures and private saving, given that the tax increase lasts for only one year.
   (c) Compute the initial change in aggregate demand that results from this combination of increases in government spending and taxes.

4. Again assume that the marginal propensity to consume out of permanent income equals 0.9 and the marginal propensity to consume out of transitory income equals 0.1. However, instead of a one-time increase in taxes, the infrastructure spending is financed by issuing a ten-year bond at the beginning of the first year. Taxes are then raised in each of the ten years to raise enough funds to retire the bond at the end of the ten years. Permanent income is reduced in each year by the amount of the tax increase in that year. The tax increases necessary to be able to retire the bond are: $15.33 billion in year 1; $15.79 billion in year 2; $16.26 billion in year 3; $16.75 billion in year 4; $17.25 billion in year 5; $17.77 billion in year 6; $18.30 billion in year 7; $18.85 billion in year 8; $19.42 billion in year 9; and $20.00 billion in year 10. (*Note:* These are net tax increases in that it is assumed that the debt is purchased domestically. Therefore any interest expense paid by taxpayers is offset as income received by taxpayers.)
   (a) Verify that the future value[a] of each year's tax increase in year 10 is $20 billion, given that the real interest rate the government can borrow at equals 3 percent. (*Hint:* Remember that the first year's tax increase can earn interest in years 2 through 10; the second year's tax increase can earn interest in years 3 through 10; and so on.)

---

[a] The future value of some amount of money A at time t in the future, given an interest rate r, is the amount of money that a person has at time t if he sets aside the amount A today, given that it earns the interest rate r between now and t. For example, the future value of $100 in ten years, given an interest rate equal to 5 percent, is $100 \times (1.05)^{10} = 162.89.

(b) Compute the amounts of consumption expenditures and private saving in each of the ten years, given that the tax increase in each year results in a decrease in permanent income.

(c) Compute the amounts that the tax increases cause consumption expenditures and private saving to change in each of the ten years when compared to the amounts prior to the change in fiscal policy.

(d) Compute the initial change in aggregate demand in each of the ten years that results from this combination of changes in taxes and government spending.

(e) Compute the present discounted value[b] of the changes in aggregate demand that result from this combination of changes in taxes and government spending, given that the real interest rate the government can borrow at equals 3 percent.

(f) Explain why the expansionary effect of the change in fiscal policy is less, both in the first year and in terms of the present discounted value of the effect of the fiscal policy over ten years, when the increase in spending is financed by debt that is paid off by a permanent tax increase rather than a one-time tax increase.

(g) What value of the marginal propensity to consume out of transitory income would make the present discounted value of the one-time tax increase equal to the present discounted value of the combination of debt financing and permanent tax increases to pay off the debt?

5. Assume that Gina's consumption decisions are consistent with the LCH. In 2008, Gina is 25 years old, expects to earn income until she is 65, and expects to consume until she dies at age 85.

(a) If Gina earns $30,000 per year and wishes to consume an equal amount each year, how much will she consume each year?

(b) What is Gina's ratio of consumption to income? What is her saving ratio?

(c) Assume that Gina has assets equal to $120,000 in 2008. Recalculate your answers for a and b.

(d) Assume that in 2028, Gina inherits $40,000. Now what are your answers to c?

6. A recent medical school graduate age 26 will intern for seven years, making $30,000 a year. Thereafter, she will make $250,000 a year for 30 years. At age 26, she also has assets of $570,000.

(a) In the absence of liquidity constraints, how much will she consume per year if she expects to live to age 83?

(b) Suppose that a collapse in the stock market reduces the value of her assets at age 26 to $285,000. How much will she now consume per year if she expects to live to age 83?

7. Suppose that Jim goes to work at age 25, earns on average $40,000 a year for 40 years. He inherits $320,000 when he starts working. He expects to live to be 75.

(a) Calculate on average how much Jim consumes per year, the ratio of his annual consumption to annual income, and his annual savings rate.

(b) Suppose now that Jim learns that he can expect to live to be 85. If Jim does not change his retirement age, compute Jim's new annual consumption, as well as the new ratio of annual consumption to annual income, and his new annual saving rate.

8. Suppose that Alan goes to work at age 22, earns on average $60,000 a year for 43 years, and inherits $300,000 the year he starts working. He expects to live to be 82.

(a) Calculate on average how much Alan consumes per year, the ratio of his annual consumption to annual income, and his savings rate.

(b) Suppose that a rise in housing prices causes Alan's inheritance to increase to $480,000. If Alan does not change his retirement age, calculate Alan's new annual consumption, as well as the new ratio of annual consumption to annual income, and his annual savings rate.

(c) Given the increase in his inheritance listed in part b, suppose that Alan decides to use the increased inheritance to finance an earlier retirement age. He does this by maintaining the same average annual consumption as in part a. At what age will Alan be able to retire?

---

[b] The present discounted value of the amount of money A at time t, given an interest rate r, is the amount of money that must be set aside today in order to have the amount of money A at time t in the future, given that it earns the interest rate r between now and t. For example, the present discounted value of $162.89 in ten years, given an interest rate equal to 5 percent, is $162.89/\left((1.05)^{10}\right) = \$100$.

 ## SELF-TEST ANSWERS

if they considered their recession-level income permanent. (4) When the U.S. economy is in a period of unusually high real GDP, a large number of people will experience above-permanent income and will consume less and save more than they would if they considered their exceptionally high income permanent.

p. 501 (1) Use the right-hand part of equation (15.7). If $A_1 = 0$, and $R/L = 30/40$, then consumption expenditures per year will be 30/40 times $50,000, or $37,500 during both the working and retirement years. (2) C/Y during working years will be $37,500/50,000, or 0.75, which of course equals R/L. (3) With initial assets of 200,000, $A_1/L = 200,000/40 = 5,000$. Consumption expenditures by equation (15.8) will then be $5,000 plus $37,500 = $42,500 during both the working and retirement years. (4) C/Y during working years will be 42,500/50,000 = 0.85.

p. 510 (1) Since the tax increase is assumed to be permanent, it will reduce permanent income by $1,000. Consumption will fall by k times $1,000 per year. (2) According to the life-cycle hypothesis as set forth in equation (15.7), Y per year will fall by $1,000, and consumption per year will fall by R/L times $1,000. (3) According to the life-cycle hypothesis, with an uncertain lifetime L, consumption per year will fall by R/L^* times $1,000. (4) According to the Barro-Ricardo equivalence theorem, consumption will not change at all, since saving will decline by the full amount of the tax increase (reflecting the lower anticipated future tax liabilities).

For additional practice and exploration, exercises that require the use of Excel are available at www.aw-bc.com/gordon.

The Economics of Investment Behavior

Whatever cannot go on forever must come to an end.
— Herbert Stein

If consumers purchased only nondurable goods and services, the permanent-income and life-cycle hypotheses predict that consumer behavior would stabilize the economy. An offsetting factor is the procyclical movement of consumer durable purchases. Although consistent with the PIH and LCH, such movement tends to aggravate booms and recessions. In this chapter we find that business fixed investment also fluctuates procyclically. Thus both durable purchases by consumers and investment purchases by businesses introduce instability into the private economy, leading policy activists to claim that an activist stabilization policy is justified.

The instability of private investment gains new relevance after the wild oscillations of the past decade. Compared to its average annual growth rate over the period 1960–2007 of 4.8 percent, nonresidential private fixed investment grew at a much faster average rate of 9.8 percent during 1996–2000 and then *declined*, exhibiting an average growth rate of −7.0 percent during 2000–02, followed by a bounce-back annual growth rate of 4.9 percent during 2002–07.

16-1 Investment and Economic Stability

In Chapter 15 we found that the permanent-income and life-cycle hypotheses of individual consumption behavior explain the partial insulation of aggregate consumption spending from changes in other types of spending in the short run. But what are the sources of changes in these other types of spending? Nominal GDP in 2007 was divided among the major types of expenditures as follows:

Personal consumption expenditures	70.3%
Gross private domestic investment	15.4
Government purchases of goods and services	19.4
Net exports	−5.1
	100.0

Having already considered consumer expenditures in Chapter 15, government spending and other aspects of fiscal policy in Chapters 5 and 12, and net exports in Chapter 6, we concentrate here on private investment.

We will review a very simple theory that explains why investment spending is likely to exhibit more pronounced fluctuations than other types of spending. According to the permanent-income hypothesis, introduced in the last chapter to explain consumer expenditures, households try to maintain a constant ratio of their consumer durable stock to permanent income. This creates sudden bursts of durable purchases when an upward revision of permanent income causes the desired durable stock to increase. In this chapter we will see that investment spending on plant, equipment, inventories, and housing is driven by the same principle and therefore is also subject to sudden bursts of purchases.[1]

16-2 Case Study

The Historical Instability of Investment

Total Investment Rises and Falls Dramatically and Procyclically

We begin by examining the historical record of investment spending since 1960. Figure 16-1 clearly shows that investment spending is far more variable than consumption spending (compare with Figure 15-1 on p. 489). The top line in the figure shows total real gross private domestic investment (GPDI). By any standard, the fluctuations in total investment are huge.

The following table shows how real GPDI has fluctuated since 1960.

Quarters			Percentage change (in lags)	
Peak	**Trough**	**Peak**	**Peak to trough**	**Trough to peak**
1960:Q1	1961:Q1	1969:Q4	−22	+61
1969:Q4	1970:Q4	1973:Q4	−7	+39
1973:Q4	1975:Q1	1980:Q1	−31	+46
1980:Q1	1980:Q3	1981:Q3	−17	+21
1981:Q3	1982:Q4	1990:Q3	−26	+47
1990:Q3	1991:Q1	2001:Q1	−11	+73
2001:Q1	2001:Q4	—	−11	—

Shown in the left part of the table are the dates of each successive business cycle peak and trough. We can see, for instance, that in the 1973–75 recession,

---

[1] Examples of plant and equipment investment include:

Nonresidential Plant (Structures)	**Equipment**
Factories	Computers
Oil refineries	Jet airplanes
Office buildings	Trucks
Shopping centers	Bar-code scanners
Private hospitals	Internet switching equipment
Hotels	Tractors

The principles developed in this chapter apply also to residential investment, construction of both single-family homes and apartment buildings.

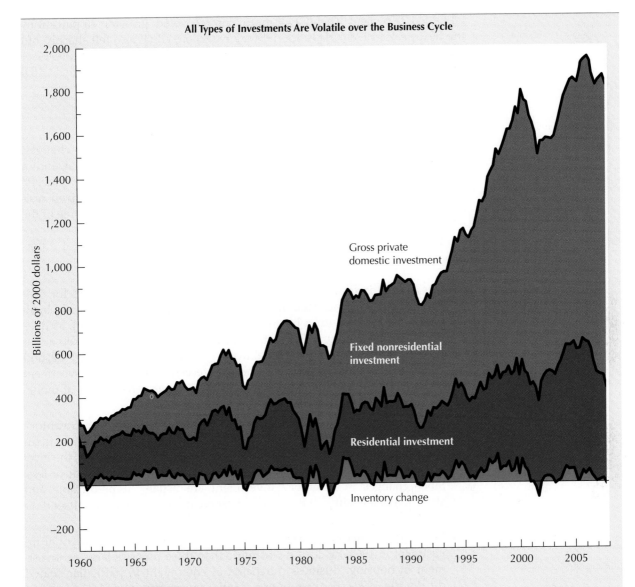

All Types of Investments Are Volatile over the Business Cycle

Figure 16-1 **Real Gross Private Domestic Investment and Its Three Components, 1960–2007**

The top line plots real gross private domestic investment and shows substantial declines in recessions. All three components contribute to this volatility, but their timing is different. There is a marked tendency for residential investment to turn down earlier than nonresidential investment and to recover earlier. Fluctuations in inventory investment are shorter-lived than fluctuations in either of the other two components The investment downturn of 2000–01 was severe by historical standards but left residential investment totally unaffected. By late 2004 total investment had surpassed the previous 2000 peak. The effect of the 2007 mortgage meltdown (see pp. 474–75) is evident in the drop of residential construction in 2007.

Source: Bureau of Economic Analysis, *NIPA Tables.*

GPDI fell 31 percent. Then GPDI more than recovered, growing 46 percent by the next peak in 1980:Q1. In the 1981–82 recession, GPDI also fell sharply, but by less than in 1973–75. After the 1991 trough, GPDI rose dramatically. Over the record-breaking ten-year expansion that ended in 2001:Q1, total real GPDI increased by 73 percent.

Behavior of the Components of GPDI

GPDI is divided into two main parts: fixed investment and inventory changes. Fixed investment is further divided into residential and nonresidential, and in turn nonresidential is divided into nonresidential structures and producers' durable equipment. For simplicity, Figure 16-1 distinguishes only fixed residential, fixed nonresidential, and inventory investment. Clearly all three of the major components contribute to the high volatility of GPDI.

Examining the three components more carefully, we note several differences among them:

1. **Residential investment turns early.** Comparing the plotted lines for residential and nonresidential investment, we note that in almost every business cycle the downturn begins earlier for residential investment, as does the subsequent upturn. For instance, residential investment peaked about a year before fixed nonresidential investment in the 1973–75, 1981–82, and 1990–91 recessions. However, in the 2001 recession, residential investment did not decline at all, responding to the Fed's aggressive easing of monetary policy (see pp. 104–105 and 474–75).

2. **Inventory change exhibits sharp but short-lived swings.** Inventory change appears as a series of small, jagged mountain peaks, with an occasional deep valley. In the mid-1970s, the early 1980s, and 2001–02, the level of inventories changed by over $100 billion over periods of a year or less. Since changes in inventory investment are usually unpredictable and short-lived, it is difficult for Federal Reserve monetary policy to offset their effects.

3. **Fixed nonresidential investment** was slightly larger than residential investment in 1960; by 2000 it was more than three times as large as investment in housing. Business purchases of equipment in particular soared during the 1990s. Because nonresidential investment constituted over 60 percent of GPDI during the past two decades, this chapter concentrates primarily on this component. ●

16-3 The Accelerator Hypothesis of Net Investment

Businesses must continually evaluate whether their buildings are the right size and have the right amount of equipment. Will they have too little capacity to produce the output they expect to be able to sell in the forthcoming year, causing lost sales and dissatisfied customers? Or will capacity be excessive in relation to expected sales, wasting expenses on maintenance workers and interest costs on unneeded plants and equipment? The **accelerator hypothesis** of investment relies on the simple idea that firms attempt to maintain a fixed ratio of their stock of capital (plants and equipment) to their expected sales.

The **accelerator hypothesis** states that the level of net investment depends on the *change* in expected output.

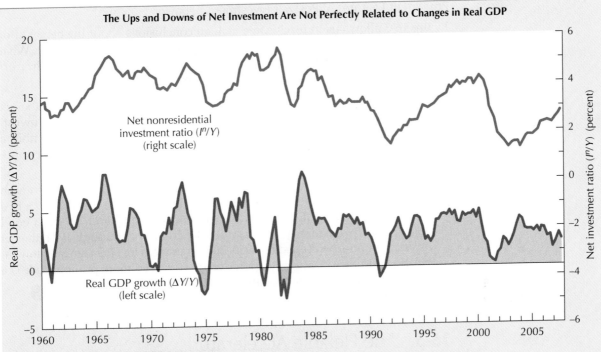

Figure 16-3 The Relation of the Net Investment Ratio (I^n/Y) to the Growth Rate of Real GDP ($\Delta Y/Y$) in the U.S. Economy, 1960–2007

The net investment ratio does not have a perfect or simple relationship with the growth rate of real GDP. But net investment was high during 1965–74 following a long period of relatively rapid real GDP growth (1961–73). And the net investment ratio was low (1960–63, 1975–76, 1981–83, 1990–92, and 2001–04) following periods of relatively slow real GDP growth. During the 1990s net investment, particularly purchases of information processing equipment, soared, but then collapsed in 2000–04.

Source: Bureau of Economic Analysis, *NIPA Tables*. Details in Appendix C-4.

It is as if an automobile's engine responded in a split second to some movements of the accelerator but took minutes to respond to other movements.

3. The overall level of net nonresidential fixed investment relative to real GDP (I^n/Y) does not have a consistent long-term relationship to real GDP growth ($\Delta Y/Y$). Although average real GDP growth was slower in the 1970s than it was in the 1960s, the ratio of net investment to GDP was higher in the 1970s than the 1960s. Further, despite the investment boom of the late 1990s, the overall average level of I^n/Y after 1990 was substantially lower than before 1990.

Period	Average $\Delta Y/Y$	I^n/Y
1960s	4.3	4.0
1970s	3.2	4.2
1980s	3.0	3.9
1990s	3.0	2.9
2000–07	2.5	2.2

Prominent Features of Postwar Investment Behavior

Figure 16-3 allows us to reach some general conclusions about the behavior of investment spending, beyond its relationship with the change in output. What do we learn from a visual inspection of the net investment ratio (I^n/Y), the purple line in Figure 16-3? Two main facts stand out in the figure:

1. **Variability**. As we saw earlier, total GPDI is highly variable, as is the net investment ratio. The past three decades have shown that the net investment ratio can shift by as much as 3 percentage points of GDP within a short period, as between 2000:Q2 and 2002:Q4. This represents a large potential shock for the economy.

2. **Persistence**. The net investment ratio does not zigzag up and down each year but often stays relatively high or relatively low for several years in a row. The period of high net investment between 1965 and 1974 is a good example of this tendency: In every quarter from 1965 through 1974, the net investment ratio exceeded its 1960–2007 average. The persistence of low investment in the Great Depression decade was even more pronounced: The net investment ratio was negative for the entire decade 1931–40.

16-5 The Flexible Accelerator

Defects of the Simple Accelerator

The simple accelerator theory of equation (16.6) depends on several restrictive and unrealistic assumptions. A more realistic version of the theory, called the **flexible accelerator,** loosens several of these assumptions.

The **flexible accelerator** theory of investment allows for gradual adjustment of sales expectations and of the capital stock. It also allows for variation in the optimal capital-output ratio.

1. The simple accelerator assumes that this period's expected output equaled last period's actual output. But the error-learning, or adaptive, hypothesis states that in general expected output is based partially on last period's actual output and partially on last period's expected output.

2. The simple accelerator assumes that the desired capital stock (K^*) equals a constant (v^*) times expected output (Y^e). But actually the desired capital-output ratio (v^*) may vary substantially, depending on the cost of borrowing, the taxation of capital, and other factors; we will postpone until the next section a detailed consideration of the factors that change v^*.

3. The simple accelerator also assumes that firms can instantly put in place any desired amount of investment in plant and equipment needed to make actual capital this period (K) equal to desired capital (K^*). Actually, some kinds of capital take a substantial length of time to construct. Buildings sometimes take two or three years between conception and completion. Some types of electricity generating stations can take as long as eight years to complete.[7] Furthermore, investing very rapidly would be excessively costly because firms supplying capital goods might raise their prices. Also, rapid installation of new buildings and equipment might disrupt normal business activities.

---

[7] At the other extreme, a shop that opens for business today in a large city could probably obtain delivery of needed equipment—cash register, computers, mobile phones, and furniture—in a day or two.

Thus, in the real world, net investment does not always close the whole gap between desired capital and last year's capital stock; more often it closes only a fraction of it.

Determinants of Gross Investment

To summarize, the relationship between economywide gross investment and output depends on at least four major factors.

1. *The fraction of the gap between desired capital and last period's actual capital that can be closed in a single period.* The higher this fraction, the more current investment responds to the change in last period's output.

2. *The response of expected output to last period's error in estimating actual output.* The higher this response, the more expected output and hence investment respond to any unexpected change in last period's actual output.

3. *The proportion of the capital stock that is replaced each year.* For long-lived types of capital, such as office buildings, only a small fraction of the stock is replaced each year. In contrast, because equipment depreciates more quickly, a larger amount of equipment investment is required annually per dollar of equipment capital to maintain the same size equipment capital stock. Firms are not forced to replace old capital on a fixed schedule. If firms delay replacement investment until expected sales are strong, total investment will respond even more than the simple accelerator model suggests.[8]

4. *The desired ratio of capital to expected output (v^*).* Investment responds more to changes in expected output in capital-intensive industries (those with a high v^*, such as electric utilities, oil refining, and chemicals) than in labor-intensive industries (those with a low v^*, such as textiles, apparel, and barber shops). Thus faster growth expected in more capital-intensive industries will spur more investment.

In the next section we investigate the determinants of the desired capital-output ratio and the policy instruments with which the government can affect the size of v^*.

16-6   The Neoclassical Theory of Investment Behavior

One of the most important contributions to the theory of investment behavior was made in the early 1960s by Dale Jorgenson of Harvard University.[9] Jorgenson's insight was to show that the user cost of capital could be derived from neoclassical microeconomic theory by examining the decision of a profit-maximizing firm. Jorgenson then demonstrated that tax policies affected how much firms invest.

---

[8] A study that confirms the procyclical behavior of replacement investment is Martin S. Feldstein and David Foot, "The Other Half of Gross Investment: Replacement and Modernization Expenditures," *The Review of Economics and Statistics*, vol. 53, no. 1 (February 1971), pp. 49–58.

[9] Dale Jorgenson, "Capital Theory and Investment Behavior," *American Economic Review*, vol. 53 (May 1963), pp. 247–57. A comprehensive review of recent theories of investment is Ricardo Caballero, "Aggregate Investment," in J. B. Taylor and M. Woodford, eds., *Handbook of Macroeconomics* (North Holland, 1999), pp. 813–62.

Tobin's *q*: Does It Explain Investment Better Than the Accelerator or Neoclassical Theories?

Both the accelerator theory of Sections 16-3 and 16-5, as well as the neoclassical theory of Section 16-6, define a desired level of the capital stock (K^*), and then assume a gradual adjustment of the actual capital stock toward the desired level. The alternative *q* theory was developed by the late Nobel Prize winner James Tobin (who also did groundbreaking work on the demand for money and whose picture appears on p. 433). Tobin's *q* theory, instead of positing a desired level of capital and a *separate* process of adjustment, merges adjustment costs directly into the firm's single calculation of the desired rate of investment at each moment of time.[a]

Tobin's theory develops an idea of Keynes's that the attractiveness of purchasing new capital equipment depends on the market value of capital in the stock market as compared with the cost of purchasing the capital. To create a quantitative measure that reflects changes in market value relative to the purchase cost, Tobin defined his variable *q* as the ratio of the firm's market value on the stock market to the replacement cost of its capital stock. Investment, then, is an increasing function of the *q* ratio.

An example of an investment equation in the *q* theory would be the following relation between gross investment relative to the capital stock (I/K), the *q* ratio (q), and the ratio of replacement investment to the capital stock (d):

$$\frac{I}{K} = j(q - 1) + d \qquad (16.7)$$

In words, this says that the I/K ratio is equal to d when Tobin's q ratio is unity. If $d = 0.1$ and $j = 0.2$, then I/K would be 0.1 when q equals unity; I/K would rise to 0.2 when q equals 1.5, and I/K would fall to zero when q equals 0.5.

In practice, the most important source of movement in q is the change in the price of a firm's shares on the stock market. During 1994–2000, for example, the change in

stock prices was at an annual rate of 19 percent, whereas in 2000–02 stock prices *declined* at an annual rate of 18 percent. Since stock prices are part of the numerator in q, such changes could change q by large amounts. As we have noted before, households' consumption spending might be affected by the stock market; higher stock prices might raise consumption by increasing households' wealth. Higher stock prices might also increase the amount of investment that firms undertake. Thus Tobin's q also suggests another channel through which changes in the stock market might affect aggregate demand.

Tobin's q theory of investment incorporates how the economic environment affects business firms' expecta-

The User Cost of Capital

The marginal product of capital (MPK) is the extra output that a firm can produce by adding an extra unit of capital.

The user cost of capital is the cost to the firm of using a piece of capital for a specified period.

Jorgenson's theory assumes that a business firm is willing to undertake an investment project only when it expects that a profit can be made. Chapter 7 showed that an extra unit of labor will not be hired unless its marginal product—the extra output it produces—equals or exceeds its real wage. Similarly, an extra unit of capital will not be purchased unless the expected **marginal product of capital (MPK)** is at least equal to the real **user cost of capital** (u):

tions of their future profitability. In addition to its theoretical appeal as a way to explain and forecast investment spending by firms, q has great practical appeal because it summarizes expectations about the level and riskiness of future profitability and thus makes unnecessary the exceedingly difficult job of estimating those expectations. Instead, Tobin's q theory states that we can simply look to the stock and bond markets for the valuation of the firm's expected future profitability, which is the numerator of q.

How does q fare in an empirical "horse race" with the accelerator and neoclassical models that we developed in Sections 16-3 and 16-6? A number of studies have tested the abilities of these three models to explain spending on fixed investment after the fact and also to forecast it.[b]

Empirical models have all been much better at explaining and forecasting business investment spending on *equipment*—so-called producers' durable equipment—than they have been at explaining and forecasting investment in nonresidential *structures*. The Oliner, Rudebusch, and Sichel study, for example, shows that investment spending on producers' durable equipment can be fairly well tracked by some of the models. They find that despite the theoretical and practical appeal of the q model of investment, both the accelerator and neoclassical models explain and forecast more accurately than do models based on q, with the accelerator model performing about as well as the neoclassical model. That is one reason why we presented both the accelerator and neoclassical models in this chapter—in practice neither is a clear-cut winner. (Findings similar to those reported by Oliner, Rudebusch, and Sichel emerge from the earlier time periods examined in other studies.)

Business investment in structures has proven more difficult to explain and forecast. In general, none of the models have demonstrated any significant ability to forecast movements in construction spending by business,

although again, the accelerator and neoclassical models tend to outperform the q model. An example of the shortcomings of all the models was their inability to forecast, or even account for after the fact, the enormous surge in commercial real estate construction during the 1980s. The large variations in business investment in structures suggest that aggregate demand for GDP may shift importantly over time. The inability to forecast those shifts suggests that it may be difficult for policymakers to anticipate and take timely action to offset them.[c]

---

[a] Most of the references on Tobin's q theory are quite technical. For the original presentation, see James Tobin, "A General Equilibrium Approach to Monetary Theory," *Journal of Money, Credit and Banking*, vol. 1 (February 1969), pp. 15–29. Important interpretations of Tobin's theory include Fumio Hayashi, "Tobin's Marginal and Average q: A Neoclassical Interpretation," *Econometrica*, vol. 50 (January 1982), pp. 213–24; and Andrew B. Abel, "A Stochastic Model of Investment, Marginal q, and the Market Value of the Firm," *International Economic Review*, vol. 26 (June 1985), pp. 305–22.

[b] See, for example, Stephen Oliner, Glenn Rudebusch, and Daniel Sichel, "New and Old Models of Business Investment: A Comparison of Forecasting Performance," *Journal of Money, Credit and Banking*, vol. 27 (August 1995), pp. 806–26, and the references cited there.

[c] A comprehensive study of the 2000–02 decline of investment and its relation to the stock market and tax policy is Mihir A. Desai and Austan D. Goolsbee, "Investment, Overhang, and Tax Policy," *Brookings Papers on Economic Activity*, no. 2 (2004), pp. 285–355.

General Form	Numerical Example	
$\mathrm{MPK} \geq u$	$\mathrm{MPK} \geq 14$	(16.8)

Both the marginal product and the real user cost can be expressed as percentages. The marginal product of capital consists of the amount of extra output produced each year by an extra piece of plant or equipment, divided by the cost of the plant or equipment. If the purchase of an extra machine costing

Figure 16-4 The Effect of a Drop in the User Cost of Capital (u) on the Desired Capital-Output Ratio (v^*)

Initially the economy is at point E_0: Firms are making a profit on their capital stock indicated by the light green area in the upper left. If the user cost falls from u_0 to u_1, the desired capital-output ratio will rise to v_1^*, the economy will move from E_0 to E_1, and the darker green area of extra profit is gained.

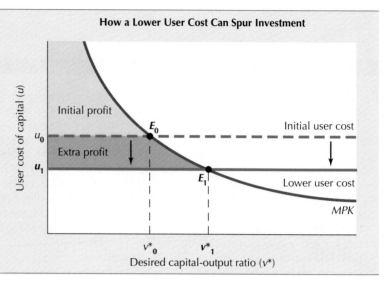

How a Lower User Cost Can Spur Investment

$100,000 allows a firm to produce $14,000 of extra output each year, then MPK would be 14 percent.[10] *The user cost of capital is the cost to the business firm of using a piece of capital for a period of time, expressed as a fraction of its purchase price. The user cost might be 14 percent, consisting perhaps of a 4 percent annual real interest rate and a 10 percent depreciation rate.*[11]

What does equation (16.8) have to do with the profitability of a business firm? When MPK is 15 percent and user cost is only 14 percent, then the extra revenue generated by a new machine exceeds its cost, and the firm's profits are increased. On the other hand, when MPK is only 13 percent and user cost is the same 14 percent, the extra revenue is insufficient to pay the costs of the new machine, and profits go down if the machine is purchased. Only if user cost falls to 13 percent or lower will the new machine be purchased.[12]

The effect of a reduction in user cost on the desired capital-output ratio is illustrated in Figure 16-4. The diminishing MPK means that each extra machine adds less output than the machine added before it, implying that the MPK curve slopes downward. Suppose each business initially faces a constant user cost u_0. Each business will then maximize its profits by choosing the capital-output ratio v_0^*, at which point the marginal benefit of the machine, its MPK, equals its marginal cost, u_0. Why? A smaller amount of capital, to the left of E_0, would mean giving up some of the profits indicated by the lighter green area that measures the difference between the marginal product of capital and the user cost. But to purchase a larger amount of capital, to the right of E_0, would cause losses. These extra units of capital have an insufficient MPK to pay for their user cost.

---

[10] As is always true in economics, the marginal product of a single input measures the extra output produced by an extra unit of that input if the quantity of other inputs is held constant.

[11] Depreciation is part of user cost, because using a machine reduces its ability to produce and thus its value.

[12] If this analysis seems familiar, in Section 3-9 on pp. 78–81 you learned that firms make investment decisions by comparing the rate of return to the interest rate. As we learn in this section, the user cost contains several components in addition to the interest rate.

Tax Incentives and Investment Behavior

The user cost of capital depends not only on the depreciation rate of capital and the real interest rate that must be paid on the funds borrowed to purchase the equipment. As derived by Jorgenson, the user cost also depends on three aspects of the tax system discussed in the next section. Thus both monetary and fiscal policy can influence the user cost—monetary policy by changing the real interest rate, and fiscal policy by affecting real interest rates and by altering tax rates and the rules of the tax system.

We can use Figure 16-4 to illustrate the effect of a change in government tax policy designed to stimulate investment. Let us assume that the government changes tax rates or rules in order to cut the user cost. For instance, the tax rate that corporations pay on their profits might be cut in half, and this reduces user cost to the firm. Additional units of capital will now be purchased to bring the desired capital-output ratio rightward to v_1^*. Increased investment is required to raise the capital-output ratio to its new, higher desired level, v_1^*. The reduction in user cost has made available extra profits, indicated by the darker green area. *By using monetary and fiscal policy instruments, the user cost of capital can be changed. Firms can thus be induced to adopt more capital-intensive methods of production, and the opposite is true as well. Just as an increase in the wage rate can cause firms to replace marginal workers with extra machines, an increase in capital's user cost can cause firms to substitute away from elaborate machines toward more labor-intensive techniques of production.*

16-7 User Cost and the Role of Monetary and Fiscal Policy

How can government policymakers affect the user cost of capital (u)? The user cost of capital depends on several factors, which can be introduced in two steps. First, let us neglect the effect of taxation. In the absence of taxation, a capital good that is purchased at a given real price imposes three types of cost on its user.

1. *An interest cost is involved in buying a capital good.* If funds are borrowed, interest at the nominal rate (i) must be paid. Alternatively, the investor loses the interest (i) that would have been received had the funds used to buy the capital good been used instead to purchase a financial asset.

2. *Physical deterioration lessens the production ability of every capital good; in addition, some capital goods become obsolete.* The **depreciation rate** indicates the annual percentage decline in value of the capital good due to physical deterioration and obsolescence.

   The **depreciation rate** is the annual percentage decline in the value of a capital good due to physical deterioration and obsolescence.

3. *The interest and depreciation cost are adjusted by price changes for capital goods.* Rapid price increases mean that used capital goods can sometimes be resold for more than their cost when new. These price increases reduce the user cost and imply that it is a *real* interest rate that matters (the nominal interest rate minus the rate of price changes for capital goods). Conversely, declines in the prices of computers, for example, raise their user costs.

Policymakers cannot easily alter the relative price of capital goods. Similarly, they cannot change the rate of physical decay and economic obsolescence summarized in the depreciation rate. But the real interest rate can be influenced by policymakers. As we learned in Chapter 4, a fiscal policy stimulus raises the real interest rate and hence crowds out investment. A monetary policy stimulus, on the other hand, reduces the real interest rate and raises investment. A change in the monetary-fiscal policy mix toward easier monetary policy and tighter fiscal policy cuts the real interest rate and user cost and thus raises investment, as shown in Figure 16-4.

Taxation and Investment Behavior

So far taxation has been ignored. But fiscal policy can have a major effect on investment by altering the user cost. Three basic fiscal tools are available:

1. *Firms invest up to the point where the marginal product of the capital stock is just sufficient to cover the user cost of capital.* Imposing a tax on a firm's income effectively adds another element to user cost, the cost of taxes. The higher the firm's income tax rate is, the greater the effective user cost it faces. Thus a higher tax rate is likely to reduce the firm's desired capital stock, and thus investment, because only with a smaller capital stock will the firm have a larger MPK.

2. *Firms can cut their corporate income tax by deducting the value of depreciation of plants and equipment.* The amount of depreciation they can deduct depends on tax laws and how the IRS implements them. Though the government cannot change the rate of physical depreciation or obsolescence directly, it can change the accounting rules used to calculate corporate income taxes. Liberalizing the tax rules regarding depreciation, for example, effectively reduces the corporate income tax rate. Whenever the depreciation tax rules are liberalized, corporate profits are protected from taxation, thus cutting the user cost of capital. The reverse happened in years when the rules were tightened.

3. *During most of the period 1962–86, a substantial part of investment in the United States was eligible for an investment tax credit.* This credit often allowed business firms to deduct 10 percent of the value of their equipment investment from their corporation income tax. Naturally this reduced the effective user cost of capital for firms making profits. The investment tax credit was rescinded in 1986 but could be reinstated if the government desired to stimulate investment. The investment tax credit may account for the fact that the net investment ratio in Figure 16-3 on p. 529 was substantially higher during 1962–86 (4.21 percent) than in 1987–2007 after the tax credit was terminated (2.70 percent).

These three fiscal tools provide much more flexibility in conducting stabilization policy than would be available if the government were limited to controlling the economy by varying the level of government spending and the personal income tax rate. For instance, government spending can be restrained and the personal income tax rate raised to slow down an economy that is experiencing too much aggregate demand. At the same time, any of the investment-related fiscal instruments can be liberalized if it is believed that the economy has too little investment and too much consumption.

Studies by economists suggest that changes in tax incentives probably have at least a modest effect on investment. However, such changes have numerous limitations and are not a promising instrument for an activist fiscal policy. First, changes in tax incentives are almost always subject to lengthy debate in Congress. Second, there is a substantial time lag between the passage of tax legislation and the resulting investment spending. Third, we are far from being able to estimate confidently how much investment will respond to tax incentives.

16-8 Business Confidence and Speculation

Confidence and the Flexible Accelerator

In Chapters 3 and 4 the terms *business* and *consumer confidence* were used as a convenient, shorthand way to refer to factors that could change output when government spending and the money supply were fixed at a given level. In the flexible accelerator theory of investment summarized here, the confidence of business firms may influence investment spending in three ways:

1. Investment depends on what fraction of the increase in last period's actual output is incorporated into expected output, and hence into desired capital and investment. When businesspeople lack confidence in the future, they may refuse to extrapolate a quarter or a year of increasing output, believing instead that any increase in output is temporary.

2. The user cost of capital (u) includes the borrowing costs that business firms *expect* to have to pay if they undertake an investment project. If businesses are pessimistic, they may underestimate how much the prices of capital goods will rise and therefore overestimate the real borrowing cost they are likely to face, making their estimate of u too high and their desired capital stock too low.

3. Perhaps most important, business firms can only guess the likely marginal product of new investment projects. It is the expected marginal product that matters. If business has recently been bad, a condition experienced by many business firms in 1930–33, or as recently as 2001, firms may already have more capital than they may desire. Some present capital may be underutilized, and future capital investments may appear unprofitable, with their expected marginal products being close to zero.

Cycles of Overbuilding

Periods of business overoptimism in U.S. history have led to overbuilding, underutilized capital, and extensive pessimism. This recurring sequence played out in the years surrounding 1970 and the years surrounding 1990, leaving the United States with billions of dollars' worth of empty apartments, office buildings, and stores. In 1996–2000 there was a new type of overbuilding consisting of excess investment in computers and telecommunications equipment. Excess capacity resulted in a collapse of this high-tech investment in 2000–01, as we will learn in Section 16-9.

Keynes placed major emphasis on the role of business confidence in determining the level of investment. In the following passage he stresses that investment decisions are based on estimates of the future yield (or marginal product) of extra capital, estimates that may be little better than a guess. Faced with identical information and uncertainty, businesspeople may go ahead with an

Investment in the Great Depression and World War II

Any event, whether political or economic, that causes a drop in business confidence can cause a sharp drop in the level of investment. In the Great Depression of the 1930s, a collapse in business confidence dropped the desired capital stock far below the actual capital stock, and business firms were so pessimistic that they did not replace depreciating capital, causing net investment to be negative year after year. The multiplier effect of the collapse of investment, together with the 1929 stock market crash and subsequent bank failures, caused consumption to decline sharply, and this fed back to a reduction in the desired capital stock and a further decline of investment spending.

The decade of the 1930s brought poverty and misery to the lives of millions of Americans. As shown in the box on pp. 224–25, the Great Depression was deeper and more severe in the United States than in any other major developed nation. The graph on the next page shows real GDP and real private domestic investment from 1929 to 1950, both expressed as an index number with 1929 equal to 100. By 1933, real GDP had declined 27 percent from its 1929 value. But even more calamitous was the decline of investment by fully 88 percent between 1929 and 1932; investment in 1932 was only 12 percent of its 1929 value!

A notable aspect of the Great Depression was not only the enormous depth of the economic decline but also its duration. Because natural real GDP grew by 53 percent between 1929 and 1941, the output ratio (actual real GDP divided by natural real GDP) remained below 100 percent until mid-1941.[a] Investment briefly regained its 1929 value in 1937 and then finally soared above the 1929 value in 1940 and 1941. After 1941, the government forced business firms to stop all investment that was not essential for the war effort, and so construction of residential housing, office buildings, hotels, and nonmilitary equipment ceased. This explains the sharp drop of investment in the years 1942–45 and the instant recovery to far above 1941 levels during the first postwar years, 1946–50.

The enormous amount of underutilized capital during the 1930s brought one benefit. When the United States became involved in World War II, initially in 1940–41 as an exporter of weapons and raw materials to Britain and the USSR, and then as a full-fledged combatant after Pearl Harbor in December 1941, it was able to put back to work all those underutilized factories and equipment. They were joined by many new factories and much new equipment paid for by the government and operated by companies such as General Motors, Ford, and Chrysler. Because this government-owned, privately operated (GOPO) capital was not counted as private investment, the red line in the graph greatly understates the amount of investment that actually took place during World War II. One example of a GOPO plant was the Ford-operated factory in Willow Run, Michigan (near Ann Arbor), that produced fourteen B-24 bombers *every day* in what

investment project when they feel optimistic but postpone the same project when they feel pessimistic:

> The outstanding fact is the extreme precariousness of the basis of knowledge on which our estimates of prospective yield have to be made. Our knowledge of the factors which will govern the yield of an investment some years hence is usually very slight and often negligible. If we speak frankly, we have to admit that our basis of knowledge for estimating the yield ten years hence of a railway, a copper mine, a textile factory, the goodwill of a patent medicine, an Atlantic liner, a building in the City of London amounts to little and sometimes to nothing; or even five

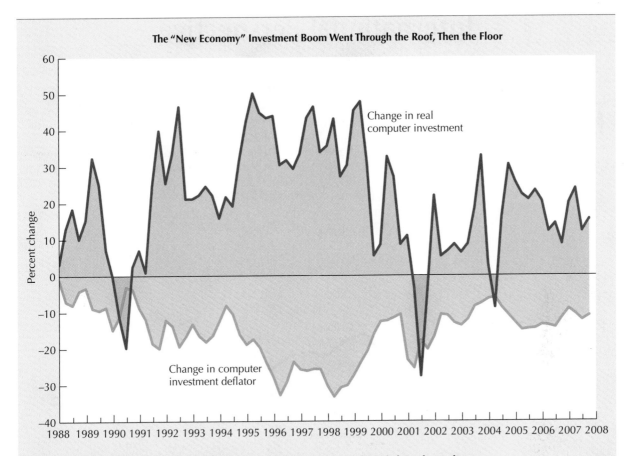

The "New Economy" Investment Boom Went Through the Roof, Then the Floor

Figure 16-5 Change in Real Investment in Computers and Peripherals and in the Computer Deflator, 1988–2007

The data shown are two-quarter average changes at an annual rate. In the bottom frame, the accelerated rate of price decline is clearly visible between 1996 and 1999, followed by a reversal in 2000–07. The top frame shows that, after erratic up-and-down movements from 1988 to 1994, the growth rate of real computer investment "took off" in 1995, registering an average growth rate of 35 percent per year from 1995 to 1999. Then came the collapse. Over the period 2000–07, real computer investment grew at 13 percent per year, substantially less than the 20 percent rate registered between 1987 and 1995.

Source: Bureau of Economic Analysis *NIPA Tables*. Details in Appendix C-4.

rushed to hire programmers to build its first Web site and make subsequent refinements. Everything seemed to explode together, including the stock prices of equipment providers and e-commerce firms.

The Collapse of the New Economy Investment Boom

When the crash came, it came rapidly. The value of the NASDAQ stock market index that specialized in high-tech stocks crashed, losing two-thirds of its value between March 2000 and March 2001. As shown in Figure 16-5, computer investment also crashed, with its growth rate suddenly dropping from an annual rate of +33 percent in the two quarters ending 2000:Q2 to −28 percent in the two quarters ending in 2001:Q3.

In retrospect, the high-tech investment boom was supported by numerous temporary factors that could not continue. First, the Web could only be invented

International Perspective

The Level and Variability of Investment Around the World

For many years, investment was much lower in the United States than in Japan or Germany. And from the mid-1980s through the early 1990s, the investment gap between the United States and Japan and Germany widened. The accompanying figure shows the share of each country's GDP that is devoted to gross investment (net investment plus depreciation) for the years 1980–2008.

However, over the period 1992 to 2000, the investment ratio in the United States rose from 17.2 to 20.8

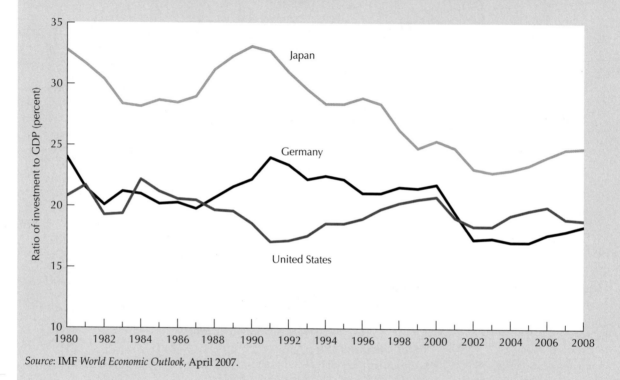

Source: IMF *World Economic Outlook*, April 2007.

once. It took much more investment in computer software and hardware to develop a firm's first Web site than to refine it and add new features in subsequent years. Second, computer columnists began to suggest in 2000–01 that the industry was no longer developing "killer applications" like the Web that would drive the next wave of computer investments. Third, many of the e-commerce companies went bust; not only did they no longer need to buy new computers, but their now unneeded computers flooded the market. Finally, the late 1990s had witnessed an additional boom in telecommunications equipment and especially in the laying of thousands of miles of fiber-optic cable intended to tie together all the office and home computers in a vast broadband network. However, like many speculative booms in the past, too many people laid too much fiber-optic cable, and by 2001 it was estimated that 97 percent of the fiber-optic capacity was not being utilized.

In summary, the new economy investment boom and collapse had some similarities with previous booms and collapses, such as the 1929–33 collapse that was led by both residential and nonresidential construction, and the 1989–92 collapse in commercial building of hotels and office buildings. The de-

percent, and exceeded Germany's ratio in 2002–08. Japan remained ahead, but the gap between Japan and the United States fell from 15 percentage points in 1991 to 4 percentage points in 2005–06.

National saving, the sum of private and government saving, always equals national investment. One reason why the investment ratio was relatively low in the United States during most of the 1970–2000 period was the low rate of U.S. national saving. During the period 1980–96 and again in 2002–08, large U.S. government deficits meant that the government surplus was negative and national saving was low. The upsurge in the U.S. investment ratio shown in the graph was made possible by heavy borrowing from foreigners, not by domestic saving.

Firms finance their investment spending in several ways. In most countries the primary source of funds for business investment in plant and equipment is retained earnings, that is, the profits that firms have not paid out in dividends but have retained inside the firms. Especially in France, Italy, and Japan, firms also rely heavily on loans from banks to finance purchases of plant and equipment. Firms in Germany, the United Kingdom, and the United States are less dependent on bank loans, obtaining relatively more of the funds they use to finance investment expenditures by issuing stocks, long-term bonds, and short-term instruments like commercial paper.

In Chapter 15 we learned that consumers sometimes face liquidity constraints, which prevent them from borrowing the full amount of funds that they would be expected to be able to repay from permanent incomes. Business firms too sometimes face liquidity constraints. Young firms, like young households, may find it difficult to borrow the amount of funds justified by their longer-term prospects. And smaller firms may find that they must reduce investment when current profits or retained earnings decline. Thus, for both households and firms, constraints on borrowing and therefore on spending may be more severe during recessions or when higher interest rates raise loan payments.

One way for firms to loosen these financing constraints may be to ally themselves with other firms. Firms in Korea sometimes belong to a *chaebol*; in Italy firms are sometimes linked by family connections; in Japan some firms belong to a group of firms called a *keiretsu*; businesses in Canada and in the United States may be owned by conglomerates; and some firms in Japan and in Germany have bankers on their boards of directors. Because the other firms in such alliances often are not in closely allied areas of business, the alliance is more likely to remain strong when one of its members may need financial support. Belonging to one of these business groups seems to provide some insulation from financing constraints, perhaps because the other firms in the group can either provide the funds needed for investment directly to a constrained firm, or can provide some assurance to an outside lender like a bank that the other firms will help repay a bank loan to the constrained firm.

cline of investment spending in 2000–01 put substantial downward pressure on the economy, which as we have seen was resisted by an easing of monetary policy by the Fed that was unprecedented in its speed of response.[14]

In 2004–05, high-tech investment finally began to revive, as shown in Figure 16-5, but not to the ebullient growth rates registered in 1996–99. In fact, over the entire period 2000–07 the annual growth rate of high-tech investment (13.1 percent) was not only far below 1996–99 (34.9 percent) but below even 1987–95 (20.4

---

[14] Three references on the high-tech investment boom are Robert J. Gordon, "Does the New Economy Measure Up to the Great Inventions of the Past?" *Journal of Economic Perspectives*, vol. 14 (Fall 2000), pp. 49–74; Dale W. Jorgenson and Kevin J. Stiroh, "Raising the Speed Limit: U.S. Economic Growth in the Information Age," *Brooking Papers on Economic Activity*, vol. 31, no. 1 (2000), pp. 125–211; and Stephen D. Oliner and Daniel E. Sichel, "The Resurgence of Growth in the Late 1990s: Is Information Technology the Story?" *Journal of Economic Perspectives*, vol. 14 (Fall 2000), pp. 3–23. A comprehensive review of the role of high-tech investment in economic growth over the 1995–2006 period is Stephen D. Oliner, Daniel E. Sichel, and Kevin J. Stiroh, "Explaining a Productive Decade," *Brookings Papers on Economic Activity*, no. 1 (2007), pp. 81–152.

percent). Notable also was that the rate of decline of computer prices slowed in 2000–07 to the same rate as in 1987–95. It appears that the investment boom of the late 1990s was a one-shot event that was not to be repeated. The post-2000 hangover of the New Economy continued to be prolonged and difficult.   ●

16-10   Investment as a Source of Instability of Output and Interest Rates

The accelerator theory resolves a favorite paradox of macroeconomics teachers. We became accustomed in Chapter 3 to associating low interest rates with high investment and high interest rates with low investment. This negative relationship between investment and interest rates has been confirmed in this chapter, because a low level of the real interest rate reduces the user cost of capital, which in turn raises the desired capital stock and hence the level of gross investment.

Yet a predominant feature of business cycles in almost every nation is a positive correlation between business investment and interest rates. U.S. business investment fluctuates procyclically, reaching peaks in years of high output and troughs during recessions or soon afterward. But, since interest rates also fluctuate procyclically, years of low interest rates are usually associated with low investment, not high investment.

How can the positive correlation between investment and interest rates be explained? The accelerator theory provides the answer. Figure 16-6 repeats the *IS-LM* analysis of Chapter 4. The *LM* curve maintains an unchanged position whenever the real money supply (M/P) and real demand for money function are fixed. The *IS* curve fluctuates whenever there is a change in the investment purchases that business firms make at a constant real interest rate.

Causes of *IS* Shifts

We have seen that many factors can make the level of gross investment, and hence the *IS* curve, shift for a given interest rate. Among them are (1) a change in the expected growth rate of output and thus sales, (2) a previous episode of

---

Figure 16-6 Effect on Output and the Interest Rate of a Shift in the Level of Investment Relative to the Interest Rate

Shifts in business confidence or in user cost (apart from those due to changes in the real interest rate) can shift the red *IS* curve back and forth between IS_0 and IS_1. The real interest rate and investment will rise and fall together. This conclusion assumes that the real money supply, which fixes the position of the *LM* curve, remains unchanged.

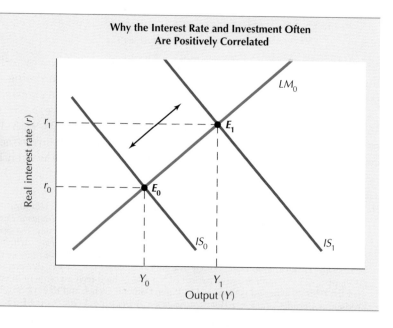

Why the Interest Rate and Investment Often Are Positively Correlated

overbuilding that makes the actual capital stock high relative to the current desired stock, (3) a shift in demand toward shorter-lived equipment, (4) a change in the relative price of capital goods, and, finally, (5) a change in fiscal incentives that alters the effective user cost of capital. A change in any of these elements shifts the level of investment that occurs at a given interest rate and, through the multiplier, shifts the *IS* curve and the level of total output.

Figure 16-6 illustrates two *IS* curves, IS_0 and IS_1. The shifts back and forth between the two *IS* curves reflect any one of the factors in the previous paragraph that cause an increase or decrease in gross investment. The positive relationship between investment and interest rates is explained in Figure 16-6 by the *IS* shifting along LM_0, which is held fixed by the fixed real money supply. That positive relationship suggests that the depressing effect of low output on investment, working through the accelerator, dominates the stimulative effect of low interest rates on investment, at least in the short run.

16-11 Conclusion: Investment and the Case For and Against Activism

We concluded in Chapter 15 that consumption spending on nondurable goods and services is relatively stable. Both the permanent-income and life-cycle hypotheses suggested that spending on nondurable goods and services tends to fluctuate less than disposable income. This stability bolsters the case for following a policy rule.

But this chapter tilts the balance in the opposite direction, toward the proposition of policy activists that the private economy contains sources of instability. The problem is epitomized by the accelerator theory of investment. Any event that causes a *permanent* increase in the desired capital stock—whether an increase in expected output or a reduction in the user cost of capital—causes only a *temporary* burst of investment spending. After the temporary burst, when net investment falls, economic instability is aggravated by the multiplier effect of Chapter 3.

Until the 1980s, the tendency for fixed investment to undergo multiyear booms and slumps formed the core of the activist case. It then became apparent, however, that net exports can be an equally important source of fluctuations in aggregate demand, as we learned in Chapters 3 and 6. The decline in net exports in the mid-1980s provided as much of a challenge for policymakers as the investment slumps of 1973–75, 1980–82, 1990–92, and 2000–02.

Investment Volatility and the Taylor Rule

The multiyear cycles in fixed investment and in net exports support the activist contention that private spending is unstable. But this does not by itself mean that policy should be entirely discretionary without any tie to a rule. On the contrary, the Taylor Rule studied in Chapter 14 is based on a formula that calls for the Fed to shift to an easier monetary policy *either* when the inflation rate drops below the Fed's target for inflation, or when the log output ratio becomes negative. Thus, under the Taylor Rule, the Fed is still able to ease policy in response to severe slumps of investment, as occurred in 2000–02, and indeed we have learned (pp. 469–71) that the Fed reduced interest rates during this period even more than is called for by a Taylor Rule. The Fed's actions after 2000 pleased adherents of policy activism who stress the need for the Fed to respond to volatile swings of investment.

Yet, as we have seen, many other observers criticize the Fed for reducing the federal funds rate too low for too long. By overreacting to the investment slump of 2000–02, the Fed created a new problem of excessive mortgage lending to borrowers who could not afford the terms of the loans that they were granted. The subprime mortgage crisis of 2007–08 (see pp. 474–75) was a direct result of the Fed's excessively easy monetary policy and of the Fed's lack of interest in regulating the mortgage brokers who unscrupulously pushed teaser rate mortgages on households that could not afford higher payments when the low rates adjusted upward.

Summary

1. The major source of instability in consumption spending is consumer expenditures on durables, which can exhibit large fluctuations in response to income changes. This chapter adds private investment spending as an additional source of instability, with the potential of causing major changes in GDP in response to small shocks.

2. The simple accelerator theory of investment relies on the idea that firms attempt to maintain a fixed relation between their stock of capital and their expected sales. Thus the level of net investment—the change in the capital stock—depends on the change in expected output. The accelerator theory explains why the gross investment of most firms is relatively unstable, at first rising and then falling in response to a permanent increase in actual sales.

3. The flexible accelerator theory recognizes that net investment in the real world usually closes only a portion of any gap between the desired and actual capital stocks. Furthermore, the desired capital-output ratio may change, altering investment with a powerful accelerator effect.

4. The accelerator theory suggests that any event that causes a permanent increase in the desired capital stock, whether arising from an increase in expected output or from a reduction in the user cost of capital, causes only a temporary rise in investment spending.

5. Government policymakers can directly alter the user cost of capital. Fiscal and monetary policy can change the real interest rate component of user cost. Taxation can affect the user cost of capital through changes in the corporation income tax, depreciation deductions,

and the investment tax credit. But the use of these policy instruments cannot eliminate all fluctuations in investment expenditures, because most policy measures operate only with lagged effects.

6. Spending on commercial construction has historically been quite variable, in part because the capital-output ratio for buildings is larger than that for other, shorter-lived types of physical capital. Because the lags between conception and completion of office buildings are long, booms and busts in spending for commercial real estate may last for several years. Changes in user costs and expected output also help explain this variability, but some of the fluctuations in construction still seem inexplicable and unpredictable.

7. Some firms face the same kinds of constraints on financing their spending that households face. Young and small firms seem particularly subject to constraints on how much investment they can undertake. In other countries around the world, firms sometimes are allied with other firms or with banks, which helps to reduce these constraints.

8. Shifts in the demand for investment spending tend to produce a positive correlation between investment and interest rates, even though the effect of higher interest rates, *ceteris paribus*, is to reduce investment spending. The former results from a shift of the *IS* curve, the latter from sliding along the *IS* curve.

9. The unpredictability of investment spending bolsters the case for policy activism. It also supports the Taylor Rule for monetary policy that reacts to booms and slumps of the output ratio caused by volatile swings of investment.

Concepts

accelerator hypothesis
flexible accelerator

marginal product of capital (MPK)
user cost of capital

depreciation rate

Questions

1. Distinguish between gross investment and net investment. Can gross investment ever be negative? Can net investment ever be negative?

2. Assume that output in the economy is growing. Does the simple accelerator model predict that net investment will also grow?

3. Discuss the role of lags in the accelerator theory. How does the existence of lags change the results of the simple accelerator model?

4. In summarizing the behavior of investment spending, the net investment ratio (I^n/Y) was described as volatile and persistent. Explain what is meant by these terms.

5. Business confidence and consumer confidence are often cited as playing a key role in the investment decision. How does business confidence enter the flexible accelerator model?

6. A capital good purchased at a given real price imposes three types of costs on its user. What are these costs? Which of these costs are subject to manipulation by policymakers?

7. What are the three tools of fiscal policy that can be used to influence the level of investment? According to the accelerator theory, are changes in these tools likely to lead to a permanent increase in the rate of investment?

8. What are the limitations to using tax incentives as a tool of activist fiscal policy?

9. Assume that the economy's output ratio equals 100 and monetary policymakers will react to any change in fiscal policy so as to prevent a rise in either the unemployment rate or the inflation rate. For each of the following changes in fiscal policy, explain what is likely to happen to the user cost of capital, the desired ratio of capital to expected output, and the level of net investment. Finally, keep in mind that any change in investment expenditures shifts the IS curve and affects aggregate demand.
   (a) Defense spending declines due to an increase in political stability across the globe.
   (b) Personal and corporate income tax rate cuts are passed in conjunction with even larger decreases in government spending.
   (c) An investment tax credit is enacted with no other changes in fiscal policy.
   (d) Federal spending on health care is increased and is only partially paid for by a higher tobacco tax.
   (e) Explain how any of your answers to parts a–d might change if the output ratio were less than 100.

10. What are the major factors that determine the relationship between gross investment and output in the economy? Briefly summarize the relationship involved.

11. Two of the functions of an economic model are to explain the behavior of economic variables and to forecast their future behavior. Using the information contained in the box on Tobin's q model, discuss how well each of the accelerator, neoclassical, and q models have explained or forecast the behavior of business spending on construction. What is the implication of this for the use of either rules-based policies or discretionary policy in efforts to stabilize the economy?

12. Use the interaction between the flexible accelerator and business confidence to explain why real private domestic investment fell so much relative to real GDP during the Great Depression. In addition, explain why real GDP rose while real private domestic investment fell during World War II.

13. Figure 16-5 shows that deflation in computer prices was much greater in the period 1996–99 than it was before and after those years. Simultaneously the amount of investment in computer equipment accelerated. Explain what the more rapid deflation in computer prices did to the real user cost of computer investment. Does that change in the real user cost of computer investment at the same time that investment in computer equipment accelerated invalidate the neoclassical theory of investment?

14. Are there other periods in the history of the U.S. economy that are similar to the collapse of the New Economy investment boom? What are some of the factors that contributed to the collapse in the boom? Finally, go to the Bureau of Economic Analysis Web site (www.bea.gov) to see if there has been a revival in investment spending on producers' durable equipment and software since the beginning of 2003.

15. According to the theory first presented in Chapter 3 and developed further in this chapter, the interest rate and investment are negatively related. Yet both business investment and interest rates tend to fluctuate procyclically, that is, are at their highest levels when the economy is at a high output level. Can you explain the paradox?

16. Using Tobin's q theory, explain what you would expect to happen to the construction of new houses as the prices of existing houses fall.

17. The procyclical nature of much investment spending tends to reduce the stability of the private economy. Suppose an investment tax credit plan is put in place under which the percentage tax credit granted to firms is negatively related to the output ratio. Would such a plan work to stabilize or destabilize the economy? Explain.

18. How does the existence of liquidity constraints affect the volatility of investment? Why might liquidity constraints be more binding on smaller firms than on larger ones and on U.S. firms than on firms in such countries as Germany and Japan?

19. Discuss how the behavior of investment described in this chapter strengthens or weakens the cases for discretionary policy and rules-based policy.

Problems

1. (a) Using the data contained in Table A-2 of Appendix A, calculate the percentage change (in logs) in real GDP from peak to trough and from trough to peak for the business cycles listed in the table at the beginning of Section 16-2's case study of the historical instability of investment.
   (b) Using your answer to part a and the data contained in the table at the beginning of the case study of the historical instability of investment, compare the volatility of real GDP with that of investment expenditures. Furthermore discuss whether the data show that the volatility of investment spending has varied over business cycles since 1960.

2. This problem uses the example in Table 16-1 (p. 525).
   (a) The economy will reach an equilibrium when expected sales no longer increase. What will net investment be at that point? What will gross investment be?
   (b) Assume that because of a new investment tax credit, the desired capital–expected sales ratio changes to 5. What would net investment be in periods 1–5?
   (c) When the economy reaches its new equilibrium, what will be the ultimate effect of the tax credits on investment?

3. This problem also uses the data in Table 16-1.
   (a) What would expected sales have to be in periods 3 to 5 for net investment to be constant at 4.0?
   (b) What would actual sales have to be in periods 3 to 5 to achieve a constant level of net investment?
   (c) What would actual sales have to be in periods 2 to 4 to achieve a steady 20 percent increase in gross investment in each of the periods 3 to 5?
   (d) At what rate do actual sales increase in part c?

4. This problem also uses the example in Table 16-1 (p. 525), except where noted. The flexible accelerator model states that net investment, I^n, equals a fraction, f, of the gap between the desired capital stock, K^*, and last period's capital stock, K_{-1} The capital stock in any period equals last period's capital stock plus last period's net investment. The equations that describe these relationships are

$$I^n = f(K^* - K_{-1}) \text{ and } K = K_{-1} + I^n_{-1}.$$

   (a) Assume that f equals 0.5. Calculate the amounts of the capital stock, net investment, and gross investment in periods 1–5.
   (b) Using the example in Table 16-1 and your answer to part a, discuss how net and gross investments differ between the simple and flexible accelerator models.

5. This problem also uses the example in Table 16-1 (p. 525) and the flexible accelerator from problem 4. Assume that f equals 0.5. Suppose that the desired capital-expected sales ratio, v^*, depends on the real user cost of capital, u. In particular, $v^* = 5.5 - 10u$.

   (a) Suppose that the real interest rate equals 5 percent (0.05) and that the capital stock lasts for 10 years, so that d equals 0.1. Calculate the real user cost of capital and the desired capital stock in periods 1–5. Explain why the amounts of the capital stock, net investment, and gross investment in periods 1–5 are the same as in part a of problem 4.
   (b) Suppose that in period 1, the real interest rate falls to 3 percent (0.03) and stays at that level for periods 2–5. Given no change in the depreciation rate, compute the new real user cost of capital, and the new amounts of the desired capital stock, the actual capital stock, net investment, and gross investment in periods 1–5.
   (c) Suppose that the real interest rate equals 5 percent (0.05), but that the capital stock depreciates more quickly, so that d equals 0.2. Calculate the new real user cost of capital, and the new amounts of the desired capital stock, the capital stock, net investment, and gross investment in periods 1–5.
   (d) Use your answers from parts b and c to discuss the effect of changes in the real interest rate and the depreciation rate on the amounts of net and gross investment.
   (e) Use your answer to part b to discuss how the flexible accelerator can be used to explain why the economy's output responds with a lag to a change in monetary policy.

6. This problem uses the Tobin q model of investment. (See the box on pp. 532–33.) Suppose that the adjustment rate, j, equals 0.2 and that the depreciation rate equals 0.1. The replacement value of the AB Corporation's capital equals 10 million dollars and the market value of its stock for the next 10 periods is listed in the table below. (The market value is listed in millions of dollars.)

Period	1	2	3	4	5	6	7	8	9	10
Market value	11	12	12	11	10	9	8	8	9	10

   (a) Calculate the value of Tobin's q for the AB Corporation in periods 1–10.
   (b) Calculate the AB Corporation's investment-to-capital stock ratio in periods 1–10.
   (c) Suppose that the Tobin q's and the investment-to-capital stock ratios for all businesses behave like that of the AB Corporation during periods 1–10. Other things being equal, explain how the economy's IS curves shift during periods 2–10.
   (d) Given your answer to part c, explain how the monetary policymakers would change the interest rate in periods 2–10 if they followed either an activist policy aimed at preventing rises in either the inflation or unemployment rate or a Taylor Rule.

SELF-TEST ANSWERS

p. **527** (1) Assuming, as in this section, that replacement investment is a fixed fraction of the previous year's capital stock, replacement investment is the most stable. Net investment, which depends on the *change* in expected output, is the least stable. Gross investment, the sum of net investment and replacement investment, is in-between. (2) The longer-lived is capital, the smaller is the fraction of the previous year's capital stock that needs to be replaced; hence, the smaller is stable replacement investment relative to unstable net investment. Thus we would expect gross investment in office buildings to be less stable than gross investment in computers.

p. **537** (1) The three potential tools are the corporation income tax, the value of depreciation deductions, and the investment tax credit. (2) If the government wants to stimulate investment, it can reduce the corporation income tax rate, or raise the value of depreciation deductions (by allowing business firms to take depreciation deductions earlier), or raise the percentage rate of the investment tax credit. If there is no investment tax credit, as in the United States after 1986, the government can introduce such a credit. (3) Monetary policy affects the user cost through its ability to change the real interest rate.

For additional practice and exploration, exercises that require the use of Excel are available at www.aw-bc.com/gordon.

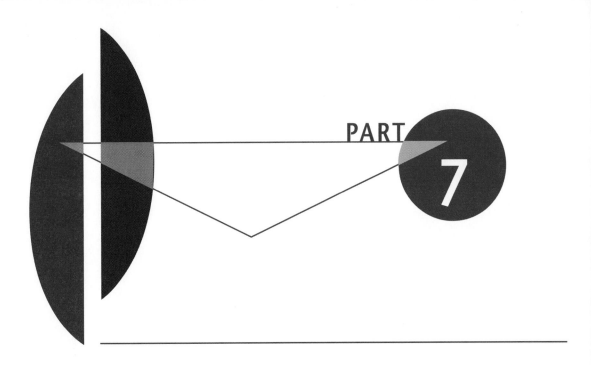

Debates at the Macroeconomic Frontier

17

New Classical Macro Confronts New Keynesian Macro

The chief cause of depressions is a want of confidence. The greater part of it could be removed almost in an instant if confidence could return, touch all industries with her magic wand, and make them continue their production, and their demand for the wares of others.
—Alfred Marshall, 1879

17-1 Introduction: Classical and Keynesian Economics, Old and New

The development of new theories in macroeconomics and the abandonment of old theories often occur in response to major macroeconomic developments. In Chapter 7 we were introduced to the classical economists whose ideas dominated macroeconomics prior to the 1930s; they believed that the price level was flexible and would shift by the amount necessary to eliminate any inadequacies in aggregate demand. We described this approach as assuming that the economy possesses strong self-correcting properties, in the form of price flexibility, that would automatically correct any tendency for real aggregate demand to be too high or too low.

In the 1930s, a calamitous macroeconomic event, the Great Depression, brought a decade-long economic slump accompanied by double-digit unemployment rates. The Great Depression discredited the old classical approach based on flexible prices and self-correction. This epochal event created among economists, journalists, policymakers, and laypeople a receptive audience for the Keynesian revolution, based on John Maynard Keynes's influential book, *The General Theory of Employment, Interest, and Income*.[1]

However, the old Keynesian approach was not without its own problems. Only a few years after the publication of *The General Theory*, economists questioned Keynes's assumption that (as in Figure 7-7 on p. 209) real wages vary countercyclically, rising in recessions and falling in expansions. Nevertheless, the old Keynesian approach dominated macroeconomics until the late 1960s. The big event that undermined its dominance was the emergence at that time of significant inflation. The old Keynesian theory based on rigid nominal wages had little to say about the causes of inflation.

New Classical Macroeconomics Versus New Keynesian Economics

Since the early 1970s, macroeconomics has been split between two basic explanations of business cycles. First to emerge as a challenge to the old Keynesian orthodoxy was the new classical approach originated by Milton Friedman,

---

[1] The late Harry Johnson examined the reasons for the success of the Keynesian revolution and developed a parallel set of reasons for the late 1960s' monetarist "counterrevolution." See his article "The Keynesian Revolution and the Monetarist Counter-Revolution," *American Economic Review*, vol. 61 (May 1971), pp. 1–14.

then at the University of Chicago, and Edmund S. Phelps of Columbia University. It was subsequently more fully developed by Robert E. Lucas, Jr., of the University of Chicago. This first approach was based on the idea that households and firms lack the full set of information needed to make their economic decisions. Later, a second strand of new classical macroeconomics emerged, based not on imperfect information but on shocks to technology and supply conditions. The second approach, the "real business cycle" model, was developed primarily by Edward Prescott of Arizona State University.

Common to all new classical models is the assumption of continuous equilibrium in labor and product markets. These markets "clear," in the sense that each worker and firm is acting as desired at the price and wage level that is expected to prevail during the period of employment or production. For Friedman, Phelps, and Lucas, business cycles emerge because workers and/or firms, while acting as desired, are doing so on the basis of incorrect information. In contrast, Prescott theorizes that business cycles emerge because a given amount of labor and capital input produces varying amounts of real GDP due to changes in the efficiency of production.

New classical macro contrasts with another recent set of theories intended in part to remedy weaknesses in the old Keynesian approach. These new theories are grouped together under the general heading of "new Keynesian" macro. Such models, examined in the second part of this chapter, accept Keynes's insight that prices and wages do not change fast enough for classical self-correction to occur. But they go beyond Keynes to examine the *reasons* why slow price and wage adjustment is often in the self-interest of workers and is consistent with profit maximization for firms. The implications of new Keynesian macro differ radically from those of new classical macro. For if prices and wages adjust slowly, no matter what the reasons, then markets do not always clear; workers are sometimes unable to obtain as many jobs as they want at the prevailing wages and prices, and firms are sometimes unable to sell as much as they would like to produce at those wages and prices.

17-2 Imperfect Information and the "Fooling Model"

One of two related theories to introduce the new classical approach was Milton Friedman's "fooling model," developed as part of his presidential address to the American Economic Association in 1967.[2]

Distinctive Features: Market Clearing and Imperfect Information

The first distinctive feature of Friedman's model is that markets clear continuously; all actions of firms and workers are voluntary. The second distinctive feature is that business cycles can occur only if workers *inaccurately perceive the price level*, hence the label "fooling model." This feature of the Friedman model is often called "imperfect information" and is a characteristic of many modern models of the market-clearing variety.

Milton Friedman (1912–2006)

Friedman, a 1976 Nobel Prize winner, was the most famous proponent of policy rules (Chapter 14) and the inventor of the permanent-income hypothesis of consumption (Chapter 15).

---

[2] Milton Friedman, "The Role of Monetary Policy," *American Economic Review,* vol. 58 (March 1968), pp. 1–17.

Friedman's fooling model is asymmetric: Firms always know the current value of the price level but workers only learn the actual price level with a time lag. The economy is initially in equilibrium with actual real GDP (Y) equal to natural real GDP (Y^N). Let us consider the effects of an increase in aggregate demand caused by a monetary or fiscal expansion. Firms are willing to produce more because the high level of aggregate demand is accompanied by a higher price level (*Review:* the economy moves from point B to point C in Figure 7-8 on p. 211). The price level might rise by 10 percent and the nominal wage by 5 percent, resulting in a 5 percent reduction in the real wage that induces firms to hire more workers. But the workers do not know that the price level has increased, and they assess the 5 percent increase in the nominal wage in terms of an unchanged expected price level. They think the real wage has increased by 5 percent, and so they willingly work more. This expectational error by the workers is what makes it possible for Y to differ from Y^N; the business cycle happens only because the workers are fooled.

Sooner or later any expectational errors will be corrected, so actual real GDP cannot remain away from natural real GDP for long. As a result, Friedman's model is sometimes called a "natural rate" model, and in fact it is Friedman who is responsible for the terms "natural real GDP" and "natural rate of unemployment." It is common to describe a model with a vertical long-run supply curve (like *LAS* in Figure 7-8 on p. 211) as obeying the **natural rate hypothesis**.

A model obeys the **natural rate hypothesis** when shifts in aggregate demand have no long-run effect on real GDP.

The Phelps Version of the Fooling Model

Simultaneously with the publication of Friedman's fooling model, Edmund S. Phelps of Columbia University developed a slightly different model in the same spirit, and he deserves equal credit for the invention of the natural rate hypothesis. In contrast to Friedman's distinction between the smart firms and the fooled workers, in Phelps's world everyone is equally fooled. Both firms and workers see the price rise in their industry and produce more, not realizing that the general price level has risen in the rest of the economy. Phelps developed one model in which firms are fooled while the workers are not. Firms see that the price of their product has increased, and they offer to hire more workers, not realizing that all other firms in the economy are experiencing the same increase in prices.

In another model, workers are isolated from information about the rest of the economy. Normally there is turnover unemployment (see Section 9-9 on pp. 308–11), as workers regularly quit one firm to go look for more highly paid work at other firms. But in a situation in which their own firm raises the wage, they stay with that firm instead of quitting. Thus the unemployment rate decreases even though, without their knowledge, all other firms in the economy have raised the wage by the same amount at the same time. The workers are fooled into a reduction in turnover unemployment, and the macroeconomic data register a decline in the unemployment rate.[3]

Edmund S. Phelps (1933–)

Phelps, a 2006 Nobel Prize winner, co-invented the natural rate hypothesis, pioneered the concept of the "golden rule" of economic growth, introduced the concept of imperfect information into many branches of economics, and helped to invent the analysis of supply shocks as summarized in Chapter 8.

---

[3] Phelps's contributions appear in two important articles. See "Phillips Curves, Expectations of Inflation and Optimal Unemployment over Time," *Economica*, vol. 34 (August 1967), and "Money-Wage Dynamics and Labor-Market Equilibrium," *Journal of Political Economy*, vol. 76 (August 1968, Part II).

Criticisms of the Friedman and Phelps Versions of the Fooling Model

How did Friedman and Phelps justify their claim that workers will hold incorrect expectations for any significant period of time? Friedman's answer was that *firms have more accurate information than is available to workers.* Firms have this informational advantage, because they have a concentrated interest in a small number of prices of particular products and monitor them continuously. Workers, on the other hand, are interested in a wide variety of prices of the things they buy and have insufficient time to keep careful track. The workers do not immediately notice when the price level rises.

The Phelps version of the fooling model does not assume any particular informational advantage of firms over workers. *Everyone* is ignorant of what is happening in the general economy, as if they were stranded on small islands completely cut off from the rest of the world. Three telling criticisms have been directed against the assumption of imperfect information that drives both the Friedman and Phelps models. First, there is no reason to single out any particular ignorance of workers, as does Friedman and one of the Phelps models. Workers and their families buy many goods, particularly food, gasoline, and drug items, on a weekly or even daily basis, and they would discover almost immediately if the general price level had risen. Second, news about the level of prices and wages is published by the government and repeated on television newscasts every month, so any ignorance could last no longer than one month, far too short to explain multiyear business cycles. Third, if periods of high real GDP and a prosperous period of economic activity were *always* accompanied by an increase in the aggregate price level, workers and firms would learn from past episodes and realize that any period of current prosperity is doubtless accompanied by higher prices.

With realistic intelligence on the part of workers and firms, there is no room in macroeconomics for any model that bases its entire explanation of business cycles on ignorance and fooling. Any change in aggregate demand will move wages and prices up or down simultaneously and the economy will remain at its natural level of output, with no business cycles at all, just as in the classical self-correcting model of Figure 7-9 on p. 215.

17-3 The Lucas Model and the Policy Ineffectiveness Proposition

The Assumption of Rational Expectations

Rational expectations need not be correct but must make the best use of available information, avoiding errors that could have been foreseen by knowledge of history.

The **Lucas model** is based on the three assumptions of market clearing, imperfect information, and rational expectations.

Despite their limitations, the Friedman and Phelps models, with their twin assumptions of market clearing and imperfect information, appealed to many economists. Preeminent among these was Robert E. Lucas, Jr., who took Friedman's model one step further by introducing an improved treatment of the way workers form their view of the expected price level (P^e). Instead of following Friedman's rather unsatisfactory assumption that workers only gradually adapted their expectations of the price level (P^e) to the actual value of the price level, allowing themselves to be fooled for weeks or even months, Lucas introduced the theory of **rational expectations.** Thus the **Lucas model** contains three basic assumptions: market clearing, imperfect information, and rational expectations.[4]

Expectations are rational *when people make the best forecasts they can with the available data.* It is important to recognize that these forecasts do not have to be correct, and so observing forecasting errors by individuals or professional economists does not constitute evidence against rational expectations. Instead, the theory of rational expectations argues that people do not consistently make the same forecasting errors.

For instance, the errors (or fooling) of the Friedman-Phelps model are not rational. If the observance of history suggested that any increase in employment had always been accompanied by a reduction in the actual real wage, then workers would learn that any offer of extra employment in the future would also be accompanied by a reduction in the actual real wage, causing these smart workers to refuse any such job offers. More generally, individuals should not make errors in the same direction week after week, especially in circumstances similar to those in history. The errors should be random, that is, independent of past forecasting errors.

The Lucas model, like those of Friedman and Phelps, makes output depend positively on a "price surprise," that is, a rise in the actual price level (P) relative to the expected price level (P^e). Lucas, like Phelps, relies on information barriers that apply equally to workers and firms. Lucas's firms are like small farmers who produce wheat or corn and are induced to produce more by an increase in the actual price. Information barriers prevent the farmers from learning that prices have gone up everywhere in the economy, raising their marginal cost of production and giving them no incentive to produce more.

Robert E. Lucas, Jr. (1937–)

Lucas, a 1995 Nobel Prize winner, is the leading developer of the new classical macroeconomics; he merged the concept of rational expectations with the assumptions of market clearing and imperfect information.

 SELF-TEST

Answer the following questions according to the Friedman-Phelps-Lucas theory of output determination:

1. Does a recession in which actual real GDP (Y) falls below natural real GDP (Y^N) require a price surprise? In which direction?

2. Does a boom in which Y rises above Y^N require a price surprise? In which direction?

3. What happens to the output gap ($Y - Y^N$) when people learn the true price level and the price surprise vanishes?

The Policy Ineffectiveness Proposition

The concept of rational expectations, which states that individuals use all available information in forming their expectations, leads to a startling prediction by Lucas and his followers. In a modern version of monetary impotence, Lucas argues that *anticipated monetary policy cannot change real GDP in a regular*

---

[4] Robert Lucas did not invent the idea of rational expectations, but rather receives credit for applying it to macroeconomics. The original idea was applied to microeconomic issues and was set forth in John Muth, "Rational Expectations and the Theory of Price Movements," *Econometrica*, vol. 29 (July 1961), pp. 315–35. Lucas's seminal contribution is contained in two articles. The more accessible of these is Robert E. Lucas, Jr., "Some International Evidence on Output-Inflation Tradeoffs," *American Economic Review*, vol. 63 (June 1973), pp. 326–34. A more technical article that motivates some of the assumed underlying microeconomic behavior is "Expectations and the Neutrality of Money," *Journal of Economic Theory*, vol. 4 (April 1972), pp. 103–24.

The **policy ineffectiveness proposition** asserts that predictable changes in monetary policy cannot affect real output.

or predictable way. Usually called the **policy ineffectiveness proposition** (PIP), Lucas's argument for monetary impotence startled the economics profession when it was developed in the early 1970s.[5]

PIP can be understood as a corollary of rational expectations together with the theory that movements of Y away from Y^N require a price surprise ($P \neq P^e$). The central bank (the Fed) can change output only if it can find some method of creating a price surprise. However, if the public knows that an increase in the money supply raises the price level, then whenever the Fed raises the money supply there will be an increase by the same amount in *both* the actual and expected price levels, no price surprise will occur ($P = P^e$), and output will remain at the natural level of real GDP ($Y = Y^N$).

> **Summary:** The policy ineffectiveness proposition states only that fully anticipated changes in the money supply cannot affect real GDP. It does not deny that a money surprise (an unanticipated change in the money supply) can alter the level of real GDP. But it implies that the Fed faces a considerable problem in creating such a money surprise, since the Fed cannot respond to economic events in the same way it has in the past.

Problem: The Prompt Availability of Information

Although PIP created a revolution that dominated macroeconomic discussion in the late 1970s, by the end of the decade several weaknesses of PIP had been pointed out. The problem was not the Lucas contribution of rational expectations. Rather, the weakness was in the twin assumptions inherited from Friedman and Phelps, continuous market clearing and imperfect information, which made deviations of the current actual price from the expected price the *only* source of business cycle movements in real GDP. The assumption of imperfect information implies that business cycles would be eliminated if we had accurate current information about the aggregate price level.

This imperfect information aspect of the Friedman, Phelps, and Lucas models has been widely criticized. Aggregate price information is easily available with short lags of a month or two. With aggregate price information easily available, why should firms or workers take any action that might move them away from labor market equilibrium?

17-4 The Real Business Cycle Model

There now appears to be general agreement that the imperfect information theory of the business cycle is unsatisfactory, since information lags are too short to be a plausible source of multiyear business cycles.[6] New classical macro-

---

[5] While Lucas receives the main credit for the basic ideas underlying the Lucas model, the formal case for PIP was made by Thomas J. Sargent and Neil Wallace in "'Rational' Expectations, the Optimal Monetary Instrument, and the Optimal Money Supply Rule," *Journal of Political Economy*, vol. 83 (April 1975), pp. 241–54.

[6] For instance, Robert Barro, who made important contributions to the development of the Lucas approach and PIP, was convinced by the problems addressed in the previous section that "the upshot of these arguments is that the new classical approach does not do very well in accounting for an important role of money in business fluctuations." See Robert J. Barro, "New Classicals and Keynesians, or the Good Guys and the Bad Guys," *Schweiz, Zeitschrift für Volkswirtschaft und Statistik*, Heft 3, 1989. More recently, Robert Lucas has admitted that "Monetary shocks just aren't that important. That's the view I've been driven to. There's no question that's a retreat in my views." See John Cassidy, "The Decline of Economics," *The New Yorker* (December 2, 1996), p. 55.

economists have turned to an alternative theory of the business cycle, one that still assumes continuous market clearing. Their new theory is the **real business cycle (RBC) model** of economic fluctuations.

The real business cycle (RBC) model assumes that the origins of the business cycle lie in real (or supply) shocks rather than monetary (or demand) shocks. The main source of shifts in output lies in swings in the aggregate supply curve (both long-run and short-run), not the aggregate demand curve. The RBC approach states that fluctuations in Y are caused entirely by fluctuations in natural real GDP itself, Y^N.

> The **real business cycle (RBC)** model explains business cycles in output and employment as being caused by technology or supply shocks.

What are these real (or supply) shocks that cause business cycles and account for the term "real" business cycle model? Shocks can include new production techniques, new products, bad weather, new sources of raw materials, and price changes in raw materials. Recall that the Lucas model failed to consider that information barriers are too short-lived to explain the *length* and *persistence* of actual business cycles. In contrast, the RBC approach assumes that these supply shocks are highly persistent, meaning that a favorable shock lasts several years, dies away smoothly, and is replaced by an adverse shock that lasts several years. It is important to note that the RBC theory simply *assumes* and does not explain the persistence of business cycles that undermined the Lucas approach.

In the RBC model, the economy responds to these persistent supply shocks according to the new classical assumption of continuous equilibrium. Firms produce the amount they desire at prices and wages that respond flexibly to changing economic conditions, and hire the number of workers they want; workers obtain exactly the number of hours of work that they desire at the market-determined real wage.[7] Our aggregate supply curve diagram introduced in Chapter 7 illustrates these aspects of the RBC model.

The Labor Market in the RBC Model

The top frame of Figure 17-1 exhibits the production function (F), which shows how much output can be produced by each additional worker.[8] An adverse supply shock leads to a downward shift in the production function, for instance from the normal curve F_0 to the bad shock curve F_1, implying a decline in the productivity of each worker. In the lower frame the labor demand curve, which shows the marginal product of labor, shifts down in response to the adverse supply shock from the line labeled N_0^d to the line N_1^d.

The effect of the adverse supply shock on both output and employment depends on the slope of the labor supply curve. If this slope is positive, as along the line labeled N_0^s, then a lower real wage induces workers to supply less labor (working fewer hours or leaving the labor force). Since the economy is always in equilibrium in the RBC model, the demand for labor shifts as a result

---

[7] Two of the most influential papers in the development of the RBC approach are Finn E. Kydland and Edward C. Prescott, "Time to Build and Aggregate Fluctuations," *Econometrica*, vol. 50 (November 1982), pp. 1345–70; and Robert G. King and Charles I. Plosser, "Money, Credit, and Prices in a Real Business Cycle," *American Economic Review,* vol. 74 (June 1984), pp. 363–80. A sympathetic exposition is Bennett T. McCallum, "Real Business Cycle Models," in Robert J. Barro, ed., *Modern Business Cycle Theory* (Cambridge, MA: Harvard University Press, 1989), pp. 16–50. A less technical introduction is Charles I. Plosser, "Understanding Real Business Cycles," *Journal of Economic Perspectives*, vol. 3 (Summer 1989), pp. 51–77.

[8] We were first introduced to the production function in Figure 10-1 on p. 325. That production function related output per worker (Y/N) to capital per worker (K/N). In contrast, the production function in Figure 17-1 relates output (Y) to the number of workers (N).

Figure 17-1 Effect of an Adverse Supply Shock on Output and Employment in the Real Business Cycle Model

In the top frame, F_0 is the normal production function. In the bottom frame, N_0^d is the normal labor demand curve. An adverse movement in supply conditions, like bad weather for growing crops, shifts the production function down to F_1 and the labor demand curve down to N_1^d. In normal times the economy operates at point B in the upper and lower frames, and in bad times at point V. The decline in employment depends on the slope of the labor supply curve; if the labor supply curve were a vertical line instead of a positively sloped line like N_0^s, the economy would move to Z instead of V. Employment would remain fixed and output would fall only from Y_0 to Y_0'.

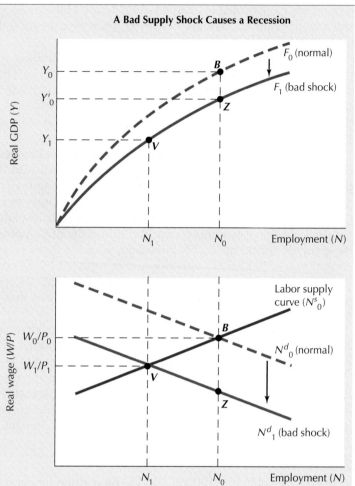

A Bad Supply Shock Causes a Recession

of the supply shock from point B to point V. Employment falls from N_0 to N_1, while output falls from Y_0 to Y_1, seen in the upper frame.

A different slope of the labor supply curve would lead to a different conclusion. Imagine that the labor supply curve, instead of being N_0^s, is a vertical line rising above N_0 through points Z and B. Then the economy's equilibrium point would be shifted downward by the adverse supply shock from B to Z. The shock would cause no change in employment, and in the upper frame there would be a much smaller decline in output, from Y_0 to Y_0'. Thus the RBC model's ability to explain why employment declines in real-world recessions requires a positive slope of the labor supply schedule, as shown by the line N_0^s.[9]

 SELF-TEST

Answer the following questions according to the RBC theory:

1. Why does output increase in a business expansion?

---

[9] The effect of an adverse supply shock in shifting the labor demand curve downward was previously shown in the upper frame of Figure 11-6 on p. 378, but there the labor supply was not shown explicitly.

2. What are examples of events that would raise output in a business expansion?

3. What are examples of events that would reduce output in a business contraction?

Labor Supply Behavior and Intertemporal Substitution

As we have seen, it is critical for the RBC model that the labor supply curve have a positive slope, as drawn in the bottom frame of Figure 17-1. The traditional microeconomic analysis of labor supply decisions stresses two conflicting effects of an increase in the real wage. A higher real wage increases the reward for work as compared to leisure (the substitution effect). But a higher real wage also raises real income and makes people want to consume more of all normal goods, including leisure, which means reducing work (the income effect). In drawing a positively sloped labor supply curve in Figure 17-1, we simply assume that the substitution effect dominates the income effect.

The RBC approach not only assumes that the substitution effect is dominant, but stresses a particular dimension of substitution that takes place over time. This type of substitution is called **intertemporal substitution.** It occurs when workers reallocate the amount of working time in response to changes in the real wage. In good times, when the real wage is high, workers choose to work more. And they take more leisure in bad times, when the real wage is low.

Students face such choices during their college years. Many students want to take one summer off to go to Europe, while planning to work in the other summers. A sophomore has two summers left before graduation. Which summer should he or she choose to go to Europe? Obviously, the summer with the best opportunities to earn relatively high wages should be chosen for work, and the European trip should be taken in the summer when high-paying jobs are scarce.

Variations in the interest rate introduce another element into the choice. If the real interest rate is high enough, it would pay to work in the first summer and postpone the trip to the second summer. Even if the wages earned in the first summer are somewhat lower than they are expected to be in the second summer, the extra interest earned on the savings account containing the earnings from the first summer would make that a better choice. In short, labor supply increases in response *either* to a high real wage or a high real interest rate.

This example highlights a problem in applying the theory of intertemporal substitution to the real world—how can students predict which future summer is likely to provide the most high-paying job opportunities? If even financial experts make major mistakes in predicting interest rates, are students any more likely to be able to predict whether interest rates will be higher or lower in future summers?

Intertemporal substitution occurs when workers work more in periods of high real wages and less in periods of low real wages. It also occurs when producers raise output in periods of high prices and reduce output in periods of low prices.

17-5 New Classical Macroeconomics: Limitations and Positive Contributions

Assessment of the Real Business Cycle Model

Both the RBC model and the conventional *AD-SAS* graphical analysis of Chapter 7 agree that supply shocks can cause business cycles. Why, then, is the RBC model so controversial? The criticisms concern the unique components of

International Perspective

Productivity Fluctuations in the United States and Japan

Productivity is simply the ratio of output to inputs and measures the efficiency with which inputs are used. Labor productivity is output per unit of labor input. As we learned in Chapter 11, a more general concept, called multifactor productivity (MFP), is output per unit of total input, including not just labor but also capital, energy, and imported materials.

Interest in the RBC model is motivated by productivity shocks that vary procyclically, that is, in the same direction as the business cycle. How important are procyclical fluctuations of MFP, that is, the ratio of output to total input? The charts on the facing page show the growth rate of output and input for the United States and Japan. Whenever output grows more rapidly than input, MFP growth is positive, as shown by the red-shaded area. Whenever output grows more slowly than input, MFP growth is negative, as shown by the blue-shaded area.

In the top frame of the figure, the data for the United States show that in booms, output growth consistently rises more than input growth (defined here as an average of growth in labor and capital input); during recessions, output growth consistently falls more than input growth. As a result, MFP growth is negative in such recession periods as 1970, 1974–75, 1980–82, and 1991. MFP growth is most strongly positive when output itself is growing most rapidly, as in 1966, 1973, 1976, 1984, 1992, 1998, and 2004.

In the bottom frame of the figure, the data for Japan show some striking differences. First, input growth is much smoother from year to year, with fewer cycles, particularly between 1975 and 1990. Because input growth was so remarkably stable, Japan was largely able to avoid the periodic episodes of massive layoffs that plagued the United States during recession periods. And, because input growth was so stable, Japanese MFP growth was even more strongly procyclical than in the United States.

The stability of Japanese input growth was very different after 1990. Input growth dropped almost to zero in 1992–94 and was negative in 1999 and 2001–02. The ups and downs of Japanese input growth after 1998 mirror output growth, much more like the U.S. pattern than in Japan before 1990.

A second difference is that output growth in Japan never fell below zero in any year between 1965 and 1998. This contrasts with the United States, where output growth turned negative in 1974–75, 1980, 1982, and 1991.

A third difference is that the pattern of MFP growth (the difference between output and input growth) is quite different in Japan from that in the United States. MFP growth in Japan was positive in every year between 1975 and 1991 except briefly and by small amounts in 1977 and 1983, with an average annual growth rate of 1.8 percent during 1975–91. In the United States, MFP growth was negative by relatively large amounts in 1974, 1980, and 1982, and by a small amount in 1991.

But after 1991 these relationships reversed. U.S. MFP growth was positive in every year after 1991 except 1995. In Japan, MFP growth was negative in six of the years after 1991, and on average Japan's MFP growth was actually negative between 1992 and 2006, with an annual growth rate of -0.1 percent. In contrast, the United States enjoyed an MFP growth revival, with an increase from an annual rate of 0.6 percent during 1975–91 to 1.2 percent during 1992–2006.

The procyclical behavior of MFP growth illustrated here is consistent with the procyclical technology shocks that drive the RBC model. However, it is also consistent with other theories, such as the idea that it is costly to hire and fire workers, with the result that firms adjust labor input only partially in response to changes in output.

the RBC analysis: the emphasis on technological shocks as the *primary* cause of business cycles, the failure to include prices or money, and the RBC interpretation of what happens in labor markets during business cycles.

Nature of technology shocks. Critics focus on two aspects of the RBC model's treatment of technology shocks. While it is plausible that *advances* in technology may occur at an irregular pace, causing cycles in the growth rate of output, the implication that recessions are caused by *retreats* in technology ("forgetfulness") strikes some critics as implausible. Defenders of the RBC model respond that there are several types of events that have the same effect as a decay in technology, even if people do not literally forget how to produce efficiently.

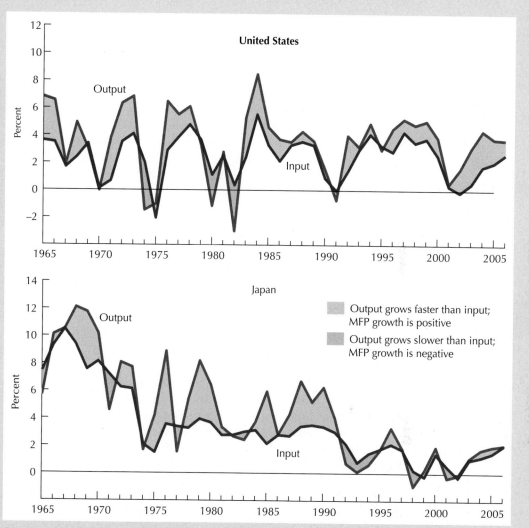

Sources: United States data from the Bureau of Labor Statistics. Japan data from EU KLEMS Database, Groningen Growth and Development Center *Total Economy Database*, and OECD *Economic Outlook*. Details in Appendix C-4.

These include bad harvests, oil price shocks, and government regulations that require heavy investment and extra workers to reduce air and water pollution.[10]

---

[10] The Great Depression is a major embarrassment for the advocates of the RBC model, since their approach forces them to interpret the massive unemployment of the 1930s as entirely voluntary, and the cause of the 27 percent decline in real GDP between 1929 and 1933 as a massive adverse supply shock, an implausible episode of "forgetfulness" in which firms and workers forgot one-quarter of the technological knowledge they had in 1929. For a contrary view that the 1930s were a period of unusually rapid technical progress, and that implicitly the Great Depression was caused by a decline in aggregate demand rather than aggregate supply, see Alexander J. Field, "The Most Technologically Progressive Decade of the Century," *American Economic Review*, vol. 93, no. 4 (September 2003), pp. 1399–1413.

Perhaps a more serious charge distinguishes between the aggregate economy and the behavior of individual industries. Unlike the *IS-LM* model of Chapter 4, the RBC model does not incorporate a multiplier effect that can magnify the impact of shocks on the economy. Therefore, to explain big recessions, the model needs big shocks. But technology is unique to particular industries. Highly distinctive technological innovations that, for instance, increase the speed of a Windows desktop computer have little impact on the productivity of coal miners. At an industry level, one would expect technological shocks (good and bad) to occur randomly, so that favorable shocks in some industries would largely cancel out adverse shocks in other industries. Any bad shock large enough to cause an economywide recession (considering that it would be partly canceled by good shocks in other industries) would be highly visible in industry data. Yet the proponents of the RBC model have as yet failed to identify any such shocks, particularly negative ones, other than the oil price shocks (see Figure 8-9 on p. 256).

Price and output changes.   Although recently there has been some attention to real demand shocks, particularly those associated with government spending, the basic RBC model is based on an alternation of good and bad supply shocks, each persisting by about as long as an average U.S. business cycle. But this leads to a troublesome implication: If business cycles occur when the aggregate supply curve shifts back and forth but the aggregate demand curve remains fixed, then prices should rise in recessions and fall in booms. The business cycle should look much like the market for wheat, with low prices and high output in years of good harvests, and with high prices and low output in years with bad harvests.

The key problem is that prices are sometimes positively related to output changes, as in the Great Depression, and sometimes negatively related to output changes, as in the supply shock episodes of the 1970s and early 1980s. This suggests that business cycles are caused both by demand and supply shocks, not just by supply shocks, just as in the *AD-SAS* model of Chapter 7 and the inflation-output model developed in Chapter 8.

Real wages and employment.   As we have seen, both the RBC model and the graphical *AD-SAS* analysis can easily explain why, due to shifts in the production function, output changes in response to supply shocks. But in order to explain why employment fluctuates in the same direction as output over the business cycle, the labor supply curve must be positively sloped, as in Figure 17-1. To support this interpretation, we should observe that real wages move *procyclically*, that is, in the same direction as output. Note that this is the opposite prediction of the Friedman fooling model, which depicts the economy as operating continuously along the labor demand curve, so that the real wage rate must fluctuate *countercyclically*.

However, most of the statistical evidence shows that (with the exception of the big oil shocks of the 1970s and early 1980s) there is no systematic movement of real wages. If anything, there is a slight tendency of prices to rise more than wages in economic booms, implying countercyclical real wages. As we saw in Table 7-1 on p. 222, real wages actually rose during the Great Depression from 1929 to 1933, even while the unemployment rate was rising from 3 to 25 percent. Thus the central mechanism that drives employment fluctuations in the RBC model is absent in most U.S. business cycles other than the oil shock episodes of the 1973–82 period.

Positive Contributions of New Classical Macroeconomics

Despite their limitations, both the Lucas and RBC versions of new classical theory have a strong appeal to a broad range of economists. What are the attractions of new classical theory?

Rational expectations: linking micro- and macroeconomics. The assumption of rational expectations appeals to economists, since it requires that people do not repeat their mistakes. Instead, people make the best use of all available information to guide their economic behavior. Such an approach is much more appealing than the alternative assumption that people make repeated mistakes in the same direction, period after period. The rational expectations hypothesis also has appeal because of its grounding in microeconomics. This means that the assumption of rational expectations in macroeconomics parallels the basic microeconomic assumptions of profit maximization and utility maximization.

The theory of efficient financial markets. Many of the ideas developed by the new classical economists have been applied successfully to markets where continuous market clearing is a reasonable assumption. This is particularly true of financial markets, including the stock market, bond market, foreign exchange market, and the markets for agricultural and crude commodities, like sugar and gold. The theory of efficient markets incorporates the assumption of rational expectations. Expectations are assumed to incorporate all available information, implying that stock prices jump the instant new information is received and that there are no opportunities to make extraordinary profits on the stock market without access to inside information.

Greater understanding of economic policy. The idea that individuals in the private part of the economy have rational expectations has improved our understanding of economic policy. Even if long-term wage and price contracts impede the flexibility of wages and prices, as discussed later in this chapter, those who negotiate contracts attempt to do so with full information on what policymakers are likely to do. For instance, wage negotiators who suspect that the government will allow rapid inflation after a supply shock are likely to demand full cost-of-living adjustments in their contracts. In contrast, past refusal of a government to allow rapid inflation following a supply shock, as in the case of the German Bundesbank in the 1970s, will increase wage negotiators' confidence that full cost-of-living protection is not necessary.

Recall that the policy ineffectiveness proposition (PIP) developed as part of the Lucas information-barrier approach implies that fully anticipated monetary policy changes have no effect at all on output. While PIP does not appear to be valid in U.S. history, a milder and more acceptable proposition is that fully anticipated policy changes have *smaller* effects than unanticipated changes. The expansionary policies pursued in the United States in the 1960s caused the output ratio to exceed 100 percent for a few years, but not permanently. In contrast, in extreme inflationary episodes (hyperinflation), radical changes in government policy seemed to halt inflation without a major decline in output.[11]

---

[11] See Thomas J. Sargent, "The Ends of Four Big Inflations," Chapter 3 in his *Rational Expectations and Inflation* (New York: Harper & Row, 1986).

Pervasive effect on economic research. Even if the new classical theories of the business cycle are subject to substantial skepticism, new techniques of analysis introduced by these theories have had a major influence on the way economists study variables such as consumption, investment, and the foreign exchange rate. The understanding of extreme episodes of inflation in places like Argentina and Brazil, as well as Turkey, is just one contribution of techniques introduced by new classical economists. The distinction between anticipated policy changes and policy "surprises" has improved our understanding of policy changes.

17-6 Essential Features of the New Keynesian Economics

Common Elements of the Original and New Keynesian Approaches

The adjective *new* distinguishes modern developments in Keynesian theory from the original Keynesian model developed during the Great Depression by Keynes and his followers and reviewed in Section 7-9 on pp. 216–21. The original Keynesian model combines a theory of shifts in aggregate demand (based on the *IS-LM* model of Chapter 4) with a theory of aggregate supply (based on the arbitrary assumption of a fixed nominal wage). Unlike the old and new classical models, with their assumptions of continuous equilibrium or market clearing, the Keynesian approach assumes that markets do not clear continuously. Hence the Keynesian model, either the original or the new variety, is often dubbed a **non-market-clearing model,** conveying the failure of prices to adjust rapidly enough to clear markets within a relatively short interval after a demand or supply shock. If slow price adjustment makes the return of the economy to natural output a long, drawn-out process, markets can fail to clear for years, as in 1929–41 or 1980–86.

In a **non-market-clearing model**, workers and firms are not continuously on their respective demand and supply schedules, but rather are pushed off these schedules by the gradual adjustment of prices.

The appeal of Keynesian economics stems from the evident unhappiness of workers and firms during recessions and depressions. Workers and firms *do not act as if they were making a voluntary choice to cut production and hours worked.* A simple thought experiment is enough. Ask yourself these questions about the real world: Can each worker during every day of a recession sell all the labor desired at the going wage and price? Would every worker in a recession refuse a job offer at the going wage and price? Then ask these related questions about business firms: Can each business firm sell all the output desired at today's prices? Would each business firm turn away customers at today's prices? The history of business cycles is punctuated by recessions and depressions lasting several years, during which workers and firms could not sell all the labor and output desired at the going wages and prices. Thus a theory of business cycles based on the failure of markets to clear, the new Keynesians believe, is more realistic than the new classical approach based on continuous market clearing.

In new classical models, business firms base their output level on news regarding their own price level, obtained from auction markets like the Chicago Board of Trade. In contrast, Keynesian non-market-clearing models turn the role of prices and output upside down. New Keynesian business firms base their choice of the price level on news regarding their own sales obtained by watching the ebb and flow of customers coming through the front door.

If the wage paid to labor and the price paid to all suppliers remain fixed, then the MC line would stay fixed as well. In this case, the profit-maximizing price is at E_2, not E_1.[15]

The most important implication is that *with sticky marginal cost, menu costs are not needed at all to explain how recessions occur.* Any factor that prevents supplying firms from cutting the price of materials, or even delays such price reductions, will tend to make marginal costs sticky, implying that E_2 is the point that maximizes profit for the firm in Figure 17-3, not point E_1.

17-8   Coordination Failures and Indexation

Our discussion of the new Keynesian model has now covered a variety of factors that may inhibit the prompt adjustment of prices in response to a change in nominal GDP, thus automatically implying a response in real GDP. Leaving aside menu costs, the full adjustment of prices to a demand shock as depicted in Figure 17-3 depends on the instantaneous response of marginal cost. Following a negative demand shock, output must fall if marginal cost declines less than marginal revenue. There are two reasons why firms may rationally expect marginal cost to move differently than marginal revenue. First, marginal revenue may move with aggregate nominal demand but marginal costs may not. This would occur if a firm believes that its costs depend on many specific factors other than the perceived level of aggregate nominal demand (for example, volatile supply conditions, price changes for imported materials, changes in cost created by exchange rate movements). Second, with a fixed nominal aggregate demand, marginal cost would also remain fixed, while a local shift in demand (for example, a decline in smoking in response to new laws banning smoking in restaurants and bars) could reduce marginal revenue, providing another reason why marginal cost may move differently than marginal revenue.

The Input-Output Approach and the Absence of Full Indexation to Nominal Demand

To explain real price rigidity, the local-versus-aggregate cost distinction must apply to a world with many different firms purchasing supplies from each other. The automaker buys headlights from a firm that buys filament from a firm that buys copper from a firm that may mine copper using trucks purchased from the automaker. The input-output model emphasizes the importance of multiple buyer-supplier relations; each firm is simultaneously a buyer and a seller.[16] With only two firms, each supplying the other, firms could easily disentangle the local-versus-aggregate components of their costs. But with

---

[15] To simplify Figure 17-3, the marginal revenue line is not shown. To draw it in, find the point halfway along the horizontal axis between the vertical axis and the demand curve. Then draw a slanted line going up and to the left; it intersects the lower required MC_1 line directly above Y_0. Point E_2 lies directly above the intersection of this marginal revenue line and the higher initial MC_0 line.

[16] The input-output approach is developed in Robert J. Gordon, "What Is New-Keynesian Economics?" *Journal of Economic Literature*, vol. 28 (September 1990), see especially pp. 1150–52. A dynamic general equilibrium version of the input-output model is presented in Kevin X. D. Huang and Zheng Liu, "Production Chains and General Equilibrium Aggregate Dynamics," *Journal of Monetary Economics*, vol. 48 (2001), pp. 437–62.

thousands of firms buying thousands of components, containing ingredients from many other firms, the typical firm has no idea of the identity of its full set of suppliers. Since the informational problem of trying to guess the effect of a demand shift on the average marginal cost of all these suppliers is probably impossible to solve, the sensible firm just "waits for the next e-mail" for news of cost increases and then passes them on as price increases.

The input-output approach provides a critical contribution to understanding not just real price rigidity, but also nominal rigidity. The standard argument against the theories of real rigidity suggested above is that they are consistent with nominal flexibility achieved through indexation to nominal demand. Yet the input-output approach emphasizes how high a fraction of a firm's costs are attributable to suppliers of unknown identity, with some unknown fraction produced in foreign countries under differing aggregate demand conditions. This environment would give pause to any firm considering nominal-demand indexation of the product price, since the failure of all suppliers to adopt similar indexation could lead to bankruptcy.

There is nothing to guarantee any confidence that supplier firms will adopt any aggregate indexation formula, for no single supplier acting alone has any incentive to do so. The rewards are too small and the penalties of acting alone are too great, *for a firm's viability depends on the relation of price to cost, not price to nominal GDP.* No individual firm has an incentive to take the risk posed by nominal GDP indexation, which would take away from the firm the required essential control of the relation of price to cost.

Coordination Failures and Daylight Saving Time

The failure of marginal cost to decline instantly and fully in response to nominal demand reflects a coordination failure. Marginal cost would drop if all workers and firms cut wages and prices together by the same percentage as nominal demand. But each is afraid to act first, since they would lose out if other workers and firms failed to act also. Daylight saving time provides a simple example of government intervention in the face of a coordination failure. All firms may want to open and close earlier in the summer to allow more time in the late afternoon for recreational activities, but none does so because each store wants to keep the same hours as other stores. By simply decreeing a shift in the clock, the government solves the failure of individual stores to coordinate their actions.

17-9 Long-Term Labor Contracts as a Source of the Business Cycle

Long-term labor contracts
are agreements between firms and workers that set the level of nominal wage rates for a year or more.

Long-term labor contracts are an important source of sticky marginal cost faced by business firms. Just as monopolistic firms impose social costs on society while maximizing profits, so too do firms and workers that enter into long-term labor contracts. Nevertheless, as the new Keynesian model emphasizes, there are good reasons why workers and firms desire such contracts. In this section, we study the features of long-term labor contracts.

Characteristics of Labor Contracts

In the United States, with few exceptions, formal labor contracts are negotiated in the union sector, which covers about 10 percent of the labor force. Industries that are heavily unionized include much of the manufacturing sector (especially autos, electrical machinery, rubber, and steel), as well as substantial parts of the construction and transportation industries (especially airlines, railroads, and trucking). Industries that tend to be nonunion include fast food and other services, retailing, and parts of manufacturing (especially apparel and textiles).

The behavior of wage rates in the union sector of the economy is more important than this 10 percent figure would suggest, since the wage rates that are negotiated in the union sector set a pattern that is imitated (although not copied exactly) by nonunion workers. The leading role of unions in moderating the flexibility of nonunion wages is evidenced by the evolution of union and nonunion wages. Nonunion wages are only moderately more flexible than union wages over the business cycle, and they exhibit a substantial degree of stickiness. One reason that unions set a pattern for nonunion wages is that nonunionized firms (such as Delta Airlines) do not want their employees to quit and join a rival unionized firm (such as American Airlines) or to vote to become unionized, and so they tend to pay wage rates similar to those in unionized firms.

Wage rigidity at colleges and universities.   Academic institutions provide ample evidence that wages and salaries can be very rigid without unionization, because few staff or faculty members are members of unions. Professors typically receive a salary that is fixed for the entire academic year, for example, from September to August, and it is typically determined in the previous spring without regard to macroeconomic conditions. Professors who are relatively young and tempted by offers from other universities receive relatively large salary increases, but only once per year, and older or less "marketable" faculty members receive small salary increases, also once per year. In some institutions the hourly rate paid to graduate student teaching and research assistants remains unchanged for several years. Macroeconomic conditions may affect university salaries only with a long lag, as when the recession of 2001 caused fiscal deficits for many state governments and they cut back budgets at state-financed universities in 2003 and 2004.

Scheduled wage changes and COLAs.   Wages negotiated under labor contracts are not completely rigid or fixed. Rather they change when a new contract is negotiated. With labor contracts, the nominal wage rate is set at the time of negotiation for the duration of the contract. Wage changes during the lifetime of the contract are allowed, but they are set in advance at the time of the negotiation. There are two types of prenegotiated changes. First, there is usually a scheduled change that takes effect in each year of multiyear contracts. Second, there is sometimes a **cost-of-living agreement (COLA)** that sets in advance the change in the nominal wage that will be allowed for each percentage point of future inflation. For instance, a contract might specify that a worker will receive a 3.0 percent increase in each of the three years of a three-year contract, plus 100 percent of the inflation that occurs in each of the three years. Thus, if the actual inflation rate turned out to be 0.0 percent in a particular year, the wage increase would be 3.0 percent. Alternatively, with an actual inflation rate of 10.0 percent, the wage increase would be 13.0 percent. A COLA contract that gives workers a fixed increase, plus 100 percent of the inflation rate, is called "full COLA protection," whereas a fixed increase plus 50 percent of the inflation rate would be "half COLA protection."

COLAs are intended to help workers maintain their real wage. Without COLAs, the real wage rate is reduced by inflation. The following table shows

Cost-of-living agreements (COLAs) provide for an automatic increase in the wage rate in response to an increase in the price level.

that a sudden change of the inflation rate from zero to 10 percent would cause a sharp decline in the real wage if the worker had no COLA protection. With full COLA protection (a nominal wage change equal to 3.0 percent plus the inflation rate), the real wage change is unaffected by inflation. With half COLA protection, the nominal wage change in the table is equal to 3.0 percent plus 0.5 times the inflation rate.

	Nominal wage change with COLA protection			Real wage change with COLA protection		
	None	Half	Full	None	Half	Full
Inflation of zero	3.0	3.0	3.0	3.0	3.0	3.0
Inflation of 10 percent	3.0	8.0	13.0	−7.0	−2.0	3.0

In this example, each of the figures for real wage change is equal to the corresponding figure for nominal wage change minus the assumed inflation rate.

 SELF-TEST

Under each of the following circumstances, tell whether or not the growth rate of the real wage is rigid, showing no response at all to a change in the rate of inflation.

1. With no COLA protection?
2. Half COLA protection?
3. Full COLA protection?

17-10 "Real" Sources of Wage Stickiness

Thus far, our discussion of the new Keynesian approach has emphasized nominal rigidities, particularly the menu costs of changing nominal prices and long-term contracts for both wages and prices that are incompletely indexed. These contracts imply that a business firm's marginal cost does not respond instantly to a decline in demand. Consequently, the contracts reinforce the role of menu costs in dissuading firms from changing their prices by the full amount needed to avoid changes in output and hence recessions. Now we turn to theories that attempt to explain real rigidities, that is, the slow adjustment of wages relative to prices or to other wages. The most prominent of these is the efficiency wage theory.

The Efficiency Wage Model

This theory explains real rigidities by stressing the reasons why firms would not want to cut the wage that they pay *relative to the wage paid by other firms*. A firm believes that the productivity of its workers will increase if the firm pays a higher wage. There will be greater effort by workers, reduced shirking or goofing off on the job, lower turnover (which reduces training costs), the ability to attract higher-quality workers, and improved morale and loyalty.

The efficiency wage result is obtained in a simple model with identical, perfectly competitive firms. Each firm has a production function in which labor input is multiplied by an efficiency factor (e) that depends on the wage rate paid relative to that paid by other firms (W), as shown in the left frame of

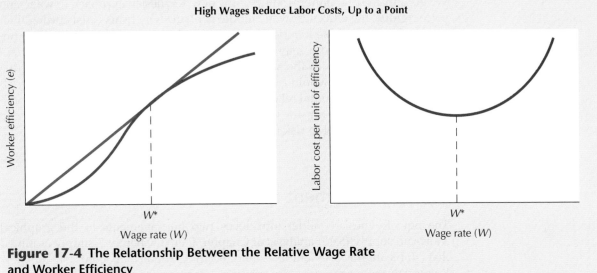

High Wages Reduce Labor Costs, Up to a Point

Figure 17-4 The Relationship Between the Relative Wage Rate and Worker Efficiency

In the left frame, worker efficiency increases faster than the relative wage up to point W^* and more slowly thereafter. As a result, labor cost per unit of efficiency reaches a minimum at W^*, as shown in the right frame.

Figure 17-4. Raising W raises labor cost by making firms pay more to workers, but reduces labor cost per unit of output by making workers more efficient. As shown in the left frame, initially a 1 percent increase in W raises e by more than 1 percent, so labor cost declines, as shown in the right frame. Firms continue raising W until it reaches the equilibrium value W^*, which occurs at the point where raising W by 1 percent raises efficiency by exactly 1 percent, thus leaving labor cost per unit of efficiency unchanged. Firms will refuse to raise W any further, since this would raise wage payments more than it would boost efficiency. The value W^* is called the efficiency wage.

Because W^* is completely fixed by whatever technological and institutional factors determine the e function, the firm's reaction to any change in demand for its product is to cut employment while maintaining the wage rate at W^*. Firms have no incentive to cut wages, since this would actually increase their wage bill per unit of output. The efficiency wage approach seems to explain numerous aspects of microeconomic labor market behavior, once we allow different groups of workers to have different levels of efficiency at any given relative wage rate. For example, the theory predicts the widely observed phenomenon that workers line up eagerly for high-paying jobs but firms hire only a few of them, maintaining the high wage in order to be able to pick and choose rather than reduce the wage rate in the face of the abundant supply of workers.

 SELF-TEST

1. According to the efficiency wage theory, how is unemployment explained?
2. Assuming that the unemployed are willing to work at a lower wage rate than existing workers, why does the firm not simply fire the existing workers and hire the unemployed in their place at a lower wage?
3. What can the unemployed workers do to obtain jobs in light of the refusal of firms to hire them?

As a theoretical underpinning of the new Keynesian approach to wage and price rigidity, the efficiency wage model explains why firms resist cutting their wage rates in response to a decline in demand, and why they do not hire unemployed workers who may be willing to work for a lower wage. This approach is still subject to the same criticism as long-term wage contracts, that full wage indexation would allow firms simultaneously to maintain worker effort by paying the optimal relative wage W^* while maintaining a flexible nominal wage rate. However, for the reasons discussed in Section 17-8, firms and workers are unwilling to risk full wage indexation.

17-11 Assessment of the New Keynesian Model

The new Keynesian model introduces two improvements to the graphical short-run supply (SAS) analysis of Chapter 7. First, Chapter 7 simply assumed that shifts in the SAS curve would occur gradually. In contrast, the new Keynesian model provides the missing reasoning for wage and price adjustment to be gradual, not instantaneous. Second, Chapter 7 suffered from *asymmetry*, in assuming that firms were always on their labor demand curve but workers were forced off their labor supply curve. In contrast, the new Keynesian model allows *both* firms and workers to operate in disequilibrium.

Contrast with other theories. The new Keynesian model seems to solve the main dilemma of the other business cycle theories examined in Chapter 7 and the first part of this chapter, that is, how to explain observed business cycles without unrealistically assuming away output fluctuations (as does classical economics), assuming complete wage rigidity (as does the original Keynesian model), assuming unrealistic fooling of firms and workers (the Friedman-Phelps model), failing to explain persistent unemployment in the presence of easily available information on prices and the money supply (the Lucas information-barrier model), or requiring procyclical real wage movements and continuous labor market equilibrium (the real business cycle model).

Workers and firms in the new Keynesian model are rational, finding it *privately advantageous* to enter into long-term agreements that may have a *macroeconomic externality*, imposing employment and output losses on other workers and firms. The other approaches fail to provide an adequate theory of the business cycle, partly because they do not distinguish between the *private interest* (for instance, signing contracts) and the *collective interest* in avoiding business cycles.

Criticisms of the New Keynesian Approach

The new Keynesian model has been criticized for suggesting *too many* reasons why wages and prices are sticky. Some of these reasons, like staggered overlapping wage and price contracts, have been criticized on the grounds that business cycles were common before the rise of labor unions in the United States in the 1930s and 1940s. To explain business cycles in eras or industries where unions are not strong, we must rely on other new Keynesian explanations that do not require written contracts. Several of these, including the input-output approach and the efficiency wage model, do not depend on the existence of organized labor unions.

New Ideas of the 1980s and Early 1990s

The real business cycle (RBC) theory (Section 17-4 on pp. 558–61) was not directly a response to events. But its introduction in the early 1980s found more ready acceptance against the background of the 1973–82 period, when supply shocks seemed a more dominant source of business cycles than demand shocks. The main debate about the RBC approach does not concern the realism of supply shocks, but rather the one-sided assumption that only supply shocks matter, while demand shocks do not.

As the 1990s began, two new strains emerged in macroeconomics, although they had not yet developed into a named "theory." First was the debate over the twin deficits (Chapters 6 and 12), which reflected a belief that fiscal policy now had more of an impact on long-term economic growth and on slow productivity growth than on the business cycle. In a sense, here the usual pattern of events-cause-ideas was reversed, since supply-side economics (Section 12-7 on pp. 400–02) was an idea that caused an event, namely, persistent budget deficits.

The second new idea of the late 1980s and early 1990s was to discredit any role for monetary aggregates (like M1) in the conduct of monetary policy by the Fed. As shown in the top frame of Figure 18-3, after 1980 there was almost no connection between the growth rate of M1 and the growth rate of nominal GDP. This continued in the 1990s, when wild fluctuations in M1 growth had no counterpart in nominal GDP growth. When M1 growth exceeds that of nominal GDP, it follows that the growth rate of velocity is negative. And the top frame of Figure 18-3 shows that velocity plummeted in 1985–87 and 1991–93, but soared in 1988–89, 1995–2001, and 2005–07. The wild gyrations of M1 growth did not make the economy unstable; on the contrary, the growth rate of nominal GDP was much more stable than that of M1, and this was particularly true in the years 1992–2000.

Economic Behavior, 1991–2007

The economic expansion of the 1990s began in March 1991. The expansion was unusual in at least three ways. First, the early part of the expansion was very weak. Employment barely grew in the first year, leading to the label "the jobless recovery." The unemployment rate peaked at 7.7 percent in July 1992, fully sixteen months after the trough of the recession. Responding to the weak growth of jobs and to high unemployment, the Federal Reserve allowed short-term interest rates to remain low well into the expansion, with the federal funds rate remaining at 3 percent from the autumn of 1992 until early 1994.

The second unusual aspect of the expansion was the behavior of inflation. Instead of accelerating as it had in 1987–90, inflation exhibited a slight deceleration from 1993 to 1998. While many economists had previously believed that the natural rate of unemployment was 6 percent or above, no acceleration of inflation occurred when the unemployment rate declined below 6 percent in late 1994. As explained in Section 8-10 on pp. 259–61, beneficial supply shocks allowed inflation to decelerate through 1998, but we can see in Figure 18-3 that during 1999–2000, inflation accelerated again, propelled both by the normal Phillips Curve mechanism related to low unemployment and also because oil prices went into reverse, converting a beneficial supply shock into an adverse shock.

One of these beneficial shocks was the post-1995 revival of productivity growth, ending the dismal record of slow productivity growth in the previous period 1973–95. This productivity growth revival constitutes the third unusual aspect of the expansion of the 1990s. Initially, the causes of the productivity growth revival seemed to be the invention of the Internet and explosion of high-tech investment in computers, software, and telecommunications equipment. But after high-tech investment collapsed during 2000–02, productivity growth soared again in 2002–04 to a rate even faster than in 1995–2000, as we learned in Section 11-6 on pp. 371–77. Rapid productivity growth helped inflation remain low but raised questions about how long the rapid growth rate could be sustained.

The fourth unusual aspect of the expansion and the subsequent 2001 recession and recovery was the behavior of monetary policy. In Section 14-7 on pp. 469–71 we were introduced to the concept of the Taylor Rule, which calls for monetary policy to set the federal funds rate based on a double target, both avoiding an acceleration of inflation and also avoiding deviations of the output ratio away from 100 percent. Compared to the hypothetical predictions of the Taylor Rule, three aspects of monetary policy stand out as unusual over the 1994–2007 period. The first was the sharp increase in the federal funds rate from 3 to 6 percent in 1994, intended by the Fed as a "preemptive strike" to avoid an acceleration of inflation as had occurred in the late 1980s. The second was the Fed's response to the 2001 recession, when it cut the federal funds rate from 6.5 to 1.0 percent in little more than a year, lowering the interest rate to a level far below that called for by the Taylor Rule. The third unusual feature was the Fed's failure to boost interest rates in 1998–2000, when the peak interest rate of 6.5 percent was virtually the same as the 6.0 percent rate of late 1994. If the Fed had raised rates more in 1998–2000, the high-tech investment boom and bust, as well as the bubble in the stock market, might have been moderated and the subsequent recession less severe.

On the surface, the 2002–07 expansion following the 2001 recession represented a remarkable episode of economic stability. The recession was so mild that real GDP never turned negative on a year-over-year basis. Real GDP growth from 2004 to 2007 was extremely stable, as was the output ratio during that period. Repeating the 1991–92 episode, negative job growth in 2001–03 repeated the earlier "jobless recovery," but after 2003 job growth returned at a robust rate. Eight million new jobs were created between 2003 and late 2007, and the unemployment rate remained below 5 percent throughout 2006 and 2007.

While the macroeconomic environment seemed on the surface to be unusually benign in 2004–07, trouble was brewing under the surface. The unusually low interest rates chosen by the Fed stimulated an unsustainable boom in residential construction and mortgage refinancing. As we have learned (pp. 474–75), mortgage brokers lured many families to sign up for mortgages that they could not afford. By 2007, housing foreclosures had reached unprecedented levels, mortgage credit had been shut off to many borrowers, and housing starts were on track to decline fully by half between 2005 and 2008. Much of this turmoil in the housing market was blamed on the Fed, both for keeping the federal funds rate too low for too long in 2001–04, and also for failing adequately to regulate the mortgage market.

New Ideas of the 1991–2007 Period

The first big puzzle involving the domestic U.S. economy was the productivity growth revival cited in the previous section. Just as economists had failed to reach a consensus about the causes of the 1973–95 productivity growth slowdown, so they had failed to converge on an explanation of the post-1995 revival and the further productivity growth explosion of 2001–04. Thus the behavior of productivity growth did not spawn any big new idea, although it motivated economists to look to the experience of other countries, for example, the failure of Europe to match the U.S. productivity achievement, in a search for explanations.

The second big puzzle was why inflation had remained so low during the expansion of the late 1990s, despite the decline in the unemployment rate to 3.9 percent, the lowest rate achieved since the 1960s. Why had the negative Phillips Curve tradeoff stopped working, in the sense that record-low unemployment rates failed to trigger the expected acceleration of inflation? What explained the even-tempered "Goldilocks economy," which was neither "too hot" nor "too cold" but rather "just right"?

The "Goldilocks" puzzle led to a new idea—that there could be regular changes in the natural rate of unemployment, often called the NAIRU (Non-Accelerating Inflation Rate of Unemployment). Macroeconomic research in the late 1990s centered on the so-called time-varying NAIRU or TV-NAIRU, an idea that was entirely an attempt to explain an empirical puzzle with no theoretical content.[10] Explanations of the decline in the TV-NAIRU during the 1990s relied on specific factual aspects of the economy, including the declining share of teenagers and the rising share of the young male population that was in prison. This led to an ironic or even cynical explanation for the Goldilocks economy, that "we had put many of our unemployed in prison."[11]

An important new idea that developed in the 1980s and spread in the 1990s was the primacy of an inflation target as the optimal rule for central bank behavior. An inflation target was adopted in the 1990s by the Bank of England and by the European Central Bank. An inflation target is a special form of the Taylor Rule in which the short-term interest rate is set entirely to keep inflation at a particular target rate; the real interest rate is raised when inflation exceeds the target and is lowered when inflation is below the target. With inflation targeting, *a zero weight* is placed on deviations of the output ratio from 100 percent.

As we learned in Section 14-7 on pp. 469–71, the Fed went in the opposite direction, away from inflation targeting. The path of the federal funds rate (shown in the bottom frame of Figure 18-3 on p. 591) demonstrated that the Fed shifted from a primary concern in the early 1980s with reducing the inflation rate, to a primary concern after 1990 with stabilizing the output ratio as close as possible to 100 percent. The failure of the Fed to boost interest rates in 1999–2000 reflected a lack of concern with the acceleration of inflation evident in the second panel of Figure 18-3 during those two years. The aggressive decline in interest rates in 2001–02 and maintenance of low interest rates in 2003–04 were consistent with the view that the Fed placed almost the entire weight of its policymaking on stimulus sufficient to bring the output ratio back up to 100 percent after the 2001 recession.

By 2005 another new idea, or rather a new theme, had emerged, and this was the revival of interest in fiscal policy, especially long-run issues

---

[10] See Robert J. Gordon, "The Time-Varying NAIRU and Its Implications for Economic Policy," *Journal of Economic Perspectives*, vol. 11 (February 1997), pp. 11–32, and other articles on the natural rate of unemployment (or NAIRU) in the same issue.

[11] See Lawrence F. Katz and Alan B. Krueger, "The High-Pressure U.S. Labor Market of the 1990s," *Brookings Papers on Economic Activity*, vol. 30, no. 1 (1999), pp. 1–65.

such as the future solvency of Social Security and alternative proposals to "fix" Social Security (see Section 12-9 on pp. 404–10). Part of the Social Security debate involved a conflict between optimistic and pessimistic assumptions about future population growth, and this helped to stimulate interest in national policies about immigration as well as the fundamental causes of the post-1995 productivity growth revival. Another part of the Social Security debate revolved around proposals for individual accounts that would allow younger workers to accumulate funds for their own retirement through investments in the stock market, and the alternative proposal that the current system be maintained but that the Social Security trust fund be allowed to invest partly in the stock market instead of entirely in government bonds.

Finally, the old idea of short-term fiscal stabilization policy was revived during the past decade. As we have seen (p. 503) tax rebates were mailed out during the middle of the 2001 recession in order to stimulate the economy, and further tax cuts were enacted in 2003. Then in February 2008, Congress and the President agreed on an even larger fiscal stimulus program with such speed that it was enacted before it was even clear whether there would be a recession at all. This prompt action appeared to overturn the belief inherited from the 1960s (see the top of p. 589) that the legislative lag of fiscal policy was so long as to make any action impractical.

An Omitted Idea

No mention has yet been made of the new Keynesian approach (Chapter 17). Almost alone among the other major macro theories covered in this book, the new Keynesians' ideas did *not* emerge as a response to an event in the economy. Rather, the development of the new Keynesian theory was mainly an intellectual event. Convinced of the continuing relevance of the original Keynesian paradigm based on sticky prices and non-market clearing, while impressed by Lucas's idea of rational expectations yet unconvinced of his reliance on continuous market clearing, the new Keynesians decided that it was time to recombine the same ingredients with a different recipe. Thus, the essential ingredient of each type of new Keynesian theory is some obstacle to instantaneous price flexibility (that is, price stickiness), justified by an analysis based on the assumptions of profit maximization and rational expectations at the level of the individual firm.

Summary: The main events of the 1971–2007 period were the two adverse supply shocks of 1974–75 and 1979–81, which created twin peaks of inflation, unemployment, and interest rates, and the beneficial supply shocks of 1996–2000, which created a "valley" of low inflation and unemployment in 1997–99. Monetary policy shifted from the accommodation of supply shocks in the 1970s, to a restrictive policy that created the Volcker disinflation of 1980–84, and finally to a policy of output ratio targeting that helped make possible a long economic expansion, from 1982 to 1990, and another long expansion from 1991 to 2001. New ideas spawned by these events included the real business cycle theory, concern over the twin deficits, discrediting of monetary aggregates, the notion of a natural rate of unemployment that varies over time, a renewed interest in long-run issues concerning fiscal policy and Social Security, and a revival of short-run stimulative fiscal policy. The new Keynesian theory developed during this period cannot be linked to any specific event but rather was a natural intellectual outgrowth of preceding theories.

18-5 The Reaction of Ideas to Events in the World Economy

Between the 1930s and mid-1960s, the United States was virtually a closed economy. In 1965 nominal exports and imports were barely 5 percent of GDP. But by 2007, foreign trade had become much more important, with nominal exports of about 12 percent of GDP and nominal imports of about 17 percent of GDP. In most other countries trade is an even larger share of GDP.

Interactions Between the World and U.S. Economies

After the Allied victory in World War II, the United States loomed large in the world economy. Its per-person GDP was far ahead of any other nation (see p. 323). Interactions between the world and the United States primarily flowed out from the United States in the form of aid programs such as the Marshall Plan (1948–53). Interactions that flowed in toward the U.S. economy consisted primarily of political events such as the Korean War, which (as we saw in Figure 18-2) destabilized the U.S. economy during the 1950–54 period.

We have described overexpansionary fiscal and monetary policies as a principal legacy of the 1960s, endowing the U.S. economy after 1970 with a higher inflation rate than would have occurred under a different policy environment. Another legacy of the 1960s was the breakdown of the fixed exchange rate Bretton Woods system, as the United States exported its inflation to other countries.

International Events Spawn Ideas: The Grass Is Greener

A simple way to summarize the international economy since the late 1960s is that the "grass is greener on the other side of the fence." This refers to the widespread enthusiasm for flexible exchange rates when the fixed (Bretton Woods) exchange rate system was breaking down, then the more recent longing for a return to fixed exchange rates, once observers noted that since 1973 flexible exchange rates were much more volatile and disruptive than had been predicted.

Flexible exchange rates had been expected to enable each country to attain monetary independence and choose the particular inflation rate that it desired. However, exchange rates turned out to be highly volatile and disruptive of the real economy, most notably when the dollar appreciated by 50 percent between 1980 and 1985, and then depreciated by the same amount between 1985 and 1987. The appreciation decimated the export markets of U.S. farms and factories. There was no doubt that businesses, jobs, and lives were disrupted by the volatility of exchange rates.

Since the late 1970s, economists and politicians have been searching for a way to return partially or completely to fixed exchange rates. The notable example is the European Monetary System, which surprised almost everyone by achieving a convergence of inflation rates within Europe (pp. 250–51). Some European countries, however, still have much higher unemployment rates than others, leading to a debate about whether the unified European currency (the euro) has now robbed individual countries of the freedom to devalue in order to revive their economies, as the United Kingdom, Italy, and other countries chose to do in 1992. Since 1999, the exchange rates of the members of the euro have been fixed against each other. As we learned from the trilemma of Chapter 6 (pp. 162, 188–89), these nations have now lost any use of domestic monetary policy and have lost the ability (enjoyed by the U.S. Fed) to stimulate their economies when output growth is slow and the output ratio is 100 percent. Two examples of an economic "basket case" handicapped by their per person membership in the euro are Germany and Italy, which in 2000–06 registered a rate of real GDP growth even slower than Japan.

International economics in the United States in the 1991–2007 period was dominated by the questions of competitiveness with Asia and the desirability of free trade, particularly with China and other East Asian countries. Questions of trade policy involve relative prices and fall within the purview of microeconomics, but there is an inevitable overlap with macroeconomics. For instance, a nation with a large trade deficit faces the alternatives of a depreciation of its foreign exchange rate or protectionist measures to reduce imports. The huge U.S. current account deficit of 2004–07 was widely expected to cause a further depreciation of the U.S. dollar beyond that which had already occurred in 2002–07. It was universally recognized that the dollar had been propped up by the seemingly unlimited appetite of the Chinese and Japanese central banks to buy up dollars in order to keep their own currencies from appreciating. The future willingness of these central banks (and others in Asia) to buy up even more hundreds of billions of dollars was a major puzzle looming over international macroeconomics.

However, a currency depreciation and protection are not the only alternatives when a nation faces a major current account deficit, as we learned at the beginning of the book with the magic equation (also called the leakages–injections identity, see p. 35) showing that the current account balance is linked to domestic saving and investment and the government budget. An improvement in the current account deficit can be achieved by any measure that increases national saving, especially measures that reduce the government budget deficit.

> **Summary:** The main international events affecting the U.S. economy were the transition to flexible exchange rates in the early 1970s and the dislocations caused by the ups and downs of the dollar in the 1980s, its further appreciation during 1995–2002, and its subsequent depreciation during 2002–07. The unexpected volatility of exchange rates and the resulting dislocation of trade patterns led to a desire by many observers to return to some version of fixed exchange rates, as had occurred in Europe, with its adoption of the euro.

18-6 Macro Mysteries: Unsettled Issues and Debates

In their professional research papers, economists (micro and macro alike) often conclude with a section called unsettled issues or agenda for future research. This macro text also concludes by reviewing six issues where the debate is still most open and lively in macroeconomics.

How Can Poor Countries Achieve Economic Growth?

As we learned in Chapter 11, many barriers prevent low-income countries from joining the rich countries in achieving high levels of per-capita income. The barriers holding back the poor countries are not the simple matters of physical and human capital investment, which are emphasized in Chapter 10. Many impoverished countries remain poor because their geography is unfavorable, their governments are corrupt, their legal systems do not protect property rights, and they do not encourage foreign trade. Some of the most fundamental barriers to economic growth are political, not a matter of simple economics.

Why Productivity Growth Ebbs and Flows

A few years ago American economists were distressed about slow productivity growth, and Europeans are still puzzled as to why their productivity growth failed to duplicate the U.S. productivity revival after 1995 and particularly after 2001. The European failure raises questions about the role of high-tech investment as a cause of the U.S. post-1995 revival, since European firms use the same types of computers and software as do American firms, and Europe is generally ahead of the United States in its use of mobile phone technology. The reasons why Europe lagged behind and the United States experienced a 2002–04 productivity growth explosion remain leading puzzles for future research and debate. A sharp slowdown in U.S. productivity growth in 2004–07 raised the question as to whether the apparent 1995–2004 productivity growth miracle was inherently a one-time event and whether U.S. productivity growth was destined to return to the slow rates of the dismal years 1973–95. Many other questions, including future U.S. economic growth and the solvency of Social Security, hinge in part on a better understanding of the productivity growth process.

Why Did the Natural Rate of Unemployment Decline?

In 1996–2000 the United States experienced a "Goldilocks" economy, with sustained real income growth, the lowest unemployment rate since 1973, and relatively low inflation. Despite low unemployment, inflation did not accelerate in response, leading economists and the Fed governors to conclude that the natural rate of unemployment had fallen substantially since the late 1980s. But why did the natural rate decline after 1990? Many suggestions were offered, including weak labor unions, worker anxiety over the fear of losing jobs, competition for jobs from immigrants, the strong dollar, and the competition of foreign workers and markets operating through imports and global competition. The invention of the Internet and the development of Web-based job search sites may have reduced the time and expense previously required for unemployed workers to find new jobs.

Should We Go for Zero Inflation?

One of the fuzziest debates in macroeconomics is over the costs of inflation and the output costs of stopping inflation. Canada and New Zealand are two nations that have made a commitment to achieving zero inflation, and so far they have been successful in achieving low inflation rates, but at the cost of persistent high unemployment. Does society reap a large benefit from, say, zero inflation as compared to 2 percent inflation? Is that benefit great enough to offset the costs of high unemployment? There is as yet no consensus on these questions.

Inflation Targeting Versus the Taylor Rule

Over the past two decades, the analysis of monetary policy has shifted from a debate between "rules versus activism" to a debate over the merits of alternative rules. A rule that targets the inflation rate has become the standard point of departure for debate and is used by the Bank of England and the European Central Bank. An alternative approach called the Taylor Rule targets *both* the inflation rate and the output ratio. Our analysis on pp. 469–71 suggests that the Fed uses a Taylor Rule rather than an inflation target and indeed has shifted to less emphasis on inflation and more on stabilizing the output ratio since 1990. Research continues on the merits of the Fed's approach compared to that in

International Perspective

How Does Macroeconomics Differ in the United States and Europe?

Europe consists of a large number of economies that in the aggregate have a larger economy than the United States, but that taken individually are smaller. Five main features differentiate European from U.S. macroeconomics; these are (1) the greater emphasis on international macroeconomic issues, (2) the continuing puzzle of high European unemployment, (3) the failure of Europe to duplicate the U.S. productivity growth revival, (4) the reversed roles of monetary and fiscal policy, and (5) the greater dominance of the Keynesian school of thought.

International Emphasis

Since foreign trade in countries such as Belgium and the Netherlands accounts for more than half of GDP, it is natural that international issues that address the interaction of different economies play a greater role in European macroeconomics, while questions of stabilization policy at the national level play a lesser role. In the 1990s, European macroeconomics was dominated by debates over the desirability of moving toward a single European currency. The 1992 Maastricht Treaty set down criteria for the maximum inflation rates and deficit–GDP and debt–GDP ratios allowed for countries to enter the new European common currency (the euro) in 1999. The transition to the euro was complete in early 2002 when euro currency and coins replaced French francs and German marks.

Unemployment Puzzle

Europeans are envious of the United States for achieving lower unemployment rates over the past 25 years. The restrictive monetary and fiscal policies adopted by many European countries attempting to meet the Maastricht criteria for joining the euro are a partial explanation of high European unemployment. Also, Europeans worry that they may have gone too far in regulating business through such devices as penalties for closing factories, restrictions on shop-opening hours on weeknights and weekends, legislation of high minimum wage levels, and the encouragement of strong unions. In contrast, many in the United States believe that our lack of regulations has pushed down the in-

Europe, and over whether the difference in approach can explain part of the faster output and productivity growth experienced in the United States than in Europe since 2001.

Differences Among Countries

The science of comparative macroeconomics is only beginning to address the many differences among countries. Why did productivity growth in the United States accelerate after 2001 while that in Europe slowed down? Why do individuals in Italy and France save so much? Why is unemployment so high in France and Germany? Why did employment grow so rapidly in Spain during 1995–2007? Why do some countries such as Chile and Argentina suffer from

comes of a large number of low-income workers, who might have done better under the European system.

The Productivity Growth Puzzle

Europeans are also envious of the U.S. productivity growth revival since 1995 and especially during 2002–04. Europe has not enjoyed the same type of revival and in fact productivity growth in Europe since 2000 has been *lower* than in the early 1990s. Europe had almost caught up to the *level* of U.S. productivity in 1995, but by one measure Europe slipped back from 97 percent of the U.S. level in 1993 to 89 percent in 2006. Explanations of this center on some of the same factors that help to explain high European unemployment, including an excess of regulation. For instance, the U.S. has surged ahead in retailing productivity thanks to big-box firms such as Wal-Mart and Home Depot, but regulations in Europe make it much more difficult for similar stores to be established, partly because of land scarcity and regulations on land use.

Reversed Roles for Monetary and Fiscal Policy

A theme of this book has been the replacement of fiscal policy by monetary policy as the U.S. government's main tool to tame the business cycle. Fiscal policy is now thought to be important mainly for discussions about foreign indebtedness and long-run economic growth. But in Europe the roles of monetary and fiscal policy are reversed. Those nations that have joined the euro have lost their monetary independence. This leaves fiscal policy as the only available tool for short-run stabilization. In most European nations the parliamentary form of government allows fiscal policy to act with a much shorter legislative lag than in the United States. Yet even fiscal policy has been handcuffed in recent years as nations struggle to reduce their deficits to meet the Maastricht criteria for joining the euro. In particular, Germany is prevented from using a fiscal policy expansion, in contrast to the aggressive U.S. tax cuts of 2001 and 2003, because to do so would push its fiscal deficit up beyond the Maastricht limit of 3 percent of GDP. Despite its slow growth since 1993, Germany is handcuffed, unable to use either monetary or fiscal policy to boost its growth rate or reduce its unemployment rate.

Keynesian Slant

As we learned in Chapter 17, the new classical macroeconomics consists both of Lucas's original version (combining market clearing, imperfect information, and rational expectations) and the real business cycle version (combining market clearing with an exclusion of demand shocks, thus relying entirely on supply shocks to explain business cycles). A notable difference in European macroeconomics in recent decades has been near-total lack of interest in new classical economics and common reliance on the Keynesian approach based on sticky prices of goods and services. The reason for this difference is not entirely clear; perhaps the emergence of persistent European unemployment since the 1980s prevented European macroeconomists from paying much attention to the new classicals. Perhaps the difference is political, since American new classicals tend to be more politically conservative than many Europeans. Or perhaps the answer is simpler: Lucas, Prescott, and other inventors of the new classical macroeconomics live in the United States, while Keynes lived on the other side of the Atlantic!

hyperinflations for a time but then enter a period of economic stability, whereas other nations cannot make the same transition, even if they implement similar policies? All these questions will remain the subject of active debate among macroeconomists for years, if not decades.

A Final Word

We have learned in this chapter about the evolution of events and ideas. Many important economic ideas respond to events, changes in economic behavior that are not compatible with previous economic theories. Virtually every theory discussed in this book has evolved in some way in response to changing macroeconomic behavior.

This book has emphasized that the United States does not stand alone. Macroeconomics makes no sense if it applies to one country but cannot explain events in other countries or differences in behavior among countries. The International Perspective boxes in this book help to introduce readers to important differences in macroeconomic behavior between the United States and other advanced countries. Some differences can be explained by our theories; others cannot. A careful study of these differences reveals some that are explained by macroeconomic theory but others that require knowledge of microeconomic theory and institutions to reach a full understanding.

As we end this book, one thing is sure. While there are many things we do not understand, there are many things that we do. Any reader of this book now qualifies as an instant critic of popular and media discussions of macroeconomics. Any reader is now equipped to dissect the many misleading journalistic statements about the economy appearing almost every day, and also to recognize those statements that reflect the remaining puzzles that truly qualify as macro mysteries.

Summary

1. Just as real-world events illustrate how theories work, sometimes real-world events make some theories obsolete and spur the invention of new theories. Many of the important theories discussed in this book evolved from an attempt to understand surprising events.

2. The big event of the interwar period was the Great Depression. This event spawned a big idea, the Keynesian revolution, with its emphasis on aggregate demand, sticky prices, and fiscal policy.

3. The big events of the 1947–69 period were the instability of aggregate demand due in part to the Korean and Vietnam wars, the overstimulation of the economy after 1964 by both monetary and fiscal policy, and the ensuing acceleration of inflation. Spawned in part by these events were several new ideas, including the Phillips Curve, the new economics, monetarism, and the natural rate hypothesis.

4. The main events of the 1970–2007 period were the two supply shocks of 1974–75 and 1979–81, which created twin peaks of inflation, unemployment, and interest rates. Also important were the Volcker disinflation, persistent budget deficits, and the Goldilocks economy of the late 1990s, which combined low unemployment with low inflation. New ideas spawned by these events included the real business cycle theory, concern over the twin deficits, and the suggestion that the natural rate of unemployment varies over time.

5. The main international events affecting the U.S. economy were the transition to flexible exchange rates in the early 1970s and the dislocations caused by the ups and downs of the dollar in the 1980s. The unexpected volatility of exchange rates and the resulting dislocation of trade patterns led many observers to desire a return to some version of fixed exchange rates.

6. The average level of unemployment includes frictional and structural unemployment. Cycles in unemployment, together with the volatility of inflation and interest rates, reflect the combined influence of demand shocks, supply shocks, and inflation inertia. The slowdown in productivity growth during 1973–95 and the subsequent revival during 1995–2004 remain partly unexplained. Volatile interest rates reflect demand and supply shocks, as well as the Fed's policy in 1979–82 of attempting to target money and ignore interest rates.

7. Remaining macro mysteries still under active research and debate include the causes of the productivity slowdown and subsequent post-1995 productivity growth revival, why productivity growth in Europe slowed while that in the United States accelerated, why the natural rate of unemployment declined after 1990, the costs and benefits of zero inflation, the merits of inflation targeting for monetary policy versus a Taylor Rule, and, finally, why macroeconomic behavior differs so much among countries.

Questions

1. Explain how the period 1923–29 was consistent with the old classical approach and how the period 1930–33 was not.

2. How did the economy in the late 1930s seem to reinforce the old Keynesian school?

3. How did the behavior of the economy during World War II support the main themes of the Keynesian revolution?

4. Explain how the Great Depression and World War II changed economists' thinking about macroeconomic policy.

5. What events caused fiscal activism to fall out of favor by the end of the 1960s?

6. Explain how the events of the late 1960s gave rise to monetarism as an approach to macroeconomic policy.

7. Explain how the events of the late 1960s gave rise to the natural rate hypothesis and changed economists' view of the trade-off between unemployment and inflation.

8. What caused the twin peaks of unemployment and inflation in 1974–75 and 1980–82? What theoretical innovations developed to explain the twin peaks?

9. Why did both unemployment and inflation decline after 1982?

10. Discuss the events that caused the discrediting of a role for a monetary aggregate in conducting monetary policy.

11. What is meant by the "Goldilocks economy" of the late 1990s? How do you explain its main features?

12. The ideas of the Taylor Rule and inflation targeting were developed in the 1980s. Inflation targeting is a special case of a Taylor Rule. Evaluate the Fed's conduct of monetary policy during 1991–2007 in terms of whether the Fed appears to have been targeting inflation or the output ratio or a weighted average of the two as implied by the Taylor Rule.

13. Which macroeconomic theories were responses to events and which were not?

14. Discuss why events in the U.S. economy since 1929 demonstrate that any theory of how the economy works must allow for both demand and supply shocks.

15. Discuss how macroeconomic policy in the United States differs from Europe.

16. What events have led to increased interest in a return to fixed exchange rates?

17. Discuss how the view of the proper role of fiscal policy in the United States has evolved since the end of World War II.

18. Discuss how events have contributed to the unresolved issues and debates about the sources of business cycles.

For additional practice and exploration, exercises that require the use of Excel are available at www.aw-bc.com/gordon.

Time Series Data for the U.S. Economy: 1875–2007

Table A-1 Annual Data, 1875–2007

	Nominal GDP (X) (B $)	GDP deflator (2000 = 100)	Real GDP (Y) (B 2000 $)	Natural Real GDP (Y^N) (B 2000 $)	Unemploy. Rate (U) (Percent)	Natural Unemploy. Rate (U^N) (Percent)	Money Supply (M1) (B $)	Money Supply (M2) (B $)	Labor Productivity (Y/N) (1992 = 100)	Nominal Interest Rate (i) (Percent)	S&P Stock Price Index (1941–43 = 10)
1875	8.9	7.3	122.9	122.9	—	—	—	2.4	11.2	4.8	—
1876	8.6	6.9	124.4	130.8	—	—	—	2.4	11.5	4.6	—
1877	8.8	6.9	128.3	139.3	—	—	—	2.3	11.7	4.6	—
1878	8.6	6.4	133.7	148.2	—	—	—	2.2	11.9	4.5	—
1879	9.4	6.3	150.1	157.8	—	—	—	2.3	12.1	4.3	—
1880	11.0	6.6	167.9	167.9	—	—	—	2.8	12.2	4.2	—
1881	11.3	6.5	173.8	172.9	—	—	—	3.3	12.2	4.0	—
1882	12.4	6.7	184.8	178.0	—	—	—	3.6	12.3	4.0	—
1883	12.2	6.4	189.5	183.3	—	—	—	3.8	12.4	4.0	—
1884	11.9	6.2	192.9	188.7	—	—	—	3.8	12.4	4.0	—
1885	11.7	6.0	194.3	194.3	—	—	—	3.9	12.5	3.9	—
1886	12.0	6.0	200.2	200.1	—	—	—	4.2	12.6	3.7	—
1887	12.6	6.0	209.2	206.0	—	—	—	4.5	12.6	3.7	—
1888	12.7	6.1	208.2	212.1	—	—	—	4.7	12.7	3.7	—
1889	13.5	6.1	221.2	218.4	—	—	—	4.9	12.8	3.6	—
1890	13.4	6.0	224.3	224.9	4.0	4.3	—	5.4	12.5	3.7	—
1891	13.8	6.0	231.6	231.6	5.4	4.3	—	5.6	12.6	3.8	—
1892	14.3	5.9	242.5	240.3	3.0	4.3	—	6.1	12.7	3.7	—
1893	14.3	5.9	242.4	249.4	11.7	4.3	—	5.9	12.9	3.8	—
1894	13.1	5.6	235.3	258.9	18.4	4.3	—	5.9	13.0	3.6	—
1895	14.5	5.5	262.8	268.7	13.7	4.3	—	6.1	13.7	3.6	—
1896	14.2	5.5	256.8	278.9	14.4	4.3	—	6.0	13.4	3.6	—
1897	15.1	5.5	277.8	289.5	14.5	4.3	—	6.4	14.0	3.5	—
1898	15.7	5.5	284.5	300.4	12.4	4.3	—	7.3	14.2	3.4	—
1899	17.8	5.6	317.5	311.8	6.5	4.3	—	8.4	14.8	3.4	—
1900	18.5	5.7	323.6	323.7	5.0	4.3	—	9.1	15.0	3.4	6.1
1901	20.9	5.8	363.2	336.2	4.0	4.3	—	10.3	16.0	3.4	7.8
1902	21.6	5.8	369.5	349.3	3.7	4.3	—	11.3	15.6	3.4	8.4
1903	22.8	6.0	380.1	362.8	3.9	4.3	—	12.0	15.6	3.6	7.2
1904	23.9	6.0	394.6	376.9	5.4	4.3	—	12.7	16.5	3.6	7.0
1905	26.1	6.1	430.6	391.5	4.3	4.4	—	14.1	17.2	3.6	9.0
1906	28.0	6.2	448.4	406.7	1.7	4.4	—	15.3	17.2	3.6	9.6
1907	28.8	6.5	441.5	422.5	2.8	4.4	—	16.0	16.6	3.7	8.1
1908	26.6	6.4	417.3	438.9	8.0	4.4	—	15.8	16.3	3.7	7.8
1909	29.8	6.4	466.0	455.9	5.1	4.4	—	17.5	17.4	3.7	9.7
1910	31.1	6.7	468.0	473.6	5.9	4.4	—	18.3	17.0	3.8	9.4
1911	32.0	6.6	482.9	492.0	6.7	4.4	—	19.4	17.2	3.8	9.2
1912	34.7	6.8	510.8	511.1	4.6	4.4	—	20.8	17.6	3.8	9.5
1913	36.4	6.9	530.9	530.9	4.3	4.4	—	21.7	18.1	3.9	8.5
1914	34.1	7.0	490.7	546.5	7.9	4.4	—	22.6	17.1	1.9	4.1

	Nominal GDP (X) (B $)	GDP deflator (2000 = 100)	Real GDP (Y) (B 2000 $)	Natural Real GDP (Y^N) (B 2000 $)	Unemploy. Rate (U) (Percent)	Natural Unemploy. Rate (U^N) (Percent)	Money Supply (M1) (B $)	Money Supply (M2) (B $)	Labor Productivity (Y/N) (1992 = 100)	Nominal Interest Rate (i) (Percent)	S&P Stock Price Index (1941–43 = 10)
1915	36.2	7.1	508.9	562.5	8.5	4.4	12.2	24.2	17.9	4.0	8.3
1916	45.9	7.8	591.5	578.9	5.1	4.4	14.3	28.9	19.3	3.9	9.5
1917	54.9	9.3	591.3	595.9	4.6	4.4	16.7	33.7	19.0	4.1	8.5
1918	69.5	10.9	636.8	613.3	1.4	4.5	18.5	36.8	20.6	4.3	7.5
1919	77.0	12.4	618.4	631.3	1.4	4.5	21.3	42.7	20.7	4.3	9.2
1920	86.9	14.4	605.2	649.8	5.2	4.5	23.2	48.0	20.0	4.9	8.3
1921	73.0	12.5	583.9	668.8	11.7	4.5	21.0	45.2	21.4	5.1	7.2
1922	72.7	11.6	625.7	688.3	6.7	4.5	21.2	46.5	21.3	4.3	8.7
1923	85.3	12.0	713.4	708.5	2.4	4.5	22.4	50.4	22.6	4.3	8.9
1924	87.6	12.0	732.3	729.2	5.0	4.5	23.2	53.2	23.7	4.1	9.4
1925	91.1	12.2	748.7	750.6	3.2	4.5	25.1	57.9	23.4	3.8	11.6
1926	97.2	12.2	793.7	772.5	1.8	4.6	25.6	60.3	24.0	3.5	13.0
1927	96.0	12.0	798.2	795.1	3.3	4.6	25.5	61.6	24.3	3.3	15.3
1928	97.0	11.9	812.9	818.4	4.2	4.6	25.8	63.9	24.5	3.3	19.4
1929	103.6	12.0	865.2	842.4	3.2	4.6	26.0	64.2	25.5	3.5	24.7
1930	91.2	11.5	790.7	872.7	8.9	4.6	25.2	63.0	24.8	3.5	19.4
1931	76.5	10.3	739.9	904.1	16.3	4.6	23.6	58.9	24.8	4.4	12.2
1932	58.7	9.1	643.7	936.3	24.1	4.8	20.7	49.6	24.3	5.7	6.3
1933	56.4	8.9	635.5	970.6	25.2	4.8	19.5	44.4	24.0	4.7	8.2
1934	66.0	9.4	704.2	1006.9	22.0	4.8	21.4	47.5	26.3	3.8	9.4
1935	73.3	9.6	766.9	1043.6	20.3	4.8	25.3	53.9	26.9	3.5	10.2
1936	83.8	9.7	866.6	1080.6	17.0	4.8	28.8	60.0	28.5	2.9	14.4
1937	91.9	10.1	911.1	1120.3	14.3	4.9	30.2	63.0	28.3	3.0	14.4
1938	86.1	9.8	879.7	1159.3	19.1	4.9	29.8	62.7	29.5	3.5	10.8
1939	92.2	9.7	950.7	1201.7	17.2	4.9	33.4	67.9	30.3	3.0	11.6
1940	101.4	9.8	1034.1	1244.5	14.6	4.9	38.8	76.1	31.3	2.8	10.8
1941	126.7	10.5	1211.1	1292.2	9.9	4.9	45.4	86.2	33.8	2.8	9.8
1942	161.9	11.3	1435.4	1338.6	4.7	4.9	54.1	98.2	37.3	2.8	8.7
1943	198.6	11.9	1670.9	1388.5	1.9	5.0	70.6	123.9	42.4	2.7	11.5
1944	219.8	12.2	1806.5	1438.2	1.2	5.0	83.3	147.2	46.6	2.7	12.5
1945	223.1	12.5	1786.3	1488.5	1.9	5.0	97.0	174.5	48.3	2.6	15.2
1946	222.3	14.0	1589.4	1543.8	3.9	5.0	104.1	191.1	38.8	2.5	17.1
1947	244.2	15.5	1574.5	1600.8	3.9	5.0	109.2	201.3	37.0	2.6	15.2
1948	269.2	16.4	1643.2	1654.5	3.8	5.1	109.7	204.1	38.0	2.8	15.5
1949	267.3	16.4	1634.6	1715.9	6.1	5.2	108.6	203.2	39.3	2.7	15.2
1950	293.8	16.5	1777.3	1779.6	5.2	5.3	111.5	207.9	41.9	2.6	18.4
1951	339.3	17.7	1915.0	1845.7	3.3	5.4	116.5	215.7	43.0	2.9	22.4
1952	358.3	18.0	1988.3	1914.2	3.0	5.6	122.3	227.4	43.8	3.0	24.6
1953	379.4	18.2	2079.5	1985.3	2.9	5.7	125.4	235.9	44.8	3.2	24.7
1954	380.4	18.4	2065.4	2059.1	5.6	5.9	127.3	244.2	45.6	2.9	30.1
1955	414.8	18.7	2212.8	2139.6	4.4	6.0	131.4	253.3	47.5	3.1	40.9
1956	437.5	19.4	2255.8	2211.8	4.1	6.0	133.0	257.6	47.2	3.4	46.5
1957	461.1	20.0	2301.1	2287.3	4.3	5.8	133.7	264.4	48.4	3.9	44.2
1958	467.2	20.5	2279.2	2367.5	6.8	5.6	135.2	277.3	49.4	3.8	46.8
1959	506.6	20.8	2441.3	2453.8	5.5	5.5	140.4	293.3	51.3	4.4	57.8
1960	526.4	21.0	2501.8	2547.2	5.5	5.6	140.3	304.3	51.9	4.4	55.6
1961	544.7	21.3	2560.0	2648.6	6.7	5.8	143.1	324.8	53.5	4.4	66.7
1962	585.6	21.6	2715.2	2758.3	5.6	5.9	146.5	350.1	55.9	4.3	62.0
1963	617.7	21.8	2834.0	2875.9	5.6	5.8	151.0	379.6	57.8	4.3	70.2
1964	663.6	22.1	2998.6	2999.8	5.2	5.7	156.8	409.3	59.6	4.4	81.5
1965	719.1	22.5	3191.1	3128.9	4.5	5.7	163.4	442.5	61.4	4.5	88.5
1966	787.8	23.2	3399.1	3260.9	3.8	5.8	171.0	471.4	63.6	5.1	84.5
1967	832.6	23.9	3484.6	3394.0	3.8	5.9	177.7	503.6	64.7	5.5	92.2
1968	910.0	24.9	3652.7	3527.7	3.6	6.0	190.1	545.3	66.9	6.2	98.5

Continued

	Nominal GDP (X) (B $)	GDP deflator (2000 = 100)	Real GDP (Y) (B 2000 $)	Natural Real GDP (Y^N) (B 2000 $)	Unemploy. Rate (U) (Percent)	Natural Unemploy. Rate (U^N) (Percent)	Money Supply (M1) (B $)	Money Supply (M2) (B $)	Labor Productivity (Y/N) (1992 = 100)	Nominal Interest Rate (i) (Percent)	S&P Stock Price Index (1941–43 = 10)
1969	984.6	26.1	3765.4	3662.3	3.5	6.0	201.4	578.7	67.0	7.0	97.6
1970	1038.5	27.5	3771.9	3798.5	5.0	5.9	209.1	601.5	68.0	8.0	83.5
1971	1127.1	28.9	3898.6	3936.9	6.0	5.8	223.1	674.4	70.7	7.4	98.2
1972	1238.3	30.2	4105.0	4077.1	5.6	5.7	239.0	758.2	73.1	7.2	109.8
1973	1382.7	31.8	4341.5	4218.4	4.9	5.7	256.3	831.8	75.3	7.4	106.5
1974	1500.0	34.7	4319.6	4361.1	5.6	5.8	269.1	880.6	74.2	8.6	81.5
1975	1638.3	38.0	4311.2	4506.9	8.5	5.8	281.3	963.5	76.2	8.8	87.1
1976	1825.3	40.2	4540.9	4655.3	7.7	6.0	297.2	1086.5	78.7	8.4	102.8
1977	2030.9	42.8	4750.5	4805.6	7.1	6.0	319.9	1221.2	80.0	8.0	97.5
1978	2294.7	45.8	5015.0	4956.9	6.1	6.1	346.2	1322.2	81.0	8.7	95.5
1979	2563.3	49.5	5173.4	5108.6	5.9	6.2	372.6	1425.7	80.7	9.6	103.3
1980	2789.5	54.0	5161.7	5261.3	7.2	6.3	395.7	1540.2	80.6	11.9	119.6
1981	3128.4	59.1	5291.7	5417.5	7.6	6.4	425.0	1679.3	81.7	14.2	127.8
1982	3255.0	62.7	5189.3	5580.2	9.7	6.3	453.0	1833.0	80.8	13.8	120.3
1983	3536.7	65.2	5423.8	5751.4	9.6	6.4	503.2	2057.5	84.5	12.0	160.7
1984	3933.2	67.7	5813.6	5930.9	7.5	6.4	538.6	2222.1	86.1	12.7	160.3
1985	4220.3	69.7	6053.7	6117.1	7.2	6.4	587.0	2419.9	87.5	11.4	189.0
1986	4462.8	71.2	6263.6	6307.1	7.0	6.4	666.3	2616.4	90.2	9.0	238.9
1987	4739.5	73.2	6475.1	6498.7	6.2	6.5	743.6	2786.5	90.6	9.4	286.0
1988	5103.8	75.7	6742.7	6692.1	5.5	6.5	774.8	2936.6	92.1	9.7	268.1
1989	5484.4	78.6	6981.4	6886.5	5.3	6.3	782.2	3059.9	92.8	9.3	326.3
1990	5803.1	81.6	7112.5	7082.4	5.6	6.2	810.6	3227.6	94.5	9.3	332.7
1991	5995.9	84.4	7100.5	7282.3	6.9	6.1	859.0	3348.3	96.1	8.8	381.5
1992	6337.7	86.4	7336.6	7489.1	7.5	5.9	965.9	3410.7	100.0	8.1	417.1
1993	6657.4	88.4	7532.7	7704.5	6.9	5.7	1078.4	3447.2	100.4	7.2	453.5
1994	7072.2	90.3	7835.5	7931.2	6.1	5.6	1145.2	3494.9	101.5	8.0	460.7
1995	7397.7	92.1	8031.7	8171.4	5.6	5.4	1143.0	3567.4	102.0	7.6	546.9
1996	7816.9	93.9	8328.9	8426.5	5.4	5.4	1106.8	3739.2	104.7	7.4	674.8
1997	8304.3	95.4	8703.5	8694.9	4.9	5.3	1070.2	3925.8	106.4	7.3	875.9
1998	8747.0	96.5	9066.9	8973.6	4.5	5.3	1080.7	4209.4	109.4	6.5	1087.9
1999	9268.4	97.9	9470.3	9258.6	4.2	5.3	1102.3	4520.1	112.5	7.0	1330.6
2000	9817.0	100.0	9817.0	9546.1	4.0	5.3	1103.6	4788.5	115.7	7.6	1419.7
2001	10128.0	102.4	9890.7	9833.3	4.7	5.4	1140.2	5207.1	118.6	7.1	1185.8
2002	10469.6	104.2	10048.8	10109.9	5.8	5.4	1196.2	5596.6	123.5	6.5	988.6
2003	10960.8	106.4	10301.0	10390.3	6.0	5.3	1273.5	5987.0	128.0	5.7	967.9
2004	11685.9	109.5	10675.8	10678.4	5.5	5.3	1344.4	6269.3	131.5	5.6	1134.0
2005	12433.9	113.0	11003.4	10974.5	5.1	5.0	1371.8	6547.8	134.1	5.2	1207.8
2006	13194.7	116.6	11319.4	11278.8	4.6	4.8	1374.7	6861.9	135.4	5.6	1318.3
2007	13843.0	119.7	11567.3	11591.6	4.6	4.8	1369.2	7268.9	137.6	5.6	1478.1

Table A-2 Quarterly Data, 1947:Q1 to 2007:Q4

	Nominal GDP (X) (B $)	GDP Deflator (2000 = 100)	Real GDP (Y) (B 2000$)	Natural Real GDP (Y^N) (B 2000$)	Unemploy. Rate (U) (Percent)	Natural Unemploy. Rate (U^N) (Percent)	Money Supply (M1) (B $)	Money Supply (M2) (B $)	Labor Productivity (Y/N) (1992 = 100)	Nominal Interest Rate (i) (Percent)	Real Federal Budget Surplus (B 2000$)	Trade-Weighted Exchange Rate (Mar 1973 = 100)
1947:Q1	237.2	15.1	1570.5	1575.2	3.9	5.1	107.8	198.0	36.5	2.6	39.1	—
1947:Q2	240.5	15.3	1568.7	1585.0	3.9	5.1	109.5	200.9	37.4	2.5	33.9	—

	Nominal GDP (X) (B $)	GDP Deflator (2000 = 100)	Real GDP (Y) (B 2000$)	Natural Real GDP (Y^N) (B 2000$)	Unemploy. Rate (U) (Percent)	Natural Unemploy. Rate (U^N) (Percent)	Money Supply (M1) (B $)	Money Supply (M2) (B $)	Labor Productivity (Y/N) (1992 = 100)	Nominal Interest Rate (i) (Percent)	Real Federal Budget Surplus (B 2000$)	Trade-Weighted Real Exchange Rate (Mar 1973 = 100)
1947:Q3	244.6	15.6	1568.0	1595.0	3.9	5.1	110.5	203.1	36.3	2.6	12.8	—
1947:Q4	254.4	16.0	1590.9	1605.0	3.9	5.2	111.0	204.9	37.8	2.8	49.4	—
1948:Q1	260.4	16.1	1616.1	1615.0	3.7	5.2	111.0	205.5	37.9	2.8	47.8	—
1948:Q2	267.3	16.3	1644.6	1625.1	3.7	5.2	110.0	204.4	37.9	2.8	31.4	—
1948:Q3	273.9	16.6	1654.1	1638.6	3.8	5.2	110.1	204.7	38.0	2.8	8.5	—
1948:Q4	275.2	16.6	1658.0	1652.3	3.8	5.2	109.7	204.2	38.2	2.8	1.2	—
1949:Q1	270.0	16.5	1633.2	1666.1	4.7	5.2	109.2	203.6	38.6	2.7	−20.6	—
1949:Q2	266.2	16.3	1628.4	1680.0	5.9	5.2	109.3	204.1	39.0	2.7	−39.8	—
1949:Q3	267.7	16.3	1646.7	1693.8	6.7	5.3	109.0	203.7	39.9	2.6	−40.0	—
1949:Q4	265.2	16.3	1629.9	1707.6	7.0	5.3	109.0	203.7	39.7	2.6	−38.1	—
1950:Q1	275.2	16.2	1696.8	1721.2	6.4	5.3	109.9	205.3	41.0	2.6	−51.8	—
1950:Q2	284.6	16.3	1747.3	1734.7	5.6	5.4	111.6	208.0	41.5	2.6	17.2	—
1950:Q3	302.0	16.6	1815.8	1751.9	4.6	5.4	112.8	209.5	42.5	2.6	81.2	—
1950:Q4	313.4	17.0	1848.9	1769.1	4.2	5.4	113.7	210.7	42.5	2.7	83.8	—
1951:Q1	329.0	17.6	1871.3	1786.3	3.5	5.5	115.0	212.5	42.6	2.7	97.8	—
1951:Q2	336.7	17.7	1903.1	1803.7	3.1	5.5	116.1	214.2	42.5	2.9	56.5	—
1951:Q3	343.6	17.7	1941.1	1821.3	3.2	5.6	117.6	217.1	43.5	2.9	29.9	—
1951:Q4	348.0	17.9	1944.4	1839.1	3.4	5.6	119.7	220.9	43.6	3.0	33.5	—
1952:Q1	351.3	17.9	1964.7	1857.1	3.1	5.6	121.3	224.1	43.7	3.0	38.6	—
1952:Q2	352.2	17.9	1966.0	1875.4	3.0	5.7	122.2	226.3	43.7	2.9	19.0	—
1952:Q3	358.5	18.1	1978.8	1894.0	3.2	5.7	123.5	229.1	43.5	2.9	6.1	—
1952:Q4	371.4	18.2	2043.8	1913.0	2.8	5.7	124.8	232.0	44.3	3.0	19.3	—
1953:Q1	378.4	18.2	2082.3	1932.1	2.7	5.8	125.3	233.7	44.6	3.1	23.7	—
1953:Q2	382.0	18.2	2098.1	1951.4	2.6	5.8	126.1	236.0	44.8	3.3	14.3	—
1953:Q3	381.1	18.3	2085.4	1970.8	2.7	5.9	126.3	237.4	45.0	3.3	19.2	—
1953:Q4	375.9	18.3	2052.5	1990.5	3.7	5.9	126.4	238.9	44.8	3.1	−17.5	—
1954:Q1	375.3	18.4	2042.4	2010.5	5.3	5.9	126.7	240.9	44.9	3.0	−18.0	—
1954:Q2	376.0	18.4	2044.3	2030.6	5.8	6.0	127.0	243.1	45.2	2.9	−10.3	—
1954:Q3	380.8	18.4	2066.9	2050.8	6.0	6.0	128.2	246.4	46.0	2.9	−7.1	—
1954:Q4	389.5	18.5	2107.8	2071.0	5.3	6.1	129.6	249.0	46.5	2.9	0.0	—
1955:Q1	402.6	18.6	2168.5	2090.9	4.7	6.1	131.0	251.8	47.4	3.0	19.4	—
1955:Q2	410.9	18.6	2204.0	2110.8	4.4	6.1	131.8	253.4	47.5	3.0	35.9	—
1955:Q3	419.5	18.8	2233.4	2130.7	4.1	6.1	132.4	254.7	47.7	3.1	26.1	—
1955:Q4	426.0	19.0	2245.3	2150.7	4.2	6.2	132.6	255.6	47.5	3.1	41.1	—
1956:Q1	428.3	19.2	2234.8	2170.9	4.0	6.1	133.1	256.3	46.9	3.1	44.4	—
1956:Q2	434.2	19.3	2252.5	2191.4	4.2	6.2	133.4	257.6	47.1	3.3	34.8	—
1956:Q3	439.3	19.5	2249.8	2212.2	4.1	6.0	133.5	258.7	47.1	3.4	39.9	—
1956:Q4	448.1	19.6	2286.5	2233.3	4.1	6.0	134.1	260.3	47.5	3.7	37.2	—
1957:Q1	457.2	19.9	2300.3	2254.7	3.9	5.9	134.4	262.5	48.1	3.7	30.7	—
1957:Q2	459.2	20.0	2294.6	2276.5	4.1	5.9	134.4	264.4	47.9	3.8	21.5	—
1957:Q3	466.4	20.1	2317.0	2296.8	4.2	5.8	134.6	266.2	48.6	4.1	21.9	—
1957:Q4	461.5	20.1	2292.5	2316.5	4.9	5.8	133.7	266.9	48.8	4.0	−7.5	—
1958:Q1	454.0	20.4	2230.2	2336.5	6.3	5.8	133.6	269.7	48.0	3.6	−15.7	—
1958:Q2	458.1	20.4	2243.4	2357.0	7.4	5.7	135.1	276.3	48.9	3.6	−40.6	—
1958:Q3	471.7	20.6	2295.2	2377.7	7.3	5.7	136.5	281.2	49.9	3.9	−31.1	—
1958:Q4	485.0	20.7	2348.0	2398.9	6.4	5.6	138.2	284.5	50.7	4.1	−16.9	—
1959:Q1	495.4	20.7	2392.9	2420.4	5.8	5.6	140.0	288.5	50.8	4.1	15.5	—
1959:Q2	508.4	20.7	2455.8	2442.4	5.1	5.6	139.3	291.0	51.5	4.4	25.1	—
1959:Q3	509.3	20.8	2453.9	2464.8	5.3	5.6	140.2	295.1	51.5	4.5	14.0	—
1959:Q4	513.2	20.8	2462.6	2487.7	5.6	5.6	142.0	298.4	51.4	4.6	10.1	—
1960:Q1	526.9	20.9	2517.4	2511.0	5.1	5.6	140.5	299.4	52.5	4.6	55.9	—
1960:Q2	526.1	21.0	2504.8	2534.8	5.2	5.7	138.4	300.0	51.8	4.5	39.0	—
1960:Q3	528.9	21.1	2508.7	2559.1	5.5	5.7	139.6	305.5	51.9	4.3	31.3	—
1960:Q4	523.6	21.1	2476.2	2583.9	6.3	5.7	142.7	312.3	51.2	4.3	10.4	—

Continued

	Nominal GDP (X) (B $)	GDP Deflator (2000 = 100)	Real GDP (Y) (B 2000$)	Natural Real GDP (Y^N) (B 2000$)	Unemploy. Rate (U) (Percent)	Natural Unemploy. Rate (U^N) (Percent)	Money Supply (M1) (B $)	Money Supply (M2) (B $)	Labor Productivity (Y/N) (1992 = 100)	Nominal Interest Rate (i) (Percent)	Real Federal Budget Surplus (B 2000$)	Trade-Weighted Exchange Rate (Mar 1973 = 100)
1961:Q1	527.9	21.2	2491.2	2609.3	6.8	5.8	142.2	317.1	51.9	4.3	11.8	117.1
1961:Q2	539.0	21.2	2538.0	2635.2	7.0	5.8	141.4	321.0	53.3	4.3	3.8	116.8
1961:Q3	549.4	21.3	2579.1	2661.6	6.8	5.9	142.0	326.5	54.1	4.4	11.7	117.7
1961:Q4	562.5	21.4	2631.8	2688.5	6.2	5.9	146.6	334.7	54.6	4.4	22.0	117.8
1962:Q1	576.0	21.5	2679.1	2715.9	5.6	5.9	146.4	341.2	55.5	4.4	11.2	118.0
1962:Q2	583.2	21.5	2708.4	2743.8	5.5	5.9	145.3	346.2	55.4	4.3	10.2	118.6
1962:Q3	590.0	21.6	2733.3	2772.3	5.6	5.9	145.0	351.6	56.1	4.3	14.4	118.7
1962:Q4	593.3	21.7	2740.0	2801.2	5.5	5.9	149.2	361.3	56.5	4.3	11.1	118.5
1963:Q1	602.4	21.7	2775.9	2830.7	5.8	5.8	149.5	369.0	56.8	4.2	19.4	118.6
1963:Q2	611.2	21.7	2810.6	2860.6	5.7	5.8	148.9	374.6	57.4	4.2	29.0	118.8
1963:Q3	623.9	21.8	2863.5	2890.8	5.5	5.8	150.1	382.2	58.6	4.3	27.1	118.8
1963:Q4	633.5	22.0	2885.8	2921.4	5.6	5.8	155.2	392.5	58.6	4.3	23.7	118.8
1964:Q1	649.6	22.0	2950.5	2952.4	5.5	5.8	155.0	398.7	59.2	4.4	9.1	118.8
1964:Q2	658.8	22.1	2984.8	2983.8	5.2	5.7	153.9	403.0	59.6	4.4	−11.8	118.8
1964:Q3	670.5	22.2	3025.5	3015.5	5.0	5.7	156.3	412.1	60.0	4.4	5.9	118.8
1964:Q4	675.6	22.3	3033.6	3047.6	5.0	5.7	162.1	423.7	59.5	4.4	14.8	118.6
1965:Q1	695.7	22.4	3108.2	3079.9	4.9	5.7	161.8	431.5	60.3	4.4	34.0	118.6
1965:Q2	708.1	22.5	3150.2	3112.4	4.7	5.7	160.6	436.1	60.6	4.4	30.3	118.8
1965:Q3	725.2	22.6	3214.1	3145.2	4.4	5.7	162.3	444.6	61.7	4.5	−1.8	118.9
1965:Q4	747.5	22.7	3291.8	3178.1	4.1	5.7	169.1	457.8	62.9	4.6	−2.6	118.8
1966:Q1	770.8	22.9	3372.3	3211.1	3.9	5.7	170.4	465.6	63.7	4.8	21.9	118.8
1966:Q2	779.9	23.0	3384.0	3244.3	3.8	5.8	170.1	468.6	63.3	5.0	15.2	118.9
1966:Q3	793.4	23.3	3406.3	3277.4	3.8	5.8	169.5	471.7	63.4	5.3	6.0	118.8
1966:Q4	807.1	23.5	3433.7	3310.7	3.7	5.8	173.8	479.6	63.8	5.4	−3.8	119.0
1967:Q1	817.9	23.6	3464.1	3344.0	3.8	5.8	173.7	486.0	64.4	5.1	−41.1	118.9
1967:Q2	822.5	23.7	3464.3	3377.3	3.8	5.9	174.2	495.7	64.6	5.3	−43.8	118.8
1967:Q3	837.1	24.0	3491.8	3410.6	3.8	6.0	178.1	509.7	64.8	5.6	−35.5	118.8
1967:Q4	852.8	24.2	3518.2	3444.0	3.9	6.0	184.7	523.0	65.0	6.0	−36.3	119.7
1968:Q1	879.9	24.5	3590.7	3477.5	3.7	6.0	185.2	530.5	66.5	6.1	−24.5	121.1
1968:Q2	904.2	24.8	3651.6	3510.9	3.6	6.1	186.7	538.2	67.1	6.3	−29.9	121.2
1968:Q3	919.4	25.0	3676.5	3544.4	3.5	6.0	190.4	549.0	67.0	6.1	6.0	121.2
1968:Q4	936.3	25.4	3692.0	3578.0	3.4	6.0	198.2	563.6	66.9	6.2	10.6	121.1
1969:Q1	961.0	25.6	3750.2	3611.6	3.4	6.0	199.6	571.8	67.5	6.7	57.0	121.3
1969:Q2	976.3	26.0	3760.9	3645.3	3.4	6.0	199.7	576.5	66.9	6.9	44.3	121.4
1969:Q3	996.5	26.3	3784.2	3679.1	3.6	6.0	200.6	580.1	66.9	7.1	21.3	122.3
1969:Q4	1004.6	26.7	3766.3	3713.0	3.6	5.9	205.8	586.2	66.6	7.5	12.0	121.0
1970:Q1	1017.3	27.1	3760.0	3747.0	4.2	5.9	205.4	587.6	66.8	7.9	−8.5	120.8
1970:Q2	1033.2	27.4	3767.1	3781.2	4.8	5.9	206.4	593.7	67.9	8.1	−57.6	120.3
1970:Q3	1050.7	27.6	3800.5	3815.5	5.2	5.9	209.0	604.3	68.9	8.2	−70.2	119.8
1970:Q4	1052.9	28.0	3759.8	3850.0	5.8	5.9	215.6	620.0	68.3	7.9	−82.5	119.7
1971:Q1	1098.3	28.4	3864.1	3884.7	5.9	5.9	217.0	641.2	70.4	7.2	−83.0	119.4
1971:Q2	1119.1	28.8	3885.9	3919.4	5.9	5.8	221.0	668.5	70.6	7.5	−104.5	118.8
1971:Q3	1139.3	29.1	3916.7	3954.3	6.0	5.8	224.7	685.2	71.2	7.6	−100.0	116.7
1971:Q4	1151.7	29.3	3927.9	3989.3	5.9	5.8	230.0	702.7	70.6	7.3	−104.4	113.0
1972:Q1	1190.6	29.8	3997.7	4024.4	5.8	5.8	231.9	725.3	71.6	7.2	−75.9	108.4
1972:Q2	1225.9	30.0	4092.1	4059.5	5.7	5.7	235.1	746.5	73.1	7.3	−92.5	107.6
1972:Q3	1249.7	30.3	4131.1	4094.7	5.6	5.7	239.9	768.4	73.5	7.2	−54.9	108.1
1972:Q4	1287.0	30.7	4198.7	4129.9	5.4	5.7	249.3	792.3	74.1	7.1	−100.2	109.0
1973:Q1	1335.5	31.0	4305.3	4165.3	4.9	5.7	251.2	812.7	75.8	7.2	−47.4	104.0
1973:Q2	1371.9	31.5	4355.1	4200.6	4.9	5.7	253.7	829.5	75.8	7.3	−46.7	99.7
1973:Q3	1391.2	32.1	4331.9	4236.1	4.8	5.7	256.7	838.0	75.1	7.6	−31.4	97.3
1973:Q4	1432.3	32.8	4373.3	4271.6	4.8	5.8	263.7	847.1	74.7	7.7	−17.4	99.9
1974:Q1	1447.0	33.4	4335.4	4307.2	5.1	5.8	264.4	863.7	74.6	7.9	−24.9	103.6
1974:Q2	1485.3	34.2	4347.9	4343.0	5.2	5.8	266.7	878.0	74.4	8.4	−31.6	99.8
1974:Q3	1514.2	35.2	4305.8	4379.0	5.6	5.8	269.3	884.5	73.6	9.0	−29.9	102.5

	Nominal GDP (X) (B $)	GDP Deflator (2000 = 100)	Real GDP (Y) (B 2000$)	Natural Real GDP (Y^N) (B 2000$)	Unemploy. Rate (U) (Percent)	Natural Unemploy. Rate (U^N) (Percent)	Money Supply (M1) (B $)	Money Supply (M2) (B $)	Labor Productivity (Y/N) (1992 = 100)	Nominal Interest Rate (i) (Percent)	Real Federal Budget Surplus (B 2000$)	Trade-Weighted Exchange Rate (Mar 1973 = 100)
1974:Q4	1553.4	36.2	4288.9	4415.3	6.6	5.8	276.4	896.4	74.3	9.0	−70.1	102.3
1975:Q1	1570.0	37.0	4237.6	4451.8	8.3	5.8	273.8	913.7	74.9	8.7	−127.4	99.4
1975:Q2	1605.6	37.6	4268.6	4488.4	8.9	5.8	278.1	951.4	76.1	8.9	−277.0	100.1
1975:Q3	1663.1	38.3	4340.9	4525.2	8.5	5.9	283.8	983.5	76.9	8.9	−161.8	104.4
1975:Q4	1714.6	39.0	4397.8	4562.2	8.3	5.9	290.0	1006.1	76.9	8.8	−161.1	105.6
1976:Q1	1772.6	39.4	4496.8	4599.3	7.7	5.9	288.7	1036.7	78.1	8.6	−132.9	105.6
1976:Q2	1804.9	39.8	4530.3	4636.5	7.6	5.9	294.3	1072.7	78.8	8.5	−120.7	106.8
1976:Q3	1838.3	40.4	4552.0	4673.9	7.7	6.0	298.0	1099.1	78.9	8.5	−128.0	106.2
1976:Q4	1885.3	41.1	4584.6	4711.4	7.8	6.0	307.7	1137.9	79.1	8.2	−133.3	107.0
1977:Q1	1939.3	41.8	4640.0	4749.1	7.5	6.0	308.9	1174.2	79.6	8.0	−108.4	107.3
1977:Q2	2006.0	42.4	4731.1	4786.7	7.1	6.0	316.0	1210.6	79.9	8.0	−92.9	106.9
1977:Q3	2066.8	42.9	4815.8	4824.5	6.9	6.0	322.0	1237.6	80.8	7.9	−105.3	106.2
1977:Q4	2111.6	43.9	4815.3	4862.3	6.7	6.1	333.1	1263.0	79.7	8.1	−106.0	103.9
1978:Q1	2150.0	44.5	4830.8	4900.1	6.3	6.1	332.7	1282.4	79.7	8.5	−104.0	100.7
1978:Q2	2275.6	45.3	5021.2	4937.9	6.0	6.1	342.3	1310.4	81.3	8.7	−56.3	99.7
1978:Q3	2336.2	46.1	5070.7	4975.7	6.0	6.1	349.9	1335.4	81.3	8.8	−42.1	94.8
1978:Q4	2417.0	47.0	5137.4	5013.7	5.9	6.1	360.4	1361.4	81.8	9.0	−31.2	93.6
1979:Q1	2464.4	47.9	5147.4	5051.7	5.9	6.2	357.0	1376.2	81.0	9.3	−12.7	94.9
1979:Q2	2527.6	49.1	5152.3	5089.6	5.7	6.2	368.5	1411.2	80.8	9.4	−12.6	96.3
1979:Q3	2600.7	50.1	5189.4	5127.5	5.9	6.2	378.6	1446.0	80.7	9.3	−23.7	94.6
1979:Q4	2660.5	51.1	5204.7	5165.5	6.0	6.3	386.7	1469.7	80.6	10.5	−40.7	96.6
1980:Q1	2725.3	52.2	5221.3	5203.6	6.3	6.3	384.5	1489.9	80.9	12.1	−59.2	96.6
1980:Q2	2729.3	53.3	5115.9	5241.9	7.3	6.3	383.9	1513.1	80.0	11.2	−102.5	96.1
1980:Q3	2786.6	54.6	5107.4	5280.4	7.7	6.4	399.2	1561.0	80.3	11.6	−125.9	93.4
1980:Q4	2916.9	56.1	5202.1	5319.1	7.4	6.4	415.3	1597.4	81.2	12.8	−107.4	95.2
1981:Q1	3052.7	57.5	5307.5	5358.1	7.4	6.4	411.4	1618.1	82.4	13.2	−68.3	98.2
1981:Q2	3085.9	58.6	5266.1	5397.4	7.4	6.3	424.1	1662.3	81.3	14.0	−74.1	104.5
1981:Q3	3178.7	59.6	5329.8	5437.1	7.4	6.4	426.9	1695.4	82.0	14.9	−85.7	109.8
1981:Q4	3196.4	60.7	5263.4	5477.3	8.2	6.3	437.3	1742.6	81.0	14.6	−130.7	106.2
1982:Q1	3186.8	61.6	5177.1	5517.9	8.8	6.3	438.8	1773.3	80.5	15.0	−163.1	110.0
1982:Q2	3242.7	62.3	5204.9	5559.1	9.4	6.3	446.1	1811.8	80.6	14.5	−170.0	114.1
1982:Q3	3276.2	63.2	5185.2	5600.8	9.9	6.4	451.8	1850.5	80.8	13.8	−227.6	118.8
1982:Q4	3314.4	63.9	5189.8	5643.1	10.7	6.4	475.3	1897.7	81.5	11.9	−277.6	120.2
1983:Q1	3382.9	64.4	5253.8	5685.9	10.4	6.4	479.9	1989.9	82.5	11.8	−269.0	117.1
1983:Q2	3484.1	64.9	5372.3	5729.3	10.1	6.3	498.7	2042.1	84.4	11.6	−261.2	119.3
1983:Q3	3589.3	65.5	5478.4	5773.1	9.4	6.4	510.0	2077.2	85.2	12.3	−283.4	122.7
1983:Q4	3690.4	66.0	5590.5	5817.5	8.5	6.4	524.1	2120.8	85.6	12.4	−248.1	122.7
1984:Q1	3809.6	66.8	5699.8	5862.3	7.9	6.4	523.4	2156.8	85.5	12.3	−230.3	123.5
1984:Q2	3908.6	67.4	5797.9	5907.7	7.4	6.4	537.3	2203.8	86.1	13.2	−243.3	124.9
1984:Q3	3978.2	68.0	5854.3	5953.6	7.4	6.4	541.6	2236.3	86.4	13.0	−252.7	131.7
1984:Q4	4036.3	68.4	5902.4	5999.8	7.3	6.4	552.2	2291.4	86.5	12.4	−267.3	134.9
1985:Q1	4119.5	69.2	5956.9	6046.4	7.2	6.4	557.1	2351.1	86.6	12.3	−212.6	142.1
1985:Q2	4178.4	69.5	6007.8	6093.4	7.3	6.4	576.5	2393.3	86.8	11.6	−283.7	138.1
1985:Q3	4261.3	69.8	6101.7	6140.6	7.2	6.4	596.3	2446.6	88.0	11.0	−249.6	131.4
1985:Q4	4321.8	70.3	6148.6	6187.9	7.0	6.4	617.8	2487.5	88.4	10.6	−257.9	122.8
1986:Q1	4385.6	70.7	6207.4	6235.5	7.0	6.4	621.2	2516.6	89.5	9.6	−255.8	116.4
1986:Q2	4425.7	71.0	6232.0	6283.2	7.2	6.4	651.8	2583.8	90.2	9.0	−284.6	110.7
1986:Q3	4493.9	71.4	6291.7	6330.9	7.0	6.4	678.8	2650.4	90.6	8.8	−290.0	106.1
1986:Q4	4546.1	71.9	6323.4	6378.8	6.8	6.4	713.6	2714.3	90.3	8.7	−241.1	106.2
1987:Q1	4613.8	72.5	6365.0	6426.7	6.6	6.4	725.8	2749.6	89.9	8.4	−249.0	100.5
1987:Q2	4690.0	72.9	6435.0	6474.6	6.3	6.4	745.0	2774.8	90.6	9.2	−172.9	96.9
1987:Q3	4767.8	73.4	6493.4	6522.7	6.0	6.5	745.0	2792.7	90.6	9.8	−183.0	98.3
1987:Q4	4886.3	74.0	6606.8	6571.0	5.8	6.5	758.0	2828.4	91.4	10.2	−188.1	92.9
1988:Q1	4951.9	74.6	6639.1	6619.4	5.7	6.5	753.4	2872.5	91.6	9.6	−190.9	89.8
1988:Q2	5062.8	75.3	6723.5	6667.9	5.5	6.5	773.3	2928.7	91.9	9.8	−174.0	88.8

Continued

	Nominal GDP (X) (B \$)	GDP Deflator (2000 = 100)	Real GDP (Y) (B 2000\$)	Natural Real GDP (Y^N) (B 2000\$)	Unemploy. Rate (U) (Percent)	Natural Unemploy. Rate (U^N) (Percent)	Money Supply (M1) (B \$)	Money Supply (M2) (B \$)	Labor Productivity (Y/N) (1992 = 100)	Nominal Interest Rate (i) (Percent)	Real Federal Budget Surplus (B 2000\$)	Trade-Weighted Exchange Rate (Mar 1973 = 100)
1988:Q3	5146.6	76.1	6759.4	6716.3	5.5	6.5	782.1	2957.0	92.2	10.0	−168.1	93.6
1988:Q4	5253.7	76.7	6848.6	6764.9	5.3	6.4	790.3	2987.9	92.7	9.5	−177.8	89.5
1989:Q1	5367.1	77.6	6918.1	6813.5	5.2	6.4	779.4	2999.4	92.4	9.7	−143.6	91.3
1989:Q2	5454.1	78.3	6963.5	6862.1	5.2	6.3	776.4	3019.6	92.6	9.5	−164.2	95.4
1989:Q3	5531.9	78.9	7013.1	6910.8	5.2	6.3	778.3	3076.8	93.0	9.0	−176.9	96.0
1989:Q4	5584.3	79.4	7030.9	6959.6	5.4	6.3	794.7	3142.9	93.2	8.9	−177.4	94.3
1990:Q1	5716.4	80.4	7112.1	7008.6	5.3	6.3	794.0	3183.7	94.0	9.2	−209.8	93.1
1990:Q2	5797.7	81.3	7130.3	7057.7	5.3	6.2	806.9	3211.1	94.7	9.4	−210.8	93.4
1990:Q3	5849.4	82.0	7130.8	7107.0	5.7	6.2	813.6	3242.2	95.0	9.4	−201.0	88.6
1990:Q4	5848.8	82.6	7076.9	7156.5	6.1	6.1	827.8	3273.7	94.3	9.3	−221.5	84.4
1991:Q1	5888.0	83.6	7040.8	7206.5	6.6	6.1	829.2	3310.4	94.5	8.9	−189.4	85.7
1991:Q2	5964.3	84.2	7086.5	7256.7	6.8	6.1	849.6	3349.8	95.9	8.9	−251.5	90.9
1991:Q3	6035.6	84.8	7120.7	7307.4	6.9	6.0	863.4	3357.1	96.6	8.8	−274.5	90.7
1991:Q4	6095.8	85.2	7154.1	7358.6	7.1	6.0	894.0	3376.4	97.2	8.4	−295.9	86.8
1992:Q1	6196.1	85.7	7228.2	7410.3	7.4	6.0	920.4	3398.5	98.8	8.3	−336.6	87.5
1992:Q2	6290.1	86.2	7297.9	7462.5	7.6	6.0	949.2	3404.5	99.5	8.3	−338.4	87.9
1992:Q3	6380.5	86.6	7369.5	7515.2	7.6	5.9	971.6	3403.3	100.4	8.0	−365.1	83.9
1992:Q4	6484.3	87.0	7450.7	7568.4	7.4	5.8	1022.6	3437.6	101.3	8.0	−337.1	88.8
1993:Q1	6542.7	87.7	7459.7	7622.2	7.1	5.8	1030.7	3418.6	100.5	7.7	−342.7	91.1
1993:Q2	6612.1	88.2	7497.5	7676.6	7.1	5.8	1062.0	3438.5	99.9	7.4	−303.9	88.2
1993:Q3	6674.6	88.6	7536.0	7731.7	6.8	5.7	1090.0	3450.2	100.3	6.9	−309.4	89.5
1993:Q4	6800.2	89.0	7637.4	7787.6	6.6	5.7	1131.3	3482.1	101.0	6.8	−282.2	90.8
1994:Q1	6911.0	89.6	7715.1	7844.3	6.6	5.7	1132.2	3481.1	101.7	7.2	−259.2	91.2
1994:Q2	7030.6	90.0	7815.7	7901.7	6.2	5.6	1142.0	3498.1	101.6	7.9	−211.6	89.7
1994:Q3	7115.1	90.5	7859.5	7960.0	6.0	5.6	1147.1	3495.7	100.9	8.2	−233.4	86.7
1994:Q4	7232.2	91.0	7951.6	8019.1	5.6	5.5	1159.5	3504.5	101.9	8.6	−236.9	86.1
1995:Q1	7298.3	91.5	7973.7	8079.1	5.5	5.5	1144.7	3498.7	101.6	8.3	−235.1	85.4
1995:Q2	7337.7	91.9	7988.0	8140.0	5.7	5.5	1145.1	3536.4	101.8	7.7	−212.6	80.7
1995:Q3	7432.1	92.3	8053.1	8201.9	5.7	5.4	1141.1	3595.4	101.9	7.4	−215.3	83.1
1995:Q4	7522.5	92.7	8112.0	8264.8	5.6	5.4	1141.4	3638.0	102.7	7.0	−192.7	84.6
1996:Q1	7624.1	93.3	8169.2	8328.6	5.5	5.4	1118.0	3675.7	103.7	7.1	−195.1	86.6
1996:Q2	7776.6	93.7	8303.1	8393.3	5.5	5.4	1117.6	3722.3	104.8	7.6	−152.8	87.5
1996:Q3	7866.2	94.0	8372.7	8458.9	5.3	5.4	1100.0	3753.1	105.1	7.6	−141.7	87.2
1996:Q4	8000.4	94.4	8470.6	8525.3	5.3	5.4	1090.5	3803.6	105.3	7.2	−115.1	87.7
1997:Q1	8113.8	95.1	8536.1	8592.4	5.2	5.3	1074.6	3849.5	104.9	7.4	−93.8	92.1
1997:Q2	8250.4	95.2	8665.8	8660.3	5.0	5.3	1064.7	3891.6	106.2	7.6	−72.6	93.4
1997:Q3	8381.9	95.5	8773.7	8728.9	4.9	5.3	1064.8	3944.0	107.1	7.2	−36.6	94.7
1997:Q4	8471.2	95.8	8838.4	8798.1	4.7	5.3	1076.4	4016.6	107.5	6.9	−31.3	95.6
1998:Q1	8586.7	96.1	8936.2	8867.8	4.6	5.3	1074.1	4093.7	108.4	6.7	13.5	98.0
1998:Q2	8657.9	96.2	8995.3	8938.0	4.4	5.3	1077.9	4165.7	108.7	6.6	30.0	99.2
1998:Q3	8789.5	96.6	9098.9	9008.7	4.5	5.3	1071.4	4225.5	109.9	6.5	62.5	100.8
1998:Q4	8953.8	96.9	9237.1	9079.7	4.4	5.4	1098.9	4350.5	110.5	6.3	54.7	95.6
1999:Q1	9066.6	97.3	9315.5	9151.1	4.3	5.4	1095.5	4433.7	111.5	6.4	81.6	96.1
1999:Q2	9174.1	97.7	9392.6	9222.6	4.3	5.4	1102.7	4490.9	111.7	6.9	107.1	98.3
1999:Q3	9313.5	98.0	9502.2	9294.4	4.2	5.3	1092.1	4538.5	112.4	7.3	110.0	97.4
1999:Q4	9519.5	98.4	9671.1	9366.2	4.1	5.3	1118.8	4617.2	114.4	7.5	124.7	95.6
2000:Q1	9629.4	99.3	9695.6	9438.1	4.0	5.3	1111.0	4695.5	113.9	7.7	214.2	97.7
2000:Q2	9822.8	99.7	9847.9	9510.1	3.9	5.3	1109.2	4763.3	116.0	7.8	181.9	100.6
2000:Q3	9862.1	100.3	9836.6	9582.1	4.0	5.3	1095.3	4803.4	115.7	7.6	190.7	102.4
2000:Q4	9953.6	100.7	9887.7	9654.1	3.9	5.3	1098.6	4893.9	116.8	7.4	171.4	105.6
2001:Q1	10021.5	101.5	9875.6	9726.1	4.2	5.3	1100.4	5029.9	116.7	7.1	154.3	105.2
2001:Q2	10128.9	102.3	9905.9	9798.2	4.4	5.3	1122.6	5151.7	118.3	7.2	120.9	108.8
2001:Q3	10135.1	102.7	9871.1	9870.5	4.8	5.3	1159.3	5256.6	118.8	7.1	−86.3	107.8
2001:Q4	10226.3	103.2	9910.0	9938.3	5.5	5.4	1178.7	5393.0	120.6	6.9	−4.6	108.7
2002:Q1	10333.3	103.6	9977.3	10006.5	5.7	5.4	1188.3	5485.6	122.7	6.6	−201.3	111.4

	Nominal GDP (X) (B $)	GDP Deflator (2000 = 100)	Real GDP (Y) (B 2000$)	Natural Real GDP (Y^N) (B 2000$)	Unemploy. Rate (U) (Percent)	Natural Unemploy. Rate (U^N) (Percent)	Money Supply (M1) (B $)	Money Supply (M2) (B $)	Labor Productivity (Y/N) (1992 = 100)	Nominal Interest Rate (i) (Percent)	Real Federal Budget Surplus (B 2000$)	Trade-Weighted Exchange Rate (Mar 1973 = 100)
2002:Q2	10426.6	103.9	10031.6	10075.1	5.8	5.4	1192.1	5527.8	122.9	6.7	−232.3	107.2
2002:Q3	10527.4	104.3	10090.7	10144.2	5.7	5.4	1189.0	5621.4	124.2	6.4	−237.0	102.8
2002:Q4	10591.1	104.9	10095.8	10213.8	5.9	5.3	1215.3	5754.2	124.1	6.3	−280.8	102.6
2003:Q1	10705.6	105.7	10126.0	10283.9	5.9	5.3	1231.4	5834.7	125.2	6.0	−274.5	97.8
2003:Q2	10831.8	106.1	10212.7	10354.5	6.1	5.3	1269.7	5961.2	126.9	5.3	−344.6	93.3
2003:Q3	11086.1	106.6	10398.7	10425.5	6.1	5.3	1288.3	6074.5	130.1	5.7	−423.4	93.1
2003:Q4	11219.5	107.2	10467.0	10497.1	5.8	5.3	1304.6	6080.2	129.9	5.7	−355.9	87.8
2004:Q1	11405.5	108.2	10543.6	10569.1	5.7	5.3	1315.2	6106.0	130.2	5.5	−380.0	85.3
2004:Q2	11610.3	109.2	10634.2	10641.6	5.6	5.3	1341.2	6258.4	131.7	5.9	−342.6	88.0
2004:Q3	11779.4	109.8	10728.7	10714.6	5.4	5.2	1346.7	6307.7	132.0	5.6	−329.6	86.4
2004:Q4	11948.5	110.7	10796.4	10788.2	5.4	5.2	1374.4	6404.8	132.2	5.5	−303.1	81.8
2005:Q1	12154.0	111.7	10878.4	10862.2	5.3	5.1	1366.0	6434.5	133.4	5.3	−266.7	81.2
2005:Q2	12317.4	112.4	10954.1	10936.7	5.1	5.1	1374.2	6508.1	133.5	5.1	−255.7	83.5
2005:Q3	12558.8	113.4	11074.3	11011.7	5.0	5.0	1368.3	6574.0	135.0	5.1	−347.7	84.5
2005:Q4	12705.5	114.4	11107.2	11087.3	4.9	4.9	1378.2	6673.9	134.5	5.4	−256.3	85.7
2006:Q1	12964.6	115.4	11238.7	11163.4	4.7	4.9	1376.9	6744.8	135.3	5.4	−190.4	84.8
2006:Q2	13155.0	116.3	11306.7	11240.0	4.7	4.9	1387.7	6824.9	135.6	5.9	−206.2	82.0
2006:Q3	13266.9	117.0	11336.7	11317.1	4.6	4.8	1362.0	6874.8	135.0	5.7	−204.4	81.6
2006:Q4	13392.3	117.5	11395.5	11394.7	4.4	4.8	1372.0	7002.3	135.6	5.4	−154.4	81.6
2007:Q1	13551.9	118.7	11412.6	11472.9	4.5	4.8	1365.2	7111.4	135.9	5.4	−184.0	81.9
2007:Q2	13768.8	119.5	11520.1	11551.7	4.5	4.8	1381.8	7243.8	136.6	5.6	−173.0	79.3
2007:Q3	13970.5	119.8	11658.9	11630.9	4.7	4.8	1361.1	7302.0	138.6	5.8	−194.1	77.0
2007:Q4	14084.1	120.6	11677.1	11710.7	4.8	4.8	1368.4	7416.9	139.2	5.5	—	73.3

International Annual Time Series Data for Selected Countries: 1960–2008

Table B-1   Canada, 1960–2008

	Nominal GDP (X) (B C$)	GDP Deflator	Real GDP (Y) (B 2000 C$)	Labor Productivity (Y/N) (C$/Hr)	Unemploy. Rate (U) (Percent)	Investment Share (Percent)	Consumer Price Index (CPI) (1995 = 100)	Long-Term Interest Rate (i) (Percent)	Labor Share (wN/X) (Percent)
1960	39.7	15.5	256.6	20.9	6.5	20.1	17.7	5.2	50.7
1961	41.2	15.6	264.5	21.0	6.7	19.7	17.9	5.1	51.5
1962	44.7	15.8	283.0	21.8	5.5	20.1	18.0	5.1	51.0
1963	48.0	16.1	298.0	22.7	5.2	19.9	18.4	5.1	50.7
1964	52.5	16.6	317.3	23.4	4.4	20.4	18.8	5.2	50.6
1965	57.9	17.2	337.5	24.2	3.6	22.3	19.2	5.2	51.1
1966	64.8	18.0	359.9	24.7	3.3	23.0	19.9	5.7	51.7
1967	69.7	18.8	370.4	24.8	3.8	21.1	20.6	5.9	53.2
1968	76.1	19.6	388.5	26.0	4.5	20.9	21.4	6.7	52.9
1969	83.8	20.5	408.0	26.7	4.4	21.7	22.4	7.6	53.8
1970	90.2	21.5	420.4	27.5	5.7	19.9	23.1	8.0	54.2
1971	98.4	22.5	437.7	28.3	6.2	20.4	23.9	6.9	54.4
1972	109.9	23.8	461.5	29.1	6.2	20.6	25.0	7.2	54.7
1973	129.0	26.1	493.7	29.8	5.6	21.7	26.9	7.5	53.7
1974	154.0	30.1	511.9	29.8	5.3	23.4	29.8	8.9	53.6
1975	173.6	33.3	521.2	30.2	6.9	22.9	33.1	9.0	55.5
1976	200.0	36.5	548.3	30.4	6.9	23.2	35.6	9.2	55.7
1977	221.0	39.0	567.3	30.9	7.8	22.4	38.4	8.7	55.8
1978	244.9	41.5	589.7	30.9	8.1	21.7	41.8	9.2	54.8
1979	279.6	45.7	612.2	30.7	7.3	23.8	45.6	10.2	54.0
1980	314.4	50.3	625.4	31.0	7.3	22.6	50.3	12.3	54.3
1981	360.5	55.7	647.3	31.6	7.3	23.9	56.6	15.0	54.6
1982	379.9	60.4	628.8	31.9	10.7	19.2	62.7	14.4	55.3
1983	411.4	63.7	645.9	32.4	11.6	19.8	66.3	11.4	53.5
1984	449.6	65.8	683.5	33.5	10.9	20.5	69.2	12.7	52.8
1985	485.7	67.8	716.1	33.9	10.2	20.9	71.9	10.9	52.7
1986	512.5	69.9	733.5	33.7	9.3	21.1	74.9	9.1	53.2
1987	558.9	73.1	764.7	34.2	8.4	22.1	78.2	9.5	53.0
1988	613.1	76.4	802.7	34.3	7.4	22.8	81.4	9.8	53.1
1989	657.7	79.8	823.7	33.9	7.1	23.3	85.4	9.8	53.3
1990	679.9	82.4	825.3	34.2	7.7	20.9	89.5	10.7	54.3
1991	685.4	84.8	808.1	34.8	9.8	18.8	94.5	9.5	55.3
1992	700.5	85.9	815.1	36.1	10.6	17.8	95.9	8.1	55.4
1993	727.2	87.2	834.2	36.2	10.8	17.8	97.7	7.2	54.3
1994	770.9	88.2	874.3	36.8	9.6	18.9	97.9	8.4	52.5
1995	810.4	90.2	898.8	37.4	8.6	18.8	100.0	8.2	51.7
1996	836.9	91.6	913.4	37.4	8.8	18.2	101.6	7.2	51.2
1997	882.7	92.7	952.0	38.1	8.4	20.7	103.2	6.1	51.3
1998	915.0	92.3	991.0	39.2	7.7	20.4	104.2	5.3	52.0
1999	982.4	93.9	1045.8	39.9	7.0	20.3	106.1	5.5	51.2
2000	1076.6	97.8	1100.5	40.7	6.1	20.2	109.0	5.9	50.6
2001	1108.0	98.9	1120.1	41.7	6.5	19.2	111.7	5.5	51.4
2002	1152.9	100.0	1152.9	42.4	7.0	19.3	114.2	5.3	51.5
2003	1213.2	103.3	1174.6	42.4	6.9	20.0	117.4	4.8	51.2
2004	1290.8	106.6	1210.7	42.5	6.4	20.7	119.5	4.6	50.7
2005	1375.1	110.2	1247.8	43.6	6.0	21.7	122.2	4.1	50.5
2006	1446.3	112.8	1282.2	43.9	5.5	22.5	124.6	4.2	51.0
2007	1536.9	116.9	1315.1	44.0	5.3	22.4	127.4	4.3	51.4
2008	1614.4	119.9	1346.0	—	5.4	23.0	129.8	4.4	52.1

Table B-2 Japan, 1960–2008

	Nominal GDP (X) (Tr ¥)	GDP Deflator	Real GDP (Y) (Tr 2000 ¥)	Labor Productivity (Y/N) (¥/Hr)	Unemploy. Rate (U) (Percent)	Investment Share (Percent)	Consumer Price Index (CPI) (1995 = 100)	Long-Term Interest Rate (i) (Percent)	Labor Share (wN/X) (Percent)
1960	16.1	21.6	74.5	755.6	1.7	22.5	18.4	7.5	40.2
1961	19.4	23.3	83.3	832.5	1.5	25.6	19.5	7.3	39.4
1962	22.0	24.3	90.5	902.0	1.3	25.2	20.8	7.5	41.4
1963	25.2	25.6	98.4	975.8	1.3	26.0	22.4	7.1	42.1
1964	29.6	27.1	109.4	1067.4	1.2	27.2	23.2	7.2	42.0
1965	33.0	28.5	115.6	1119.6	1.2	26.6	24.8	7.2	43.9
1966	38.3	30.0	127.5	1205.1	1.4	27.3	26.0	6.8	43.8
1967	44.9	31.7	141.6	1305.1	1.3	29.8	27.0	6.9	42.9
1968	53.1	33.5	158.5	1434.1	1.2	31.9	28.5	7.0	42.3
1969	62.4	35.2	177.4	1603.3	1.1	33.1	30.0	7.0	42.3
1970	73.6	37.6	195.7	1757.4	1.2	35.9	32.4	7.0	43.3
1971	81.0	39.6	204.3	1831.7	1.3	34.6	34.4	7.1	46.5
1972	92.7	41.9	221.4	1981.6	1.4	35.1	36.0	6.9	47.4
1973	112.9	47.2	239.2	2100.6	1.3	36.2	40.2	7.1	48.8
1974	134.7	57.0	236.3	2143.1	1.4	34.4	49.5	8.2	52.0
1975	148.8	61.1	243.6	2246.3	1.9	31.8	55.4	8.5	54.9
1976	167.1	66.0	253.3	2283.7	2.0	31.7	60.6	8.6	55.0
1977	186.2	70.4	264.4	2344.9	2.0	31.3	65.5	7.5	55.1
1978	205.1	73.7	278.3	2433.7	2.3	31.9	68.3	6.4	54.0
1979	222.3	75.7	293.6	2528.1	2.1	32.2	70.8	8.3	53.7
1980	241.0	79.8	301.9	2571.0	2.0	31.1	76.3	8.9	53.8
1981	259.0	83.4	310.7	2643.8	2.2	30.9	80.1	8.4	54.1
1982	271.9	85.1	319.3	2692.0	2.4	29.9	82.3	8.3	54.5
1983	282.8	87.2	324.5	2701.6	2.7	28.3	83.8	7.8	55.1
1984	300.9	89.9	334.6	2752.8	2.8	28.2	85.7	7.3	54.6
1985	323.5	92.0	351.6	2892.9	2.7	28.7	87.5	6.5	53.1
1986	338.7	93.6	362.0	2949.5	2.8	28.5	88.0	5.1	52.9
1987	352.5	93.8	375.7	3032.8	2.9	29.0	88.1	5.0	52.5
1988	379.3	94.5	401.2	3190.2	2.5	31.2	88.7	4.8	51.7
1989	408.5	96.7	422.4	3329.9	2.3	32.3	90.7	5.1	51.5
1990	440.1	99.0	444.4	3501.2	2.1	33.1	93.4	7.0	51.6
1991	468.2	102.0	459.3	3609.0	2.1	32.7	96.6	6.3	52.5
1992	480.5	103.6	463.7	3666.7	2.2	31.0	98.2	5.3	52.8
1993	484.2	104.2	464.9	3783.3	2.5	29.6	99.5	4.3	53.5
1994	486.6	103.5	470.0	3837.2	2.9	28.4	100.1	4.4	54.3
1995	493.6	103.0	479.2	3939.0	3.2	28.4	100.0	3.4	54.5
1996	504.3	102.4	492.3	4012.1	3.4	28.9	100.1	3.1	54.1
1997	515.2	103.0	500.1	4091.5	3.4	28.4	102.0	2.4	54.1
1998	504.8	103.1	489.8	4082.3	4.1	26.3	102.6	1.5	54.5
1999	497.6	101.7	489.1	4180.8	4.7	24.8	102.3	1.7	54.2
2000	503.0	100.0	503.1	4285.3	4.8	25.4	101.5	1.7	53.9
2001	497.7	98.7	504.0	4346.0	5.1	24.8	100.8	1.3	54.1
2002	491.3	97.2	505.4	4440.8	5.4	23.1	99.9	1.3	53.4
2003	490.3	95.7	512.5	4512.1	5.3	22.8	99.6	1.0	52.7
2004	498.3	94.6	526.6	4657.6	4.8	23.0	99.6	1.5	51.5
2005	501.3	93.4	536.5	4755.2	4.5	23.4	99.3	1.4	51.6
2006	507.5	92.6	548.1	4813.7	4.2	24.1	99.6	1.7	51.9
2007	514.4	92.1	558.4	4882.9	4.1	24.1	99.6	1.7	51.6
2008	520.9	91.8	567.1	—	4.1	24.1	100.1	1.9	51.3

Table B-3   France, 1960–2008

	Nominal GDP (X) (B euro)	GDP Deflator	Real GDP (Y) (B 2000 euro)	Labor Productivity (Y/N) (euro/Hr)	Unemploy. Rate (U) (Percent)	Investment Share (Percent)	Consumer Price Index (CPI) (1995 = 100)	Long-Term Interest Rate (i) (Percent)	Labor Share (wN/X) (Percent)
1960	47.7	12.5	382.6	9.2	1.5	21.2	13.1	5.7	44.4
1961	51.7	12.9	401.6	9.6	1.2	21.5	13.3	5.5	45.8
1962	57.9	13.5	429.2	10.1	1.4	21.9	14.0	5.4	46.2
1963	65.0	14.2	456.3	10.7	1.6	22.2	14.8	5.3	47.1
1964	72.1	14.8	486.1	11.2	1.2	23.6	15.2	5.4	47.4
1965	77.6	15.2	509.3	11.6	1.6	23.5	15.7	6.2	47.5
1966	84.0	15.7	535.9	12.1	1.6	24.3	16.0	6.6	47.3
1967	90.7	16.2	561.0	12.7	2.1	24.4	16.5	6.7	47.2
1968	98.6	16.9	584.9	13.4	2.7	24.7	17.3	7.0	48.6
1969	112.5	18.0	625.7	14.3	2.3	25.8	18.3	8.2	48.7
1970	125.6	19.0	661.6	15.2	2.5	25.6	19.3	8.6	49.4
1971	140.0	20.2	693.3	15.9	2.8	25.4	20.4	8.4	50.0
1972	156.4	21.6	724.0	16.6	2.9	25.6	21.7	8.0	50.0
1973	178.8	23.4	763.4	17.5	2.8	26.7	23.3	9.0	50.3
1974	206.2	26.2	787.1	18.2	2.9	27.0	26.4	11.0	52.2
1975	232.4	29.6	784.9	18.7	4.2	22.9	29.5	10.3	54.7
1976	269.2	32.9	818.2	19.8	4.6	24.2	32.4	10.5	54.9
1977	303.6	35.9	844.5	20.4	5.2	23.3	35.4	11.0	55.4
1978	345.5	39.6	872.8	21.2	5.4	22.3	38.7	10.6	55.1
1979	393.4	43.5	904.3	21.9	6.1	22.9	42.8	10.8	54.9
1980	444.9	48.3	920.7	22.4	6.5	23.2	48.6	13.8	55.8
1981	500.5	53.8	930.6	23.0	7.6	21.3	55.1	16.3	56.4
1982	574.0	60.1	954.4	24.7	8.3	21.7	61.7	16.0	56.4
1983	636.2	65.8	967.3	25.3	8.6	20.0	67.6	14.4	55.9
1984	693.0	70.5	983.2	25.7	10.0	19.3	72.7	13.4	55.1
1985	744.4	74.3	1001.9	26.8	10.5	19.3	77.0	11.9	54.3
1986	802.5	78.1	1027.7	27.5	10.6	19.8	78.9	9.1	52.9
1987	845.2	80.1	1054.5	27.9	10.8	20.4	81.5	9.5	52.4
1988	910.2	82.5	1103.3	28.8	10.3	21.6	83.7	9.1	51.4
1989	981.2	85.2	1151.8	29.7	9.6	22.5	86.7	8.8	50.7
1990	1033.7	87.4	1182.7	30.4	8.6	22.5	89.6	9.9	51.4
1991	1070.7	89.6	1195.2	30.8	9.1	21.7	92.5	9.0	51.8
1992	1106.7	91.4	1210.4	31.4	10.0	19.9	94.7	8.6	52.1
1993	1114.3	92.8	1200.5	31.8	11.3	17.4	96.6	6.8	52.6
1994	1153.9	94.0	1227.1	32.6	11.9	18.3	98.3	7.2	51.8
1995	1195.5	95.2	1255.2	33.5	11.3	18.5	100.0	7.5	51.8
1996	1227.7	96.7	1269.1	33.7	11.8	17.6	102.1	6.3	51.8
1997	1267.3	97.7	1297.3	34.4	11.7	17.4	103.4	5.6	51.5
1998	1324.1	98.6	1343.4	35.3	11.2	18.7	104.1	4.6	51.2
1999	1367.2	98.6	1386.7	35.9	10.5	19.3	104.7	4.6	51.8
2000	1442.8	100.0	1442.8	37.3	9.1	20.4	106.6	5.4	51.8
2001	1497.5	102.0	1468.3	37.6	8.4	20.0	108.5	4.9	52.2
2002	1549.8	104.4	1484.2	38.8	8.8	19.0	110.6	4.9	52.5
2003	1595.8	106.4	1500.1	39.3	9.6	18.9	113.0	4.1	52.5
2004	1657.8	108.1	1534.0	39.4	9.8	19.5	115.6	4.1	52.3
2005	1715.8	110.0	1560.4	40.1	9.9	20.2	117.8	3.4	52.2
2006	1793.7	112.5	1594.9	40.6	9.7	21.0	120.1	3.8	51.9
2007	1867.6	114.9	1624.8	40.8	8.8	21.1	122.0	4.3	51.9
2008	1942.4	117.5	1653.3	—	8.2	20.9	124.2	4.3	51.8

Table B-4   Germany, 1960–2008

	Nominal GDP (X) (B euro)	GDP Deflator	Real GDP (Y) (B 2000 euro)	Labor Productivity (Y/N) (euro/Hr)	Unemploy. Rate (U) (Percent)	Investment Share (Percent)	Consumer Price Index (CPI) (1995 = 100)	Long-Term Interest Rate (i) (Percent)	Labor Share (wN/X) (Percent)
1960	150.8	23.3	648.3	8.8	1.1	—	31.3	6.3	55.0
1961	164.4	24.2	678.2	9.2	0.6	—	32.0	5.9	56.9
1962	183.6	25.9	709.9	9.7	0.6	—	32.9	6.0	56.4
1963	205.9	28.2	729.8	10.2	0.5	—	33.9	6.1	53.9
1964	228.3	29.3	778.4	10.7	0.4	—	34.7	6.2	53.1
1965	245.8	30.0	820.1	11.3	0.3	—	35.8	6.8	54.7
1966	266.1	31.6	843.0	12.1	0.3	—	37.2	7.8	54.4
1967	287.4	34.2	840.4	12.8	1.3	—	37.7	7.0	50.3
1968	312.4	35.2	886.3	13.5	1.1	—	38.3	6.7	49.7
1969	345.5	36.3	952.3	14.5	0.6	—	39.0	7.0	50.6
1970	390.9	39.1	1000.3	15.1	0.5	28.7	40.4	8.2	53.0
1971	433.8	42.1	1031.7	15.7	0.6	28.0	42.5	8.2	54.1
1972	473.0	44.0	1076.0	16.5	0.7	27.7	44.8	8.2	55.0
1973	526.8	46.7	1127.5	17.4	0.7	27.5	47.9	9.4	56.2
1974	570.2	50.1	1137.5	18.0	1.6	24.6	51.3	10.6	57.5
1975	597.2	53.0	1127.6	18.6	3.4	22.7	54.3	8.8	57.3
1976	647.5	54.7	1183.4	19.3	3.4	23.9	56.7	8.2	57.2
1977	690.0	56.4	1223.1	20.2	3.4	23.5	58.8	6.7	57.6
1978	735.9	58.4	1259.8	20.9	3.3	23.6	60.3	6.3	57.7
1979	799.2	60.9	1312.1	21.0	2.9	24.8	62.8	7.7	57.5
1980	854.7	64.2	1330.6	21.7	2.8	24.0	66.2	8.6	58.4
1981	895.1	66.9	1337.7	21.9	4.0	21.5	70.4	10.2	58.5
1982	932.4	70.0	1332.4	22.0	5.6	20.1	74.1	9.1	57.9
1983	973.6	71.9	1353.3	22.5	6.9	21.2	76.6	8.2	56.7
1984	1021.0	73.4	1391.5	23.5	7.1	21.0	78.4	8.1	56.2
1985	1067.0	74.9	1423.9	24.1	7.2	20.2	80.1	7.2	55.9
1986	1124.2	77.2	1456.5	24.4	6.6	20.3	80.0	6.3	55.9
1987	1154.5	78.2	1476.9	24.8	6.3	19.8	80.2	6.4	56.9
1988	1217.5	79.5	1531.7	25.5	6.3	20.7	81.2	6.6	56.2
1989	1301.4	81.8	1591.4	26.5	5.7	21.6	83.5	7.1	55.0
1990	1416.3	84.6	1675.0	27.8	5.0	22.2	85.7	8.7	54.7
1991	1534.6	87.2	1760.6	29.4	5.6	24.0	87.2	8.5	55.1
1992	1646.6	91.5	1799.7	30.2	6.7	23.4	91.6	7.9	55.6
1993	1694.4	94.9	1785.3	30.7	8.0	22.2	95.7	6.5	55.4
1994	1780.0	97.2	1831.9	31.6	8.5	22.5	98.3	6.9	54.0
1995	1849.3	99.0	1868.2	32.4	8.2	22.2	100.0	6.9	54.0
1996	1877.0	99.5	1886.7	33.2	9.0	21.1	101.2	6.2	53.7
1997	1917.3	99.8	1921.6	34.0	9.9	21.1	102.7	5.7	52.8
1998	1963.2	100.3	1956.8	34.3	9.3	21.6	103.4	4.6	52.6
1999	2007.1	100.7	1993.6	34.8	8.5	21.5	104.0	4.5	52.9
2000	2062.8	100.0	2062.9	35.8	7.8	21.8	105.5	5.3	53.4
2001	2116.3	101.2	2091.1	36.5	7.9	19.5	107.5	4.8	53.0
2002	2146.4	102.6	2091.2	37.0	8.6	17.3	108.9	4.8	52.6
2003	2166.8	103.9	2086.4	37.4	9.3	17.4	110.1	4.1	52.3
2004	2203.5	105.0	2098.3	37.4	10.3	17.1	112.0	4.0	51.6
2005	2240.9	105.8	2118.6	38.0	11.2	17.1	114.2	3.4	50.5
2006	2323.3	106.4	2183.9	39.0	10.4	17.8	116.2	3.8	49.5
2007	2428.0	108.3	2241.8	39.4	8.3	18.3	118.7	4.2	48.7
2008	2512.9	110.2	2281.3	—	8.1	18.6	120.8	4.2	48.5

Table B-5 Italy, 1960–2008

	Nominal GDP (X) (B euro)	GDP Deflator	Real GDP (Y) (B 2000 euro)	Labor Productivity (Y/N) (euro/Hr)	Unemploy. Rate (U) (Percent)	Investment Share (Percent)	Consumer Price Index (CPI) (1995 = 100)	Long-Term Interest Rate (i) (Percent)	Labor Share (wN/X) (Percent)
1960	13.2	4.1	322.7	6.9	3.7	30.9	5.8	5.3	40.0
1961	14.6	4.2	349.2	7.5	3.2	31.8	5.9	5.0	40.0
1962	16.4	4.4	370.9	8.2	2.8	32.2	6.2	5.0	41.5
1963	18.8	4.8	391.7	8.9	2.4	32.0	6.7	5.2	44.1
1964	20.6	5.1	402.7	9.3	2.7	28.8	7.0	5.7	45.1
1965	22.2	5.3	415.8	10.0	3.5	26.0	7.4	5.4	44.3
1966	24.0	5.5	440.7	11.0	3.7	25.7	7.6	5.5	43.8
1967	26.5	5.6	472.3	11.8	3.4	27.0	7.8	5.6	43.8
1968	28.7	5.7	503.3	12.8	3.5	26.8	8.0	5.6	43.9
1969	31.7	5.9	533.9	13.9	3.5	28.1	8.1	5.8	43.9
1970	35.6	6.3	562.3	14.8	3.2	28.7	8.5	7.7	45.6
1971	38.9	6.8	573.2	15.5	3.3	26.3	9.0	7.0	47.8
1972	42.5	7.2	591.3	16.1	3.8	26.1	9.5	6.6	48.8
1973	51.2	8.1	630.0	17.1	3.7	27.7	10.5	6.9	49.2
1974	64.7	9.8	663.2	18.0	3.1	28.9	12.5	9.6	48.3
1975	73.8	11.4	649.6	17.8	3.4	24.4	14.6	10.0	51.3
1976	92.7	13.4	692.0	18.8	3.9	25.7	17.1	12.7	49.9
1977	112.6	15.9	708.4	19.5	4.1	23.6	20.0	14.7	50.4
1978	132.5	18.0	734.2	20.3	4.1	23.4	22.5	13.1	50.1
1979	162.1	20.9	774.8	21.2	4.4	23.8	25.8	13.0	49.0
1980	203.6	25.4	801.8	21.8	4.4	24.8	31.2	15.3	48.2
1981	243.4	30.1	808.0	22.0	4.9	22.5	36.8	19.4	49.1
1982	287.0	35.4	810.6	22.2	5.4	22.0	42.9	20.2	48.4
1983	334.9	40.8	821.8	22.5	5.9	21.2	49.2	18.3	47.7
1984	382.9	45.1	848.2	23.9	5.9	21.8	54.5	15.6	46.5
1985	429.9	49.3	872.4	24.2	6.0	21.9	59.5	13.7	46.3
1986	475.8	53.0	898.3	24.8	7.5	21.6	63.0	11.5	45.2
1987	519.3	56.2	924.8	25.5	7.9	22.0	66.0	10.6	44.9
1988	577.6	59.9	964.5	26.1	7.9	22.1	69.3	10.9	44.3
1989	634.8	63.6	998.2	26.8	7.8	22.3	73.7	12.8	44.2
1990	701.5	68.9	1017.7	26.9	7.0	22.3	78.2	13.5	44.7
1991	766.0	74.1	1033.3	26.9	6.9	22.0	83.0	13.3	44.9
1992	804.8	77.4	1039.8	27.9	7.3	21.4	87.2	13.3	44.8
1993	828.8	80.4	1030.6	28.3	9.8	18.9	91.1	11.2	44.3
1994	877.9	83.3	1054.1	29.5	10.7	18.7	94.9	10.5	42.8
1995	948.2	87.4	1084.8	30.4	11.3	19.8	100.0	12.2	41.2
1996	1003.5	92.0	1091.2	30.4	11.3	19.2	104.0	9.4	41.4
1997	1049.3	94.3	1112.7	30.8	11.4	19.4	106.0	6.9	41.6
1998	1090.6	96.7	1127.3	30.9	11.5	19.6	108.1	4.9	39.7
1999	1125.9	98.0	1148.6	31.2	11.0	20.1	109.8	4.7	39.8
2000	1191.9	100.0	1191.9	32.0	10.2	20.7	112.7	5.6	39.2
2001	1248.7	103.0	1212.5	32.3	9.2	20.6	115.3	5.2	39.5
2002	1295.1	106.5	1216.5	32.0	8.7	21.1	118.3	5.0	39.8
2003	1336.2	109.7	1217.8	31.7	8.5	20.7	121.6	4.3	40.1
2004	1388.9	112.9	1230.3	31.9	8.1	20.8	124.4	4.3	40.0
2005	1423.4	115.4	1233.1	32.0	7.8	20.6	127.1	3.6	40.8
2006	1476.7	117.5	1257.0	32.4	6.9	21.2	130.0	4.0	41.2
2007	1542.9	120.6	1279.4	32.7	6.6	21.6	132.4	4.5	40.8
2008	1598.7	123.4	1295.5	—	6.6	22.0	134.8	4.5	41.0

Table B-6   United Kingdom, 1960–2008

	Nominal GDP (X) (B £)	GDP Deflator	Real GDP (Y) (B 2000 £)	Labor Productivity (Y/N) (£/Hr)	Unemploy. Rate (U) (Percent)	Investment Share (Percent)	Consumer Price Index (CPI) (1995 = 100)	Long-Term Interest Rate (i) (Percent)	Labor Share (wN/X) (Percent)
1960	26.0	6.6	394.8	7.7	2.2	19.6	8.4	5.9	58.5
1961	27.4	6.8	403.9	7.9	2.0	19.8	8.6	6.3	59.9
1962	28.7	7.0	408.1	8.0	2.7	18.3	9.0	5.8	60.4
1963	30.4	7.1	425.6	8.2	3.3	18.4	9.2	5.2	60.0
1964	33.2	7.4	448.9	8.6	2.5	21.7	9.5	5.7	59.6
1965	35.8	7.8	459.0	8.8	2.1	21.2	10.0	6.6	59.6
1966	38.1	8.1	467.8	9.1	2.3	20.7	10.3	6.9	60.0
1967	40.2	8.4	479.4	9.5	3.3	21.7	10.6	6.7	59.3
1968	43.5	8.7	499.4	10.0	3.2	22.3	11.1	7.5	58.6
1969	46.9	9.2	509.8	10.2	3.1	21.7	11.7	8.8	58.2
1970	51.6	9.9	521.2	10.7	3.1	21.0	12.5	8.6	59.4
1971	57.5	10.8	531.8	11.2	4.2	20.2	13.6	7.9	58.4
1972	64.4	11.7	550.8	11.8	4.4	19.2	14.6	8.4	58.9
1973	74.1	12.6	590.0	12.3	3.7	21.7	15.9	10.6	59.3
1974	83.9	14.4	582.0	12.3	3.7	21.4	18.5	14.2	62.6
1975	105.9	18.3	578.3	12.6	4.5	18.3	22.9	13.2	64.9
1976	125.3	21.1	593.6	13.1	5.4	19.8	26.7	13.6	62.4
1977	145.8	24.0	607.8	13.4	5.6	20.1	31.0	12.0	59.4
1978	168.1	26.8	627.5	13.8	5.5	19.8	33.5	12.1	58.8
1979	197.8	30.7	644.4	14.3	5.4	20.3	38.0	12.9	58.6
1980	231.2	36.6	631.0	14.2	6.9	17.4	46.5	13.9	59.7
1981	253.6	40.8	621.8	14.7	9.7	15.6	52.2	14.9	59.1
1982	277.7	43.8	633.7	15.3	10.8	17.0	56.6	13.1	57.2
1983	303.6	46.3	656.0	16.0	11.5	17.8	59.6	11.3	56.0
1984	325.3	48.4	672.8	16.2	11.8	18.7	62.2	11.1	55.9
1985	356.1	51.1	696.6	16.5	11.4	18.5	65.5	11.0	55.4
1986	382.8	52.9	724.3	17.1	11.4	18.4	67.8	10.1	55.6
1987	421.6	55.7	757.5	17.6	10.5	19.4	70.6	9.6	54.6
1988	470.7	59.2	795.3	17.8	8.6	21.7	73.8	9.7	54.6
1989	517.1	63.6	812.7	17.8	7.3	22.5	77.7	10.2	55.3
1990	560.9	68.5	819.0	17.9	7.1	20.5	83.1	11.8	56.3
1991	589.7	73.0	807.8	18.4	8.9	17.5	89.3	10.1	56.9
1992	614.8	75.9	809.5	19.2	10.0	16.6	93.1	9.1	56.5
1993	645.5	78.0	827.9	19.9	10.4	16.2	95.5	7.5	55.2
1994	684.1	79.2	863.6	20.5	8.7	16.9	97.4	8.1	53.9
1995	723.1	81.3	889.0	20.8	8.7	17.4	100.0	8.2	53.3
1996	768.9	84.1	913.8	21.3	8.1	17.2	102.4	7.8	52.5
1997	815.9	86.6	942.2	21.7	7.0	17.5	104.3	7.1	52.7
1998	865.7	88.9	973.7	22.1	6.3	18.6	105.9	5.6	53.8
1999	911.9	90.9	1003.4	22.5	6.0	18.4	107.3	5.1	54.4
2000	958.9	92.1	1041.5	23.2	5.5	18.0	108.3	5.3	55.5
2001	1003.3	94.1	1066.2	23.5	5.1	17.7	109.5	4.9	56.2
2002	1055.8	97.0	1088.1	24.1	5.2	17.4	110.9	4.9	55.6
2003	1118.2	100.0	1118.2	24.8	5.0	17.1	112.4	4.5	55.2
2004	1184.3	102.6	1154.7	25.5	4.8	17.5	114.0	4.9	54.8
2005	1234.0	104.9	1175.9	25.8	4.8	17.5	116.3	4.4	55.6
2006	1301.9	107.7	1209.4	26.4	5.5	18.0	119.0	4.5	55.4
2007	1385.3	111.1	1246.7	27.2	5.5	18.5	121.9	5.0	54.3
2008	1447.9	113.9	1271.2	—	5.5	18.5	124.3	4.9	53.3

APPENDIX C

Data Sources and Methods

C-1   Annual Variables (Sources and Methods for Table A-1)

1. Nominal GDP (X):

   1875–1928: Data from Nathan S. Balke and Robert J. Gordon, "The Estimation of Prewar GNP: Methodology and New Results," *Journal of Political Economy*, vol. 97 (February 1989), pp. 38–92, Table 10. Linked in 1929 to:

   1929–2007: Data from U.S. Department of Commerce, Bureau of Economic Analysis. National Income and Product Accounts: Table 1.1.5 on the BEA Web site: www.bea.doc.gov

2. Implicit GDP Deflator (P):

   Same as Nominal GDP (X), except Table 1.1.9 for 1929–2007.

3. Real GDP (Y):

   Same as Nominal GDP (X), except Table 1.1.6 for 1929–2007.

4. Natural Real GDP (Y^N):

   1875–1955: Y^N is the geometric interpolation between real GDP for the benchmark years 1869, 1873, 1884, 1891, 1900, 1910, 1924, and 1949 and the value of natural real GDP in 1955 (see below).

   1955–2007: Average annual values of the natural real GDP series described in Appendix C-2.

5. Unemployment Rate (U):

   1890–1899: Lebergott's series copied from Christina Romer, "Spurious Volatility in Historical Unemployment Data," *Journal of Political Economy*, vol. 94 (February 1986).

   1900–1946: Series B1 in Long-Term Economic Growth, 1860–1970 (Washington, D.C.: U.S. Department of Commerce, 1973).

   1947–2007: Series LNS14000000 from http://stats.bls.gov, Bureau of Labor Statistics, Department of Labor. Average of quarterly values.

6. Natural Unemployment Rate (U^N):

   1890–1901: Assumed to be the same level as in 1902, 4.1 percent.

   1902–1954: U^N is the linear interpolation between the U^N values of the benchmark years of 1902, 1907, 1913, 1929, and 1949 and is calculated as $U^N = B*(U/UA)$ where UA is the published unemployment rate that adjusts for self-employment. UA equals the number of unemployed divided by the civilian labor force net of self-employed persons. The long-run equilibrium rate for UA ("B") reflects the value of UA observed in late 1954 when the economy was operating at its natural

   rate of unemployment. Changes in U^N before 1954 reflect only changes in the U/UA ratio.

   1955–2007: Time-varying NAIRU for chain-weighted GDP price index-based deflator with standard deviation = 0.2 from Robert J. Gordon, "Time-Varying NAIRU," *Journal of Economic Perspective*, vol. 11, pp. 11–34, extended to 2007 using unpublished research. For recent unpublished research papers on time-varying NAIRU, see http://faculty-web.at.northwestern.edu/economics/gordon/researchhome.html

7. Money Supply (M1):

   1915–1946: *Historical Statistics of the United States: Colonial Times to 1970* (Washington, D.C.: U.S. Department of Commerce, 1975), series 414. Linked in 1947 to:

   1947–1958: *Federal Reserve Bulletin* (Washington, D.C.: Board of Governors of the Federal Reserve System), various issues. Linked in 1959 to 1959–2007: Data from FRED, Federal Reserve Bank of St. Louis.

8. Money Supply (M2):

   1875–1907: Milton Friedman and Anna J. Schwartz, *Monetary Statistics of the United States* (New York: National Bureau of Economic Research, 1970), pp. 61–65. Linked in 1907 to:

   1908–1946: *Historical Statistics*, series 415. Linked in 1947 to:

   1947–1958: *Federal Reserve Bulletin* (Washington, D.C.: Board of Governors of the Federal Reserve System), various issues. Linked in 1959 to:

   1959–2007: Data from FRED, Federal Reserve Bank of St. Louis.

9. Labor Productivity (Y/N):

   1875–1946: Data computed by dividing real output from item 3 above by series A173 from *Long Term Economic Growth*, 1860–1970. Linked in 1947 to:

   1947–2007: Series PRS85006093 from http://stats.bls.gov, Bureau of Labor Statistics, Department of Labor. Average of quarterly values.

10. Nominal Interest Rate (i):

    1875–1939: The yield on corporate bonds from Robert J. Gordon, ed., *The American Business Cycle* (Chicago: University of Chicago, 1986), Appendix B.

    1940–2007: Corporate bonds (Moody's Aaa) from the Board of Governors of the Federal Reserve System.

11. S&P Stock Price Index:
    1875–1939: The index of all common stocks from Gordon, *The American Business Cycle*, Appendix B. Linked in 1940 to:

    1940–2004: Standard and Poor's Composite Index (1941–43 = 10) from the *2008 Economic Report of the President* (Washington D.C.: United States Government Printing Office, 2008).

C-2 Quarterly Variables (Sources and Methods for Table A-2)

1. Nominal GDP (X):
   1947:Q1–2007:Q4: Data from U.S. Department of Commerce, Bureau of Economic Analysis. National Income and Product Accounts: Table 1.1.5 on the BEA Web site: www.bea.gov.
2. Implicit GDP Deflator (P):
   Same as Nominal GDP (X) except Table 1.1.9.
3. Real GDP (Y):
   Same as Nominal GDP (X) except Table 1.1.6.
4. Natural GDP (Y^N):
   1947:Q1–2007:Q4: Data from Robert J. Gordon, "Exploding Productivity Growth: Context, Causes, and Implications," *Brookings Papers on Economic Activity*, 2003, no. 3, data underlying Figure 3, p. 227, updated in unpublished research.
5. Unemployment Rate (U):
   1947:Q1–2001:Q1: Series LNS14000000 from http://stats.bls.gov, Bureau of Labor Statistics, Department of Labor.
6. Natural Unemployment Rate (U^N): See Appendix C-1, line 6.
7. Money Supply (M1):
   1947:Q1–1958:Q4: *Federal Reserve Bulletin* (Washington, D.C.: Board of Governors of the Federal Reserve System), various issues. Linked in 1959 to:
   1959:Q1–2007:Q4: Data from FRED, Federal Reserve Bank of St. Louis.

8. Money Supply (M2):
   1947:Q1–1958:Q4: *Federal Reserve Bulletin* (Washington, D.C.: Board of Governors of the Federal Reserve System), various issues. Linked in 1959 to:
   1959:Q1–2007:Q4: Data from FRED, Federal Reserve Bank of St. Louis.
9. Labor Productivity (Y/N):
   1947:Q1–2007:Q4: Series PRS85006093 from http://stats.bls.gov, Bureau of Labor Statistics, Department of Labor.
10. Nominal Interest Rate (i):
    1947:Q1–2007:Q4: Corporate bonds (Moody's Aaa) from the Board of Governors of the Federal Reserve System.
11. Real Federal Budget Surplus in 2000 Dollars:
    1947:Q1–2007:Q4: Calculated by dividing the nominal federal government surplus from the U.S. Department of Commerce by the implicit price deflator using Tables 3.2 and 1.1.9.
12. Trade-Weighted Exchange Rate:
    1961:Q1–1966:Q4: Effective exchange rate (MERM) from various issues of *International Financial Statistics* (Washington, D.C.: International Monetary Fund). Linked in 1967:Q1 to:
    1967:Q1–2007:Q4: Trade-weighted exchange value of U.S. dollar versus Major Currencies from FRED, Federal Reserve Bank of St. Louis.

C-3 International Variables (Sources and Methods for Appendix B, same sources for all countries)

1. Nominal GDP (X):
   Gross domestic product (expenditures) from *Organization for Economic Cooperation and Development, National Accounts, Volume 1: Main Aggregates*, and *OECD Economic Outlook* no. 82, December 2007. Both are available at *OECD.Stat* online database.
2. Implicit GDP Deflator (P):
   Equals X/Y.
3. Real GDP (Y):
   Same sources as in 1. Nominal GDP.
4. Labor Productivity (Y/N):
   Real output (real GDP, Y) divided by total manhours, N (the product of total employment and hours

worked per employee). Total manhours are from *The Conference Board and Groningen Growth and Development Centre, Total Economy Database*, January 2008, www.conference-board.org/economics.
5. Unemployment Rate (U):
   Unemployment rate from Bureau of Labor Statistics, *Comparative Civilian Labor Force Statistics, Ten Countries, 1960–2006, Table 2*, and International Monetary Fund *World Economic Outlook*, October 2007.
6. Investment share:
   Alan Heston, Robert Summers, and Bettina Aten, Penn World Table Version 6.2, Center for International Comparisons of Production, Income

and Prices at the University of Pennsylvania, September 2006, and IMF *World Economic Outlook,* October 2007.

7. Consumer Price Index (CPI):
   International Financial Statistics Yearbook, 2001 (Washington, D.C.: International Monetary Fund, 2001). Updated using IMF *World Economic Outlook,* October 2007.

8. Long-term Interest Rate (*r*)
   OECD Economic Outlook, no. 82, December 2007.

9. Labor Share (*wN/ X*):
   Calculated by dividing compensation of employees by national income in *OECD Economic Outlook No. 82,* December 2007, and *National Accounts, Volume I: Main Aggregates,* found at *OECD.Stat.*

C-4 Sources and Methods for Figures in Chapters

Please note: Many of the figures contain complete source notes. The following sources, listed in order by page number, refer to the subset of figures that require more complete or detailed source notes than can be included underneath the figures.

Some sources are abbreviated as follows:

FRB: The Board of Governors of the Federal Reserve System

BEA: U.S. Department of Commerce *Bureau of Economic Analysis*

NIPA Tables: *National Income and Products Accounts Tables* obtained from www.bea.gov

BLS: U.S. Department of Labor *Bureau of Labor Statistics*

GGDC: The Conference Board and Groningen Growth and Development Centre

Historical Statistics: *The Historical Statistics of the United States: Millennial Edition Online*

IMF: International Monetary Fund

OECD: The Organization for Economic Cooperation and Development

1. Figure 1-6 (p. 13):
   1900–2007: See Appendix C-1, lines 3–6

2. Figure 1-7 (p. 15):
   1929–41 and 1995–2007: See Appendix C-1, line 5

3. Figure 1-8 (p. 16):
   Thomas J. Sargent, "The Ends of Four Big Inflations," in Robert E. Hall, ed., *Inflation: Causes and Effects,* University of Chicago for NBER, 1982, Table G1, pp. 74–75

4. Figure 1-9 (p. 18):
   GDP per capita is a linear average of GK and EKS PPP GDP measures
   1960–2007: GGDC, Total Economy Database, January 2007, www.ggdc.net
   2007–2008: GDP per capita growth is population growth subtracted from real GDP growth
   South Korea and the Philippines population estimates
   U.S. Census Bureau, International Data Base www.census.gov/ipc/www/idb/
   GDP growth rates and U.S. implicit GDP deflator estimates
   IMF, World Economic Outlook, April 2007

5. International Perspectives box (pp. 20–21):
   Labor Productivity
   1960–2007: GGDC, Total Economy Database, January 2007
   EU-15 Unemployment
   1960–2007: OECD Labour Force Statistics—Summary tables Vol. 2007 release 03. SourceOECD Employment and Labour Market Statistics
   EU-15 Civilian Labor Force
   1960–2007: OECD Labour Force Statistics—Summary tables Vol. 2007 release 03. SourceOECD Employment and Labour Market Statistics
   U.S. Unemployment
   1960–2007: See Appendix C-1, line 5

6. Figure 2-4 (p. 40):
   1900–2007: See Appendix C-1, lines 1–3

7. Figure 2-5 (p. 45):
   Current Population and Employment Statistics Surveys
   1990–2007: BLS Series Ids: LNS12000000 and CES0000000001
   For accurate comparison, requires: Employment in Agriculture, Forestry, and Fishing
   1990–2007: BEA *NIPA* Table 6.8

8. Figure 3-1 (p. 58):
   Real GDP
   1950–2007: See Appendix C-2, line 3

9. Figure 3-3 (p. 65):
   Personal Consumption Expenditures and Personal Disposable Income
   1929–2007: BEA *NIPA* Table 2.1

10. Box of Special Interest (p. 81)
    Consumer Sentiment
    1960–2007: Surveys of Consumers, Reuters and the University of Michigan
    www.sca.isr.umich.edu/
    Real GDP:
    1960–2007: See Appendix C-2, line 3

11. International Perspective Box (pp. 118–19)
    GDP per-capita
    1980–2007: GGDC, Total Economy Database, January 2007
    2007–2008: Forecasts use data from OECD Economic Outlook no. 81, Annex Table 1 and the U.S. Census Bureau, International Data Base
    Interest rates (see detailed source note on p. 119)

Intermediate good (2-3)   A product resold by its purchaser either in its present form or in an altered form.

Intertemporal substitution (17-4)   Workers work more in periods of high real wages and less in periods of low real wages. Also occurs when producers raise output in periods of high prices and reduce output in periods of low prices.

Intervention (6-5)   Under the flexible exchange rate system, the buying or selling of a nation's money by domestic or foreign central banks in order to prevent unwanted variations in the foreign exchange rate.

Inventory investment (2-4)   All changes in the stock of raw materials, parts, and finished goods held by business.

IS curve (3-10)   The schedule that identifies the combinations of income and the interest rate at which the commodity market is in equilibrium; everywhere along the *IS* curve the demand for commodities equals the supply.

Keynes Effect (7-9)   The stimulus to aggregate demand caused by a decline in the interest rate.

Labor productivity (11-2)   Real GDP per hour of work, or output per hour of work.

Large open economy (6-8)   An economy that can influence its domestic interest rate. A high domestic interest rate generates a steady stream of capital inflows that are not great enough to eliminate an interest rate differential between the domestic and foreign interest rate; a low domestic interest rate generates a steady stream of capital outflows.

Leakages (2-5)   The portion of total income that flows to taxes or saving rather than into purchases of consumer goods.

Life-cycle hypothesis (LCH) (15-1)   Conjecture that households base their current consumption on their total lifetime incomes and their wealth.

Liquidity constraint (15-6)   Occurs when households cannot borrow as much as they wish, even though there is sufficient expected future income to repay the loans.

Liquidity trap (4-8)   Situation in which the central bank loses its ability to reduce the interest rate.

LM curve (4-4)   The schedule that identifies the combinations of income and the interest rate at which the money market is in equilibrium; on the *LM* curve the demand for money equals the supply of money.

Long-run aggregate supply curve (LAS) (7-1)   A vertical line drawn at the natural level of real GDP; it shows the amount that business firms are willing to produce when the nominal wage rate has fully adjusted to any changes in the price level.

Long-run equilibrium (7-7)   A situation in which labor input is the amount voluntarily supplied and demanded at the equilibrium real wage rate.

Long-term labor contracts (17-9)   Agreements between firms and workers that set the level of nominal wage rates for a year or more.

Lucas model (17-3)   Economic model based on the three assumptions of market clearing, imperfect information, and rational expectations.

M1 (13-3)   The U.S. definition of the money supply that includes only currency, transactions accounts, and traveler's checks.

M2 (13-3)   The U.S. definition of the money supply that includes M1; savings deposits, including money market deposit accounts; small time deposits; and money market mutual funds.

Macroeconomic externality (17-7)   A cost incurred by society as a result of a decision by an individual economic agent (worker or business firm).

Macroeconomics (1-1)   The study of the major economic totals, or aggregates.

Magic equation (2-5)   Private saving plus net tax revenue must by definition equal the sum of private domestic investment, government spending on goods and services, and net export.

Marginal leakage rate (Appendix to Ch. 3)   The fraction of income that is taxed or saved rather than being spent on consumption.

Marginal product of capital (MPK) (16-6)   The extra output that a firm can produce by adding an extra unit of capital.

Marginal propensity to consume (3-3)   The dollar change in consumption expenditures induced by a dollar change in disposable income.

Marginal propensity to save (3-3)   The change in personal saving induced by a dollar change in disposable income.

Market-clearing model (7-9)   Theory that the economy is always in equilibrium at the intersection of supply and demand curves, particularly in the labor market.

Medium of exchange (4-2)   Units used for buying and selling goods and services; a universal alternative to the barter system.

Menu cost (9-3, 17-6)   Any expense associated with changing prices, including the costs of printing new menus or distributing new catalogues.

Mismatch unemployment (9-7)   Structural unemployment; one of the two components of the natural rate of unemployment (the other being turnover, or frictional unemployment); it occurs when the present location or skills of members of the labor force do not match location or skill requirements of job vacancies.

Monetarism (14-3)   A school of thought that opposes activist or discretionary monetary policy and instead favors a fixed rule for the growth rate of high-powered money or of the money supply.

Monetary impotence (7-9)   Failure of real GDP to respond to an increase in the real money supply.

Monetary policy (1-7)   Changes made in the money supply or interest rates or both in order to try to influence target variables.

Money market instruments (13-2)   Assets sold in financial markets that have short maturities, usually less than one year, small fluctuations in price, and minimal risk of default.

Money multiplier (13-4)   The ratio (M/H) of the money supply to high-powered money. There is a separate money multiplier for each definition of the money supply, e.g., $M1/H$ and $M2/H$.

Money-multiplier shock (13-5)   Any event that causes the money multiplier to change, such as a change in the public's demand for currency relative to deposits, or a shift between deposits having different reserve requirements.

Money supply (4-2)   Currency and transactions accounts, including checking accounts at banks and thrift institutions.

Multifactor productivity (10-5)   The growth in multifactor productivity is the growth rate of output per hour of work, minus the contribution to output of the growth in the quantity of other factors of production per hour of work, notably capital but sometimes including energy, raw materials, or other factors of production.

Multiplier (3-6)   The ratio of the change in output to the change in autonomous planned spending that causes it; also 1.0 divided by the marginal propensity to save (the fraction of an extra dollar of income that is not spent on consumption).

Multiplier uncertainty (14-4)   The lack of firm knowledge regarding the change in output caused by a change in a policy instrument.

National Income and Product Accounts (2-3)   Official U.S. government economic accounting system that keeps track of GDP and its subcomponents.

National saving (5-5, 12-2)   The sum of private saving (by both households and business firms) and government saving (the government budget surplus).

Natural employment surplus (NES) or **deficit (NED)** (5-4)   The government budget surplus or deficit at the natural level of real GDP.

Natural rate hypothesis (17-2)   The hypothesis that shifts in aggregate demand have no long-run effect on real GDP.

Natural rate of unemployment (1-3)   The level of unemployment at which the inflation rate is constant, with no tendency to accelerate or decelerate.

Natural real GDP (1-3)   The level of real GDP at which the inflation rate is constant, with no tendency to accelerate or decelerate.

Net (2-6)   Economic aggregate excluding capital consumption allowances.

Net domestic product (2-6)   GDP minus depreciation.

Net exports (2-4)   Exports minus imports.

Net foreign investment (2-4)   Equal to exports minus imports.

Net international investment position (5-7)   The difference between all foreign assets owned by a nation's citizens and domestic assets owned by foreign citizens.

Neutral policy (8-9)   Attempt by government or central bank, following a supply shock, to maintain nominal GDP growth so as to allow a decline in the output ratio equal to the increase of the inflation rate.

New Keynesian economics (17-6)   Approach that explains rigidity in prices and wages as consistent with the self-interest of firms and workers, all of which are assumed to have rational expectations.

Nominal (2-7)   An adjective that modifies any economic magnitude measured in current prices.

Nominal anchor (14-8)   A rule that sets a limit on the growth rate of a nominal variable, for instance, high-powered money, the money supply, the price level, or nominal GDP, to prevent inflation from accelerating without limit.

Nominal GDP (2-7)   The value of gross domestic product in current (actual) prices.

Nominal interest rate (9-3)   The market interest rate actually charged by financial institutions and earned by bondholders.

Nominal rigidity (17-6)   A factor that inhibits the flexibility of the nominal price level due to some factor, such as menu costs and staggered contracts. Such factors make it costly for firms to change the nominal price or wage level.

Non-market-clearing model (7-9, 17-6)   Workers and firms are not continuously on their respective demand and supply schedules, but rather are pushed off these schedules by the gradual adjustment of prices.

Okun's Law (8-12)   A regular negative relationship between the output ratio (Y/Y^N) and the gap between the actual unemployment rate and the average rate of unemployment.

Open economy (1-8, 5-5)   An economy that exports (sells) goods and services to other nations, buys imports from them, and has financial flows (capital flows) to and from foreign nations.

Open-market operations (13-5)   Purchases and sales of government securities made by the Federal Reserve in order to change high-powered money.

Output ratio (8-1)   The ratio of actual real GDP to natural real GDP. In the absence of supply shocks, the inflation rate remains constant when the output ratio is 100 percent, accelerates when the output ratio is above 100 percent, and decelerates when the output ratio is below 100 percent.

Parameter (3-5)   A value taken as given or known within a particular analysis.

Perfect capital mobility (6-8)   A condition that occurs when investors regard foreign financial assets as a perfect substitute for domestic assets, and when investors respond instantaneously to an interest rate differential between domestic and foreign assets by moving sufficient assets to eliminate that differential.

Permanent income (15-4)   The average income that people expect to receive over a period of years in the future.

Permanent-income hypothesis (PIH) (15-1)   Conjecture that consumption spending depends on the long-run average (or permanent) income that people expect to receive.

Persistent unemployment (7-9)   A situation in which a high level of unemployment can last for many years, as in the United States in 1929–41 and 1980–85.

Personal disposable income (2-6)   Personal income minus personal income tax payments.

Personal income (2-6)   Income received by households from all sources, including earnings and transfer payments.

Personal saving (2-4)   That part of personal income that is neither consumed nor paid out in taxes.

Pigou Effect (real balance effect) (7-9)   The direct stimulus to aggregate demand caused by an increase in the real money supply; does not require a decline in the interest rate.

Policy activism (14-1)   Active use of instruments of monetary and fiscal policy to offset changes in private sector spending.

Policy credibility (14-6)   The belief by the public that the policymakers will actually carry out an announced policy.

Policy ineffectiveness proposition (17-3)   Assertion that predictable changes in monetary policy cannot affect real output.

Policy instruments (1-7, 14-2)   Elements that government policymakers can manipulate directly to influence target variables.

Policy mix (4-10)   The combination of monetary and fiscal policy in effect in a given situation.

Policy rule (14-1)   Requirement of a fixed path of a policy instrument like the short-term interest rate, of an intermediate variable like the money supply, or a target variable like inflation or unemployment. Also requirement of a specified response of a policy instrument to a given change in a target variable.

Private investment (2-4)   The portion of final product that adds to the nation's stock of income-yielding physical assets or that replaces old, worn-out physical assets.

Production function (10-3)   A relationship, usually written algebraically, that shows how much output can be produced by a given quantity of factor inputs.

Productivity (1-1)   Average output produced per hour.

Purchasing power parity (PPP) theory (6-4)   Theory that the prices of identical goods should be the same in all countries, differing only by the cost of transport and any import (or customs) duties.

Quantity theory of money (7-8)   Theory that actual output tends to grow steadily, while velocity is determined by payment practices such as the use of cash vs. checks, and that as a result a change in the money supply mainly affects the price level and has little or no effect on velocity or output.

Rate of return (3-9)   Annual earnings of an investment project divided by its total cost.

Rate of time preference (12-2)   The extra amount a consumer would be willing to pay to be able to obtain a given quantity of consumption goods now rather than a year from now.

Rational expectations (15-6, 17-3)   Forecasts of future economic magnitudes based on information currently available about the past performance of the economy and future government policies.

Real balance effect (Pigou Effect) (7-9)   The direct stimulus to aggregate demand caused by an increase in the real money supply; does not require a decline in the interest rate.

Real business cycle (RBC) model (17-4)   Explanation attributing business cycles in output and employment to technology or supply shocks.

Real exchange rate (6-4)   The average nominal foreign exchange rate between a country and its trading partners, adjusted for the difference in inflation rates between that country and its trading partners.

Real GDP gap (output gap) (1-4)   The percentage difference between actual and natural real GDP.

Real interest rate (9-3)   The nominal interest rate minus the inflation rate.

Real money balances (4-3)   Total money supply divided by the price level.

Real rigidity (17-6)   A factor that makes firms reluctant to change the real wage, the relative wage, or the relative price.

Redistribution effect (7-9)   The decline in aggregate demand caused by the effect of falling prices in redistributing income from high-spending debtors to low-spending savers.

Required reserves (13-5)   The reserves that Federal Reserve regulations require depository institutions to hold.

Reserve requirements (13-5)   Rules, which apply only to transactions accounts, that stipulate the minimum fraction of deposits that must be held as reserves.

Residual (10-5)   The amount that remains after subtracting from the rate of real GDP growth all of the identifiable sources of economic growth.

Revaluation (6-5)   A nation's raising of the value of its money when its foreign exchange reserves become so excessive that they cause domestic inflation.

Rigid rule (14-3)   A rule for policy that sets a key policy instrument at a fixed value as in a constant growth rate rule for the money supply.

Rigid wages (7-9) The failure of the nominal wage rate to adjust by the amount needed to maintain equilibrium in the labor market.

Sacrifice ratio (8-7) The cumulative loss of output incurred during a disinflation divided by the permanent reduction in the inflation rate.

Seignorage (9-5) The revenue the government receives from inflation; equal to the inflation rate times real high-powered money.

Self-correcting forces (7-8) The role of flexible prices in stabilizing real GDP under some conditions.

Shoe-leather cost (9-3) Occurs when inflation raises interest rates, inducing people to keep more of their funds in interest-bearing bank accounts and less in pocket cash.

Short-run aggregate supply (SAS) curve (7-1) Graph of the amount of output that business firms are willing to produce at different price levels, holding constant the nominal wage rate.

Short-run equilibrium (7-7) The point where the aggregate demand curve crosses the short-run aggregate supply curve.

Short-run Phillips *(SP)* **Curve** (8-2) The schedule relating real GDP to the inflation rate achievable given a fixed expected rate of inflation.

Small open economy (6-8) An economy with perfect capital mobility but with no power to set its domestic interest rate at a level that differs from foreign interest rates.

Solow's residual (10-5) Growth in multifactor productivity.

Stabilization policy (1-7) Any policy that seeks to influence the level of aggregate demand.

Staggered contracts (17-6) Wage contracts that have different expiration dates for different groups of firms or workers.

Standard of living (11-2) Real GDP per member of the population, or output per capita.

Steady state (10-3) A situation in which output and capital input grow at the same rate, implying a fixed ratio of output to capital input.

Stock (2-2) An economic magnitude in the possession of a given economic unit at a particular point in time.

Store of value (4-2) A method of storing purchasing power when receipts and expenditures are not perfectly synchronized.

Structural deficit (5-4) What the government budget deficit would be if the economy were operating at natural real GDP.

Structural surplus (5-4) What the government budget surplus would be if the economy were operating at natural real GDP.

Supply inflation (8-8) An increase in prices that stems from an increase in business costs not directly related to a prior acceleration of nominal GDP growth.

Supply shock (8-1) Caused by a sharp change in the price of an important commodity.

Supply-side economics (12-7) Theory predicting that a reduction in marginal income tax rates will create an increase in the supply of output, that is, in natural real GDP.

Target variables (1-7, 14-2) Economic aggregates whose values society cares about—society's goals.

Taylor Rule (14-7) This rule calls for the central bank to move the real short-term interest rate away from its desired long-term value in response to any deviation of actual inflation from desired inflation and in response to any deviation of real GDP from natural real GDP.

Thrift institutions (13-2) Financial intermediaries such as savings and loan institutions, mutual savings banks, and credit unions.

Time inconsistency (14-6) Policymakers' deviation from a policy after it is announced and private decision-makers have reacted to it.

Time series (15-3) Data covering a span of time of one or more series (e.g., disposable income or consumption spending).

Total factor productivity (10-5) The growth rate of output per hour of work, minus the contribution to output of the growth in the quantity of other factors of production per hour of work, notably capital but sometimes including energy, raw materials, or other factors of production.

Total labor force (2-9) The total of the civilian employed, the armed forces, and the unemployed.

Transfer payments (2-3) Payments for which no goods or services are produced in return.

Transitory income (15-4) The difference between actual income and permanent income; it is not expected to recur.

Trilemma (6-1) The impossibility for any nation of maintaining simultaneously (1) independent control of domestic monetary policy, (2) fixed exchange rates, and (3) free flows of capital with other nations.

Turnover unemployment (frictional unemployment) (9-7) One of the two components of the natural rate of unemployment (the other being mismatch, or structural unemployment), it occurs in the normal process of job search.

Unanticipated inflation (9-3) Situation in which the actual inflation rate (p) differs from the expected (or anticipated) inflation rate (p^e).

Unemployed (2-8) Persons without jobs who either are on temporary layoff or have taken specific actions to look for work.

Unemployment rate (1-1, 2-8) A percentage that expresses the ratio of the number of jobless individuals actively looking for work or on temporary layoff divided by the total employed and unemployed in the labor force.

Unintended inventory investment (3-5)   The amount business firms are forced to accumulate when planned expenditures are less than income.

Unit of account (4-2)   A way of recording receipts, expenditures, assets, and liabilities.

User cost of capital (16-6)   The cost to the firm of using a piece of capital for a specified period.

Value added (2-3)   The value of the labor and capital services that take place at a particular stage of the production process.

Wage indexation (cost-of-living agreements) (9-6)   An automatic increase in the wage rate in response to an increase in a price index.

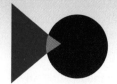

Index

Guide to Symbols

[*Note:* For most variables, the level is indicated by an uppercase letter (X) while the growth rate is indicated by a lowercase letter (x). Each such variable is listed only once in this list by the appropriate uppercase letter (X).]

Symbol	Chapter Where Introduced	Definition
Δ	3	The change in a magnitude
A	3	Real autonomous expenditure
A	10	Autonomous growth factor; multifactor productivity
A	15	Assets held in life-cycle hypothesis
b	4–Appendix	Dollar change of A_p in response to a one percentage-point change in the interest rate
b	10	Elasticity of output with respect to capital input
b	13	Broker's fee in Baumol's theory of money demand
B	9	Dollar amount of government bonds outstanding
c	3	Marginal propensity to consume
c	13	Fraction of bank deposits held as currency by the public
C	2	Real personal consumption expenditures
C	13	Currency held by the public
d	10	Depreciation rate
D	12	Nominal government debt (ΔD = nominal government deficit)
D	13	Demand deposits (accounts at banks or thrift institutions that allow checks to be written)
e	6	Real foreign exchange rate
e'	6	Nominal foreign exchange rate
e	13	Fraction of deposits that banks hold as reserves
E	2	Real expenditures ($E = C + I + G + NX$)
f	4–Appendix	Dollar change of the demand for real money in response to a one percentage-point change in the interest rate
F	2	Real government transfer payments
g	8–Appendix	Slope of the short-run Phillips curve (SP)
G	2	Real government purchases of goods and services
h	4–Appendix	Dollar change of the demand for real money in response to a one-dollar change in real income, holding the interest rate constant
h	8–Appendix	Response of unemployment to the output ratio
h	17	Response of output to a price surprise in the Friedman-Lucas supply function
H	9	High-powered money (same as the monetary base; consists of currency plus bank reserves)
i	9	Nominal or market interest rate
I	2	Real gross private investment
j	8–Appendix	Coefficient of adjustment of expectations
k	3	Spending multiplier
k_1	4–Appendix	Multiplier for autonomous spending in *IS-LM* model
k_2	4–Appendix	Multiplier for real money supply in *IS-LM* model
k	15	Marginal propensity to consume out of permanent income
K	10	Capital stock
L	4	Money demand function
L	15	Age at death in life-cycle hypothesis
M	4	Nominal money supply

Symbol	Chapter Where Introduced	Definition
nx	3–Appendix	Response of net exports to a change in real income
N	7	Labor input, usually measured in person-hours
NX	2	Real net exports
P	4	Price index or price deflator
r	3	Real interest rate
R	2	Real government tax revenue
R	15	Age at retirement in life-cycle hypothesis
s	3	Marginal propensity to save ($s = 1 - c$)
s	10	Average propensity to save; ratio of saving to income
S	2	Real private saving, including business firms and households
t	3–Appendix	Income tax rate
t	5	Ratio of net government tax revenues to GDP
T	2	Real government tax revenue net of transfers ($T = R - F$)
u	16	Real user cost of capital
U	2	Actual unemployment rate
v	16	Capital-output ratio in accelerator theory of investment
V	4	Velocity of money ($V = PY/M$)
W	7	Nominal wage rate
X	8	Nominal GDP ($X = PY$)
$\hat{x}$	8–Appendix	Excess nominal GDP growth ($\hat{x} = x - y^N$)
Y	2	Real income, real output, real GDP
$\hat{Y}$	8–Appendix	Log of ratio of actual to natural real GDP expressed as a percent
z	8–Appendix	The contribution of supply shocks to the inflation rate

Frequently used superscripts

d	4	Demand, as in demand for real balances $(M/P)^d$
e	7	Expected, as in expected rate of inflation (p^e)
f	6	Foreign, as in foreign interest rate (r^f)
N	5	Natural, as in natural rate of unemployment (U^N) or natural real GDP (Y^N)
s	4	Supply, as in the nominal money supply (M^s)

Frequently used subscripts

0	4	Initial situation prior to a change
1	4	New situation after a change
a	3	Autonomous, as in autonomous consumption (C_a)
p	3	Planned, as in planned expenditures (E_p)
u	3	Unplanned, as in unintended inventory investment (I_u)